THE SOVIET POLITY

THE SOVIET POLITY

Government and Politics
in the USSR

THIRD EDITION

JOHN S. RESHETAR, Jr.
University of Washington

HARPER & ROW, PUBLISHERS, New York
Cambridge, Philadelphia, San Francisco, London,
Mexico City, São Paulo, Singapore, Sydney

1817

Sponsoring Editor: Lauren Silverman
Project Editor: Eric Newman
Cover Design: 20/20 Services
Cover Photo: Moscow: view of the Kremlin from the Grand Stone (Tass from SOVFOTO)
Production Manager: Willie Lane
Compositor: ComCom Division of Haddon Craftsmen, Inc.
Printer and Binder: R. R. Donnelley & Sons Company
Cover Printer: Lynn Art

The Soviet Polity: Government and Politics in the USSR, Third Edition

Library of Congress Cataloging-in-Publication Data

Reshetar, John Stephen.
   The Soviet polity: government and politics in the USSR/John S.
Reshetar, Jr.—3rd ed.
   p.   cm.
   Bibliography: p.
   Includes index.
   ISBN 0-06-045398-2
   1. Soviet Union—Politics and Government—1917–   I. Title.
JN6511.R37 1989
320.947—dc19   88-15421
                                       CIP

89 90 91 9 8 7 6 5 4 3 2

Contents

Preface

Although the first and second editions of this work were well received, in this third edition I have made improvements by giving close attention to the dramatic and difficult developments in the Soviet Union since 1978, including the revealing pronouncements of M. S. Gorbachev and the numerous challenges that confront the Soviet polity. Greater attention has been given to the Russian condition and to the costs and burdens of empire. As in the previous editions, I have attempted to provide an essentially eclectic approach to the subject, emphasizing institutional structures, functional analysis, the nature of the Soviet leadership, the principal components of Soviet political life, and the definition of the major problems confronting the Soviet polity. I have also sought to convey something of its ethos and have endeavored to deal with the question of the Soviet political culture. An effort has been made to enable the reader to characterize the Soviet polity and relate it to other political systems—especially in Chapter 12, where six relevant systemic models are analyzed and compared.

Where possible and relevant I have attempted to treat the Soviet polity in terms of problems and issues that are comparable to those confronted by other political systems. However, I have eschewed the direct imposition of a single mode of analysis, or of conceptual schema or a set of analytical categories that are derived essentially from the study of certain Western political systems. Although there is now a vast fund of knowledge regarding Soviet politics, there remain serious lacunae of the kind that do not burden the student of American politics, who is with unfailing regularity inundated by ever-increasing bodies of new empirical data, the results of survey research, efforts at theory-building, and the never-ending revelations of innumerable participants and observers. But few if any governments have published so much and revealed so little as has the Soviet government. Unfortunately there are certain significant closed aspects of the Soviet polity, and some sources of data are denied the investigator. Two examples will suffice. (1) Important, indeed vital, sources of personal testimony are lacking. Prominent Soviet politicians have not published memoirs written from the detached perspective of honorable retirement. Khrushchev's reminiscences, though valuable and unprecedented, were prepared under difficult circumstances and without access to his own official papers and Party archives. (2) Field research in the Soviet Union by Western political scientists is severely circumscribed and can be conducted only on innocuous subjects and in the face of numerous obstacles. There are many barriers to understanding the Soviet Union, and, unfortunately, they are to a large extent a consequence of the policies and attitudes of Soviet authorities.

It is always easier to raise questions than it is to provide acceptable answers. I have undertaken to deal with certain controversial aspects of the Soviet polity that have not received adequate attention. Thus I have dealt with certain aspects of Russian political experience that some might ignore or minimize, and in doing so I have advanced certain hypotheses. However, my purpose has been neither to denigrate nor to justify the Soviet polity but only to attempt to explain it.

In matters of transliteration I have generally followed Library of Congress usage, except for certain minor modifications, and have employed commonly accepted spellings of certain Russian proper names in English (Trotsky, Berdyaev). I have sought to avoid anglicizing plural forms of Russian names and have usually employed the Russian plural form instead.

During the several decades that I have concerned myself with the study of Soviet political phenomena, I have benefited from the counsel, research, and example of far more colleagues than can be acknowledged in a brief preface. To some extent my debt is recognized in the citation of various works. In particular, I wish to thank certain of my colleagues in the Russian and East European Studies Program of the Henry M. Jackson School of International Studies at the University of Washington for advice on various matters. Professor John A. Armstrong of the University of Wisconsin provided valuable counsel from the very beginning of this enterprise. Advice for the revised editions was also provided by Professors Yaroslav Bilinsky, Alexander Groth, Joseph L. Nogee, Rolf H.W. Theen, and Dean C. Myers and is much appreciated. Dr. James P. Nichol of the Library of Congress was especially helpful in obtaining certain source materials. I am also grateful to members of the editorial staff of Harper & Row for their aid. Helene Reshetar, my wife, contributed immeasurably to each edition and patiently bore with the many inevitable disruptions and inconveniences inflicted upon our household as a result of this enterprise. However, I alone am responsible for all sins of omission and commission and for any errors of fact or judgment that may be found in the pages that follow.

John S. Reshetar, Jr.

chapter 1

The USSR: A Multinational Empire

There are compelling reasons for studying the political system of the Union of Soviet Socialist Republics. The world's third most populous country, the Soviet Union emerged from World War II a great power. When it subsequently obtained a nuclear-weapons and missile capability and embarked upon space exploration, it acquired still greater importance. Recognition by the United States of "strategic parity" with the Soviet Union in 1972 meant that the Soviet leadership would henceforth play a role in nearly every important international crisis or negotiation. As possessor of the world's largest nuclear warheads and the heaviest intercontinental ballistic missiles, the Soviet Union can be ignored only at great peril. It has also developed formidable naval power and has deployed the largest submarine fleet in the history of seapower.

For political scientists the Soviet Union is also significant as the first of the twentieth-century dictatorships and as the prototype of the totalitarian regime. Furthermore, as a type of industrial system and as an urbanized society, the Soviet Union offers an area of investigation for all the social sciences. Because it is a multinational entity, the Soviet Union is important for what it reveals (or conceals) regarding its special form of ethnic relations. Its claim to represent "scientific socialism" (Marxism-Leninism) and to offer a developmental model for Asian, African, and Latin American peoples also makes the study of Soviet domestic politics and Russian political behavior relevant. The twentieth century has been confronted with the challenge of communism both as a doctrine and as a political system. Since the Soviet Union is the world's oldest communist regime, the study of Soviet political practice is essential to an understanding of what communism is and what it has to offer its adherents and subjects. The Soviet

Union is a creation of Russian political figures and a reflection of certain Russian cultural attributes and characteristics. Study of the Soviet polity provides a means of understanding the Russians as a people—who they are, the kinds of values that they profess to represent, the objectives that they pursue, and the behavioral traits that they manifest.

In order to have a broader and more profound understanding of the contemporary Soviet Union, it is necessary to be cognizant of its origins and of the nature and development of the Russian Empire from which it emerged. It is all too simple—and erroneous—to treat the Soviet polity as a homogeneous and fixed entity when, in fact, it is the result of a protracted process of development that involved the "gathering together" of diverse lands and peoples. In order to appreciate the complex composition and substance of the Soviet polity, it is important to view it initially with reference both to its precursor and its ethnic composition.

THE SOVIET UNION: SUCCESSOR TO THE RUSSIAN EMPIRE

The uninformed frequently equate the entire Soviet Union exclusively with Russia and incorrectly identify Soviet citizenship with being "Russian." In fact, the Russians constitute but a plurality of the USSR's population. Prior to World War I, the Russians had only a plurality of 43 percent of the population of the Russian Empire. The millions of non-Russians who have retained their sense of national identity despite Russian rule represent a broad variety of cultures, languages, and distinctive historical development. However, as the most numerous and dominant nationality in the Soviet Union, the Russians have always attracted greater attention.

The term *Russian* has at times been used indiscriminately (and incorrectly) to refer to all persons under Russian rule. Strictly defined, the term refers to the most numerous of the Slavic peoples, who began to emerge as an identifiable entity in the northern part of Eastern Europe in the period between the ninth and eleventh centuries. The Russians originated as an offshoot of the earlier Eastern Slavic population that had come to inhabit much of the central forested part of Eastern Europe, mingling with the indigenous Finnish population and acquiring other ethnic admixtures as well. The Eastern Slavs were originally divided into a number of different tribes to which the term *Russian* can hardly be applied. The term *Rus'* (probably of Scandinavian or Varangian origin), applied to the territory of the Eastern Slavs, was originally used in a territorial rather than an ethnic sense. Thus *Rus'* should not be confused or equated with *Rossiia,* the term for Russia. Indeed, in the basic chronicle *The Tale of Bygone Years (Povest' vremennykh let),* there is no reference to a Russian language (but in the entry under the year 1037, it is stated that translations were made from Greek into "Slavic writing"). The early Eastern Slavs did not constitute a homogeneous entity, let alone something that can be termed "Russian." Nor did they possess a single political jurisdiction. The chronicles make it clear that the Eastern Slavic tribes and the various principalities were often in conflict.

There was no political unity in *Rus',* despite the existence of a single dynasty of Varangian origin (the successors of Rurik or Hrörekr); the various princes frequently engaged in fratricidal conflict. In 1169 Andrei Bogoliubsky, prince of Vladimir-Suzdal, sacked Kiev, the original seat of the Rurik dynasty and source of culture, thus demonstrating the lack of unity. As the tribes abandoned paganism, the sole unity that *Rus'* acquired was based on a single Orthodox Christian ecclesiastical jurisdiction (the Kiev metropolitanate), usually headed by a Byzantine Greek.

Growth of the Russian Empire

Russia as a distinctive ethnic and political entity can be said to have developed in the area of the Vladimir-Suzdal principality, in which Muscovy (first referred to in the chronicles in 1147) emerged as the cradle of the Russian state and nation. The phenomenal growth of the Russian Empire from a territory of 15,000 square miles in the fifteenth century to a vast domain 570 times its original size four centuries later, furthermore, had its origins in the emergence and rise of the principality of Muscovy. Indeed, the Russian historian Vasilii O. Kliuchevsky has stated that Muscovy in the time of Ivan Kalita (1328–1340) hardly extended over 500 square miles.[1] This process of expansion began with the acquisition by Muscovy of other Russian principalities as a result of the advantageous position that it had enjoyed during the latter part of the so-called Tatar yoke. Novgorod, whose unique political system is discussed in the following chapter, was annexed by Muscovy in 1478 after having lost its northern and eastern colonies. Tver was seized in 1485, Viatka in 1489, Pskov in 1510, Smolensk in 1514, and Riazan in 1517. Ivan IV ("the Terrible") not only annexed other ethnically Russian territories, but in 1552 also commenced the process of seizing non-Russian territory in conquering Kazan, capital of the Volga Tatars. By 1554 Russian rule was established at the mouth of the Volga at Astrakhan and access to the Caspian Sea obtained.

The stage was now set for the great eastward push across the Urals through Siberia to the Pacific Ocean. By the late 1580s Western Siberia had been conquered to the Ob' and Irtysh rivers, largely as the result of the activities of Yermak Timofeievich, an energetic adventurer in the employ of the Stroganovs, a wealthy landowning and commercial family. Expansionism in Siberia persisted—the Sea of Okhotsk was reached in 1638—and by the end of the seventeenth century, the Russians had discovered the Kamchatka Peninsula.

Russian expansionism was to persist across the North Pacific and the Bering Sea, as well as in Eastern Europe during the seventeenth and eighteenth centuries. Eastern Ukraine (east of the Dnieper River) was acquired in 1654 and Kiev in 1667. Unable to gain much territory in southern Ukraine at the expense of the Ottoman Empire, Peter I concentrated his expansionist efforts on the Baltic coast and challenged Sweden's supremacy in that area by building a navy. The process of successfully breaking through to the Baltic, attempted in vain by Ivan the

---

[1] V. O. Kliuchevsky, *Kratkoe posobie po russkoi istorii,* 5th ed. (Moscow, 1906), p. 67.

Terrible during a quarter-century of conflict against Sweden and Poland, commenced in 1701–1704 with the seizure of Ingria (the area southwest of what is today Leningrad), along with the cities of Narva and Tartu. This acquisition enabled Peter to begin to build his new "western" capital on the marshlands at the mouth of the Neva River. By 1710 the Finnish city of Vyborg (Viipuri) and all of Karelia were annexed; Estonia and Livonia were also taken, along with the city of Riga. By carrying the war into Swedish waters and raiding the Swedish mainland (the first Russian naval victory was won in 1714), Peter was able to compel Sweden to recognize his Baltic territorial gains in the Treaty of Nystadt (1721), which concluded more than two decades of intermittent but bitter warfare (the "Great Northern War"). Russia could now claim to be a European power, and her coarse and willful ruler proclaimed himself "the Great" and emperor as well. Prior to 1721 Russia had not existed as a juridical entity; it was officially known as the Muscovite State *(Moskovskoe Gosudarstvo),* which Peter renamed the Russian Empire *(Rossiiskaia Imperiia).*

Apparently unsatiated with warfare and having his appetite for more non-Russian territory whetted by the Nystadt settlement, Peter turned to the Caspian Sea to wage war against Persia. Taking advantage of internal turmoil in Persia, he obtained the western and southern shores of the Caspian (including Baku) in 1722; after his death the coastal area was returned to Persia, but the western shore of the Caspian was reannexed by Alexander I. The Ottoman Empire had prevented Peter from breaching the Caucasus.

The growth of the Russian Empire during the reign of Catherine II (1762–1796) resulted from two wars against Turkey (1770–1774 and 1787–1792) and the three successive partitions of the Polish State. By the Treaty of Kuchuk-Kainardji (1774), Catherine gained most of the northern shore of the Black Sea; and the Crimean Tatar Khanate was removed from Ottoman Turkish suzerainty and became nominally independent (an independence terminated by Russian annexation in 1783). The second Russo-Turkish war ended with Turkey's recognition of Catherine's annexation of the Crimea, and Russia also acquired a new frontier along the lower reaches of the Dniester River. Imperial Russia now became a Black Sea power, building a naval base at Sevastopol and founding the new port city of Odessa in 1794. The partitioning of the Polish State (1772, 1793, and 1795) enabled Catherine to gain Lithuania, part of Latvia, Belorussia, and a large part of Western Ukraine.

As a result of the Napoleonic Wars, Alexander I changed sides—joining Napoleon in 1807—and took Finland from Sweden, making it a Russian Grand Duchy in 1809. Bessarabia was obtained from the Ottoman Empire in 1812. By being on the winning side against Napoleon in 1815, Russia acquired "Congress Poland," along with Warsaw.

The eighteenth century witnessed a Russian push across the North Pacific and the establishment of "Russian America";[2] by the 1760s, the Russians had

---

[2]See Frank A. Golder, *Russian Expansion on the Pacific, 1641–1850* (1914; reprinted Gloucester, Mass.: Peter Smith, 1960). Cf. George V. Lantzeff and Richard A. Pierce, *Eastward to Empire;*

established themselves as fur traders in the Aleutian Islands and in the southern coastal part of Alaska. The ruthless individual traders (who mistreated the natives in the search for sea otter pelts) soon formed companies; and in 1799 the Russian American Company, a semigovernmental firm, was granted a hunting and commercial monopoly extending southward from Alaska to 55° N. The company was authorized to maintain armed forces and to claim lands south of 55° N as Russian possessions.[3]

In 1812 the Russian American Company established Fort Ross on the California coast seventy miles north of San Francisco in order to provide a base for hunting sea otter and to serve as a source of food supply for the Russians in Alaska. Spain, in possession of San Francisco, protested the Russian settlement and demanded its abandonment, and the Mexicans also protested the Russian presence when they replaced the Spaniards. As more Americans arrived in California, the Russians abandoned Fort Ross in 1841.

The sale of Alaska and the Aleutian Islands was considered by the Russians as early as 1853, but the American Civil War caused its postponement until 1867. The Russian decision to sell to the United States for $7.2 million was prompted by a number of factors. The land was remote from Russia, and the Crimean War (1853–1856) had revealed Russian military weakness and an inability to defend an overseas empire. The Polish revolt of 1863 demonstrated the weakness of Russia's fleet when it had to seek refuge in New York and San Francisco because of the possibility of an international crisis resulting from Russia's suppression of the revolt.[4] Alaska had become an economic liability and was requiring an annual government subsidy of 200,000 rubles; the fur resource had become seriously depleted. The decision to sell to the United States was also due, in part, to Russian antipathy toward Great Britain. Russia's commitments in North America had apparently exceeded her capabilities, and a retreat was in order.[5]

Despite the retreat in North America, the claim to a larger Russian empire

---

Exploration and Conquest on the Russian Open Frontier to 1750 (Montreal and London: McGill–Queen's University Press, 1973).

[3]In 1810 Russia attempted to claim the Pacific Coast as far south as the Columbia River, despite the fact that it had been claimed by Lewis and Clark in 1804; and in September 1821, Russia attempted to claim the American coast to 51° N. See Samuel Flagg Bemis, *John Quincy Adams and the Foundations of American Foreign Policy* (New York: Knopf, 1950), pp. 173–174. For a general account of the Russian occupation of Alaska's southern coastal area, see Stuart R. Tompkins, *Alaska, Promyshlennik and Sourdough* (Norman, Okla.: University of Oklahoma Press, 1945); also see Clarence A. Manning, *Russian Influence on Early America* (New York: Library Publishers, 1953), Howard L. Kushner, *Conflict on the Northwest Coast; American-Russian Rivalry in the Pacific Northwest, 1790–1867* (Westport, Conn.: Greenwood Press, 1975), and S. Frederick Starr, ed., *Russia's American Colony* (Durham, N.C.: Duke University Press, 1987).

[4]Many Americans misinterpreted this act as "proof" of Russian friendship for the Union cause. See Frank A. Golder, "The Russian Fleet and the Civil War," *American Historical Review,* XX (July 1915), pp. 801–812.

[5]A clumsy effort by a representative of the Russian American Company to annex Hawaii in 1815–1817 ended in failure due to the tsarist government's unwillingness to support it. See Klaus Mehnert, *The Russians in Hawaii, 1804–1819* (Honolulu: University of Hawaii Occasional Papers No. 38, 1939) and Richard A. Pierce, *Russia's Hawaiian Adventure, 1815–1817* (Berkeley: University of California Press, 1965).

was pressed in Asia and in the Caucasus. By 1801 much of Georgia was reduced to the status of a Russian province. The hardy, freedom-loving Moslem peoples of the Caucasus fought Russian encroachment for a quarter-century under the leadership of Shamil, but by 1859 Russian rule was established in the Eastern Caucasus. By 1864 the Russians were in control of the Western Caucasus, but only after resettling large numbers of Circassians and permitting 200,000 to immigrate to Turkey.

A renewed campaign to conquer Turkestan came in the wake of Russia's defeat in the Crimean War. Tashkent was taken in 1865, and when Samarkand was captured in 1868, the Emir of Bukhara became a vassal of the tsar. In 1873 the Khiva Khanate was conquered, and the khan also became a Russian vassal. The Kokand Khanate, which had become a vassal state in 1866, was abolished in 1876 following suppression of a revolt and was annexed as a Russian province. In January 1881, the taking of the fortress of Geok Tepe was followed by a massacre of Turkmens. The Russian annexation of Central Asia was completed with the acquisition of Kushka from Afghanistan in 1885 and the recognition of the Pamir area as a Russian possession in 1895.

In the Far East, Northern Sakhalin was occupied in 1853, and in 1875 Japan ceded Southern Sakhalin to Russia in return for the Kurile Islands.[6] The Amur Region and the territory east of the Ussuri River, which Russia had recognized as being Chinese in the Treaty of Nerchinsk (1689), were seized from a weakened China in 1858. Recognition of this conquest by local Chinese authorities in the Treaty of Aigun (1858) was confirmed by the hard-pressed Chinese government in the Treaty of Peking (1860) but disputed a century later by China's communist rulers.

The city of Vladivostok ("Ruler of the Orient") was founded in 1860 at the southern extremity of this territory annexed from China. It was only the Russo-Japanese War of 1904–1905 that halted the Russian advance and prevented Russia from obtaining control of Southern Manchuria and Korea.

The Soviet regime regained most of this vast empire of the tsars, although Poland, Finland, Estonia, Latvia, Lithuania, and Bessarabia went their separate ways as a result of the Russian revolution of 1917. However, in September 1939, the Soviet Union annexed Western Ukraine and Western Belorussia, which had been part of the Polish State created in 1919. In 1940 the three Baltic States lost their independence and became soviet republics; Bessarabia was also retaken by Moscow after having been under Romanian rule. The Ukrainian territory of Northern Bukovina, which had never been under Russian rule, was also annexed in 1940. The Carpatho-Ukraine was taken from Czechoslovakia in June 1945. World War II resulted in the annexation by the USSR of an additional non-Russian population of at least 22 million. In addition, the war enabled the Soviet Union to seize the Karelian isthmus from Finland, along with the city of Vyborg as well as the Petsamo (Pechenga) region—the loss of which deprived Finland of access to the Barents Sea. In 1945

---

[6]Japan regained Southern Sakhalin in 1905, following the Russo-Japanese War, but the Soviet Union seized the entire island as well as the Kurile Islands in 1945 after declaring war on Japan.

Russia also acquired the northern half of East Prussia, including the German city of Koenigsberg (renamed Kaliningrad).

Motive Factors in Russian Expansionism

The record of Russian expansionism is significant because of its continuity over more than four centuries and its relentless nature in spite of having suffered certain setbacks. It is unique also in that the Russians have been able to retain their multinational empire, contiguous with their own ethnic territories, while the overseas empires of the European powers, in contrast, have been liquidated with the granting of independence to the colonies. No single factor can explain the phenomenon of Russian expansionism, but it undoubtedly was facilitated by Muscovy's absolutist political order.

Another factor was the relative weakness of the conquered peoples. Thus, the Russian acquisition of Siberia was effected by relatively small forces that had firearms, while the vanquished were armed with bows and arrows. In Europe the extent of Russia's acquisitions depended upon the international balance of power: Sweden, Poland, Lithuania, the Livonian (Teutonic) Knights, and Denmark had been able to prevent Ivan the Terrible from acquiring an outlet to the Baltic, but Peter I succeeded in this endeavor as a result of a shift in the balance of power to Muscovy's advantage. Furthermore, weak neighbors, incapable of defending themselves, invited aggression. Poland's internal weakness led to intervention and to her partition, for example, as some Poles, members of the ruling class, could always be found to look to Russia for support and would do its bidding in the shortsighted hope of promoting their own interests. The weakness of the Ottoman Empire and of China also invited Russian expansion.

The search for security has been cited as an important cause of Russian expansionism—with Muscovy reacting to Tatar, Polish, Lithuanian, and Swedish neighbors and protecting itself against a supposedly hostile non-Russian world. The difficulty in explaining the *entire* process in terms of this single cause lies in the fact that Russia frequently annexed peoples who constituted no threat to her security. In addition, it should be pointed out that the search for security knows no limits and can be used to justify any aggression, because each new acquisition usually requires another aggression if it, too, is to be in turn made "secure." Indeed, it might be contended that the very vastness of Russia's empire complicated its defense and simultaneously promoted new acquisitions.

A geopolitical interpretation of Russian expansionism stresses the lack of natural barriers confronting Muscovy and the relative ease and rapidity with which the eastward movement was accomplished. However, geographical determinism does not explain very well the fact that the Russian eastward movement, beginning in the fifteenth and sixteenth centuries, was a dramatic reversal of the earlier, centuries-long westward movement of alien populations that had been emerging from Asia to invade and populate parts of Europe in successive waves. If the plains and lack of natural frontiers left Russia open to foreign incursions, they also facilitated Russian expansionism once the necessary power base arose in the form of the autocratic Muscovite State.

It has also been contended that the Russians had an inexorable compulsion to reach the sea.[7] This provocative thesis is based on a geographical determinism that holds that in Russian expansionism rivers were followed to their mouths and, with the use of numerous portages and the construction of forts, provided trade routes. A similar point of view has endeavored to justify Russian expansionism in terms of a desire for warm-water ports.

However, to argue that the Russian urge to colonial expansion resulted primarily from a desire to reach the sea is to oversimplify. This explanation appears to be applicable only in the drive to reach the Baltic and in Catherine's wars against Turkey. Prior to the eighteenth century, Russia had neither a navy nor a naval tradition, and Peter had to hire foreigners in order to establish a fleet. The bulk of Russian expansionism occurred long before Russia undertook to become a maritime power. Indeed, the Russians had reached the Kola Peninsula and the ice-free open sea as early as the thirteenth century but did not develop maritime interests until much later; they did not bother to build a port at Murmansk until they were compelled to do so in 1915 as a result of the Central Powers' blockade of the Baltic and Black seaports. The port of Arkhangelsk, closed two-thirds of the year by ice, had been founded in 1584 at the request of Dutch traders and was Russia's great port during the seventeenth century, serving her modest foreign commercial needs very adequately. Nor can the eastward expansion across Siberia be explained in terms of a desire to reach the sea; Yermak did not have this as his motive when he pushed across the Urals in search of personal gain. The original Russian acquisition of Eastern Ukraine cannot be explained in terms of a need for ports, either. Likewise, Russian expansion into the Caucasus and the acquisition of Poland and of Turkestan cannot be explained in terms of a need to reach the sea.[8]

More important as a motive—especially for eastward expansion—was the quest for furs, gold, and commercial routes to the Orient. The quest for gold and a route to India motivated Peter I in his sending of an ill-fated expedition to Turkestan in 1715–1717. Furs were also a motive in the Russian attempt to establish an overseas empire in North America. Tribute in the form of furs *(iasak)* was frequently imposed by the Russians upon subjugated peoples; in fact, furs constituted the most important single Russian export in the seventeenth century, although Russia was not a significant participant in world trade at that time.[9] The lure of rapidly acquired wealth in the fur trade and the rate of depletion drove Russian traders, hunters, and trappers from the Urals to the Pacific within eighty years.

---

[7]See Robert J. Kerner, *The Urge to the Sea, The Course of Russian History* (Berkeley and Los Angeles: University of California Press, 1942).

[8]For a refutation of the thesis that Russian expansionism can be explained by Russia's need for access to the seas, see John A. Morrison, "Russia and Warm Water: A Fallacious Generalization and Its Consequences," *United States Naval Institute Proceedings,* LXXVIII (November 1952), pp. 1169–1179.

[9]See Raymond H. Fisher, *The Russian Fur Trade, 1550–1700* (Berkeley and Los Angeles: University of California Press, 1943).

However, Russian expansionism was not in all instances due to official policy. When strong monarchs like Ivan III, Ivan IV, Peter I, and Catherine II reigned, expansion was the order of the day. Yet the beginning of the conquest of Siberia occurred as a result of the activity of the brigand Yermak; originally frowned upon by Ivan IV as a risky enterprise, the conquest was viewed approvingly once its relative ease and its lucrative aspects became apparent. Another Russian who initiated expansionist policy was Nikolai Murav'ev, the governor-general of Eastern Siberia, who moved forces into the Amur region without waiting for official approval. The Russian military, probing into Turkestan in the nineteenth century, exceeded its orders on occasion and accelerated the process of empire-building in its desire for decorations and promotions. Indeed, over the centuries Muscovite absolutism and serfdom provided a host of rough and ready pioneers who, along with religious dissenters, preferred flight to the established order and who were prepared to risk their lives on some distant new frontier.

If empires have frequently grown as a result of a combination of governmental policy, individual daring, the quest for adventure, and the desire for personal gain and glory, they have not been lacking in pretense and rationalization. Thus, the Russians could claim that they had fulfilled a "civilizing mission" in bringing the Orthodox faith to the Aleuts, in introducing domestic animals into Alaska, and in "pacifying" the nomads of Turkestan. Russian concern over the fate of the Orthodox Christians of the Balkans also provided a convenient pretext for an anti-Turkish policy and "liberation wars" that served the interests of Russian expansionism. The preoccupation with acquiring Constantinople, dating back at least to the eighteenth century, reflected a Russian tendency to adopt a messianic role.[10]

THE NON-RUSSIAN NATIONALITIES

Although the diverse non-Russian peoples have often been termed "national minorities" and their territories "Russian provinces" or "borderlands," most of them constitute a substantial majority of the population of their own territories

---

[10]In 1782 Catherine II proposed, without success, to the Austrian emperor Joseph II that the Turks be driven out of the Balkans and that a Greek Empire (including Bulgaria, Macedonia, and Albania) be established with Constantine, her grandson, on the throne. The Russian preoccupation with the Straits and Constantinople began to bear fruit in the secret agreements of February–March 1915, negotiated by the tsarist foreign minister, S. D. Sazonov, under which Britain and France conditionally agreed to transfer the Straits, along with adjacent territories and the Turkish capital, to Russia. Not satisfied, the Russians in April 1916 claimed all of Eastern Turkey (Erzerum, Trabzon, Van, Bitlis) and much of Kurdistan as well. Russia also obtained "complete freedom" in delimiting its western frontier, which would have enabled it to annex Western Ukraine. The Russian Provisional Government, despite its democratic pretensions, did not renounce these claims in 1917; if Russia was unable to obtain the spoils of World War I, it was, in large part, due to Lenin's destruction of the Provisional Government. See Iu. V. Kliuchnikov and Andrei Sabanin, eds., *Mezhdunarodnaia politika noveishego vremeni v dogovorakh, notakh i deklaratsiiakh* (Moscow: NKID, 1926), Part II, pp. 25–27, 38–39, 69. Also see Sergei D. Sazonov, *Vospominaniia* (Paris, 1927), pp. 292–322. After World War II Stalin unsuccessfully demanded a military base on the straits and territories in northeastern Turkey.

(see Table 1.1).[11] The presence of numerous smaller ethnic groups, many of whom are in the Russian Republic, makes it possible to discuss here only the more numerous non-Russian peoples.

The *Ukrainians* are the second most numerous Slavic people and also the second most numerous nationality in the Soviet Union. Possessing a distinctive language with a rich melodious quality and a substantial literary tradition, the Ukrainians inhabit a republic that has Kiev (*Kyiv* in Ukrainian) as its capital. Historically, they trace their origins to the Kiev *Rus'* of the ninth to the thirteenth centuries. The Ukrainians received Christianity from Byzantium in A.D. 988, and what was subsequently to become Muscovy accepted Christianity from Ukraine more than a century later. The Kievan missionary Saint Kuksha was martyred in 1113 by the Viatichi tribe—ancestors of the Russians. The Kiev State was followed by the Galician-Volynian State in Western Ukraine in the thirteenth century, but was ultimately absorbed into the Lithuanian State, which flourished in the fourteenth and fifteenth centuries; the Western Ukraine was annexed by the Polish State. The Union of Poland and Lithuania in 1569 then brought almost all Ukrainians under Polish rule. During this lengthy period, the Ukrainians had no contact with the Russians.

As a result of the presence of Tatars in the Crimea, it became necessary—in a significant development—to defend the southern Ukrainian frontier. This responsibility was fulfilled in the sixteenth and seventeenth centuries by the Zaporozhian *Kozaks* of Eastern Ukraine, who bore arms, in addition to engaging in agriculture, and over whom the Polish government could not usually exercise authority. The term *kozak* (cossack) is of Turkic origin and refers to a guardian, a free and independent man; it was not, as is sometimes assumed, an exclusively Russian term—although Cossacks (*kazaks,* in Russian) in Russian service to the east of Ukraine performed a similar function.

The Ukrainian kozaks, who possessed their own administration and elected their commander *(hetman),* revolted against Polish rule in 1648 under the leadership of Hetman Bohdan Khmelnytsky. Finding it difficult to defend their independence in the face of Polish and Crimean Tatar opposition, the Ukrainian kozaks turned to the tsar of Muscovy for aid. They concluded with Muscovy the Treaty of Pereiaslav (1654), which they thought signified an alliance but which the tsar regarded as an act of submission.[12] In this way Eastern Ukraine came under Russian rule, during the eighteenth century losing its rights under the treaty (including the right to have diplomatic relations and impose tariffs) as well as its separate military establishment; the hetmanate was abolished in 1764 by Catherine II, who also introduced serfdom into Ukraine.

The attempt of Hetman Ivan Mazepa in 1709 to ally with Sweden and

---

[11]Major exceptions are the Kazakhs and the Kirghiz (who are minorities in their own republics) and the Jews, who do not possess their own republic but are dispersed throughout various parts of the Soviet Union. The more numerous Tatars are also denied a union republic but have autonomous republics—with the exception of the Crimean Tatars who were forcibly dispersed.

[12]For the various interpretations of the Pereiaslav Treaty, including shifting Soviet interpretations, see John Basarab, *Pereiaslav 1654: A Historiographical Study* (Edmonton: Canadian Institute of Ukrainian Studies, University of Alberta, 1982).

Table 1.1 PRINCIPAL NATIONALITIES OF THE SOVIET UNION

Nationalities	1959 Census (thousands)	Percentage of total population	1970 Census (thousands)	Percentage of total population	1979 Census (thousands)	Percentage of total population	Percentage declaring given language as native in 1979	Percentage of population of own republic in 1979	Portion of nationality living outside of own republic in 1979 (percentage)
Russians	114,114	54.6	129,015	53.4	137,397	52.4	99.9	82.6	17.4
Ukrainians	37,253	17.8	40,753	16.9	42,347	16.1	82.8	73.6	13.8
Uzbeks	6,015	2.9	9,195	3.8	12,456	4.7	98.5	68.7	15.2
Belorussians	7,913	3.8	9,052	3.7	9,463	3.6	74.2	79.4	20.0
Tatars	4,968	2.4	5,931	2.5	6,317	2.4	85.9	—	—
Kazakhs	3,622	1.7	5,299	2.2	6,556	2.5	97.5	36.0	19.3
Azerbaidjanis	2,940	1.4	4,380	1.8	5,477	2.1	97.9	78.1	14.0
Armenians	2,787	1.3	3,559	1.5	4,151	1.6	90.7	89.7	34.4
Georgians	2,692	1.3	3,245	1.3	3,571	1.4	98.3	68.8	3.9
Moldavians	2,214	1.1	2,698	1.1	2,968	1.1	93.2	63.9	14.9
Lithuanians	2,326	1.1	2,665	1.1	2,851	1.1	97.9	80.0	4.9
Jews	2,268	1.1	2,151	0.9	1,811	0.7	14.2	—	—
Tadjiks	1,397	0.7	2,136	0.9	2,898	1.1	97.8	58.8	22.8
Germans	1,620	0.8	1,846	0.8	1,936	0.7	57.0	—	—
Chuvash	1,470	0.7	1,694	0.7	1,751	0.7	81.7	—	—
Turkmens	1,002	0.5	1,525	0.6	2,028	0.8	98.7	68.4	6.7
Kirghiz	969	0.5	1,452	0.6	1,906	0.7	97.9	47.9	11.5
Latvians	1,400	0.7	1,430	0.6	1,439	0.5	95.0	53.7	6.6
Mordovians	1,285	0.6	1,263	0.5	1,192	0.5	72.6	—	—
Bashkirs	989	0.5	1,240	0.5	1,371	0.5	67.0	—	—
Poles	1,380	0.7	1,167	0.5	1,151	0.4	29.1	—	—
Estonians	989	0.5	1,007	0.4	1,020	0.4	95.3	64.7	7.1
Others	7,215	3.3	9,016	3.7	10,343	4.0			
Total	208,827	100.0	241,720	100.0	262,400	100.0			

Sources: Tsentral'noe Statisticheskoe Upravlenie SSSR, *Itogi Vsesoiuznoi perepisi naseleniia 1970 goda*, Vol. IV, *Natsional'nyi sostav naseleniia SSSR* (Moscow: "Statistika," 1973), and *Naselenie SSSR. Po dannym Vsesoiuznoi perepisi naseleniia 1979 goda* (Moscow: Politizdat, 1980).

regain Ukrainian independence failed, and the partitioning of the Polish State brought many more Ukrainians under Russian rule. The Western Ukrainians in Galicia, who were of the Catholic faith (as distinct from the Orthodox Eastern Ukrainians) but who employed the Slavonic rite, exchanged Polish for Austrian rule in 1772. Bukovina came under Austrian rule in 1775.

Despite these vicissitudes, a nationalist movement grew among the Ukrainians. When the Russian government endeavored to destroy Ukrainian nationalism during the second half of the nineteenth century, the movement found more favorable conditions in the Ukrainian lands under Austrian rule. Despite oppressive conditions of Russian rule during this period, Eastern Ukraine developed a national literature and produced the greatest Ukrainian poet, Taras Shevchenko (1814–1861)—a prophet of national liberation—and Professor Mykhailo Hrushevsky (1866–1934), the nation's most prominent historian. With the collapse of the Russian Empire in 1917, the Ukrainians finally proclaimed their independence (the anticommunist Ukrainian People's Republic led by Symon Petliura) but lost it to the superior military forces of the Soviet regime after three years of bitter struggle. While the national movement won a victory of sorts in the establishment of the Ukrainian Soviet Socialist Republic, severe repressions against the Ukrainian intelligentsia and peasantry followed in the 1930s. World War II led to the unification of almost all Ukrainian territories as a result of Soviet annexations. In its level of industry, agriculture, and population, the Ukrainian S.S.R. surpasses most other European countries and is comparable to France. Ukraine is also a charter member of the United Nations and holds membership in a number of international bodies.

The *Belorussians* or *White Ruthenians* are not Russians despite the similarity in name, since they are known as *Belarusy* while the Russians are *russkie.* Their homeland lies between Russia and Poland, and their language is distinct from those of their Slavic neighbors. The economy, agricultural to a significant degree, includes such industries as textiles and lumber; other industries, including heavy truck and tractor assembly plants, are based largely on imports from other parts of the Soviet Union.

Historically, the *Belarusy* are descended from such early Slavic tribes as the Western Krivichi, Dregovichi, and Radimichi. Later the Polotsk Principality in Belorussia was an important center in the ancient *Rus'.* Between the fourteenth and eighteenth centuries, the *Belarusy* were united with the Lithuanians in the Great Lithuanian Principality and, as a result of the union of Lithuania and Poland, were later included (along with the Ukrainians) in this unique East European multinational state. The partitioning of the Polish State (which was far larger in size than ethnic Poland) brought the *Belarusy* under the rule of Imperial Russia. Catholic influences were suppressed by the tsarist regime as part of the effort to russify the *Belarusy.* Although World War I and the Russian Revolution enabled the *Belarusy* to proclaim their independence, their country was partitioned in 1921—Poland receiving the western part and the eastern part becoming the Belorussian S.S.R., with Minsk as the capital. Poland's military defeat in 1939 led to the Soviet annexation of Western Belorussia. Although the national consciousness of the *Belarusy* has not been equal to that of their neighbors, this sturdy people has remained attached to its homeland.

The *Turkic* (or *Turco-Tatar*) peoples in the Soviet Union are related to the Osmanli Turks of Turkey. The area populated by Turkic peoples extends from Iakutia in the Lena River basin in Siberia to the Mediterranean. Although differing racially, the Turkic peoples are closely related linguistically, despite the existence of various idioms. Another unifying factor has been their Moslem faith, the overwhelming majority being of the Sunni branch. The Turkic settlement of Central Asia began as early as the sixth century; and the Arab conquest of Samarkand in A.D. 712 led to the removal of Chinese influence and to the introduction of Islam. The rise of the Mongols in the thirteenth century meant the subjugation of the various Turkic peoples and their inclusion in the Mongol Empire. Although various Turkic tribes were in contact with the Eastern Slavs since the earliest times, the Tatars are the Turkic people who have left the most recent mark upon European Russia. Their subjugation by the Russians began in the sixteenth century, and the process of acquiring Turkic peoples for the Russian Empire was not completed until the latter half of the nineteenth century with the conquest of Turkestan in Central Asia.

The *Uzbeks,* who inhabit the south central part of Turkestan bordering on Afghanistan, are the most numerous of the Soviet Turkic peoples. Uzbekistan, with its capital at Tashkent, is the leading Soviet cotton-producing center and also has an impressive industrial establishment specializing in textiles, chemicals, and metallurgy. The ancient capitals of Bukhara and Samarkand are also located in Uzbekistan. The *Kirghiz* live to the east of the Uzbeks, bordering on Xinjiang, or Chinese Turkestan. Traditionally, the Kirghiz were nomadic horsemen who tended their herds in mountain pastures. In 1916 they participated in a revolt of the Turkestanis against the tsarist regime's efforts to conscript native manpower for labor (after requisitioning flocks and imposing heavy taxes); the Kirghiz suffered heavy losses in the repression that followed. The revolt, which began among the Uzbeks, led tens of thousands of Kirghiz to flee across the border into China to escape punishment.

The *Kazakhs* are a Turkic people who should not be confused with the Russian term (of Turkic origin) *kazak* (cossack). They are a formerly nomadic people who have inhabited the plains to the north of Kirghizia and Uzbekistan, and many of them experienced the same fate in the suppression of the 1916 revolt. The Kazakhs have been reduced to a minority in their own republic as a result of a great influx of Russians and Ukrainians connected with the development of agriculture, mining, and industry and intensified after 1955 by Moscow's decision to cultivate the vast, dry virgin lands of the Kazakhs.

To the west of Uzbekistan live the *Turkmens,* whose land—which lies north of Iran and Afghanistan—is largely desert. The bulk of the population lives in the foothills near the Iranian frontier and is engaged in irrigated agriculture; industry is based on oil and gas, minerals, and chemicals.

The *Azerbaidjanis* inhabit the western shores of the Caspian Sea. Unlike the other Turkic peoples, who are Sunni Moslems, the Azerbaidjanis are Shi-ite and partly Sunni Moslems. Although both Persians and Anatolian Turks had an interest in Azerbaidjan prior to its annexation by the Russians early in the nineteenth century, the Azerbaidjanis were able to reestablish their independence in May 1918, only to lose it two years later as the result of a Russian communist invasion. Petroleum at Baku (Azerbaidjan's capital), cotton, rice, tea, fruits, fisheries, and caviar have figured prominently in the Azerbaidjan economy.

The *Tatars* constitute another Turkic group.[13] The *Volga Tatars* live along the middle reaches of that river and to the east of it and include the Kazan Tatars (descended from the Kazan Khanate). The *Siberian Tatars* are found in Western Siberia north of Kazakhstan in the Tiumen', Tobolsk, and Tara regions and near Tomsk. The *Crimean Tatars,* who lived in the Crimea from the thirteenth century until World War II, were forcibly resettled in Central Asia because of their opposition to the Soviet regime. They have sought unsuccessfully by means of protests and petitions to obtain permission to return to the Crimea. The *Bashkirs* live on the southern slopes of the Urals and on the adjacent steppe. The discovery of petroleum on their territory led to an influx of outsiders, but the number of Bashkirs has increased, as has the percentage declaring Bashkir to be their native language. The *Chuvash* are related to the Turkic peoples linguistically, although they are mostly Christian rather than Moslem and have been subjected to russification; their homeland lies to the southeast of the great bend in the Volga River, and their capital is at Cheboksary. Other Turkic people are the *Iakuts* (also Christianized), the *Kara-kalpaks* (who live in northwestern Uzbekistan), the *Tuvinians* (of the Mongolian border area), the *Karachais* and *Balkarians* of the Northern Caucasus, and the *Gagauzy* (a Christianized Turkic minority living in Bessarabia).

The *Tadjiks* are linguistically an Iranian people who are often associated with Turkestan because they inhabit its southeastern corner on the Afghan frontier and are Moslems. The Tadjiks live in a land of high peaks in the Pamirs, and in addition to mining they engage in agriculture and animal husbandry in the valleys. Their capital, Diushambe, was named Stalinabad from 1929 to 1961.

Mongol peoples of Buddhist culture in the Soviet Union include the *Buriats* of the Lake Baikal region (related to the people of the Mongolian Peoples Republic) and the *Kalmyks,* who live west of the mouth of the Volga river, having settled there in the eighteenth century.

The *Armenians* in the Soviet Union are the heirs of an old Christian culture that was flourishing and had a written alphabet long before the development of the Russian nation. When Christianity was introduced in A.D. 303, Armenia became the world's first Christian state; later it developed a unique national church, which has its center at Etchmiadzin. Situated to the north of Iran and

---

[13]The term *Tatar* originally was a popular and imprecise name used for the Mongols by the Chinese, Moslems, and Europeans. Certain Turkic peoples acquired the name when they were subjugated by the (non-Turkic) Mongols and became allied with them in military campaigns. The army of the Golden Horde, which subjugated much of Russia in the mid-thirteenth century, had a Mongol nucleus but was composed largely of Turkic warriors. The Horde's Slavic subjects called both the Mongols and the Turkic invaders "Tatars."

Turkey, Armenia was long exposed to Persian and Turkish influences. The arrival of Russian military forces in the area south of the Caucasus Mountains and the Russian acquisition of Armenian territory from Persia in 1828 (Treaty of Turkmanchai) caused the Armenians to seek Russian protection against their non-Christian neighbors and to become pawns in Russia's efforts to defeat the Ottoman Empire. The collapse of the Russian Empire enabled the Armenians, who had been under Russian rule, to proclaim their independence in May 1918, under the leadership of the Dashnak Party; Soviet Russia invaded Armenia in November 1920 and established a small Armenian Soviet Republic with its capital at Yerevan. However, many Soviet Armenians live outside the boundaries of Armenia, mostly in neighboring Azerbaidjan and Georgia.

The *Georgians,* whose country on the eastern shores of the Black Sea south of the Caucasus is more correctly known as *Sa-kartvel-o* in Georgian (*Gruziia* in Russian), possess an ancient and unique language and culture far older than that of the Russians. Converted to Orthodox Christianity by Saint Nina in the fourth century, the Georgians—like the Armenians—were subjected to numerous foreign incursions, often accompanied by pillaging and devastation. However, the ancient capital of Mtskheta (with its extant great cathedral, Sveti Tskhoveli, behind fortress walls) remained a bastion of Georgian culture, as did Tbilisi, the capital since the fifth century. In the late twelfth and early thirteenth centuries, during the reign of Queen Tamara, Georgia experienced a cultural flowering personified by the poet Shota Rustaveli. The hostility of Turkey and Persia caused the Georgians to seek Russian protection at the end of the eighteenth century, which led to annexation in 1801. In May 1918, Georgia seceded from Russia; and its independence was recognized by Moscow in a treaty of May 7, 1920. However, in February 1921, Soviet Russia invaded Georgia and established a Georgian Soviet Republic after defeating the Social Democratic government, which had proclaimed the country's independence. One of the reasons for the Soviet invasion was Georgia's rich manganese deposits at Chiatura, as well as its tea, citrus fruits, viticulture, and fine wineries. Georgia is a colorful land whose people are proud of their heritage and have a high degree of national consciousness.

The *Lithuanians* are the most numerous of the three Soviet Baltic peoples. Like the Estonians and Latvians, they belong neither to the Slavic nor to the Germanic worlds but constitute a separate ethnic entity. Lithuanian is an old Indo-European language related to ancient Sanskrit and is of great interest to philologists. The Lithuanians have been predominantly Roman Catholic since 1386, when their king, Jogaila, married the Polish Queen Jadwiga and a union of the two countries resulted.

The *Latvians* speak a language that is related to Lithuanian (although subjected to Germanic and Russian lexical influence). German influence among the Latvians was very considerable as a result of their having been under the rule of the Teutonic Order, a body of military crusaders sent ostensibly to convert the Baltic peoples to Christianity in the twelfth century but which established a harsh system of rule and cruelly exploited the native Latvians. Riga, the capital, early emerged as the commercial, ecclesiastical, and political center. The presence of

German rulers caused the Latvians to embrace Lutheranism early in the sixteenth century, although Latgallia remained Catholic. By 1561 the Order was secularized and the descendants of the knights became powerful, landowning laymen ("Baltic Barons"). The attempt of Muscovy's Ivan the Terrible to break through to the Baltic in the second half of the sixteenth century and the developing conflict between Muscovy and the Polish-Lithuanian State led to the establishment of Polish suzerainty over most of Latvia. This was followed in the seventeenth century by Swedish rule, which ended in 1721 when the Russian Empire annexed Latvia.

The *Estonians* speak a Finno-Ugrian language and are related to their neighbors, the Finns.[14] They are of the Lutheran faith. Estonia's history has paralleled that of Latvia—with seven centuries of foreign rule by Danes, German crusading knights and nobles, Poles (in southern Estonia), Swedes, and Russians. The rule of the Swedish Vasa kings was the most enlightening, in relative terms, and led to the founding of the University of Tartu in 1632. Imperial Russian rule left intact the privileged position of the German nobles and even enhanced it—as in Latvia—and also brought attempts at russification. Estonia, Latvia, and Lithuania enjoyed two decades of political independence between the two world wars, only to be annexed by the Soviet Union in 1940 and reduced to the status of soviet republics.

The *Jews* were originally regarded with suspicion and hostility by the Muscovite State, which excluded them from permanent residence. The Jewish population under Russian rule was acquired by Catherine II as a result of the partitions of the Polish State. Most of this population had originally left the German lands and Bohemia during the twelfth and thirteenth centuries and settled in Poland, Lithuania, Ukraine, and Belorussia. The Jews played an important role in the development of commerce and industry in the areas under Polish rule. Annexation by Russia meant that almost all Jews were confined to the Pale of Settlement in Ukraine and Belorussia and experienced various forms of official discrimination. Although the Soviet regime initially provided many opportunities for Jews, their involvement in the system was subsequently circumscribed, and many have sought to emigrate.

The Soviet *Moldavians* are actually Romanians, most of whom live in Bessarabia, which lies between Ukraine and Romania. They differ from the Romanians principally in having been compelled to use the Slavic Cyrillic alphabet rather than the Latin alphabet in their language. Prior to 1812 Bessarabia was part of the greater Moldavian Principality (now Eastern Romania) under Ottoman Turkish suzerainty. From 1812 to 1917 Bessarabia was part of the Russian Empire, and from 1918 to 1940 it was included in Romania. The Soviet Union seized Bessarabia from Romania in June 1940. Soviet Moldavia's capital is at

---

[14]Other Finno-Ugrian peoples in the Soviet Union include the Udmurts, Mordovians, and Mari—each of whom has an autonomous republic in the area of the great bend in the Volga River east of Moscow. These peoples have been under extensive Russian pressure—as have the related Komi people in the Far North.

Kishinev (Chisinau) and its population has been traditionally Orthodox Christian.

Other peoples who live in the USSR include Germans, Poles, Bulgars, Koreans, Greeks, Hungarians, Gypsies, and Kurds; they do not have their own politico-administrative units, as they are dispersed over various parts of the Soviet Union. The Volga Germans had an autonomous republic until their deportation to Central Asia in September 1941 as a preventive measure. They were "rehabilitated" in August 1964, but their republic was not restored and they could not return to the Volga region. Most of the major nationalities of the Soviet Union have separate union republics that, together with the Russian S.F.S.R., constitute the USSR.

FORMATION OF THE SOVIET UNION

With the formal proclamation of the Russian Socialist Federated Soviet Republic in July 1918, at the time its first constitution was adopted,[15] the world's first communist regime was formally established by V. I. Lenin and was to become the future nucleus of the USSR. The Russian communist regime—in an effort to distinguish itself from Imperial Russia—had already promulgated a "Declaration of the Rights of the Peoples of Russia" on November 2 (15), 1917.[16] This document, signed by Lenin and Stalin, promised the non-Russian nationalities complete equality and sovereignty and the right of self-determination, including the right to secede and establish independent states.[17] The non-Russian nationalities accepted this document at face value and proceeded to secede from the defunct Russian Empire and its Soviet successor state. Thus, the Soviet regime granted recognition to the anticommunist Ukrainian People's Republic on December 4 (17), 1917, and to independent Finland's new government on December 18 (31), 1917.[18] However, in each case the Russian communists endeavored (with the aid of such non-Russian communist support as they could find) to overthrow these regimes and replace them with communist regimes. Finland succeeded in preserving her independence from Russia (proclaimed after 108 years of Russian rule), while Ukraine, Belorussia, Georgia, Armenia, Azerbaidjan, and Turkestan were invaded by Moscow's forces and had Soviet rule imposed upon them by 1920–1921.

However, the fiction of independent Soviet republics had to be preserved.

---

[15]Following the seizure of power by the communists in central Russia in November 1917, the regime was first known as that of the Russian Soviet Republic or as the Republic of Soviets of Workers, Soldiers, and Peasants Deputies. With the adoption of the 1936 Constitution, the words *socialist* and *soviet* were transposed to read Russian Soviet Federated Socialist Republic.

[16]The use of two dates for events occurring prior to February 1 (14), 1918, is due to the fact that Russia until that time adhered to the Julian calendar, which in the twentieth century was thirteen days behind the Gregorian calendar. The Russian Orthodox Church has continued to observe the Julian calendar, but the Gregorian calendar has replaced it in all aspects of public life.

[17]*Istoriia Sovetskoi Konstitutsii, sbornik dokumentov, 1917–1957* (Moscow: Akademiia Nauk SSSR, 1957), pp. 19–20.

[18]*Ibid.*, pp. 32–33, 36. Also see D. L. Zlatopol'skii, and O. I. Chistiakov, *Obrazovanie Soiuza SSR* (Moscow: "Iuridicheskaia literatura," 1972), pp. 26–27.

By 1921 the Russian, Ukrainian, and Belorussian Soviet republics had entered into treaty relationships that governed military and economic affairs. In foreign affairs there was nominal independence, reflected in the participation of the Ukrainian S.S.R. along with the Russian S.F.S.R. in the negotiation of the Treaty of Riga with Poland (March 18, 1921). However, on February 22, 1922, the non-Russian Soviet republics as well as the so-called Far Eastern Republic signed a protocol in Moscow that authorized the Russian S.F.S.R. to represent them at the Genoa Conference.[19] This act presaged the formal absorption of these republics into the Soviet Union.

With the liquidation of the Far Eastern Republic in November 1922 and its annexation by the Russian S.F.S.R., the stage was set.[20] The Union of Soviet Socialist Republics was formally established on December 30, 1922, with four constituent parts (union republics): the Russian S.F.S.R., the Ukrainian S.S.R., the Belorussian S.S.R., and the Transcaucasian Socialist Federated Soviet Republic (consisting of Armenia, Azerbaidjan, and Georgia). The Russian S.F.S.R. in 1923 included much of Turkestan; but the remainder of that region was organized as two "soviet people's republics," Khorezm and Bukhara, populated largely by Uzbeks. In October 1924, two new union republics were created—the Uzbek and Turkmen—and all of Turkestan was divided into separate so-called national states. In December 1929, the number of union republics increased to seven when the Tadjik Autonomous S.S.R. was elevated in status (largely in the hope of enabling Moscow to influence developments in neighboring Afghanistan). The adoption of the 1936 Constitution saw the number of union republics increase to eleven as a result of the dissolution of the Transcaucasian Federation and the transformation of the Kazakh and Kirghiz autonomous republics into union republics. World War II added four more union republics to the USSR with the annexation of Estonia, Latvia, Lithuania, and Bessarabia (Moldavian S.S.R.).[21]

The establishment of the Soviet Union as a nominal federation of national republics, one which has grown in size, resulted from a number of causes. The Soviet Union was a means of replacing the Russian Empire under a new name, with an apparently different form of multinational structure harnessed to the objectives of communist political action. In view of the fact that communist regimes were established in the non-Russian lands largely as a result of the

---

[19]Mikhail I. Kulichenko, *Obrazovanie i razvitie Soiuza SSR* (Yerevan: "Aiastan", 1982), pp. 198–199. The Soviet republics were Ukraine, Belorussia, Georgia, Azerbaidjan, Armenia, Bukhara, and Khorezm.

[20]The Far Eastern Republic was formally established in April 1920, exercising authority over Eastern Siberia; its capital was at Chita. It served as a convenient, communist-controlled Russian buffer state between the Russian S.F.S.R. and the part of Siberia occupied by the Japanese, as well as a means of misleading opinion and of bringing about an end to Japanese military intervention.

[21]Between 1940 and June 1956—as a result of the existence of the Karelo-Finnish S.S.R.— there were sixteen union republics. This republic, located between the White Sea and Lake Ladoga and inhabited largely by Russians, became a union republic in March 1940, following the Soviet war against Finland, and included depopulated territory seized from that country. The decision taken in 1956 to reduce this republic to its former status as the Karelian Autonomous S.S.R. (and to eliminate the reference to a Finnish population) was due, in part, to the small number of Finns living in the Soviet Union. See Zlatopol'skii and Chistiakov, *op. cit.* (above, n. 18), pp. 286–287.

preponderance of Russian arms, it followed that these regimes had no choice but to accept full union with Soviet Russia. Since the non-Russian Communist parties were treated as subordinate units of the Russian Communist Party, it was logical that centralism in Party structure and rule by a single party should be accompanied by governmental centralism, in lieu of the earlier treaty relationships between the republics. The subjugated status of the non-Russian Communist parties became evident when they were denied membership in the Third Communist International (Comintern), founded by Moscow in March 1919.

The official name of the Russian S.F.S.R. reveals a significant lexical distinction in the Russian language. It is, in Russian, called the *Rossiiskaia* republic and *not* the *Russkaia* republic. The choice is revealing because the adjective *russkaia* means "ethnically Russian," while the adjective *rossiiskaia* includes both ethnic Russians and non-Russian subject peoples, reflects the imperial obsession, and was also the name of the Russian Empire. In (mis)translating *rossiiskaia* into English as "Russian," one loses its true meaning. Since Moscow is the capital of both the Russian S.F.S.R. and the USSR, the Soviet Union can be seen as a Russian creation ruled from Russia's traditional capital. Thus the Soviet Union is *not* a nation-state, but it cannot be understood apart from the Russian political heritage that is discussed in Chapter 2.

Before proceeding to a consideration of the major components of the Soviet polity, it is essential to examine certain aspects of the physical and social environment within which the polity functions. To this end it is important to consider at least briefly the country's geography and climate and certain essential facts regarding its economy and social strata, as well as some of the distinguishing features that make the Soviet Union unique.

THE LAND AND CLIMATE

The vastness of the Soviet Union, with its 8.6 million square miles of territory, makes it the world's largest area under a single political regime. From the Baltic Sea to the Bering Sea and the North Pacific, this one-sixth of the earth's landmass extends a distance of more than 6000 miles over 150 degrees of longitude. Thus, when it is noon on the Soviet-Polish frontier, it is 11:00 P.M. in the easternmost extremities of this far-flung modern empire. From north to south, exclusive of the bleak Soviet island possessions in the Arctic, it extends, in varying width, from 1800 to 2600 miles.

Although the Soviet landmass is more than twice the size of the United States, a simple comparison based on area is misleading. A demographic map of the Soviet Union makes it clear that large parts of the country are not conducive to protracted habitation for sizable populations. In certain areas, such as the Ukrainian and Moldavian Soviet Republics, the density of population approaches that of parts of Western Europe; but the USSR as a whole has an average population density only one-ninth that of Western Europe. Thus, there is a large area of high concentration of population in the western and southwestern parts of the Soviet Union, while to the east there is a long, thin, sparsely settled belt extending along the Trans-Siberian Railway to the Maritime Region north of

Vladivostok. The entire eastern half of the country has but 10 percent of the total population.

Zones

Although the USSR (with its population of more than 282 million in 1987) is the world's third most populous country, it is not a large population for such an enormous area. This is due to the quality of Soviet territory and to climatic conditions. The land is divided into a series of zones based on soil, vegetation, fauna, topography, and climate. In the Far North the *tundra zone,* constituting nearly 15 percent of the USSR, extends from the Murmansk area in the northwest across to the northern part of the Kamchatka Peninsula. It is treeless and supports only mosses, lichens, and berries; in winter it is a frozen wasteland, and in the brief, pale summer surface-thawing creates marshy conditions in which gnats and mosquitoes abound. The *forest zone* is the world's largest and covers 52.5 percent of Soviet territory. It extends in a broad belt from Finland and the Baltic Sea across the entire central portion of the European USSR and Siberia. Coniferous forests cover the northern part of this zone and most of Siberia (the *taiga*); in the southern part mixed deciduous and coniferous forests predominate.

The forest zone gradually gives way to the *steppe zone,* covering approximately 17 percent of the USSR and extending from the Ukrainian Republic in the west to the Altai Mountains, which border on the Mongolian People's Republic. The treeless steppe includes the rich black earth *(chernozem)* area with its soil of high humus content. The arable part of the Soviet Union is limited largely to this belt, in which the quality of the soil and dependability of rainfall decline as one moves eastward. To the south of the steppe zone lie the *semidesert* and *desert zones,* which comprise approximately 13 percent of Soviet territory and extend from the northern and eastern shores of the Caspian Sea to the valleys and high mountains of Soviet Central Asia (Turkestan), where China, Afghanistan, and Iran border on the USSR. Irrigation has made possible the cultivation of parts of these zones having better soils. The Amur and Ussuri areas in the Soviet Maritime Region east of Manchuria, along with the eastern part of Kamchatka, constitute a special maritime zone with cold winters and cool, moist summers. Two small *subtropical zones* extend over 2 percent of the country. These include the southern tip of the Crimean Peninsula, the eastern coast of the Black Sea, and the area south of the Caucasus Mountains. These areas are exceptional in that they receive rather heavy rainfall and enjoy a mild climate because of their sheltered location between mountain ranges and the sea.

In marked contrast to the subtropical zones is the 43 percent of Soviet territory that is affected by permafrost. This special zone, which includes the entire tundra zone and most of the eastern half of the country, extends far south of the Arctic Circle and is distinguished by the failure of the subsoil to thaw during the brief summer. In the Soviet Far North the subsoil is perpetually frozen to depths of several hundred feet. Although the depth of the permafrost diminishes as one moves southward in Siberia, it creates difficulties in construction and agriculture.

Most of the Soviet Union is a vast plain extending from Poland and the Baltic Sea to the Yenisei River in Central Siberia. This plain is interrupted by the Ural Mountains, which are old and rounded and form a low barrier between European Russia and Siberia. The average altitude of the great East European plain is 600 feet. Beyond the Urals lies the West Siberian Lowland, which is centered on the Ob' River basin. The forested lowlands contain the world's largest bog and have poor drainage because the Ob' River has a very slight gradient, sluggishly descending only 295 feet in the 1860 miles between Novosibirsk and its mouth. The Central Siberian Plateau, between the Yenisei and Lena rivers, varies in altitude from 1300 to 1900 feet. Eastern Siberia beyond the Lena River is mountainous and includes such ranges as the Verkhoiansk, Cherskii, Kolyma, and Anadyrskii (or Chukotsk) Mountains, which reach heights of from 6000 to 9750 feet. In southeastern Siberia the Iablonovyi, Stanovoi, and Dzhugdzhur ranges extend from the area east of Lake Baikal to the Sea of Okhotsk. The nature of Eastern Siberia also manifests itself in the rugged topography of the Maritime Region, Sakhalin, and Kamchatka.

Much of the southern frontier of the Soviet Union lies within mountainous areas bordering on the Mongolian Peoples Republic, China, Afghanistan, Iran, and Turkey. This chain of frontier mountain ranges commences in the area west of Irkutsk and Lake Baikal with the Saian Range and continues in the Tannu Ula and Altai ranges. The highest mountain ranges in the Soviet Union are the Tien Shan and Pamir ranges, which lie in the Kirghiz and Tadjik Soviet Republics. The highest peak, Mount Communism—formerly Mount Stalin—(24,590 feet) is in the Pamirs. Farther to the west, between the Caspian and Black seas, lie the Caucasus Mountains. The main range of the Caucasus includes Mount Elbrus (18,470 feet), Europe's highest peak.

Climate

The absence of mountain ranges on the Soviet Union's northern frontier comparable to those in the south exposes the great Eurasian Soviet landmass to the frigid climate of the Arctic. Another factor that causes the Soviet Union to have a severe, extremely continental climate is its distance from oceans, other than the Arctic, which would have a moderating effect—warming the land in winter and cooling it in summer. Thus the climate is for the most part harsh and intemperate and is characterized over much of the area by extremes of heat in the short summer and cold in the long winter. In Leningrad the mean temperature in January is 15° F and in July it is 64° F. In Iakutsk in Eastern Siberia the mean temperature in January is −46° F, while in July it is 66° F. Snow remains on the ground in most of Siberia for at least seven or eight months of the year, yet the heat of summer is often intense.

Much of the Soviet Union has limited rainfall, receiving well under twenty inches of precipitation annually. The Soviet Union lies in the high northern latitudes and extends northward to a greater degree than does North America, so that a far greater part of Soviet territory lies within the Arctic Circle. Leningrad at 60° N is in the same latitude as Seward, Alaska, while Moscow at 55° N would correspond to Edmonton, Alberta, at 54° N. Murmansk at 69° N lies as far north as the middle range of Baffin Island or northwestern Alaska but has an ice-free port. Correspondingly, the southern parts of the Soviet Union also lie rather far north. The Ukrainian capital of Kiev at 50.5° corresponds to Winnipeg, Manitoba, in latitude, while the southernmost point in the Soviet Union at Kushka in Turkmenistan (35° N) is in the latitude of Memphis, Tennessee. Irkutsk and Novosibirsk in Siberia correspond, respectively, to Saskatoon, Saskatchewan, and to the southern shores of Hudson's Bay. Vladivostok, the southernmost port in the Soviet Far East, lies in the latitude of Portsmouth, New Hampshire. The Soviet Union is unusual in being located in such high northern latitudes, and this imposes certain limitations on its development.

INDUSTRY, AGRICULTURE, AND TRANSPORT

Well endowed with natural resources—all of which are state-owned, as is the entire Soviet industrial establishment—the Soviet Union emerged after World War II as the world's second-ranking industrial power. This feat was accomplished as a result of governmental direction of the economy by means of heavy taxation and human deprivation, controls over allocation of labor, and the skewed and forced development of heavy industry (production of the means of production) at the expense of light industry (consumer goods). Thus, between 1940 and 1987 steel production rose from 18.3 million to 162 million metric tons. Coal production, including lignite, more than doubled between 1951 and 1987, reaching a level of 760 million metric tons. Soviet production of electricity during the 1951–1987 period rose from 117 to 1665 billion kilowatt hours. Petroleum output increased phenomenally from 47 to 624 million metric tons between 1951 and 1987 as a result of the exploitation of the newer Volga-Urals and West Siberian oil fields.

Much of this economic growth was facilitated by the development of a new economic heartland in the Urals, southwestern Siberia, and Kazakhstan based on coal and iron deposits of these inner regions. Furthermore, mammoth and costly hydroelectric dams have been constructed on the Angara River at Bratsk and Ust-Ilimsk and on the Yenisei River at Krasnoiarsk and Saiano-Sushensk, although the Soviet Union must still rely primarily on thermal generation of electric power. The development of a formidable industrial establishment has thus enabled the Soviet Union to make great strides in the manufacture of machine tools, a key sector in any modern economy. Yet Soviet industrial development has depended over the years on the continued importation of Western European and American technology. Entire factories—including textile mills, factories for the manufacture of dinnerware and household items, and huge automobile and truck assembly plants—have been imported into the Soviet Union. Large-scale imports of technology enabled the country to concentrate on the further development of military and naval power.[22]

However, the spectacular successes of Soviet industry have not been matched in agriculture. This has been due in large part to natural conditions, such as limited rainfall in the areas of better (chernozem and chestnut) soils, the limited growing season due to the Soviet Union's location in northern latitudes, and the need to use costly fertilizers in the areas of poor, ashlike soils. The amount of arable land, therefore, is limited in spite of the vast territory. Extensive, rather than intensive, agriculture has been the rule—the tendency being to bring marginal land under cultivation instead of increasing crop yields.

In view of the fact that 20 percent of the Soviet labor force is committed to it, Soviet agriculture has been an expensive undertaking. This is a rather wasteful disposition of the labor force for a country with such a high level of industrial development. Another distinctive characteristic of Soviet agriculture has been its organization in terms of gigantic (and often inefficient) farms. Less than half of Soviet agricultural land is cultivated by the collective farms (kolkhozy), which are cooperatives in theory, with the state holding ultimate title to the land. More than half of the agricultural land is held by state-owned farms (sovkhozy), on which the laborers are paid a fixed wage in contrast to the collective farm method of basing members' income on the individual member's labor contribution and on the farm's earnings.

In spite of the resources and large amounts of manpower committed to agriculture, the Soviet Union has had only moderate success in adequately feeding its growing population. It has had difficulty in developing livestock and dairy industries of sufficient quality because of fodder shortages and poor animal husbandry. The need to close the protein gap in the Soviet diet and to compensate for the livestock shortage has led to the establishment of large, modern deep-sea fishing fleets, which operate in waters remote from the Soviet Union.

The establishment of large Soviet fishing and whaling fleets has accompanied the Soviet Union's emergence as a maritime power possessing an impressive merchant marine—much of it constructed in foreign shipyards. This development has occurred in spite of the fact that most of the Soviet ports are icebound for several months of each year. Exceptions include the ports of Murmansk on the Barents Sea; Poti, Batumi, Sukhumi, and Novorossiisk on the Black Sea; and Liepaja and Ventspils (in Latvia), Klaipeda (in Lithuania), and Kaliningrad (Koenigsberg) on the Baltic Sea. Two new ports, Nakhodka and Vostochnyi (east of Vladivostok), are virtually ice-free.

River transport has been limited not only by the fact that Soviet rivers are frozen two or more months of the year in the south and six months in the north, but also by the location and direction of flow. The principal rivers flow in a northerly or southerly direction, while the country's great longitudinal extent

---

[22]The detailed record of Soviet importation of technology between 1917 and 1965 is documented in Antony C. Sutton, *Western Technology and Soviet Economic Development,* 3 Vols. (Stanford: Hoover Institution Press, 1968, 1971, 1973).

creates a demand for transport that the rivers cannot fulfill. Thus, European Russia and Siberia are not linked by a network of waterways except for the Arctic maritime link provided by the Northern Sea Route. However, this waterway can be traveled only during the short summer navigation season and often requires the use of icebreakers. In the European part of the USSR, navigable rivers and a system of canals link the White and Baltic seas with the Black and Caspian seas. Yet river transport, though increasing in tonnage over the years, has declined relative to rail transport.

The state-owned railways remain the prime mode of transport and have been carrying the greater part of Soviet freight. The Soviet railroad network is far less dense than that of the United States and corresponds generally to the population pattern. Soviet railroads cover enormous distances and are used extensively. The country leads the world in electrified rail lines. The widely dispersed location of Soviet natural resources, industrial establishments, and markets has resulted in high transportation costs and in high traffic density. There is no hard-surfaced, all-weather network of highways linking the various parts of the Soviet Union, and a motor trip across the country would not be recommended. As a result, the trucking of freight is confined largely to the more densely populated areas.

The absence of a modern highway system and the vastness of the country have necessitated the development of an extensive network of airways. In addition, the Soviet civil air fleet has military significance, as well as usefulness in cartography, in crop-dusting, and in aerial reconnaissance—as, for example, in guiding vessels through the pack ice on the Northern Sea Route. Soviet interest in transpolar flight was demonstrated as early as 1937, when two nonstop flights were made from Moscow to Vancouver, Washington, and San Jacinto, California, in single-motor aircraft. Governmental direction and a willingness to ignore the cost factor in selected cases enabled the Soviet Union to inaugurate the first successful international jet civilian passenger service in August 1956, with the Tupolev-104. However, it failed with the TU-144 supersonic transport, which was apparently based on an imprecise model of the successful British-French *Concorde*. The state-owned airline, Aeroflot, enjoys a monopoly and claims to be the world's largest air carrier.

SOCIAL STRUCTURE

Communist ideology has required the Soviet leadership to claim that the Soviet Union is in the process of establishing a "classless" society. This assertion is based upon the assumption that exploitation of man by man and the resultant class differences derive solely from precommunist societies and are to be found only in "bourgeois" or "capitalist" countries. However, it is a fact that marked differences exist between the various strata of the Soviet population. While claiming that the entire Soviet population consists of "toilers," the regime was compelled to recognize the existence in the Soviet Union of two "friendly" classes—the workers and peasants—and a "stratum" in the case of the intelligentsia.[23] However, the 1977 Constitution, in its Preamble, refers to "social strata" and to the "union of the working class, the collectivized peasantry, and the people's intelligentsia." Soviet society is said to be characterized by "sociopolitical unity" and the working class is said to be its "leading force." Yet the Preamble asserts that "the highest goal of the Soviet state is the building of a classless communist society." The 1986 Communist Party Program reaffirmed these social distinctions and proclaimed the "indestructible alliance" of the three strata and also predicted that "the formation of a socially homogeneous society will be completed in the highest phase of communism."

The criteria for distinguishing between classes include income differentials (reflected in housing, clothing, education, and living standards), status and prestige and the varying degrees of deference accorded certain groups and occupations, and the degree of influence and self-expression enjoyed by various groups; all are applicable to Soviet society and its class structure. Indeed, among the factors that have led to distinct social stratification is the industrial and urban Soviet economy—which has required an extensive hierarchy, a complex division of labor, and various kinds of technical expertise. The elitist nature of the Communist Party, with its political hierarchy and its use of various incentives in an economy characterized by various scarcities, has also been an important cause of stratification.

The total Soviet population of 277.4 million in 1985 was 65.3 percent urban and 34.7 percent rural (as contrasted with 48 percent urban in 1959). Females outnumbered males in 1985 by 17.2 million and constituted 53.1 percent of the population. However, Soviet data on social classes are hardly revealing because they refer to broad categories that embrace more than one stratum. Such categories as "workers" or "employees" are not homogeneous. A more realistic image of the class structure of the Soviet population requires that it be viewed in terms of the following strata: the Soviet ruling class, the "middle class," the intelligentsia, the urban working class, and the peasantry.

The ruling class cannot be equated with the entire membership of the Communist Party of the Soviet Union, but only with its leading cadres, which in turn must be viewed in terms of gradations of status and degrees of influence. Even all members of the Party's Central Committee are not equal in status and influence, and this pattern persists downward through the hierarchy of Communist Party officialdom. Another definition of the communist ruling class or elite is found in the "new class" concept of the disillusioned Yugoslav communist, Milovan Djilas (a former vice-president of Yugoslavia). According to Djilas, the new class of owner-exploiters consists primarily of certain members of the party and state bureaucracy and is said to be the principal beneficiary of the country's economy. Thus, in spite of the myth that all natural resources and the means of

---

[23]Iakov N. Umanskii, *Sovetskoe gosudarstvennoe pravo* (Moscow: Gosiurizdat, 1959), p. 95. Cf. "Sotsial'naia osnova SSSR" in B. N. Topornin, ed., *Konstitutsiia strany sovetov, slovar'* (Moscow: Politizdat, 1982), pp. 243–244.

production belong to the "people," the "fruits of the revolution" go to this elite that, says Djilas, enjoys the "right of profit and control" of nationalized enterprises. The new class, having at its disposal the entire state machine, replaces the former capitalists and employs "socialist ownership" as a disguise for its having arrogated to itself the right to enjoy and dispose of nationalized property as it pleases.[24] An example of ostentatious wealth was the Soviet leader Leonid Brezhnev's collection of foreign automobiles.

Yet the Communist Party leaders, government officials, and managers do not directly own the means of production and cannot bequeath them to their heirs, although they do control them, exercising a form of custodial "ownership" and enjoying many perquisites. These include country homes, automobiles, vacations at the best resorts, discounted purchases at special closed stores that purvey imported goods, superior medical care, and opportunities to travel abroad. Their heirs can be given distinctive higher education, social status, personal property, valuables, bank accounts, automobiles and homes—all signs of privilege—and they can also be provided with well-paying and prestigious positions in the Soviet academic and scientific establishments.

The term *nomenklatura* has been used synonymously with the "new class" or elite to refer to the scores of thousands of Soviet officials whose appointments require the approval of the Communist Party apparatus. The nomenklatura system is based on lists of responsible positions that cannot be filled without the approval of the appropriate Communist Party officials or whose incumbents are selected directly by those officials. Thus the nomenklatura represents the most privileged part of the Soviet elite.[25]

The Soviet "middle class" includes both Party members and non-Party members who serve the regime and benefit from it. It differs from the old petit bourgeoisie in that it is state-created. This stratum includes managerial and technical personnel, accountants, clerks, and persons performing various kinds of semiprofessional or specialized functions that in the West would be termed "white-collar" positions. Although it is regarded as part of the Soviet working class, the middle class is frequently distinguished as "salaried" or as "employees" *(sluzhashchie)*. In 1987 it was said to constitute 26.2 percent of the population.

This class overlaps with the intelligentsia, which in its broadest and hardly meaningful definition formerly included nearly all persons engaged in mental labor.[26] Defined more precisely, the intelligentsia can be said to engage in mental work of a complex and creative nature in the various professions and especially in education, literature, the arts, economic management, engineering, and the

[24]Milovan Djilas, *The New Class; An Analysis of the Communist System* (New York: Praeger, 1959), pp. 27, 35, 39f., 42, 44, 45, 47, 49f., 61f., 81, 82.

[25]See the work of the historian and former Soviet citizen Mikhail Voslensky, *Nomenklatura: The Soviet Ruling Class* (Garden City, N.Y.: Doubleday, 1984), which provides a penetrating first-hand account of the perquisites and vices of the Soviel elite. A sociologist and former Soviet citizen has estimated the Soviet privileged class to number as many as 12–13 million, including family members. See Ilya Zemtsov, *The Private Life of the Soviet Elite* (New York: Crane Russack, 1985), pp. 52–54.

[26]*Politicheskii Slovar'*, ed. B. N. Ponomarev, 2nd ed. (Moscow: Gospolitizdat, 1958), p. 211.

sciences. The intelligentsia has grown steadily, as have the ranks of skilled manual workers, but the role of the intelligentsia is especially important as technologies have become more complex and as more of the Soviet political leadership comes from this stratum and must rely upon the advice and specialized knowledge that it can provide.

The urban working class can be divided into three substrata: the highly skilled manual and mental workers in special sectors of industry, some of whom are paid on a better scale than professional persons and constitute a "labor aristocracy"; the semiskilled and rank-and-file workers possessing medium skills; and the disadvantaged, who are grossly underpaid and who perform simple kinds of operations or menial tasks. The Soviet peasantry is distinguished from the urban working class because much of it is employed in "cooperative collectives" (as the collective farms are regarded in communist theory), although the government insists that both classes have common interests as a result of their presence in a "socialist" society that is "building communism." The Soviet regime has, in fact, sought to liquidate the differences between town and country, seeking in the end to convert collective-farm peasants into agricultural laborers devoid of individual plots, livestock, and farm household animals.[27] This class includes such diverse groups as collective-farm administrators, machine operators, herders, milkmaids, and field hands.

The income of peasants has varied with the particular collective farm and depends upon many factors, including the quality of farm management, the price paid by the state for agricultural commodities, climatic conditions, and the location of the farm. Thus the peasantry has been viewed by the regime as an indispensable part of the population but not entirely trustworthy to the extent that it retains the "village capitalist" mentality as reflected in its traditional desire to cultivate land individually. By 1987 it had declined to 12.1 percent of the population—the least numerous of the three officially recognized social classes.

Smaller but distinct strata or substrata of society are to be found in the secret police and security forces, in the professional military officer corps, and among those working on state farms. Those Soviet citizens who have at one time or other been charged with political (or economic) offenses and whose loyalty has been questioned also constitute a distinct group—but one whose opportunities have been limited.

Finally, however—if one discounts the factors of political unreliability and disadvantaged status resulting from lack of ability or opportunity—there nevertheless had been a relatively high degree of mobility in Soviet society. This was due to the expanding nature of the economy and the resultant demand for persons with skills. However, social mobility has been restricted in the 1980s as a result of declining economic growth rates and reduced educational opportunity that favors the children of the privileged. The study of social mobility and opportunity has become the concern of Soviet sociologists, whose discipline was officially recognized in 1958. They are fully aware of differences within the traditional

---

[27]Umanskii, *op. cit.* (above, n. 23), p. 96. Also see V. I. Lenin, *Polnoe Sobranie Sochinenii,* 5th ed., (Moscow: Gospolitizdat, 1961), XXXIX, pp. 15 and 276–277.

threefold classification and are giving attention to the study of class differences and social inequality.

DISTINCTIVE FEATURES

There is much that distinguishes the Soviet Union from other countries and from other political systems. It is the world's only Eurasian country (apart from Turkey) and borders on twelve neighboring states—more than any other country—in a wide arc extending from Norway and Finland to China and Korea. It shares maritime frontiers with Japan and the United States. The Soviet Union has assumed a variety of roles. It is a one-party system as well as a multinational state, but it also serves as a device for what are perceived to be the interests of the dominant, ethnically Russian population. It is a superpower negotiating with the United States, the countries of Western Europe, Japan, and the People's Republic of China, but it also claims to be the center of international communism for a number of ruling and nonruling Communist parties. It professes to be a source of inspiration and material support for the "liberation struggle" of various peoples and is also the center of a military and economic alliance system of Communist states.

In addition to its multiple roles, the sheer size of the Soviet Union has fostered an obsession with bigness that is evident in the gross, large-scale nature of so many aspects of Soviet life. Illustrative of this phenomenon are the gigantic collectives and state farms, the world's largest steel production, and the largest submarine fleet; the Soviet Union also boasts the heaviest nuclear warheads with the greatest megatonnage of detonative power and the largest missiles. The Nobel laureate Aleksandr Solzhenitsyn, in his *Letter to the Leaders of the Soviet Union* of September 5, 1973, referred to the "political gigantism" that has prompted the Russians to involve themselves with the fate of "other hemispheres . . . and the warm oceans."[28] Thus the Soviet Union stands apart from almost all other countries in terms of the scale on which it functions, its efforts to influence other peoples, and the pretentious claims that it puts forward.

Yet vast portions of the country, including certain large cities, have been closed to foreigners. Foreign tourists must travel only on approved routes and may not deviate from them without special permission. Most foreigners who reside in the Soviet Union are kept under surveillance, and long-term residents often live in guarded housing compounds—reminiscent of an earlier Russian practice of the old Muscovite State. The automobiles of resident foreigners bear special license plates that make them readily identifiable. Travel beyond one's place of residence is severely limited. If a foreign resident in Moscow wishes to visit even a part of the country that is "open," permission must be obtained and arrangements made with Intourist, the Soviet travel organization or, in the case of diplomats, with the Foreign Ministry. Foreign embassies are kept under surveillance. With very few exceptions, non-Soviet publications are not available for

---

[28]Aleksandr Solzhenitsyn, *Letter to the Soviet Leaders* (New York: Harper & Row, 1974), p. 55.

sale in the Soviet Union; foreign-language publications that are sold are usually published by foreign Communist parties or organizations.

Detailed and accurate maps of Soviet cities are not published; schematic maps are available for the tourist, but these often omit important information. A telephone directory for any large city is difficult to obtain, and there are no commercially published city directories providing names, addresses, and occupations of residents. However, addresses are available from municipal information offices. The authorities are kept apprised of the movement of persons through the ordinary police *(militsiia)*. Soviet citizens receive an internal passport at the age of 16 that is of indefinite validity. The new internal passport, introduced between 1976 and 1981 in exchange for that introduced by Stalin in December 1932, has three pages for photographs of the bearer at ages 16, 25, and 45. It contains the bearer's surname, given name, and the Russian form of patronymic. It also contains information regarding place and date of birth, nationality, children, family status, military service, and place of residence. There is no provision for social status as in the earlier passport because of the alleged achievement of "socio-political unity."[29] The issuance of passports is administered by the ministries of internal affairs at the republic level. The movement of citizens and tourists within the country is monitored by the ordinary police, and passports must be registered with them even though one is only visiting a city. By withholding residence permits, the authorities are able to limit the size of local populations. Soviet citizens must be prepared at all times to establish their identity and their right to be in a particular place.

It is difficult to obtain access to Communist Party and governmental offices without a pass *(propusk)* or special permission. Soviet politicians—apart from infrequent public appearances—tend to remain aloof and do not indulge in informalities. They prefer the formal statement made from the platform and rarely grant interviews to foreign or Soviet correspondents or hold press conferences. Thus foreign journalists who report on Soviet developments from Moscow must rely mostly on official handouts and on the Soviet press. They cannot engage in in-depth reporting and are limited to interviewing minor officials, and then only with permission. Foreign correspondents are subjected to self-censorship and the fear of expulsion by the authorities. Some correspondents have even been physically assaulted or made victims of various kinds of provocations either to serve as a warning or to prompt their voluntary departure. The Soviet authorities are secretive about many things, including the incidence of crime in Soviet society, the suicide rate, and the personal lives of members of the leadership and the perquisites that they enjoy.

One of the peculiar attributes of the Soviet system is the refusal to acknowledge and honor signed statements of political prisoners formally renouncing their Soviet citizenship. Expression of the desire to emigrate has been equated with

---

[29]The new passport was described by the Minister of the Interior of the Ukrainian SSR, I. Kh. Holovchenko, in an article published in *Molod' Ukrainy,* January 9, 1975. For the full text see *Digest of the Soviet Ukrainian Press,* Vol. XIX, No. 3, March 1975, pp. 7–8. Cf. "Pasport" and "Pasportnaia sistema" in *Iuridicheskii Entsiklopedicheskii Slovar',* ed. by A. Ia. Sukharev et al (Moscow: "Sovetskaia Entsiklopediia," 1984), pp. 242–243.

disloyalty. In certain instances individuals have been permitted to go abroad and have then been deprived of their Soviet citizenship. Soviet authorities have often endeavored to discourage and even prevent marriages between Soviet citizens and foreigners and have at times kept spouses separated for years by insisting that the foreign national leave the Soviet Union and refusing to permit the Soviet spouse to emigrate. Regulations of the USSR Council of Ministers that took effect in January 1987 provided for emigration based on invitations from close relatives residing abroad legally (not in violation of Soviet law). However, they also provided numerous grounds for denying exit visas, including any "reasons affecting the security of the state."

These attributes can be understood in terms of the relevance of past practices and experience as well as the values and self-perceived roles professed by the Russian communist rulers. These fundamental sources of Soviet political conduct are discussed in Chapters 2 and 3 and serve as an essential introduction to the study of the functioning institutional structures of the Soviet polity.

chapter 2

Soviet Political Culture and the Russian Political Tradition

The study of political culture is based on the assumption that peoples are not necessarily alike and that the political ethos varies from one people to another. Each people is regarded as having a distinctive set of political values that determines the form and substance of its political structures and practices. A political culture embodies the "way of life" of a people—its ideals, beliefs, attitudes toward authority, and the norms that serve to condition political behavior, although overt behavior may at times vary from these norms. It reflects the means by which a country was formed as well as the kinds of expectations its subjects have regarding the role of government and relations between rulers and ruled. Political culture involves the sources of loyalty to, and psychological identification with, the prevailing system; it determines the degree of commitment to a country's rulers, the trust that they enjoy, and what they can and cannot do. Among its manifestations is the perceptual factor—the particular ways in which those who share a culture perceive what is transpiring both within and beyond it. Thus, a people's self-image and their image of the outside world are of primary concern to the student of political culture.

The study of political culture is important for an understanding of why Marxism-Leninism has assumed different forms in communist-ruled countries. Communism has developed in divergent ways in Albania, China, Kampuchea under the infamous Pol Pot dictatorship, and Yugoslavia. If Roman Catholicism is a vital component of Poland's culture with which its communist rulers have had to reckon, while the Russians, in contrast, have to a large degree succumbed to the official preachments of "scientific atheism," this profound difference can be explained only in the different values and perceptions of the two peoples. Yet if the Soviet system and Marxism-Leninism were to disappear for some reason, there would not be a total void, because the political culture of the Russians would survive in some form.

The study of Soviet political culture is complicated by a number of factors in addition to those that are usually encountered in this area of investigation. It cannot be confined to the "operational code" of the Politburo or Soviet elite (as derived from Bolshevik Party experience and doctrinal writings and from the pre-Soviet intelligentsia). The modus operandi and the values of the political elite must instead be distinguished from the mass culture; and this is especially necessary in the case of the USSR, where the rulers have sought to impose upon their subjects a particular set of beliefs associated with Marxism-Leninism. The ideas and values professed by the Soviet elite are dealt with in the following chapter, while the concern of this chapter is the impact of the Russian political tradition upon Soviet political culture.

In view of the country's vast size and diversity and the common conflict between overt and normative behavior, it would be erroneous to assume that there is a single, homogeneous Soviet political culture. Rather, there are various subcultures based on region (as those of Leningrad and the Soviet Far East), social class, the rural versus the urban milieu, and the traditional versus the modern outlook. There are also numerous distinctive non-Russian cultures or subcultures in the various republics that often compete with the dominant culture. Yet if the Soviet Union is a cultural mosaic of contrasting and interacting components that has at times experienced extensive fragmentation, it also embodies certain dominant traits that are the central concern of this chapter.

It should be noted at the outset that certain caveats are in order. Although this area of investigation was originally derived from "national character" studies, it should in no sense be regarded as biological (or racist); the subject matter deals, rather, with *learned* behavior that is transmitted over time through succeeding generations but that is also subject to change. Thus, the presence over time of certain recurring cultural traits or behavioral syndromes does not in itself make them innate or immutable. If there is a danger that this area of study can become a vehicle for prejudice, stereotyped views, sweeping generalizations, and polemics directed against particular cultural traits, there is an equal danger in ignoring the impact upon the Soviet regime of Russian attitudes and traditional political practices. To study Russian (and Soviet) cultural traits, furthermore, does not necessarily imply acceptance of a mystical "Russian soul," nor does it mean adoption of a pessimistic view of the Russians.

The investigation of a political culture involves use of a wide variety of data and the astute observations of highly experienced and sophisticated interpreters and students of a people's development.[1] Where possible, mass political culture

---

[1] The relevant literature, methodological problems, and kinds of data are surveyed in Alex Inkeles and D. J. Levinson, "National Character: The Study of Modal Personality and Sociocultural Systems," in Gardner Lindzey, ed., *Handbook of Social Psychology* (Reading, Mass.: Addison-Wesley, 1954), II, pp. 977–1020; in Arvid Brodersen, "National Character: An Old Problem Re-examined," in James N. Rosenau, ed., *International Politics and Foreign Policy* (New York: Free Press of Glencoe, 1961), pp. 300–308; John S. Reshetar, Jr., *Problems of Analyzing and Predicting Soviet Behavior* (New

is studied by means of survey research and public opinion polls, attitude measurement, and intensive interviews. Although these methods have not as yet been applied extensively to Soviet studies, direct observation and oral inquiry of a limited nature have been possible in the Soviet Union since Stalin's death. However, political culture can also be observed "at a distance" by study of historical data, classical literature, folk literature, contemporary fiction, personal documents (including memoirs and life history interviews), proverbs ("collective documents"), language patterns and changing vocabulary, and child-rearing methods. As is to be expected, the use of such a variety of data has led to diverse hypotheses dealing with Russian (and Soviet) political culture.

The discussion of political culture that follows is deliberately eclectic and seeks to present a broad range of theory and interpretive analysis and a variety of evidence. We are dealing with hypotheses and tentative formulations rather than with definitive statements. Our knowledge of what distinguishes Russians from other peoples is not so profound or extensive to permit us to summarily discard any particular theory simply because it might be controversial or discomfiting. A theory or hypothesis can be discarded only if there is a manifestly superior substitute that explains more, is based on a more substantial body of data, and enjoys *more than equal* validity with other attempts at explanation.

THEORIES OF RUSSIAN POLITICAL BEHAVIOR

Attempts to explain the Russian character have ranged from geographic and climatic theories to psycho-cultural and historical ones. For example, the advocates of environmental determinism have emphasized the influence of the harsh Russian climate, the melancholic forests, and the seemingly endless plains.[2] Such speculative hypotheses cannot readily be tested empirically, but they do prompt observers to search for underlying explanations of certain behavioral syndromes.

Interpretive Theories

This body of theory is based largely upon personal observation and the study of historic development, linguistic pecularities, and overt group behavior. Among the most prominent of such observers was the Russian philosopher Nicolas Berdyaev, who described the Russians as a "polarized people to the highest degree, a combination of opposites." He noted that: "One can become enchanted and disenchanted with them; from them one can always expect the unexpected; they are to the highest degree capable of inspiring intense love and intense hatred.

York: Doubleday, 1955). Also see Alex Inkeles, "National Character and Modern Political Systems," in Francis L. K. Hsu, ed., *Psychological Anthropology, Approaches to Culture and Personality* (Homewood, Ill.: Dorsey Press, 1961), pp. 172–208, and Alfred G. Meyer, "Communist Revolutions and Cultural Change," *Studies in Comparative Communism,* Vol. V, No. 4 (Winter 1972), pp. 345–370. For a discussion of definitional problems and methods, see Archie Brown, ed., *Political Culture and Communist Studies* (London: Macmillan, 1984), especially the chapters by Mary McAuley, John Miller, Stephen White, and Archie Brown.

[2]See the Russian historian V. O. Kliuchevsky, *Kurs russkoi istorii* (Moscow: Sotsekgiz, 1937), I, pp. 57–60.

This is a people that evokes the uneasiness of the peoples of the West."[3] Berdyaev contended that the Russian character was formed on the basis of two sets of fundamental opposites: "a native, pagan Dionysiac element and ascetic-monastic [Christian] Orthodoxy." He observed in his own people a series of contradictory characteristics or antinomies:

> despotism, the hypertrophy of the state *and* anarchism, license; cruelty, a disposition to violence *and* kindliness, humanity and tenderness; belief in ritual *and* truth-seeking; individualism, a heightened consciousness of individual personality *and* faceless collectivism; nationalism, self-praise *and* universalism, identification with humanity *(vsechelovechnost');* eschatological-messianic religiosity *and* outward piety; God-seeking *and* militant atheism; humility *and* impudence; slavery *and* rebellion.[4]

Berdyaev, who possessed one of the most brilliant minds of the twentieth century, knew Russia and the West well. He saw the Russians as a contradictory people characterized by dualism that had resulted from long historical experience—a conflict between Eastern and Western cultural influences in Russia and the inability of the Russians to identify fully with either. Although the Russian educated classes did endeavor to assimilate Western ideas, Berdyaev could not regard the Russians as a Western people. The Russian variant of Marxism was transformed into Leninism; and a knowledge of classical Marxism is not of great help in providing one with an understanding of Soviet politics. Berdyaev saw Russian communism as having national roots and regarded Leninism as a Russian phenomenon.[5] Russia's history has been painful and unhappy in Berdyaev's view, involving much suffering. The expansive nature of the Russian—as contrasted with Western conciseness—Berdyaev explained in terms of the boundlessness and formlessness of the Russian landscape. He contended that the "Russian people fell a victim to the immensity of its territory."[6] Having acquired the world's largest empire, it had to impose a despotic regime in order to retain and organize its vast territorial possessions.[7] Ironically, however, this huge empire did not give the Russians the security that they ostensibly sought.

Another interpretive theory—expounded in the early 1950s by the Russian émigré historian of art Wladimir Weidlé—sees Russia as being an integral part of Europe and desiring to identify with the West.[8] Byzantium, from which Eastern Slavdom received Christianity, is regarded by Weidlé as having been part of

---

[3]Nikolai Berdyaev, *Russkaia ideia* (Paris: YMCA Press, 1946), p. 5.

[4]*Ibid.,* pp. 6–7.

[5]The thesis is developed and documented in Nicolas Berdyaev, *The Origin of Russian Communism* (London: Geoffrey Bles, 1948).

[6]*Ibid.,* p. 9.

[7]This view was held by Empress Catherine II, who, on the basis of Montesquieu's writings, contended that the size of her domain required absolutist rule. Montesquieu had held that large states and despotic rule went hand in hand. See Thornton Anderson, *Russian Political Thought, An Introduction* (Ithaca, N.Y.: Cornell University Press, 1967), p. 139.

[8]See Wladimir Weidlé, *Russia: Absent and Present,* trans. by A. Gordon Smith (New York: Random House (Vintage Books) 1961), *passim.* (The English translation was originally published by John Day Company in 1952.)

Europe. The presence of numerous foreigners in Russia's ruling class (including the dynasty founded by Rurik and the successor House of Romanov after the eighteenth century) is cited as proof for this thesis, along with evidence of Russian cultural and scientific borrowing from the West on a vast scale. The reforms of Peter I are also cited as evidence of Russian desire to be part of the West. According to Weidlé, Marxism was viewed by its Russian adherents as a European phenomenon to be adopted in the name of modernity and progress.

The basic question in assessing Weidlé's thesis is how extensive and profound the desire to identify with the West actually has been in Russian society. In fact, it was the Russian aristocracy that spoke French (Russian was the language of the peasants), vacationed at European spas, and built homes and Russian Orthodox churches on the Côte d'Azur. If part of the intelligentsia desired to embrace certain European ideas and ways, another part of this class was no less certain in its rejection of Europe. Finally, Weidlé readily concedes that the Russian peasantry traditionally could not be absorbed into the nation or made to appreciate the meaning of national unity and pride.[9] He also observes that the Russians failed to produce a unified and stable culture. In Weidlé's view Russian culture lacked continuity, completeness, and cohesion and was not comparable to the cultures of France, England, or Italy. Russian history has not been a "success" and has been characterized by upheaval and disruption.[10]

It is Weidlé's contention that the Soviet regime has rejected the values of the West and has reduced its ties with Europe. Indeed, he defines the Soviet Union as an "anonymous" Eurasian empire that has broken with Russia's past. Weidlé's interpretation raises many questions, and his assertion that the Soviet regime is devoid of much Russian content can be doubted. He defines the Russians as a people endowed with humility and charity but incapable of accepting authority, and he contends that the Russians have succumbed to a "fatal antithesis" that has tragically negated what has allegedly been dearest to them. By failing to seek a compromise between supreme ideals and earthly virtues, the Russians have left themselves vulnerable to the very things that they have despised and resisted: hierarchies, command, obedience, injustice, pharisaism, empty rhetoric, and an excess of form.[11] Thus, according to this definition the Russians are the antithesis of most of what they have claimed to profess and to desire. They have fallen victim to harsh rule in an effort to "avoid all rule." Russian history in this view is a series of antinomies resulting from the Russians' apparent inability to achieve self-mastery, overcome their amorphousness, limit their excesses, and pursue modest and attainable goals rather than some "supreme good."

A somewhat different interpretation of the Soviet regime sees it as a reflection of Russia's traditional peasant culture that has been blended with an overlay of modernism. Although Bolshevism was spawned by a segment of the Russian intelligentsia, the Soviet regime and the Communist Party were subsequently taken over by opportunistic Russian peasant types who left the village, became

---

[9]*Ibid.,* p. 115.
[10]*Ibid.,* pp. 17–18, 26, 47, and 117.
[11]*Ibid.,* pp. 168 and 171–172.

Party members, and made careers for themselves in the large cities, stamping the peasant imprint upon the regime. In this view, expounded by Nicholas Vakar in his *The Taproot of Soviet Society* (New York: Harper & Row, 1961), the Soviet regime came to embody the triumph of ruthless, hardheaded, and power-conscious rustics, who, under other circumstances, would probably have been *kulaks* (tightfisted, resourceful peasants who acquired wealth initially through usury).

The traditional Russian peasant society promoted conformity through the system of communal landholding and periodic redistribution of the land, and by means of the patriarchal family. The maintenance of paternal authority, based on tradition and on physical beating, bred resentment—but it also made acceptance of a political leader more likely. The peasant family was an autocratic order that came close to being a totalitarian dictatorship in microcosm. Peasant life was characterized by hostility and tension resulting from conflict with the father, quarrels with neighbors, and the presence of a landlord and of overbearing officials. It existed in cultural isolation and allowed little personal privacy; it was a closed society that provided little room for individualists, although the peasant still retained a certain sense of pride and was suspicious of strangers.

Thus, the Russian village—or at least part of it—emerged triumphant when it took over Lenin's party of disaffected intellectuals and effected a second revolution under Stalin. Harsh, covetous, calculating, cunning, and ruthless peasant types and their scions became the new Soviet ruling class. This thesis relegates Marxist-Leninist ideology to a secondary place and subject to modification as Soviet society becomes increasingly urban and is modernized. It is especially applicable to the Communist Party leadership from 1953 to 1985 as represented by N. S. Khrushchev, L. I. Brezhnev, and K. U. Chernenko. However, the significance of the thesis lies in its view that the communist model for revolution is inevitably subject to the demands of the native culture, even though that culture is itself subject to change.

The Contribution of Historicism

The emergence in the fifteenth century of an autocratically ruled Russian state based upon Muscovy has prompted the search for its origins in external influences. These have been attributed to two sources: the 240 years of Mongol rule to which the Eastern Slavs were subjected (1240–1480); and the cultural impact of the Byzantine Empire, from which the Slavs received Christianity and other cultural attributes.

The influence of the Mongols upon Russian development has been recognized by prominent Russian historians including Nikolai Karamzin, Paul Miliukov, and the so-called Eurasian School of Russian émigré historians led by Prince N. S. Trubetskoy. The Mongols, leading a large Turco-Tatar force (the two were later referred to as the Golden Horde—from the Turkic *urdu*, "the tent and residence of the khan"), easily succeeded in mastering the steppe and in overrunning and subjugating the Eastern Slavic peoples, who were divided into numerous principalities and could not mount an effective resistance. The Mongols (who were not numerous but who had great mobile military power as armed cavalrymen) not only exacted tribute from their Slavic subjects but exercised a profound impact upon their institutions and statecraft. To the Mongols can be attributed an influence in the system of effective taxation, military organization, census taking, postal system, and intelligence service.[12] Not least of all, Mongol rule—although it recognized religious toleration and granted churches and clergy exemption from taxes and tribute—taught the Russians submission to secular rulers and promoted the rise of Muscovite political absolutism.

The case for making the Mongols responsible for the introduction of "Oriental despotism" into Russia has been stated most forcefully, and with much erudition, by Professor Karl A. Wittfogel. According to his explanation, Oriental despotism emerged in arid or semiarid regions that required the construction of large-scale water-conservancy works and irrigation facilities; it was also present in humid areas in which aquatic plants, such as rice, were cultivated. The need to erect and maintain such facilities led to the establishment of a "single-centered system," in which the despot and his bureaucracy were able to acquire "total power" based on heavy taxation, corvée labor, service to the state, and terror.[13] Although private property existed, in such a system its ownership does not entail political power. In this hydraulic-bureaucratic system, the population is atomized; it exists in villages that are isolated and offer no effective resistance to the single center, the seat of total power. China, to the study of which Wittfogel devoted much of his academic career, provided the classic model of a self-perpetuating Oriental despotism, although Kampuchea in 1975–1979 provided an example based on the construction of water-conservancy works by mass forced labor. However, Wittfogel has also applied the concept of a "hydraulic society" to India, the Near East, and to the Incas. In each case, the state is stronger than society, and both ruler and ruled are alienated and lonely. In contrast, a "multi-centered society" is stronger than the state.

Post-Mongol Muscovy and the Russian Empire that emerged from it are viewed by Wittfogel as a "marginal agrarian despotism" based on the Oriental model, although Russia has a rainfall agriculture and did not develop a "hydraulic economy." The Mongols are said to have introduced into Russia methods of despotic rule that they acquired in China.[14] The kind of state that developed in Muscovy was an absolute service state in which land was distributed and retained conditionally on the basis of service to the ruler (the *pomestie* system). Although Muscovy did not adopt such Oriental institutions as polygamy and political eunuchism, its rulers remained unlimited autocrats until well into the twentieth century. Although pre-Muscovite Russia, by comparison, was not a single-

---

[12]On the Mongol-Tatar impact on Muscovy, see Charles J. Halperin, *Russia and the Golden Horde* (Bloomington: Indiana University Press, 1985). The Russian language was enriched by such Turco-Tartar words as *den'gi* (money), *khalat* (robe), *kreml'* (kremlin), *karakul'* (karakul), *kazna* (treasury), and *kazak* (cossack). The state monopoly of alcoholic beverages, retained under the Soviet regime, was originally adopted from Tatar practice. The culinary meat dumpling specialty known as *pel'meny* was adopted from the Tatars.

[13]See Karl A. Wittfogel, *Oriental Despotism, A Comparative Study of Total Power* (New Haven: Yale University Press, 1957).

[14]See the discussion of "Russia and the East" published in the *Slavic Review,* XXII, No. 4 (December 1963), pp. 627–662.

centered society, Imperial Russia, based on the Muscovite model, was an atomized society of isolated villages lacking roads; and the tsarist bureaucracy could not be effectively challenged by other classes.

It is profoundly ironic that the concept of Oriental despotism was developed and actually applied to Russia by Marx and Engels in the 1850s and that this designation was accepted by such Russian Marxists as Plekhanov and Lenin.[15] Marx, writing in the summer of 1856, described the Mongol impact on Muscovite Russia in the following terms:

> The bloody mire of Mongol slavery, not the rude glory of the Norman epoch, forms the cradle of Muscovy, and modern Russia is but a metamorphosis of Muscovy. . . . [Ivan] Kalita's whole system may be expressed in a few words: the machiavellism of the usurping slave. . . . It is in the terrible and abject school of Mongolian slavery that Muscovy was nursed and grew up. It gathered strength only by becoming virtuoso in the craft of serfdom. Even when emancipated, Muscovy continued to perform its traditional part of the slave as master.[16]

Originally Marx and Engels recognized a distinctive "Asiatic mode of production" apart from their three-stage model for explaining Western historical development in terms of slaveholding, feudal, and capitalist periods. Thus, Marxism originally denied the notion of unilinear development, so widely held during the nineteenth century. In repeatedly referring to Russia as an "Oriental despotism" and as an "Asiatic" country, Marx and Engels expressed an initial awareness of development as a multilinear phenomenon occurring in more than one pattern. Lenin also referred to Russia as "Asiatic" and "savage" and expressed concern that an "Asiatic restoration" might take place despite modernization. The original Marxist-Leninist view of Russia was abandoned by Lenin in 1916 when it became an embarrassing obstacle to the politically expedient notion of unilinear historical development. Under Stalin, the concept of a distinctive Asiatic society was purged from the communist historical and ideological lexicon and was replaced with "feudalism."[17]

The other external influence in Russian development was that of Byzantium, which also had several centuries in which to make itself felt. In Wittfogel's

---

[15]This is amply documented in Karl A. Wittfogel, "The Marxist View of Russian Society and Revolution," *World Politics,* XII, No. 4 (July 1960), pp. 487–508. See also Chap. 9 in Wittfogel's *Oriental Despotism.*

[16]Karl Marx, *Secret Diplomatic History of the Eighteenth Century* and *The Story of the Life of Lord Palmerston,* Lester Hutchinson, ed. (New York: International Publishers, 1969), pp. 111, 112, 114, 121.

[17]By 1884, in *The Origin of the Family, Private Property and the State,* Engels had abandoned the concept of "Oriental despotism," probably because of its disturbing implications for a movement (Marxism) that sought to attain its ends by means of political dictatorship and state ownership of the economy. In the post-Stalin period, largely due to the impact of Wittfogel's research and the developing dispute with the People's Republic of China, Soviet writers were compelled to deal with the problem of the Asiatic mode of production. However, the concepts of a single-centered society and of total power wielded by a state bureaucracy that controls the means of production have had discomforting implications for those who view the Soviet regime as the embodiment of a new order.

view, the Byzantine Empire was an Oriental despotism whose influence on the Eastern Slavs was primarily cultural and did not affect political relationships. Yet a case can be made for Byzantine influence on Russian political thought and values. Byzantium provided a model for the Russian ruler both as a defender of religious faith and dogma and as its propagator; the notion of a state church meant that rulers would be selected on the basis of divine guidance and meant also the general absence of conflict between religious and secular life. Byzantium also served as an example of centralism and of a hierarchic conception of politics. If Byzantium gave the Eastern Slavs and Russians Orthodox Christian religious dogma, liturgical forms, church architecture, and religious art, it also taught them that Europe (Rome) was heretical. Byzantine influence meant that the Russians were to live in cultural isolation, cut off from Roman Catholicism, the Renaissance, and the Reformation. Russian culture was largely clerical (and monastic) and suffered from a lack of respect for secular learning; the clergy did not usually learn Greek or Latin. Byzantium also provided Russia with a static view of truth, so that orthodoxy extended beyond the religious sphere.

Psycho-Cultural Theories

The body of theory that deals with the relationship between Russian culture and personality attempts to identify and explain modal personality traits. While such traits might not be found in all Russians, their presence is regarded as sufficiently widespread, despite the existence of subgroups, to make possible a tentative definition of a modal personality pattern. Personality traits are generally regarded as being derived from child-rearing experiences, preadult learning, and the personal experiences of adult individuals with the regime and with political figures. Personality is viewed as a product not only of the social system but of the political culture as well. Thus, various types of data can be used in the search for modal personality traits and their sources.

One of the more controversial psycho-cultural theories is based on the swaddling hypothesis associated with Geoffrey Gorer and Dr. John Rickman, a physician who practiced medicine in Russia from 1911 to 1918; this theory was also espoused by Dr. Margaret Mead. In an effort to explain the psychology of the Russian national character (in which guilt and group pressure and moral responsibility were all seen as playing a role), Gorer and Rickman concluded that the Russian peasant practice of swaddling infants for all or most of the first year of life provides some possible clues to Russian behavior. According to the practice, still employed in the Soviet Union, the infant is tightly swaddled or wrapped in strips of cloth with its legs straight and its arms at its sides; this involves complete constraint and absence of gratification, alternating with complete freedom and total gratification while the infant is breastfed or bathed and given attention. The swaddled infant can express its emotions only by moving its eyes or by screaming if its mouth is not stuffed with a pacifier. Complete inhibition of movement is followed by its opposite, and the absence of inhibition is then followed by its reimposition when the infant is once again wrapped like a parcel in being swaddled.

The swaddled infant is said to experience "intense and destructive rage" as a result of the complete inhibition of movement. By means of "projection" the infant is said to attribute its own thoughts and wishes to vague figures in its environment and to fear retaliation if it should attempt to gratify its own destructive wishes. However, swaddling makes it impossible for the infant to gratify such destructive wishes, and he is spared the retaliation that he allegedly fears. Central to the hypothesis is the notion that hostility is accompanied by a profound and diffused guilt feeling as well as by fear as a result of this child-rearing practice. Swaddling also allegedly induces in the infant a feeling of "complete loneliness and helplessness" after having exhausted itself both physically and psychologically in expressing rage. Yet the restraint is also seen as preventing gratification of the infant's destructive wishes and as serving to protect the infant from "the fancied perils of retaliation."[18]

Central to the hypothesis is the argument that most Russians manifest a diffuse unconscious feeling of guilt and fear, which originates with the projection of infantile hostility and is subsequently reinforced. In support of this contention, Gorer cites the role of sin and guilt in the Russian Orthodox Church and the relief provided to believers by the ritual of absolution. The importance of enemies and of "dark and sinister forces" is stressed both in traditional Russian folklore and in the Soviet view of historical development ("capitalists," "fascists," "imperialists," "Trotskyites," "Maoists," "neocolonialists," "monopolists"). Public shaming, used in the traditional peasant community, has been employed by the Soviet regime to induce compliance as has the practice of "criticism and self-criticism." Thus, guilt-feeling has been perpetuated.[19] The alleged presence of a "free-floating unfocused hostility" in the Russian people is said to have been reinforced by the Soviet regime in directing popular hatred toward various countries, class enemies, alleged aggressors, warmongers, and reactionary forces.

If "all-pervasive unconscious hostility and guilt" have been attributes of the Russians, then it is understandable that the Russian people have had a tendency to idealize their leadership (whether that of the autocracy or of the Communist Party). Gorer contends that the psychological well-being of the Russians has depended upon their preserving one figure that is supposedly uncontaminated by suspicion, fear, and guilt. Thus, an idealized and strong leadership has been acceptable to Russians, ostensibly to protect them from anarchy and from their own guilt.

---

[18]For Gorer's exposition of his hypothesis and its genesis, see Geoffrey Gorer and John Rickman, *The People of Great Russia, a Psychological Study* (New York: Chanticleer Press, 1950), pp. 93–153, 197–226. The hypothesis was not claimed by Gorer to be more than "one of a presumably large number of antecedents" to the development of the Russian character. He conceded that he undoubtedly overemphasized the possible derivatives of the practice of swaddling and stated explicitly that "it is a clue, not a cause of Russian behavior" (p. 198; cf. pp. 128f.).

[19]*New York Times* correspondent David K. Shipler, while stationed in Moscow in the late 1970s, observed that "Russians move always in a diffuse mist of vague guilt and vulnerability" because of widespread illegality and corruption. He noted that the "sense of perpetual sin is very strong" and is advantageous for the authorities, as it constantly keeps citizens on the defensive and promotes outward compliancy. See David K. Shipler, *Russia: Broken Idols, Solemn Dreams* (New York: Penguin Books, 1984), p. 224.

The polarity that Berdyaev saw in the Russians was also evident to Gorer as an oscillation syndrome that could have had its prototype in the swaddling experience, with its alternating of constraint and gratification. Thus, he, too, noted sudden switches in Russian behavior: total gratification (orgiastic feasting and drinking) followed by fasting and deprivation; violence changing to gentleness; kindness followed by cruelty; and activity followed by passivity. Similarly, "friends" could suddenly be unmasked as "enemies." Such profound changes of feeling, "swings in mood," and manifestations of instability and inactivity were often evident in the conduct of the Russian intelligentsia and in Russian literature; and—it should be noted—they have been condemned by the communists. The Bolshevik "operational code" as defined by Dr. Nathan Leites has advocated control of the emotions and feelings and has condemned "emotional incontinence," fatalism, and passivity.[20]

The apparent tendency to alternate between diametrically opposite extremes has also been seen as originating in the traditional Russian patriarchal family structure. The alternations of kindness and severity, gentleness and brutality, rebelliousness and resignation have been noted; outbursts of feverish activity and euphoria have alternated with inertia, apathy, and despair; Russian tyranny has bred demands for absolute liberty, and these, in turn, have led to reimposition of harsh rule. It is possible that these traits could be attributed originally to Russian child-rearing practices and to familial relationships. It has been contended that the traditional family structure bred persons (especially males) with such traits as dependence, fear, a sense of guilt, mistrust, power-seeking, duplicity, and emotional instability.[21] Traditionally the male has dominated the female, and submission and fear have characterized the father-child relationship. Children experienced different treatment from the father and the mother: the father tended to demand and receive unquestioning obedience while the mother treated children with warmth and solicitude but also exercised firm and sometimes unpredictable authority. The father-son relationship, one of dominance-submission

---

[20]See Nathan Leites, *A Study of Bolshevism* (Glencoe, Ill.: The Free Press, 1953), pp. 186–275 and 314–340 *passim.* Lenin acknowledged "mood swings" in the Russians in a speech on June 12, 1920, in which he identified as a "trait of the Russian character" the inability to sustain an effort and persevere, which leads to "fragility and flabbiness." Thus, military strength, he complained, is transformed into weakness and into "laxity, slovenliness" because a Russian "becomes undisciplined" *(raspuskaetsia)* before a task is completed and a goal attained. V. I. Lenin, *Polnoe sobranie sochinenii,* 5th ed. (Moscow: Gospolitizdat, 1963), Vol. 41, pp. 144–145. Apparently M. S. Gorbachev expressed a similar concern to the Central Committee in June 1987 when he warned against "becoming enraptured with each success but also not falling into despondency *(unynie),* let alone panic, when certain negative phenomena are revealed." *Pravda,* June 26, 1987, p. 3.

[21]This hypothesis has been advanced in Dinko Tomasic, *The Impact of Russian Culture on Soviet Communism* (Glencoe, Ill.: Free Press, 1953), pp. 77–120. Evidence for this hypothesis can be found in Russian folk literature and proverbs and in the *Domostroi,* the sixteenth-century code for family life compiled by the priest Sylvester, counselor and confessor to Ivan the Terrible.

Yet it can also be contended that Russian male assertiveness has been of a compensatory nature concealing an actual male dependence upon the female, who is seen as supportive and as more resilient, persevering, and constant than the male. Feminine strength is reflected in a century of classical Russian and Soviet literature. See Vera Sandomirsky Dunham, "The Strong-Woman Motif" in Cyril E. Black, ed., *The Transformation of Russian Society* (Cambridge: Harvard University Press, 1960), pp. 459–483.

often characterized by physical beating and abusive treatment, is said to have resulted in much tension and mutual hostility. This, in turn, fostered self-pity, along with a sense of insecurity, inadequacy, and guilt feeling, and produced a personality type that is both domineering and/or servile—depending upon circumstances—and one capable of destructive aggressiveness. Insofar as Russian regimes have been based on arbitrariness and coercion, they may be said to have perpetuated and reinforced these traits.

An attempt to identify the traits of the Russian modal personality on the basis of psychological interviewing has provided a degree of confirmation for certain of the statements offered above. Such a survey was undertaken by the British psychiatrist Dr. Henry V. Dicks, who conducted intensive interviews with a group of twenty Russian male defectors, most of whom had served in the Soviet armed forces during World War II. Dr. Dicks observed in his Russians a conflict between oral and anal personality traits characterized by ambivalence and by oscillation in large swings between extremes of behavior. The gratification of oral traits is said to be an important aspect of Russian "need systems." Included here are the Russian preoccupation with food and its acquisition, the fondness for vodka as a means of alleviating tensions, the fondness for talk and singing, and the desire to gratify other impulses quickly and fully. Such outbursts of prodigality, spontaneity, and "manic omnipotence feeling" are succeeded by apathy, hostility, melancholy, and self-depreciation. It is not unusual for feelings of superiority and contempt to alternate with expressions of self-abasement and inferiority.[22]

Dr. Dicks also observed in his respondents a diffuse guilt feeling and a "ruminative self-doubt" as well as a reluctant recognition of a need for an authority that is arbitrary and capable of limiting self-indulgence and providing a "coercive moral corset." Authority *(vlast')* is viewed as something that is to be feared but regarded as necessary; it is expected to be severe and arbitrary, capricious and deprivational, and is resentfully obeyed as well as inwardly resisted, admired, and disliked. The ambivalent attitude toward authority is related to the generally recognized role of the political elite as promoting mastery over the gratification of impulses, mass organization of purposeful activities such as economic growth and achievement of communist goals, and the ability to withstand deprivation. The oral-anal conflict seen in the Russian character means that the subject often recognizes the need for restrictions imposed by those in authority in order to combat anarchic tendencies, depressive apathy, other forms of impulse gratification, paranoid hatred, and self-hatred. Guilt feeling and doubt are coped with through outbursts of organized effort and by the psychological mechanisms of displacement and projection. However, such anal traits as the acquisition of property, punctuality, orderliness, and discipline have not been congenial to the

---

[22]Henry V. Dicks, "Observations on Contemporary Russian Behavior," *Human Relations,* V, 2 (1952), pp. 111–175. Also see Dicks's "Some Notes on the Russian National Character," in Cyril E. Black, ed., *The Transformation of Russian Society* (Cambridge: Harvard University Press, 1960), pp. 636–652; and cf. the related papers in the same volume, especially those of Robert C. Tucker ("The Image of Dual Russia"), Frederick C. Barghoorn ("Some Russian Images of the West"), and J. S. Reshetar, Jr. ("Russian Ethnic Values"), as well as the summary and review by Hans Speier.

Russian culture pattern and have had to be instilled in the population by the regime. Thus, the Soviet regime has literally waged war against the Russian modal personality and has also been affected by it.

The Soviet political elite is said to be generally characterized by the presence of anal (and compulsive) personality traits. This is understandable in ambitious officials who have risen from humble peasant origins. Anal traits are also related to, and lend credence to, the viewpoint of Bolshevism as a "reaction formation." In this interpretation Lenin and his fellow Bolsheviks are seen as having reacted in opposition to certain qualities of the Russian intelligentsia that they regarded as harmful.[23] Yet Dicks has contended that the less attractive features of the Soviet regime have been made tolerable by means of "backsliding" and various forms of oral gratification (including the use of alcohol). Even a harsh and demanding authority can be accepted and tolerated by Russians if it does not become devoid of the paternalistic and human quality and if it does not indulge in *izdevatel'stvo* (mockery and humiliation).

At the same time there is a related Russian tendency to impassiveness reflected in apathy, patience, endurance, and a willingness to bear pain and to accept much with fatalism (the *nichevo* syndrome). There is an apparent need in the Russian to see authority as a source of truth and initiative, and this helps to induce submissiveness. Adjustment to the regime is facilitated also if it permits a degree of personal autonomy. Submissiveness is made acceptable by the Russian need for affiliation and the desire to confide in someone who is safe and friendly. According to Dicks, there is a need to be loved by the group and to be accepted.

Certain key findings of Dr. Dicks's study were confirmed by a survey based on clinical psychological research conducted by the Harvard Project on the Soviet Social System. This investigation involved the interviewing of 51 former Soviet citizens, nearly all of whom were Russians and most of whom (41) were males. The respondents were also given a battery of psychological tests—as was a matched sample of Americans.[24] The results confirmed Dicks's discovery of a Russian need for affiliation and dependence and a strong desire to interact with other people and to enjoy affection. There is also confirmation of orality as a need and preoccupation with food and drink, volubility, and singing. By contrast, the American matched sample stressed achievement (not evident in the Russian group) and need for approval, as well as autonomy without being isolated from the group. The Russians were found to manifest "emotional aliveness" and expansiveness and to be very much aware of their impulses, willing to give in to them but also to be highly cognizant of the need to control them. Yet such impulse-control is not seen as emerging from within the person but as resulting from "guidance and pressure exerted by higher authority and by the group."

The Russians were seen as manifesting behavior or viewpoints of a polarized nature and as being concerned with the choices represented by such alternatives.

---

[23]See Leites, *op. cit.* (above, n. 20), pp. 21–22, 148–165, 201–231.
[24]See Alex Inkeles, Eugenia Hanfmann, and Helen Beier, "Modal Personality and Adjustment to the Soviet Socio-Political System." *Human Relations,* XI, No. 1 (1958), pp. 3–22. Reprinted in Alex Inkeles, *Social Change in Soviet Russia* (Cambridge: Harvard University Press, 1968), Chap. 6.

This tends to confirm Dicks's conclusions regarding the contradictoriness and ambivalence of the Russian character. The Harvard clinical study found its Russian subjects to be consciously concerned with conflicts between trust versus mistrust in relation to others, faith versus despair, and activity versus passivity. Russians are seen as desiring leaders to be warm, nurturant, and considerate of their subjects' welfare. Authority is expected to give orders, require obedience, and exercise initiative; it is also expected to employ coercion and other sanctions to "control bad impulses in individuals" and to be stern and demanding. Whether or not a government is properly elected or follows exact legal procedures is not seen as important; a "good" government is one that provides what Dicks termed an "external moral corset" and is not arbitrary, unjust, and unapproachable. Russians appear to rely less on self-control in curbing emotions and impulses than Americans do. They tend to accommodate themselves passively to difficult situations, while also being "capable of great bursts of activity." Relations between ruled and rulers are seen in terms of a "we"–"they" dichotomy that reflects a basic incompatibility between the political elite and its subjects.

Although the psycho-cultural data from which the modal personality traits of the Russians are derived are not as plentiful in a quantitative sense as one would desire, they nonetheless do provide significant hypotheses and tend to confirm some of the interpretive theories and impressionistic observations discussed elsewhere in this chapter. Ultimate confirmation, refutation, or modification of these psychocultural hypotheses could only be had if a larger sample of Russians (and subsamples from various strata and non-Russian republics) were to be studied *in the Soviet Union* with the same clinical-interview instruments. Such social-science-survey research would not only be very costly but could not be undertaken without the consent of the Soviet regime—an unlikely occurrence.

PERSISTENT SYNDROMES

A political culture—which, as has been shown, can be studied in terms of the behavior and character of a people—can also be studied in terms of the relationship and interaction between national cultural traits and political structures and practices by viewing the latter in the context of their historical development. A functioning polity can remain the product of a people's political tradition even when a revolutionary regime seeks to remake a system and its people on the basis of an official ideology. Political structures and action reflect attitudes and values; and institutions, once established, can also instill or reinforce certain traits.

Political experience, attitudes, and values are transmitted over generations; and historical experience, in turn, influences attitudes and values. Each political culture can be said to have been shaped by the problems that have confronted the country's rulers and to which solutions have been sought over time. The presence of persistent issues and conflicts and the preference for one type of solution to another inevitably have a profound impact upon the political culture. Norms of political conduct, the sources and nature of alienation from the system, and the conditions under which departure from norms is more likely—all must be considered in any attempt at a definition of a people's political culture.

A political culture consists of a set of interrelated traits. While it is possible to find a particular trait in more than one political culture (e.g., Russia, England, and France experienced royal absolutism at particular times), it is the degree to which the trait manifests itself and its intensity over time that are important. Thus, it is the particular combination of traits and their total configuration that are significant and that distinguish one polity from another.

Centralization of Power and the Denial of Autonomy

Probably the most significant fact regarding Russian political culture has been that it spawned an autocratic order and then perpetuated it over a period of four and a half centuries. The advent of Russian autocracy was an outgrowth of the emergence of the principality of Muscovy (Moscow) initially as a modest center in a remote part of the zone of mixed forests during the period of Mongol suzerainty. The princes of Muscovy obtained an advantageous position by pursuing a policy of collaboration with the Mongol rulers and by serving as collectors of tribute from other Russian principalities. They also scored a gain by 1326 in attracting the Metropolitan (Archbishop) of the Orthodox Church to Moscow and causing him to abandon the principality of Vladimir-on-the Kliaz'ma as his see. Although the hierarch was formally subordinate to the Byzantine Patriarchate at Constantinople, his presence in Muscovy and the close relationship between religious and secular authority gave its princes a decided advantage. Soon they appropriated for themselves the title "of all Rus' " that had hitherto been limited to the ecclesiastical jurisdiction of the Kiev metropolitans. Muscovy's rulers also acquired Mongol-Tatar techniques of statecraft and took the lead in resisting the Golden Horde but only when circumstances were propitious. Thus submission and collaboration alternated with guile and various forms of resistance. The policy of collaboration was adopted initially by (Saint) Alexander Nevsky, Prince of Vladimir-Suzdal, who resisted the German Teutonic Knights and the Swedes but who submitted to the Golden Horde. Muscovy took advantage of the errors of other principalities in their relations with the Horde and, in subjugating them, itself became the successor to the Golden Horde.

The leading rival of Muscovy was Novgorod (usually referred to in the Chronicles as "Lord Novgorod the Great"), a principality located to the north and west of Muscovy. The significance of Novgorod lay in its older tradition (it antedated Moscow by approximately three centuries), its role as a great commercial center having ties with the German Hanseatic cities, and its unique political order. Novgorod developed as a republic ruled largely by the commercial and land-owning class. Although it had princes, they were not hereditary princes and were ultimately compelled to consent to having their powers circumscribed on the basis of a written agreement. Occasionally a prince was ousted. Novgorod had as elected officials the mayor *(posadnik),* the head of its militia, and even its bishop after 1156. Sovereignty reposed in the popular assembly *(veche),* the meetings of which (held in the marketplace) were often tumultuous; authority was actually exercised by a small number of local magnates.

If Novgorod rather than Muscovy had become the center of Russian political development in the post-Mongol period, it is likely that Russian political culture would have acquired a very different character from that given it by Muscovy. Instead, Novgorod was subjugated by Ivan III and annexed by Muscovy in 1478. The prince of Muscovy had been able to intervene in Novgorod's internal affairs as a result of conflict within the city's population. Following annexation, Ivan III abolished Novgorod's *veche* and removed to Moscow the great bell that had been used to summon the citizens to this popular assembly. Those in Novgorod who resisted Muscovite rule—numbering more than 7000— were deported, and their homes and lands were given to Muscovites who were sent to replace them. Muscovy was to employ this practice also in subjugating other Russian principalities.[25] The historian Kliuchevsky described the early princes of Muscovy as "shameless plunderers" unhindered by any traditions, lacking any sense of propriety, and guided solely by the desire for self-aggrandizement.[26]

The emergence of absolutist rule in Muscovy occurred in several stages as its rulers extended their domain and claimed more grandiloquent titles and more remote antecedents. In succeeding the rulers of the Golden Horde and also in subsequently claiming the Mongol-Tatar lands, the rulers of Muscovy sought to "legitimize" their self-aggrandizement in various ways. One means was to replace the title of prince *(kniaz')* with that of *tsar',* a Russian version of *caesar.* Ivan IV (the Terrible) was the first ruler to be crowned with this title, in 1547, and he subsequently claimed by conquest the important Mongol-Tatar successor states by proclaiming himself to be "tsar of Kazan" and "tsar of Astrakhan."[27]

The effort to create ties with Byzantium's former rulers and to claim to be the successor to the "Second Rome" had occurred earlier, during the reign of Ivan III—who in 1472 married Sophia Paleologa, a niece of the last Byzantine emperor. Ivan III also assumed the title of *Gosudar'* (sovereign) and was referred to as "autocrat." During the reign of Ivan III there was introduced the so-called cap of Monomakh, which the autocrat placed on his grandson's head. This "crown"— probably of Turkic origin—subsequently became the subject of a legend to the effect that it had been given to Vladimir Monomakh, the Grand Prince of Kiev (1113–1125), by the Byzantine Emperor. The absurdity of this claim, in view of the fact that the hat did not even remotely resemble a Byzantine crown, testifies to the penurious nature of Muscovite legitimacy. The effort to embellish the claim continued when the Abbot Philotheus of Pskov early in the sixteenth century asserted Moscow's claim to be the "Third Rome"—the succes-

---

[25]More than four centuries later, the Soviet regime was to adopt a similar practice in some of the non-Russian republics, deporting large numbers of the indigenous population to Russia and introducing Russians in their place, especially in urban centers.

[26]V. O. Kliuchevsky, *Kurs russkoi istorii* (Moscow, 1937), II, p. 13.

[27]On the Muscovite annexation of Kazan and the questionable claims on which it was based, see the discussion in the *Slavic Review,* Vol. 26, No. 4, December, 1967, pp. 541–583 by Ihor Sevčenko, Edward L. Keenan, Jr., Jaroslaw Pelenski, and Omeljan Pritsak.

sor to Rome and Byzantium. According to this theory both the western and eastern Roman empires had fallen because of heresy, and the task of preserving true religious faith now fell to the Muscovite tsar. As the sole independent Orthodox Christian ruler, the tsar could claim to possess special virtue and demand unqualified obedience.

Muscovite monarchical authority was enhanced during the half-century reign of Ivan IV (the Terrible) (1533–1584), as the power of the aristocratic boyars declined and the tsar's domains increased as a result of foreign acquisitions and domestic confiscation.[28] Ivan's move against his opponents came in January 1565, after he withdrew from Moscow with a military force; when he was asked to return he stipulated conditions, including the right to arrest those whom he deemed disloyal. He launched a policy of terror, torture, exile, and executions; and by confiscating the estates of his victims, he broke the power of the boyar class. He established a royal reserve of land, the *Oprichnina,* from which he rewarded loyal followers. He also established a royal guard, the members of which were known as *oprichniki;* this 6000-man force wore black uniforms, rode black horses, and had a dog's head and broom as its emblem, depicting the sweeping out of traitors. The excesses of this royal force and the increased royal prerogative were a marked departure from earlier practice, in which the grand prince relied on the advice of his boyars. Instead, the tsar regarded his domain as his personal estate, and the boyars and others had little choice but to submit or flee.

Among those who fled was Prince Andrei Kurbskii, who sought refuge in Lithuania-Poland in 1564 after serving Ivan IV for many years. Kurbskii—who, like Ivan, was a member of the Riurikide house—exchanged letters with the tsar, and this correspondence figured prominently in Russian political thought. The Prince attempted to reason with Ivan and to persuade him to recognize the value of wise counsel and to avoid "foul parasites and adulators" who told the ruler what he wished to hear. Ivan responded with an unqualified defense of autocracy and rejected the very thought of taking counsel with others, who by definition were his inferiors. The autocrat was responsible only to God and was God's instrument.

Although autocracy experienced a setback during the "Time of Troubles" early in the seventeenth century, after the Riurikide dynasty came to an end, it reasserted itself with the establishment of the Romanov dynasty in 1613. In the middle of the century the Church was again subordinated to the crown, with the failure of the efforts of Patriarch Nikon to claim for the Church superiority or at least coequal status with the state. The autocratic order was also vastly strengthened during the reign of Peter I (the Great) in the first quarter of the eighteenth century. Peter decapitated the Orthodox Church by abolishing the

---

[28]Ivan IV's search for legitimacy as a ruler is reflected in the fact that he actually placed a member of the Chinggisid dynasty, Simeon Bekbulatovich, on the Muscovite throne in 1574. This unusual act was performed in order to acquire for the Muscovite throne the charisma of this dynasty and of Kazan, the Crimea, and Astrakhan. See Omeljan Pritsak, "Moscow, the Golden Horde and the Kazan Khanate from a Polycultural Point of View," in *Ibid.,* pp. 577–583.

Patriarchate and replacing it with a collegial body, the Holy Synod, headed by a layman. He ignored the Assembly *(Duma)* of Boyars, but he used his enhanced powers to introduce reforms and especially foreign technical skills.

The presence of a strong monarch made possible the extensive utilization and even enhancement of autocratic power. When the monarch was a weak person or a minor, the autocracy functioned through the bureaucracy (rule by arbitrary and uncontrolled officialdom) or—in earlier periods—through the boyars, as during Ivan the Terrible's childhood or during the "Time of Troubles." Russian monarchs crowned themselves at their coronations as if to demonstrate that their powers were not derived from any human source apart from the autocracy itself. Autocracy remained the basis of the Russian political order until October 1905, when it was partially modified to allow for a quasi-parliamentary body, the State Duma, to which government ministers were *not* responsible.

It is significant that the Russian word *vlast'* has multiple meaning, being used to express such different terms as *regime, authority, dominion,* and *power.* Thus, the distinction between arbitrary rule based on force and that based on legitimized authority is blurred in this word. Indeed, the blurring may be a semantic reflection of the lack in Russia of adequate countervailing forces to check autocratic power and the absence of effective institutional restraints to prevent its growth. Neither the Church nor the boyars were, in the long run, able to check the autocracy. Although the *Zemskii Sobor* (Assembly of the Land) emerged in the middle of the sixteenth century and included clergy, nobles, and merchants, it did not limit the tsar's prerogatives either. He could hear its advice but did not have to heed it. The fact that the Assembly elected the first Romanov tsar in 1613 did not make the Romanovs limited monarchs. Finally, because it was a purely consultative body and did not meet regularly, the Assembly could not be independent. It did not survive the seventeenth century. The *pomestie* system, which lasted until the eighteenth century (1762), provided for a gentry based on land tenure conditional upon service to the state and meant that those who enjoyed its benefits were dependent upon the absolute monarch. Serfs—who constituted more than ninety percent of the population—and landowners were equally subject to, and in the service of, the state.

The observation of the Russian historian Kliuchevsky that "the state expands, the people grow sickly" reflects the Russian failure—as a result of having nurtured an absolutist polity—to develop a pluralistic or multicentered society. Thus, even the traditional rights of cities assured under the Magdeburg Law to such urban centers as Riga and Tallin—and to Kiev, Poltava, Chernigov, and other Ukrainian cities—were abolished. The failure to develop effective institutional restraints on autocratic power was to have profound consequences.

It is not surprising that the CPSU adapted to its own ends the centralist order of the Russian autocracy. The communist ruling class—which claims a monopoly on truth and political power and claims to be the source of wisdom, justice, and moral good—provides a collectivized modern counterpart to the Russian tsars, who were supposedly all-wise and all-powerful and who ruled on the basis of divine right. The tsars were responsible only to God and to their own consciences, while the communist rulers have claimed to be responsible only to "history," as conveniently understood in terms of their own philosophy.

Resistance, Sectarianism, and Anarchic Tendencies

If the centralist syndrome and the denial of autonomy were the sole dimensions of the Russian political tradition, the task of defining that tradition would be far less complicated. For there is a wealth of evidence indicating that Russians have never submitted totally or permanently to their rulers. The gulf separating rulers from ruled in Russia had been both broad and deep. Rulers have often represented alien forces and have endeavored to impose foreign ways. This applies to the original Riurikide dynasty and to the Mongols and Tatars, as well as to the later House of Romanov, which became German after 1762. The imposition of Christianity, the reforms of Peter I, and the modernization introduced by Stalin and his successors testify to the presence of rulers who have sought to change traditional ways.

Authority has been distrusted and challenged when the opportunity has presented itself. The *veche,* or popular assembly, in the pluralistic Eastern Slavic society of *Rus'* in the pre-Mongol period, opposed the princes, especially in Kiev and Novgorod. The requirement of unanimity was often satisfied by recourse to violence and under duress, while the emergence of absolutism and serfdom led to the flight of serfs to the frontier areas. It also resulted in the great peasant revolts of Bolotnikov (1606–1608), Sten'ka Razin (1670–1671), and Emilian Pugachev (1773–1774). The burning of manor houses persisted into the twentieth century, and the 1917 revolution was accompanied by an outburst of peasant wrath. It is such events that prompted Russia's greatest poet, Pushkin, to refer to Russian rebellion as "senseless and ruthless."

The Russians have a rich tradition of religious sectarianism, despite the earlier presence of a regime dedicated to the propagation of a state religion and the Soviet polity's dedication to secular salvation, human reformation, and economic and social reorganization. An early sect was that of the "Judaizing heresy," which denied the trinity and the divinity of Christ and refused to venerate icons; early in the sixteenth century it was suppressed. The most profound schism occurred in the mid-seventeenth century and was prompted by a revision of sacred texts and religious practices by Patriarch Nikon, which reforms the dissident Old Ritualists (Old Believers) refused to accept. Nikon, with the support of the state, succeeded in imposing the Greek forms in place of the corrupted Russian practices, but at great cost. The Old Ritualists awaited the advent of Antichrist; and when they objected to the reforms of Peter I, they saw the tsar as assuming this role. The Old Ritualists divided into two groups, the "Priestists" and the "Priestless"; the former retained a clergy and ultimately reacquired a religious hierarchy and episcopate, while the latter took a separate path, due to the shortage of anti-Nikonian priests. The Priestless also abandoned traditional Orthodox Christian religious ritual because they had believed at the time of the schism's origin that the end of the world was imminent and hence there would be little need for ritual.

Persecuted by the tsarist government, the Priestless Old Believers, their lay readers, and preachers fled from Antichrist (Peter I) and sought refuge in the northern forests and in Siberia, even engaging in acts of mass self-immolation, especially during the regency of Sofia (1682–1689).[29] The Priestless, in time, divided into special sects.

That religious sectarianism was in the Russian tradition is testified to by the emergence of a number of exotic sects. The *Khlysty* (Flagellants) developed at the end of the seventeenth century; various branches developed, with some advocating different forms of abstinence and the abolition of marriage, while others engaged in orgies on the assumption that succumbing to the desires of the flesh would contribute to its mortification. As a reaction in the latter half of the eighteenth century, there emerged the *Skoptsy* (Emasculates), who at times sought to overcome lust, sin, and temptation by the drastic means of castration. Another sect, the *Dukhobory* ("Spirit Fighters"), rejected the notion of private property and refused to pay taxes, perform military service, or recognize political authority. With the aid of the novelist Lev Tolstoy, many immigrated to Canada, where a branch of the sect has at times been a source of difficulty for the authorities in British Columbia because of its anarchist views. One offshoot of the Dukhobory, who also regarded themselves as "Spiritual Christians," were the *Molokane* (Milk Drinkers), whose name was derived from their refusal to observe fasting. In the Soviet period the Russian Orthodox Church was itself divided as a result of the emergence of a reform movement, the Living (or "Renovationist") Church, which sought to modernize it, challenge the Moscow Patriarchate, and come to terms with the Soviet regime. More recently, such groups as the Seventh Day Adventists, Pentecostalists, and Jehovah's Witnesses have also made their appearance in the Soviet Union.

It is highly significant that, in defiance of the established church prior to 1917 and in opposition to the regime's ideology since then,[30] millions of Russians have embraced religious sectarianism. Frequently the religious sectarian fled from political authority in order to get beyond its reach and because he regarded it as being of the devil. However, what might be termed the "sectarian syndrome" has also manifested itself in Russian politics, despite the existence of autocratic regimes, organizational "monolithism," and an official creed or ideology. Indeed, Russian absolutist rule, in its various manifestations, can be viewed as a reaction

[29]Mussorgsky's opera *Khovanshchina* depicts the faith and sufferings of the Old Ritualists. Religious sectarianism also serves as a theme in Andrei Belyi's novel *The Silver Dove*.

[30]It is revealing that the Soviet Communist Party, prior to the establishment of the Soviet regime, when it was known as the Bolshevik faction, attempted to utilize the various sectarian movements in its revolutionary struggle against the tsarist regime. The Party's specialist on religious sects, Vladimir D. Bonch-Bruevich, conducted extensive research and published various studies on the sects. The principal works on Russian sectarians are Frederick C. Conybeare, *Russian Dissenters* (Cambridge: Harvard University Press, 1921; New York: Russell & Russell, 1962); Serge Bolshakoff, *Russian Nonconformity* (Philadelphia: Westminster Press, 1950); and Paul Miliukov, *Outlines of Russian Culture*—Part I, *Religion and the Church* (Philadelphia: University of Pennsylvania Press, 1943), Chaps. 3–6. See also Ethel and Stephen P. Dunn, "Religion as an Instrument of Cultural Change: The Problem of the Sects in the Soviet Union," *Slavic Review*, XXIII, No. 3 (September 1964), pp. 459–478 and Christel Lane, *Christian Religion in the Soviet Union* (Albany: State University of New York Press, 1978), Chaps. 4–8.

to this syndrome and as a means of restraining the Russian tendency to rebel and to embrace *vol'nost'* (excessive liberty or license). It is significant that much of the Soviet Communist Party's history has consisted of efforts to suppress deviant factions.

It is probably not coincidental that Russians have contributed much to the doctrine of anarchism and that they produced more than one generation of atheistic revolutionaries. Such Russian aristocrats as Mikhail Bakunin, Count Lev Tolstoy, and Prince Peter Kropotkin expounded various kinds of anarchist teachings. Tolstoy's anarchism, nonviolent and religious, was based on pacifism and the alleged virtues of the rural way of life. Bakunin's was violent and atheistic, dedicated to "creative" destruction and to the establishment of supposedly voluntary communes. Kropotkin's anarchic communism was to be based on the principle of mutual aid and the rejection of both the wage system and the state.

Berdyaev contended that anarchism was principally a Russian creation and that Russians tend not to like the state and to regard it as something alien to be revolted against or meekly accepted as circumstances dictate or permit.[31] Georgii Fedotov, in discussing Russian *buntarstvo* (rebelliousness), noted that Russians have an "organic antipathy to all completeness of form."[32] If these contentions have validity, they help to explain why Russian regimes have often been harsh and repressive and why they have been challenged by alienated and restless subjects. The one reinforced the other by means of mutual reaction and fed its opposite. The fear of anarchy may explain why the Soviet leaders constantly insist that the country enjoys "sociopolitical unity." Their obsession with total consensus may serve to conceal their fears of the consequences of any significant relaxation of Soviet rule. The popular fear of disorder *(besporiadok)* has tended to prompt acquiescence in the Soviet system and has worked to the rulers' advantage.

The Alienated Intelligentsia

One of the few Russian words absorbed into foreign languages has been "intelligentsia," although the term originally had a very special meaning. It was used to refer to the numerically small but vocal stratum that emerged in the nineteenth century from various classes, consisting of "men of ideas" given to critical thought. Indeed, some of the members of the intelligentsia frequently became so enamored of certain abstract ideas and so committed to their fulfillment that they ceased to be thinking men and, instead, became dedicated fanatics devoted to revolutionary action.[33] Lacking a developed sense of political realism, they frequently pursued grandiose dreams based on a few simple tenets. The intelligentsia was frequently alienated from the Russian state, church, na-

---

[31]Nicolas Berdyaev, *The Russian Idea* (London: Geoffrey Bles, 1947), pp. 142–144.

[32]Georgii P. Fedotov, *Novyi grad, sbornik statei,* ed. by Iu. P. Ivask (New York: izd-vo im. Chekhova, 1952), p. 79.

[33]For a discussion of the psychological attitudes and sociological attributes of the nineteenth-century Russian intelligentsia, see Vladimir C. Nahirny, *The Russian Intelligentsia, From Torment to Silence* (New Brunswick, N.J.: Transaction Books, 1983).

tion, and way of life; its members were often alienated from their parents and families. Its rootlessness and restless nature prompted it to embrace, variously, German idealist philosophy, philosophical materialism, populism (the "going to the people" movement that the suspicious peasantry rejected), nihilism, socialism, scientific rationalism, Slavophilism, and Marxism. It advocated the ideologization of literature and the arts and did not recognize private interests or individual rights.

The intelligentsia was frequently melancholic or pessimistic and given to dreaming, apathy, and helplessness; it often manifested feelings of guilt. Yet it could also organize conspiratorial groups in testimony to its alienation from Russian society, its rejection of values, and its determination to remake Russia. The organization of such groups compounded the existing cleavages between rulers and ruled, between the peasantry and the rest of Russian society.

It is significant that prominent members of the intelligentsia should have had to seek refuge abroad: Herzen, Bakunin, Lavrov, Plekhanov, Lenin, Gorky, to name but a few. Such prominent Russians as the Nobel literary prize winner Ivan Bunin, the composers Rakhmaninov, Stravinsky, and Gretchaninov, as well as the novelist Merezhkovsky, Berdyaev, and the basso Chaliapin, could not accept the Soviet regime and chose exile instead. In continuation of the tradition were the defections of numerous Soviet citizens during and after World War II. The crowning irony was the defection in 1967 of Svetlana Alliluyeva, daughter of the late Soviet dictator Joseph Stalin, who has spoken and written very critically of the regime. The alienation of such prominent writers as Anatolii Kuznetsov, Andrei Siniavsky, and Aleksandr Solzhenitsyn and the cellist-conductor Mstislav Rostropovich testifies to the persistence of the phenomenon.

The Soviet regime has created an intelligentsia of specialists—in contrast to the "generalists" who constituted the original Russian intelligentsia—and has endeavored to control it by the discipline imposed on the Communist Party membership and by threatening to withhold material satisfactions. By increasing the size of the intelligentsia and by giving it vital tasks to perform, the Soviet regime has also made that class potentially more significant. Even specialists can pose critical questions, however, and while some members of the Soviet intelligentsia have joined the "internal emigration" by becoming immersed in their professions, others have persisted in manifesting the restlessness and dedication that characterized their predecessors.

Identity, Appropriation, and the "Search" Syndrome

Both the question of Russian identity and the conflict between indigenous values and foreign ways have figured prominently in the country's development. Russians have long been concerned with the question of their relationship to Europe and with the ways in which their country differs from the West. The great debate between Westerners and the so-called Slavophiles in the nineteenth century reflected this concern. The question persisted in the conflict between the anticapitalist Populists *(Narodniki),* who idealized the Russian peasantry, and the early Russian Marxists, who argued that the country's development on the basis of the European economic model was inevitable. The question "What is Russia?" and the search for identity in terms of a special role, and a unique mission and way of life, have troubled generations of Russian thinkers as well as rulers.

The problem of identity has been greatly complicated and extended by the superficial attraction to the West experienced during the eighteenth century. The journey of Peter I to Holland and England to learn Western techniques—especially in shipbuilding—his contacts with Germans who lived in a segregated community in Moscow suburbs, and his decree in 1702 ordering the hiring of foreigners had a profound impact on Russian life. His new city of St. Petersburg, moreover, when compared with Moscow, provided a vivid contrast architecturally and culturally between Russia and Europe. Peter's lead was followed to an extent by his successors. Catherine II, who conducted a correspondence with Voltaire, attempted to play the role of the "enlightened despot" but abandoned the flirtation with Europe as a result of the excesses of the French Revolution. Alexander I also endeavored to play the liberal monarch, granting the Poles a constitution that he would not give his other subjects and subsequently becoming an advocate of monarchical legitimacy.

Some Russians were attracted to Freemasonry, which acquired a following among members of the Russian gentry during the eighteenth century. The Decembrists, who endeavored to establish a constitutional order by their rebellion in 1825, had been influenced by their contacts with Europe during the Napoleonic Wars and by Freemasonry.

The Russian elite contained many non-Russian elements, in fact, and foreigners frequently contributed to Russian development. Peter I, following his annexation of the Baltic territories, recruited Baltic Germans as trustworthy instruments of reform. Indeed, the Russian ruling family, the House of Romanov, became German after 1762 during the reigns of Catherine II (a minor princess of Anhalt-Zerbst) and her ill-fated husband Peter III (of the House of Holstein-Gottorp, although a grandson of Peter I).

The impressive contribution of foreigners to Russia is evident in many of the leading architectural and historical monuments. Thus, Ivan III had the Italian architect Fioravanti construct the Cathedral of the Dormition (*Uspenskii Sobor*) in the Kremlin (1475–1479), and he commissioned two other Italians to erect the Hall of Facets (*Granovitaia palata*). A Venetian architect built the Archangel Cathedral, and another Italian was summoned to build the high Belltower of Ivan the Great. Although Russian architects were erecting smaller structures of distinctive style, only foreigners were entrusted with the building of the imposing structures in Peter I's new capital of St. Petersburg. These included Rastrelli, Rossi, Quarenghi, de la Mothe, von Klenze, de Thomon, Trezzini, Stakenschneider, and many others. Indeed, very few of the principal historical structures of St. Petersburg (Leningrad) were designed and executed by Russians.

The number of foreigners or persons of non-Russian origin who attained positions of great responsibility in public life or prominence in Russian culture is truly remarkable. In Russian literature there are such figures as Pushkin (of African ancestry), Lermontov, Gogol', Blok, Gippius, Korolenko, Kuechelbeker, Del'vig, Fonvizin, Dostoevsky, and Akhmatova. Russia's leading lexicographer,

Vladimir Dal', was of Danish origin. The prominent Russian choreographer, Marius Petipa, was French by origin. Explorations undertaken by Russia were usually conducted by foreigners such as Vitus Bering, I. F. (Adam) Kruzenstern, F. P. Litke, Otto Kotzebue, and Thadeus Bellingshausen.

The presence in modern Russian political life of persons of foreign origin was evident in such figures as Czartoryski, Plehve, and Stürmer and among such tsarist ministers of finance as Witte, Bunge, and Reutern. Russian diplomacy utilized the talents of such non-Russians as A. I. (Heinrich) Ostermann and his son Ivan A. Ostermann (in the eighteenth century), Count Karl V. Nesselrode, Nikolai Karlovich Giers, Baron F. I. Brunnow, N. Hartwig, Count John Capodistrias, Count N. D. Osten-Saken, O. M. Shtakel'berg, A. F. Benckendorff, and Baron R. R. Rosen.[34]

The willingness of Russians, since the eighteenth century, to adopt those foreign techniques and practices that proved effective testifies to their abilities as appropriators.[35] The presence in the Russian language of large numbers of English, French, and German loan words as common nouns testifies to the Russian capacity to borrow. Such words as *metro, trolleybus, carousel, trailer, jeans, limit, start, finish, know-how, sidewalk (trottoir), overcoat (paletot), scarf (cache-nez), greenhouse (orangerie), mouthpiece (mundstück), sandwich (butterbrot), bathtub (wanne), lampshade (abat-jour),* and numerous others serve as examples. The Soviet regime's importation of Western technology and vocabulary in the thirties and seventies confirms the tendency to borrow.

By borrowing on an extensive scale and by annexing foreign lands and non-Russian populations, the Russians have inevitably complicated and made more acute the question of their identity. Appropriation of foreign ways and peoples led to fear of "contamination" and tended to promote the threat of fragmentation of the Russian polity. The diverse, complex, and synthetic nature of Russia's "unity" and the fact that the writing of a Russian history developed only in the eighteenth century—and that with the help of Germans—have prompted concern over the questions "what is Russia?" and "where can the 'true' Russia be found (in which social class)?" There has also been concern over the question of Russia's ultimate goals and her role in history.

Self-preoccupation has remained a favorite Russian concern, but it has been

---

[34]It was the use of numerous non-Russians that prompted Friedrich Engels to assert, in his essay on "The Foreign Policy of Russian Czarism" (1890), the following rather harsh judgment of Imperial Russia's diplomats: "It is this secret society, recruited originally from foreign adventurers, which has raised the Russian empire to its present plenitude of power. With iron perseverance, eyes set fixedly on the goal, not shrinking from any breach of faith, any treason, any assassination, any servility, distributing bribes lavishly, never overconfident following victory, never discouraged by defeat, over the dead bodies of millions of soldiers and at least one Czar, it is this gang—as talented as it is without conscience—rather than all the Russian armies put together which has extended the Russian boundaries . . . ; it is this gang which has made Russia great, powerful and feared, and has opened up for it the way to world domination." Karl Marx and Friedrich Engels, *The Russian Menace to Europe,* ed. Paul W. Blackstock and Bert F. Hoselitz (Glencoe, Ill.: Free Press, 1952), p. 26.

[35]For a popular but extensively documented treatment of Russian appropriation of Western knowledge and techniques, see Werner Keller, *East Minus West = Zero* (New York: Putnam, 1962). Although Keller has overstated his thesis—as is evident in the work's unfortunate title—he has provided a mass of evidence regarding Russia's cultural debt. Also see Donald W. Treadgold, *The West in Russia and China, Religious and Secular Thought in Modern Times.* Vol. I, *Russia, 1472–1917* (New York: Cambridge University Press, 1973).

complicated by the contradictory nature of the Russian self-image and the search for a viable identity. Thus Russians were not able to resolve the question of whether to be truly Russian meant being Orthodox Christian. The polyglot empire, in which the Russians were a minority, in the end made the task of establishing a conventional national identity quite impossible. The identity problem was due to the commitment to pursue empire and to the fact that Muscovy was transformed into a multi-national empire before the emergence of a Russian national consciousness. The national and imperial constituents became mingled in a strange entity that was Russia and that was not Russia. This circumstance, in turn, resulted in the unusual claim of some of the Slavophiles that the Russians, while rejecting the West and claiming moral superiority, were capable of identifying with other peoples. The great Russian writer Fedor Dostoevsky, in particular, expressed this view of the Russians as bearers of the doctrine of "human universality" *(obshchechelovechnost')* who were destined to embrace humanity and reconcile differences among peoples. The modern counterpart to Dostoevsky's dream is the Soviet claim that the Russians are exponents and practitioners of "internationalism" which entitles them to condemn every form of (non-Russian) nationalism while employing the concept of "internationalism" as a means of promoting the Russian language and culture and glorifying Russia's past and future.[36] Russians have been hostile to the nationalism of other peoples in the name of universalism and fraternalism that are dialectically transformed into a unique kind of Russian nationalism that denies its form while retaining much of its substance.

The persistence of the identity issue can be seen in the question of who the Soviet leaders have been and are: Khrushchev, Brezhnev, Andropov, Chernenko, and Gorbachev as well as Lenin have all given their nationality as "Russian"—as has the preponderant majority of members of the Soviet oligarchy. Yet Aleksandr Solzhenitsyn, in his *Letter to the Leaders of the Soviet Union* (1973), contended that their policies were detrimental to Russia's best interests and appealed to them to settle for authoritarian rule, abandon Marxism-Leninism, restore traditional Russian values, and withdraw from the claims and burdens of empire. The Soviet leaders rejected Solzhenitsyn's counsel and apparently have their own views concerning what Russia is, what its purposes are, how it should be ruled, and what is required to sustain it.

Implicit in this disagreement is the perplexing question of Russian identity

---

[36]The Soviet political dictionary defines nationalism as "bourgeois ideology, politics and psychology in the nationality question" that is associated with capitalism and that allegedly advocates the superiority of some nations and the inferiority of others. See "Natsionalizm" in *Kratkii politicheskii slovar'*, ed. by L. A. Onikov and N. V. Shishlin, 3rd ed. (Moscow: Politizdat, 1983), p. 211. "Internationalism" in Soviet usage is qualified with the adjectives "proletarian" and/or "socialist." Even as astute and critical observer of the Russians as Berdyaev at times empathized with Dostoevsky's view of "human universality" as a Russian attribute. Thus, in an essay on "Nationalism and Imperialism" published in 1918, Berdyaev asserted that "Russian imperialism has a national basis, but in its tasks it transcends all purely national tasks" and might unite "West and East, Europe and Asia." According to Berdyaev, "Russian policy can only be imperialistic and not nationalistic, and our imperialism . . . must be generously beneficent and not predatorily deprivational." Quoted in Nikolai P. Poltoratzky, *Berdiaev i Rossiia* (New York: Obshchestvo Druzei Russkoi Kul'tury, 1967), p. 132. See also Nicolas Berdyaev, *Dream and Reality, An Essay in Autobiography* (New York: Macmillan, 1951), pp. 250 and 265.

and why Russians cannot be regarded as a conventional nationality. Russians, as evidenced by their leaders and thinkers, remain a troubled people searching for some ultimate fulfillment that appears to escape them and constantly seeking to prove their worthiness and greatness to the world and to history.

"Truth-Seeking" and Maximalism

Russian political thought did not develop under the influence of rationalism but in an environment dominated by modes of thought that can be termed "mystical." Russian philosophy and the role in Russia of superstition and of "dark" and "impure" forces, as well as the obsession with "enemies" and with the sense of mission, testify to this. Thus, "devil" theories have tended to enjoy currency, and Russian political parties have more often than not been doctrinal and sectarian rather than pragmatic and broadly based. There has been a tendency to idealize Russian society and to indulge in self-glorification.[37] Traditionally political power in Russia has been wedded to ideology, a pattern promoting the appeal of the total, ready-made solution and of all-embracing dicta, absolute values, and official truth. The pursuit of maximal goals tended to discourage moderation and to rule out the "bourgeois" politics of compromise.

The preoccupation with political orthodoxy and the perceived need to protect the official truth have resulted in censorship both under the Russian Empire and the Soviet Union. The suppression of political dissent by the authorities is a practice of long standing. Thus Alexander Radishchev was sentenced to death by Catherine II for his book, *A Journey from Petersburg to Moscow* (1790), but the sentence was commuted to ten years in Siberian exile. Nicholas I had the philosopher Peter Chaadaev declared "insane" in 1836 for his critical (pro-Western) views of Russia, but Chaadaev subsequently recanted. The Soviet security police have continued these practices and have gone to great lengths to obtain public recantations from political prisoners. Carried to the extreme, the preoccupation with "truth" has resulted in over-reactive harshness in response to even the most minor of (mis)perceived threats. It has led to incessant searches, obsession with the security of frontiers and illegal border crossings, rigid visa requirements, searches for contraband literature, and systematic surveillance. "Truth" must be protected by intimidation.

If Berdyaev was correct in describing the Russians as an "apocalyptic people"—one concerned with ends and with the prophetic in life—it is not to be wondered that Marxism, with its facile predictions, held an attraction for some thinking Russians.[38] Many reasons can be cited to explain this attraction. Marxism was European and modern and claimed to be "progressive" and scientific. It also gave Russians, especially Lenin and his followers, the opportunity to claim that Russia had saved Marxism from corruption and betrayal by the West, which has been depicted as an unworthy guardian of the doctrine. Russians could also claim to have "enriched" Marxism with Lenin's teachings and subsequent theoretical embellishments. Marxism also had appeal in Russia because it was a

---

[37]Tibor Szamuely, *The Russian Tradition* (London: Secker and Warburg, 1974), pp. 60–61.
[38]See Nicolas Berdyaev, *The Russian Idea* (above, n. 31), Chap. 9.

Western doctrine that Russians could use against the West that they envied and despised. Marxism was compatible with the Russian intelligentsia's affinity for maximalism in that it provided a "historiology" (a science of history) and a total solution that was utopian and that claimed to assure social justice and be of universal application. Marxism had credibility in the Russian experience because class conflict, central to Marxism, was important in Russian history and was relevant for Russians. Capitalism—against which Marxism had declared war— had failed to acquire much popularity in Russia because it disrupted the traditional way of life and was disliked by both the landed nobility and the governmental bureaucracy. The Russian bourgeoisie was weak, as was the system of private enterprise. Marxism's futurism was attractive because it gave new substance to Russian messianism, which depicted Russia as a savior of humankind.

Marxist teachings in Russian hands provided a new secular orthodoxy, a new form of official truth seen as supplanting Russian Orthodox Christianity. The concept of the *collective* had a precedent in the Russian doctrine of *sobornost'*, or religious conciliarism. Marx's use of the dialectic was compatible with the alleged polarity of the Russian character with its emphasis on opposites. If Russians have had an affinity for thinking in holistic terms, Marxism was acceptable because of its emphasis on relationships, connections, and mutual dependence in development. Marxism was also compatible with anarchic tendencies in the Russian political culture because it promised a stateless society and removal of restraints. The internationalist professions of Marxism attracted support as a reaction to Russian imperialism and to the tsarist regime's mistreatment of the non-Russian nationalities. Finally, Marxism—together with its Russian variant, Leninism—also gave new form to the Russian seeking of purposefulness and commitment to principle *(ideinost')*.

Recurring Problems

Russian governments have functioned in a particular context and have had to confront certain basic problems. For instance, although Russian rulers have promulgated many legal codes, those codes have not been subjected to the kinds of legal restraints associated with constitutional regimes. Spying and exile have traditionally been elevated to the status of established institutions. Coups, depositions, and assassinations have played a significant role in Russian political life. Ivan the Terrible killed his son, and Peter I had his son executed. Catherine II had her husband, Peter III, killed. Catherine's son, Paul I, was assassinated and was succeeded by Alexander I, who apparently knew of the plot. Alexander II and various ministers and officials were assassinated, and Nicholas II and his immediate family as well as the sinister Rasputin were murdered. Attempts were made on Lenin's life, and numerous Soviet leaders were purged; Kirov and Trotsky were assassinated. The practice of deposing weaker rulers and of exiling them (or incarcerating them in monasteries in the tsarist period—as Peter I deposed and banished his half-sister, Sofia, who had served as regent) has persisted in the more recent Soviet period, with the removals of various members of the leadership.

The use of fear and degradation or of swift removal and consignment to oblivion, if not to death, has characterized Russian politics all too frequently. The appeal to violence and the use of repression have reflected a tendency to ignore genuine expressions of public opinion. The tendency to rely excessively upon an elite has contributed to the frequent estrangement of Russian regimes from the masses. Thus, the cleavages within Russian society have reflected the uneven race between needed reform that would basically change the system and revolution that would bring its collapse. If Russian rulers have often been reluctant to effect reforms and if reforms, when undertaken, have been nullified or eroded, it is probably in testimony to the persistence of cultural traits.

A key problem has been that of coming to grips with reality, especially regarding goals, rather than relying upon verbal incantations in the form of lengthy official resolutions and rhetorical pronouncements that reflect official truth (for example, the Communist Party Program and Central Committee resolutions). Yet the truth is manipulable, as is evident in the Russian distinction between two forms of truth: *pravda,* the lower and more prosaic form that can be manipulated and played with, and *istina,* the higher, noble, and pure truth that presumably is inviolable. It has been noted that, correspondingly, there are also two forms of mendacity in Russian: *vranyo* and *lozh.* Vranyo is usually defined as the ordinary, commonplace lie that is more an art form or performance and that may be quite harmless and that is designed to relieve drabness and boredom. Vranyo can be likened to a fib or blarney. Lozh is often seen as a more serious lie uttered for a sinister purpose. Dostoevsky, in his *Diary of a Writer,* wrote an essay entitled "Something on Lying" (1873) in which he posed the unusual question: "Why does everyone among us [in Russia] lie *(lgut)* and without exception?" Dostoevsky contended that in Russia even honorable people engage in vranyo and do so "out of hospitality" by exaggerating artistically in order to "create an aesthetic impression." He noted that the truth is "for us too boring and prosaic, insufficiently poetic, too commonplace." Dostoevsky saw lying as principally a male phenomenon in Russia; Russian women were far less likely to engage in it and were said to be "more persistent, more patient . . . [and] more *serious.* "[39]

It has also been noted that there is a Russian tendency to engage in *pokazukha,* or showmanship—a continuation of the "Potemkin villages" consisting of stage-prop scenery used by Prince Potemkin to impress Catherine II during a journey in Southern Ukraine. Vranyo or pokazukha can take various forms such as the claims made regarding Soviet elections or some of the imaginative assertions and explanations offered on occasion by Intourist guides.[40] This is not to suggest that Russians have any monopoly on prevarication or that they are among its most consummate practitioners. Mendacity in various forms and degrees can be found in all political systems. However, it can be contended that Russian political experience and practice have tended to color or distort reality in various

---

[39]"Nechto o vran'ye" in Fedor M. Dostoevsky, *Polnoe sobranie sochinenii* (St. Petersburg: izd. A. F. Marksa, 1895), Vol. 9, pp. 320–322 and 330.
[40]For an extended discussion of *vranyo* and related matters, see Ronald Hingley, *The Russian Mind* (New York: Charles Scribner's Sons, 1977), pp. 90–104.

ways and that this has affected the recognition and perception of problems. Aleksandr Solzhenitsyn has observed that the suppression of the hideous record of Stalin's crimes was itself a lie; he noted sadly that "no one in our country ever remembers anything, for memory is the Russians' weak spot, especially memory of the bad."[41] This raises the basic question of how a people can overcome its past if it cannot come to terms with it. The avoidance syndrome found confirmation in the speech of General Secretary M. S. Gorbachev to the 27th Party Congress on February 25, 1986, in which he called for "the lesson of truth" and conceded that various "negative processes" had been ignored during the preceding fifteen years.

The Soviet leaders have sought to impose different values and create a new culture based on a world outlook discussed in Chapters 3 and 10. Yet such attempts inevitably provoke resistance with the old culture endeavoring to reassert itself. Such phenomena as religious belief and nationalism have persisted along with other traditional ways. For example, the Soviet leaders have had to accommodate to the Christmas (now New Year's) tree and to the figure of Grandfather Frost (the Russian counterpart of Santa Claus) and the Snow Maiden. They have had to tolerate the small private agricultural plot, the sale of vodka and other spirits, and horse racing and betting. The attention given to Lenin's cadaver and the transformation of his mausoleum in Red Square, the heart of the Soviet capital, into a shrine can be understood principally as a vestige of the traditional Russian attitude regarding religious relics. The persistence of bribery in the Soviet Union also testifies to the difficulty of changing established ways. Lenin, in a speech to political education specialists delivered on October 17, 1921, referred to "such a truly Russian phenomenon as bribery";[42] and Lenin's successor, M. S. Gorbachev, at the 27th Communist Party Congress in 1986, denounced "all sorts of bribe-takers and self-seekers who are not averse to using their official positions for mercenary purposes."[43] Thus it would appear that bribery has a cultural basis (although it might also perform an economic function) and is perceived by Russians as a "gift" for a favor rendered. The persistence of high levels of alcohol consumption in the Soviet Union can be understood in cultural terms despite official efforts to promote sobriety. These examples illustrate how a culture reflects tensions, contradictions, and compromises in the society and how it represents an uneasy and changing synthesis.

Political culture is not static, though it can be highly durable. However, it can be modified when a people undergoes a trauma or a unique experience over time that is incompatible with established patterns of conduct and ways of perceiving reality. Continuity does not mean immutability, and change, when it occurs, is in turn limited and modified by a people's debt to its past.

---

[41]Aleksandr I. Solzhenitsyn, *The Gulag Archipelago, 1918–1956* (New York: Harper & Row, 1975), Parts III–IV, p. 121.

[42]V. I. Lenin, *Polnoe sobranie sochinenii,* 5th ed. (Moscow: Gospolitizdat, 1964), Vol. 44, p. 171.

[43]*Kommunist,* March 1986, No. 4, p. 35.

chapter *3*

The Ideological Heritage

When communists insist that they are serious about their convictions and that their actions and policies are motivated by ideological considerations, such claims cannot be taken lightly. If on occasion certain ideological tenets have been revised, it should not be concluded from this that the Soviet rulers are mere pragmatists or cynical opportunists. An ideology, in its political meaning, is a set of axioms or a scheme of systematic ideas based upon a particular interpretation of observed phenomena. In the communist case it has also involved a special mode of thinking and method of political analysis, in addition to being a *Weltanschauung* or world outlook (*mirosozertsanie* in Russian)—a system of thought that seeks to explain or rationalize the totality of reality in a convincing manner and also seeks to provide a vision of a vastly improved future designed to influence human behavior. If the ideology frequently has provided a distorted image of reality, it is no less significant as a force that has motivated and inspired men and women.

COMMUNISM AS A CREED

The intensity of communist belief cannot be adequately explained if communism is regarded as nothing more than a conventional political or economic theory. Far too many of its attributes are those of a sectarian or quasi-religious movement. While differing from theistic religious movements in rejecting the existence of the supernatural and in preaching a militant atheism, communism promises a species of secular salvation (by which the bulk of humankind is supposedly to be saved from evil) and in its name has demanded and exacted great sacrifices from its

60

adherents. Like a surrogate religion, it has sought to provide a set of ultimate goals, to give meaning to life, and to inspire action; it has also insisted that much be accepted on faith. While claiming to be "scientific," it has often conducted itself like a pseudochurch combining a messianic faith with a supposedly rational view of humanity and the cosmos.

If communism were nothing more than a political or economic theory, it would not claim to explain all historical development and the totality of human experience. It would not claim to be the sole, true philosophy and would not dismiss all other theories, doctrines, and philosophies as harmful and incorrect. If communism were but a theory, it would be neutral toward religious belief instead of attempting to destroy it and to claim for itself the right to decide all fundamental questions of human existence.

Among the quasi-religious attributes of communism are the reliance upon doctrine, catechism, conversion, and the notion of redemption.[1] The Party, in its original, less numerous membership, in certain respects resembled a secular "priesthood," which was expected to be dedicated to dogma and to proselytize on its behalf. It has preached a doctrine of human "salvation" in this world based upon the worship of work, economic development, and the supposedly predestined triumph of communist ideology and political rule. It has viewed humankind as having been corrupted by the "original sin" of exploitation (resulting from the ownership of various forms of property), which supposedly brought to an end the "primitive communist" stage of history regarded by communists as characterizing the natural state. In condemning "exploitation" and private or group ownership of the means of production as evil, communism has based itself on a moral judgment while simultaneously denying that persons of antagonistic social classes can be bound by a common morality.

The struggle between communism and its antagonists is viewed as inevitable, and the victory of the former is regarded as the triumph of "good" over "evil." This belief is comparable to the aspect of religious thought known as eschatological—pertaining to the doctrine of final things. Communist leaders have also insisted upon orthodoxy in ideology and have condemned and excommunicated the members of many deviationist movements—the communist counterpart of religious heresies. Communism has its own "scriptural" works in the frequently cited writings of Marx, Engels, and Lenin. The god-substitute of the communist cult is its doctrine of historical inevitability, with the world divided into believers and unbelievers, those who are saved and those who are doomed to perdition. It has venerated Lenin's embalmed body in the Red Square mausoleum as a surrogate religious relic. The Communist Party has employed the hierarchical principle—but without any explicit counterpart of spiritual grace—and has demanded of its members unfailing obedience. It has utilized a probationary period of candidacy for membership similar to the religious novitiate and

---

[1]The analogy between communism and religion was first systematically developed by Nicolas Berdyaev in *The Russian Revolution* (1931; republished in 1961 by University of Michigan Press, in Ann Arbor Paperbacks for the Study of Communism and Marxism). Berdyaev contended that Russian socialism and atheism were essentially an inversion of religion in that they rejected God in the name of justice and human welfare.

employs continuing indoctrination. Above all, it has endeavored to explain humanity's relationship to society and to the entire physical universe.

SOCIALISM AND COMMUNISM

The "socialist" label has been adopted by the USSR and constitutes part of the country's official name. For communists, socialism is the first stage of communism, but it must be socialism instituted by a ruling Communist Party. Although socialism actually preceded the emergence of communism (the *Communist Manifesto* was published in 1848), communists have insisted that so-called scientific socialism first made its appearance in the writings of modern communism's founder, Karl Marx.[2] The earlier socialist theories were dismissed by them as utopian. These included the theories of two Frenchmen, the Comte de Saint-Simon (1760–1825) and Charles Fourier (1772–1837), and of the Englishman Robert Owen (1771–1858), theories that stressed cooperative (group) rather than state ownership. The anarchism expounded by Pierre Joseph Proudhon (1809–1865) included establishment of syndicates, or producers cooperatives. Earlier theories include the communism in the consumption of goods that Plato advocated for the ruling class in *The Republic*, as well as the agrarian communism of the Diggers in seventeenth-century England.[3]

If pre-Marxian socialism advocated a more equal distribution of property and cooperative economic enterprises, modern socialism has been a protest against the excesses of pure laissez-faire capitalism. Although communism also protested against an early form of capitalism (no longer existing in industrialized countries), democratic socialism has differed from communism in a number of respects. Socialists are much less doctrinaire than communists and do not attempt to explain the cosmos. Communists usually insist upon complete nationalization or state ownership of the economy; socialists, on the other hand, vary in the degree of state ownership they advocate but usually favor a mixed economy lying between the two extremes of classical capitalism and the near-total state ownership demanded by doctrinaire communists. Socialists usually compensate for nationalized property, while communists usually confiscate it. Socialists recognize that state ownership, with government officials managing industry, is not a panacea, as it frequently leads to bureaucracy and waste; they therefore usually

[2]The term "communist" came into use in 1847 with the founding of an international Communist League in London. The *Communist Manifesto*, drafted largely by Marx with the help of Friedrich Engels, provided the league with a program distinguishing it from the other contemporary socialist movements, which the communists regarded as "conservative or bourgeois." For a general study of the development of modern socialist and communist thought, see Edmund Wilson, *To the Finland Station* (New York: Doubleday, 1940; 1953 Anchor Book edition). The most exhaustive study is that of G. D. H. Cole, *History of Socialist Thought*, 5 Vols. (London: Macmillan, 1953–1960). Also see Eduard Bernstein, *Evolutionary Socialism* (New York: Schocken Books, 1961), Karl R. Popper, *The Open Society and Its Enemies*, 4th ed. (Princeton, N.J.: Princeton University Press; London: Routledge and Kegan, 1962), and Albert S. Lindemann, *A History of European Socialism* (New Haven: Yale University Press, 1983).

[3]See Eduard Bernstein, *Cromwell and Communism, Socialism and Democracy in the Great English Revolution* (New York: Schocken Books, 1963).

limit state ownership to certain public utilities, transportation, communications media, certain natural resources, and medical and social insurance.

In addition to economic policy, socialists and communists differ in their political mores and practices. Democratic socialists achieve their ends by constitutional means, eschewing the violence and coercion that have been standard communist tactics. Democratic socialists respect basic civil liberties and do not suppress other parties; unlike communists, they are willing to hold free elections and relinquish power if they lose. Genuine socialists have hesitated to enter a coalition government with communists because of fear that the latter will subvert the coalition. Communists have an elitist conception of their movement, while democratic socialists have operated as a conventional political party. In all these ways socialists must be distinguished from communists, who at times freely employ the "socialist" label. The condescending Soviet attitude was expressed by General Secretary M. S. Gorbachev at the Twenty-seventh Party Congress in February 1986 in the following terms: "It goes without saying that the ideological differences between communists and social democrats are profound and their experience and achievements are dissimilar and not of equal value."[4]

BASIC CATEGORIES OF COMMUNIST BELIEF

Communist doctrine is based upon certain broad tenets and basic assumptions that were developed and applied by Karl Marx (1818–1883) and Friedrich Engels (1820–1895). Both men emerged from a German environment and were influenced by certain movements in German philosophy. Ironically, neither man came from a working-class milieu. Marx was the son of a middleclass Jewish lawyer converted to Christianity; Engels was the son of a textile manufacturer and was himself a successful businessman.

Marx received a doctorate in philosophy from the University of Jena in 1841; by 1843, he had taken refuge in Paris after a brief experience in journalism in Cologne led to the suspension of the newspaper by the authorities. Expelled from France in 1845, he spent three years in Brussels. Upon being expelled from Belgium, Marx returned to Germany during the revolution of 1848, engaged in radical journalism, and was arrested; acquitted when tried for sedition, he went into exile again in 1849. The remaining three decades of his life were spent in London as a political émigré. Isolated from British life, he engaged in journalism, in polemics, and in scholarship.

Marx and his family suffered many privations in England. However, he was able to persist in his activities largely due to Engels' generosity and to two legacies. In addition to the *Manifesto* and newspaper articles, Marx wrote analyses of French politics and his lengthiest work, *Capital.* The first volume of *Capital* appeared in 1867 and attracted only limited attention; the other two volumes appeared after Marx's death and were completed by Engels. While

---

[4]*Kommunist,* March 1986, No. 4, p. 62.

Marx's ponderous writings dealt principally with economic and political analysis, Engels' more readable works dealt with a variety of historical and philosophical questions.[5] Both men developed their doctrines in response to the abysmal living conditions that characterized urban life during the industrial revolution: the factory system, child labor, unemployment, low wages, and extremes of wealth and poverty.

Marx and Engels claimed that their teachings were scientific and that they had discovered laws that explained the entire historical process. In part, these claims were due to their desire to distinguish themselves from the alleged senti-mentalism of utopian and Christian (or ethical) socialism. By claiming to offer a rational analysis of history and by assuming the inevitability of events that would validate their predictions, Marx and Engels sought to endow their system with the guise of scientism. Also, since their system was based upon materialism, it was regarded as being "scientific" by definition because it gave the appearance of dealing with the material world in empirical terms. Unfortunately, however, the distinction between hypothesis and dogmatic assumption or belief became blurred in Marxist thought.

Philosophical and Historical Materialism

The concept of philosophical materialism is at the very core of communist doc-trine. It is based on the assumption that thought, mind, and consciousness are reflections of the objective reality of the material, physical world. The assertion of the primacy of matter over thought is a denial of what communists condemn as the philosophical idealist view, which holds that existence, nature, and matter are a reflection of the spirit or of the Absolute Idea. In the communist ontology, being is defined exclusively in material terms and is said to determine conscious-ness. For philosophical idealists it is the spirit or consciousness that is primary and that determines being and the material world. Communists, as philosophical materialists, see the mind as a reflection of the material world (being) and as secondary to, and dependent upon, matter. Matter to communists is the "totality of material things"—the "objective reality" that is perceived by the sense organs and that exists independently of the human mind, consciousness, and perception. This viewpoint tends to limit all experience to the perceptible physical world. It also assumes that the totality of reality can be known and that absolute truth is ultimately ascertainable. Since it is only the material world that exists in reality, atheism is an essential element in communist belief.

The emphasis on materialism and atheism in communism resulted largely from the influence upon Marx and Engels of the German philosopher Ludwig Feuerbach (1804–1872), who held that nature exists independently of philosophy and is the source of all knowledge. Feuerbach held that philosophy must be based

---

[5]For detailed accounts of the relationship between Marx and Engels and their thought, see Sir Isaiah Berlin, *Karl Marx, His Life and Environment* (London: Oxford University Press, 1948), Franz Mehring, *Karl Marx* (Ann Arbor: University of Michigan Press, 1962), and David McLellan, *Karl Marx, His Life and Thought* (New York: Harper & Row, 1973).

on the observation of nature and on practical experience, not on ratiocination and abstract ideas; he held man to be little more than a biological entity. Feuerbach's denial of God, expressed in his *Essence of Christianity* (1841), was based on his assumption that religion results from man's unconscious efforts to deify himself and to endow God with qualities that man values. Theology was to be replaced by anthropology, with the latter becoming a secular humanist movement based on love and the achievement of man's supposed potentialities.[6]

Although Feuerbach called himself a "communist," certain aspects of his philosophy have been criticized by communists. Feuerbach, for example, advocated a "religion" of love and of humanity; he recognized the power of religious ideas and wished to unite what he regarded as the "positive" aspects of religion with philosophy. In contrast to this, communists have denied the existence of positive features in modern religion. Feuerbach's materialism was philosophical and not historical. He saw men as part of nature but not in relationship to social class, political party, or revolution. He distinguished between various historical epochs on the basis of the criterion of religion and not in terms of the economic system or class structure. Thus, Feuerbach did not apply his philosophical materialism to the study of society. This task was undertaken by Marx and Engels.

Marxists view history as a single process of development conforming to certain laws that, in turn, reflect identifiable social forces. At the bottom of this scheme is the assumption that human relationships and political behavior are determined fundamentally by the ways in which men obtain their livelihood. Thus, politics is seen as a function of the "mode of production" and of the material and social conditions corresponding thereto. Technology, the nature of tools, and the uses to which man puts resources are said to determine the mode of production. This, in turn, is said to determine the "relations of production"— or the property (and social) relationships that result from ownership of tools and resources, as well as from the ways in which production and labor are organized and managed. In time, the relations of production conflict with the mode of production. The process was described by Marx in the Preface to his *Contribution to the Critique of Political Economy* (1859), in the following terms:

> In the social production of their means of existence men enter into definite, necessary relations which are independent of their will, productive relationships which correspond to a definite stage of development of their material productive forces. The aggregate of these productive relationships constitutes the economic structure of society, the real basis on which a juridical and political superstructure arises, and to which definite forms of social consciousness correspond. The mode of production of the material means of existence conditions the whole process of social, political and intellectual life. It is not the consciousness of men that determines their existence, but, on the contrary, it is their social existence that determines their consciousness. At a certain stage of their development the material productive forces of society come into contra-

---

[6]On Feuerbach and other precursors of Marx and Engels, see Sidney Hook, *From Hegel to Marx* (published originally in 1936; reissued in Ann Arbor Paperbacks for the Study of Communism and Marxism, University of Michigan Press, 1962).

diction with the existing productive relationships, or, what is but a legal expression for these, with the property relationships within which they had moved before. From forms of development of the productive forces these relationships are transformed into their fetters. Then an epoch of social revolution opens. With the change in the economic foundation the whole vast superstructure is more or less rapidly transformed.[7]

The personal motives of men are irrelevant, for men are held to act as they do because they are seen as the instruments of the socioeconomic forces that have produced them.

Base and Superstructure

There are two inseparable parts of an attempt to explain human activity in terms of historical materialism. The "base" represents the combination of "production relations" that constitutes the economic structure of society corresponding to a particular stage of development. The "superstructure" represents for communists the particular form of social consciousness, political institutions, and legal norms corresponding to the economic base and determined by it. Thus, the superstructure is said to include politics, constitutions, law, religion, morality, political theory, philosophy, the arts, and literature as well as all ideologies. This scheme of analysis holds that ethical judgments and principles of right, liberty, and justice do not exist in the abstract but are tied to the economic system (base), which is the ultimate determinant of history. A philosophy or ideology must be partisan and can serve only as a rationalization of an existing order or as a reflection of "progressive" opposing forces developing in the base.

In theory, communists—especially under Engels' influence—have recognized that the superstructure can exercise some influence upon the base, retarding or accelerating development. Engels, in some of his correspondence in 1890 and in 1894, conceded that noneconomic factors could have a secondary role. In a letter to Heinz Starkenburg, dated January 25, 1894, Engels declared:

> Political, juridical, philosophical, religious, literary, artistic, etc. development is based on economic development. But all these react upon one another and also upon the economic base. It is not that the economic position is the *cause and alone active,* while everything else only has a passive effect. There is, rather, interaction on the basis of the economic necessity, which *ultimately* always asserts itself.[8]

---

[7]Emile Burns, ed., *Handbook of Marxism* (New York: International Publishers, 1935), pp. 371–372. In contrast to the emphasis on the forces of production in the later Marx and in Soviet Leninism, a more recent Marxist school has stressed the concept of alienation as reflecting the "true" (earlier) Marx. Alienation of humanity from its true nature is seen in economic production, the state, social class, and religion. See Bertell Ollman, *Alienation: Marx's Conception of Man in Capitalist Society* (New York: Cambridge University Press, 1971) and Istvan Meszaros, *Marx's Theory of Alienation* (New York: Harper & Row Torchbook, 1972).

[8]Karl Marx and Friedrich Engels, *Selected Correspondence, 1846–1895* (New York: International Publishers, 1942), p. 517.

In the end, for communists, it is economic relations that are decisive, and it is economic necessity rather than historical accident or free will that determines a people's fate.

Surplus Value

If economic determinism plays the key role in communist belief, its most essential component is the concept of "surplus value." This economic category is related to commodity production, which is production for exchange rather than for consumption by the producer. As a result of economic development and increased division of labor, commodity production becomes characteristic of the entire capitalist economy and ceases to be a mere exchange of goods. Purchase for the purpose of selling at a profit converts money into capital—another form of property with a new and higher value. Money has "grown" into capital—a new value based upon surplus value. Value of this kind exceeds the producer's costs.

The notion that value has its source in labor (the labor theory of value) was first developed by the seventeenth-century political theorist John Locke and later by the classical economists David Ricardo and Adam Smith. This viewpoint was originally based on the assumptions that manufacturing by artisans involved no more than the investment of their labor (as they owned their tools) and that therefore the product of their labor did not have to be shared with others. It remained for Marx to take Ricardo's political economy (and that economist's failure to explain profit adequately) and derive from it his theory of surplus value.

Marx contended that capitalist commodity production differs from simple commodity production (exchange of goods) because capitalism treats labor power itself as a commodity. The introduction of steam-driven machinery and the rise of the factory system compelled formerly self-employed artisans to become wage-laborers, as they could not compete with machinery. The capitalist purchased labor power for a specific period of time, paying it only the bare minimum it cost to subsist and reproduce itself (the "iron law of wages"). The surplus results from the difference between the value of the commodities produced by this labor and the value paid to it and constitutes profit. For Marx the value of a commodity was based exclusively upon the labor embodied in it. The surplus product allegedly produced by labor power alone was not paid for by the capitalist but was appropriated as an unearned increment.

The theory of surplus value assumes incorrectly that the worth of an object is determined by labor alone. In fact, value results from many sources: the skill of those who perform manual functions or operate machines, the machines and tools not themselves furnished by the worker, the capital invested in an enterprise, land, and the managerial abilities of the entrepreneur. Indeed, how is investment achieved under any system if not by profits and invested savings (whether forced or voluntary)? The theory also ignores the fact that use-value is a variable that changes through time and often cannot be expressed in monetary terms. Thus, a priceless painting or piece of sculpture or a classical symphony has a value quite apart from the number of hours the artist or composer devoted to it and the initial compensation, if any. Conversely, as the quality of labor varies, much labor and effort can be expended upon something of little worth. The notion of value, then, is a highly elusive concept that Marx endeavored unsuccessfully to reduce to a simple formula.[9]

Exploitation

Closely related to the concept of surplus value is that of "exploitation," which plays a key role in the communist view of the so-called capitalist order. In the Marxist scheme, "constant capital" is defined as the value of the means of production, such as machinery, tools, and raw materials. "Variable capital" is that expended for labor (wages). The value of commodities produced is equal to constant capital plus variable capital plus surplus value. The "degree of exploitation," finally, is the ratio of surplus value to variable capital. Thus, the owners of the means of production who receive income from rents, interest from investments, and profits from manufactures are accused of exploiting the remaining, nonowning part of society.

Exploitation and the tendency to drive down wages in order to maximize profits (the ratio of surplus value to total capital) are said to be accompanied, under capitalism, by the so-called industrial reserve army of the unemployed. In addition, as competition between capitalists intensifies—with the weaker competitors absorbed by the stronger, leading to a concentration of capital (and ultimately monopoly)—the need for new and more expensive machinery increases the value of constant capital and reduces variable capital. With rising costs as a result of the supposed need to increase profits, the rate of profit and of surplus value is said to actually decline as expensive machinery supplants human labor. The working class is supposedly further impoverished as production costs and output rise, while wages are said to fall. The increased misery of the proletariat, it is alleged, inevitably leads to political crises and proletarian revolution.

The Ruling Class and the State

Basic to communist doctrine is the notion of a ruling class that in varying form characterizes each stage of historical development. This class owns the means of production and as a result is said to exercise political control in the interest of perpetuating its position of dominance. In accordance with the base-superstructure relationship, ideas, law, ethics, morality, religion, philosophy, and aesthetics are seen exclusively as partisan weapons employed at various stages by slaveowners, landowners, and the industrial bourgeoisie to justify their privileged status. Marx and Engels in *The German Ideology* (1846) gave expression to this thesis in the following terms:

---

[9]For the classic critique of Marx's theory of value, see Eugen von Böhm-Bawerk, *Karl Marx and the Close of His System* (1896), republished with an introduction by Paul M. Sweezy (New York: Augustus M. Kelly, 1949).

The ideas of the ruling class are in every epoch the ruling ideas; i.e. the class, which is the ruling material force of society, is at the same time its ruling intellectual force. The class which has the means of material production at its disposal, has control at the same time over the means of mental production, so that thereby, generally speaking, the ideas of those who lack the means of mental production are subject to it.[10]

It follows logically, in the communist view, that the state is nothing more than an instrumentality of a particular ruling class designed to serve the interests of that class. Thus the *Communist Manifesto* asserts that "the executive of the modern [capitalist] state is but a committee for managing the common affairs of the whole bourgeoisie." It also declares that "political power, properly so called, is merely the organized power of one class for oppressing another."

The Class Struggle

Communist doctrine explains social classes exclusively in terms of their relationship to the means of production, their role in the social organization of labor, and the particular share of social wealth accorded them. Classes are said to have emerged as a result of the division of labor and the introduction of private ownership of the means of production. Each historical epoch is supposedly characterized by a distinctive social structure that reflects the conflict of classes. Irreconcilable class antagonism between "exploited" and "exploiters" is said to result from private ownership of the means of production. The *Communist Manifesto* asserts categorically that:

The history of all hitherto existing society is the history of class struggles.

Freeman and slave, patrician and plebeian, lord and serf, guild-master and journeyman, in a word, oppressor and oppressed, stood in constant opposition to one another, carried on an uninterrupted, now hidden, now open fight, a fight that each time ended, either in a revolutionary reconstruction of society at large, or in the common ruin of the contending classes. . . .

Our epoch, the epoch of the bourgeoisie, possesses, however, this distinctive feature: it has simplified the class antagonisms. Society as a whole is more and more splitting up into two great hostile camps, into two great classes directly facing each other—bourgeoisie and proletariat.[11]

Although the class struggle is a political struggle, it does not manifest itself with equal intensity at all times. Thus Engels recognized that "there are periods when the warring classes so nearly attain equilibrium that the State power, ostensibly appearing as a mediator, assumes for the moment a certain indepen-

---

[10]Karl Marx and Friedrich Engels, *The German Ideology, Parts I and III* (New York: International Publishers, 1947), p. 39.

[11]Emile Burns, *op. cit.* (above, n. 7), pp. 22–23.

dence in relation to both."[12] The state, in addition to being the instrument of the ruling class, is a means of holding class antagonisms in check, at least temporarily, so that the conflicting classes "may not consume themselves and society in sterile struggle."[13] Of course, conflict must and will occur, but in a form that will supposedly assure historical "progress." The class struggle is regarded as the prime motive force in historical development during the periods characterized by antagonistic class structures.

Once communists consolidate their rule in a country, such antagonistic relationships between classes supposedly become "friendly" and nonantagonistic. With the alleged liquidation of the exploiters, the class struggle is transferred to the international arena, where it occurs between communist and noncommunist states or, in the Marxist-Leninist terminology, between the "socialist" and "capitalist" systems.

Stages of Historical Development

Communist doctrine endeavors immodestly to explain the entirety of human history in terms of "laws" reflecting philosophical materialism, economic determinism, the class struggle, and the dialectic. For the communist this combination of concepts comprises modern "social science," although it is in fact no more than a philosophy of history. The notion of historical inevitability is based on the assumption that the relations of production and the economic base determine historical events. Historical periods emerge as a result of socioeconomic forces that people cannot resist but are "free" to recognize.

All of human history is reduced by communist doctrine to five stages, each of which is characterized by a particular socioeconomic structure, base and superstructure, and set of production relations. The *original stage* is defined as a primitive, supposedly communist, society in which there is said to have been communal ownership of the means of production—simple tools and stone implements. There supposedly were no social classes in this original stateless society. The *second historical stage* is defined as the slaveholding stage, with private rather than common ownership of the means of production (including slaves). The class struggle manifested itself in the antagonism between slaveowners and slaves. The *third stage* is that of feudalism, which supposedly resulted from a different mode of production but which, like the slaveholding stage, involved private ownership of the means of production. The class struggle in the third stage was between landowning nobles and serfs and between nobles and burghers. The *fourth stage* is that of capitalism, with its large, privately owned factories and its struggle between owning and exploiting bourgeoisie and exploited proletariat, resulting from a system of wage labor. The *fifth stage* is that of communism (preceded by a "socialist" transitional stage), with supposedly public or common ownership of

---

[12]Friedrich Engels, *The Origin of the Family, Private Property and the State, ibid.*, p. 330. As examples, Engels cited the absolute monarchies of the seventeenth and eighteenth centuries, "which balanced the nobles and burghers against each other," and the First and Second French Empires of the Bonapartes, which "played off the proletariat against the bourgeoisie."

[13]*Ibid.*, p. 328.

the means of production and no class struggle. In stages two, three, and four, there are ruling classes, while in the first and fifth stages, there are said to be none.

This highly simplified scheme resulted from an effort at historical retrojection, under the influence of the indisputably revolutionary transformation that society had undergone in the nineteenth century as a result of industrialization. Marx and Engels, having witnessed the profound changes caused by these new forces of production, sought to persuade others that a comparable pattern had occurred in previous epochs. In general, Marx dealt with the capitalist system of his day and said little of the slaveholding and feudal societies. The references to primitive communal society in Marx's and Engels' writings are vague.

Marx's and Engels' views regarding the existence of communal property and the absence of a state or social classes among primitive peoples were based on the work of the American ethnologist Lewis Henry Morgan (1818–1881), who, ironically, was an upstate New York railroad attorney, a capitalist, and a Republican. Marx and Engels were much impressed with Morgan's principal work, *Ancient Society* (1877), which was inspired by his contacts with the Iroquois Indians and was limited largely to the American Indians, Greeks, and Romans. Morgan contended that private property was preceded by primitive communism in the process of historical development "from savagery through barbarism to civilization." Private property, in Morgan's opinion, arose in an evolutionary process as a result of technological development and new inventions. Although Morgan's views prompted Marx and Engels to greet his work with enthusiasm, Morgan was not a socialist—let alone a communist—and he did not believe in the class struggle as the mover of history. He recognized historical materialism, but he was neither a philosophical materialist nor a dialectical materialist. Subsequent research in anthropology has cast doubt on Morgan's contention regarding the existence of primitive communism.[14] However, communists have persisted in their mythology regarding a primitive communal society in order to make it appear that they are restoring humankind to a previous "uncorrupted" state that was supposedly enjoyed prior to the advent of private property.

The Dialectic

Where the doctrine of historical materialism has been associated primarily with Marx, the use of the dialectic in Marxism as applied to natural phenomena has been attributed largely to Engels' influence. The dialectic is regarded as the embodiment of the "laws of development" or as the "science of the general laws of motion—both of the external world and of human thought." In its original Greek sense, dialectics refers to the art of disputation by means of which the arguments of one's opponent are exposed and truth is discovered as a result of

---

[14]The existence of individual and family-owned hunting territories, fishing locations, and other forms of wealth as well as social castes and slavery among peoples whom Morgan would have regarded as "savages"—had he been acquainted with them—has been adequately documented. See Bernhard J. Stern, *Lewis Henry Morgan, Social Evolutionist* (Chicago: University of Chicago Press, 1931), pp. 179–181. Also see Carl Resek, *Lewis Henry Morgan, American Scholar* (Chicago: University of Chicago Press, 1960; reprint edition, 1974).

the clash of opposing arguments. Taken from the philosopher Georg Wilhelm Friedrich Hegel (1770–1831), the dialectic as employed by Marx, Engels, and Lenin was divested of its Hegelian philosophical idealism and combined with historical materialism to form "dialectical materialism"—put simply, a combination of belief in movement with belief in the notion that only matter is real. Hegel saw history as the constant development and enrichment in time of the absolute idea of World Spirit *(Weltgeist)*. Development of the "Idea of Spirit" occurred in terms of the Hegelian triad of thesis, antithesis, and synthesis. Thus, a concept was said to inevitably generate its opposite, and as a result of the mutual interaction of the two concepts, a new synthesis would emerge. Marx, in the Preface to the second edition of *Capital* (1873), asserted that in Hegel the dialectic was "standing on its head" and had to be "turned right side up again, if you would discover the rational kernel within the mystical shell." In reality Marx merely substituted "matter" for Hegel's "idea." Yet the "rational kernel" has endowed communist thought and practice with a highly elusive character.

Basic to the dialectic are the notions of contradiction and conflict and of a phenomenon being transformed into its opposite. Among the "laws" of dialectics or the general characteristics of the dialectical method, as interpreted by communists, are the following:

1. All phenomena and objects are interrelated and interdependent. The dialectical method condemns as "metaphysical" the view that regards phenomena as isolated; for the dialectic, only the totality is real. All events, objects, and phenomena must be viewed in terms of their interconnectedness and mutual dependence.

2. The dialectic is based upon constant movement and development from the lower to the higher, from the simple to the complex; movement is progressive, and development is not simply cyclical or linear but proceeds in a spiral pattern. The dialectic condemns as "metaphysical" all attempts to view phenomena as static and immutable and holds that only matter and motion are constant.

3. *The "law" of interpenetration, unity, and strife of opposites* holds that every phenomenon or object is not a homogeneous mass but is, instead, a changing unity of contradictory parts. Although the constituent parts of a phenomenon—or of the social order itself—are in conflict, they also constitute a unity of interacting parts that cannot be divorced from each other until protagonist and antagonist have played out their predetermined roles on the stage of history. Development occurs as a result of the struggle of opposites, and the source of movement is internal, resulting from the "contradictions" that are inherent in the object or phenomenon. Conflict is regarded as "progressive." Thus, social classes in their conflict and interaction determine the course of historical development.

4. *The "law" of the transformation of quantity into quality and vice versa* sees development as resulting from gradual, often imperceptible, incremental *quantitative* changes that occur in every phenomenon and that lead to abrupt and readily perceptible *qualitative* changes. The new qualitative state is the result of a "leap," which occurs with the crossing of a "nodal line."

A frequently cited example of this formulation is the transformation of water into ice or steam (qualitative change) as a result of changes in temperature (quantitative change). Communists also view political changes in terms of this "law"—quantitative changes resulting from the contradictions that characterize the socioeconomic order thus lead to qualitative political changes.

5. *The "law" of the negation of the negation* reflects the incessant change that characterizes the dialectic in its pure form. The new qualities that result from quantitative changes are, in turn, subjected to new quantitative changes and are replaced by subsequent qualitative states. Thus development is said to occur in stages, and each new synthesis, which has negated its predecessor as a result of the thesis-antithesis formula, is, in turn, negated by a new synthesis. In this way the negation is itself negated. The historical epochs of Marxism serve as an illustration: the feudal stage was the negation of the slaveholding stage and was itself negated by capitalism, which, in turn, was said to be negated by communism. The new replaces the old in optimistic testimony to inevitable progress.[15]

Dialectical development is based on internal movement, self-generated as a result of the internal contradictions that allegedly result from the struggle of opposites within a unity. Thus the predicted doom of capitalism is seen as resulting from the clash of bourgeoisie and proletariat (thesis and antithesis), which leads to a new synthesis. Proponents of dialectical materialism—that combination of mystical movement and mundane matter—distinguish it from mechanistic materialism or from so-called vulgar materialism that they reject. Mechanistic materialism is said to diverge from the dialectic in not giving adequate recognition to change, in stressing external rather than internal sources of movement, in recognizing only quantity instead of quality, in denying historical "leaps," and in rejecting the notion of progressive development from the lower to the higher. Vulgar materialism is said to neglect the role of ideas, voluntarism (will), and consciousness.

The dialectic holds that opposites cannot be separated or reconciled: life and death, positive and negative, action and reaction, war and peace, offense and defense, and conflicting classes cannot be understood apart from each other. By this doctrine anything can turn into its opposite, just as friends can become enemies and stability can abruptly be transformed into instability. Thus, dialecticians regard as inadequate the law of identity in formal logic where $A = A$ and presumably cannot be anything other than A. Dialectics regards A as having within itself the potential to become something other than A in the course of its development. Since contradiction is the essence of the dialectic, it enables communists to make numerous distinctions. Thus they readily distinguish between the "progressive" or beneficial aspects of slavery or of capitalism (in terms of the

---

[15]The dialectic is featured prominently in the curriculum for Party schools prepared by the Academy of Social Sciences of the Central Committee. See B. I. Siusiukalov and L. A. Yakovleva, eds., *Marksistsko-Leninskaia filosofiia, Uchebno-metodicheskoe posobie po dialekticheskomu i istoricheskomu materializmu* (Moscow: "Mysl' ", 1984), pp. 75–105.

development of productive forces) and the evil and oppressive aspects. The *Communist Manifesto* provides eloquent testimony to this dualism: it praises the bourgeoisie and capitalism for promoting unprecedented economic development in their time but denounces each as doomed for the future. When compared with its negation and with that which it negated, the same phenomenon can have two contradictory characteristics at different stages in its development. Capitalism is "progressive" in its earlier stages when compared with feudalism but ceases to be so as soon as it begets its antithesis. Yet the communists claim that they preserve the "positive" features and achievements of capitalism.

The dialectic is an analytical concept that endows communists with a high degree of flexibility because it thrives on paradox and defies logic. Dialectical materialism claims to furnish ready explanations for all events and to be an accurate reflection of "objective reality." It also enables communists to believe that the course of development is predetermined in their favor as the dialectical dance of history unfolds.

The Ultimate Society

The classics of communism have had little to say regarding the specific nature of communist society except to assert that social classes will cease to exist and the state will "wither away." Such formulas as "an association in which the free development of each is the condition for the free development of all" *(Communist Manifesto),* "the government of persons is replaced by the administration of things and the direction of the process of production" (Engels' *Anti-Dühring*), and Lenin's "from each according to his ability, to each according to his needs" are hardly helpful signposts on the road to communism. Indeed, it is difficult to escape the conclusion that the future communist society is both mythical and utopian in its avowed egalitarianism and in its boundless optimism regarding humanity's future.

Commencing with the base-superstructure relationship, communists have believed that a change in the economic base—nationalization of industry plus economic development—will lead to the "expropriation of the expropriators" and pave the way for the new society. This change will also produce a new humanity, since the suppression of one class by another will ultimately be eliminated— although the majority of the formerly exploited will still need to suppress the minority of former exploiters during a transitional period. In 1917 Lenin expressed this vague and naive hope in this way:

> We are not utopians, and we do not in the least deny the possibility and inevitability of excesses on the part of *individual persons,* nor the need to suppress *such* excesses. But, in the first place, no special machinery, no special apparatus of repression is needed for this; this will be done by the armed people itself, as simply and as readily as any crowd of civilized people, even in modern society, parts a pair of combatants or does not allow a woman to be outraged. And, secondly, we know that the fundamental social cause of excesses . . . is the exploitation of the masses, their want and their poverty. With

the removal of this chief cause, excesses will inevitably begin to *"wither away."* We do not know how quickly and in what succession, but we know that they will wither away. With their withering away, the State will also *wither away.*[16]

By the simple act of making the whole of society "one office and one factory, with equal work and equal pay," it was assumed by Lenin that ultimately all persons will "become accustomed to observe the fundamental rules of social life, and their labor is so productive, that they voluntarily work *according to their ability.* "

For decades communists have been confronted with the task of attempting to define in concrete terms the nature of the future communist society. Yet the 1919 and 1961 Programs of the Communist Party of the Soviet Union were singularly disappointing in their detailing of the communist future. The 1986 Program was even more reticent.[17]

Its Contribution

Marx and Engels have been placed in the unenviable position of being associated with the varied interpretations of their teachings offered by their successors. Irrespective of how one views these teachings and their denunciation of private property, recognition must be accorded their contribution to the social sciences. They provided an impetus to the study of economic history and recognized the role of social classes and of property and class relationships in political life. In studying the consequences of the use of labor-saving machinery (the factory system), they promoted awareness of the impact of technology on society. Their concern with the problem of human alienation created interest in the question of its sources and how it can be overcome. In offering an appraisal of the capitalism of their time and in challenging it with their dire prophecies, they contributed to vast social changes. By applying the dialectic to the study of history and society, they demonstrated its usefulness in promoting an understanding of the complex and contradictory nature of development and the need to study the whole of society.

LENINISM

The Russian version of Marxism, known as Leninism, provided twentieth-century communism with many of its distinctive characteristics—the result of Vladimir Ilyich Lenin's efforts to apply the nineteenth-century doctrines of Marx and Engels to Russian conditions. Lenin, a Russian lawyer who reorganized the Marxist movement into the Communist Party, saw the growth of capitalism as inevitable in Russia and saw it also as providing for the triumph of his brand of

---

[16]V. I. Lenin, *The State and Revolution* (1917) in Burns, *op. cit.* (above, n. 7), p. 747. For a highly critical discussion of Lenin's understanding of the nature of politics, see A. J. Polan, *Lenin and the End of Politics* (London: Methuen & Co., 1984).

[17]For the texts of the 1919 and 1961 Programs, see Leonard Schapiro, ed., and Albert Boiter, assoc. ed., *The U.S.S.R. and the Future* (New York: Praeger, 1963), pp. 255–324. For the text of the 1986 Program see the December 1986 supplement to the *Current Digest of the Soviet Press.*

socialism. He corrected the failure of Marx to address himself to the political form that communist doctrine would assume. Much of Leninism constitutes a blend of practical considerations, along with certain theoretical refinements, designed to obtain and retain political power. The principal tenets of Leninism deal with very specific problems.

A Party of Professional Revolutionaries

Lenin's principal contribution, expounded in his *What Is to Be Done?* (1902), lay in his advocacy of a unique type of political party, composed of a limited number of dedicated, disciplined, tested, and trained communists fully conscious of their role. This elite was to be enrolled in a centralized organization, a substantial part of which was to remain conspiratorial in nature. Since it was unwise, in Lenin's view, to rely upon the revolutionary initiative and spontaneity of the proletarian masses, the Party organization was to serve as the vanguard of the working class. That this vanguard was to be mostly of intellectual and bourgeois origin did not trouble Lenin, for he assumed that the conduct of the revolutionary struggle was a task for full-time professionals and not for naive amateurs, however well intentioned. Thus, the Communist Party was to understand the "true interests" of the proletariat far better than the proletariat itself could.

The Need to Seize Power

Lenin's writings abound with admonitions concerning the dangers of settling for economic reforms within the framework of capitalism. In place of trade unionism and reformism, Lenin unceasingly advocated the primacy of political struggle directed against the bourgeois state. This preoccupation led to the advocacy of violent seizure of power, combined with appropriate agitational measures and slogans and a ready willingness to capitalize upon any and all issues useful in defeating the "class enemy." While revolutions were said to result from "objective conditions," it was also possible to accelerate the process by means of revolutionary action. Thus, Lenin believed that the "bourgeois epoch" in Imperial Russia— and elsewhere—could be abbreviated and the advent of communism expedited. This reflected the voluntarist element in Lenin's thinking that resulted from the importance given by Marxists to *consciousness*—that is, to thorough and rational knowledge and awareness of the role one is playing. The Communist Party, claiming to be endowed with such consciousness, assumed responsibility both for making the workers class conscious and for promoting the class struggle. Thus, the dialectical process of development could be "accelerated," and revolution could occur even in the underdeveloped and semicolonial countries that constituted the "weakest link" in capitalism.

The Dictatorship of the Proletariat

The class struggle was seen as culminating in the "democratic dictatorship of the proletariat"—a contradiction in terms that was inaccurate also because the Party was viewed as its embodiment. To this formula, in practice, the peasantry was added by Lenin—although it was recognized that the peasantry was unstable and contained petit-bourgeois elements. The dictatorship was to assure the establishment of socialism and the destruction of the class enemy and all counter-revolutionary forces. Although Marx originally employed this term ("the democratic dictatorship of the proletariat") in his *Critique of the Gotha Program,* it was Lenin who gave it practical expression by equating it with rule by the Communist Party.

Tactical Flexibility

Since circumstances could change, Lenin recognized the need to postpone achievement of goals should that be necessary. Thus, tactical retreats were regarded as proper, as when he decided to sue for peace with the Central Powers in 1918, to adopt the New Economic Policy in 1921 as a concession to small-scale capitalism, and to abandon the effort to communize Poland in 1920 and instead sign the Treaty of Riga. Such retreats were permissible so long as the basic purpose was kept in mind and it was known when to abandon a given tactic and turn a retreat into a new offensive. One of Lenin's best treatments of political tactics is to be found in his *"Left Wing" Communism, An Infantile Disorder* (1920), written for the benefit of European communists to whom he recommended a variety of tactics, including the use of bourgeois parliaments.

Partiinost' (Party-Mindedness)

The notion of partisanship in philosophy and in the social sciences—disciplines defined exclusively in terms of their service to the Party and its cause—was derived by Lenin from dialectical materialism. This principle was developed in Lenin's *Materialism and Empirio-Criticism* (1909). For Lenin, man's sense perceptions reflected "objective reality"—as perceived by the Party in terms of its ideology. Perception that did not correspond to this image of reality was therefore to be denounced as "idealist," "subjectivist," "relativist," and the like. Underlying *partiinost'* is the assumption that the Communist Party is the repository of philosophical truth *(istina)* in its understanding of history.[18] It is said to represent a "class approach" to all phenomena of social and political life.

A Theory of Imperialism

Unlike Marx and Engels, Lenin lived to witness World War I—an event that he attempted to explain in terms of historical and dialectical materialism. Lenin ignored such explanations as the breakdown of the balance of power, nationalism, or the miscalculations of rulers and diplomats caught in a crisis of their own making. Instead he contended (in his *Imperialism, the Highest Stage of Capitalism*) that war resulted from the efforts of a "ripening" capitalism to cope with its internal contradictions and to forestall a revolution. According to Lenin, a new

---

[18]B. I. Siusiukalov and L. A. Yakovleva, *op. cit.* (above, n. 15), pp. 153–154.

kind of finance capitalism characterized by monopoly and a merger of banking and industry was said to export capital abroad (because of declining profits and shrinking markets at home) to areas possessing raw materials and an abundant, cheap labor supply. The export of capital was followed by colonialism, in the form of annexation of these territories of new investment. Once all colonial territories were annexed, only redivision was possible, and this redivision allegedly led to military alliances and wars. The class struggle then entered the international arena in the form of the conflict between exploited colonial nations and the exploiting imperialist powers. The alleged contradictions within capitalism were said to be intensified as a result of the conflict between imperialist powers over colonial spoils. On the basis of these assertions and very limited historical evidence, Lenin concluded that wars are inevitable so long as capitalism exists.

THE STALINIST VARIANT

As dictator of the Soviet Union and leader of world communism from the late 1920s to his death in 1953, Iosif Vissarionovich Stalin claimed only to be Lenin's pupil and the faithful executor of his teachings. Yet the one-time theological student and professional revolutionary did enrich the body of Marxist-Leninist thought in his own inimitable way by demonstrating how the ideology could be modified and manipulated.

The doctrine of "socialism in one country" was adopted by Stalin in 1924 in his struggle for power with Lev Trotsky. Stalin contended that the building of socialism in the Soviet Union could be accomplished without the communist revolution in Western Europe that Trotsky was depicted as claiming to be essential to socialism's triumph. However, Stalin did not deny the desirability of communist victories in other countries. It is significant that Stalin was able to buttress his argument with an appropriate quotation from Lenin, who in August 1915 asserted that "uneven economic and political development is an absolute law of capitalism. Hence the victory of socialism is possible first in several or even in one capitalist country, taken singly."[19] Yet Stalin was to reaffirm as late as 1938 in his "Letter to Ivanov" that the victory of socialism in the USSR could not be final, as "we are living not on an island but 'in a system of states,' a considerable number of which are hostile to the land of socialism and create the danger of intervention and restoration."[20]

It followed logically from this last position that Stalin placed great emphasis upon the doctrine of "capitalist encirclement" of the Soviet Union. He concluded that it would be necessary to launch a program of forced development of heavy industry (production of the means of production rather than of consumer goods) as an essential part of the building of socialism, along with the collectivization of agriculture. These policies led to increased internal tension in the Soviet Union and to Stalin's March 5, 1937, assertion that the remnants of the defeated exploiting classes would become more desperate and dangerous as they grew weaker and

---

[19]V. I. Lenin, *Polnoe sobranie sochinenii,* 5th ed. (Moscow: Gospolitizdat, 1961), XXVI, 354.
[20]J. V. Stalin, *A Letter to Ivanov* (New York: International Publishers, 1938), pp. 12–13.

as the Soviet regime scored greater successes; this development would intensify the class struggle in spite of the fact that the establishment of socialism in the Soviet Union had been proclaimed.[21] Stalin believed firmly that no dying ruling class departs voluntarily from the stage of history. Only a fierce class struggle waged under Lenin's "dictatorship of the proletariat" would destroy the remnants of the old ruling class once and for all. Thus the Soviet state could not be expected to "wither away" under conditions of "capitalist encirclement."

Stalinism came to be associated with blood purges and the adulation of the *vozhd'* (leader) as well as with Russian chauvinism, the supremacy of the Communist Party apparatus, and the subordination of the international communist movement to the interests of Soviet foreign policy. Yet Stalin did introduce certain refinements into communist theory. In 1950 in his *Marxism and Problems of Linguistics,* he declared that the superstructure does not merely reflect the base in a passive, neutral manner but is an "exceedingly active force" helping to reshape the base. Stalin exempted language from the superstructure and declared that it had permanent features; it was not dependent upon the base but transcended historical epochs and the class struggle, serving various ruling classes, including the Communist Party, without changing fundamentally. Stalin also asserted that the law of the transformation of quantity into quality did not necessarily involve an abrupt change (an explosion or "leap") in a society not divided into hostile classes—and, of course, the Soviet Union had become such a society by official definition. Basic changes were said to occur in the Soviet Union without "explosions" by means of "revolution from above." However, leaps would still occur under capitalism with its numerous antagonistic contradictions.

These "contradictions" loomed large in Stalin's last theoretical work, *Economic Problems of Socialism in the U.S.S.R.* (1952). In it, he asserted that the contradictions between the various capitalist countries were greater and more acute than the contradictions between capitalism and socialism (the communist camp). Thus, while wars *between* capitalist states were still inevitable—as a result of the "struggle for markets" and the desire to "crush competitors"—a capitalist war against the Soviet Union was not very likely. Stalin held out the hope that the "peace movement" that arose in the 1940s would develop under communist influence into a "struggle for socialism." Yet he also declared that, to eliminate the inevitability of war, it would be necessary to abolish "imperialism" (i.e., capitalism).

As a ruler, Stalin did much to advance the cause of communism. In 1952, for instance, he stipulated certain conditions necessary for the achievement of communism. Among these was the disappearance of commodity exchange (by means of purchase and sale) in the collective farms, whose property was to be raised under communism to the level of public property, as "products exchange" replaced "commodity circulation" and money relations. With the achievement of communism, Stalin asserted, the law of value would disappear along with com-

---

[21]Stalin advanced this thesis as early as April 1929 in his campaign against the Right Deviation and as late as May 4, 1948, in a letter to the Communist Party of Yugoslavia.

modity production, and "society's demand for goods" would supposedly regulate production. Commodity production was to disappear once the "essential distinction" between industry and agriculture, between city and country was eliminated and replaced by a single "all-embracing production sector." Although Stalin was vague as to how this was to be accomplished, he did recognize that, in the Soviet Union, there were contradictions between the "relations of production" (including the peasantry) and the nationalized "forces of production." Such "nonantagonistic" contradictions would have to be eliminated by the abolition of "commodity circulation" (trade based on a money economy) and its replacement by "products exchange," which is essential to the development of a communist society.

Stalin also recognized the need to modify doctrine to fit changing conditions, since a formulation that is correct for one set of circumstances may be incorrect in a different situation. To illustrate this in the 1950 Linguistics Controversy, Stalin referred to the "socialism in one country" formula that, he contended, was rejected by Marx and Engels and accepted by Lenin as a result of differing conditions. Stalin offered the following explanation:

> As is obvious, we have here two different conclusions on the question of the victory of socialism which not only contradict but exclude each other.
>
> Some exegetes and Talmudists, who, without probing into the essence of the matter, quote formally, in isolation from historical conditions, may say that one of these conclusions, being absolutely incorrect, must be discarded, and the other conclusion, being absolutely correct, must be extended to all periods of development. But Marxists must know that the exegetes and Talmudists are mistaken; they must know that both of these conclusions are correct—not categorically so, but each in its time: the conclusion of Marx and Engels for the period of premonopoly capitalism and the conclusion of Lenin for the period of monopoly capitalism.[22]

Stalin concluded the entire discussion with the assertion: "Marxism does not recognize immutable conclusions and formulas obligatory for all epochs and periods. Marxism is the enemy of every kind of dogmatism."[23] Thus, the groundwork was laid for greater ideological flexibility with the accession to office of Stalin's successor, Nikita Sergeievich Khrushchev.

THE KHRUSHCHEV VARIANT

Although both Stalin and Khrushchev claimed to be Leninists, Khrushchev in 1956 launched a full-scale campaign against the "cult of personality"—a euphemism employed to refer to certain of Stalin's excesses—and did this in the name of a restoration of Leninism. While not denying the Communist Party's claim to possess truth and wisdom and its mastery of the "laws of historical development,"

---

[22] *Bolshevik,* No. 14, 1950, p. 4.
[23] *Ibid.,* p. 6.

Khrushchev's denunciation of the "cult of personality" and the adulation of Stalin indicated that the Party need not be led by a dictator or despot. Khrushchev's "Secret Speech," delivered late at night on February 24, 1956, at the Party's Twentieth Congress, inevitably led to controversy over the correctness of many beliefs and practices that had been taken for granted in Stalin's time but that were now questioned. It also evoked the antagonism of those communists who were discomforted by change and who regarded Khrushchev's iconoclasm as providing aid and comfort to the enemy.

Certain aspects of communist ideology dealing with foreign relations were modified by Khrushchev in February 1956 when he declared that World War III was "not fatalistically inevitable." Although this declaration was based on Stalin's 1952 pronouncement on contradictions between capitalist states and the communist world, it was followed by Khrushchev's explicit proclamation of the end of the "capitalist encirclement" of the Soviet Union—a key concept in Stalin's thinking. The end of encirclement was said to be due to the emergence of a world socialist system and to the enhanced position of the Soviet Union as a great power. As part of the new Soviet international posture, Khrushchev refurbished the doctrine of "peaceful coexistence." In lieu of a world war waged with nuclear weapons, peaceful coexistence would be based on a relentless economic competition between communism and capitalism, with an intensification of the ideological struggle. Rejecting any notion of a permanent status quo, this doctrine recognized the inevitability and desirability of local "wars of liberation," waged either to destroy alleged remnants of colonialism or to establish communist regimes or regimes more vulnerable to communist infiltration and take-over. Thus, the two systems were said by Khrushchev to be diametrically opposed, and the march of the world to communism was declared to be proof of *the irrevocable fact that the historic process is irreversible.*[24]

Khrushchev also reaffirmed the Leninist doctrine of various "roads to socialism," along with the belief that ruling classes do not surrender power voluntarily. However, in 1956 he held out hope for a "parliamentary" road to socialism, along which communists by some unusual means would obtain a majority of the seats in a "bourgeois" parliament—which they would then proceed to save from itself. At the same time, "national communism" was condemned on the grounds that the struggle waged by the various communist parties should be a common one based on a fund of common experience.

Although Khrushchev's claim to be a systematic theoretician could not compare with Stalin's, certain of the latter's doctrines applicable to Soviet internal policy were revised by Khrushchev. The Stalinist dictum regarding the intensification of the class struggle as the class enemy grows weaker was officially repudiated. Stalin's 1952 injunction forbidding the sale of agricultural machinery to collective farms was violated when Khrushchev sold the state-owned machine-tractor stations. In the 1961 Party program the Soviet Union was declared to be no longer a "dictatorship of the proletariat" but a "state of the whole people"—as

---

[24]Nikita S. Khrushchev, "On Peaceful Coexistence," *Foreign Affairs,* XXXVIII, No. 1 (October 1959), p. 15. Italics in original.

a result of the achievement of socialism and the transition to "full-scale construction of communism."

The image of the communism of the future promised by Khrushchev had much in common with Stalin's 1952 pronouncement regarding basic conditions for its establishment: economic abundance, a dramatic rise in real wages, and improved housing. Khrushchev promised but did not achieve the world's highest living standard, making it conditional upon increased labor productivity, national income, an improved international situation, and the future of the arms race. He also insisted that the oft-discussed stateless communist society would be "highly organized" and that the Soviet state would survive intact until the complete victory of communism.

SOVIET IDEOLOGY AFTER KHRUSHCHEV

Khrushchev's successors contributed less to Soviet ideology in terms of striking formulations, although they did introduce some substantial revisions. Initially, Leonid Brezhnev ignored Khrushchev's formula regarding the Soviet "state of the whole people" but found it necessary to restore the concept in the 1977 Constitution. Brezhnev's principal contribution was to define the Soviet Union as representing "developed, mature socialism" rather than being on the threshold of communism. The Communist Party, while claiming to have retained the essence and ideology of the working class, was correspondingly defined as the "party of all the people." Under Brezhnev the "scientific-technical revolution" was given much attention as a source of Soviet development and as the handmaiden of Marxism-Leninism.

In 1981 Brezhnev had the Party's Twenty-sixth Congress adopt a decision to revise Khrushchev's 1961 Program. This was necessary because the document had become a source of embarrassment as a result of its specificity and its unrealistic (fantastic) promises and claims regarding Soviet achievements. Especially embarrassing was the bold, actually reckless, concluding assertion: "THE PARTY SOLEMNLY PROCLAIMS: THE PRESENT GENERATION OF SOVIET PEOPLE SHALL LIVE IN COMMUNISM!"[25] This sentence proved to be one of the more notable overstatements of the twentieth century. The circumstances of the Soviet Union in 1981 rendered this claim patently false and required the issuance of an essentially new document.

The adoption of the 1986 Party Program was explained by General Secretary M. S. Gorbachev at the Twenty-seventh Congress. He conceded that in the 1961 Program "certain miscalculations were made in the timetables" and that "not all of the assessments and conclusions have been confirmed." Yet it was decided to issue a revision of the Third (1961) Program instead of a Fourth Program because each new program in the past had been adopted as a result of the attainment of certain goals. The tone of the 1986 revision reflects a somewhat more subdued militancy, and its language is somewhat less strident. Its emphasis

---

[25]*Programme of the Communist Party of the Soviet Union* (Moscow: Foreign Languages Publishing House, 1961), p. 128.

is on the "acceleration of social and economic development" and the need to avoid a world war. Yet it optimistically asserts: "For all its unevenness, complexity and contradictory nature, humanity's movement toward socialism and communism is inexorable."[26]

However, the 1986 Program states that there is "no sharp boundary" between socialism and communism, but there must be sufficient "productive forces that open up opportunities for the complete satisfaction of the reasonable requirements of society and the individual." Communism is to be a "classless social system with a single form of public ownership of the means of production" but is not to be stateless, and the phrase "withering away of the state" is not included in the 1986 Program. It is to be "a highly organized society" with "communist public self-government." It is claimed that "the activity of state agencies will acquire a non-political nature, and the need for the state as a special political institution will gradually disappear."[27] However, Gorbachev warned that "a time frame for the achievement of programmatic goals is not warranted." He estimated the advent of communism in the following cautious terms: "The errors of the past are a lesson for us. The only thing that can be definitely said today [in 1986] is that the fulfillment of the present program extends beyond the confines of the current century."[28]

EVALUATION OF THE IDEOLOGY'S ASSUMPTIONS

Since historical materialism is an essential element of Marxist-Leninist doctrine, the question of its validity looms large in any evaluation of the ideology. Historical materialism embodies the fallacy inherent in any monistic view of history and is based upon highly selective data. Man's history is far too vast and diverse to be subsumed under a single doctrine or explained by a single theory. How can the entirety of recorded history be reduced arbitrarily to three stages (slaveholding, feudal, and capitalist)? Is it not highly questionable to base an entire theory of historical development on three cases and then proclaim it to be "scientific"? How can all of history be subordinated to the single principle that human behavior is a function of the mode of production, with everything attributed to a people's tools and the way in which they earn their living? Indeed, it can be argued in refutation of the Marxian view that the economic base—the mode of production that supposedly determines the superstructure—is actually determined by the superstructure, for the methods of production are the result of human inventiveness and not vice versa.

Historical materialism is based on the debatable assumption that a human being is primarily an economic animal. It conveniently ignores the fact that this same being is also political and religious. Why should the economic determinants—tools and food—be more important than philosophical creeds, ethnic identity, personality, sex, chance, or accident? The error of Marxism-Leninism

---

[26]*Kommunist,* March 1986, No. 4, p. 112.

[27]*Ibid.,* pp. 113–114.

[28]*Ibid.,* p. 78.

lies in the fact that Marx and Engels devoted their energies and talents to an investigation of their own era—one in which they thought they discerned a certain pattern of inevitable development based on the conflict between the "mode of production" and the "relations of production." Influenced by the technology of the Industrial Revolution and its resultant social dislocations, they posited a historical scheme based upon a particular mode of production by applying the distinctive character of capitalism retrojectively to the stages that preceded it.

Yet one can ask: what "changes in the methods of production and exchange" marked the transition from the slaveholding to the feudal stage? In actual fact the changes in the techniques of agriculture and the crafts employed by ancient slaves and medieval serfs were very slight compared to the changes that characterized the transition from feudalism to capitalism. Thus, one can ask, what contradiction resulting from a new mode of production could have led to the fall of the slaveholding society? In reality, two different "relations of production" (slaveholding and feudal) resulted from essentially similar "modes of production." In a similar manner, the allegedly different relations of production that are said to distinguish communism from capitalism are based on industrial techniques and processes common to both systems. Clearly the political and social changes in question cannot be fully explained in terms of economic determinism. In addition, Marx and Engels dealt with ancient and medieval societies superficially and neglected non-Western societies in general and the "Asiatic" mode of production ("oriental despotism") in particular.

Marxism's obsession with class has led to certain inconsistencies in the ideology. The class concept claims to embrace millions of persons said to be conscious of their class affiliation and possessed of a single will that is capable of determining the outcome of history. Yet in practice it is the Communist Party that is truly class conscious, substituting its own consciousness and will for the ghost class that it claims to represent. Thus, in practice, Communist parties have frequently tended to be parties of disaffected intellectuals and bourgeois sympathizers rather than of workers and peasants. The theory of class hardly explains the appearance of Marx and Lenin as leaders of the proletariat, in view of their nonproletarian background. Moreover, class solidarity often fails to materialize, as when a supposedly exploited class refuses to revolt or when some members of the bourgeoisie or proletariat betray the interests of their class and serve its enemies. In basing morality on class interests, furthermore, communism ignores the fact that a moral code usually transcends class lines and can unite supposedly inimical classes. For communist doctrine the morality of the class that is winning is superior to that of the class that is on the way out. By this doctrine, what is "moral" is determined by what is successful.

In communist theory, history is the record of class struggle and the future is said to belong to the exploited class. Yet the slaves of ancient society did not overthrow their exploiters and become the ruling class (the feudal lords) of the new epoch. Similarly, it was not the serfs of the feudal epoch who as a class inherited the dominant role in the capitalist epoch as the new bourgeoisie. Thus it is doubtful that the proletariat—supposedly the "gravedigger" of capitalism— will succeed the bourgeoisie as the new postcapitalist ruling class in accordance with communist predictions. Indeed, Marxism errs in reducing social relationships to two classes, for society in reality is far more complex. In positing a doctrine of historical inevitability, communism ignores the fundamental fact that predictions are conditional—since people can frequently invalidate them by deliberately changing the conditions that it was erroneously assumed would persist. Thus it must be asked why class war and a communist victory must be regarded as inevitable. Communists, moreover, do not distinguish between their predictions and their actions designed to bring about the events whose occurrence they have predicted. In confusing determinism with voluntarism, they fuse the inevitable with the (to them) desirable. Communism is therefore not a science but a revolutionary reformism whose advocates predict crises and then—thanks to Lenin's influence—do everything in their power to bring them about.

The predictions of communists have often been incorrect. Marx and Engels predicted the progressive impoverishment of the industrial proletariat. In fact, the working class improved its living standard by means of free trade unions, cooperatives, the ballot box, social insurance, the graduated income tax, and other measures that demonstrated that the chain of inevitability can be broken. The middle class was not impoverished and proletarianized, as forecast by communists, but flourished and attracted members of the proletariat. Similarly, communism did not take hold in the industrialized countries in which the "contradictions" of capitalism were supposedly most highly developed but rather in certain agrarian countries whose conditions did not readily fit the Marxist scheme of analysis. Marxists also incorrectly predicted the decline of nationalism as a result of the growing internationalism of trade and communications and of economic institutions (trusts, cartels) and practices.

If the accuracy of communist prognoses has left something to be desired, the doctrine of dialectical materialism with its emphasis upon contradiction makes these failures palatable. At issue here is not the proposition that a society's ideas have been influenced—communists would say determined—by the conditions of material existence but rather the blind assumption that historical development occurs exclusively in terms of class conflict in accordance with the rhythmic dissonance of the dialectic. The concept of the dialectic can be a very useful analytical tool, since contradiction and conflict characterize many phenomena and the world is not static. However, when this concept is abused and elevated by communists to an all-embracing principle that purports to explain all development in terms of a struggle of opposites *leading to a preordained outcome,* certain questions arise. How can we really be certain of the outcome? Does the dialectic not involve the danger of being a method of analysis by definition, in which the results obtained depend upon the user? Is not proof of this provided by the fact that both Hegel and Marx employed the dialectic with different results and for different purposes? In fact, the dialectic is a process of thought that does not adequately explain the *ultimate* cause and origins of the events it seeks to interpret.

An even greater difficulty arises from the Marxist forced marriage of the dialectic with philosophical and historical materialism, which recognizes only a material world based on sensory perception and assumes that matter is eternal and is its own cause developing by self-movement. Indeed, "matter," as employed by communist philosophers, is never really explained but is defined as "objective reality" (Lenin) or as the "totality of material things" (Engels). This viewpoint ignores the question of the source of matter; it simply assumes the material world as given and does not inquire into the cause of the order that characterizes the universe. The reliance upon self-movement to explain development dialectically assumes that the causes of change are inherent in everything as a result of internal contradictions and bear no reference to external factors. Thus dialectical causation does not really explain why events develop in a given direction, but when invoked by communists it has provided reassuring confirmation of their conviction that history is developing in their favor along a generally predetermined course.

A fundamental weakness in communist thought is in its treatment of ideology, which classical Marxism regards as ephemeral false consciousness and as a rationalization of class interests. Thus ideologies come and go in accordance with the pattern of class struggle and are simply a part of the superstructure, which is determined by the economic base. However, an inconsistency arises here because of the refusal of Marxists to apply this Marxist concept to the ideology of Marxism. Thus, instead of viewing their own ideology as transitory and relative—like all other ideologies—communists see themselves as the great exception: for the first time in all history, absolute truth is said to have been discovered. A related inconsistency is that the Soviet definition of ideology is highly positive and differs from the classical Marxist definition of it as false perception.

The illogic and the simplistic nature of communist philosophy are evident when one asks why the dialectic, social classes, and the class struggle should cease to be operative (once communists are victorious) if they have been motive forces in all of human history. Why should the class struggle be replaced by a "classless" society? Why should contradictions be "antagonistic" under capitalism and "nonantagonistic" under a communist regime? Indeed, the analytic categories of Marxism-Leninism do not provide adequate explanations of such phenomena as Stalin's cruel dictatorship or the bitter ideological dispute that developed between the Soviet Union and the People's Republic of China.

Dubious aspects of communist belief include the assumption that nearly everything can be known, the blind belief in inevitable progress, the utopian nature of professed communist goals, and the willingness to justify the use of any means in the pursuit of these ends. It is ironic but revealing that communists should simultaneously preach humanism and class hatred. Indeed, communists have failed to understand that ends are influenced by the means chosen to achieve them. Indeed, the use of base means—so frequently advocated by Lenin and Stalin—served to corrupt noble ends and to debase the entire socialist movement. A basic fallacy in the doctrine has been the a priori assumption that state (communist) ownership of the means of production is the source of moral conduct and will create justice, remake humanity, society, and guarantee human happiness.[29] The pursuit of these goals has led to the sacrifice of the individual on the altar

---

[29]One of the errors of Marx and Engels was their apparent inability to distinguish between the evils of a developing industrial economy and early capitalism. By attributing the characteristics of early industrialism to capitalism, they failed to recognize that the fact of ownership itself does not change the character of the industrial system and the hierarchical relationships resulting from it.

of the collectivity in accordance with communism's sociocentric nature. This is a reflection of Marx's Sixth Thesis on Feuerbach: "But the human essence is no abstraction inherent in each separate individual. In its reality it is the ensemble of the social relations." Thus the humanism professed by communists is not defined in terms of individual rights but by equating the alleged interests of a single class (and party) with those of humanity.

FACTORS PROMOTING BELIEF

Although the basic premises and conclusions of communist ideology can be questioned, they have attracted those who seek to believe and are predisposed to accept the doctrine.[30] Belief in the ideology has been reinforced by the fact that Soviet communism is embodied in a functioning political system that has achieved successes in rapid industrialization, nuclear weapons, space exploration, and in international politics. The fact that communism made significant political gains after World War II, bringing more than one-third of humanity under the rule of various Communist parties, provided "proof" of the correctness of the ideology for those who wished to accept it. Confirmation was provided by subsequent communist gains in Cuba, South Vietnam, Laos, and Kampuchea.

In the noncommunist world, communists have chosen to single out those events that give them comfort and appear to confirm their prognoses. These have included unrest in the former colonial areas, the competition between capitalist states for markets, the emergence of a number of neutralist countries, and the nationalization of foreign-owned properties in various lands. In the industrialized capitalist countries, communists have found confirmation of their beliefs in strikes, unemployment, inflation, increased crime, and the presence of prominent businessmen in high political office as well as in business failures, corporation mergers, and the alleged growth of monopoly as a result of the elimination of smaller competitors. In each case communists have isolated such events from the total environment and interpreted them in accordance with their own rigid scheme of analysis while ignoring contrary evidence. Criticism of "bourgeois society" by disaffected Western writers and public figures has been used to give credence to Marxism-Leninism.

Acceptance of the basic premises of the ideology fulfills the desire for dedication and commitment. Sharing common values, beliefs, enemies, and goals, its adherents see proof enough in the very existence of a mass movement that embraces tens of millions and rules over hundreds of millions. Indeed, if communists do not find the meaning of life in their ideology, it is unlikely that they will obtain it outside of the Party because alternative philosophies of history and politics are excluded. Thus pragmatism, positivism, and existentialism are rejected as "bourgeois" philosophies. Soviet philosophy claims to provide answers

---

[30]For an incisive discussion of the attractions and defects of communist ideology, see Robert G. Wesson, *Why Marxism? The Continuing Success of a Failed Theory* (New York Basic Books, 1976). See also Robert L. Heilbroner, *Marxism: For and Against* (New York: Norton, 1980) and Thomas Sowell, *Marxism: Philosophy and Economics* (New York: William Morrow, 1985).

to all questions or dismisses certain questions as "irrelevant."[31] Communist beliefs provide a rationale for the regime's existence and a sense of legitimacy and destiny; anyone having a stake in the Soviet political order must accept them or repress their doubts.

RELEVANCE TO SOVIET POLITICS

Communism has been described by C. E. M. Joad as a "philosophy in action." Its concern with uniting theory and practice was expressed by Marx in the eleventh of his *Theses on Feuerbach:* "Philosophers have only *interpreted* the world in various ways; the point, however, is to *change* it." Thus, communist philosophy is reflected in political practice. The refusal to share power and to tolerate other political parties or private economic organizations, the insistence upon forced industrialization, collectivized agriculture, and the propagation of "scientific atheism" in schools and universities—all testify to the influence of ideological requirements. Indeed, the claim to possess "truth" has enabled communists to rationalize their use of repressive measures and their demands for great sacrifices from their subjects in the name of a happy future.

The requirements of ideology have tended to exclude certain policies. Thus, large-scale private cultivation of land and liquidation of the collective and state farms are rejected. Financial incentives and the individual's ability to innovate in return for a generous payoff have been restricted because of the fear that someone's income might be "unearned" or "excessive." Historians are not permitted much latitude in the writing of history and must even suppress certain historical facts as "non-events." For example, the Norman theory regarding Scandinavian influence on the Eastern Slavs is banned; the Soviet Union's status as a quasi-ally of Nazi Germany in 1939–1941 and its willingness to join the Rome-Berlin-Tokyo Axis on certain conditions have been expunged from the Soviet historical record. Soviet historians receive from the Communist Party's Central Committee official theses to be used in interpreting particular historical events.

The dialectic—with its emphasis upon contradictions, abrupt changes, and the transformation of phenomena into their opposites—has influenced Soviet political behavior. It has facilitated sudden shifts in the policies and general line of the Communist Party. Thus, the New Economic Policy, with its concessions to petty capitalism and commerce, could replace War Communism in 1921 and be replaced, in turn, by its antithesis in the First Five Year Plan of 1929. Veteran Party leaders have been praised and decorated only to be denounced and publicly disgraced. The posthumous denigration of Stalin following his adulation during his lifetime provides a graphic example of the transformation of something into its opposite. The dialectic has also enabled Soviet politicians to advocate unabashedly contradictory formulae. Accordingly, Stalin could declare in June 1930:

---

[31]For a reaffirmation of the validity of Soviet ideology and a criticism of its critics, see Lev N. Moskvichov, *The End of Ideology Theory: Illusions and Reality. Critical Notes on a Fashionable Bourgeois Conception* (Moscow: Progress Publishers, 1974).

> We are for the withering away of the state. And at the same time we stand for the strengthening of the dictatorship of the proletariat, representing the strongest and most powerful authority of all existing state authorities up to the present time. The higher development of state authority for the purpose of preparing the conditions *for* the withering away of state authority—there you have a Marxist formula. Is it "contradictory"? Yes, it is "contradictory." But contradiction is a part of life, and it fully reflects Marxist dialectics.[32]

Persons trained in the dialectic with its concern for contradiction and change tend to view the truth as a variable depending upon circumstances. Yet truth must further the communist cause and must therefore be official and subject to censorship and change. Since in this view the inevitable future is more important than the prosaic present, it is permissible to utter a statement that is false today but is *potentially* true. Conversely, what is true today may be false tomorrow. In addition, the dialectic with its emphasis upon antagonism and struggle promotes a brand of politics preoccupied with enemies and seeing life as characterized by conflict rather than by moderation and compromise. Thus political dissenters have been subjected to cruel treatment and regarded as being in the service of the "class enemy."

Yet the essentially dogmatic character of communist ideology should not blind one to its instrumentalist and manipulative aspects. Lenin modified and developed the teachings of Marx and Engels in applying them to Russia. Stalin modified Lenin's teachings, and Khrushchev revised certain of Lenin's and Stalin's doctrines. Yet each Soviet leader claimed that he was remaining faithful to the basic belief. It was possible for Stalin to remove language from the Marxist superstructure; he could also decide to tolerate formal logic and even introduce it as a subject of instruction after it was denounced for years as being contrary to dialectics. In 1955 Einstein's relativity theory was found to be acceptable after first having been rejected on the grounds that it represented philosophical idealism in physics, was not based on dialectical materialism, and denied absolute space and time as reference systems. Its acceptance was made possible by treating energy (into which mass is transformed) as a form of matter in motion. This change was prompted by practical considerations and the need to exploit nuclear energy. A similar change occurred in the case of cybernetics—the science of control and communications in machines and living organisms—which was denounced in 1953 as a "pseudoscience" and later accepted (without its possible ideological or philosophical implications) because of its relevance to computers, automation, and guidance systems. Soviet leaders do adopt certain decisions on purely pragmatic grounds, modifying or circumventing the ideology.

While it is incorrect therefore to view ideology as static or immutable, its pragmatic aspects should not blind one to such of its axiomatic bases as atheism, historical materialism, historical necessity, the role of the class struggle in history, the supposedly evil nature of private ownership of the means of production, and the belief in inevitable progress and in the leading role of the Communist Party

---

[32]I. V. Stalin, *Sochineniia,* XII, pp. 369ff.

as the chosen instrument of the will of history. These tenets have constituted the hard core of doctrine. The practice of combining basic truth with pragmatic truth was well expressed in Engels' assertion that "our doctrine is not a dogma but a guide to action." Thus, all ideological pronouncements are not of equal significance; some are crucial. Khrushchev succinctly summarized the blending of doctrine and policy when he reminded the Twentieth Congress of the Communist Party of the Soviet Union that "Marxism-Leninism teaches that theory divorced from practice is dead, and practice which is not enlightened by revolutionary theory is blind."[33]

Ideology has dictated intervention by the Party in a variety of fields, including literature, the arts, pedagogy, genetics, psychology, historiography, architecture, the social sciences, and philosophy. In many of these fields the Party has issued directives banning certain kinds of activities and prescribing specific teachings and practices. Yet such fields as geology and mathematics were not affected by ideological dictates, and physics was not severely affected. Genetics as a science suffered the worst depredations in the forties at the hands of the ideologists and their collaborators in biology (who insisted on the inheritance of acquired characteristics in the short run). It managed to re-emerge as a scientific discipline in the sixties.[34]

The ideology has required the use of official textbooks in all disciplines and has dictated their revision in more sensitive areas. Power struggles and policy debates have been conducted in doctrinal terms as conflicts between orthodoxy and deviation. There are ideologically "correct" and "incorrect" policies. Communists, it should be remembered, believe that ideas are important and that they have consequences. They take great pains to distinguish between what they regard as "true" and "false" philosophies. Their beliefs have provided a rationale and justification for the acts of the Soviet government and the Communist Party.

Vast amounts of public funds are spent to propagate Marxism-Leninism in the Soviet Union and abroad. Yet there is ample evidence from a variety of Soviet and non-Soviet observers—and even a degree of official admission—that Soviet ideology is expressed in stereotyped forms, is boring, and provides unsatisfactory answers to important questions. Alain Besançon has contended that the Soviet system has ceased to be the *ideocracy* (government based on a system of ideas) that it originally was and has become a *logocracy*—a system of rule based on the propagated word.[35] Ideology is not believed so much as it is talked about and invoked. Thus ideology is seemingly reduced to verbal terms. The "correct" answers and explanations are learned and expressed "for the record," although the same person might be a "private dissenter" and strictly separate public

---

[33]*XX S"ezd Kommunisticheskoi Partii Sovetskogo Soiuza, Stenograficheskii otchet* (Moscow: Gospolitizdat, 1956), I, p. 112.

[34]On the fate of genetics, see Zhores Medvedev, *The Rise and Fall of T. D. Lysenko* (New York: Columbia University Press, 1969), David Joravsky, *The Lysenko Affair* (Cambridge, Mass.: Harvard University Press, 1970), and Mark Popovsky, *The Vavilov Affair* (Hamden, Conn.: Archon Books, 1984).

[35]Alain Besançon, *The Soviet Syndrome* (New York: Harcourt Brace Jovanovich, 1978), pp. 20–21.

utterances and private inner thoughts. It may be that the Soviet rulers are prepared to settle for this form of verbal outward compliance. However, there undoubtedly are "true believers" in the Party membership, although the Soviet rulers themselves do not know their exact number.

Thus, the fabric of Soviet ideology may have become thin and threadbare, as Besançon has contended, but it is being mended and kept intact. The vast sums spent by the Soviet leaders on this effort testify to the importance they give to ideology, although they are finding it increasingly difficult to impose ideological conformity. Because of the difficulties and the shortcomings of Marxist-Leninist ideology, there is the question of whether or not there is a more suitable replacement. The apparent dearth of alternatives is eloquent and remarkable. One possibility—which has been invoked and utilized as a supplementary "ideology"—is "Russianism."

Indeed, there is the concern that communism or Sovietism has become a vehicle for "Russianism" and is being absorbed by it. However, the problem with "Russianism" as a formal alternative is its limited appeal. It appeals to ethnic Russians (but not necessarily to all Russians) and to those among non-Russians who would serve the Russians in order to obtain rewards and bask in their reflected glory. "Russianism" can be defined in the following terms: belief in the superiority of the Russians as a people; recognition of their cultural and scientific achievements; praise of their alleged virtues and their role as a new "chosen people" destined to identify with and deliver humanity from all evil; and expression of unbounded gratitude to the Russians for their "sacrifice" in redeeming humanity and in preserving and enhancing world civilization. "Russianism" does serve as a form of background music to the Kremlin's professions of "internationalism" and "humanism." Non-Russians in the Soviet Union are required to praise the Russians and express their gratitude for being ruled by Moscow. However, non-Russians are likely to be repelled in the end should the implicit "Russianism" become totally explicit. Thus, "Russianism" is at best a less effective alternative to Marxism-Leninism and would serve as a poor bonding agent for an imperial system.

The status of Soviet ideology might be more readily understood if it is likened to the condition of the Russian Orthodox Church as the state religion of the Empire. Russian Orthodoxy enjoyed official status, and even unbelievers had to comply with certain of its requirements, insofar as civil acts necessitated religious dispensation or ecclesiastical participation. Despite this privileged position, there was much questioning and rejection of religion, and much of the Russian intelligentsia was known for its atheism or agnosticism despite the officially cultivated and politically useful image of a "Holy Russia." Lip service and minimal outward conformity proved to be poor substitutes for genuine devoutness and religiosity. This uneasy, uncertain coexistence of official religion with private and censored public irreligion or skepticism persisted in the Russian Empire for many decades. It may have a modern analog in the condition of Marxist-Leninist ideology in the Soviet Union.

chapter 4

The Communist Party of the Soviet Union: Development and Organization

The Communist Party, although mentioned only briefly in the Soviet constitution, has provided the lifeblood of the Soviet regime in the form of the cadres or key personnel that operate the political system. The Party recruits and trains persons and defines the conditions of advancement for political and administrative positions of responsibility. It determines the regime's basic policies, which are then adopted by the Soviet government. It endeavors to persuade Soviet citizens to accept its special role and view of history and has defined itself as a "party of a new type." Because of the Party's dominant role, the Soviet political system has been referred to as a "partocracy." The Party's membership of more than 19 million is committed to propagating its values and prescriptions for the communist version of the "good life" and is the embodiment of the attitudes and beliefs that are termed "communist ideology." In brief, the Party sees itself as exercising a tutelary role in relationship to its subjects, and the Party leaders view their relationship to the rank-and-file membership in a similar fashion. Billboards and banners frequently proclaim the slogan, "Glory to the CPSU."

This remarkable organization began to take shape soon after the turn of the century as a result of the activities of a small number of compulsive and dedicated persons who had embraced Marxism and endeavored to give it substance in the context of the Russian Empire's autocratic political order. To a significant degree the Party was the brainchild of Vladimir Ilyich Lenin (Ulianov), who imposed upon it his organizational blueprint and who abused, chastised, and excommunicated those of its members who would not accept his leadership, ideological formulas, and tactics. The son of a provincial school inspector and by consequence a member of the appointive nobility, Lenin abandoned legal practice and engaged in full-time political agitation in behalf of Marxism.

THE EMERGENCE OF LENINIST BOLSHEVISM

The Russian version of a Marxist political party came into being as a reaction against the peasant-oriented Populist movement *(Narodnichestvo)* of the last quarter of the nineteenth century. It was also a response to earlier ineffective efforts to establish such a party. The Marxists of the Russian Empire parted company with other Russian revolutionaries in insisting on the desirability and inevitability of Russia's experiencing capitalism and industrial development with a bourgeoisie and proletariat. They opposed the Populist efforts to socialize Russia on the basis of a rural commune and contended, instead, that Russia's future lay with the urban industrial working class.

The founding in 1883 (the year of Marx's death) of the "Emancipation of Labor" Group in Geneva, Switzerland, by Georgii Plekhanov and other Russian political émigrés was not consequential, although it reflected the break with Populism. Initially, the Russian Marxist movement began in the late 1880s and early 1890s with a few small clandestine study groups confined principally to genuine or would-be intellectuals, as well as a few small workers' circles. In December 1895, the Union for the Struggle for the Emancipation of the Working Class was formed in St. Petersburg. However, most members of this group of Marxist intellectuals, including Lenin, were soon arrested. Lenin was kept in prison during all of 1896 and spent the three subsequent years in exile in Siberia.[1]

In March 1898, several unions for emancipation and other Marxist groups held the founding congress of the Russian Social Democratic Labor Party (RSDLP) in Minsk. This Congress had no practical results, and eight of the nine delegates were arrested soon after it adjourned. Lenin, in exile, determined that the Party would have to be based on particular organizational principles. Upon completing his sentence in 1900, Lenin joined several Russian political émigrés in Western Europe and established *Iskra (The Spark),* a Marxist newspaper that was smuggled into Imperial Russia. Lenin's method was to employ the newspaper to propagate Marxism and also to use its agents and subscribers in Russia as organizers of local groups that would affiliate with the revived Party. The agents would also raise funds and transmit them along with information to the Party center in Western Europe.

Lenin insisted on organizing a new kind of party based upon professionalism and iron discipline and the use of various methods of struggle, including

---

[1]For the early period of Russian Marxism, see Richard Pipes, *Social Democracy and the St. Petersburg Labor Movement, 1885–1897* (Cambridge: Harvard University Press, 1963) and Leopold H. Haimson, *The Russian Marxists and the Origins of Bolshevism* (Cambridge: Harvard University Press, 1955). Also see Donald W. Treadgold, *Lenin and His Rivals: the Struggle for Russia's Future, 1898–1906* (New York: Praeger, 1955; reprint edition, Greenwood Press, 1976). On Lenin's childhood and youth, see Rolf H. W. Theen, *Lenin: Genesis and Development of a Revolutionary* (Princeton, N.J.: Princeton University Press, 1980).

conspiracy. He used the pages of *Iskra* for expressing his views on Party organization and in 1902 published a work, *What Is to Be Done?*, in which he explained his plans in greater detail.[2]

Lenin advocated these views with considerable success at the Party's Second Congress, held in Brussels and London during August 1903. *Iskra* became the Party's central organ, with Lenin as editor, and a Central Committee was elected. However, the Congress was marked by controversy over the definition of a Party member (Lenin advocated an inelastic definition), how much autonomy local Party organizations would have (Lenin demanded complete centralism), and the issues of national self-determination and cultural development of non-Russian nationalities. When seven delegates walked out of the Congress, Lenin and his followers were able to claim a "majority"; and as a result of this fateful act, Lenin's faction became known as the *Bolsheviks* (members of the majority). The opponents who remained at the Congress were called *Mensheviks* (members of the minority), and Lenin subsequently was to claim that his Bolsheviks were the majority even when they were in the minority in a badly divided Party.

Lenin also sought to reduce the editorial board of *Iskra* from six to three members, with the Mensheviks having but one representative, L. Martov. When Martov refused to serve, the other member (Plekhanov) deserted Lenin and advocated the reinstatement of the ousted Menshevik members of the editorial board. Lenin, outmaneuvered, resigned as editor of *Iskra* and had himself appointed to the Central Committee; he soon began publishing another newspaper, *Vperyod (Forward),* organ of the Bolshevik faction. In April and May of 1905 the Bolsheviks held their own Party Congress in London, which was boycotted by the Mensheviks. Efforts to heal the breach at the Stockholm "Unity" Congress in April–May of 1906 were unsuccessful when the Bolsheviks were outvoted and Lenin was not even elected to the Central Committee. A subsequent Congress (the Fifth by Bolshevik count), held in London in May 1907 and attended by both factions, did not end the schism in the Party.

The division between Bolsheviks and Mensheviks involved differences of degree on many issues, which subsequently became differences in kind. Both factions were Marxist and socialist and believed that capitalism, although temporarily beneficial for Russia, would be replaced by the revolutionary order. However, the Mensheviks did not share the impatience of the Bolsheviks to overthrow the regime and were willing to let the bourgeois capitalist epoch run its course and fulfill its purpose in Russia by establishing conditions conducive to the advent of socialism. The Bolsheviks emphasized illicit conspiratorial organization and a tightly organized party of professionals, while many of the Mensheviks favored a mass party of workers, less centralism, and reliance upon legal means. The two factions also disagreed over tactics toward and within the Russian quasi-parliament, the State Duma, and on the issue of electoral alliances with other parties. Another source of controversy was the Bolshevik method of obtaining funds by

---

[2]For a slightly abridged English translation of Lenin's *What Is To Be Done?* see the edition prepared by S. V. Utechin, which also has a lengthy introduction and notes by S. V. and Patricia Utechin (London: Oxford University Press, 1963).

means of armed raids; on one occasion they also arranged a fictitious marriage in order to gain control of an inheritance. The Mensheviks objected to such methods, as well as to the Bolshevik faction's practice of maintaining its separate treasury, apparatus, and newspaper. Thus the factions in the RSDLP disagreed largely over methods and tactics rather than over ultimate socialist goals.

Lenin had no genuine desire to repair the breach with the Mensheviks. He was able to acquire funds from wealthy donors and from other sources, including foreign governments; in general, he kept the various sources of funds secret even from many of his closer followers. The tsarist secret police (the *Okhrana*) succeeded in infiltrating Lenin's Bolshevik movement and was fully aware of his activities in Switzerland, France, and Austria; they even placed a spy in the Central Committee. The police were also interested in promoting the Bolshevik-Menshevik split, with the intention of weakening the social democratic movement. Lenin obliged them while promoting the interests of his own faction. In January 1912, he gathered his followers in Prague for a conference, as a result of which his organization came to be called the **Russian Social Democratic Labor Party (of Bolsheviks)** and the division of the Russian Marxists into two parties was consummated. In 1912 each group was publishing its own daily newspaper—and that of the Bolsheviks was named *Pravda (Truth)*. Subsequent efforts to unite the factions were unsuccessful.

By November 1917, Lenin was in a position to wrest the reins of power from a weak and indecisive Russian Provisional Government, which did not exercise full powers in its own capital but had to share them with the Petrograd Soviet of Workers and Soldiers Deputies; the latter body gradually came under Bolshevik control. Lenin's success in 1917 was due to several factors. In addition to being ruthless and dedicated, he was preaching a simple and readily understood doctrine in a time of general confusion and despair.[3]

The Provisional Government, under the leadership of Alexander Kerensky, was bent upon prosecuting an unpopular war effort, while Lenin advocated immediate peace and promoted disaffection among the troops. Lenin also promised bread to those who were in need and land to the land-hungry peasantry. He had succeeded in creating for the Bolsheviks a private army (the "Red Guard") and in winning over or demoralizing and neutralizing the troops in the capital, thus depriving the Provisional Government of armed support. The Provisional

---

[3]Lenin had returned to Russia from Switzerland in April 1917 with the aid of the Imperial German Government, which had clandestinely financed the Russian revolutionary movement (but especially the Bolsheviks) and defeatist elements during World War I in an effort to weaken the Russian political order and compel the tsarist regime to sue for peace. Millions of German marks were invested in this operation, and although Lenin took support from wherever he could find it and crossed Germany by rail on his return to Russia, he was no one's agent but his own and was serving the interests of Bolshevism. See Z. A. B. Zeman, ed., *Germany and the Revolution in Russia, 1915–1918: Documents from the Archives of the German Foreign Ministry* (London and New York: Oxford University Press, 1958) and Stefan T. Possony, *Lenin: The Compulsive Revolutionary* (Chicago: Henry Regnery, 1964). Other studies of Lenin are Louis Fischer, *The Life of Lenin* (New York: Harper & Row, 1964); Robert Payne, *The Life and Death of Lenin* (New York: Simon & Schuster, 1964); and Bertram D. Wolfe, *Three Who Made a Revolution* (New York: Dial Press, 1948; Stein and Day, 1984). Certain aspects of Bolshevik conspiratorial activity are dealt with in Michael Futrell, *Northern Underground* (New York: Praeger, 1963).

Government also lacked an effective intelligence service and police organization, since the tsarist secret police had been dissolved.

Other parties could obtain more votes in Russia's last free election but could not compete with the Bolsheviks' demagogic appeals nor with their organizational talents. Lenin's paramilitary force seized power on the night of November 6–7, 1917 (October 24–25 according to the then-official Julian calendar), by taking the Winter Palace, the seat of the weak Provisional Government, and other key points in the capital.

STAGES IN THE PARTY'S DEVELOPMENT

Lenin's Leadership (1917–1922)

After having spent a decade and a half in Western Europe as an émigré, Lenin was to have but four and a half years to leave his mark upon the Soviet regime, which had now become synonymous with Bolshevism. The Party grew rapidly from approximately 20,000 members in March 1917 at the time of the monarchy's collapse to ten times that number by the year's end. It attracted left-wing Mensheviks and renegade Socialist Revolutionaries, and as it grew, it acquired an appearance far different from that intended by Lenin when he first expounded the notion of an exclusive, tightly knit group of dedicated conspirators and agitators.[4]

The Party seized power in a demoralized and war-weary country beset with innumerable problems. The collapse of the army made it impossible to resist the advancing armies of Germany and Austria-Hungary. Thus, it was imperative for Lenin to conclude a peace treaty and dissociate his regime from an unpopular war, in this way improving its chances for survival. With the signing of the Brest-Litovsk Treaty, however, Russia lost certain of her Western non-Russian territories and had to recognize Ukrainian independence. Lenin encountered considerable difficulty in getting the treaty ratified by the Party's Seventh Congress (March 1918); he had to contend with the opposition of his fellow Bolsheviks (the "Left-Communists"), who objected to the treaty, contending that it was a surrender to imperialism and a denial of revolutionary war. The treaty also caused the fellow-traveling Left Socialist Revolutionaries to resign from Lenin's government.

The peace treaty, which enabled Russia to withdraw from World War I, was but the prelude to a renewed internal armed struggle between Bolshevism and its Russian and non-Russian opponents. The Party, which had adopted the communist label at the Seventh Congress, recruited a new army and imposed a harsh secret-police system upon its subjects. It nationalized industry and banking, conscripted labor, imposed rationing, and requisitioned food from the peasants, whom it could not compensate with consumer goods. Yet the policy of War

---

[4]For a general treatment of the Party's development under Lenin, Stalin, and Khrushchev, see J. S. Reshetar, Jr., *A Concise History of the Communist Party of the Soviet Union,* rev. ed. (New York: Praeger, 1964).

Communism did not prevent Lenin from using tsarist army officers and bourgeois (non-Communist) managers and technical specialists. Such concessions evoked much antagonism among diehard orthodox Bolsheviks, who were not placated by the adoption of a new program at the Eighth Congress in March 1919. The Congress upheld Lenin's policies and also established a Political Bureau (Politburo)—a body capable of superseding the Central Committee. The Congress also authorized the first full-scale purge (verification and "cleansing") of the membership, which resulted in the ouster of approximately half of the members; however, the admission of new members raised the level to 350,000 by late 1919.

The Soviet regime's ability to retain control of the country's vital core made it possible for Lenin to engage in ineffective efforts to foment world revolution. The Comintern or Communist (Third) International was founded in 1919, just prior to the Party's Eighth Congress, but the failure to establish a communist regime in Poland by military means during the summer of 1920 led to renewed preoccupation with internal problems. The Ninth Congress (March–April 1920), for instance, witnessed a controversy over the role of trade unions and their relationship to the Party. It was decided that the communist trade union leadership would be subordinate to the Party apparatus and that civilian labor would be mobilized and disciplined. Idealistic communists—members of the Democratic Centralist Opposition—were becoming disillusioned as a result of the growth of a Party bureaucracy, the appointment rather than the election of many Party officials, and the arbitrary transfer of dissident members as a form of administrative "exile." Lenin defeated the Democratic Centralist Opposition, but he was soon confronted with strikes and famine as well as an armed rebellion (at the Kronstadt Naval Base), which demanded free elections to the soviets and an end to the Party's monopoly of political power.

The Tenth Congress, in March 1921, saw the defeat of a new dissident movement—the Workers' Opposition—which was dissatisfied with the influx of nonproletarian elements into the Party. Lenin was incensed by the charge that the Party was losing its character as a workers' organization and denounced his former followers as a "petit-bourgeois anarchist element." He employed several drastic measures: he had the Tenth Congress adopt a resolution forbidding factional and opposition movements; he ordered the suppression of the Kronstadt rebellion; and he obtained adoption of the New Economic Policy (NEP). This last measure signaled a relaxation of controls in an effort to restore production; small-scale "capitalism" and private retail trade were to be permitted, but the regime retained ownership of heavy industry and large-scale manufacturing, transport, communications, and natural resources; in lieu of the hated agricultural requisitions, the peasants were permitted to sell any surplus they had after paying a tax in kind. The NEP was accompanied by a new purge of the Party in 1921, which led to the expulsion of 170,000 members.

At this time Lenin began to show symptoms of the arteriosclerosis that was to cause his death on January 21, 1924. The first of three strokes occurred in May 1922 and left Lenin an invalid for the remaining twenty months of his life. Unable to exercise leadership, Lenin could only ponder what he had wrought in a lifetime of agitation, polemical activity, and conspiracy combined with utopian visions and a significant appreciation of political realities.

From Collective Leadership to Stalinist Dictatorship (1923–1929)

During 1922 and 1923, as Lenin lay ill, leadership of the Party was assumed by a triumvirate that consisted of Iosif V. Stalin (Dzhugashvili), Lev B. Kamenev (Rosenfeld), and Grigorii E. Zinoviev (Radomyslskii). Stalin had been elected General Secretary of the Party on April 3, 1922, following the Eleventh Congress (he had become a Marxist in 1898, had been appointed to Lenin's Central Committee in 1912, and had served as a member of the Soviet government since 1917). Kamenev headed the Moscow Soviet, while Zinoviev headed the Leningrad Party organization and was the leading figure in the Comintern. All three were Politburo members. Lenin did not designate a successor in his Testament (December 25, 1922) but in a postscript of January 4, 1923, called for Stalin's removal from the General Secretaryship on the grounds that he was too rude and capricious and not sufficiently tolerant, loyal, or polite. However, Stalin's fellow triumvirs had Lenin's Testament suppressed and saved Stalin's career. (The Testament was not published in the Soviet Union until 1956.)

A fourth leader, Lev Trotsky (Bronstein), figured prominently in the power struggle that occurred after Lenin's death. Trotsky had had disagreements with Lenin since 1903 and did not, in fact, join the Bolsheviks until the summer of 1917. However, he acquired fame as a Politburo member, as the principal organizer of the regime's Red Army, and as its Bolshevik civilian head. Trotsky was Stalin's principal rival, although a bitter personal feud between Trotsky and Zinoviev obscured this conflict—a feud beneficial to Stalin because it assured him of Zinoviev's support during a crucial period. Stalin enjoyed an important advantage as General Secretary because of his control of Party personnel. He also could give the appearance of having had better relations with Lenin—so long as the Testament was suppressed—while the other three leaders had been publicly criticized by Lenin at various times. Indeed, Stalin was able to pose as an advocate and interpreter of Leninism in his publications and speeches by quoting his teacher and by taking an oath at Lenin's funeral to remain faithful to his teachings.

It is ironic that in the 1923–1925 period it was Trotsky who was thought by many to present a greater danger of aspiring to the role of dictator. Stalin skillfully dissimulated his character and appeared to be a moderate. The exaggerated fear of Trotsky as a Bolshevik Bonaparte held the triumvirate together until the summer of 1925. Kamenev and Zinoviev, in their feud with Trotsky, had acquiesced to the strengthening of the Party's administrative apparatus in Stalin's hands. The Twelfth Congress in April 1923 and the Thirteenth in May 1924 resulted in the enlargement of the Central Committee to nearly twice its size (from 27 to 53 members); this gave Stalin an opportunity to reward loyal followers and to use this enlarged (and supposedly more "democratic") body to reduce the influence of his colleagues in the Politburo.

Trotsky challenged the triumvirate only in a spasmodic and ineffective manner. He had failed to oppose Stalin openly on the issue of nationality policy at the Twelfth Congress, when the dying Lenin had asked him to do so in the winter of 1922–1923. Instead, Trotsky criticized the bureaucratic regime in the Party and endeavored to rally the Party youth against Stalin's machine. He also criticized Zinoviev for Comintern failures and was unhappy about the NEP. Finally, in January 1925, the triumvirate removed Trotsky from his post as Commissar of War. Stalin was now ready to adopt a rightist orientation in agricultural policy by reducing the tax on those peasants who did not hire labor. This course won the support of other Politburo members—the theoretician Nikolai Bukharin, the head of government Aleksei Rykov, and the trade union chief Mikhail Tomsky. Stalin was now able to dispense with Kamenev and Zinoviev, who disapproved of these concessions and who had belatedly become aware of the General Secretary's growing power. The triumvirate was replaced by a quadrumvirate, and Stalin's influence was greater in the latter than it had been in the former. Kamenev and Zinoviev, joined by Lenin's widow (Krupskaia), challenged Stalin ineffectively at the Fourteenth Congress in December 1925 by criticizing the NEP. Stalin defended the NEP as a Leninist policy, while Trotsky remained aloof from the spirited debate after having falsely denied the authenticity of Lenin's Testament (which had been published abroad in 1925).

By the spring of 1926 Kamenev, Zinoviev, and Trotsky belatedly joined forces against Stalin—who accused them of being "unprincipled" because they had put aside their earlier disagreements to unite against his rule. However, by now Kamenev had been demoted to the rank of a candidate-member of the Politburo. Zinoviev had been removed from the leadership of the Leningrad Party organization in February and was expelled from the Politburo in July. Although the oppositionists capitulated in the autumn of 1926, they renewed their campaign against Stalin during the summer and autumn of 1927. Demonstrations in the streets of Moscow on November 7, 1927, were broken up by Stalin's supporters; and the oppositionists were expelled from the Party. The Fifteenth Congress in December 1927 reaffirmed Stalin's victory.

Stalin's triumph over the Trotskyite "Left Deviation" was possible because he had obtained the support of the Right (Bukharin's group), which favored a continuation of the NEP and a slower rate of industrialization based on a prosperous peasantry. The defeated Left had condemned the NEP, the Party bureaucracy, and the *kulaks* ("wealthy" peasants) and had advocated rapid industrialization. While Trotsky had argued the necessity of extending the revolution (communist rule) to other countries, Stalin had responded by insisting that socialism could be built in one country. The disagreement, however, was over tactics and methods and not over goals, for Stalin never rejected world revolution as the ultimate objective, defending "socialism in one country" as the most realistic means of achieving this end.

After Stalin had disposed of the Left in 1927, he was able to dispense with his allies of the Right, who mistakenly thought that he had adopted their policy of less rapid industrialization—financed by an increased agricultural output made possible by granting concessions (and paying adequate prices) to the middle ranks of the peasantry. Instead, Stalin adopted a policy of forced collectivization of agriculture, under which the peasants would deliver agricultural products to the state at low prices and pay for the program of rapid forced industrialization. By 1929 the NEP was replaced by the First Five Year Plan, Bukharin was expelled from the Politburo, and some of Trotsky's followers had begun to recant and support Stalin now that he had adopted Trotsky's program of industrialization and collectivization. Stalin had changed direction so rapidly that the Right was disarmed and divided before it could coalesce into a well-defined faction. The Secretary General was now in an unassailable position.

Stalinist Socialism and Purges (1930–1939)

The development of a state-owned heavy industry involved the accumulation of capital on a vast scale by means of expropriation of the peasantry; forced savings in the form of compulsory government loans; inflation; and deprivations in consumption. It also led to an artificial famine in 1932–1933, which claimed millions of peasant victims, especially among the Ukrainians, while Stalin exported grain at depressed world prices in order to pay for machinery imports. Increased emphasis was placed upon technical skills as well as upon acceptance of the Party line as laid down by Stalin's Secretariat and Central Committee. Thus at the Sixteenth Congress in June 1930, there was no debate, but the delegates heard recantations uttered by the members of the defeated Right Opposition.

At the Seventeenth Party Congress in January 1934, Stalin warned against "enemies both internal and external" and stressed the selection of personnel and "verification of fulfillment" in organizational work. Within a year he launched the first of a series of blood purges that, ironically, took place under the regime's slogan, "Life has become better, life has become happier." In reality, life had only become cheaper. The mysterious assassination of the Leningrad Party leader, Sergei Kirov, on December 1, 1934, provided the pretext for the first wave of blood purges, many of whose victims did not even know Kirov. Stalin erected monuments to Kirov but may also have played some role in his death.

The blood purges were to last four years and, upon attaining their most intensive stage, were to be termed the *Yezhovshchina*—in dubious honor of Nikolai Yezhov, the chief of Stalin's secret police from September 1936 to December 1938. After he had performed his gruesome task and Stalin no longer required his services, Yezhov also perished. Three "show trials" were staged in Moscow in August 1936, January 1937, and March 1938. The defendants were old Party leaders and oppositionists and included Kamenev, Zinoviev, Bukharin, Aleksei Rykov, Christian Rakovsky, Karl Radek, and others—as well as certain obscure persons who were probably provocateurs. The defendants, almost without exception, confessed to having committed treasonable acts and frequently made fantastic and false admissions. The overwhelming majority were sentenced to death and executed. A secret trial of eight leading Soviet generals, including Marshal Tukhachevsky, was held in June 1937; all of the accused were executed.[5]

The rank-and-file membership also felt the blow of the purges. The membership decreased by more than 1.6 million between 1933 and 1938; but the number purged was greater because new members were admitted after November 1936. (Prior to that—beginning in December 1932—admission of new members was suspended.) Nor were members of the Central Committee immune. It was reported in 1956 that 98 of the 139 Central Committee members and candidate-members elected at the Seventeenth Congress in January 1934 were executed; ironically, it had been called the "Congress of Victors."[6] Loyal Stalinists perished along with those who had made an unfortunate statement or association in the past. Nor did Trotsky—the star defendant *in absentia* at the Moscow trials—escape Stalin's reign of terror. Exiled from the Soviet Union in 1929, the Red Army's founder took refuge in Turkey, France, Norway, and, finally, in Mexico. There on August 20, 1940, an assassin drove an ice axe into Trotsky's skull. Stalin had destroyed the last of his old opponents.

War and the "Cult of Personality" (1940–1953)

The failure of Stalin's efforts to avoid involvement in World War II had a profound impact upon the Party. Its losses were great, and new members had to be admitted not only to compensate for the wartime losses, but also to obtain a greater degree of support for the regime—especially in the armed forces. In 1945, Party membership reached a new high of nearly 4 million members and 1.8 million candidate-members. Much of the new membership consequently had to be screened and part of it expelled during the postwar years. At the same time the educational level rose as the Party acquired intellectuals, technicians, and members of the managerial class.

Beginning in 1946, the Party launched a campaign for ideological purity under the direction of the Leningrad Party leader, Andrei Zhdanov. Philosophers, writers, poets, geneticists, and alleged advocates of "rootless cosmopolitanism" came under attack. Stalin later issued pronouncements on linguistics and economics, which at the time were accepted by the professors and ideologists. The General Secretary was now head of the government, generalissimo of the armed forces, author (or so credited) of the official textbook on Party history, and dictator of tastes in music and architecture. Celebrated as a "genius," as the

---

[5]The Stalinist era is treated extensively in John A. Armstrong, *The Politics of Totalitarianism* (New York: Random House, 1961). On the purges, see F. Beck and W. Godin, *Russian Purge and the Extraction of Confession* (New York: Viking Press, 1951). For the transcript of the March 1938 show trial, see *The Great Purge Trial,* ed. and with notes by Robert C. Tucker and Stephen F. Cohen (New York: Grosset & Dunlap, 1965). For biographies of Stalin, see Isaac Deutscher, *Stalin: A Political Biography* (New York: Oxford University Press, 1949); Boris Souvarine, *Stalin, A Critical Survey of Bolshevism* (New York: Alliance Book Co., 1939); Leon Trotsky, *Stalin, An Appraisal of the Man and His Influence* (London: Hollis and Carter, 1947); and Adam Ulam, *Stalin, the Man and His Era* (New York: Viking Press, 1973); for an appraisal of the Stalinist era, see Robert C. Tucker, ed., *Stalinism: Essays in Historical Interpretation* (New York: Norton, 1977).
[6]*Current Soviet Policies II,* ed. Leo Gruliow (New York: Praeger, 1957), p. 176.

"father of peoples," and as the "Lenin of today," Stalin was adulated and became the object of what his successor termed the "cult of personality." In his last years Stalin gave some indication of suffering from some form of dementia. He became increasingly suspicious and allegedly would "look at a comrade with whom he was seated at the same table and say: 'Your eyes are shifty today.' "[7]

Shortly before his death Stalin convoked the Party's Nineteenth Congress— in October 1952—and eliminated the term "Bolshevik" from the Party's name. The All-Union Communist Party (of Bolsheviks) now became the Communist Party of the Soviet Union (CPSU). The aging dictator installed a large number of new lieutenants and made ready to eliminate some of his senior lieutenants who had survived the purges of the thirties and whose careers had benefited from the resultant vacancies.[8]

In January 1953, the arrest of nine physicians for allegedly having committed medical murder on orders of United States intelligence was announced. Andrei Zhdanov, the Leningrad Party leader who died in 1948, and Alexander Shcherbakov, former political chief of the Soviet Army, were said to have been the victims of this fantastic "doctors' plot." Six of the arrested physicians were Jewish. Fear gripped the entire population and the Party as events pointed to the unleashing of a massive blood purge. Thus, Stalin's death on March 5, 1953, left his subjects both bewildered and relieved. An era of spectacular achievements and of unsurpassed despotism had come to an end.

Collective Leadership Again (1953–1957)

In formally announcing Stalin's death, the senior lieutenants implored the public not to succumb to "disorder and panic" and then proceeded to divide the heritage of the late dictator. Georgii Malenkov, who had served in the Party Secretariat under Stalin, became head of government, but he soon had to relinquish his post as a Party Central Committee Secretary. This left Nikita S. Khrushchev in the most advantageous position within the Secretariat, and he soon adopted the title of "First Secretary" of the Party (as distinct from Stalin's title of "General Secretary"). Lavrentii Beria, a deputy premier, was made head of a reunified secret police organization, as interior minister, and also controlled an internal security army. This collective leadership was to lose one member in late June 1953 when Beria was arrested and subsequently executed. The secret police chief, who had endeavored to gain support by freeing the physicians accused in the "doctors' plot" and by advocating concessions to the non-Russian nationalities and to the collectivized peasantry, had presented a threat to the others.

---

[7]*XXII S"ezd Kommunisticheskoi Partii Sovetskogo Soiuza, stenograficheskii otchet* (Moscow: Gospolitizdat, 1962), II, p. 583. Khrushchev quoted Stalin as telling the Politburo at the time of the "doctors' plot": "You are blind like young kittens; what would happen without me? The country would perish because you do not know how to recognize enemies." *Current Soviet Policies,* II, p. 183.

[8]Khrushchev, in his secret speech at the Twentieth Congress, asserted that Stalin "evidently had plans to finish off the old members of the Political Bureau." He also observed that "had Stalin remained at the helm for another several months, Comrades Molotov and [Anastas] Mikoyan would probably not have delivered any speeches at this Congress." *Current Soviet Policies II,* p. 187.

Beria's place in the collective leadership was taken by Viacheslav M. Molotov, an old Bolshevik and head of government during the 1930s, who had succeeded in having himself restored to the post of foreign minister after Stalin's death. The collective leadership lost another member with the removal of Malenkov from the chairmanship of the U.S.S.R. Council of Ministers in February 1955; he was replaced by Nikolai Bulganin, former defense minister. In September 1955, Molotov was accused of an "ideological error" and issued a reluctant recantation; in June 1956, he was compelled to resign from his post as foreign minister. Khrushchev, as Party chief, and Bulganin, as premier, were seemingly inseparable members of a duumvirate in 1955 and 1956.

The membership of the collective leadership had changed as a result of differences over domestic and foreign policy issues and ideological questions (often closely related to policy). Khrushchev and Malenkov disagreed, for instance, over the rate of development for heavy industry versus light industry and the amount of consumer goods that the regime could afford. The extent and nature of the Soviet Union's nuclear deterrent and the consequences of World War III also entered into this debate, which concealed a power struggle.[9] Among the foreign-policy issues was the decision to sign the Austrian State Treaty in May 1955 and to terminate the Soviet military occupation of Eastern Austria. Molotov opposed this decision, as well as the visit of Khrushchev and Bulganin to Belgrade to attempt a reconciliation with Marshal Tito and the excommunicated Yugoslav Communist Party. Domestic policy issues causing disagreement included the decision to denigrate Stalin's memory in the "secret speech" at the Twentieth Congress and in more moderate terms in public addresses at the Congress. Khrushchev's policy of bringing millions of acres of virgin lands under cultivation (in Western Siberia and Kazakhstan) and his scheme to cultivate corn aroused opposition—as did his plan to reorganize economic management in 1957.

The period of collective leadership culminated in an unsuccessful attempt to oust Khrushchev from his post as First Secretary in June 1957. A majority of seven of the eleven members of the Central Committee's Presidium favored Khrushchev's removal. The wily and ruthless First Secretary, fighting for his political life, contended that he could only be removed by the Central Committee and succeeded in calling a plenary session of that body, at which he rallied his supporters and defeated his opponents.[10] Significantly, these opponents had united against Khrushchev despite their disagreements over policies. Malenkov, Molotov, Lazar Kaganovich (an old crony of Stalin's and a deputy premier), and the former foreign minister, Dmitrii T. Shepilov, were then expelled from the Central Committee and denounced as the "anti-Party group." Within eighteen months four other opponents of Khrushchev, including Premier Bulganin and

---

[9]For a discussion of these matters, see Herbert S. Dinerstein, *War and the Soviet Union,* rev. ed. (New York: Praeger, 1962).

[10]On Khrushchev's rise to power, see Lazar Pistrak, *The Grand Tactician: Khrushchev's Rise to Power* (New York: Praeger, 1961) and Myron Rush, *The Rise of Khrushchev* (Washington, D.C.: Public Affairs Press, 1958). For an appraisal of Khrushchev's career, see Roy A. and Zhores Medvedev, *Khrushchev: The Years in Power* (New York: Columbia University Press, 1976) and Roy A. Medvedev, *Khrushchev* (Garden City, N.Y.: Anchor Press/Doubleday, 1983).

Marshal Kliment Voroshilov, were demoted and publicly denounced. The June 1957 crisis and Khrushchev's assumption of the premiership on March 27, 1958—while retaining his post as Party First Secretary—marked the end of the period of collective leadership.

The Khrushchev Era (1958–1964)

Many of the reforms introduced by Khrushchev reflected an effort to revitalize a regime that showed the effects of having been in power for four decades. As First Secretary and Premier, he adopted a distinctive style of visiting the various union republics and making state visits abroad—in contrast to Stalin's self-imposed isolation in the Kremlin. Khrushchev readily granted impromptu interviews, employed earthy language, expressed concern for his subjects' welfare, and occasionally engaged in studied clowning. His volubility—like Stalin's laconism—served to conceal a cunning that had enabled him to plot and fight his way to the top. However, Khrushchev was not able to utilize the secret police as the punitive organ of his personal secretariat in the way in which Stalin had. The demise of Beria and many of his aides (termed collectively the "Beria gang" in official parlance at the time) had enabled the Party as a whole—if not individual members—to acquire a degree of independence from the security police.

During Khrushchev's tenure, Party membership (including candidate-members) increased from 7.2 million in 1956 to 11.7 million in 1964. An effort was made to recruit more factory workers and peasants as members. Khrushchev departed from the Stalinist pattern of rule by holding regular Party congresses and convening the Central Committee in regular sessions. The Twentieth Congress—in February 1956—was significant in that it elected a new Central Committee and indicated an effort to dissociate the Party from Stalin's despotism, blaming the regime's failures, cruelties, and shortcomings on the late dictator. The Twenty-first Congress—January–February 1959—did little more than approve the Seven Year Plan (1959–1965) and denounce the defenseless members of the anti-Party group of Malenkov, Molotov, et al., who had attempted to oust Khrushchev in 1957.

The Twenty-second Congress—in October 1961—adopted a new Party Program and new statutes in an effort to convey the impression of Party "legality" and the "restoration of Leninist norms of Party life." The attacks on the anti-Party group were intensified. The Congress ordered the removal of Stalin's body from the Lenin-Stalin mausoleum in Red Square and its interment in a simple grave near the Kremlin wall—a petty gesture that could hardly eradicate the impact of the quarter-century of Stalin's rule. The Congress was also significant in providing a forum for the excommunication of Albania from the Soviet communist camp. This action, taken by Khrushchev, prompted a public expression of disapproval by the Chinese communist delegation headed by Premier Chou En-lai, who left the Congress prematurely.

The deterioration of the Sino-Soviet relationship became a principal feature of Khrushchev's regime, with the two leading communist powers engaging in undignified mutual recrimination. Khrushchev was denounced as a "revisionist" by the Chinese because of his ideological pronouncements and policies, and the primacy of the CPSU was challenged. The disarray in international communism was paralleled by a host of Soviet domestic problems to which Khrushchev responded with improvised and ineffective solutions. His numerous administrative reorganizations and his vaunted but abortive policies, especially in agriculture, resulted in frustration and confusion.

The abrupt removal of Khrushchev on October 14, 1964, by what was said to have been a plenary session of the Central Committee, coincided with the detonation of China's first nuclear device. Initially, it was announced by the Central Committee in *Pravda* on October 16 that it had only complied with Khrushchev's "request" that he be relieved of his duties as First Secretary, Presidium member, and Chairman of the U.S.S.R. Council of Ministers (Premier) "in view of his advanced age and deteriorating health." Although Khrushchev had turned seventy in April of 1964, the falsity of the "reasons of health" explanation soon became apparent on October 17 when *Pravda* attacked him by innuendo in denouncing "hare-brained schemes, premature conclusions, hasty, unrealistic decisions and actions, boasting and idle talk, a preoccupation with administration, and an unwillingness to consider what has already been proven by science and practical experience. . . ." The Party was said to oppose "subjectivism" and "the ideology and practices of the personality cult," implying, it would appear, that Khrushchev had violated the "collective leadership" principle. At the March 1965 plenary session of the Central Committee, Khrushchev was criticized implicitly in references to "errors of leadership" in the field of agriculture.

The coup that resulted in Khrushchev's ouster was well planned and had the character of a palace revolution. The First Secretary had been staying at his palatial retreat near the Black Sea resort of Sochi. When he learned what was afoot, his efforts to offer a defense and to prevent his removal were in vain. Participants in the coup included Leonid Brezhnev, Khrushchev's successor as First Secretary, and Party Secretaries Mikhail Suslov and Aleksandr Shelepin. Khrushchev's colorful career of ten eventful years at the very top of the Soviet pyramid ended where it had begun—in the Central Committee.

Khrushchev was a contradictory figure given to bombast, the sober recognition of problems, and the adoption of unusual measures, including the unprecedented decision to import grain from abroad. He was also an improviser who sought desperately to re-revolutionize the Soviet Union by reviving Leninism and undertaking a renewed antireligious campaign and an anticolonial offensive designed to enhance Soviet influence in the former colonial countries of Asia and Africa. Although Khrushchev was removed from office by a conspiracy, his various efforts at reform had a profound impact. The relatively "liberal" period of the late 1950s that accompanied the de-Stalinization campaign prompted many Soviet citizens to become more emboldened. Although Khrushchev had served Stalin loyally, he also had developed a profound distaste for Stalin's despotic rule.

Khrushchev's iconoclastic act administered a potent catharsis to the Soviet polity, after which it could never be quite the same again.

The Brezhnev Era (1964–1982)

The collective leadership that took control in October 1964 was characterized by greater internal stability than the two previous experiences with collective rule. Brezhnev became the leading Party Secretary and Aleksei Kosygin became head of government—thus separating the two positions held by Khrushchev. The perpetrators of the coup undertook to undo certain of Khrushchev's administrative reforms and to assure republic and provincial Party secretaries lengthier tenure in contrast to Khrushchev's efforts at systematic renewal of cadres with limited right of succession.

Brezhnev abruptly terminated Khrushchev's anti-Stalin campaign and ordered the rehabilitation of much of Stalin's reign, tempering it with restrained criticism of certain "errors and distortions associated with the cult of personality." In 1970 a monument was erected over Stalin's grave. Khrushchev became an "unperson" when he was ousted; his portrait was removed from all public places, and his published works were withdrawn from circulation. When Khrushchev died on September 11, 1971, he was not given a state funeral and was denied burial near the Kremlin Wall. Troops were used to prevent Soviet citizens from attending the funeral at Moscow's Novo-Devichii Cemetery. None of his former associates and political protégés came to pay their respects.

In retrospect, certain aspects of Khrushchev's decade of rule appeared "liberal" when compared with Brezhnev's domestic policies. Centralism of the economy was reaffirmed after 1964 with the reestablishment of a large number of central governmental ministries in Moscow. Stalinist nationality policy was restored more fully, with more repressive measures aimed at controlling non-Russian dissidents. Internal dissent, in general, was suppressed with several show trials and numerous secret trials of dissidents and the use of large numbers of forced labor camps, many of them located in the Mordovian Republic. While restoring repressive measures and controls domestically, the Brezhnev regime undertook large-scale importation of Western technology.

Brezhnev assumed Stalin's title of CPSU General Secretary but did not acquire Stalin's powers. He undertook a re-registration of Party membership between 1973 and 1975, expelling at least 347,000 members, and attempted to raise the requirements for admission. Brezhnev contributed little of consequence to Communist ideology apart from the so-called Brezhnev Doctrine that is attributed to him by foreigners. The doctrine resulted from the Soviet occupation of Czechoslovakia in 1968 and condones armed intervention by one socialist (communist) state in the internal affairs of another deemed to be departing from socialist teachings. Such intervention need not be requested and is justified on the grounds that international law and the sovereignty of states are subordinate to the class struggle. The Brezhnev Doctrine was invoked again in December 1979, when Soviet forces occupied Afghanistan and killed the communist president, Hafizullah Amin. In lieu of any significant contribution to Marxist-Leninist theory, Brezhnev published his collected speeches and articles (carefully omitting those delivered prior to October 1964) in several volumes under the title *On the Leninist Course.*

Brezhnev's political style differed markedly from that of Khrushchev. While Khrushchev was willing to experiment and reorganize and to decanonize Stalin, Brezhnev opted for the more cautious course. He was not impulsive and sought to protect his position by not saying more than necessary and by seeking to establish consensus in the Politburo and making certain to obtain its approval prior to any major undertaking. Brezhnev relied on several personal aides and was also willing to obtain the advice of specialists. Turnover in the oligarchy was reduced, and Party and government officials were assured tenure in contrast with Khrushchev's practice of transferring personnel and creating uncertainty. The internal stability in the Party that characterized Brezhnev's tenure was accompanied by his promotion of men who had been associated with him previously in Ukraine, Moldavia, and Kazakhstan. It resulted in cronyism and stagnation accompanied by an increase in corruption as the leadership adopted an attitude of tolerance on the apparent assumption that a public campaign against corruption would tarnish the Party's image. Brezhnev developed a cult of his own person, published vanity memoirs that embellished his wartime military activities (he was a political officer), and gave himself the military rank of marshal and nominal command of the Soviet armed forces. Brezhnev's tenure of 18 years was of far longer duration than many observers had originally expected it to be. However, it had its long-term costs that heavily taxed the abilities of his several successors. Even Brezhnev's successes in foreign policy—the SALT I Agreement and the ABM Treaty, which gave the Soviet Union strategic parity with the United States—were tarnished as a result of the breakdown of detente following the failure to ratify SALT II and the costly Soviet invasion of Afghanistan.

Gerontocratic Rule (1978–1985)

In the late 1970s and early 1980s, the Soviet Union was quite literally a gerontocracy—a geriatric oligarchy. This period began with a stroke suffered by Brezhnev in 1975 and the subsequent decline of his health, which affected his speech and movement.[11] The Soviet Union experienced three political successions and three state funerals of Communist Party General Secretaries in a period of 28 months (November 1982 to March 1985).[12] This would appear to indicate the presence

---

[11]On the suppressed information concerning Brezhnev's health and the struggle for power, see Zhores A. Medvedev, *Andropov* (New York: Penguin, 1984), pp. 5–9.

[12]This condition appeared to lend credence to what the late Bertram D. Wolfe termed the "law of diminishing dictators"—the contention that each Soviet leader has been of lesser stature than his immediate predecessor. Thus Stalin was less than Lenin, and Khrushchev was less than Stalin. Brezhnev was less than Khrushchev, and Andropov was less effective than Brezhnev. Each leader was of lesser stature, had less personal power, and had diminished initiative. The diminution in status may also be due to each General Secretary being less of a dictator and more a leader with varying capacities and opportunities. Diminished stature may also be due to the greater complexity of the problems confronting each leader. Yet Wolfe wisely conceded, in an addendum to his "law": "To be sure, there is always the possibility of surprises." Thus a leader might, on occasion, be of greater

(continued)

of serious flaws in the Soviet leadership selection process and the inability to disqualify or remove a leader who is in poor health or is suffering from a physical disability.

Yuri Andropov became General Secretary despite Brezhnev's clear efforts for several years to groom and designate as his successor Konstantin Chernenko, a member of the CPSU Secretariat. To this end Brezhnev had Chernenko included as a member of the Soviet delegation to the Vienna SALT II summit conference in 1979, and the two leaders were frequently photographed together for the Soviet media. Andropov was the first Soviet leader to come from the security police, the KGB, which he had headed for 15 years. Thus he overcame this apparent disadvantage and succeeded where Lavrentii Beria had failed in 1953. However, the apparent disadvantage was also an advantage, insofar as it gave Andropov access to important political intelligence that he used in the struggle for power. If he was feared by the other oligarchs, it was to his advantage so long as they were not capable of removing him. Andropov had also served in the Secretariat from 1962 to 1967 and had more seniority than Chernenko. He took advantage of Brezhnev's physical debility and was brought back into the Secretariat to replace Mikhail Suslov, who died in January 1982 (at the age of 79). Andropov is said to have contributed to Suslov's death by engaging in a campaign to discredit Brezhnev by means of a criminal investigation directed against his daughter Galina and various persons with whom she associated. This whole matter was presented to Suslov for his approval and resulted in his death. It also led to the death (possibly by suicide or murder) of the KGB first deputy chairman, General Simeon Tsvigun, who was also Brezhnev's brother-in-law and who, presumably, was incapable of protecting the Brezhnev family by quashing the investigation.[13]

Thus Andropov became the dominant figure in the Secretariat (and is said to have become a de facto regent) nearly a year prior to Brezhnev's death, which occurred on November 10, 1982. Andropov, with the aid of Secretariat member Mikhail Gorbachev, undertook important personnel changes, removing provincial Party secretaries, and also removed Chernenko from his position as head of the important General Department of the Central Committee, though he remained in the Secretariat. CPSU Secretary Andrei Kirilenko was forced out of the Politburo at the age of 76. Andropov undertook a campaign against corruption, tardiness, absenteeism, and alcoholism. However, his health soon failed, and, after only nine months in office, he was last seen in public on August 18, 1983, when he received a group of U.S. senators. Soviet authorities repeatedly issued false statements concerning Andropov's activities, his "complete recov-

---

stature than his predecessor. See Bertram D. Wolfe, *An Ideology in Power, Reflections on the Russian Revolution* (New York: Stein and Day, 1969), p. 36.

[13]Zhores Medvedev, *Andropov* (above, n. 11), pp. 91–97. The Tsvigun obituary was published in *Izvestiia* on January 22, 1982. Significantly, it was *not* signed by Brezhnev, presumably because he could not endorse the official version of the cause of his brother-in-law's death. The obituary was signed by Andropov, Gorbachev, and a host of KGB officials including Viktor Chebrikov.

ery," and his impending return to official duties. Andropov died on February 9, 1984, as a result of renal failure and other ailments.

Konstantin Chernenko was now finally able to become General Secretary at the age of 72—the oldest man to assume that position. His election was probably due to the inability of his two principal rivals, M. S. Gorbachev and Grigorii Romanov, to obtain sufficient support. Chernenko was a weak figure whose poor health made his tenure very uncertain. His election was the last collective act of the "old guard" (Moscow Party Secretary Viktor Grishin, Foreign Minister Gromyko, Premier Tikhonov, and Defense Minister Dmitrii Ustinov) in the Politburo. It also provided a respite for the officials who had felt threatened by Andropov's anticorruption campaign. Andropov, with the help of his protégé Gorbachev, had removed more than one-fifth of the USSR government ministers and nearly half of the CPSU Central Committee department heads. Gorbachev, at age 53, could sit out Chernenko's limited tenure as General Secretary (13 months) and use the interval to his own advantage. Chernenko died on March 10, 1985, from cardiac arrest. He had suffered from pulmonary emphysema and chronic hepatitis that resulted in cirrhosis of the liver.

Gorbachev

The election of Mikhail Sergeievich Gorbachev as General Secretary on March 11, 1985, represented an important leadership change in several respects. At the age of 54, Gorbachev could provide the vigor and determination needed to effect at least a partial transformation of the Soviet system. His election was unique in that he was a graduate of the juridical faculty of Moscow State University (in 1955) and was the first lawyer to head the Party since Lenin, although he did not engage in the practice of law. His decision to pursue a career in politics rather than law was evident in his having become a Party member as a student at the age of 21. Immediately upon graduating from law school, Gorbachev became the Komsomol (Young Communist) city committee first secretary for Stavropol', the center of his native Stavropol' Territory *(krai)*. He was also unique in having his entire career as a Party official limited to the Stavropol' Territory prior to his being called to Moscow in 1978 to serve as Central Committee secretary in charge of agriculture. After having spent seven years in the Komsomol organization, Gorbachev in 1963 became, successively, a department head in the *kraikom* (territorial Party committee), first secretary of the Stavropol' Party city committee, second secretary of the kraikom, and (in 1970) first secretary of the Stavropol' kraikom at the age of 39. This position—as unquestioned leader of the territory— entitled Gorbachev to full membership in the CPSU Central Committee. Thus, Gorbachev's early career was limited largely to his native territory, and he lacked the regional experience possessed by Khrushchev, Brezhnev, Andropov, and Chernenko. Gorbachev had no administrative experience in any non-Russian republic, and this again set him apart from his predecessors. Furthermore, Gorbachev had limited experience in Moscow, as he was a Politburo member for only five years prior to becoming General Secretary.

Gorbachev had certain advantages upon assuming office apart from his age and apparent vigor. The advanced age of much of the Politburo membership meant that he was the beneficiary of attrition. Earlier, death had claimed such aged communist stalwarts as Mikhail Suslov and Dmitrii Ustinov. Nikolai Tikhonov, at age 80, could be replaced as head of government by Nikolai Ryzhkov. Foreign Minister Andrei Gromyko, at age 76, could be replaced by the Georgian Party Secretary Eduard Shevardnadze; Gromyko was retained in the Politburo as a senior member and was made head of state—a position in which he would have less influence on foreign policy. Thus Gorbachev could preside over a generational change, bringing in new faces and removing older members with relative ease. He was also able to remove two opponents: Central Committee Secretary Grigorii Romanov and Moscow Secretary Viktor Grishin. Romanov, former Leningrad Party leader, had aspired to the General Secretaryship, but he proved to be a weak contender because of personal failings and indiscretion, lack of polish, and lack of experience and the ability to learn quickly in the area of foreign policy. Grishin had been a close associate of Chernenko and was instrumental in obtaining for him the General Secretaryship in 1984. Grishin was also vulnerable because of his age and the numerous problems that had developed in the large Moscow Party organization under his lackluster leadership. Thus Gorbachev obtained the post of General Secretary almost by default.[14]

Gorbachev also had the distinct advantage of being able to organize and preside over the Party's Twenty-seventh Congress within a year after becoming General Secretary. This opportune event added to the media campaign designed to enhance his status by depicting him as a decisive and articulate leader. Gorbachev also used to his advantage the summit meeting in Geneva with President Ronald Reagan in November 1985. The Twenty-seventh Congress gave Gorbachev the opportunity to influence the composition of a new Central Committee, 44 percent of whose voting members were newly elected. He was also able to reshape almost entirely the membership of the Central Committee Secretariat, including the innovative appointment of Ambassador Anatolii Dobrynin as head of the International Department and as a close adviser on foreign policy— especially important because of Dobrynin's vast experience. Gorbachev also appointed to the Secretariat Aleksandra Biriukova, the second woman to serve in that body in its entire history.

The Twenty-seventh Congress gave Gorbachev the opportunity to issue a revised Party Program and provided a platform from which he could identify and speak frankly of major problems facing the Soviet Union. He conceded that "problems in the country's development grew faster than they were solved" and advocated "a very important restructuring of the socialist economic mechanism." However, Gorbachev did not have the Congress adopt a complete blueprint for reform but offered a number of suggestions and measures that indicated a piecemeal and patchwork approach. Yet even his limited proposals served to challenge the Soviet governmental and economic bureaucracy. Gorbachev's leadership in

---

[14]For a brief treatment of Gorbachev's earlier career, see Zhores A. Medvedev, *Gorbachev* (Oxford: Basil Blackwell, 1986).

its second year was tarnished by the catastrophe at the nuclear power station at Chernobyl' in the Ukrainian S.S.R. This horrendous and costly disaster symbolized the failings of the Soviet economy and technology and the legacy of unresolved problems bequeathed to Gorbachev by his predecessors.

Gorbachev's vigorous but controversial reform efforts prompted him to publish *Perestroika, New Thinking for Our Country and the World* (Harper & Row, 1987). Designed to appeal to foreign readers, the book was also available to the Soviet public. Though less candid than some of Gorbachev's speeches, the work reflected the leader's shrewdness and considerable sophistication as well as his determination to make the Soviet system more effective. Yet Gorbachev's leadership style, demanding policies and reorganizations, inevitably elicited uncertainty, skepticism, and resistance among critics while inspiring hope among his supporters. The crucial need for change and "new thinking" meant that the Soviet system confronted serious difficulties.

CENTRAL PARTY ORGANIZATION

The central Party bodies and the administrative apparatus stand at the top of a vast hierarchical structure. At the bottom are more than 440,000 primary Party organizations that are expected to do the bidding of the Party apparatus in government offices, economic enterprises, institutions, farms, and military units. The primary Party organizations are subordinated to district *(raion)* or city *(gorod)* Party organizations, which are in turn subordinated—except in the case of the largest cities—to province *(oblast')* or territory *(krai)* Party organizations. The latter organizations number approximately 150, and in the case of the larger non-Russian republics (Ukraine, Belorussia, Kazakhstan, and Uzbekistan) are subordinated to the central committees of the respective republic Party organizations, which, in turn, are subordinated to the CPSU Central Committee and its Secretariat in Moscow. The oblast' and krai Party organizations within the Russian SFSR are subordinated directly to the CPSU Central Committee. Each non-Russian republic has its separate Party organization with a central committee, politburo, and secretariat and its own republic Party congress. At the apex of the entire CPSU structure are the central Party bodies: the CPSU Congress, the Central Committee, the Politburo, the Secretariat, the Committee of Party Control, and the Central Auditing Commission.

The CPSU Congress

Although the Party statutes define the Congress as the Party's "supreme organ," in practice it is much less than that. The large numbers of delegates and the relative infrequency of Congresses have made this body subsidiary to the Central Committee and to the Politburo and Secretariat. Regular Congresses are convened by the Central Committee "at least once every five years" according to the statutes. Extraordinary Congresses can be called during the intervening periods—as was the case with the Twenty-first Congress in 1959.

The first six Congresses were held prior to the establishment of the Soviet regime, and only the First in 1898 and the Sixth in 1917 were held on the territory of the Russian Empire. All Congresses since the Eighth have been held in Moscow. From 1917 until 1925 Congresses met annually in accordance with a statutory provision. Stalin initially violated the provision when he convened the Fifteenth Congress in 1927 rather than in 1926. Subsequent violations occurred, and in 1934 the statutes provided for the Congress to meet "at least once every three years." This new provision was first violated in 1937, when Stalin postponed the Eighteenth Congress until 1939. No Congress was held between 1939 and 1952, despite the provision in the 1939 statutes for convening a Congress at least once every three years. The 1952 and 1961 statutes provided for a Congress to be held at least once every four years. Under Khrushchev's leadership a degree of regularity in the convocation of Party Congresses was restored, but his successor failed to convene the Twenty-third Congress in the autumn of 1965 or the Twenty-fourth Congress in the spring of 1970 as provided for in the statutes. The convocation of the Twenty-fourth Congress in March–April 1971 was a year overdue, but subsequent congresses were held at five-year intervals.

Spirited debates over leadership, policies, and organizational matters distinguished nearly all Congresses prior to the Fifteenth in 1927. The growth in the size of the Congress and the ability of the Secretariat to control the election of delegates then eliminated the last vestiges of debate and deliberation. After 1925 the Congress became a vast spectacle used to register unanimous support for the General Secretary and his policies and to proclaim his (and the Party's) wisdom and achievements. Various oppositionists and factionalists were also denounced in accordance with the propaganda requirements of the day. Leadership changes have not occurred at Party congresses, which are carefully planned. However, unexpected events have taken place at congresses, as in 1956, when Stalin was denounced, and in 1961, with the surfacing of the Soviet-Albanian and Sino-Soviet disputes.

The Congress meets in Moscow's Kremlin in a large modern auditorium, the Palace of Congresses (built by Khrushchev), that contrasts sharply with the traditional Kremlin structures. It follows a tested format that reflects the circumscribed role defined in the Party's statutes for this "supreme organ." The Congress "hears and approves" the reports of the Central Committee and of the Central Auditing Commission and also elects these two bodies; it "reviews, amends, and approves" the Party's Program and statutes; it "determines the Party line on questions of domestic and foreign policy and examines and decides on the most important problems of Party and state life and of the building of communism."

The principal document of a Congress is the Report of the Central Committee, which is usually delivered by the leading figure in the Party. Thus, Lenin presented these reports from 1918 to 1922. Zinoviev and Stalin shared the task in 1923, offering separate political and organizational reports. Stalin delivered political reports at the five Congresses between 1925 and 1939. In 1952, at the Nineteenth Congress, Malenkov presented the report under Stalin's watchful eye. Khrushchev, during his tenure as First Secretary, presented the report in 1956,

1959, and 1961; and Brezhnev and Gorbachev subsequently performed this task as General Secretary. The Central Committee's Report is really the report of the Secretariat and the Politburo of the Central Committee. It is a lengthy document and provides much information in its three parts, which deal with the general international situation and the Soviet Union's foreign policy, the domestic situation and problems of Soviet economic development, and ideological questions and the general condition of the Party.

The various Party leaders address the Congress on matters for which they are primarily responsible; secretaries from the non-Russian union republic Party organizations speak on problems within their respective jurisdictions. A carefully planned and controlled agenda also permits a select few of the rank-and-file delegates to deliver brief statements. The Congress also provides a pretext for bringing to Moscow representatives of foreign Communist parties, who consume much time speaking of their activities and who usually praise the Soviet leadership and the Soviet Union's way of life.

The delegates are elected on the basis of a norm of representation and in accordance with procedures set by the CPSU Central Committee prior to each Congress; the ratio of delegates to members has varied considerably since 1934 (see Table 4.1). Delegates are elected at oblast' and krai party conferences in the Russian SFSR and at oblast' conferences in the larger non-Russian republics. Delegates from the smaller non-Russian republics are elected at republic Party congresses. Party organizations in military units stationed abroad elect delegates at their own conferences, while those in units on the territory of the USSR and in internal security, frontier, and convoy troop units participate in the conference of the local territorial Party organization. Delegates are "elected" by means of a list system, and their nomination is carefully controlled by the Party secretaries responsible for organizing the electing conference or republic congress.

It would appear from the occupational and other data in Table 4.2 that some effort has been made to change the weight of different groups and categories. Thus, there has been a steady effort to increase the number of female delegates. Prior to the Twenty-second Congress, the largest single occupational group among the delegates was that of full-time Party officials. In 1961, however, the industry, transport, construction, and agricultural categories together constituted nearly half of the delegates at the Twenty-second Congress; this resulted in a decline in other categories (including that of higher education). The Twenty-second Congress, the largest the Party had seen, had 2825 more voting delegates than the previous Congress of record size. Apart from Party officials and certain well-known public figures, delegates are not likely to be elected to two or more congresses. Thus 74.4 percent of the delegates at the Twenty-fourth Congress in 1971 were attending their first congress; at the 1976 Congress 73.5 percent were first-time delegates. In 1986, at the Twenty-seventh Congress, 76.5 percent of the delegates were attending their first (and probably for most of them, their only) congress.

Despite the lack of genuine debate and the pro forma nature of the voting, the Congress serves a number of functions. In fulfilling the ritual of "electing"

Table 4.1 PARTY CONGRESSES

Congress	Number of delegates		Party membership	Ratio of delegates to members	Duration (days)	Size of central committee	
	Voting	Nonvoting				Members	Candidate-members
Seventh March 6–8, 1918	46	58	ca. 300,000 (170,000 represented at Congress)	None because of wartime conditions	3	15	8
Eighth March 18–23, 1919	301	102	313,766	1:1,000	6	19	8
Ninth March 29–April 5, 1920	554	162	611,978	1:1,000	8	19	12
Tenth March 8–16, 1921	694	296	732,521	1:1,000	9	25	15
Eleventh March 27–April 2, 1922	522	165	532,000	1:1,000	7	27	19
Twelfth April 17–25, 1923	408	417	386,000	1:1,000	9	40	17
Thirteenth May 23–31, 1924	748	416	735,881 643,000	1:1,000	9	53	34
Fourteenth December 18–31, 1925	665	641	445,000[a] 887,233	1:1,000	14	63	43
Fifteenth December 2–19, 1927	898	771	348,957[a] 1,260,874	1:1,000	18	71	50
Sixteenth June 26–July 13, 1930	1,268	891	711,609[a]	1:1,000	18	71	67

Congress	Date	Voting delegates	Consultative delegates	Members	Candidate members	Ratio			
Seventeenth	January 26–February 10, 1934	1,225	736	1,874,488	935,298[a]	1:1,500	16	71	68
Eighteenth	March 10–21, 1939	1,569	466	1,588,852	888,814[a]	1:1,000	12	71	68
Nineteenth	October 5–14, 1952	1,192	167	6,013,259	868,886[a]	1:5,000	10	125	110
Twentieth	February 14–25, 1956	1,349	81	6,795,896	419,609[a]	1:5,000	12	133	122
Twenty-first	(Extraordinary) January 27–February 5, 1959	1,269	106	7,622,356	616,775[a]	1:6,000	10	none elected	
Twenty-second	October 17–31, 1961	4,394	405	8,872,516	843,489[a]	1:2,000	15	175	155
Twenty-third	March 29–April 8, 1966	4,619	323	11,673,676	797,403[a]	1:2,500	11	195	165
Twenty-fourth	March 30–April 9, 1971	4,740	223	13,810,089	645,232[a]	1:2,900	11	241	155
Twenty-fifth	February 24–March 5, 1976	4,998	not applicable	15,058,017	636,170[a]	1:3,000	11	287	139
Twenty-sixth	February 23–March 3, 1981	4,994	not applicable	16,763,009	717,759[a]	1:3,350	9	319	151
Twenty-seventh	February 25–March 6, 1986	4,993	not applicable	18,309,693	728,253[a]	1:3,670	10	307	170

[a]Candidate-members.

Compiled from data in: *KPSS v rezoliutsiiakh i resheniiakh*, 7th ed. (Moscow: Gospolitizdat, 1960); *Politicheskii slovar'*, ed. by B. N. Ponomarev, 2d ed. (Moscow: Gospolitizdat, 1958); and stenographic reports for select Party Congresses.

Table 4.2 DATA ON DELEGATES TO PARTY CONGRESSES

	Twentieth Congress (1956)	Twenty-first Congress (1959)	Twenty-second Congress (1961)	Twenty-third Congress (1966)	Twenty-fourth Congress (1971)	Twenty-fifth Congress (1976)	Twenty-sixth Congress (1981)	Twenty-seventh Congress (1986)
Voting delegates	1355	1269	4408	4619	4740	4998	4994	4993
Occupational groups								
Party workers	506 37.3%	432 34.0%	1158 26.3%	1204 26.0%	1205 24.3%	1114 22.2%	1077 21.5%	1074 21.5%
Government employees	177 13.1%	147 11.6%	465 10.5%	539 11.6%	556 11.2%	693 13.8% }	691 13.8%	682 13.6%
Trade union and communist youth officials	20 1.5%	19 1.5%	104 2.3%	126 2.7%	126 2.5%	}		
Industry, transport, and construction	251 18.5%	355 28.0%	1391 31.5%	1577 33.0%	1195 24.0%	1703 34.1%	1370 27.4%	1375 27.5%
Agriculture	187 13.8%	175 13.8%	748 16.9%	874 18.9%	870 17.5%	887 17.7%	877 17.5%	872 17.5%
Military	incomplete data	91 7.2%	305 6.9% incomplete data	352 7.6%	—	314 6.3%	—	—
Arts, sciences, and culture	incomplete data	50 3.9%	incomplete data	—	354 7.0%	272 5.4%	269 5.4%	270 5.4%
Female delegates	193 14.2%	222 17.5%	1073 22.3%	1154 23.3%	1204 24.3%	1255 25.1%	1329 26.6%	1352 27.0%
Education								
Completed higher education	758 55.9%	708 55.8%	2312 52.5%	55.5%	58.0%	nearly 90% }	94% }	more than 98% }
Incomplete higher education	116 8.5%	67 5.3%	230 5.2%	24.0% }	27.0% }	}	}	}
Secondary education	169 12.4%	155 12.2%	665 15.1%	}	}	ca. 10% }	ca. 6% }	
Incomplete secondary or elementary	312 23.2%	339 26.7%	1201 27.2%	20.5%	15.0%	}	}	
Age								
40 or under	20.3%	21.1%	38.6%	40.2%	31.8%	70.5% }	62.6% }	30.5%
41–50	55.7%	47.8%	37.9%	34.3%	41.6%	}	}	34.7%
over 50	24.0%	31.1%	23.5%	25.5%	26.6%	29.5%	37.4%	34.8%

Sources: (Table is based on data in reports of chairmen of Credentials Commissions at Party Congresses) *XX S"ezd KPSS* (Moscow, 1956), I, 232–239; *Vneocherednoi XXI S"ezd KPSS* (Moscow, 1959), I, 258–262; *XXII S"ezd KPSS* (Moscow, 1962), I, 421–431; *XXIII S"ezd KPSS* (Moscow, 1966), I, 278–285; *XXIV S"ezd KPSS* (Moscow, 1971), I, 330–335; *Izvestiia,* February 28, 1976, p. 3; *Pravda,* February 26, 1981, p. 3; *Pravda,* February 28, 1986, p. 5.

a Central Committee, it periodically endows the Party leadership with a degree of apparent legitimacy. It also serves as an important medium for promulgating and approving new policies, programs, and economic plans and launching propaganda appeals. These are then propagated by the delegates when they return to the subordinate Party organizations. The Congress provides delegates with a sense of participation—however passive and modest it may be—and with an opportunity to see and hear (if not question) the Party's leaders.

The institution of the Party *conference,* held in the intervals between Party congresses, was revived by M. S. Gorbachev with the decision to convene the Nineteenth Conference in June 1988—the first Party conference to be held in 47 years. Gorbachev's Central Committee decided to have the conference delegates elected by secret ballot by the oblast' and krai Party committees and by union republic central committees in the smaller union republics. The decision was prompted by Gorbachev's desire to use the conference to appraise and promote his policy of "restructuring."

The Central Committee

The Party has had a Central Committee since its founding Congress in 1898, when three of the nine delegates were elected to serve as its members. Subsequent Central Committees reflected the various divisions within the Party and at times also shared authority with the editorial staff of the Party organ prior to 1917. Under Lenin's leadership, however, the Central Committee developed into the principal instrument for ruling the Party. Stalin enlarged the Committee substantially (see Table 4.1), rewarding his followers with membership but also demeaning the Central Committee membership by convening joint plenary sessions with the much larger Central Control Commission. In the first years of the Soviet regime, Central Committee meetings were to be held twice a month, but the 1922 statutes reduced their frequency to once every two months. By 1934 the statutes provided for meetings once every four months, and in 1952 this was fixed at once every six months. However, the Central Committee fell into a state of desuetude during the latter part of Stalin's rule, when plenary sessions were infrequent and brief, occurring at intervals of several years. Following Stalin's death, plenary sessions were convened at least twice a year, although as many as six sessions were held in 1958.

The Central Committee, which is elected by each regular Party Congress, "directs all Party activities and local Party bodies" during the lengthy intervals between Congresses. It also includes representation from various key groups in Soviet society, and its plenary sessions are used to publicize certain information and developments and to promote new policies. The Central Committee elects a Politburo and a Secretariat that act in its name. The Secretariat, for its part, selects and assigns Party personnel (leading cadres) and directs the work of governmental and public organizations through the Party members within them. It controls the Party's press organs and journals and appoints and removes their editors. It has at its disposal the central Party fund and allocates expenditures. The Central Committee also "establishes various Party organs, institutions and enterprises and directs their activities." It represents the CPSU in its relations with other parties.

Plenary sessions of the Central Committee usually last a day or two and have dealt with a wide range of subjects, including governmental and economic reorganization, economic plans, agricultural policy, the chemical industry, "ideological work," control of the intelligentsia, technical progress, Party organization, internal power struggles, foreign policy, and relations with other Communist parties. Some sessions called by Khrushchev were enlarged to include planning officials, local government heads, factory directors, local Party secretaries not included in the Committee's membership, and scientific workers. Such enlarged plenary sessions confirmed the usefulness of the Central Committee as a means of promoting the regime's policies and programs, although Khrushchev was later criticized for this practice.

Central Committee plenary sessions are usually announced in advance and are carefully planned. However, there have been secret plenary sessions, in which heated debates have occurred in the course of a life-and-death political struggle. Such sessions occurred in January 1955, when it was decided to remove Malenkov from the premiership; in June 1957, when Khrushchev defeated the members of the anti-Party group; and in October 1964, when Khrushchev himself was ousted. What were said to be stenographic reports of Central Committee plenary sessions first began to be published following the December 1958 session (except for the publication of Committee proceedings for a brief period preceding and following the seizure of power in 1917). However, these records reflected the prearranged nature of most Central Committee proceedings, in which speakers vied with each other to do the bidding of those in command of the Party's administrative apparatus. Brezhnev reverted to the old practice of not publishing Central Committee stenographic reports and simply had the press report on who addressed the plenary session along with a list of decisions taken and the texts of certain important resolutions.

The Central Committee has become too large and meets too infrequently to be a continuing decision-making body. Yet its importance in the crisis situations of 1955, 1957, and 1964 and the need for the Party's rulers to act in its name at all times indicate that it is a significant body. Its formal confirmation of the Soviet oligarchy is essential. The General Secretary must enjoy the confidence of the Central Committee if he is to lead the Party, and he must obtain its approval of his actions and policies.

The Central Committee consists of voting members and candidate-members; the latter attend plenary sessions and can speak but not vote. The Committee's membership, as indicated in Table 4.3, is derived from several categories of officials. The largest group of members consists of Party secretaries of the central Party organization and of the union and autonomous republics and includes the large group of oblast' and krai Party committee first secretaries. *Oblasti* consistently represented in the Central Committee—in addition to Moscow and Leningrad—have included Saratov, Gorky, Volgograd (Stalingrad), Tula, Kuibyshev, Ivanovo, Smolensk, Kaliningrad (Koenigsberg), Perm (Molotov), Irkutsk, and Novosibirsk. In 1961 the oblast' contingent was increased with the addition of

Table 4.3   MAJOR CATEGORIES IN VOTING MEMBERSHIP OF THE CENTRAL COMMITTEE

Year Elected	1956 (133 members)		1961 (175 members)		1966 (195 members)		1971 (241 members)		1976 (287 members)		1981 (319 members)		1986 (307 members)	
Oblast' and *krai* committee secretaries	41	30.8%	46	26.2%	45	23.0%	58[a]	24.0%	83[b]	28.9%	86[d]	26.9%	79[e]	25.7%
USSR government ministers	31	23.8%	28	16.0%	37	18.9%	54	22.4%	66	23.0%	81	25.4%	67	21.8%
Union Republic Central Committee secretaries	16	12.0%	19	10.9%	19	9.8%	20	8.0%	19	6.6%	21	6.5%	20	6.5%
CPSU Central Committee secretaries and department heads	11	8.0%	15	8.6%	13	6.6%	14	5.8%	15[c]	5.2%	28[c]	8.7%	28[c]	9.1%
Union Republic premiers and deputy premiers	5	3.8%	8	4.6%	9	4.6%	8	3.3%	11	3.8%	11	3.4%	9	2.9%
Military	6	4.5%	14	8.0%	15	7.8%	20	8.0%	20	7.0%	20	6.2%	23	7.5%
Female members	4	3.0%	6	3.4%	5	2.5%	6	2.5%	8	2.7%	8	2.5%	13	4.2%

[a] Includes three city committee secretaries and eight secretaries of Party committees of autonomous republics.
[b] Includes six city committee secretaries and 11 secretaries of Party committees of autonomous republics.
[c] Includes two aides to the CPSU General Secretary.
[d] Includes four city committee secretaries and 11 secretaries of Party committees of autonomous republics.
[e] Includes four city committee secretaries and 12 secretaries of Party committees of autonomous republics.

Compiled from data in: *Current Soviet Politics I,* ed. Leo Gruliow (New York: Praeger, 1953), pp. 237–240; *Bulletin, Institute for the Study of the USSR,* Supplements for May 1956; November 1961; and September 1966; *Current Soviet Policies VI* (Columbus, Ohio: AAASS, 1973) pp. 186–191; U.S. Central Intelligence Agency, Publication CR 76-11259; Publication CR 81-11349; Publication LDA 86-10123; and Radio Liberty Research Report RL 145/86.

119

eight Ukrainian oblast' secretaries; in 1952, in contrast, only one Ukrainian oblast', Kiev, was represented in the Central Committee. The krai Party Secretaries in the Central Committee are usually from the Altai, Stavropol, Krasnoiarsk, Maritime, and Krasnodar territories. The first secretaries of the central committees of the Party organizations in the non-Russian union republics are *de facto, ex officio* members of the CPSU Central Committee.

Among the most influential members of the Central Committee are its own secretaries and certain of the Secretariat's department heads. The membership also includes the Soviet Union's premier, its chief of state, and the premiers of the leading non-Russian republics. A few workers and a collective-farm chairman are included for the sake of appearance. The Central Committee has also never included many females among its membership (see Table 4.3). Non-Russian nationalities, especially the non-Slavic peoples, have been underrepresented.

The election of the Central Committee takes place at the closed penultimate session of the Party Congress, and the published stenographic reports reveal nothing concerning the procedures employed. It is usually claimed that the voting is by secret ballot. However, there apparently have been only as many names on the list of candidates to be elected as there are seats in the Central Committee. Thus all members of the Central Committee may not receive the same number of votes. The Party Secretariat (possibly with the approval of the Politburo) determines who shall be nominated.[15]

There has always been a turnover in Central Committee membership, although the rate has varied. The Central Committee elected in 1934 had a survival rate of only 22.5 percent when its successor body was elected in 1939; only 16 of the 71 voting members elected in 1934 were reelected in 1939 as a result of Stalin's purges. The Committee elected in 1939 had a survival rate of 47 percent, with 33 of its members reelected to the enlarged Central Committee of 125 members in 1952. Sixty-four percent of the 1952 Central Committee was reelected in 1956, 49.6 percent of the 1956 Central Committee was reelected in 1961, and 78.4 percent of the 1966 Central Committee was reelected in 1971. However, only 54 percent of the 1981 Central Committee was reelected in 1986. The rate of turnover, as reflected in the percentage of *newly elected* members, is indicated in Table 4.4. The steady increase in the size of the Central Committee has allowed the number of new members to be larger than the number not reelected. Tenure of a Central Committee member may be uncertain because it usually depends upon his holding a particular position that gives entitlement to membership but that is held at the discretion of the Secretariat.

The 1961 Party statutes provided for the "systematic renewal" of the membership of Party bodies. In the case of the Central Committee and its Politburo,

---

[15]Khrushchev in his reminiscences described the use of a list system in the election of the Central Committee at the Seventeenth Congress in 1934 and stated that six votes were cast against Stalin's and his own candidacies at that time. A negative vote was cast by crossing out the candidate's name. See *Khrushchev Remembers* (Boston: Little, Brown, 1970), pp. 48–49.

Table 4.4 **NEW MEMBERS IN CENTRAL COMMITTEE**

Year committee elected	Number of newly elected full members	Percentage of total membership
1918	2	13.3
1919	7	36.8
1920	6	31.6
1921	10	40.0
1922	7	25.9
1923	16	40.0
1924	16	30.2
1925	14	22.2
1927	19	26.8
1930	14	19.7
1934	15	21.1
1939	55	77.5
1952	92	73.6
1956	53	39.8
1961	109	62.3
1966	48	24.6
1971	88	36.5
1976	85	29.6
1981	88	27.9
1986	135	43.9

Source: Adapted, with modifications, from Zbigniew Brzezinski and Samuel P. Huntington, *Political Power: USA/USSR* (New York: Viking Press, 1964), Table 10, p. 179.

"at least one-fourth" of the membership was to be replaced at each regular Party Congress and a limit of three consecutive terms was adopted. However, an exception was provided for "Party workers [who] by virtue of their recognized authority, high political, organizational or other qualities" could be elected for more than three terms if they received three-quarters of the votes cast in the election of the Central Committee at the Congress. In practice the Central Committee was renewed at a rate in excess of 25 percent. In 1966 the statutes were amended to eliminate the fixed rate of turnover in membership while affirming the "principle of systematic renewal . . . and continuity of leadership" for all Party bodies from the bottom to the Central Committee.

The Central Committee's size and composition are not defined in the Party statutes; and the degree to which various geographic areas, institutions, and interests will be represented in it is a political issue of great importance in the Soviet Union and one that is resolved behind the scenes. Committee meetings are not scheduled at any fixed time on the Soviet calendar, as the convoking of a plenary session depends upon when the leadership summons the members to Moscow. However, sessions have usually been held in the late spring and in late autumn or early winter prior to the semiannual sessions of the USSR Supreme Soviet. The Committee's proceedings can be secret or published in part or in what is purported to be their entirety—all at the discretion of the leadership. The statutes' vague and laconic provisions regarding the Central Committee reflect its unstructured nature, as well as its instrumental role in behalf of whoever controls the Committee's apparatus. As its size has increased, the prestige value and the influence of membership may have correspondingly declined. In apparent awareness of the problem of size, Gorbachev in 1986 reduced the number of full (voting) members from 319 to 307, but increased the number of candidate members.

The Politburo of the Central Committee

This body—called the Presidium from October 1952 until April 1966—is elected by the Central Committee "to direct the work of the Party" during the lengthy intervals between Committee plenary sessions. Such a body first came into being in 1917 on the eve of the seizure of power. It was made permanent in March 1919 by the Eighth Congress; and its size gradually increased to ten full members and five candidate-members in 1934. As in other Party bodies, candidate-members do not vote but can participate in discussions. For many years the Politburo's size remained relatively constant at 11 or 12 full members and 6 to 9 candidate-members—with the exception of the five-month period between the Nineteenth Congress and Stalin's death, when there were 25 full members and 11 candidate-members. A slight increase occurred again after the June 1957 crisis—when there were as many as 15 full members and 10 candidate-members—and again in 1971. It appears that, in general, experience has reflected a preference for a Politburo of 11 to 13 full members and 6 or 7 candidate-members as optimal in size.

Under Stalin the Politburo-Presidium atrophied; it met rarely in the last years of his life. During World War II it was superseded by the State Committee for Defense (GKO). Stalin divided the Politburo membership into small specialized committees and in this way retained the ability to act as arbiter and adopt decisions independently. Khrushchev stated that the Politburo members other than Stalin were "just errand boys."[16]

After Stalin's death the Presidium was reconstituted with ten members and four candidate-members. It became the setting for a fierce inner-Party struggle for power, but it also began to meet regularly (often at weekly intervals) and to adopt policy decisions by majority vote while seeking unanimity.

The Politburo membership includes the General Secretary of the Party, the head of government (premier or chairman of the U.S.S.R. Council of Ministers), and the chief of state (chairman of the Presidium of the U.S.S.R. Supreme Soviet). It usually includes several Central Committee secretaries (under Khrushchev the number varied from two to nine) and a U.S.S.R. first deputy premier. The First Secretary of the Ukrainian Communist Party is usually a member. The chairman

---

[16]*Khrushchev Remembers, The Last Testament* (Boston: Little, Brown, 1974), p. 357. In the 1970 volume (p. 281) he stated that the 25-member Presidium never met.

of the Party Control Committee has held Politburo membership. Other Politburo members have held a variety of positions.

Although the Politburo is, in practice, the highest Soviet policy-making body, relatively little is known about it apart from its membership and the fact that specific decisions of great import obviously originate within it. It meets secretly, and its minutes are not published. Andropov in 1983 introduced the practice of publishing in the press brief, but probably incomplete, accounts of Politburo meeting agendas and of certain actions taken. Brezhnev told a group of American journalists in June 1973 that the Politburo meets every Thursday afternoon at 3:00 P.M. for several hours and usually arrives at decisions by consensus after discussion rather than by voting. He subsequently informed the Twenty-sixth Congress in 1981 that the Politburo held 236 meetings during the previous five years—approximately four meetings per month. Some members are not always in Moscow, since they hold positions in the union republics; in all probability some Politburo meetings are held in their absence. Prominent members have been demoted abruptly and consigned to oblivion.

Central Committee resolutions usually reflect Politburo decisions, and the Politburo also issues directives to various government ministries and agencies. It takes up urgent problems brought before it by the departments of the Party Secretariat, a ministry, or the Council of Ministers. Individual Politburo members often have a field of specialization for which they are responsible, deciding matters of lesser import independently and referring difficult cases to the entire Politburo. On occasion the Politburo has discussed matters that would appear to be trivial in other political systems. There have been occasions when the Politburo has been undecided or deadlocked, and decisions have simply had to be postponed. When the Politburo has not been able to resolve internal conflicts involving a struggle for power, those conflicts have been taken to the Central Committee. The presence of a dominant personality such as Lenin or Stalin (or even Khrushchev at certain times during the height of his career) has determined the way in which the Politburo would function and has restricted its freedom of action. In the absence of such a dictator, arbiter, or strong personality, decisions have been arrived at "collectively" with more deliberation and less dispatch.

The Secretariat

The Party's administrative apparatus, with approximately 250,000 full-time officials and employees, is directed by the Central Committee's Secretariat, which is headed by the General Secretary (between 1953 and 1966, by the First Secretary). Party administration is in the hands of the Secretariat, and it is second only to the Party's Politburo in importance. The Party statutes say almost nothing about this body and did not even mention the powerful post of General Secretary prior to 1966. The Secretariat is elected by the Central Committee and is authorized "to direct current work, chiefly the selection of cadres and the verification of the fulfillment of Party decisions." In practice, this means that the Secretariat serves as the Party's executive arm and controls the activities and key personnel of all union republic, province, city, and district Party organizations. It issues directives to them and receives their reports.

Lenin never held the position of Party secretary. As principal founder of the Party, his position was that of leading member of the Central Committee and Politburo. The first person to serve as Party secretary during 1918 was Iakov Sverdlov, who was also chairman of the Soviet legislature (the Central Executive Committee of the Congress of Soviets). Sverdlov relied more on the well-financed governmental machinery than on the small central Party staff. His death in March 1919 resulted in the appointment of Nikolai Krestinsky, who was succeeded by Molotov in 1921. Their inability to organize the Secretariat effectively led to the election of Stalin as General Secretary in April 1922. Originally the Secretariat was to have been a service organization and a records department subordinate to the Organizational Bureau (Orgburo), established in March 1919, along with the Politburo. While the Politburo was to decide policy, the Orgburo was to decide organizational questions and allocate the Party's forces. The appointment of two additional Secretaries in March 1920 made the Secretariat a potential rival of the Orgburo.

Stalin's appointment as General Secretary made him a member of all four leading Party bodies: the Central Committee, the Politburo, the Orgburo, and the Secretariat. Under his command the Secretariat became a power unto itself and overshadowed the other bodies. The abolition of the Orgburo in October 1952 gave belated recognition to its having been superseded by the Secretariat. Since Stalin's time the Secretariat has served as the principal vehicle for determining the Soviet leadership in the person of the General Secretary or for advancing one's career as a political lieutenant. Yet this most important position does not have its powers or term of office defined in the CPSU statutes, which only state that "the Central Committee elects the General Secretary of the Central Committee of the CPSU" (article 38 of the 1986 statutes).

The Secretariat has varied in size from three to as many as fourteen members. Rarely—as in the winter of 1952–1953 and from July 1957 to 1959—have all or most of the Secretariat members been members or candidate-members of the Party Presidium-Politburo. Usually the Secretaries have been in a minority in the Politburo, although the General Secretary and certain subordinate Secretaries exercise substantial influence in that body.[17] The Secretariat's responsibility for detail and the careful screening of policy options is reflected in the fact that the 1977 Soviet draft constitution was discussed twice by the CPSU Central Committee, five times by the Politburo, and eighteen times by the Secretariat.[18]

The Secretariat is organized into a number of departments *(otdely),* each of which is headed by one of the Secretaries or by a department head. The division

---

[17]On Secretariat influence in the Politburo, see John H. Kress, "Representation of Positions on the CPSU Politburo," *Slavic Review,* p. 39, (2), (June 1980), pp. 218–238.

[18]Konstantin U. Chernenko, *Voprosy raboty partiinogo i gosudarstvennogo apparata,* 2nd ed. (Moscow: Politizdat, 1982), p. 172.

of responsibilities between Secretaries is usually not revealed but is often evident from their activities and pronouncements. Usually the designation of a department head is made public in an indirect manner and after the fact rather than by formal announcement. The number of departments has varied but has always included a group devoted to various sectors of industry and to agriculture, construction, transport, and communications. The Organizational and Party Work Department (formerly known as the "Party Organs" Department) is responsible for supervising the subordinate party organizations, the Komsomol (Communist Youth), and trade unions; it is also charged with staffing these and governmental organizations; and it keeps dossiers on all of the regime's leading officials. The Administrative Organs Department exercises guidance and control over the courts, prosecuting agencies, and the police. The Department of Propaganda is responsible for the communications media and ideological training. A separate department is in charge of science and education, and there is also a department for culture. Relations with ruling Communist parties in other countries and with foreign parties not in power are the responsibility of separate departments. A department for cadres abroad must give its approval to governmental appointments for service outside the Soviet Union and must approve all Soviet persons, delegations, and groups traveling abroad. The Main Political Administration of the Armed Forces, although formally in the Defense Ministry, is regarded as a branch of the Secretariat. A separate department is responsible for the defense industry. The General Department is responsible for archives, the disposition of complaints, internal security, and probably the preparation of Politburo agendas. The Administrative (Affairs) Department functions as a general services and housekeeping organization responsible for the Party's many office buildings and other properties, including housing and health and vacation facilities.

There is hardly any sector of Soviet life for which some branch of the Secretariat cannot claim responsibility. It receives reports from subordinate Party bodies and monitors their performance as well as the functioning of a wide range of institutions and enterprises. The Secretariat issues, in the name of the Central Committee, directives with criticisms and instructions for specific province or city Party organizations or for a ministry, industrial enterprise, or scientific institute. These directives are published and a specific time set for the fulfillment of their provisions. The Secretariat prepares reports for the Politburo as well as background papers on current problems, policy proposals, and recommendations. It oversees the entire Party machine and is responsible for the execution of Party policy decisions. It allocates the Party's manpower and controls its resources. It mobilizes the rank-and-file membership and enables the Party to act with a high degree of unity.

Control Bodies

The Central Committee also elects a Party Control Committee. The precursor of this latter committee was the Central Control Commission, which came into being in 1921 along with local and regional control commissions established in the autumn of 1920. These bodies were responsible for the enforcement of Party discipline and were to be independent of the Party committees that functioned at their level. In practice they became adjuncts of the Party bureaucracy. The Central Control Commission began to meet with the Central Committee in joint plenary session in October 1923 and was used by Stalin to combat critics and oppositionists. The Commission's membership was increased to 50 in 1923 and to 151 in the following year; by 1925 it had 163 members. In 1934 it was renamed the Party Control Commission, and after 1939 it was elected by the Central Committee rather than by the Congress. In 1952 it became the Party Control Committee. The function of the Committee is to verify and enforce Party discipline and to hear appeals regarding penalties or the expulsion of members by union republic and province Party organizations.

The Central Auditing Commission

This committee of inspection is elected by the Congress. Its responsibilities were stated in greater detail in the 1986 CPSU statutes (article 36). It "verifies the observance of the established order of the conduct of affairs, work regarding the examination of letters, statements and complaints of workers to the central organs of the Party, correctness in the fulfillment of the Party budget, including the payment, collection and accounting of members' Party dues, and also the financial and economic activities of enterprises and institutions of the CPSU Central Committee."[19] The Commission's chairman reports to each regular Congress on the conduct of the Party's business in a speech that is not particularly informative. Since the Party is very secretive about its finances and expenditures (as has been the case since Lenin's time), the Auditing Commission's report is correspondingly vague and incomplete. Although most unsatisfactory as a financial statement, the report does include references to the Party's publishing enterprises and the payment of dues. Income from dues constituted 57 percent of the Party's total income in 1985 (compared with 65 percent in 1976 and 85 percent in 1952). Income from the sale of Party publications has risen; in 1986 it was reported that the Party had 114 publishing enterprises, 78 of which had their own printing plants. A chronic complaint is that local Party secretaries are lax in collecting dues and do not deposit funds promptly and that this leads to cases of embezzlement. There are also cases of ineffective use of funds, as when it was necessary to "establish order" in the *Pravda* publishing house as a result of various financial irregularities.[20] The Auditing Commission has usually criticized local Party officials for delays in dealing with letters of complaint and proposals, while giving the Central Committee apparatus a clean bill of health in such matters. It was stated at the 1986 Congress that the Central Committee headquarters received more than 3.5 million letters from citizens between 1981 and 1985 and that many such letters

---

[19]"Ustav KPSS," *Kommunist,* No. 4 (March 1986), p. 161.
[20]*Pravda,* February 26, 1986, p. 11.

were prompted by the fact that local Party, governmental, and economic bodies are not sufficiently attentive to citizens' complaints.

SUBORDINATE BODIES

The Primary Party Organizations

These bodies, called "cells" prior to 1939, are the foundation stones on which the Party structure stands. They number more than 440,000 and are to be found in every Soviet enterprise and institution—including government ministries, factories, schools and universities, economic enterprises, farms, military units, and Soviet embassies. Wherever three Party members are similarly employed, a primary party organization (p.p.o.) is formed. Less than one-fifth of the p.p.o.'s are territorial and are to be found in some villages and in cities; the latter are in housing developments and consist of Party members who are housing officials, pensioners, or housewives. Thus most of the p.p.o.'s are organized on the *functional* principle (as in a steel mill or university) in contrast with higher Party bodies, which are organized exclusively on a *territorial* basis. Thus, the authority of the p.p.o. is limited to the particular functional enterprise, while the jurisdiction of a local Party committee extends over a district or city and embraces a number of primary party organizations.

Every Party member must belong to a p.p.o. Those having at least fifteen members elect a "bureau" or committee for two or three years to conduct the Party business in the particular enterprise; the bureau meets two or three times each month. Those having fewer than 15 members elect only a secretary and a deputy for one year. If the p.p.o. has more than 150 members, one or more secretaries are relieved of all regular duties within the enterprise to concentrate on Party work as full-time employees who work for the Party but are kept on the enterprise's payroll. This practice increases the size of the CPSU apparatus greatly at no cost to the Party. The members of smaller p.p.o.'s hold a closed Party meeting once a month, but in larger organizations meetings of the entire membership are called less frequently.

The p.p.o. serves as the eyes and ears of the Party in every enterprise, institution, or public organization. In organizations engaged in industry, transport, trade, communications, agriculture, construction, scientific research, education, and medical care, the p.p.o.'s "have the right of control over the activities of administrations" (article 59 of the 1986 Statutes). By "control" is meant the right to monitor and verify performance. In governmental bodies and in organs of economic administration, the p.p.o. "must actively influence the perfecting of the work of the apparatus" and must inform the "corresponding Party organs" of any "shortcomings" rather than intervene directly. Thus, each p.p.o. can intervene actively in the operations of the particular enterprise and must be reckoned with. The p.p.o. enlists new members and is responsible for their training in Marxism-Leninism. It can also expel members by a two-thirds vote of those present at a duly constituted general meeting of the p.p.o.; before coming into force, expulsions must be approved by the district or city Party Committee to which the p.p.o. is subordinate. Lesser penalties, such as a reprimand with or without a recorded entry in the member's file, can be imposed by the p.p.o. without the approval of the appropriate district or city Party committee. The p.p.o. can investigate the personal life of a Party member and can expose and censure his or her conduct.[21] The p.p.o. must engage in mass agitation and propaganda in support of Party decisions and public appeals; it must mobilize the masses to fulfill economic plans, combat waste and laxity, and strengthen both labor and state discipline. It must "struggle against any manifestations of bourgeois ideology, revisionism and dogmatism, backward views and attitudes" (article 58) and improve productivity and product quality.

The *Raikom* and *Gorkom*

At the district *(raion)* level, which is comparable to a small rural county or an urban ward or borough, the Party is organized on the territorial principle. All p.p.o.'s in the *raion* are subordinated to the Party's raion committee (*raikom* is the Russian acronym for this body), which places an "instructor" in charge of each group of p.p.o.'s. Larger cities are divided into *raiony,* each of which also has a Party raikom. At the municipal *(gorod)* level there is a Party committee that is called a *gorkom.* The raion and gorod (city) Party committees are elected at conferences held every two or three years (twice in five years) to which the p.p.o.'s send representatives. The raikom and gorkom are elected at the district or city conference for a two- or three-year term and meet in plenary session at least once every three months. The daily work of the Party is conducted by a bureau or smaller committee, in which the raikom secretaries play the key role.

The *Obkom* and *Kraikom*

At the provincial level (including the autonomous soviet republics), there are approximately 150 oblast' Party committees and six krai Party committees. The oblast' is a basic administrative-territorial unit that varies in area and population. Approximately half of the oblasti are in the Russian S.F.S.R., and another twenty-five are in the Ukrainian S.S.R. The krai is generally larger than the oblast', though often more sparsely populated; is more remote from the center of Soviet power; and is generally located in the Russian S.F.S.R. Oblasti can vary significantly in area and in population, with some, especially in remote regions, having a population well below one million. Some oblasti have populations of

---

[21] Arkady N. Shevchenko, a former Soviet diplomat and Under Secretary General of the United Nations, has noted that the p.p.o. in the USSR Ministry of Foreign Affairs was passive and neither challenged nor initiated anything. He states that its principal function was to "ensure discipline," see that orders were carried out, and interfere in the personal lives of Party members who had engaged in misconduct such as "heavy drinking, philandering, and . . . smuggling Western consumer goods." However, "the higher the transgressor's rank . . . the greater the tendency to cover up his misdeeds." He noted that "the pettier the subject, the longer the discussion of it." Arkady N. Shevchenko, *Breaking with Moscow* (New York: Ballantine Books, 1985), pp. 111–112.

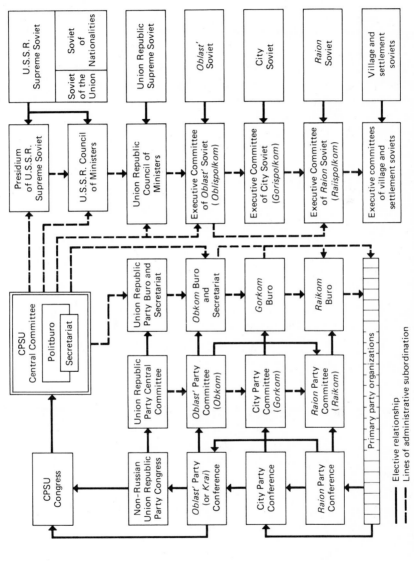

Figure 4.1 Party and governmental bodies. [*Source:* Michael Curtis (ed.), *Introduction to Comparative Government* (New York: Harper & Row, Publishers, Inc., 1985).]

Elective relationship

Lines of administrative subordination

several million. The "ideal" oblast' might have 1.5 million people and be fairly well developed economically, with some diversity but with a predominant economic specialty. The average oblast might be likened to a smaller-sized state in the United States, although there are several oblasti that are very large in area (Tiumen, Irkutsk, Kamchatka, and Magadan), but these are remote from the center. The relative stability of the oblast' system indicates that for both Party and governmental purposes, it is a tested and optimally sized jurisdictional unit that facilitates monitoring of performance.

The typical oblast' Party headquarters is a very recognizable and often quite impressive edifice that rivals that of the government and represents the Soviet political order. The oblast' committee *(obkom)* and the krai committee *(kraikom)* of the Party are elected every two or three years at conferences to which the raion Party organizations elect delegates. The obkom and kraikom meet at least once every four months; the daily business of the Party is conducted by the bureau. The obkom bureau includes the several obkom secretaries, leading officials of the oblast' government (soviet), and a Communist Youth (Komsomol) representative, along with a trade union leader, the editor of the oblast' newspaper, the oblast' security police (KGB) chief, the oblast' center gorkom first secretary, and several raikom secretaries.[22] The Party apparatus at this level mirrors much of the Central Committee Secretariat apparatus in Moscow with its various departments.[23] The first secretary of the obkom or kraikom is usually the most influential person in the province, his authority is usually unquestioned, and he is held responsible for performance.

The Union Republic Central Committee

Each non-Russian union republic Communist Party has a Central Committee, which is elected by the republic Party congress. However, in the smaller union republics, which are not divided into oblasti, the Central Committee is treated by Moscow as the equivalent of an obkom. The non-Russian union republic Party congresses are held every five years. The Russian Republic does not have a separate Central Committee, nor does it hold its own Party congress. The dominance of the CPSU Central Committee and Congress by the Russian oblast' Party organizations makes a Russian Republic Party organization with its own congress and central committee unnecessary.

The organizational scheme described above has served the Party well and

---

[22]See Joel C. Moses, *Regional Party Leadership and Policy-Making in the U.S.S.R.* (New York: Praeger, 1974), pp. 160–161, as well as "Functional Career Specialization in Soviet Regional Elite Recruitment," by Joel C. Moses in T. H. Rigby and Bohdan Harasymiw, eds., *Leadership Selection and Patron-Client Relations in the USSR and Yugoslavia* (London: George Allen & Unwin, 1983), pp. 20 and 33.

[23]A typical *obkom* or *kraikom* headquarters includes the following departments: Party-organizational work, industry and transport, light and food industry, construction, science and education, general department, agitation and propaganda, agriculture, administrative organs, commercial-financial organs, financial and economic, as well as specialized industrial departments (e.g., petroleum, chemicals, wood products) depending on the nature of the *oblast'* economy. See *Politicheskaia organizatsiia sovetskogo obshchestva, nagliadnoe posobie,* 2nd ed. (Moscow: Politizdat, 1972), p. 73.

has enabled it to impose its will upon millions of subjects. It has kept the Party leadership sufficiently informed of conditions throughout the land to permit it to cope with dissident elements, to satisfy or suppress enough of the demands emanating from the population, and to control its own officials. When the Party's leadership has erred—as it has egregiously on occasion—it has been able to retain power largely because of its ability to command the numerous forces available to the Party apparatus. The ability to deploy Party cadres and to obtain the support of the rank-and-file membership has been due in large measure to the organizational machine.

chapter 5

The Communist Party
and the Structure
of Power

The quasi-monopoly of power enjoyed by the Soviet Communist Party has been jealously guarded, and it has not been prepared to share power. In the 1936 Constitution the Party defined itself as the "leading core of all organizations of the working people, both public and state" (article 126). In the 1977 Constitution (Article 6), the CPSU is described as "the leading and directing force of Soviet society, the nucleus of its political system, of all state and public organizations." The Party is not bound by any constitutional requirements; it can change the constitution of the Soviet polity at will, reorganizing the government, replacing or abolishing existing agencies or practices, or even writing a new constitution. The Party retains control of the government and gives direction to its administrative machinery, determining which Party leaders will hold particular governmental positions. Yet it seeks to avoid administering the government and economy directly and relies on the Soviet governmental bureaucracy to carry out its policies. The Party recruits, trains, and advances (or demotes) members of the Soviet political class. The Party develops public policies and defines goals; Party decisions have the force of law. It attempts to resolve the conflicting interests of various subordinate organizations and segments of Soviet society, often counterposing and weakening them to its own advantage.

GENERAL CHARACTERISTICS
Centralism and Antifederalism

Under Lenin's leadership the Bolsheviks in 1903 adopted a position opposed to federalism based on ethnic distinctions. The walkout of the Jewish Social Democrats (the Bundists) from the Second Congress had been precipitated by Lenin's rejection of the proposal that the Marxist movement in the Russian Empire be based on coequal organizations representing the various nationalities. Lenin's professed "proletarian internationalism" provided the theoretical basis for what was to become, in practice, a Russian-dominated central Party apparatus. Bolshevism's founder was acutely aware of the centrifugal forces inherent in an ethnic conglomerate such as the Russian Empire and hoped to prevent their operating within the Party. A federal type of organization would, in Lenin's view, concede too much to non-Russian national interests and would be a denial of what he chose to call the international solidarity of the working class. If, subsequent to the seizure of power, separate Communist Party organizations were established for the various non-Russian nationalities, they were nevertheless strictly subordinated to the Party's center in Moscow.

The principle of "democratic centralism," which reflects this subordination, was first defined in the Party statutes in 1919, although the term was first introduced but not explained in the 1906 statutes. The centralist side of the coin is evident in the provision for "periodic accountability of party organs to their Party organizations and to higher organs" and in the stipulation that "the decisions of the higher organs are absolutely binding on lower organs" (article 19 of 1986 Statutes). The Party statutes (article 2) obligate members to combat "localism" *(mestnichestvo)*—that is, the tendency to place local or regional interests ahead of those of the center or other areas. Local Party organizations "are autonomous in deciding local matters provided that these decisions are not contrary to Party policy" (article 21)—a very broad qualification.

Antifactionalism

From its beginnings, Bolshevism was plagued with opposition, from within the ranks, of Russian Marxists who adopted different views regarding tactics and priorities. In the late 1890s Lenin did battle with the "Economists," who advocated economic reforms by means of trade unionism, strikes, and boycotts for the purpose of improving the workers' lot. Lenin insisted upon the primacy of the political struggle over economic demands, fearing that the latter would become an end in itself rather than a means of promoting political conflict. The Mensheviks—whom Lenin called "Liquidators" because of their desire to abandon illicit conspiratorial activity and dissolve the underground apparatus—were another factional group that was regarded as harmful.

However, factionalism broke out among the Bolsheviks themselves after the 1905 revolution. When Lenin decided in June 1906 to end his boycott of the tsarist quasi-parliament, the Duma, and to sponsor Bolshevik candidates for legislative seats, he was confronted with a movement among those of his followers who opposed such "bourgeois" methods. These Recallists *(Otzovisty)* and Ultimatists were more "Bolshevik" than Bolshevism's founder in their desire to pursue a purely leftist policy of boycotting the Duma. Lenin, on the other hand, wished to employ the bourgeois parliament as a tribune for revolutionary agitation, using legal means along with conspiratorial methods. Disagreements over philosophical questions—especially regarding the nature of cognition and perception—in 1908 and 1909 prompted Lenin to denounce some of his followers as Machists (followers of Ernst Mach's Empiriocritical philosophy) and as philosophical "idealists" and betrayers of dialectical materialism. An effort to deify human potential in the form of a humanistic quasi-religion resulted in the "God-building" movement led by the Bolshevik A. Lunacharsky; this, too, aroused Lenin's ire. When several of these factionalists organized a Party school on the island of Capri with the help of the writer Maxim Gorky, Lenin denounced the effort and succeeded in disrupting the school's work.

The pattern of factionalism persisted after the Bolsheviks came to power. "Left-Communists," led by the theoretician Nikolai Bukharin, opposed Lenin's decision to sign a peace treaty with the Central Powers in March 1918. In 1919 a Military Opposition expressed dissatisfaction with Lenin's policy of organizing a standing army and hiring tsarist officers rather than relying on an armed popular militia. In 1920 the Democratic Centralist Opposition unsuccessfully took issue with the growing centralism and authoritarian practices of the Party apparatus. The Workers' Opposition of 1920–1921 objected to the limited role of industrial workers in the Party, to its increased bureaucratization, and to the policy of hiring bourgeois technicians and specialists. These opposition movements prompted Lenin to adopt harsh measures at the Tenth Congress in March 1921, including a resolution that outlawed all factions and provided for the expulsion of offenders from the Party. Although factionalism was outlawed, it could not be prevented; there subsequently emerged such factions as the Left Opposition (Trotsky, Kamenev, and Zinoviev), the Right Opposition (of Bukharin, Rykov, and Tomsky), and the so-called anti-Party group of 1957.

The 1986 Party statutes, like earlier such documents, declare that "any manifestation of factionalism and group activity is incompatible with Marxist-Leninist party principles and party membership." The preamble refers to "the ideological and organizational unity and monolithic cohesion" of the Party's ranks as an "immutable law of the [Party's] life." Thus, dissent is forbidden once a policy has been adopted and the current line laid down. Although the "free and businesslike discussion of the questions of Party policy" (article 26) is said to be "an important principle of inner-party democracy," it would be unwise for the rank-and-file member to question the wisdom of the current leadership. If the statutes grant to members the supposed right "to criticize at Party meetings, conferences, congresses, and committee meetings any Party body, any Communist, irrespective of the post he occupies" (article 3), it is difficult to reconcile this provision with the outright condemnation of factionalism. In practice the Party line is laid down by those in control of the central apparatus, who are able to equate criticism with factionalism.

Obligations of Membership

The statutory definition of the Party as "the militant, tried, and tested vanguard of the Soviet people" implies a highly selective approach to the recruitment of members. Although the Party inevitably attracts many careerists, it also imposes obligations upon its members.[1] Applicants undergo a one-year period of candidacy during which they familiarize themselves with the Party's program and statutes and with the current official version of its history. Each candidate must obtain recommendations from three members of at least five years' standing who have been acquainted with him or her professionally and socially for at least one year.

Members' duties include the following: "to struggle to create the material-technical base of Communism," increase labor productivity and master technology, and "safeguard and augment public socialist property"; to "carry out Party decisions firmly and undeviatingly" and strengthen ties between the Party and the people; to participate actively in "political life" and in "economic and cultural construction," setting an example in the fulfillment of public duty; "to master Marxist-Leninist theory, raise the ideological level [and] . . . combat resolutely any manifestations of bourgeois ideology, vestiges of a private-property psychology"; to promote "socialist internationalism and Soviet patriotism, combat the survivals of nationalism and chauvinism"; to protect the Party's "ideological and organizational unity," to guard against the penetration of the Party by those "unworthy of the high title of Communist," and to "display vigilance and keep Party and state secrets."

Members are required to "develop criticism and self-criticism" (limited in practice to means rather than to policies) and to combat "ostentation, conceit, complacency and localism . . . [and] oppose any activities prejudicial to the Party and state and report them to the Party bodies up to and including the CPSU Central Committee." Other obligations include the observance of "the Party line in the selection of cadres [key personnel] on the basis of their political and professional work *(delovye)* qualifications," the observance of "Party and state discipline," and the strengthening of the "defensive might" of the USSR. Members and candidate-members are also required to pay monthly dues ranging from 0.5 percent to 3.0 percent of their income.

The Party is a harsh taskmaster, viewing itself—in Lenin's definition of September 1917—as "the intelligence, honor, and conscience of our epoch."[2] It is a jealous ruler, brooking no rivals and exacting many demands as well as offering the possibility of real rewards along with the prospect of some hazards and risks. Members are not only required to propagate convincingly the rationale for current Party policies, but are expected to carry out decisions even if they do

---

[1] Khrushchev conceded that among the Party's members there are "many people without principle, lickspittle functionaries and petty careerists" who "seek to get much more out of our society than they put into it." It is no longer a party of self-sacrificing idealists. See *Khrushchev Remembers* (Boston: Little, Brown, 1970), pp. 17, 57, 182. At the Twenty-sixth CPSU Congress in 1981, Brezhnev conceded that "at times unworthy people by chance find their way into the ranks of the CPSU," and he noted that during the previous five-year period "nearly 300,000 persons" had been expelled for "acts incompatible with the title of communist." *Izvestiia*, February 24, 1981, p. 8.

[2] V. I. Lenin, *Polnoe sobranie sochinenii* (Moscow: Gospolitizdat, 1962) 5th ed., XXXIV, p. 93.

not approve of them. This is the price of discipline.[3] Members of a "minority"—
by definition those who may be in disagreement with the Party's administrative
apparatus—have no recourse but to accept the current line and remain silent or
risk expulsion for continuing their activities. Party discipline may even require
that members condemn themselves, as the victims of the Moscow purge trials did
in the 1930s. The members of the anti-Party group in 1957 voted *for* the resolution of censure and *for* their expulsion from the Central Committee—with the
exception of Molotov, who abstained but would not cast a solitary vote in his own
defense. Khrushchev, upon being summarily ousted in October 1964, could offer
no public defense of his policies and conduct but had to retire in humiliating
silence. The strange spell cast by one's affiliation with the Party has frequently
paralyzed the will to resist those who act in its name.

With a steadily growing Party membership that exceeded 19 million in
1987, it has become very difficult to monitor the conduct of members and to
adequately screen applicants. Many join the Party simply in order to advance
their careers, qualify for a promotion, or be cleared for travel abroad. At the
Twenty-seventh Congress it was proposed that a general purge of the membership
be undertaken to cleanse the Party of persons whose conduct and life-style were
not compatible with the Party's requirements. Gorbachev rejected the proposal
for a "special campaign to purge the ranks of the CPSU" and claimed that it was
a "healthy organism" improving itself. Such reassurances were negated by the
attention given by Gorbachev to shortcomings in the work of Party cadres and
in the methods and style of work.

"KREMLINOLOGY"

The study of the current alignment of forces within the Soviet ruling circle and
the significance of the promotion or demotion of individual leaders and aides have
sometimes been referred to as "Kremlinology." However, the struggle for power
and influence, and the elimination of actual and potential rivals, occurs irrespective of what it may be called. Although frequently only the surface manifestations
of this struggle are evident, its consequences (in the form of ousters, personnel
transfers, and shifts in policy) ultimately provide confirmation of its having
occurred. Thus, the student of Kremlinology is compelled to rely on fragmentary
data and clues that must be interpreted cautiously, with a full awareness of the
many pitfalls to be encountered. Indeed, Kremlinology is a consequence of the
secretive nature of the Soviet political system.

Various criteria and clues reflecting prestige and protocol have proved
useful in determining the relative positions of individual Soviet politicians. In
addition to the order in which leaders are listed (if not alphabetical) in public
pronouncements and the order of their portraits, status can be revealed by their
absence or presence at official functions and by their positions in group photo-

---

[3]As early as September 1902, Lenin likened the Central Committee's role to that of an
orchestra conductor who knows "who is playing which violin where . . . who is playing false notes
where and why . . . and who should be transferred where and how in order to correct a dissonance,
etc." *Ibid.,* VII, p. 22.

graphs that appear in the Soviet press. Who sees whom off and who is in the welcoming delegation usually indicate current standing in the leadership. The Party Congress has provided one means of distinguishing between leaders: the adjectives used to describe the amount and quality of applause given to individuals as recorded in the official stenographic report.[4] The length of a leader's speech at the Congress and its subject matter also serve as a status index. Who quotes whom is important and bears watching. Appointment to certain positions—such as first secretary of an important oblast' Party organization or of a large union republic central committee—is usually a sign of advancement in the Party hierarchy.

Leaders who are advancing often promote subordinates with whom they were associated in the past. The careers of these subordinates become dependent upon that of their sponsor, at least for a time. The number of lieutenants and aides who obtain higher positions as a result of their sponsor's support is an index of his influence. However, past associations may not be durable, and it is possible for lieutenants to shift allegiance if their mentor's star is declining and that of a rival is ascending. Although the charting of personal relationships between Soviet leaders in terms of past associations is subject to many provisos, it can serve as one indicator of the shifting currents of Kremlin politics.

Another index of status is the number of honorary nominations received by leading Soviet politicians at the time of elections to the U.S.S.R. Supreme Soviet. In the end each leader declines all nominations but one, although the ritual has been indicative of the relative standing of the various leaders, which is subject to rapid change. Thus, in the 1954 election Premier Malenkov received 50 nominations, as compared with 43 for Khrushchev; in 1958 Khrushchev received 84 nominations, while Marshal Voroshilov was second with 31; in 1962 Khrushchev was nominated in 136 constituencies, and Leonid Brezhnev was second with 39 nominations. In 1966 Brezhnev led the field with 170 nominations, followed by Kosygin with 94 and Podgorny with 52; Suslov had 41, Voronov 34, Kirilenko 31, and Shelepin 29. In the 1984 elections Andropov led (only days prior to his death) with 39 nominations; Chernenko was second with 13; Tikhonov had 12, Gorbachev 8, Romanov 7, Aliev and Gromyko 6, Chebrikov and Shevardnadze 3, and Rvzhkov 2. Still another criterion for determining status is the treatment accorded to prominent Party leaders in successive editions of the frequently revised official Party history.

Critics of Kremlinology have disparaged the study of power relationships within the Soviet inner elite as being overly deterministic, to the exclusion of chance and contingency. The critics contend that Kremlinologists read far too

---

[4]Thus, at the Twentieth Congress in 1956, there were the following gradations: "applause"; "continued applause"; "stormy applause"; "stormy, continued applause" (Molotov, Malenkov, Voroshilov, Suslov); "stormy, prolonged applause" (Mikoyan); "continued, lasting applause. All rise." (Premier Bulganin); "Stormy, prolonged applause transforming itself into an ovation. All rise." (Khrushchev). Following Khrushchev's ouster, the gradations became less pronounced, although the length of applause continued to have significance. The Twenty-seventh Congress in 1986 had five categories: "applause"; "continued applause"; "Continued applause, all rise"; "Stormy, continued applause"; and "Stormy, continued applause. All rise."

much significance into minor events. Yet such events as the transfer of Khrushchev from Kiev to Moscow in December 1949 and the return of Brezhnev to the Secretariat in June 1963 had far-reaching consequences that were not perceived at the time. It is difficult to determine which events, at the time of their occurrence, are of minor or major significance, but the Kremlinologist is acutely aware of the possibility that an obscure and seemingly unimportant piece of information may be of great potential significance. He or she proceeds on the basis of theoretical constructs and hypotheses, fully aware of the possibility that the regime may falsify some data as well as suppress information.[5]

Another criticism of Kremlinology is based on the contention that Soviet politics are determined, not by personalities, but by sweeping socioeconomic forces. These are identified as industrialism, urbanization, a state-operated economy, the existence of a technical intelligentsia and a managerial class, the possession of nuclear weapons, and a capability in rocketry and space flight. Thus, in this view, policies and problems that result from such forces are far more important than the personalities dealing with them. Yet if one concedes both the importance of socioeconomic forces and the technical apparatus that accompanies those forces, it does not follow from this that personalities can be ignored. Indeed, the proponents of the socioeconomic-forces thesis may be said to ignore the role of individual leaders in a quasi-Marxist manner. They neglect the possibility that the winner in the Soviet power struggle may have a very different political style, method, and program from those of the loser. It is quite likely that the Soviet Union would have developed along different lines had Bukharin rather than Stalin emerged as the victor; or had Beria, Molotov, or Malenkov defeated Khrushchev; or had Shelepin rather than Brezhnev prevailed. The study of the careers and power relationships of the Soviet leadership, if it is pursued to the exclusion of other factors, can obscure the purposes for which power is sought. However, to ignore the means by which individual Soviet leaders place themselves in a position to determine ends and adopt policies is to neglect the essence of Soviet politics.

THE SOVIET GAME OF POLITICS

That Soviet politics involves anomalies, surprises, and irony is seen in the fact that two men—Stalin and Khrushchev—who together ruled the Soviet Union for more than forty years, subsequently fell into disgrace. Their successor, Brezhnev, was criticized posthumously for tolerating corruption and stagnation. Only Lenin, who ruled less than five years, remained as an uncorrupted figure worthy of praise as the regime's founder and posthumous holder of Party membership card number one. In this context it would appear that the process for recruiting

[5]See the excellent study by Robert Conquest, *Power and Policy in the U.S.S.R.; The Study of Soviet Dynasties* (New York: St. Martin's Press, 1961). For a "Kremlinological" study that deals with the fierce rivalry between Andrei Zhdanov and Georgii Malenkov, see Werner G. Hahn, *Postwar Soviet Politics, The Fall of Zhdanov and the Defeat of Moderation, 1946–53* (Ithaca, N.Y.: Cornell University Press, 1982).

the top Soviet leadership and the general political environment have left something to be desired. Indeed, leading Soviet politicians do not often retire voluntarily. If charged with failures and errors, they have no opportunity to call a press conference and explain their actions or to publish memoirs in their own defense.[6]

The Soviet game of politics is played for high stakes and is essentially what theorists have termed a zero-sum game—one in which the winner takes all and the loser receives nothing. It involves a fierce struggle in which no holds are barred; and it makes possible the rise of vigorous and resourceful men, although some may later be demoted or disgraced and suffer silent degradation or even live under virtual house arrest. Those who are removed make way for ambitious men seeking to rise in the hierarchy. Yet at times it has also promoted excessively long tenure.

Various weapons are employed in the game at the highest level. One of these has been ideology and the charge of ideological deviation used to compromise one's opponents. Power struggle cannot be depicted officially as a clash of personalities but only as a conflict between orthodoxy and deviation, between the "correct" Party line and the proponents of "factionalism" or "distortion" of "Leninist norms of Party life." Soviet politicians who emerge triumphant can claim that they are pursuing ideologically "correct" policies, although such "correct" policies cannot be adopted without first obtaining office. Thus Malenkov was accused by Khrushchev of advocating a "Rightist" line in 1954–1955 and was removed from the premiership. The "anti-Party group" of 1957 was said to have opposed the Twentieth Party Congress and the campaign against the "cult of personality." Khrushchev could claim that his policies were "correct" after he was able to oust his opponents, and Brezhnev could claim that his was the true "Leninist course." Gorbachev could criticize Brezhnev and yet claim that his own course was "Leninist."

At various times in the past—especially during Stalin's regime—opponents have been executed, although political blackmail can also serve as an effective method of silencing one's opponents. It is probable that the large volume of information gathered by the Soviet Party apparatus and the secret police has provided much material that those with access to the files have been able to use effectively at times. Thus Khrushchev could implicate Malenkov, Molotov, and Kaganovich in Stalin's crimes while giving himself a not entirely deserved clean bill of health. The opportunities for intrigue and blackmail have not usually been missed in Soviet politics. The Soviet security police (KGB) provides bodyguards for members of the oligarchy and learns much about their private lives and vulnerabilities. The fact that important Soviet political personages (such as Shele-

---

[6]Khrushchev's reminiscences, dictated in isolation, had to be tape-recorded without benefit of any access to state papers or Party records or even to library facilities and could only be published abroad. The authenticity of the tapes has been verified by voiceprint analysis. The Party's Control Committee compelled Khrushchev to issue a statement, released on November 16, 1970, in which he denied only that he himself had "passed on" any memoirs for publications abroad and "did not turn over such materials to the Soviet publishing houses either." In branding such reports a "fabrication," he did not deny the existence of the memoirs. See *Khrushchev Remembers, The Last Testament* (Boston: Little, Brown, 1974), pp. xiv–xv.

pin, Podgorny, Romanov, and Grishin) could be required to retire from political life in silence inevitably raises questions regarding how this is accomplished and what inducements or forms of persuasion are used.

The practice of "criticism and self-criticism," in addition to giving support to the pretence of intraparty democracy, permits officials to be singled out for allegedly ineffective performance of their duties. Central Committee members who are associated with a losing individual or group in the Politburo may therefore find themselves subjected to criticism on performance grounds and may subsequently be removed. The ability of the Secretariat to shift personnel and effect periodic shake-ups and reorganizations gives it a powerful weapon in dealing with opponents. The system of *nomenklatura* gives the Secretariat—and at lower levels the corresponding Party officials—the right to control the appointment of all persons to a stipulated series of positions.[7] It has been estimated that the total number of nomenklatura listings for the various jurisdictions include two million or more positions.[8]

The practice of systematic transfers serves as a convenient cover for removals and appointments, which can affect the distribution of forces within the Central Committee. The tenure of an obkom first secretary's appointment varies considerably, and what may appear to be routine transfers may in fact have political consequences at Party headquarters in Moscow. The economic reorganization of 1957 was used by Khrushchev to remove many of the supporters of the anti-Party group from Moscow. Involuntary exile abroad by appointment to Soviet ambassadorships has at times also been a means of removing prominent politicians from the Moscow scene. Stalin employed this device in the 1920s, and Khrushchev and Brezhnev also used it.[9]

---

[7] These positions range from Party secretary or department head to Soviet government executives, oblast' secret police chief, newspaper editor, and factory or state farm director. Even "elective" posts are included in the nomenklatura system. Each Party committee has a list, and persons filling positions on it must be approved by the next higher Party committee (secretariat). Thus positions on the lists affecting the raikom or gorkom can be filled only with the approval of the obkom. Positions at the obkom level can only be filled with the approval of the union republic or CPSU Central Committee Secretariat. There are also lists of supposedly qualified and politically reliable persons who are acceptable for certain categories of positions. The entire nomenklatura system has its origins in Leninist practice. See Bohdan Harasymiw, *"Nomenklatura:* The Soviet Communist Party's Leadership Recruitment System," *Canadian Journal of Political Science* II, No. 4, (December 1969), pp. 493–512.

[8] See "Introduction" by T. H. Rigby in T. H. Rigby and Bohdan Harasymiw, eds., *Leadership Selection and Patron-Client Relations in the USSR and Yugoslavia* (London: George Allen & Unwin, 1983), pp. 3–4, 9–10, n. 10.

[9] Thus Molotov was sent to the Mongolian People's Republic and to the International Atomic Energy Agency in Vienna. Pervukhin, also a member of the anti-Party group, was named ambassador to East Germany. P. K. Ponomarenko, one of Malenkov's supporters and a former Central Committee Secretary, was sent successively to Poland, India, and the Netherlands as ambassador. Brezhnev had the Leningrad obkom First Secretary, Vasilii S. Tolstikov (a protégé of his late rival Frol Kozlov), appointed ambassador to China in September 1970. In 1967 Brezhnev demoted one of his critics, Nikolai G. Yegorychev, Moscow gorkom First Secretary, to Deputy Minister of Tractor and Agricultural Machinery Construction; in April 1970 he was appointed Ambassador to Denmark and in 1971 was dropped from the Central Committee. Dmitrii Poliansky was appointed Ambassador to Japan in 1976 and subsequently to Norway after being removed from the Politburo. Vitalii Vorotnikov, as Russian Republic first deputy premier, was "exiled" as ambassador to Cuba (1979–1982) and was subsequently brought back by Andropov and became premier of the Russian Republic and a full member of the Politburo.

Party officials do not enjoy fixed terms of office, and even Politburo and Central Committee members are subject to uncertain tenure. The standing of a Politburo member can become untenable should that member be transferred by administrative fiat to a lesser position that would clearly not be commensurate with continual membership in the Party's highest policy-making body. Thus the Ukrainian Party's first secretary, Petro Shelest, though supposedly holding an "elective" office, was arbitrarily demoted in May 1972 to one of the deputy premierships in the U.S.S.R. Council of Ministers. He remained in the Politburo, but in a completely untenable position, until April 1973, when he was forced into retirement.

The Party Secretariat wields enormous power in being able to appoint to, or demote from, positions that may entitle incumbents to membership in the Central Committee. Thus, the road to power is not based on facing the electorate—or even the Party membership—in an actual contest or obtaining a fixed term of office or on the possession of wealth or influence. It is based exclusively upon one's standing in the political and administrative elite and upon appointive position held at the discretion of whoever is in control of the Party apparatus and can use its power over cadres.

Transfers and removals of personnel are prompted not only by personal associations but by disagreements within the Soviet leadership on policy issues. In Stalin's time such issues were usually debated in a rather cryptic manner, although in the 1920s they were discussed quite openly (the future of the NEP). After World War II differences existed among Stalin's lieutenants regarding the appropriate labor unit in agriculture—the smaller "link" (zveno) or the larger "brigade"—and over whether or not collective farmers should be permitted to manufacture their own construction materials. A somewhat abstract discussion in the Soviet leadership in 1948–1949 on the "law of value" under socialism reflected very real disagreement over the degree of rigidity in economic planning and the role of profit in determining what should be produced.

Disagreements in Khrushchev's time dealt with the anti-Stalin campaign, the virgin-lands program, the economic reorganization of 1957, the Party reorganization of 1962, the sale of state-owned agricultural machinery to the collective farms, the level of steel production, and investment allocations for the various sectors of the economy (agriculture, heavy industry, and consumer goods production).[10] Foreign-policy issues such as nuclear deterrence, arms reduction, the nuclear test ban, the Austrian State Treaty of 1955, and the problem of Germany also provoked differing viewpoints within the leadership. During Brezhnev's leadership, disagreements developed over economic reform and reliance upon

---

[10]For a series of case studies, see *Soviet Policy-Making,* ed. Peter H. Juviler and Henry W. Morton (New York: Praeger, 1967). See also Sidney I. Ploss, *Conflict and Decision-Making in Soviet Russia: A Case Study of Agricultural Policy* (Princeton, N.J.: Princeton University Press, 1965) and Thane Gustafson, *Reform in Soviet Politics, The Lessons of Recent Policies on Land and Water* (New York: Cambridge University Press, 1981). Disagreement among Soviet leaders is often revealed—or poorly concealed—by criticism of anonymous persons ("certain comrades," "certain theoreticians," "some people") or by the fact that a member of the leadership deliberately remains silent on a particular issue. Differences in emphasis or in the choice of an adverb or adjective may appear to be slight but may also reflect disagreement. Thus, the careful study of verbal formulae is an important concern of those who seek clues indicating disagreements within the Soviet leadership.

profit incentives. The 1977 constitution was repeatedly debated and postponed apparently because of lack of consensus regarding its provisions. A related controversy persisted over the question of the rights of the union republics and assimilationism (of non-Russians) as opposed to a genuine commonwealth or some synthetic compromise. The conditions of détente have also prompted disagreement, as have questions on arms limitations and Soviet policy toward various communist and Third World countries.

Oligarchical decision making is not always likely to produce genuine unanimity, although oligarchies have been necessary whenever one man or several have had to rule by means of a coalition—in the absence of a strong dictator. Yet an oligarchy or "collective leadership" usually requires a spokesman and arbiter in the person of its leading member, and the composition of its coalitions is subject to change. The more weakly structured the oligarchy, the more likely it is to result in disequilibrium as coalitions shift from one issue to another. The addition or removal of one or more members can affect the relationships among the oligarchs. Alliances within the oligarchy were not stable in the coalitions of the 1920s, 1950s, and 1960s in the Soviet Politburo. Under Brezhnev's leadership there was greater stability for more than a decade, although the Politburo was increased from 11 to 16 (later 15) members, six of whom—Gennadii Voronov, Petro Shelest, Aleksandr Shelepin, Dmitrii Poliansky, Nikolai Podgorny, and Kiril Mazurov—were ousted between 1973 and 1978. If the various groups in the Politburo can be kept in balance, stability can be maintained.

However, one cannot always be sure of one's allies and lieutenants, especially in the absence of the sanction of terror as wielded by a dictator with a personal secretariat of the kind Stalin had. Thus, Beria aroused the suspicions of his fellow oligarchs in 1953. Molotov and Kaganovich supported Khrushchev in the ouster of Malenkov from the premiership, but they were later to break with Khrushchev and join forces with Malenkov. Premier Bulganin deserted Khrushchev in 1957 and joined the "anti-Party group." Dmitrii Shepilov, one of Khrushchev's most trusted aides, also turned against his mentor in 1957; originally in the Malenkov camp, he then joined Khrushchev and finally rejoined Malenkov. In the end Khrushchev placed too much trust in his subordinates, who ousted him in October 1964 and demonstrated the ephemeral and conditional nature of personal loyalty among Soviet politicians. The First Secretary had spent too much time away from Moscow, and by not employing terror within the Party, he was to seal his political fate by being unable to prevent the coalescence of the conspiracy that removed him from office.

The tactic of playing off lieutenants and associates against each other, developed most fully by Stalin, has been an important feature of Soviet politics. Stalin, for example, encouraged a rivalry between the Leningrad Party leader Andrei Zhdanov and Malenkov in 1946–1948. Following Zhdanov's death, Stalin brought Khrushchev to Moscow from Ukraine in 1949, presumably to check the ambitions of Malenkov.[11] Khrushchev attempted to employ the same tactic in

---

[11]See Myron Rush, *Political Succession in the U.S.S.R.* (New York: Columbia University Press, 1965), p. 137. Khrushchev provided confirmation in his reminiscences, wherein he noted his suspicion that "one of the reasons Stalin had called me back to Moscow was to influence the balance of power

1963 when he brought the Ukrainian Party secretary, N. V. Podgorny, to Moscow in an apparent effort to counterbalance the growing influence of Brezhnev. Although Brezhnev eliminated such rivals as Podgorny and Shelepin from the Secretariat, he benefited from the arrangement by which younger ambitious Secretariat members were kept out of the Politburo. Andropov employed the tactic when he brought Leningrad Party Secretary Grigorii Romanov into the CPSU Secretariat in 1983, presumably to serve as a check on Gorbachev, whom he had also promoted. The rivalry of lieutenants, if cultivated and utilized successfully, can enhance the position of the Party's leading figure; but it also means that no lieutenant can be entirely sure of his position. A lieutenant who is too closely associated with the leader, as Chernenko was with Brezhnev, can actually find this to be a disadvantage as the leader's power erodes. Thus Chernenko had to experience the dual humiliation of having to nominate his rival, Andropov, as General Secretary in an address to the Central Committee on November 12, 1982, and as head of state before the Supreme Soviet on June 17, 1983.

Oligarchy, by its very nature, tends to promote jockeying for advantage. It has been noted that various kinds of "behind the scenes conflicts and intrigues" occur in the Kremlin.[12] Although there are cases of remarkable longevity of tenure, there is also much vulnerability, and full membership in the Politburo can be lost in short order. The loyalty of lesser members of the oligarchy, and of the elite generally, is constantly subject to testing and must be demonstrated by affirmations and compliance.

TYPES OF CAREER PATTERNS

A political career in the Soviet Union depends upon the fulfillment of certain prerequisites. Apart from membership in the Party, one who aspires to high political office must be associated with a person who is rising in the hierarchy. Each Soviet leader since Stalin has had a mentor or sponsor who took notice and was instrumental in promoting the novice at some crucial point in his career. Khrushchev was first noticed by Lazar Kaganovich and took advantage of his having been selected to study in the Industrial Academy in Moscow. As a student he became secretary of the Academy's Party organization and attracted the attention of Stalin's wife—a fellow student who concealed her identity and who apparently informed Stalin that Khrushchev was a loyal Stalinist. Khrushchev subsequently characterized this crucial episode in his career as his "lucky lottery ticket" and even attributed to it his having survived Stalin's purges.[13] Brezhnev's mentor was Khrushchev, under whom Brezhnev served as an obkom first secretary when Khrushchev headed the Ukrainian Communist Party. Khrushchev subsequently brought Brezhnev into the CPSU Secretariat in Moscow. Andropov apparently came to the attention of Stalin's lieutenant Otto Kuusinen, who probably took notice of him in Karelia and was instrumental in obtaining for him

. . . and to put a check on Beria and Malenkov." Nikita S. Khrushchev, *Khrushchev Remembers, op. cit.* (above, n. 1), p. 250.

[12]Arkady N. Shevchenko, *Breaking with Moscow* (New York: Ballantine Books, 1985), p. 199.

[13]Nikita S. Khrushchev, *Khrushchev Remembers, op. cit.* (above, n. 1), p. 44.

a position as an inspector in the CPSU Central Committee apparatus. Chernenko was a protege of Brezhnev, with whom he was first associated when Brezhnev headed the Communist Party organization of the Moldavian S.S.R. Gorbachev was brought to Moscow as a CPSU Central Committee Secretary by Brezhnev but probably on the recommendation of Andropov and Kosygin.

In contrast with many other political systems, lawyers are not only few in number, but their chances of having a political career are very limited. Although Lenin was a lawyer by training and Stalin made use of Andrei Vyshinsky in the purge trials and as foreign minister, the Soviet legal profession has been a source of legal technicians rather than of politicians and policymakers. The fact that Gorbachev received legal training (but did not practice law) is an exception. In addition, the chances of a woman's pursuing a political career are severely limited, despite the claim that the Soviet regime promotes women's rights. Only Madame Furtseva succeeded in attaining full membership in the Politburo in 1957, for example, and served there only four years, although continuing as U.S.S.R. Minister of Culture until her death in 1974.

A political career is likely to begin with an individual's attracting attention in a primary party organization and achieving a work record of some distinction. Some obtain experience in a Communist youth raikom secretaryship, from which they move quickly into the Party raikom and may also serve briefly in the raion government. Success at the raion level or in industrial management may lead to appointment as an obkom department head, as secretary and ultimately as first secretary. It is necessary to break through the obkom level to a union republic secretaryship or to a position in the CPSU Central Committee apparatus that may lead to the Secretariat; this may qualify one for Politburo membership. However, many Politburo members have slipped into obscurity.[14] Once a leading Soviet politician has been downgraded, a comeback is unlikely. The exceptions to this rule are mostly officials of middle rank who have managed to survive a setback along with their mentor or who have found a new sponsor among the top leadership.

The need to have an elder or two in the leadership as a sign of legitimacy and as a tie with the Party's past brought to, or kept in, the Politburo such figures as Otto Kuusinen (who entered it in 1957 at the age of 76), Anastas Mikoyan, Nikolai Shvernik, Kliment Voroshilov, Arvid Pel'she, and Andrei Gromyko. However, since Stalin's time there has been an increased emphasis upon demonstrating technical competence at least at some stage in one's political career. Leonid Brezhnev, for instance, was a metallurgical engineer before becoming a Party official; Madame Furtseva began her career as a chemical engineer; her

---

[14]A survey of the 95 full and candidate-members of the Politburo between 1917 and 1971 indicated that 63 served as candidate-members, while 32 became full members without first serving as candidate-members. Of the 63 candidate-members, 26 (2 out of 5) failed to achieve full membership. See Kenneth N. Ciboski, "Ambition Theory and Candidate Members of the Soviet Politburo," *The Journal of Politics,* XXXVI, No. 1 (February 1974), pp. 172–183. A comparison of obkom secretaries under Stalin and the post-Khrushchev leadership indicates a slower promotion; this is apparently due to specialized training and increased rigidity in recruitment and promotion. See Robert E. Blackwell, Jr., "Career Development in the Soviet Obkom Elite: A Conservative Trend," *Soviet Studies* XXIV, No. 1 (July 1972), pp. 24–40.

successor as minister of culture (1974–1986), Petr Demichev, was also a chemical engineer in addition to having had professional military training and being a graduate of the Central Committee's Higher Party School. N. V. Podgorny graduated from the Kiev Institute of Food Industry Technology and served as engineer in Ukrainian sugar refineries before becoming a Party official and head of state. Party Secretary Anatolii Dobrynin was trained as an aeronautical engineer prior to becoming a diplomat. Mikhail Gorbachev found it advantageous to graduate from the Stavropol Agricultural Institute while serving as a provincial Party official. Ukrainian Party First Secretary V. V. Shcherbitsky was trained as a chemical engineer. KGB chief Viktor Chebrikov graduated from the Dnipropetrovsk Metallurgical Institute. Russian Republic premier Vitalii Vorotnikov graduated from the Kuibyshev Aviation Institute.

In addition to attaining a measure of success in one's nonpolitical field of specialization, a career in Soviet politics requires appropriate openings, a mentor-sponsor, and good fortune; it is usually disadvantageous to be a non-Russian. Designation as a representative for an important region or city may also improve one's career opportunities. For those who aspire to the highest ranks, it is essential to have a personal following, consisting of former associates who can be brought into the Central Committee and placed in key posts. Thus, it is highly advantageous to have Party field experience.

Gorbachev's career demonstrates the advantages of combining ability, opportunity, the proper connections, and good fortune. Gorbachev was fortunate in serving as Party secretary in a reasonably well-endowed agricultural region that was given enough investment capital to assure him relative success. This was made possible as a result of the fact that the former Stavropol kraikom first secretary, Fedor Kulakov, had become the Central Committee Secretary responsible for agriculture. The fact that such leaders as Andropov and Kosygin vacationed at the Kislovodsk spa in the Stavropol krai brought Gorbachev to their attention. In addition, it was advantageous that both Andropov and Gorbachev were natives of Stavropol krai. It was also advantageous for Gorbachev that the Politburo member Mikhail Suslov had once served as Stavropol kraikom first secretary. The death in 1978 of Fedor Kulakov created the opportunity for Gorbachev to be summoned to Moscow as Party secretary responsible for agriculture. Gorbachev was also fortunate in being able to redirect his Secretariat responsibilities away from agriculture.

There are *four broad types* of career patterns, although there are also subgroups within these patterns. The *first type* is that of the *central Party apparatus official,* whose rise is attributable to his obtaining a responsible position in the Central Committee's administration and then becoming a member of the Secretariat. The case of Malenkov provides a classic example; he joined the Central Committee apparatus in 1925 immediately upon graduating from a technical school. Beginning in 1934 Malenkov headed the important Department of Leading Party Organs, and in 1939 he became a member of the Secretariat; by 1941 he was a candidate-member of the Politburo, becoming a full member in 1946 and remaining such until his ouster in 1957. The career of Aleksandr N. Shelepin is another example of one based on the Moscow apparatus. His career began in the

Komsomol organization, of which he was first secretary. He subsequently headed the KGB and served as a Central Committee secretary, attained full membership in the Politburo in 1964, and was removed from it in 1975. The careers of Malenkov and Shelepin illustrate the pitfalls in this type of career and the apparent limits it presents for acquiring a personal following.

The career of Yuri Andropov can be placed in this category, as he held only lesser positions in the Karelian Republic before being brought to Moscow in 1951 as an inspector in the Central Committee apparatus. From 1953 to 1957 he served as Soviet ambassador to Hungary and attracted attention for his role in the suppression of the Hungarian rebellion of 1956. In 1957 he became head of the Secretariat department for relations with socialist countries, and in 1962 he became a member of the Secretariat. As head of the Soviet security police (KGB) from 1967 to 1982, he attained full membership in the Politburo and also belatedly completed his higher education, graduating from the Higher Party School. Andropov, as a result of his control of the KGB, could overcome the apparent disadvantages of the Moscow-based career type.

Other examples of this career type are provided by Petr Demichev and Ivan Kapitonov. Demichev, with an uncommon variety of higher education and after seven years of professional military service, commenced his career in the Moscow city Party organization at the raion level in 1945. After service in the Central Committee apparatus, he served in the Moscow obkom. In 1958 he served briefly in the government as Administrator of Affairs in the U.S.S.R. Council of Ministers, where he presumably carried out Khrushchev's administrative reorganization. In 1959 he became Moscow obkom first secretary, entered the Central Committee Secretariat in 1961, and became a candidate member of the Politburo in 1964. After serving 12 years as U.S.S.R. Minister of Culture, Demichev in 1986 became first deputy head of state—a largely ceremonial post—but retained his Politburo seat.

Ivan Kapitonov's career also began in the Moscow Party organization under Stalin and Malenkov. However, from 1959 to 1964 he was sent to Ivanovo to serve as obkom first secretary (probably due to corruption charges). Following Khrushchev's ouster, Kapitonov served in the Central Committee Secretariat for two decades and headed the Organizational Party Work Department until he was made chairman of the Central Auditing Commission in 1986. His career indicates that one can spend many years in the Secretariat and be a member of the oligarchy and not even attain candidate membership in the Politburo.

The *ideocrat* represents a *second type* of career pattern. His career is made primarily in Moscow—although it might commence in the provinces—and it is distinguished primarily by the fact that in his training and experience he is primarily a power-oriented ideologist-theoretician. He can serve as a propaganda expert and speech writer or as part of the Central Committee "brain trust" developing ideological arguments to justify current policies or as an ideological guardian and specialist on the international communist movement. The career of Mikhail A. Suslov (1902–1982) offers an example of this species of Soviet politician. Suslov, following a brief academic career in economics, entered Party work in 1931 and participated actively in Stalin's purges. Following service as Stavropol kraikom first secretary from 1939 to 1944, he conducted purges in Soviet-occupied Lithuania. In 1947 he was brought into the Central Committee Secretariat—probably with the help of Andrei Zhdanov—and remained in it until his death in 1982. He became a full member of the Politburo under Khrushchev, supported Khrushchev against the "anti-Party group" in 1957, engineered the ouster of Khrushchev in 1964, and served as "kingmaker" in arranging for Brezhnev to become General Secretary. Suslov's responsibilities included supervision of propaganda campaigns, enforcement of ideological purity, control of Soviet journalism and culture, and relations with foreign Communist parties (including the Chinese). Suslov's tenure of 35 years in the Secretariat and 27 years in the Politburo was paralleled only by that of Stalin.

Another example of the ideocratic career is that of Boris N. Ponomarev, which matched Suslov's in longevity. Ponomarev joined the Party in 1919 at age 14 and entered propaganda work after graduating in history from Moscow State University in 1926. He graduated from the Institute of the Red Professorate in 1932 and worked for the Comintern from 1937 until 1943. After joining the Central Committee apparatus, he became head of its International Department in 1955 and Secretary in 1961 with responsibility for nonruling Communist parties. He held Politburo candidate membership from 1972 to 1986, when he was retired from the Secretariat. He supervised the writing of Party history for Khrushchev and its rewriting for Brezhnev. Khrushchev obtained for him full membership in the U.S.S.R. Academy of Sciences in 1962. Ponomarev was a lieutenant under Suslov and had a reputation as an old-time ideological hardliner and opponent of Communist polycentrism and Eurocommunism.

The career of Konstantin Chernenko (1911–1985) can also be typed as essentially ideocratic. His early career in Siberia was in the Krasnoiarsk kraikom as a minor Party functionary. From 1948 to 1956 he headed the Propaganda and Agitation Department in the Communist Party of the Moldavian S.S.R. There in 1953, at the age of 42, he graduated from the Kishinev Pedagogical Institute—his only other education having been earlier at the Moscow Higher School for Party Organizers. In Moldavia he developed a close association with Leonid Brezhnev, who in 1956 brought him to Moscow, where he initially headed the mass propaganda sector in the Central Committee's Agitprop Department. When Brezhnev served as head of state in the early 1960s, he made Chernenko chief of the Secretariat of the Presidium of the Supreme Soviet. When Brezhnev succeeded Khrushchev as Party chief, Chernenko was made head of the General Department; he became a Secretary in 1976 and a full member of the Politburo in 1978 at the age of 67. Apart from being a Party administrator and propagandist, Chernenko was also a publicist and a faithful lieutenant of Brezhnev, whom he frequently quoted and praised.

Other examples of the ideocrat are the Central Committee secretaries Vadim A. Medvedev and Aleksandr N. Yakovlev. Medvedev came into Party work from an academic background, having graduated from Leningrad State University and attained the degree of doctor of economic sciences and the title of professor. He joined the Central Committee Propaganda Department in 1970, and in 1978 he became rector of the Party's Academy of Social Sciences of the

Central Committee. In 1983 he became head of the Science and Educational Institutions Department of the Central Committee; he was made a Secretariat member under Gorbachev and placed in charge of the Department for Liaison with Communist and Workers' Parties of Socialist Countries.

Aleksandr N. Yakovlev acquired academic credentials, having graduated from the Central Committee's Academy of Social Sciences, and obtained the degree of doctor of historical sciences and the title of professor. He entered the Central Committee apparatus in 1953. From 1973 to 1983 he served as ambassador to Canada in a Soviet effort to influence Canadian foreign policy. In 1983 he became director of the Institute of World Economics and International Relations of the U.S.S.R. Academy of Sciences. Gorbachev brought him into the Secretariat and placed him in charge of the Central Committee's Propaganda Department. In June 1987 Yakovlev became a full member of the Politburo—apparently as a counter to Secretariat and Politburo member Yegor Ligachev. Thus, the newer type of ideocrat, armed with academic credentials and experienced in the field of propaganda, remains an important part of the Soviet oligarchy.

A *third type* of career pattern is that of the *specialist or administrator* who does not serve in the Secretariat or in the Central Committee apparatus but whose value to the Party guarantees membership in the Central Committee or even in the Politburo. A prominent example of such a career was that of Anastas Mikoyan, an Armenian who graduated from a theological seminary and joined the Party in 1915. Following a career as a revolutionary in the Caucasus, he held various regional Party posts and headed the U.S.S.R. Commissariat of Foreign and Internal Trade. He subsequently was responsible for food supply, food industry, and foreign trade; in 1937 he became a deputy premier. He became a Central Committee full member in 1923. Stalin brought him into the Politburo in 1926 as a candidate-member; he achieved full membership in 1935, survived purges and power struggles, and retired in April 1966. Had Mikoyan been in the Secretariat or less adept as a communist businessman, his career in the leadership would probably have been of shorter duration.

Soviet heads of government (premiers) have frequently been specialists. Aleksei Kosygin, who headed the U.S.S.R. Council of Ministers from 1964 to 1980, began his career in Leningrad, where he graduated from a textile institute and was director of a textile factory. In 1938, as a result of the purges, he moved into Leningrad Party and government work and served as mayor of the city. In 1939, at the age of 35, he assumed the first of a number of positions in the U.S.S.R. government: Minister of the Textile Industry, deputy premier, Minister of Finance, Minister of the Consumer Goods Industry, and head of the State Planning Commission *(Gosplan)*. He was a full member of the Politburo from 1948 to 1952 but fell into disfavor with Stalin (Khrushchev revealed that in 1949 Kosygin's "life was hanging by a thread").[15] He regained Politburo candidate membership in 1957 and full membership in 1960. Although his association with Leningrad nearly led to his undoing in 1949, he managed to remain essentially outside of

---

[15] N. S. Khrushchev, *Khrushchev Remembers, op. cit.* (above, n. 1), p. 257.

Party struggles within the Party apparatus and to fulfill the role of technocrat and chief governmental bureaucrat.

Kosygin's successor, Nikolai A. Tikhonov, who headed the U.S.S.R. Council of Ministers from 1980 to 1985, had a similar career. Trained as a metallurgical engineer, he managed a tube mill in Ukraine, and in 1950 he was summoned to Moscow to head a branch of the U.S.S.R. Ministry of Ferrous Metallurgy, becoming a deputy minister in 1955. From 1957 to 1960 he headed the regional economic council in Dnipropetrovsk. In 1960 he returned to Moscow to serve as deputy chairman of the State Scientific and Economic Council and of *Gosplan*. Under Brezhnev—whom he knew in Ukraine—he became deputy premier in 1965 and first deputy premier in 1976 and served as a check on Kosygin. In 1979, at the age of 74, he became a full member of the Politburo; and at the age of 75, he became head of the Soviet government. Tikhonov became a member of the Soviet ruling oligarchy without having ever held a position in the Party apparatus.

Another Soviet premier, Nikolai Bulganin, headed the government from 1955 to 1958 and prior to that served in a variety of non-Party positions as mayor of Moscow, head of the U.S.S.R. State Bank, and as Minister of Defense. He was a Politburo member from February 1948 until his ouster in 1958. The protection that the role of "specialist" gave Bulganin ceased when he became involved in the attempt to unseat Khrushchev in June 1957. Thus, this type of Soviet politician can have a relatively "safe" career so long as he does not choose the losing side in a crucial division within the Politburo.

Specialists in the Politburo under Gorbachev have represented a variety of fields. Andrei Gromyko was only the second Soviet foreign minister to attain Politburo membership; he was able to do so in 1973 by having cultivated Brezhnev and having aided him when the future General Secretary was head of state in the 1960s and had to fulfill certain diplomatic functions. Geidar Aliev, an Azerbaidjanian, was brought to Moscow by Andropov in 1982 to serve as first deputy premier and as a check on Tikhonov. A graduate of the Azerbaidjanian State University in history, Aliev began his long career in the police and state security organs in 1941, when he was 18 years of age. In 1967 he became head of the Azerbaidjanian Republic KGB; in 1969 he became first secretary of the Azerbaidjanian Communist Party, and this enabled him to become a candidate member of the CPSU Politburo in 1976. He became a full member of the Politburo in November 1982 following the death of Brezhnev but lost his seat in October 1987. Nikolai I. Ryzhkov, who succeeded Tikhonov as Chairman of the U.S.S.R. Council of Ministers, graduated from the Ural Polytechnic Institute. From 1950 to 1970 he rose from shift foreman to director of the Ural Machine Plant. In 1975 he became first deputy minister of heavy and transport machine construction and, in 1979, first deputy chairman of *Gosplan*. From 1982 to 1985 he held his sole Party post as a member of the Secretariat and as head of the Central Committee's Economic Department. He was made head of government by Gorbachev and became a full member of the Politburo in April 1985.

A *fourth type* of career is that of the *Party official* who attains a responsible position in the Secretariat and/or Politburo *following field experience* in oblast' and/or union republic Party and governmental organizations. The careers of both Khrushchev and Brezhnev are representative of this type of politician. Khrushchev gained invaluable field experience as head of the Ukrainian Communist Party and developed a following of subordinate Party officials; he also had the advantage of heading the Moscow oblast' and city Party organizations.

Leonid Brezhnev joined the Party in 1931, the same year in which he entered the metallurgical institute in his Ukrainian home city of Dnieprodzerzhinsk. Following employment as an engineer from 1935 to 1937, he became deputy mayor of Dnieprodzerzhinsk. In May 1938, he left local government for a Party post as department head in the Dnipropetrovsk obkom, and as a result of the purges he became a secretary of that obkom in 1939. During World War II he served as a political officer and attained the rank of major general. In 1946 he became first secretary of the Zaporozhe obkom, and in 1947 he headed the Dnipropetrovsk obkom under Khrushchev's tutelage. He followed Khrushchev to Moscow in 1950 and served in the Central Committee apparatus, but from July 1950 to October 1952, he was first secretary of the Moldavian Communist Party. He attained Central Committee membership in October 1952 at the age of 45; he also became a candidate-member of the Politburo-Presidium and a Central Committee Secretary, but he lost both positions four months later following Stalin's death. Brezhnev spent most of 1953 as deputy chief of the Main Political Administration of the Armed Forces. In February 1954, Khrushchev appointed Brezhnev second secretary of the Kazakhstan Communist Party, and in August Brezhnev became First Secretary, with responsibility for the republic's virgin-lands program. In February 1956, he regained the positions he had lost in March 1953—candidate-member of the Politburo and Central Committee Secretary. He became a full member of the Politburo in June 1957, following the expulsion of the anti-Party group. Although he was out of the Secretariat from May 1960 until June 1963 (he served as chief of state from May 1960 until July 1964), he returned to that body and within sixteen months helped engineer the ouster of Khrushchev. (Brezhnev's reappointment to the Secretariat was made possible by the illness of Frol Kozlov.) The varied nature of Brezhnev's career experiences in the field and in Moscow, in Party and in government, provided him with skills and associations that he put to effective use.

Gorbachev's career also qualifies for this category, although his field experience was limited exclusively to the Stavropol krai and included no service in any of the non-Russian republics. Central Committee Secretary Yegor K. Ligachev, who was brought into the Secretariat by Andropov in 1983, graduated from the Moscow Aviation Institute and the Higher Party School. He served only one year as a plant engineer and in 1944 became a Komsomol raikom secretary in Novosibirsk; by 1949 he was first secretary of the Komsomol obkom. He then held a variety of Party gorkom and obkom positions in Novosibirsk and became an obkom secretary. From 1961 to 1964 he held various positions in the Central Committee apparatus. From 1965 to 1983 he was first secretary of Tomsk obkom. He became a Central Committee member in 1976 and a full member of the Politburo in April 1985 under Gorbachev.

Boris N. Yeltsin, first secretary of the Moscow gorkom in 1986–87, was trained as a construction engineer at the Ural Polytechnic Institute. From 1955 to 1963 he was employed by a construction trust; and after joining the Party in 1961, he was promoted to head a large housing construction firm in Sverdlovsk. In 1968 he entered Communist Party work and soon became a secretary and, in 1976, first secretary of the Sverdlovsk obkom (which qualified him for Central Committee full membership in 1981). He was appointed first secretary of the Moscow gorkom by Gorbachev, replacing Viktor Grishin, and became a candidate member of the Politburo in February 1986. When Yeltsin rashly clashed with Gorbachev over the slowness of reform, he was replaced as Moscow secretary by Lev Zaikov and was removed from the Politburo in February 1988.

The appointment of Lev N. Zaikov to the Secretariat in July 1985 and his election to full membership in the Politburo in March 1986, at the age of 63, represented a rapid rise as well as a late entry into Party work. Zaikov, having graduated from the Leningrad Economic Engineering Institute, acquired a reputation as an economic specialist. He joined the Party in 1957 and rose from a skilled laborer to general director of a unified complex of enterprises. In 1976 he became chairman of the executive committee of the Leningrad city soviet (mayor) and was made first secretary of the Leningrad obkom by Andropov in 1983. Historically Leningrad Party leaders have not fared well in the CPSU central leadership—as demonstrated by the careers of Grigorii Zinoviev, Sergei Kirov, Andrei Zhdanov, Frol Kozlov, and Grigorii Romanov (all of whom were losers). Zaikov entered the Soviet oligarchy with less Party work experience and involvement and may have been selected as much for his economic expertise and supervisory skills as for his representing Leningrad (along with Leningrad obkom first secretary Yuri F. Soloviev, whom Gorbachev brought into the Politburo as a candidate-member).

The examples of Ligachev, Yeltsin, and Zaikov indicate that the period of professional work experience prior to entering full-time Party work can vary greatly. Once an upward-bound Party official attains the rank of obkom first secretary, the record achieved and the contacts acquired at that post become crucial in determining future advancement.

THE SYSTEM OF PARTY SCHOOLS

Millions of Soviet citizens, including non–Party members, are exposed to political instruction as a result of the regime's trained use of propagandists. An extensive network of "universities of Marxism-Leninism" provides a two-year program of evening courses in which dialectical and historical materialism and the Party's history and program are studied. Party functionaries require more thorough and advanced training, which is provided by a system of inter-oblast' and union republic Party schools. At the apex of the system is the Academy of Social Sciences attached to the CPSU Central Committee, which trains officials for the Party and the Soviet government at the central, republic, krai, and oblast' levels and also for the ideological, trade union, and Komsomol organizations. However, its special responsibility is to train Party secretaries and department heads for republics and oblasti and chairmen and deputy chairmen of the (governmental) executive committees of oblast soviets.

Prior to 1978 the Central Committee's Higher Party School and its correspondence-course branch existed as a separate entity; but as a result of a reorganization, they were merged into the Academy of Social Sciences. The organization was said to be prompted by the need to raise the level of the Party's ideological work and relate the Academy's activities to Soviet foreign-policy objectives. The Academy also performs a scientific-research function and serves as a social science "think tank" based on Marxism-Leninism; the Academy is expected to analyze processes occurring under developed socialism and in international relations and to provide solutions to concrete socioeconomic problems.

Applicants with higher education are accepted up to the age of 40 by the Academy on the recommendation of the union republic central committee, the obkom or kraikom, or the central organizations and ideological institutions. An entrance examination is also required of those who seek the *aspirantura* (the degree of "candidate"). The Academy has a regular course of study for students in residence as well as a program of correspondence study; it also accepts students from other communist countries. It has departments *(kafedry)* of CPSU history, Marxist-Leninist philosophy, political economy, scientific communism, party structure, soviet state structure and law, ideological work, economy and organization of production, conduct of socioeconomic processes, social psychology and pedagogy, history, journalism, socialist culture, international communist movement, and international relations and foreign policy. It also has an Institute of Scientific Atheism.

PARTY MEMBERSHIP: SOCIAL AND ETHNIC VARIATIONS

The CPSU membership can be divided into four main groups. The top- and middle-rank leadership consists of Central Committee members, responsible Central Committee apparatus officials, and influential members of union republic central committees and of oblast' Party committees; this leadership numbers several thousand. A second group, which is both dependent upon, and indispensable to, the first group, consists of the Party apparatus itself and includes Party officials at the raion and city levels. Estimates of its size have varied from 200,000 to 250,000. A third group consists of the well-rewarded members of the "new class" who are not Party officials but who are active in the professions, in economic management, in the military, and in governmental ministries. Millions of rank-and-file members constitute a fourth group; many members are not privileged and often have a living standard below that of those members of the "new class" who are not Party members.

The Party recognizes three social categories of members: workers, peasants, and employees (salaried persons). The size and relative weight of these three groups have varied. Following the establishment of the regime, the Party in January 1918 claimed the following social origin for its membership: worker, 56.9 percent; peasant, 14.5 percent; employees, 28.6 percent. During the 1920s, the employee category declined to a low of 16.8 percent, while the membership of

Table 5.1   SOCIAL COMPOSITION OF THE PARTY

	January 1956	January 1966	January 1976	January 1987
Workers	32.0%	37.8%	41.6%	45.3%
Collective farmers	17.1	16.2	13.9	11.6
Employees and others	50.9	46.0	44.5	43.1

Compiled from data in: Merle Fainsod, *How Russia Is Ruled,* rev. ed. (Cambridge: Harvard University Press, 1963), p. 276; *XXIII S" ezd KPSS, stenograficheskii otchet* (Moscow: Politizdat, 1966), I, 86; *Partiinaia zhizn'* No. 10 (May 1976), p. 14; and *Partiinaia zhizn'* No. 21 (November 1987), p. 9.

worker *origin* rose to a high of 61.4 percent. The peasant category ranged from 19.0 to 28.8 percent during the first decade of Soviet rule. However, the percentage of Party members actually *employed* as workers engaged in production never exceeded 48.8 percent (in 1930).[16] The 1930s witnessed a decline in the worker component because the Party membership card has served as a ticket to social advancement. As the demands of economic growth required more technicians and managers, the employee (salaried) group grew steadily at the expense of the worker and peasant categories. The social composition of the Party has varied as shown in Table 5.1.

Women have always been a minority within the Party membership. They constituted 8.2 percent of the membership by 1924; 15.9 percent in 1932; 14.9 percent in January 1941; 17 percent in January 1945; 20.7 percent in July 1950; 24.3 percent in 1976; and 29.3 percent in 1987.

The ethnic composition of the CPSU membership has not accurately reflected the ethnic composition of the Soviet Union (see Table 5.2). Russians for years constituted more than 60 percent of the Party membership, although their percentage of the population is less. Russians constituted 72 percent of the membership in 1922 and 65 percent in 1927. The percentage of Russians in the CPSU first fell below 60 percent in 1981. Although Georgians have been overrepresented in the Party, non-Russians have tended to be underrepresented in varying degrees, and the Turkic peoples, the Tadjiks, and the Moldavians have been significantly underrepresented. The largest city and provincial Party organizations in the Russian Republic are those of the city of Moscow; the oblasti of Leningrad, Moscow, Rostov, Gorky, and Sverdlovsk; and that of the Krasnodar krai. The largest non-Russian union republic Party organizations are, in order of size, those of Ukraine, Kazakhstan, Belorussia, Uzbekistan, Georgia, and Azerbaidjan.

THE MASS AUXILIARY ORGANIZATIONS

The CPSU has in its ranks 9.7 percent of the adult population and must also rely on a series of auxiliary mass organizations. These bodies are designed to serve as transmission belts to win popular support for the Party's policies, although each of these organizations also performs functions peculiar to it. These organizations

---

[16]Merle Fainsod, *How Russia Is Ruled,* rev. ed. (Cambridge: Harvard University Press, 1963), pp. 250–252.

Table 5.2 ETHNIC COMPOSITION OF PARTY MEMBERSHIP

	Membership January 1, 1976	Percentage of party membership	Membership January 1, 1986	Percentage of party membership	Percentage of population (1979 census)
Russians	9,481,536	60.6	11,241,958	59.1	52.4
Ukrainians	2,505,378	16.0	3,041,736	16.0	16.1
Belorussians	563,408	3.6	726,108	3.8	3.6
Uzbeks	321,458	2.1	465,443	2.4	4.7
Jews	294,774	1.9	—	—	0.7
Georgians	259,520	1.7	321,922	1.7	1.4
Armenians	234,253	1.5	291,081	1.5	1.6
Kazakhs	282,471	1.8	387,837	2.0	2.5
Azerbaidjanis	232,223	1.5	337,904	1.8	2.1
Lithuanians	106,967	0.7	147,068	0.8	1.1
Latvians	65,116	0.4	78,193	0.4	0.5
Tadjiks	63,611	0.4	87,759	0.5	1.1
Moldavians	67,707	0.4	110,715	0.6	1.1
Kirghiz	49,542	0.3	78,064	0.4	0.7
Estonians	49,739	0.3	61,277	0.3	0.4
Turkmens	48,021	0.3	76,786	0.4	0.8
Others	1,013,171	6.5	1,550,527	8.2	9.9
Total Members and Candidate-Members	15,638,891		19,004,378		

Source: Based on "KPSS v tsifrakh," *Partiinaia zhizn'* No. 10 (May 1976), p. 16, and No. 14 (July 1986), p. 24.

enable the regime to mobilize millions of its subjects who are beyond the sanctions and inducements of Party membership. Although they are said to be non–Party organizations—and are such in the strict sense of the term—their leadership consists of Party members whose task it is to make certain that the auxiliary bodies remain in a subordinate role and perform their assigned functions. A new provision in the 1986 CPSU Statutes (article 61) obligated the Party members in such organizations to "carry out Party policy . . . strengthen Party and state discipline, struggle against bureaucratism, verify the fulfillment of Party and state decisions."

The Soviet trade union movement embraces nearly all workers and salaried employees in the USSR and is based on the production principle. A countrywide congress elects the All-Union Central Council of Trade Unions (VTsSPS),[17] which serves as a counterpart of the Party's Central Committee; the Council elects a Presidium and Secretariat. The trade unions promote Soviet patriotism as well as fulfillment of the economic plan by sponsoring "socialist emulation" among workers (the word "competition" has invidious connotations in the Soviet lexicon and, when used, is associated with "capitalism"). The trade unions administer part of the state's social insurance program and sponsor a variety of facilities and activities, including athletic and sports contests, "palaces of culture," libraries, clubhouses, resorts and camps, cinemas, excursions, and lectures on atheism and other subjects. The Council publishes the newspaper *Trud* (Labor) and also operates its own publishing house, *Profizdat*. Decisions of the CPSU Central Committee are approved at Council plenary sessions, and the entire trade union movement provides an effective means of mobilizing mass support.

The *Komsomol* (VLKSM, or All-Union Leninist Communist League of Youth) brings more than 40 million of "progressive Soviet youth" under Communist influence. It was founded in October 1918 and by the 1930s had become a mass organization useful to the regime in the collectivization of agriculture and in the anti-*kulak* campaign (directed against more prosperous peasants who opposed collectivization), as well as in World War II. Its membership embraces youth from 14 through 28 years of age, although the Komsomol leadership is often beyond the maximum age. The Komsomol includes student membership as well as employed youths. Despite official assertions that the Komsomol is non-Party, its organizational structure parallels that of the CPSU from primary party organization to central committee. The First Secretary of the Komsomol is a member of the CPSU Central Committee. The Party closely supervises the youth organization and recruits many of its own members from the Komsomol.[18] The

---

[17]*Vsesoiuznyi Tsentral'nyi Sovet Professional'nykh Soiuzov.* For a somewhat uncritical but useful study, see Emily Clark Brown, *Soviet Trade Unions and Labor Relations* (Cambridge: Harvard University Press, 1966). See also Blair A. Ruble, *Soviet Trade Unions; Their Development in the 1970s* (New York: Cambridge University Press, 1981), which gives attention to the international activities of the VTsSPS.

[18]For the history of the Party-Komsomol relationship, see Ralph T. Fisher, Jr., *Pattern for Soviet Youth; A Study of the Congresses of the Komsomol, 1918–1954* (New York: Columbia University Press, 1959). A general treatment of the Party's youth organizations is provided in Allen Kassof, *The Soviet Youth Program, Regimentation and Rebellion* (Cambridge: Harvard University Press, 1965).

Komsomol's official organ is *Komsomolskaia pravda,* which is published daily on weekdays.

The Komsomol is used in the attempt to control the social and political behavior of youth and to guide its energies into channels useful to the regime. It promotes labor productivity among its members in factories and on farms, combats antisocial attitudes and conduct, and aids in the dissemination of propaganda. Study of the works of Marx and Lenin is encouraged in terms of their relationship to the current Party line. The Komsomol mobilizes "volunteer" labor for special projects, as in bringing the virgin and fallow lands under cultivation in the late 1950s and aiding collective and state farms during harvesting seasons or in special construction projects. The Komsomol is closely related to secondary and, especially, higher education; it is nearly impossible to obtain admission to a university unless one is a member. Social control is high on its list of objectives, and it has sought to impose orthodox tastes not only in political attitudes but in dress, the arts, dancing, and in personal conduct.

The Pioneers, also officially named in honor of Lenin, is the mass communist organization of children of the Soviet Union. Its ranks consist of more than 20 million Soviet schoolchildren from the ages of 10 through 15, and it serves as a training and recruiting ground for the Komsomol. It was founded in 1922 as a result of the Party's concern over child-rearing practices and its desire to limit familial influence in the interests of indoctrination. In the Pioneer organization the child is subordinated to the group pressures of the "collective" and conditioned to accept public shaming and civic rituals at an early age.

Pioneers wear special uniforms and an emblem with a hammer and sickle emblazoned upon a star and inscribed with the organization's slogan, *Vsegda gotov!* ("Always ready"). They take a ceremonial pledge upon being initiated.[19] The children are organized into brigades *(druzhiny)* by schools; each grade in a school is organized into a detachment *(otriad);* and at the classroom level there is the "link" *(zveno),* which is the basic unit of the Pioneers and consists of from 5 to 12 children. Older Komsomol members are assigned to work with Pioneer detachments and brigades, and the teachers and school director also supervise their activities.

The Pioneers serve as the Soviet Union's answer to the scouting movement, which is regarded as bourgeois and counterrevolutionary—although Pioneers and scouts share certain common characteristics. Pioneers are not concerned primarily with recreational activities, although the organization does operate camps with the financial support of the trade unions and has "Pioneer palaces" used for handicrafts, study courses, and work in the various arts. More important are the organization's efforts to inculcate discipline, seriousness, punctuality, and respect for work. Socially useful labor is performed, as, for example, tree planting and the collecting of scrap metal when required. Excursions are organized, and, in accordance with the slogan "the Pioneer is an example for all children," children

---

[19]For a description of the Pioneer induction ceremony and the text of the oath, see David K. Shipler, *Russia: Broken Idols, Solemn Dreams* (New York: Penguin Books, 1984), pp. 118–120.

are urged to excel in schoolwork. Each Pioneer detachment has a banner, and a drum and bugle are used in marching exercises; commands are conveyed by means of the bugle.

The work of the Pioneers organization embraces one of the vital periods in the process of political socialization experienced by Soviet youth. No opportunity is lost to introduce children to a favorable view of Soviet history, the life of Lenin, and to group observance of political holidays. Pioneers are told that they live in the best of all possible societies and that bourgeois society is evil and corrupt.[20] Nature studies are conducted in a manner designed to propagate the materialist-world outlook and atheistic belief. Children are prepared for membership by spending three years in the Little Octobrists (Oktiabriata), which embraces the seven-to-nine age group. A semiweekly newspaper, Pionerskaia pravda, is published by the organization. The relationship to the Party is evident in the practice of having a delegation of Pioneers appear at each Party Congress; marching into the auditorium and filling the aisles and stage before the dais, the children greet the delegates and leadership and extol the Party by reciting especially composed verses.

The mass civil defense organization, DOSAAF (Voluntary Society for Assistance to the Army, Air Force, and Navy),[21] is said to have more than 100 million members. Its organization closely parallels that of the Party but is subordinate to the Ministry of Defense. It publishes a newspaper, The Soviet Patriot, as well as several journals and maintains close ties with the Komsomol. DOSAAF is a paramilitary organization that trains its members in physical culture, marksmanship and weapons, skiing, parachuting, gliding, diving, and military history as well as in the operation of aircraft, motorcycles, trucks, and radio and electronic equipment. It also promotes interest in the breeding of dogs for military use. However, it is concerned primarily with manning evacuation and shelter facilities, anti-air defense, and fire fighting and decontamination. Members receive training and, in turn, train nonmembers in the population. DOSAAF's activities indicate the seriousness with which Soviet leaders regard civil defense; they also provide a means of promoting patriotism and disseminating a variety

---

[20]Pioneers have for years been told of the "heroism" of Pavlik Morozov, a boy who betrayed family loyalties during the collectivization campaign when he informed on his father; the father was shot and villagers then killed the son in vengeance in September 1932. On the Morozov case, see Pionerskaia organizatsiia imeni V. I. Lenina (Moscow: Uchpedgiz, 1950), pp. 25–27 and Kassof, op. cit. (above, n. 18), pp. 37ff. See also Bol'shaia Sovetskaia Entsiklopediia, 2nd ed. (1954) XXVIII, 310 and 3rd ed. (1974) XVI, p. 580.

[21]Dobrovol'noe obshchestvo sodeistviia armii, aviatsii i flotu—formed in 1951 as the result of a merger of the civil defense organizations of the three services, which existed separately after 1948. The predecessor organization was Osoaviakhim (Obshchestvo sodeistviia oborone i aviatsionno-khimi-cheskomu stroitel'stvu SSSR), the Society for Assistance in the Defense and Aviation-Chemical Construction of the U.S.S.R., founded in 1927. Activities of DOSAAF are discussed in Leon Gouré, Civil Defense in the Soviet Union (Berkeley and Los Angeles: University of California Press, 1962) and in his War Survival in Soviet Strategy, USSR Civil Defense (Coral Gables, Fla.: University of Miami, Center for Advanced International Studies, 1976). On its predecessor see William E. Odom, The Soviet Volunteers, Modernization and Bureaucracy in a Public Mass Organization (Princeton, N.J.: Princeton University Press, 1973).

of skills. Much of the numerically large membership may be nominal or passive, and members may be motivated more by a desire to drive a vehicle, acquire various skills, or obtain access to special equipment.

THE SECURITY POLICE

From its inception the Soviet regime has employed a special political police force to suppress its internal enemies and to frighten potential opponents into compliance. This organization—known since March 1954 as the Committee of State Security or KGB *(Komitet Gosudarstvennoi Bezopasnosti)*—had its origins in the *Cheka,* which was established on December 20, 1917. The name Cheka was derived from the Russian term *Chrezvychainaia Komissiia;* its full title was the Extraordinary Commission for the Struggle against Counter-Revolution, Sabotage, and Breach of Duty by Officials. In February 1922, it was renamed the GPU *(Gosudarstvennoe Politicheskoe Upravlenie)* or State Political Administration, although members of the secret police continued to be called "Chekists." With the establishment of the Soviet Union at the end of 1922, the GPU formally became the OGPU—the additional initial standing for the word "Unified" *(Ob-'edinennoe).* In July 1934, it was renamed the NKVD (People's Commissariat for Internal Affairs) and became a ministry (MVD) when the new designation was adopted in March 1946.

However, a separate Commissariat of State Security (NKGB) was established in April 1943, probably because of the special security police responsibilities resulting from Soviet reoccupation of territories held by the Nazis during the war. The NKGB had the task of uncovering wartime collaborators, as well as agents left behind by the Nazi forces; it was also necessary to establish a new and larger network of Soviet secret police informers *(seksoty),* who were often recruited by blackmail to spy upon the population. The ordinary police functions have been performed by the militia under the jurisdiction of the Ministry of Internal Affairs (MVD), which is responsible for combating crime, maintaining public order, regulating traffic, and administering the internal passport system. The MVD also has within its jurisdiction the fire departments, automobile and driver licensing, the state archives, and the registry of vital statistics (conducted by civil registry offices known as ZAGS—*Zapis' aktov grazhdanskogo sostoianiia).*[22]

The division of functions between MGB and MVD was terminated in March 1953—following Stalin's death—when a unified Interior Ministry (MVD)

---

[22]The history of the Soviet secret police is described in Simon Wolin and Robert M. Slusser, eds., *The Soviet Secret Police* (New York: Praeger, 1957). On the Cheka and GPU see Lennard D. Gerson, *The Secret Police in Lenin's Russia* (Philadelphia: Temple University Press, 1976) and George Leggett, *The Cheka: Lenin's Political Police* (Oxford: Clarendon Press, 1981). See also Robert Conquest, *The Great Terror; Stalin's Purges of the Thirties,* rev. ed. (New York: Macmillan, 1973). On the development and activities of the KGB, see Boris Levytsky, *The Use of Terror: The Soviet Secret Police, 1917–1970* (New York: Coward, McCann & Geoghegan, 1972).

was created under Lavrentii Beria. It was subsequently redivided on March 13, 1954, with the establishment of the KGB.

The Soviet regime has, in general, preferred to rely upon constraint and terror only as means of last resort; to obtain compliance it has also utilized indoctrination and psychological conditioning, social inducements, and material incentives. However, it has not hesitated to employ repressive measures, and under Stalin at times the organs of terror were permitted to run rampant. The reliance upon secret police methods had its origins in the Bolshevik experience with the *Okhrana* (the tsarist secret police) and in the fear of factionalism and penetration that Lenin bequeathed the Party. Revolution was to breed various forms of counterrevolution and justify their elimination by whatever means regarded as necessary. The Party leadership long viewed itself as commanding a fortress under siege and repeatedly issued calls for "vigilance."[23] The fear of being contaminated by the non-Soviet world and the need for the Party to protect its claim to a monopoly of power have served to rationalize the perpetuation of the regime's political police apparatus. The police have also had a certain utility in keeping officials alert and citizens cautious and submissive.

Under Stalin the NKVD became the country's largest "employer," using millions of persons in forced labor camps for lumbering, gold and coal mining, and construction projects (including canals, roads, and railways). Nor did the Party itself escape the toils of the secret police. Although originally the Cheka and OGPU were directed against the former ruling class and the old intelligentsia, oppositionists within the Party felt its oppressive hand in the late 1920s, and many of them perished in its execution chambers during the 1930s. Khrushchev revealed that during the purges, all Party elections, promotions, and transfers of personnel had to be screened and candidates approved by the NKVD, indicating that the Party apparatus was subordinate to the police as an instrument of Stalin's personal dictatorship.[24]

The secret police also played the leading role in uncovering so-called wrecking (sabotage) activities allegedly engaged in by Soviet engineers in behalf of foreign powers. The political police spearheaded the collectivization of agriculture, arresting and deporting millions of recalcitrant peasants who were arbitrarily classified as *kulaks* (wealthy peasants). The NKVD also prepared the defen-

---

[23]The 1961 CPSU Program included the following provision regarding the use of repressive measures: "The general trend of class struggle within the Socialist [i.e., Communist-ruled] countries in conditions of successful Socialist construction leads to consolidation of the position of the Socialist forces and weakens the resistance of the remnants of the hostile classes. But this development does not follow a straight line. Changes in the domestic or external situation may cause the class struggle to intensify in specific periods. This calls for constant vigilance in order to frustrate in good time the designs of hostile forces within and without. . . ." *Programme of the Communist Party of the Soviet Union* (Moscow: Foreign Languages Publishing House, 1961), p. 24. The 1986 CPSU Program is less explicit regarding the "safeguarding of state security" but links it with military power. It asserts that "the armed forces and the state security agencies should display a high degree of vigilance and should always be prepared to curb imperialism's intrigues against the U.S.S.R. and its allies." *Partiinaia zhizn'*, No. 6–7 (March–April 1986), p. 125.

[24]*Khrushchev Remembers, op. cit.* (above, n. 1), pp. 81–82.

dants for Stalin's three show trials of Old Bolsheviks held between August 1936 and March 1938.[25]

The NKVD developed a variety of techniques for breaking people, including the writing of autobiographies, the practice of holding prisoners incommunicado for lengthy periods, and the alternating of threats with blandishments during protracted interrogations often held at night.[26] Its methods have included the "conveyer method" of interrogation, by which a succession of interrogators would confront the isolated and fatigued prisoner, who has been systematically deprived of sleep. The practice of having prison cells constantly illuminated and of having guards maintain frequent surveillance of prisoners through cell doors— at least in Moscow's infamous Lubianka Prison—is indicative of the kind of regime maintained in prisons of the secret police. Nor have the police hesitated to employ outright fabrications and provocateurs and to prompt prisoners to compromise each other.

There are also two known instances of mass murder perpetrated by the NKVD—the massacre of more than 10,000 Ukrainians in 1937–1938 in the city of Vinnytsia and the mass execution of 4,000 Polish army officers in the Katyn Forest, west of Smolensk, in 1940.[27] The number of other such mass atrocities perpetrated by the Stalinist regime remains buried with the victims.

The use of the secret police by Stalin was one of the most important elements in his dictatorship. Yet the men who have headed the security police have usually not held very high positions within the Party leadership. The

---

[25]For the incomplete stenographic record of the March 1938 trial of Bukharin, Rakovsky, Grin'ko, and others, see *The Great Purge Trial,* ed. Robert C. Tucker and Stephen F. Cohen (New York: Grosset & Dunlap, 1965).

[26]There is a very substantial literature dealing with the practices of the Soviet security police. Among the knowledgeable authors are F. Beck and W. Godin, Margarete Buber, Rev. Walter J. Ciszek, David J. Dallin, Peter Deriabin, Alexander Dolgun, Rev. Gerhard Fittkau, Evgeniia S. Ginzburg, Jerzy Gliksman, Albert Konrad Herling, Victor Herman, Valentin Gonzalez ("El Campesino"), N. N. Krasnov, Jr., Aino Kuusinen, Edward Kuznetsov, Elinor Lipper, Anatoly Marchenko, Allan Monkhouse, Valentyn Moroz, John Noble, Unto Parvilahti, Vladimir Petrov, A. Pidhainy, Nicholas Prychodko, David Rousset, Joseph Scholmer, Zbigniew Stypulkowski, Alexander Weissberg, and Pyotr Yakir.

Aleksandr I. Solzhenitsyn's *The Gulag Archipelago, 1918–1956,* 3 Vols. (New York: Harper & Row, 1974–1976), is based on the personal experiences of the author and testimonies of 227 former prisoners of the Soviet forced labor camp system. See also Robert Conquest, *Kolyma, The Arctic Death Camps* (New York: Oxford University Press, 1980).

[27]The Vinnytsia massacres have been accorded little attention as compared with Katyn. See *The Crime of Moscow in Vynnytsia* (Edinburgh: Scottish League for European Freedom, 1952) as well as testimony heard by the Committee on Un-American Activities of the United States House of Representatives, 86th Congress, First Session, on September 9, 1959, *The Crimes of Khrushchev* (Washington, D.C.: Government Printing Office, 1959), pp. 17–37. Also see Zbigniew K. Brzezinski, *The Permanent Purge* (Cambridge: Harvard University Press, 1956), pp. 109 and 228. For an account by a journalist who witnessed the grisly mass exhumations at Vinnytsia and obtained testimonies from the relatives of victims, see Anthony Dragan, *Vinnytsia: A Forgotten Holocaust* (Jersey City, N.J.: "Svoboda" Publishers, The Ukrainian National Association, 1986). On Katyn, see J. K. Zawodny, *Death in the Forest,* 2nd ed. (Notre Dame, Ind.: University of Notre Dame Press, 1972) and the volumes of testimony and documentation amassed by the Select Committee of the U.S. House of Representatives, 82nd Congress, Second Session (1952). Apart from the Katyn Forest victims, more than 10,000 additional Polish officers disappeared in the Soviet Union in 1940 as prisoners of war, their fate unknown.

Cheka's founder, Felix E. Dzerzhinsky, was a Central Committee member from 1917 to his death in July 1926; he attained Politburo candidate-membership only in 1924. His successor and deputy, Viacheslav R. Menzhinsky, headed the OGPU from 1926 until his death in 1934 and became a full member of the Central Committee in December 1927. Menzhinsky was succeeded as NKVD chief by Genrikh G. Yagoda, a bookkeeper who had joined the Cheka in 1920 and became deputy chief in 1924. Yagoda was removed in September 1936 and stood trial in March 1938 on fantastic charges of having killed Menzhinsky, the writer Maxim Gorky, and Valerian Kuibyshev; he was condemned to death. Yagoda's successor was Nikolai Yezhov, a Central Committee secretary who had headed the Cadres Department. Yezhov attained Politburo candidate-membership in October 1937 and had the dubious distinction of having the most sanguinary Soviet purge, the *Yezhovshchina,* named for him in the popular lexicon. After serving his purpose, Yezhov was removed in December 1938 and perished.

Yezhov's successor was Lavrentii Beria, who served in the secret police during the 1920s and headed the Party apparatus in Transcaucasia in the 1930s. Beria headed the NKVD until 1945 and in that year also attained full membership in the Politburo. He was also a deputy premier and continued to supervise police activities. Thus Beria rose higher in the Party leadership than any prior Soviet secret police chief. Although he was nearly purged in the last period of Stalin's reign, he succeeded in retaining control of the secret police following Stalin's death. Beria, as Minister of Internal Affairs, was a threat to Stalin's other heirs, and he was executed in 1953 even though previously he had been decorated with the Order of Lenin on five occasions. Following Beria's demise, the unified MVD was headed by General Sergei N. Kruglov until the KGB was established.

The KGB was headed by General Ivan Serov from its inception in March 1954 until December 1958. Serov began his career in the military but became a professional police officer in the 1930s; although a Russian, he headed the Ukrainian NKVD in 1940–1941, when he developed an association with Khrushchev that proved to be advantageous. In 1952 he attained Central Committee candidate-membership; as KGB chief he became a full member in 1956.[28] When Serov was appointed chief of the Military Intelligence Directorate (GRU), he was succeeded in the KGB by a Party apparatus official, Aleksandr Shelepin, who had served as First Secretary of the Komsomol from 1952 to 1958. Shelepin's successor as Komsomol First Secretary, Vladimir Semichastny, also succeeded him as KGB head in November 1961. Semichastny was removed in May 1967, and was succeeded by Yuri Andropov, a Secretariat member who became a Politburo candidate-member in June 1967 and a full member in April 1973. Andropov was also given the rank of General of the Army in 1976.

---

[28]Serov was subsequently compromised as a result of his associations with Colonel Oleg Penkovskiy, Soviet military intelligence General Staff officer who served Anglo-American intelligence organizations in 1961 and 1962. Serov was expelled from the Party in 1965. See *The Penkovskiy Papers* (Garden City, N.Y.: Doubleday, 1965), pp. 70, 90–91, 188–191, 210–211, 239, 279, 282.

The decision to place the secret police under the direction of professional Party officials was undoubtedly related to the shakeup that the police organs had experienced following the execution of Beria and his aides. Yet the police have not been able to play an independent role in Soviet politics. The military has served as a counterforce and check on the police, and the Party has never hesitated to deal harshly with its police chiefs. Beria, while head of the police, enjoyed full Politburo membership, while Shelepin obtained a post in the Secretariat and later in the Politburo only after leaving the KGB chairmanship. However, Andropov's promotion to full membership in the Politburo indicated the importance of the security police in the Soviet system. Viktor M. Chebrikov, who became head of the KGB in December 1982, had served under Andropov as head of the KGB cadres administration since 1967; prior to 1967, he had been a Party official. Chebrikov attained full membership in the Politburo in 1985 and holds the rank of General of the Army.

Although Soviet security police chiefs have been quite expendable and at a disadvantage, historically, in competing for power, Andropov's ability to become CPSU General Secretary testifies to the potential of the KGB leadership. The position entails great responsibility and tends to elicit fear and distrust because of the opportunities it provides for collecting information of a compromising nature that can be used against opponents. Although the police representation on the Central Committee is limited, it could prove to be decisive during an internal crisis. If the role of the police is circumscribed within the leadership and kept under Party control, it nevertheless remains an indispensable component of the Soviet system.

The Soviet secret police organization exercises vast powers and has at its disposal personnel numbering in the hundreds of thousands. The KGB includes foreign intelligence, counterintelligence, and the political police who deal with offenses against the state, censor the mails, and guard the Soviet leadership. The border guards control the world's longest frontier, preventing persons from entering the country illegally and Soviet citizens from leaving it without permission. The border troops, who number as many as 200,000, are fully trained for combat and can be regarded as part of the Soviet armed forces. They share responsibility with the air defense force in guarding the Soviet frontiers, which are 60,000 kilometers in length. The border troops maintain a frontier zone of varying width (it includes the twelve-mile belt of territorial waters) in which the movement of persons is strictly controlled. Soviet citizens who live in the frontier zone are identified as residents in their internal passports. Nonresidents can enter the zone only with the permission of the MVD. The width of the zone is not defined in law and can vary greatly in practice. A narrower frontier belt *(pogranichnaia polosa)* that directly parallels the Soviet border has even stricter controls. It is frequently plowed so that new footprints will be easy to see, and it contains watchtowers, guard dogs, and sensing devices. The border troops use ships, helicopters, light aircraft, armored vehicles, and horses where necessary. They control international airports, river and seaports of entry, and rail and highway frontier crossing points. A Soviet law of November 24, 1982, empowers the border troops to seize printed matter, matrices, manuscripts, videotapes, audiotapes, and photographic materials from travelers.[29]

The police (MVD) also control the Army of Internal Security, a special force used to maintain order in the event that the militia cannot do so; it also serves as a counterforce to the regular army and as a means of suppressing internal revolt. This force numbers several hundred thousand and is used to guard special facilities and structures regarded as having strategic significance. The KGB includes the Kremlin Guards, and it is also responsible for guarding the Soviet leaders. The KGB maintains its own communications facilities and operational air force. It has even been known to reach out into foreign lands in order to dispose of persons regarded as enemies of the Soviet regime.[30] An organization of this type also of necessity conducts many operations that remain unknown to the general public.

The political importance of the KGB is not measured exclusively by the extent of KGB presence in the Politburo—as, for example, under Gorbachev with Chebrikov and Aliev as full members. The Soviet oligarchy depends on the KGB to cope with domestic opponents, as demonstrated by Andropov's repressive measures against political dissidents. The KGB performs a variety of covert operations abroad. It is used to prepare and disseminate disinformation and to forge documents designed to confuse and deceive the Soviet Union's principal adversaries and to discredit or compromise persons or groups regarded as opponents.[31] It monitors the activities of émigré organizations and groups and endeavors to use them or weaken them as circumstances permit. Most important is the KGB's role as the principal, but not sole, Soviet intelligence-gathering organization. The intelligence function gives the KGB the ability to influence important Politburo decisions affecting domestic and foreign policy. To the extent that the

---

[29]*Izvestiia,* November 26, 1982. See also B. M. Klimenko and A. A. Pork, *Territoriia i granitsa SSSR* (Moscow: "Mezhdunarodnye otnosheniia," 1985), pp. 170–175. The previous statute *(polozhenie)* of August 5, 1960, dealing with Soviet frontiers limited the frontier belt *(polosa)* to a width of two kilometers, but the 1982 law did not specify any width—in conformity with its purpose of enhancing the powers of the border troops. Although these powers are extensively detailed in the 1982 law, the border forces are authorized to issue additional regulations.

[30]Illustrations are provided by the kidnapping of the Russian émigré General Paul Kutepov off a Paris street by Soviet police agents on January 26, 1930 (see the admission by Colonel-General N. Shimanov in *Krasnaia zvezda,* September 22, 1965, p. 3) and by the assassinations in Munich of the Ukrainian émigrés Lev Rebet and Stepan Bandera (in October 1957 and October 1959 respectively) by the Soviet agent Bogdan Stashinsky. The confessed assassin was tried in the Supreme Court of the Federal Republic of Germany in Karlsruhe. The German Foreign Ministry protested to the USSR on April 23, 1963; see the *Bulletin des Presse und Informationsamtes der Bundesregierung* of April 25, 1963, No. 73. On these assassinations, see *The Service, The Memoirs of General Reinhard Gehlen* (New York: World Publishing-Times Mirror, 1972), pp. 240–244, and John Barron, *KGB, The Secret Work of Soviet Secret Agents* (New York: Reader's Digest Press, 1974), pp. 313–319.

[31]See Richard Shultz and Roy Godson, *Dezinformatsia, Active Measures in Soviet Strategy* (New York: Pergamon-Brassey's, 1984) and Ladislav Bittman, *The KGB and Soviet Disinformation, An Insider's View* (New York: Pergamon-Brassey's, 1985). For examples of Soviet forgeries, see *Soviet Active Measures,* Special Reports numbers 88 (October 1981), 101 (July 1982), and 110 (September 1983), published by the Bureau of Public Affairs of the U.S. Department of State. See also Jeffrey T. Richelson, *Sword and Shield: The Soviet Intelligence and Security Apparatus* (Cambridge, Mass.: Ballinger, 1986), Chap. 7.

Party remains preoccupied with security, constant vigilance, and the monopoly of power and retains a hostile or suspicious view of the non-Soviet world, its dependence on the KGB is likely to continue.

THE MILITARY

Most polities—with the possible exception of long-established constitutional systems—are confronted with the problem of preventing the military from challenging civilian control. In numerous Afro-Asian and Latin American countries, civilian politicians have been ousted and replaced by juntas or by a single dominant military figure. The role of the armed forces vis-à-vis the Party has troubled the Soviet leadership since Lenin's time. The problem has been one of utilizing the military, with its indispensable professional knowledge and its weaponry, in order to enhance Soviet power while simultaneously preventing it from challenging the Party.

Initially, Lenin favored establishment of a nonprofessional people's army and the abolition of standing armies. The Soviet regime had owed its establishment to the demoralization of the old army and the organization of the Party's own paramilitary force, the Red Guard. However, the need to employ substantial military force to preserve the regime and extend its domain necessitated the establishment of the Red Army, based on conscription and the hiring of approximately 50,000 commissioned officers and more than 200,000 noncommissioned officers of the tsarist army. This fact, together with the Party's fear that it might lose control of its new military forces, led to the establishment of the system of political commissars. These officials were instructed to prevent the defection of army officers, to sign orders and reports along with the commander, and to conduct propaganda among the troops.

The system led to friction, but it enabled the regime to defeat its domestic enemies by 1921. Subsequently, professional army officers who joined the Party and gained its confidence were given independent authority to make military decisions ("single command" or *edinonachalie*), while non–Party members were checked by the commissars. These gains made by the professional military were quickly eroded with the establishment of Stalin's dictatorship, although the armed forces were increased in size and given larger appropriations. The purges of the 1930s resulted in the ouster or elimination of fully half of the officer corps; eight of the leading officers, including Marshal Tukhachevsky, were executed in June 1937.[32] Stalin also enhanced the role of the political commissars, making them coequal with commanding officers in August 1937. The system of dual command did not function well during the Soviet-Finnish war of 1939–1940; it was modified in August 1940, when the office of commissar was replaced with that of the deputy commander for political affairs *(zampolit),* who dealt with propaganda and morale while the commander was responsible for military deci-

---

[32]For a personal account of a Soviet officer who was arrested and released only during World War II when trained commanders were in great demand, see the memoirs of General A. V. Gorbatov, which appeared in an abridged English translation, *Years Off My Life* (New York: Norton, 1965).

sions. Stalin's lack of confidence in the military was testified to in July 1941, following the Nazi invasion of the Soviet Union, when the commissar system was reintroduced. However, the zampolit system was restored in October 1942. Although the Soviet Army was given much latitude during World War II, stringent controls were reimposed in 1945.

Party-military relations have followed an uneven course that has depended upon the degree to which the Party has had to rely on military support.[33] In order to maintain its traditional dominance over the military, the Party developed a variety of controls and techniques. Foremost among these has been the effort to recruit nearly all officers as Communist Party members and bring them within the sphere of party discipline through the primary Party organizations in military units. A classic example of the kind of control the Party exercises was provided in the case of M. V. Frunze, who in 1925, as Commissar of the armed forces, was ordered by the Politburo to undergo surgery—from which he never recovered. A second method is that of political indoctrination, which is part of professional military training and is conducted under the supervision of the Main Political Administration (MPA) or *Glavnoe Politicheskoe Upravlenie* (GlavPU) of the Soviet armed forces. The MPA, although housed in the Ministry of Defense, is subordinate to the Party's Administrative Organs Department in personnel matters. It is charged with evaluating the political reliability of responsible military personnel. It directs the work of the deputy commanders for political affairs *(zampolity)*, who function at the divisional, brigade, regimental, and battalion levels. Through them it monitors the primary Party organizations and the Komsomol units in the armed services. A third method used at various times is to have the territorial Party organizations check on the military units within their jurisdiction. Related to this type of control is the institution of the military council—established by Stalin in May 1937—which functions at the regional level. This body includes the regional commander and his chief of staff, representatives from the local (oblast' or krai) party organizations, and usually a member from the security police. The commander's decisions must have the Council's approval.

Other techniques of control include the practice of promoting those officers who are "politically reliable," the implicit threat of demotion or transfer to the reserves with loss of privileges, and the use of personal rivalries between leading military figures (as between marshals Zhukov and Konev). The Party has also employed political generals among the professional military. It has introduced secret police informers into the armed services in order to promote conformity and uncover the disaffected.[34] The Soviet practice of "criticism and self criticism" *(kritika-samokritika)* at Party meetings, in which one can criticize others but

---

[33]For a thorough historical treatment of the Soviet military, see John Erickson, *The Soviet High Command: A Military-Political History, 1918–1942* (New York: St. Martin's Press, 1962). The system of political control and the Party-military relationship are treated in Roman Kolkowicz, *The Soviet Military and the Communist Party* (Princeton, N.J.: Princeton University Press, 1967). See also Timothy J. Colton, *Commissars, Commanders, and Civilian Authority: The Structure of Soviet Military Politics* (Cambridge, Mass.: Harvard University Press, 1979).

[34]See Amy W. Knight, "The KGB's Special Departments in the Soviet Armed Forces," *Orbis,* XXVIII, No. 2 (Summer 1984), 257–280.

must also admit one's own errors, is used to pit one military rank against another; in this way a state of tension is institutionalized, and Party meetings are used to mix ranks and to cut senior officers "down to size." The regular army is also held in check by the separate army of the interior, which is armed with heavy weapons and also performs internal-security functions.

However, direct and indirect controls and indoctrination are accompanied by inducements and rewards. The officer corps of the Soviet armed services constitutes a privileged class valued by the regime. At the same time measures must be exercised to prevent the military from becoming a caste that could dictate policy to the Party leadership.

The degree of latitude permitted the military within the system of controls and the degree of influence on policy exercised by the leading generals depend upon the state of the Party leadership and the extent to which the regime is *immediately* dependent upon military support. If the Party oligarchy is divided and one or another faction seeks the backing of the armed forces leadership, the military is in a position to exact concessions. The varying degree to which controls have been applied in relationship to the domestic political situation is reflected in the direction of the MPA. Its heads have been "political generals" during periods of intensified control, and the post has been sensitive to changes in Party leadership.[35] The head of the MPA is usually a Central Committee member. Yet the MPA may be too heavily staffed with professional military personnel and too closely associated with the military to serve as a fully effective agency for the Party.

Marshal Georgii K. Zhukov was the first professional army officer to attain full membership in the Politburo-Presidium (and that briefly, from July to October 1957); he was soon regarded as a threat to the Party and to Khrushchev's

---

[35]As early as 1924 Stalin removed Antonov-Ovseenko, a Trotskyite, as head of PUR *(Politicheskoe Upravlenie Raboche-Krestianskoi Krasnoi Armii),* the precursor of MPA, thus indicating the importance of the post in the developing power struggle with Trotsky and in the system generally. A. S. Bubnov, a Stalinist and nonmilitary figure, held it until 1929. Bubnov's successor was Jan B. Gamarnik, a Party official and army commissar, who held the post until 1937, when he committed suicide at the time of the execution of eight of the Soviet Union's leading generals. From 1937 to 1940 the MPA was headed by Lev Z. Mekhlis, a former Party official and member of the editorial board of *Pravda,* who presided over the purging of the officer corps. From 1942 to 1945 the MPA was headed by Aleksandr S. Shcherbakov, a member of the Party Secretariat and a veteran official of its apparatus. Shcherbakov, unlike his predecessor, remained a Central Committee Secretary while heading MPA, in addition to serving as Moscow city and obkom secretary; he also attained candidate-membership in the Politburo.

Controls were tightened in the postwar period, when Iosif V. Shikin headed MPA from 1946 to 1949, and leading military figures were given obscure posts. Shikin, a protégé of Andrei Zhdanov, was removed in 1949, along with other of Zhdanov's followers; but he made a comeback after Stalin's death and served as ambassador to Albania in 1960. The MPA was subsequently headed by a military man, Colonel General F. F. Kuznetsov, and in the same year Marshal Vasilevsky replaced the political Marshal Bulganin as Defense Minister. Following Stalin's death the MPA was headed by Colonel General Zheltov, who remained at the post until January 1958, when he was succeeded by General (later Marshal) F. I. Golikov. Both of these chiefs presided over a weaker MPA; but in May 1962, Golikov, a professional army officer, was succeeded by Aleksei A. Yepishev, a political general who tightened controls. Yepishev had served with Khrushchev in the Ukrainian Party apparatus after

rule.[36] His summary removal from the post of Minister of Defense and from the Central Committee was accomplished in October 1957, when he was sent to Yugoslavia and Albania on an official mission. Zhukov was later accused of pursuing a "Bonapartist policy." His rapid advance had been due to the fact that the Party needed the support of the army against Beria. Khrushchev also required it in his struggle for power with Malenkov, which led to the latter's removal from the premiership. The military did not approve of Malenkov's budget cuts or his views in 1954, which regarded Soviet nuclear deterrence as adequate to deal with any external threat and advocated the diversion of resources from heavy industry to the production of consumer goods. The military also favored the rewriting of Soviet history in 1956–1957 to take into account its role, in contrast to that of Stalin, in achieving victory in World War II. Zhukov insisted, moreover, that the Party posthumously rehabilitate the generals executed in 1937. While the military had supported Khrushchev against the "anti-Party group" in 1957, Khrushchev's victory made it possible for the Party to reassert its control over the armed forces. The improved conditions and the emancipation from indoctrination obtained for the military by Zhukov were thus short-lived.

Zhukov's successor as Minister of Defense, Marshal Rodion Malinovsky, did not attain Politburo membership. However, Malinovsky's successor, Marshal Andrei Grechko, was made a full member of the Politburo in April 1973 and enjoyed longer tenure than Zhukov. Grechko owed his advancement initially to Khrushchev, with whom he was associated in Ukraine while serving as commander of the Kiev Military District. He was appointed First Deputy Minister of Defense in 1957 after Zhukov's ouster and commanded Warsaw Pact forces prior to becoming Minister of Defense in 1967. Grechko was brought into Brezhnev's Politburo presumably to associate him with the policy of détente or to muffle criticism of it within the military. However, when Grechko died in April 1976, he was replaced as defense minister by a Politburo and Secretariat member Dmitrii F. Ustinov, an armaments and heavy-industry specialist, who, though a civilian, was placed in military uniform and given the rank of Marshal. As if to reinforce civilian and Party control over the military, Brezhnev also became a Marshal in 1976.

Ustinov's death in December 1984 raised the question of who should suc-

World War II and was brought to Moscow in 1951, apparently by Khrushchev, to be Deputy Minister of State Security (MGB). He left that post in 1953 and became first secretary of the Odessa obkom in Ukraine; in 1955 he was appointed ambassador to Romania and in 1961 ambassador to Yugoslavia. Yepishev's career illustrates the kinds of political qualifications and experience that the Party requires of the MPA chief when it has wished to reimpose more rigid controls over the military. Yepishev headed the MPA from 1962 to July 1985, when he was replaced by General Aleksei D. Lizichev, a professional army officer and a graduate of the Lenin Military-Political Academy who served as political chief of Soviet forces in Germany.

[36]Although Marshal K. Voroshilov was in the Politburo from 1926 to 1960, he was less a representative of professional military interests and more of a crony of Stalin. His military experience was limited, and his advancement was due more to his revolutionary past than to military expertise. Voroshilov's appointment as Soviet chief of state, following Stalin's death, was probably designed to accord greater recognition to the military.

ceed him as defense minister. The aggressive and articulate Chief of Staff of the Armed Forces, Marshal Nikolai V. Ogarkov, had been removed from his post in September 1984 and placed in command of the Western Military Region apparently for having advocated policies and levels of military expenditure that the Party leadership found unacceptable. Instead, it appointed as defense minister Marshal Sergei L. Sokolov, a professional officer with more than a half century of military service, who at age 73 was only given candidate membership in the Politburo—an apparent indication of the Party's intent to subordinate the military. Sokolov and other leading military figures were replaced as a result of the sensational and embarrassing overflight of the Soviet Union by a small West German private aircraft that reached Moscow's Red Square and landed nearby—having penetrated Soviet anti-air defenses (ironically, on May 28, 1987—Soviet Borderguards' Day). A lesser-ranking figure, General of the Army Dmitrii T. Yazov, was named minister of defense and given candidate-membership in the Politburo in June 1987. M. S. Gorbachev's Central Committee Report to the Twenty-seventh Congress included an especially striking statement: "Militarism is becoming inordinately swollen on the arms race, and is seeking, step by step, to seize the political levers of power as well. It is becoming the ugliest and most dangerous monster of the twentieth century."[37] Although this forceful warning was offered in the context of a discussion of bourgeois capitalism, it could also have a broader application.

The military's sense of professionalism and exclusiveness and its awareness of how important a role it might play still lead to disagreements with the Party leadership. The military often dislike political controls and ideological indoctrination, which consume much time and detract from professional activities and interests. The military may sometimes represent views that conflict with those of Party leaders regarding military policy, questions of strategy, and estimates of risk and capabilities. Khrushchev revealed that it was the Politburo that decided which kinds of naval vessels would be constructed—over the opposition of Admiral N. G. Kuznetsov.[38] Khrushchev's military reforms involving reduction in conventional forces aroused opposition in the officer corps and prompted the military to view his ouster with approval. Marshal Grechko as defense minister is said to have clashed with Foreign Minister Gromyko over détente and SALT I and to have advocated a punitive and preventive nuclear strike against China in 1969.[39]

Both Party and military leaders have views regarding the country's defense needs, what the size and nature of the defense establishment should be, how resources and investments should be allocated, and what the level of defense expenditures should be. There are opportunities, in other words, to differ over the extent to which international tension can be reduced and over what the conditions

---

[37]*Pravda,* February 26, 1986, p. 2.
[38]See *Khrushchev Remembers, The Last Testament* (Boston: Little, Brown, 1974), Chap. 2. Admiral Kuznetsov was demoted twice, first by Stalin and then by Khrushchev, and also deprived of his rank.
[39]Arkady N. Shevchenko, *Breaking with Moscow* (New York: Ballantine Books, 1985), pp. 200, 218–219, 268–269.

of deterence and détente might be. The military does not always trust the judgment of Party leaders in military matters; it wishes to apply its professional expertise and has a natural distrust of the amateur or of the politician whose policies might lead to a war for which the military is not prepared. Yet the Party leaders seek to define military doctrine and have the final word in establishing strategy. The 1977 Soviet Constitution introduced a novel provision (article 32): "The state ensures the security and defense capability of the country, and supplies the Armed Forces of the USSR with everything necessary for that purpose." Such an assertion can be interpreted either as an alleged statement of fact or as a pledge.

Although there are disagreements *within* the military, which the Party can often manipulate to its own advantage, the Party must constantly act to preserve its monopoly of authority and its system of controls. By means of a skillful granting and retraction of concessions, as well as by keeping the military under close surveillance and encouraging personal and interservice rivalries, the Party has been able to maintain its dominant position. The military and the secret police are among the more influential interest groups in Soviet politics, but they are also indispensable attributes and instruments of Party rule. The Party is dependent on the military and the security police to preserve its domain and all that is subordinate to it. It relies on them for its claim to be a superpower and for the promotion of patriotism and the preservation of public order. They are needed to maintain the Soviet alliance system and to keep reluctant allies compliant. The task of preventing this dependence from being transformed into military or police dominance is one that the Party leadership continually faces and cannot claim to have resolved in any final sense.

chapter 6

The Central Government

Knowledge of the Communist Party's leadership and organization, while indispensable for a thorough understanding of Soviet political structures, is not in itself adequate for that understanding. For while it is commonplace to assert that the Soviet regime and its Communist Party are synonymous, in practice, the Party and government are distinct organizational entities. Within the government there are bodies that fulfill many functions not performed by the Party organization. And while the Party apparatus exercises vast powers and ultimate decision-making ability, it lacks juristic authority; this requisite of its rule it obtains only by means of the vast governmental structure that it originally created.

THE SOVIETS: ORIGIN AND MEANING

It is indicative of the nature of language and of the mutable nature of semantics that the ordinary and politically neutral Russian word *soviet,* denoting "council," should have acquired a highly specific political meaning. For many, the term has come to be synonymous with communist dictatorship and is at times even used interchangeably (though incorrectly) with the adjective *Russian.*

The term *soviet* was used by the Imperial Regime in naming the State Council *(Gosudarstvennyi Sovet),* a purely advisory body established by Alexander I in 1810. With the proclamation of the Duma in 1906, the State Council became the upper house of the Imperial legislature. The tsarist regime also had a Council (soviet) of Ministers. However, the term began to acquire a politically tendentious meaning, originally as a result of the 1905 Revolution. In October of that year, there emerged in St. Petersburg a Soviet of Workers' Deputies, which assumed leadership of the general strike that prompted concessions from Nicholas II. The most important of these were the establishment of the Duma and the recognition of circumscribed freedom of expression. The 1905 Soviet vainly proclaimed the eight-hour workday and advocated a constituent assembly and a republic. When its chairman, a lawyer, was arrested, the Menshevik Trotsky became its spokesman. The tsarist government arrested the entire Executive Committee of the Soviet when it issued a financial manifesto calling upon the public not to pay taxes.

The soviet as a revolutionary institution made its appearance again in the Russian capital in 1917, with the establishment of the Petrograd Soviet of Workers' and Soldiers' Deputies. This was a spontaneous body whose members were not elected in accordance with any established procedures. In the period following the tsar's abdication, the Petrograd Soviet and the Provisional Government, which had emerged from the Duma, constituted a dyarchy. The Soviet, initially consisting largely of Socialist Revolutionaries and Mensheviks, had vague objectives, such as defending the revolution, but would not enter the Provisional Government. While refusing to accept the responsibility of governing, the Soviet succeeded in paralyzing the Provisional Government and in bringing about the collapse of authority in the Russian capital. The assumption was that authority would be assumed by the All-Russian Constituent Assembly, but the Provisional Government was dilatory in organizing the popular election of that body. Soviets were organized in other cities and in peasant communities; factory committees and soldiers' committees added to the general confusion.

The return of Lenin to Russia in April 1917 prompted the Bolsheviks to utilize the Petrograd and other soviets. Lenin declared war on the Provisional Government and advocated the slogan of "All Power to the Soviets." Although the Bolsheviks were a small minority in the principal soviets, Lenin gradually built up a following in factory committees and in the Petrograd garrison. By using street mobs Lenin succeeded in pressuring both the Provisional Government and the Petrograd Soviet. As the Provisional Government, headed by Alexander Kerensky, lost strength and prestige in the early autumn of 1917, both the Bolsheviks and the Soviets (which included many non-Bolsheviks) gained ground. In September, Trotsky, who had now joined the Bolsheviks, succeeded in becoming chairman of the Petrograd Soviet after the Menshevik Chkheidze resigned ill-advisedly and helped preempt the situation.

The Bolshevik seizure of power occurred as the Second All-Russian Congress of Soviets of Workers' and Soldiers' Deputies was being convened. The Bolsheviks did not have a clear majority in the Congress, but Lenin seized power in the name of the soviets rather than relying upon the Congress to determine Russia's future. Lenin succeeded in gaining control of the Congress when most of the Mensheviks, the Socialist Revolutionaries, and the Jewish Bundists walked out—again preempting the situation rather than resisting the Bolsheviks. While claiming to have seized power in behalf of the Congress of Soviets, the Bolsheviks had it acclaim their new, supposedly provisional, government—a soviet of people's commissars *(sovnarkom)*. The rump Congress also approved a Bolshevik-dominated Central Executive Committee, which was to serve as an interim legislative body.

Thus began the long association of the Russian Communist Party (of Bolsheviks) and the institution of soviets, which has enabled the ruling party to claim that it is not actually the government of the USSR and that, rather, its regime is "soviet power." Indeed, when Lenin dispersed at bayonet point the popularly elected All-Russian Constituent Assembly on January 19, 1918, he justified his action as a defense of "soviet power." His regime would submit its policies for approval only to Congresses of Soviets, whose membership it would control. Thus, at the Third Congress of Soviets, which met in late January 1918, Lenin's Bolsheviks had 61 percent of the seats. In subsequent convocations of soviets at all levels of government, the Bolsheviks were to fashion ready instruments to transform their Party decisions into law.

In Lenin's theory the system of soviets was to serve as communism's answer to "bourgeois parliamentarism" and was to provide the organs of "proletarian power." Although soviets are nothing more than elected councils, it was claimed that they provided a "state of a new and higher type" that would lead to socialism. Soviets did, in fact, give to the communist regime a mass-participation basis while not permitting the masses any choice in the matter of Communist Party rule. Yet it is claimed that "state authority" resides in the "soviets of people's deputies"—although they do not participate directly in the decision-making process of the CPSU.

THE FUSION OF POWERS

The system of soviets extends from the U.S.S.R. Supreme Soviet (the country's bicameral legislative body) to the unicameral supreme soviets of the union republics and of the autonomous republics, down through the province and city soviets to the rural and urban district level, and to the smallest village and hamlet. At each level, from the highest to the very lowest, there is an elected soviet that serves to legitimize governmental authority. Yet all of the soviets, irrespective of their territorial jurisdiction, are said to constitute a single unified system that supposedly gives substance to the claim regarding the unity of the Soviet state and people. The centralism that characterizes Communist Party organization has thus been extended to the government, and the lower soviets are "strictly subordinate" to the higher soviets. At the same time, all soviets, including the U.S.S.R. Supreme Soviet, are in fact subordinate to the Communist Party organization at each jurisdictional level.

The soviets embody the principle of the fusion of legislative and executive power that is a basic characteristic of the Soviet political system. Thus, Lenin is quoted approvingly as having asserted in 1917 that "there *cannot be* two powers *(vlastei)* in a state."[1] While a differentiation of functions and competence is

---

[1] V. I. Lenin, *Polnoe sobranie sochinenii,* 5th ed. (Moscow, 1961), XXXI, 155; italics in original. See B. N. Ponomarev, ed., and A. E. Bovin et al., *Konstitutsiia SSSR, Politiko-pravovoi kommentarii,* (Moscow: Politizdat, 1982), pp. 26–27, 292–294. Lenin's rejection of the separation of powers is seen

recognized as existing between legislative, administrative, and judicial bodies, it is still claimed that state authority is unified. The soviets are said to "control" the executive because the executive bodies (the councils of ministers of the USSR and of the various republics and the executive committees of the soviets below the republic level) are elected by them and consist of persons from their membership. However, legislative initiative rests with the executive and, ultimately, with the Party organization, which is the embodiment of the fusion of powers.

SOVIET CONSTITUTIONS

The first Soviet constitution was adopted in July 1918—for the Russian Socialist Federated Soviet Republic—and, by Lenin's admission, was not drafted by jurists or based on any other constitution. Instead, it was said to be based on the experience of revolutionary struggle and did, in fact, give evidence of having been drafted hastily. It proclaimed the "dictatorship of the proletariat" and claimed to have replaced "bourgeois democracy" with "proletarian democracy." The land, resources, and banking system were nationalized, and the factories, mines, railways and other means of production and transport were placed under "workers' control" and under the Supreme Soviet of the Public Economy (VSNKh) as the first step toward complete state ownership. The 1918 Constitution provided for "universal labor service" as a means of "destroying the parasitic strata of society." It also endeavored to have international appeal by vowing to "deliver humanity from the claws of finance capital and imperialism."[2]

The soviets were proclaimed to be truly popular organs of government, and the norms of representation established in 1918 were to persist until 1936. Thus, the "bourgeoisie" and "exploiters" (including persons hiring labor for profit or living on unearned income, tradesmen, clergymen, tsarist police officers, and employers) were denied the right to participate in such direct elections as were held. Lenin justified this prohibition as providing "proof" that the soviets were "not organs of petit bourgeois compromise with the capitalists and [were] not organs of parliamentary chatter."[3] Why such discriminatory denial of suffrage should have been necessary when the bourgeoisie was but a small minority in Russia was not explained.

A second Soviet constitution was adopted in January 1924 as a result of the formation of the Union of Soviet Socialist Republics and the need to restructure the political order in accordance with the Union's multinational nature. The Ukrainian and Belorussian communist regimes, whose nominal independence had been recognized by Moscow, adopted their own constitutions in 1919; that of Azerbaidjan did so in 1921; and those of Armenia and Georgia followed suit in 1922. Although the non-Russian communists expressed preference for a

---

in his statement on the Paris Commune, in which he asserted that "legislators must themselves work, must carry out their own laws, must verify that which occurs in life. . . ." Lenin, *op. cit.*, XXXIII, 47–48. See also L. A. Grigorian, *Narodovlastie v SSSR* (Moscow: "Iuridicheskaia Literatura," 1972), pp. 290–292.

[2]*Sovetskie konstitutsii, spravochnik* (Moscow: Gospolitizdat, 1963), p. 130.

[3]Lenin, *Polnoe sobranie sochinenii, op. cit.* (above, n. 1), XXXVII, p. 290.

confederation in 1923 during the drafting of the constitution, Moscow succeeded in imposing a federal order characterized by a high degree of centralism.

The 1924 Constitution consisted of two principal parts: a declaration of an ideological nature that reflected the "two camps" doctrine ("capitalism" and "socialism," with the latter purporting to represent "mutual confidence and peace, national freedom and equality, peaceful coexistence and the fraternal collaboration of peoples")[4] and a treaty between the Russian S.F.S.R. and the Ukrainian S.S.R., the Belorussian S.S.R. and the Transcaucasian S.F.S.R. (Azerbaidjan, Georgia, and Armenia). The treaty contained the actual U.S.S.R. constitution, which was modeled on the 1918 R.S.F.S.R. constitution.

The 1924 Constitution established an All-Union Congress of Soviets (as the previous All-Russian Congress had functioned only on the territory of the R.S.F.S.R.), but the norms of representation were fixed to the advantage of the urban population. Delegates to the All-Union Congress of Soviets were elected indirectly (by provincial and republic congresses of soviets) on the basis of one delegate per 25,000 *voters* in the cities, while for the rural areas there was one delegate per 125,000 *inhabitants.* Official commentators have endeavored to justify these ratios of representation on the grounds that they were adopted in 1917 for the elections to Congresses of Soviets prior to the establishment of Lenin's regime. However, the Bolsheviks were not bound to retain such discriminatory norms of representation except for the fact that they were advantageous for a regime that distrusted the peasantry.

The All-Union Congress of Soviets, which functioned until 1936, was to meet annually until 1927 and, subsequently, biennially. Its voting membership ranged from 1540 to more than 2000 and was elected for each specific congress. The All-Union Congress was said to be the "supreme organ of authority," but during the lengthy intervals when it was not in session, its authority was exercised by the All-Union Central Executive Committee (CEC). The CEC was bicameral; the Council of the Union was elected by the Congress itself on the basis of the population of each republic; the Council of Nationalities was elected by the congresses of soviets of the union republics, autonomous republics, and autonomous oblasti on the basis of fixed representation.

The CEC was to hold at least three sessions during each of its convocations between the All-Union Congresses of Soviets. During the lengthy intervals between CEC sessions, "supreme legislative, executive and administrative" authority was vested in the Presidium of the CEC, which issued decrees. The Presidium's membership varied from 21 to 27. The CEC elected both its Presidium and the Council of People's Commissars at a joint session of the Council of the Union and the Council of Nationalities, with both chambers voting separately. Under the 1924 Constitution, the Council of People's Commissars was responsible to the Presidium of the CEC and to the CEC when that body was in session. The Presidium, although a continuously functioning body, was said to be responsible to the CEC, and the latter, in theory at least, was responsible to

---

[4]*Sovetskie konstitutsii, spravochnik* (above, n. 2), p. 183.

the All-Union Congress of Soviets. This elaborate pyramid of indirectly elected bodies was retained by Stalin until 1936, when the All-Union Congress of Soviets was abolished and the CEC was replaced by the U.S.S.R. Supreme Soviet.

The Stalin Constitution was adopted by the Extraordinary Eighth Congress of Soviets on December 5, 1936, but only after the Central Committee of the CPSU had initiated the proposal at its February 1935 plenary session. Although Stalin presided over the constitutional commission, Nikolai Bukharin and Karl Radek contributed much to its drafting. The new document was supposedly the "constitution of victorious socialism" and reflected the profound changes that had occurred in the country's class structure and economy—with the proclaimed liquidation of "exploiting classes," the development of technology and heavy industry, and the collectivization of agriculture. The draft constitution was approved by the Party's Central Committee and by the Presidium of the CEC of the Congress of Soviets in June 1936. There followed five months of controlled public discussion in which more than 50 million persons were said to have "participated."

The 1924 Constitution was declared to have been a document for the transitional period from capitalism to socialism. With the proclaimed achievement of socialism, it was expedient, therefore, under the 1936 Constitution to provide for general, equal, and direct suffrage in the election of all soviets, from the village to the U.S.S.R. Supreme Soviet. Secret suffrage was introduced in lieu of the open voting used previously, although the absence of a choice between candidates hardly required secrecy at the polls. The previously disfranchised classes (clergy, entrepreneurs, and persons said to have been privileged under the tsarist regime) were henceforth permitted to participate in elections.

Although all Soviet constitutions have probably concealed more than they have revealed regarding the true nature of the Soviet polity, this does not mean that they can be ignored. The nature of the Soviet constitutions reflects certain of the polity's characteristics. All of the constitutions have been permeated with Marxist-Leninist ideology. The 1936 Constitution proclaimed work to be a duty and declared that "He who does not work neither shall he eat" (article 12)—but without attributing the quotation to Holy Writ (II Thess 3:10). Soviet spokesmen have repeatedly claimed that their constitution has "enormous international significance," supposedly offering the world an ideal and providing an inspiration to all "progressive humanity."

The instrumental nature of the Soviet constitution is seen in the assertion that "new constitutions are adopted when substantial changes occur in the relationship of class forces in the country."[5] Thus, a constitution is not regarded as a repository of certain sacrosanct political norms and principles but simply as a device designed to fulfill the alleged needs of a particular stage of historical development. The Soviet constitution has been amended with great ease (the 1977 Constitution, like that of 1936, has provided for amendment by a two-thirds majority of both chambers of the Supreme Soviet); amendment has been frequent

---

[5]*Ibid.,* p. 216.

and at times has even been initiated by executive decree. Soviet constitutions have little relationship to constitutionalism, for they have not effectively restrained the country's rulers.

The 1977 Constitution, the fourth adopted by the Soviet regime, was promulgated by Leonid Brezhnev after a protracted drafting process. Nikita Khrushchev had asserted that the 1936 Constitution was "obsolete" and did not reflect the numerous changes that had occurred in the country. A constitutional commission was established in April 1962, under Khrushchev's chairmanship, to draft a new document. Following the ouster of Khrushchev in October 1964, the chairmanship was assumed by Brezhnev. The new constitution was still not promulgated in 1972 on the fiftieth anniversary of the establishment of the USSR. The lengthy delay was undoubtedly due to both disagreements regarding proposed changes and (especially) the division of powers between Moscow and the union republics.

The decision to publish the draft of the 1977 Constitution, 15 years in preparation, was made by the CPSU Central Committee on May 27, 1977. Several factors may be said to have prompted the decision to issue the new constitution. Undoubtedly Brezhnev, upon entering his eighth decade, wished to bequeath to the country an important document comparable to Stalin's 1936 Constitution and Khrushchev's 1961 Party Program. Apart from personal vanity, the adoption of the 1977 Constitution coincided with the sixtieth anniversary of the Soviet regime and would reflect the profound changes of the previous four decades. The new constitution was said to reflect a "developed, mature socialist society" and to raise Soviet state and economic activity to a "qualitatively new level." The constitution's lengthy recital of promised social and economic benefits would enable the Soviet Union to claim to offer more in the way of human rights at a time when Brezhnev and his associates were being criticized abroad for denying human rights and for incarcerating political dissidents and other domestic critics.

The 1977 Constitution does not provide a new blueprint for the building of communism. Portions of the document have the character of promotional advertising, with the Soviet regime praising itself and its achievements and yet promising to do better.[6] The Constitution does not circumscribe the role of government

---

[6]The 1977 Constitution is a more lengthy and detailed document than the 1936 Constitution and has 174 articles instead of 146. It has an extended preamble that is ideological in tone and reminiscent of the 1924 Constitution. Portions of the 1977 Constitution are repetitious and even redundant. There are three articles that deal with the protection of the environment (articles 18, 42, and 67). Increased labor productivity and labor discipline are stressed repeatedly. Article 19 asserts that the "Soviet state promotes the intensification of the social homogeneity of society . . . elimination of important differences between city and countryside, [between] mental and physical work. . . ." Among other unique provisions is Article 66, which obligates citizens "to rear children properly, prepare them for socially useful work, and train worthy members of a socialist society." Article 53 asserts that "the family is under the protection of the state." The 1977 Constitution is also distinctive in having numerous articles dealing with the general principles and goals of the Soviet economy and three articles on professed goals of Soviet foreign policy. Although the 1977 Constitution did not change the structure of the Soviet political system, it did extend to the Soviet state the "democratic centralism" principle of CPSU organization. Article 3 asserts that the decisions of superior bodies are binding upon subordinate bodies and that a "single leadership" is combined with "local initiative and creative activity."

with any list of specific acts forbidden to authorities that one would expect to find in a genuine bill of rights based on the British and American models. The rights that the 1977 Constitution confers on Soviet citizens are largely social and economic and deal with such matters as housing, medical care, education, and material security in retirement or in the event of illness or disability. Vague in nature, these statements of rights do not provide for specific levels of benefits. There are various lacunae, exceptions, and qualifications. Thus, the right to employment (Article 40) states that wages and the choice of employment must be "in accordance with . . . due regard for the needs of society." The right to rest and to an annual paid vacation does not specify a minimum length of the vacation but does provide for a 41-hour work week.

Rights of a political nature are carefully circumscribed or even nullified. Article 47 provides for "freedom of scientific, technical and artistic creativity" but only "in accordance with the goals of communist construction." The fundamental freedoms of "speech, press, assembly, meetings, street processions and demonstrations" can be exercised only "in accordance with the interests of the working people and for the purpose of strengthening and developing the socialist system" (Article 50). The citizens' right to unite in public organizations must be "in accordance with the goals of communist construction" (Article 51). The personal life of citizens and the secrecy of correspondence, telephone conversations, and telegraphic communications are not protected by any absolute guarantees but are simply "protected by law"—which can provide for violation of such rights by authorities.

Ten articles in the 1977 Constitution impose obligations on Soviet citizens, and it is specifically stated that the "realization of rights and freedoms is inseparable from the fulfillment by citizens of their obligations" (Article 59). There is a duty to work and to observe strictly labor and production discipline. Citizens are required to respect socialist property and to "combat the embezzlement and squandering of state and public property" (Article 61). There is an "honorable obligation" to perform military service and a duty to aid in the preservation of public order. Apart from the specific qualification, there is a general qualifier clause (Article 62): "The citizen of the U.S.S.R. is obliged to defend the interests of the Soviet state and to promote the strengthening of its might *(mogushchestvo)* and authority." This blanket provision leaves no room for dissent. As if one such clause were not sufficient, Article 39 includes the following provision: "The exercise by citizens of rights and freedoms must not cause harm to the interests of society and the state, [to] the rights of other citizens." Although Article 49 grants a right to "present to state organs and public organizations proposals for improving their activities and to criticize shortcomings in [their] work," this obviously does not include criticism of basic Communist Party and governmental policies.

Various Soviet constitutional provisions have had a decidedly hollow ring, including Article 2 of the 1977 Constitution, which asserts that "all power in the U.S.S.R. belongs to the people" (under Stalin's 1936 Constitution, "all power" belonged to the "working people of town and country"). The 1924 Constitution (Article 4), the 1936 Constitution (Article 17) and the 1977 Constitution (Article

72) have granted to union republics the right to "freely secede from the U.S.S.R.," but an attempt to exercise this right is treated as treason. Union republics are empowered to enter into diplomatic relations with other countries (Article 80), but none has been permitted to exercise this "right."

The inclusion of such passages of low credibility has prompted some critics to regard the Soviet constitution as little more than a sham and fraud and an exercise in pretense. Yet even a Soviet constitution can be said to fulfill certain functions. Although it does not lay down the ground rules for the Soviet game of politics as practiced in the CPSU Politburo and Central Committee, it does clarify the Party's exclusive role and defines the basic governmental structures and the kinds of demands that are made on Soviet citizens.

Any constitution—even one that is violated—can serve as a useful device in giving a regime the appearance of a conventional political order and in pre- scribing certain formalities. A constitution is also a mark of respectability, serving as a symbol of "moral and political unity" and as a source of legitimation, even if only in a contrived manner. In the case of the 1936 Constitution, its adoption was also designed to impress gullible foreigners, who mistook constitutional provisions for Soviet political reality. It was also issued at a time when Moscow was seeking allies among the Western democracies. Stalin and his successors unabashedly proclaimed their constitution to be the "world's most democratic." Brezhnev could contend that the 1977 Constitution would have "enormous inter- national significance," allegedly demonstrating to the entire world the nature of Soviet "socialist democracy" and "enriching the common treasure-house of expe- rience of world socialism."

THE U.S.S.R. SUPREME SOVIET

Although the Supreme Soviet is referred to in the 1977 Constitution as the "highest organ of state power in the U.S.S.R." (article 108), this can be said to be true only in a highly formal and legalistic sense. It is a meaningful statement only insofar as all acts of the Soviet government are done in the name of the Supreme Soviet and are ultimately given blanket approval by that body. The largely honorific role of the Supreme Soviet in Russian political practice is seen in the fact that it meets for but a few days each year—usually meeting for approximately one week out of the year. Indeed, probably the most significant fact regarding the Supreme Soviet is that it consists of part-time, nonprofessional legislators. Soviet spokesmen endeavor to justify this unusual but highly revealing fact by claiming it to be a virtue. By not being professional legislators, Supreme Soviet deputies are said to be closer to their constituents; and it is seriously argued that, as amateur legislators, they can retain their jobs in the regular economy, can observe the laws in action, and remain closer to the electorate. "Bourgeois par- liamentarians" are said to form a "caste of officials divorced from the people."[7]

---

[7]V. Kotok, *The Soviet Representative System* (Moscow, n.d.), pp. 34 and 36. P. S. Romashkin, ed., *Fundamentals of Soviet Law* (Moscow, n.d.), p. 70. David L. Zlatopol'skii, *Verkhovnyi Sovet SSSR—vyrazitel' voli sovetskogo naroda* (Moscow: "Iuridicheskaia literatura", 1982), pp. 245–247.

Why the CPSU should have a professional officialdom when professional full-time lawmaking by a legislative assembly is frowned upon has never been satisfactorily explained by Soviet spokesmen.[8]

The anomalous nature of the Supreme Soviet and its modest role should not prompt its being dismissed as irrelevant or as redundant. Potentially it could serve as a conventional parliament under the relevant provisions of the Soviet Constitution—if the duration of its meetings were lengthened and made more frequent and if freedom of debate and of legislative initiative were permitted. The Supreme Soviet is probably the most representative body in the Soviet political system and is certainly far more representative than the Party's Central Committee because of its large size, the broader nature of its membership, and its closer relationship to the constituencies.

Organization and Procedure

The U.S.S.R. Supreme Soviet consists of two chambers, the Soviet of the Union and the Soviet of Nationalities, that have equal powers under the Constitution (see Figure 6.1). The deputies of both chambers are elected at the same time for five-year terms under the 1977 Constitution in place of the four-year term provided in the 1936 Constitution. The newly elected Supreme Soviets are numbered consecutively, and each such convocation *(sozyv)* is divided into sessions, the numbering of which begins anew with each new convocation. The duration of each session has varied from a day or two to approximately one week. Ordinarily the Supreme Soviet meets twice a year, but prior to 1953, it was meeting hardly more frequently than once a year (five sessions in the course of four years). Both chambers commence their sessions and adjourn simultaneously.

The Soviet of the Union was originally elected under the 1936 Constitution on the basis of population, in accordance with a provision that set a ratio of "one deputy for every 300,000 of the population." Consequently, the Soviet of the Union increased in size every four years, reflecting increased population. This occurred in all elections between 1937 and 1962, when the Soviet of the Union's membership rose from 569 to 791. The process was then reversed and the constitutional provision violated in the election of the Seventh Convocation in 1966, when the size of the Soviet of the Union was reduced to 767 deputies. The membership of the Soviet of Nationalities, on the other hand, is based on fixed representation for the various national territorial units. Each of the fifteen union republics has had 32 deputies since 1966 (25 prior to that); each autonomous republic has 11 deputies, each autonomous oblast' has 5, while each national area *(okrug)* has 1. The Soviet of Nationalities increased in size from 574 deputies in 1937 to 750 in 1966 as a result of the establishment of new union republics and

---

[8]Stalin asserted in an "election speech" following the adoption of the 1936 Constitution (on December 11, 1937) that "bourgeois deputies" (legislators) are "independent" of the voters once they are elected (after allegedly "fawning before them [the voters], swearing loyalty to them, and making a heap of promises"). By contrast, the Soviet deputy would have no such "independence." Although Stalin misunderstood—or chose to misunderstand—the relationship of the legislator and constituency in a democracy, he established a precedent regarding the deputy's dependence that was to survive his rule. I. V. Stalin, *Sochineniia* (Stanford, Calif.: The Hoover Institution, 1967), I [XIV], p. 261.

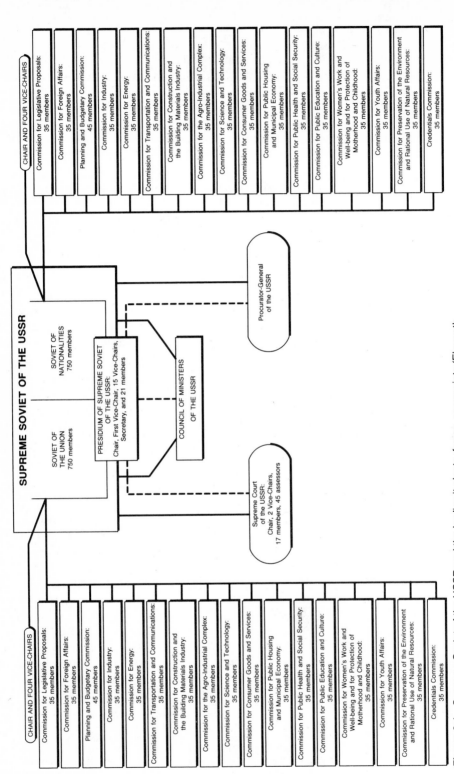

Figure 6.1 Supreme Soviet of the USSR and the bodies it elects, forms, or appoints (Eleventh Convocation, 1984–1989). Adapted from *The Soviet Parliament* (Moscow: Progress Publishers, 1967), facing pp. 68–69; and *Pravda*, April 12, 1984, pp. 2 and 4.

the increase in the number of union republic deputies in 1966. As a result of the regime's preference for chambers of approximately equal size, the number of deputies in the eighth and ninth Convocations, elected in 1970 and in 1974, remained at 767 in the Soviet of the Union and 750 in the Soviet of Nationalities. The 1977 Constitution provides for an equal number of members in both chambers and for constituencies of equal size in electing deputies to the Soviet of the Union.

The two chambers have equal, if limited, rights, and neither exercises any special prerogatives. Both chambers employ the same procedures and organization and sit jointly as well as separately. Joint sessions are held to elect the Presidium of the Supreme Soviet and the U.S.S.R. Supreme Court and to appoint the U.S.S.R. Council of Ministers. The two chambers also meet jointly to hear reports on the economic plan, the state budget, and "important sociocultural questions" as well as the report of the U.S.S.R. foreign minister. The Chairman of the Council of Ministers addresses joint sessions. These reports are discussed by the chambers meeting separately; if a law is adopted at a joint session, the chambers vote separately. Joint sessions are held in the large conference hall of the Great Kremlin Palace.

However, voting in the U.S.S.R. Supreme Soviet is, significantly, by show of hands only. Every vote in the Supreme Soviet has been said to be unanimous, and it has been seriously—if not very convincingly—claimed that this practice is indicative of the country's "moral-political unity."[9] Actually it demonstrates the readily admitted fact that the Supreme Soviet conducts its business under the close direction of the Central Committee of the CPSU.[10] The Central Committee frequently meets prior to a session of the Supreme Soviet. More than 70 percent of the deputies are Party members, and this proportion has persisted in each of the elections. Thus, the Party effectively dominates the so-called electoral bloc of communists and non-Party people. The unanimity in open voting renders irrelevant the provision in the Constitution that calls for the use of a conciliation commission in the event of disagreement between the two chambers. The 1936 Constitution provided for dissolution of the Supreme Soviet and the ordering of new elections by its Presidium if conciliation should fail, but no comparable provision was included in the 1977 Constitution. The 1977 Constitution provides for a country-wide referendum in the unlikely event of a disagreement between the two chambers.

Disagreements do not arise in the plenary sessions of the chambers because of the Party's use of the Council of Elders and the committee system. A Council of Elders (Sovet Stareishin) is formed in each chamber in accordance with custom and not on the basis of any constitutional provision. It has approximately 150 members and consists of leaders of groups of deputies from the various republics, territories (kraia), and provinces (oblasti). This body recommends to its chamber

---

[9]A. I. Lepeshkin, A. I. Kim, N. G. Mishin, and P. I. Romanov, *Kurs sovetskogo gosudarstvennogo prava* (Moscow, 1962), II, p. 395.

[10]*Ibid.*, II, 399–400, 412. See also D. L. Zlatopol'skii, *op. cit.* (above, n. 7), pp. 114–117, 201–202.

the candidates who are elected as chair and as vice-chairs (four) and the candidates who are elected to membership in the various standing committees. It also determines the agenda and approves the candidates of the various bodies and officials elected by the Supreme Soviet. Each Council of Elders is presided over by the chair of the respective chamber.

The committees—termed "commissions"—are identical in both chambers, although from 1957 to 1966 the Soviet of Nationalities alone had an Economic Commission, designed to take into account the particular needs of the republics in economic planning. The number of commissions was substantially increased in 1966 and made more specialized. Prior to 1966, both chambers had commissions on credentials, legislative proposals, the budget, and foreign affairs. The enlarged roster of standing commissions is indicated in the diagram on page 180. Most of the commissions deal with economic matters, although the Legislative Proposals Commission deals with all matters that do not come within the jurisdiction of other commissions. The commissions, which because of their large size also rely on subcommissions, are used to review bills that usually originate elsewhere. It is at the commission stage that amendments to a bill are more likely to be made and that additional relevant information is assembled and government officials and specialists are consulted. A unique feature of the Soviet commission system is the practice of referring a bill to more than one commission of the same chamber. Commissions often meet between sessions of the Supreme Soviet and have been given more attention in the media since the 1970s. The presence of identical commissions in each chamber enables them to hold joint sessions.[11]

The work of the commissions is "coordinated" by the Supreme Soviet's Presidium, and the two chambers can adopt legislation not considered by their commissions. Deputies do not initiate legislation as individuals. The vast majority of bills adopted by the Supreme Soviet are initiated by its Presidium or by the Council of Ministers (at times formally in conjunction with the Party's Central Committee) and by the Council of Elders. Very few bills have been initiated either by the commissions or by the union republics.[12] Informally, it is the Communist Party that determines whether any of these is to initiate a particular bill. Three quarters of the deputies serve as members of the standing commissions, and it is at this stage in the legislative process that actual debates can occur. However, Party Central Committee officials hold key positions on the standing commissions to make certain that Party policy prevails.

---

[11]For a discussion of the commissions' enhanced role, see Robert W. Siegler, *The Standing Commissions of the Supreme Soviet, Effective Co-optation* (New York: Praeger, 1982).

[12]Lepeshkin et al., *op. cit.* (above, n. 9), II, 411. On the controversy surrounding commission jurisdiction, see D. Richard Little, "Soviet Parliamentary Committees after Khrushchev: Obstacles and Opportunities," *Soviet Studies,* XXIV, No. 1 (July 1972), pp. 41–60. Article 113 of the 1977 Constitution authorizes initiation of legislation by the following: the two chambers, the Presidium of the U.S.S.R. Supreme Soviet, the U.S.S.R. Council of Ministers, union republic governments, commissions of the two chambers, deputies, the U.S.S.R. Supreme Court, the U.S.S.R. Procurator General, and the All-Union organs of mass public organizations. Such generous and all-inclusive provisions prompt comparison with Article 49 in the 1936 Constitution, which provided for country-wide referenda to be held and became a dead letter. The 1977 Constitution (Article 5) also includes such a provision for referenda for draft laws if invoked by the Supreme Soviet or by a union republic.

The process of enactment involves the presentation of the bill by a rappor-teur *(dokladchik),* and at times also by a co-rapporteur, who speaks on behalf of the initiating body. In the case of important bills sponsored by the Council of Ministers, they are presented by its chair or by ministers. All legislation concerning the budget is presented by the minister of finance. Voting on a bill becomes a mere formality in view of the practice of requiring unanimity; voting is on the bill in its entirety rather than on each article. The discussions on bills can hardly be characterized as a full-dress legislative debate, for the speeches of deputies are usually of a stereotyped nature.

Membership

The large membership of the Supreme Soviet would in itself severely limit the role of the deputy even if it were not circumscribed by the rigors of Party controls and by the brevity of the sessions. A person who is not a Party member has a very limited chance to become a deputy in view of the practice of electing approximately 70 percent of the 1,500 deputies from the ranks of the CPSU officialdom and membership. Thus, in the Supreme Soviet elected in 1984, 71.5 percent of the deputies were Party members, and another 15 percent were Komsomol members. Thus, the overwhelming majority of the Soviet population who do not belong to either the CPSU or the Komsomol are allotted only 13.5 percent of the seats in the Supreme Soviet. However, Soviet spokesmen can claim that no "bourgeois" legislative body has so many women in its membership as does the Supreme Soviet. The percentage of female deputies has risen from 16.3 percent in the Supreme Soviet elected in 1937 to 32.8 percent in the Eleventh Convocation elected in 1984.

The Supreme Soviet membership consists of persons from nearly all of the Soviet Union's non-Russian nationalities and from a great variety of occupational fields. In the Eleventh Convocation (1984–1989), 35.1 percent of the deputies were said to be workers, 16.1 percent were collective farmers, 13.2 percent of the deputies were government officials, and 3.7 percent represented the military. Party and Komsomol officials held nearly 17 percent of the seats. Usually a very high percentage of the deputies—three-quarters or more—have been decorated with orders and medals; this indicates that deputies are carefully recruited in the nominating process and that an effort is made to select persons of some distinction, including outstanding milkmaids, crane-operators, tractor drivers, coal miners, and factory workers.

Yet, the tenure of the average deputy is not at all secure. Only the Communist Party leaders and officials, high government officials, or nonpolitical eminent persons are likely to be reelected to the succeeding convocation of the Supreme Soviet. If the Soviet Union's rulers have quotas for the election of various groups of deputies, they have also established a high rate of turnover, eliminating as many as two-thirds of the deputies at successive elections by denying them nomination. Thus, in 1958, 62.3 percent of the Supreme Soviet deputies were newly elected; in 1966, the deputies who had not been previously elected constituted 65.4 percent of the membership. In 1984, 58.9 percent of the deputies were newly elected.[13]

It is evident that the position of deputy is viewed as an award that should be rotated in the case of rank-and-file deputies and conferred repeatedly only in the case of the regime's luminaries. Thus the renewal rate has been higher among female deputies and those who have less formal education and are not Party members, while older male Party members are more likely to be reelected.[14]

The honorific nature of the deputy's position is also confirmed by the modest emolument that is awarded. Deputies continue to receive their salaries at their place of employment while attending Supreme Soviet sessions or committee meetings. They are also reimbursed for certain of their expenses. Deputies wear an emblem that entitles them to immediate service; they need not wait in line anywhere. In addition, deputies are given free rail, water, bus, and air transportation throughout the country but must pay for taxis. However, they are subject to recall by the electorate in their constituency. Thus, if deputies should conduct themselves improperly or in some way lose the confidence of the Communist Party leaders who arranged their nominations, recall meetings are organized quickly, and removal from office is effected without difficulty. When Gorbachev removed important officials in 1986–1987, he also had them resign as Supreme Soviet deputies and held new elections for their successors.

Functions of the U.S.S.R. Supreme Soviet

Although Supreme Soviet deputies are hardly the "masters of the country" that the regime's pronouncements claim them to be, the Supreme Soviet performs certain important functions. Like the constitution, it serves as a source of legitimation by giving its approval to the acts and policies of the Soviet government. The Supreme Soviet enacts laws including constitutional amendments, organic laws that define the structure and jurisdiction of state organs, and a variety of ordinary laws. In addition, it enacts economic planning and budgetary laws, including tax measures. The Soviet government's fiscal year coincides with the calendar year; the state budget is usually adopted by December, although in Stalin's time it was adopted as late as the summer, when more than half of the fiscal year had expired. The annual and long-range economic plans have the force of law, even though the goals are not always fulfilled.

The Supreme Soviet also has the task of approving but not discussing the numerous decrees *(ukazy)* issued by, or in the name of, its Presidium during the lengthy periods when the "Soviet parliament" is not in session. The decrees are issued and signed by the Chairman and Secretary of the Presidium, are published within seven days, and have the force of law. The Supreme Soviet is thus presented with a series of *faits accomplis;* its approval of the decrees, while appar-

---

[13]V. Kotok, *op. cit.* (above, n. 7), p. 35, *The Soviet Parliament, A Reference Book* (Moscow: Progress Publishers, 1967), p. 41, and *Pravda,* April 12, 1984, p. 4.

[14]See Ronald J. Hill, "Continuity and Change in USSR Supreme Soviet Elections," *British Journal of Political Science,* II, Part 1 (January 1972), pp. 47–67.

ently necessary, can hardly be said to add appreciably to their legal force. Yet such formalities can be important, and the Supreme Soviet gives its approval with the usual unanimous vote. Often as many as half or more of the laws enacted by the Supreme Soviet are Presidium decrees that it summarily approves.[15]

The Supreme Soviet must give its approval to the appointment of the Council of Ministers (ratifying the entire slate of ministers at once) and to the establishment of new ministries and government agencies, along with the definition of their competence and jurisdiction. It approves the appointment of the Procurator-General of the USSR, the country's leading legal official, for a five-year term; it also elects the U.S.S.R. Supreme Court every five years. The Presidium of the Supreme Soviet must also be elected every five years so that the parent body's "supreme authority" can be readily exercised on a permanent proxy basis.

The infrequent sessions of the Supreme Soviet provide an opportunity for the public criticism of individual ministers and ministries whom the Party leadership has singled out for embarrassment. While this practice hardly demonstrates that the Supreme Soviet exercises initiative in performing a "control" function, it provides a useful means of occasionally calling an administrator to account without directing embarrassing questions to the Soviet executive or to the Party leadership. Although relatively few deputies are able to obtain recognition to address the Supreme Soviet, those who do so can use the opportunity to place in the stenographic record specific requests emanating from their constituencies. Such requests frequently deal with budgetary items, and they provide a means of bringing to the attention of particular ministries the needs and complaints of a republic, oblast', or city. The greater participation of deputies in the work of the standing commissions since 1966 has also provided opportunities for making officials in the Moscow ministries more aware of the concerns of the deputies' constituencies.

The deputy's post is not necessarily a sinecure, because constituents bring many complaints and requests to deputies in the hope of obtaining some support in their struggles with the Soviet bureaucracy. The conscientious deputy who can find the time must intercede with ministries and other departments and agencies in an effort to satisfy constituents' needs. The writer Ilya Ehrenburg, who served as a Supreme Soviet deputy from several constituencies, recounted how he obtained ambulances and buses for the city of Engels only after much effort, which he described as "trials and tribulations" *(khozhdenie po mukam)*. He would receive constituents on Sundays in the building of the municipal soviet, to which "hundreds of unfortunates" would come with every conceivable kind of request— grievances against the procuracy, housing needs, or a request for help to obtain an artificial limb. Yet Ehrenburg conceded that he was often unable to aid constituents.[16]

The Supreme Soviet provides a medium through which the regime can issue

---

[15]D. L. Zlatopol'skii, *op. cit.* (above, n. 7), p. 136.

[16]Ilya Ehrenburg, *Liudi, gody, zhizn', Sobranie sochinenii* (Moscow: "Khudozhesvennaia literatura," 1967), IX, pp. 678–680.

foreign-policy pronouncements and serves as a sounding board for its foreign minister. Joint sessions of the Supreme Soviet have approved declarations, appeals, statements, and messages dealing with particular problems and issues, expressing support for Soviet foreign policy, and denouncing the alleged "aggressive actions of international reaction." The usefulness of the Supreme Soviet in this respect has been especially evident since June 1955 with its participation in the Inter-Parliamentary Union. Soviet membership in that international body has given the regime greater respectability at home and abroad and has led also to the establishment of the Parliamentary Group of the USSR. Thus, although this organization of deputies mainly attempts to promote the Soviet Union's foreign policy objectives in the annual conferences of the Inter-Parliamentary Union, it also provides a means of promoting among its members greater awareness of their role as deputies.

The modest enhancement of the Supreme Soviet's role that has occurred in the post-Stalin period has not enabled it to compete effectively with the Communist Party apparatus as an initiator of legislation or as a source of authority to whom the highest office-holders are directly responsible.[17] The June 1988 CPSU Conference resolved that a new body, the U.S.S.R. Congress of People's Deputies, be established. It is to meet annually and have 1500 elected members and approximately 750 representing Communist Party, trade union, youth, and other organizations. It is to elect from its membership a standing bicameral Supreme Soviet of lesser size to legislate and direct administrative bodies. M. S. Gorbachev also obtained a strengthened executive (presidency) as part of the political "restructuring" of the system. The Supreme Soviet, in its enhanced role, could serve as a more effective monitoring and interest-representational body.

THE PRESIDIUM OF THE SUPREME SOVIET

The Soviet regime is somewhat unique in possessing a collegial chief of state or titular executive in the form of the U.S.S.R. Supreme Soviet's Presidium. This body—elected from its membership by the Supreme Soviet at a joint session for the duration of the convocation—consists of a chairman, one first vice-chairman, 15 vice-chairmen, a secretary, and 21 members (16 prior to 1966)—a total of 39 members. It performs many different functions and illustrates well the fusion in the Soviet system of legislative, executive, and even quasi-judicial powers in a single body.

The Presidium's role as a legislative body is exercised on the basis of powers delegated to it by the Supreme Soviet, although the 1936 Constitution solemnly proclaimed that "the legislative power of the U.S.S.R. is exercised exclusively by the Supreme Soviet" (Article 32) and the 1977 Constitution (article 108) states that "laws of the U.S.S.R. are adopted by the U.S.S.R. Supreme Soviet or by a

---

[17]For a discussion of the development of the Supreme Soviet and changes in membership, see Stephen White, "The USSR Supreme Soviet: A Developmental Perspective," *Legislative Studies Quarterly,* V, No. 2 (May 1980), pp. 247–274; reprinted in Daniel Nelson and Stephen White, eds., *Communist Legislatures in Comparative Perspective* (London: Macmillan, 1982), pp. 125–159.

referendum." The delegation of legislative authority is necessitated by the fact that the Supreme Soviet is in session but twice a year for only a few days. During the lengthy intervals between sessions, the Presidium can issue decrees (*ukazy*) and even amend the Constitution—as it did on October 10, 1945, when it raised the age requirement for deputies from 18 to 23 years, or whenever it would hastily create a new ministry or executive agency. It can provide instant legislation by issuing decrees on any matter, including taxation, economic policy, organization of industry, agriculture and transportation, and law enforcement. The Chairman and Secretary sign all decrees. The Presidium also issues ordinances *(postanovleniia),* which are designed to reinforce its actions in organizational and administrative questions. At times important decisions are adopted and enacted jointly by the Presidium and the U.S.S.R. Council of Ministers and the Central Committee of the CPSU. Although in theory the Presidium is accountable to the Supreme Soviet, in practice it exercises independent powers much of the time.

In addition to acting as an interim legislative body, the Presidium performs such functions as convoking regular and extraordinary sessions of the Supreme Soviet and in general supervising the work of the parent body and its commissions. It calls for new elections upon expiration of the deputies' five-year terms; it determines the constituencies for both chambers and approves the composition of the Central Election Commission. It appoints and dismisses ministers at the suggestion of the Chairman of the Council of Ministers when the Supreme Soviet is not in session. The Presidium also appoints and recalls ambassadors and receives foreign envoys accredited to the Soviet Union; it ratifies and denounces treaties, although this is a formality. The Presidium grants Soviet citizenship and can deprive persons of it or permit its renunciation; it can grant asylum. It also establishes and confers awards, decorations, and titles of honor.

The executive function of supervising the military is conducted by the Presidium. It appoints and removes the high command of the armed services, although the relevant decisions are initiated in the Party apparatus dealing with personnel. It establishes the U.S.S.R. Defense Council and confirms its membership. The Presidium fixes the order of service ranks and confers the rank of Marshal of the Soviet Union. It is empowered to order general or partial mobilization and can proclaim a state of war or martial law in all or part of the country in the interests of defense, public order, or state security.

The Presidium receives petitions for justice, exercises the right of pardon, and can issue partial or full amnesties. It performs an important function in receiving letters, appeals, complaints, and requests from ordinary citizens. Many of these communications are simply transmitted to the administrative agency concerned. The Presidium is in a position to collect a variety of information and proposals useful to the leadership of Party and government. It also serves as a means of ultimate resort by which the ordinary citizen might obtain redress of a grievance.

Although the Presidium is primarily a legislative and executive body, it also performs quasi-judicial functions. The Constitution states that the Presidium "gives interpretations of the laws of the U.S.S.R." (Article 121). In practice it is simpler for the Presidium to interpret laws by issuing new laws by decree. According to the Law on the Supreme Court of the U.S.S.R. of November 30, 1979 (articles 10 and 35), the Court "is responsible to and reports to the Supreme Soviet" and must also "report systematically" on its activities to the Presidium. The Court is also obligated to refer to the Presidium suggestions on matters that should be determined by legislative procedure and suggestions on questions of the interpretation of the laws.[18] The Presidium is empowered to annul acts of the USSR and union republic councils of ministers as well as orders and instructions of the U.S.S.R. Procurator-General that it finds contrary to law.

The Presidium publishes all of its own decrees and the laws adopted by the Supreme Soviet. These are to be found in the *Gazette of the Supreme Soviet of the USSR (Vedomosti Verkhovnogo Soveta SSSR);* the Presidium also publishes the newspaper *Izvestiia,* official organ of the Soviet government. The Presidium's staff records all changes in the laws, including those decrees and laws that have been rescinded or superseded.

In practice the Presidium is supposed to meet at least once in two months, although it is said to be a "continuously acting" body. Its meetings are not public, and little is known about them, although accounts of plenary sessions are published in *Vedomosti.* On occasion it has functioned through committees. It is very likely that when decrees have had to be issued without delay, they have simply been signed by the Presidium's Chairman and Secretary and have subsequently been approved by the entire body as a formality. It is evident that the Presidium's staff and its various departments (legal, awards and decorations, complaints) function on a permanent basis.

The Presidium's membership is rather diverse and is intended to reflect that of the parent body. It usually includes several women as well as members from ordinary walks of life (as, for example, a weaver, tractor driver, collective farm official), in addition to a number of republic and regional Party officials. The Presidium also includes a substantial number of non-Russian members as well as members and candidate-members of the CPSU Central Committee. However, tenure can be insecure, as demonstrated by the abrupt replacement of members who have lost important Party posts.

The leading Party Secretary (General Secretary of the CPSU prior to 1953 and since 1966) is a member of the Presidium if he is not also head of government as Chairman of the U.S.S.R. Council of Ministers. Thus, Khrushchev was a Presidium member until he became head of government in 1958, and Brezhnev remained a Presidium member after becoming First Secretary of the CPSU in 1964. This practice is designed to provide the Party chief with a nominal but quasi-prestigious position in the government so that he can participate in purely state and diplomatic functions as the occasion may warrant. On May 24, 1977, the CPSU Central Committee decided "in complete unanimity" that General Secretary Brezhnev should also hold the post of Chairman of the Presidium.

---

[18]*Konstitutsiia SSSR i razvitie sovetskogo zakonodatel'stva* (Moscow: "Iuridicheskaia literatura", 1983), pp. 272, 285. See also the Judiciary Law of February 12, 1957, in N. T. Savenkov, comp., and A. P. Kositsyn, ed., *Obrazovanie i razvitie Soiuza Sovetskikh Sotsialisticheskikh Respublik (v dokumentakh)* (Moscow: "Iuridicheskaia literatura," 1973), p. 543.

Although this decision was not publicized until the following month, it was announced in May that the Central Committee had "released Comrade N. V. Podgorny from the duties of Politburo member." Podgorny resigned the Presidium chairmanship, and on June 16, 1977, the Supreme Soviet unanimously elected Brezhnev to succeed him. The unusual step of combining the General Secretaryship with the position of Soviet head of state created a new precedent.

The precedent was adopted by Iuri Andropov and Konstantin Chernenko, each of whom became Chairman of the Presidium within a few months of becoming CPSU General Secretary. During the interim in each instance following the death of the General Secretary, the first vice-chairman of the Presidium fulfilled the responsibilities of head of state. However, Mikhail Gorbachev chose not to become head of state in 1985 upon becoming General Secretary and, instead, elevated Andrei Gromyko to the post of Chairman of the Presidium.[19]

The Chairman of the Presidium performs many of the ceremonial functions of a President, including, more recently, state visits to foreign countries. However, the use of a collegial body to fulfill the functions of chief of state places certain limitations on the Chairman's role. The Presidium is collegial because of the Soviet rationalization that collegiality is the equivalent of "democracy"—a position that conveniently ignores the crucial criterion of the accountability of a popularly elected president.[20] The multinational nature of the Soviet Union, however, provides a more practical reason for a collegial executive. The fifteen vice-chairmen of the Presidium represent the union republics; by custom they are the chairmen of the presidiums of the republic supreme soviets.

The Chairman of the Presidium, although a member of the Party's Politburo on what might be termed in practice an ex officio basis, has not always exercised the same power and influence. Such chairmen as Mikhail I. Kalinin (1938–1946), Nikolai M. Shvernik (1946–1953), and Kliment Voroshilov (1953–1960) were not members of the inner ruling circle, despite being Politburo members and chiefs of state. Certain Presidium chairmen such as Leonid I. Brezhnev (1960–1964 and 1977–1982), Anastas I. Mikoyan (1964–1965), and Nikolai V. Podgorny (1965–1977) have played important roles in policy making. Although the chairmanship has served both as a sinecure and as a figurehead post for a somewhat benign Party leader useful to the oligarchy as a front, its real and

---

[19]Such are the anomalies of the Soviet polity that American presidents have found themselves dealing with the principal Soviet leader who is neither head of government nor head of state. This occurred at summit meetings at Geneva in 1955 and 1985; at Moscow in 1972 and 1974; at Washington, D.C., and San Clemente, California, in 1973; at Vladivostok in 1974; at Reykjavik in 1986 and at Washington, D.C. in 1987. In each case the First or General Secretary of the CPSU held only a nominal governmental position as an ordinary member of the Presidium of the U.S.S.R. Supreme Soviet. This did not prevent him, however, from signing important international agreements in 1972, 1973, 1974, and 1987.

[20]During the discussion preceding the adoption of the 1936 Constitution, Stalin displayed a certain sense of humor when he expressed opposition to the popular election of the Presidium's Chairman on the grounds that such a president might counterpose himself to the supposedly omnipotent Supreme Soviet. Stalin reasoned that a collegial executive would be "most democratic" and subordinate to the Supreme Soviet. I. Stalin, *Voprosy Leninizma,* 11th ed. (Moscow: Gospolitizdat, 1952), p. 569. On the anomalous aspects of the Presidium's role, see D. Richard Little, "Legislative Authority in the Soviet Political System," *Slavic Review,* XXX, No. 1 (March 1971), pp. 57–73.

potential significance should not be ignored. In a highly formalized regime, any chief of state is in a position to exercise some degree of influence, and if the role of the Supreme Soviet should be enhanced, it is likely that the Chairman of the Presidium would gain as a result. However, enhancement of the authority of a governmental body would be at the expense of the Party apparatus; and the Soviet chief of state would, moreover, have a rival beneficiary within the central government in the person of its head, the Chairman of the Council of Ministers. The 1977 decision to have Brezhnev resume the post of head of state while retaining the top leadership position in the CPSU undoubtedly reflected the Party's concern over retaining control of the Soviet state and its governmental apparatus to prevent its developing into a rival force. The CPSU, while advocating some expansion of the role of the republic and local soviets, wishes to make certain that the unified system of soviets will serve its purposes.

THE U.S.S.R. COUNCIL OF MINISTERS

The government of the Soviet Union is usually equated with the Council of Ministers, which, according to the 1936 and 1977 Constitutions, is said to be the "highest executive and administrative organ of state authority." It is appointed by the Supreme Soviet at a joint session at the beginning of the first session of each new convocation, although ministers are obviously initially selected by the Party leadership and apparatus officials responsible for personnel. The practice of having the Council of Ministers go through the motions of resigning and of being formally reappointed is designed to provide an innocuous means of demonstrating its "responsibility" to the U.S.S.R. Supreme Soviet. Stalin, during the most frightening years of his brutal dictatorship, would perform this ritual of "resigning" as head of government as if to mock his subjects and "their" deputies, who had no choice but to sanction his reappointment.

While in terms of constitutional theory the Council of Ministers appears to function like a cabinet under the parliamentary system, in reality it has little to do with the "Soviet parliament." It oversees the functioning of a vast state bureaucracy and is supposed to carry out the Party's policies at the administrative level. It resolves legal problems in cooperation with the Presidium of the Supreme Soviet, and it initiates much legislation, although undoubtedly this is usually done at the Party's behest. The Council of Ministers supervises the development and fulfillment of the economic plan and the budget and is also responsible for credit, monetary, and price policies. It carries out the Party's policies in cultural and in military matters as well as in relations with foreign states. It also supervises a substantial part of the activities of the councils of ministers of the union republics and can annul those of their acts that it can claim fall within its own competence. It is responsible for public order and state security.

The Council of Ministers is empowered to issue ordinances *(postanovleniia)* and regulations *(rasporiazheniia)* based on its decisions in the areas within its competence. Ordinances are generally normative acts and are said to be collegial, while regulations usually are nonnormative, have a more specific and concrete application, and are simply signed by the Chairman or his deputy. Both kinds of acts are supposedly based on law, have the same juridical standing, are enforceable over the entire territory of the Soviet Union, and provide one of the bases for enactments of the governments of the union republics. Highly important matters are dealt with by joint ordinances adopted by the Central Committee of the CPSU and by the U.S.S.R. Council of Ministers.

The Council of Ministers is a large and unwieldy body and is required to meet at least once every three months. It is headed by a Chairman and includes one or more First Deputy Chairmen and as many as eight or nine Deputy Chairmen and numerous ministries, state committees, and other administrative agencies. The total membership has reached more than ninety. It includes as ex officio members the chairmen of the councils of ministers of the fifteen union republics; this unusual practice is based on a constitutional amendment of May 10, 1957, and was also incorporated into the 1977 Constitution. The types and varieties of ministries and government agencies are discussed in the following chapter.

The size of the Council of Ministers has made necessary the establishment of an "inner cabinet"—the Presidium of the Council of Ministers—which consists of the Chairman, First Deputy Chairmen, and Deputy Chairmen. Although such a body and its Bureau apparently existed in Stalin's time after 1946, the present Presidium was established in March 1953. Its relationship to the Council of Ministers was clarified in the law of July 5, 1978, which defines the Presidium as a "permanent organ of the Council of Ministers" (article 17). The Presidium directs the Council's work, determines its organization and composition, and exercises a special role in economic matters. It also operates through committees that confer with particular ministries before recommending the issuance of regulations by the Presidium. It is authorized by law to meet as frequently as circumstances require. The Presidium functions with considerable flexibility, and it frequently acts in the name of the entire Council of Ministers. There is also an Office of Administration of Affairs *(upravlienie delami),* which serves as a secretariat and monitors the work of the various ministries and considers complaints.[21]

The Chairman of the Council of Ministers is in a sense the "premier" or "prime minister" of the Soviet Union. However, the one-party system and the fact that the incumbent Chairman need not be the leading figure in the CPSU render the use of the term misleading. The Chairmanship has been held by Lenin, Stalin, and Khrushchev as well as by secondary leaders. As the first Chairman of the Council of People's Commissars (renamed Council of Ministers in March 1946), Lenin exercised great influence because of his generally undisputed role in the Party Politburo. His successor as head of government was Aleksei Rykov, who held the post from 1924 to 1929, when he was ousted from the Party for having participated in the "Right Opposition." Rykov was succeeded by Viacheslav Molotov, who served as Chairman from 1930 to 1941 and as foreign minister from 1939. (It suited Stalin's purposes to have the Soviet government headed by a colleague during the 1920s and 1930s, while he established and consolidated his

---

[21]N. A. Volkov, *Vysshie i tsentral'nye organy gosudarstvennogo upravleniia SSSR i soiuznykh respublik v sovremennyi period* (Kazan: izd-vo Kazanskogo universiteta, 1971), p. 34.

personal dictatorship as the Party's General Secretary.) Stalin retained the highest Party post and also headed the government from 1941 to his death in 1953. Georgii Malenkov held the Chairmanship from March 1953 to February 1955, when he was succeeded by Nikolai Bulganin, who served until March 1958. Nikita Khrushchev was Chairman and also CPSU First Secretary from 1958 to October 1964, when he was succeeded as head of government by Aleksei Kosygin.

Kosygin's tenure was nearly as lengthy as that of Brezhnev, with whom he shared power, extending from 1964 to 1980. Brezhnev selected as Kosygin's successor Nikolai Tikhonov, who had considerable ministerial experience and who headed the Council of Ministers from 1980 to 1985. Gorbachev as Party chief brought in a younger head of government, Nikolai Ryzhkov, who had managerial and ministerial experience and had also served in the Party Secretariat.

The Chairman is a member of the Politburo. Although he nominally heads the government apparatus, his position is not necessarily secure because of that fact. His influence in the Politburo may be limited, and his position may become untenable should he align himself with an unsuccessful opposition group within the leadership—as happened to Rykov and Bulganin. Chairmen have been summarily removed or demoted, as they do not have fixed terms of office. A Party chief who simultaneously heads the government undoubtedly has enhanced powers as well as greater prestige (and responsibility) than one who does not head the government. The head of government who has not made his career in the Party apparatus (Rykov, Molotov, Bulganin, Kosygin) may be especially vulnerable. He can be accused of opposing the government to the Party, of advocating or pursuing policies that are inimical to the Party, or of having perpetrated administrative failures.

The Chairmanship is potentially a powerful position if the incumbent should succeed in mobilizing the interests of the administrators and economic managers. It is also a position that could possibly retain its viability and prestige in the event that the party leadership were to experience a degree of fragmentation that would prove fatal. The Party apparatus seeks to prevent any independent development of the government by providing for an interlocking arrangement, under which most members of the Council of Ministers are also members or candidate-members of the Central Committee. Brezhnev, as Party Secretary after 1970, took to addressing the U.S.S.R. Council of Ministers in person, thus upstaging Chairman Kosygin while also playing the leading role in foreign policy. Party leaders have also assigned a Party official as a first deputy premier in order to keep the head of government under close surveillance and to serve in a liaison capacity. While such practices do not guarantee an identity of interests between Party and government apparatus, they appear to be based upon Lenin's advice to the Party's Tenth Congress to foster a "fusion" of the Party and soviet "summits."[22]

The Party's claim to primacy was reflected in the fact that Nikolai Tikhonov's letter of resignation (as premier) was addressed to General Secretary Gorbachev and not to Gromyko (to whom, as chairman of the Presidium, the

---

[22]V. I. Lenin, *Polnoe sobranie sochinenii, op. cit.* (above, n. 1), XLIII, p. 15.

premier is legally responsible). Yet it is the Presidium that had to formally accept the resignation and approve Ryzhkov as the new premier. The actual appointment or selection of the new premier was made by the Politburo, and the formal presentation of the nomination to the Presidium was made by Gorbachev.[23] This ritual reflected the formal as well as the actual subordination of the head of state to the General Secretaryship and of the Presidium to the Politburo.

SOVIET ELECTIONS: THEIR CONDUCT AND MEANING

Although the results of Soviet elections are already known prior to election day, the regime has nevertheless developed what is probably the most elaborate electoral system known to any one-party system. That this is not entirely a matter of sham and political ritual can be seen from the rationale for Soviet elections offered at the conclusion of this section. Soviet spokesmen and political writers frequently attack the electoral systems of Western European countries and the United States, presumably on the assumption that such attacks will somehow make the obvious fundamental defects in the Soviet system of elections less evident or more acceptable. They cite the phenomenally high percentage of voter participation in Soviet elections (uniformly claimed to be no less than 99 percent) as contrasted with other countries and contend that bourgeois elections are often determined by pluralities rather than by absolute majorities and that the suffrage is limited by residence and other requirements as well as by gerrymandering. The Soviet argument ignores the fact that Russian elections provide no incentive to gerrymander constituencies because the outcome is determined in advance through the nomination process. Advocates of the Soviet system, in effect, have asserted that a "genuinely democratic" electoral system is one that, like theirs, permits no choice between political parties or even between two candidates from the single ruling party.

The Soviet rulers have made suffrage general, equal, direct, and secret since 1937. Prior to the adoption of the 1936 Constitution, the suffrage was unequal (at the expense of the rural population), a small percentage of the population was disfranchised, only the lowest soviets were elected directly, while the higher soviets were elected indirectly and voting was open and by lists and not by secret ballot for individual candidacies; voting prior to 1937 was in electoral assemblies often convened in production enterprises. The right of suffrage now applies to all persons who are 18 years of age. The sole restriction in law is that mentally ill persons are denied the right to vote on the basis of legal certification of such a condition. There is no literacy test, although the Soviet Union is a country having a high rate of literacy. Persons under court sentence for crimes are not formally disfranchised, although they were denied the right to vote prior to a constitutional amendment adopted on December 25, 1958. Yet in practice prisoners are still denied the right to vote while serving sentences despite the abandonment of the constitutional provision providing for their disfranchisement.

---

[23]For the text of the letter of resignation and other statements, see *Pravda,* September 28, 1985, p. 1.

The nearly all-inclusive electorate votes for deputies to the various local soviets and to the republic and U.S.S.R. supreme soviets; it also votes for the judges of the courts of first instance, the People's Court. All other officials are appointed or elected by the various soviets. Under the 1936 Constitution, as amended, deputies to the U.S.S.R. Supreme Soviet had to be at least 23 years of age, while those elected to republic supreme soviets had an age requirement of 21 years and deputies to local soviets had to be at least 18 years of age. The 1977 Constitution fixed the age of eligibility at 21 years for deputies to the U.S.S.R. Supreme Soviet and at 18 years for lesser soviets.

The election of deputies to the various soviets is based on the single-member district, with one deputy from each constituency or election district *(izbiratel'nyi okrug).* In view of the fact that more than 2.3 million deputies are elected to more than 50,000 soviets ranging from villages to the U.S.S.R. Supreme Soviet, the number of overlapping constituencies is very great.[24] A voter must vote for one deputy to each of the two chambers of the U.S.S.R. Supreme Soviet and for one deputy to the unicameral supreme soviet of the union republic in which he lives. If he lives in an autonomous republic, he must vote for a deputy to its supreme soviet. He will also vote for a deputy to his oblast' or krai soviet, and if he lives in a city, he will vote for a deputy to the city soviet; if the city is large enough to be divided into boroughs *(raiony),* he must also vote for a deputy to the raion soviet. If he lives in a rural area, he will vote for the deputy to the oblast' or krai soviet but will also vote for a deputy to the rural raion (district) soviet and for one to his village soviet.

Nomination is tantamount to being elected and is accomplished not through primary elections but by means of a unique process. An individual cannot simply file for a deputy's seat and present the voters with his candidacy. Only "public organizations" such as the Communist Party's local organizations, trade unions, cooperatives, the Komsomol (Communist youth organization), "workers collectives," and military units can propose candidates for nomination, although in the less populous constituencies the individual's role may be somewhat less circumscribed by the nominating process. The qualifications of potential candidates are discussed in factory and other nominating meetings. The process, always conducted under the watchful eyes and pervasive tutelage of the responsible Communist Party officials, leads to an official public nominating meeting. This is a very formal public meeting in the large constituencies, complete with ceremony and entertainment. The candidate who has the Party organization's approval is nominated by acclamation, the matter having been decided in advance.

The nomination is then presented to the election commission for the particular constituency. The officials of the nominating meeting certify that it was conducted in accordance with the election statute, and the nominee agrees in

---

[24]The origins of the Soviet system of elections are discussed in George B. Carson, Jr., *Electoral Practices in the USSR* (New York: Praeger, 1955). For the results of a field study of Soviet elections, see Max E. Mote, *Soviet Local and Republic Elections* (Stanford, Calif., 1965). Also see Jerome M. Gilison, "Soviet Elections as a Measure of Dissent: The Missing One Percent," *American Political Science Review,* LXII, No. 3 (September 1968), pp. 814–826. Subsequent evidence revealed a higher percentage of dissent by means of election avoidance.

writing to accept the candidacy. In practice there has been but one candidate for each position. A major exception is the practice of also nominating prominent members of the Party leadership as supreme soviet deputies in certain constituencies. The number of such honorary nominations that a particular leader receives is significant, but all such nominations are declined, except for the one in the constituency that the leader will represent. Soviet election laws do not exclude the possibility of electoral contests within a single electoral district, but political practice has served to prevent the registration of more than one candidate for each position.

Registration of candidates is one of the functions of the election commission that is found in every constituency. Election commissions are also established in every precinct and are charged with the actual conduct of the particular election; their membership is unpaid, and thus elections cost very little. The commissions are appointed by the executive body of the soviet that is being elected; their volunteer membership comes from the same public organizations that participate in the nominating process and numbers more than 9.26 million persons for the entire country. Their administration of the electoral machinery is supervised by the All-Union Central Election Commission for elections to the U.S.S.R. Supreme Soviet and by republic central election commissions for the elections to republic supreme soviets and to local soviets.

The size of constituencies varies. The largest are for the election of deputies to the two chambers of the U.S.S.R. Supreme Soviet. The smallest has fewer than one hundred voters in the case of an average village or settlement soviet. The size of the constituencies for the Council of Nationalities varies with each republic, as does the size of the constituencies for the republic supreme soviets. The boundaries of the constituencies for each soviet are determined prior to each election by the executive body of the soviet that is being elected.

The lack of electoral contests does not preclude election campaigning. The network of agitators is fully activated during the ten days preceding the election. Agitators must visit voters in the precinct and explain the virtues and qualifications of the candidates. The mass media publicize the biography of each candidate to the larger soviets and urge a resounding vote of confidence for the regime. The candidate spends no money campaigning but holds meetings with voters; in the smaller constituencies the voters are able to apprise the candidates of their needs and expectations, although the latter cannot usually offer very effective assurances that such wishes will be heeded during their term of office. While such meetings do provide one means of determining the grievances of a particular constituency, they are also used to explain and justify the Party's policies.

The voting is administered by the electoral commission of several members that functions in each precinct *(uchastok)*. Lists of voters prepared by the commission on the basis of local records are posted in public prior to the election and are subject to correction. Elections, which are held on Sunday, have a festive quality. The voter's identity is ascertained by means of the domestic passport, the possession of which is required by law, and he or she is given as many ballots as there are candidates (and positions to be filled). The printed form of the ballot provides space for more than one candidate, and the voter is instructed to cross out all names except that of the candidate for whom he or she is voting; but in practice each ballot has had only one name. Thus, the voter has no need to go into a booth, except possibly to cross out the name of the sole candidate as an act of protest or to inscribe a message to the Soviet leadership—and this can attract unfavorable attention. Indeed, the ballot need not be marked but can simply be deposited in the ballot box; very few Soviet voters use the booths. A write-in candidacy as an alternative to the Communist Party's candidate would be futile and is not recognized by law because only organizations can nominate candidates and each nomination must be registered by the appropriate election commission. Crossing out the name of the candidate and writing in the name of another is regarded as invalidating the ballot.

The high percentage of voter participation in Soviet elections is due to the practice of checking off the names of those on the list of voters who have voted (thus the authorities know who has not voted). Usually most persons vote by mid-afternoon; but if it is evident that the voting is slow, activists are dispatched to call on those who have not yet voted and remind them of their civic obligation. Refusal to vote is regarded as an unpatriotic act. Even the sick are expected to vote, and ballot boxes are brought to the bedsides of hospital patients. Voting occurs on ships that are at sea on election day if there are at least twenty-five voters aboard; the votes are added to those cast in the ship's home port. Passengers on long-distance trains vote in special precincts while in transit.

A unique feature of Soviet elections is the provision for absentee voters, who, before embarking on their journey, apply for a certificate that they present at the polls wherever they may be on election day. Thus, the absentee voters vote not for the candidates in the several constituencies in which they actually reside but for the candidates on the ballot in the precinct in which they happen to present themselves. Election commissions in resort areas have had to print additional ballots in order to accommodate the influx of voting tourists. Under such a system it is possible for the candidate to obtain more than 100 percent of the (registered) vote in a constituency. The practice of being able to vote in a constituency in which you do not reside obviously demeans the concept of a mandate conferred on a deputy by constituents. In the view of the Soviet rulers, whom one votes for is not important; what is important is that a person votes somewhere to register support of the regime.

In practice the Soviet system of absentee voting provides a means of election avoidance that has been revealed by former Soviet citizens. This is accomplished by the voter's requesting an absentee voting form and then not using it. Such an absentee voter is not listed among participating voters in his or her place of residence but is not added to the list in any other constituency. Such election avoidance reflects a refusal to participate in elections that are regarded as a sham and that are viewed with indifference, cynicism, or contempt. Confirmation has been provided by the substantial statistical discrepancy between the number of persons of voting age and the number of persons reported as voting. The size of the nonvoting population has been conservatively estimated to be at least 2.5 percent of the electorate but is probably higher, especially in the larger urban areas.[25] Apart from the absentee voters who choose not to vote, there is a large group that probably does not vote but that is reported as having voted. Election officials apparently have no difficulty in stuffing the ballot box on behalf of nonvoters, as voting consists simply of placing unmarked ballots in the box.[26] Thus, it is evident from firm statistical evidence that there is some degree of falsification of official Soviet election results and that voter participation, while high by any standards, is not as high as officially reported.

Despite the fact that candidates are unopposed and are reportedly favored by 99 percent of the voters, a minute fraction of the candidates fails to obtain a majority of the votes cast. This usually occurs only in small constituencies at the village or settlement level where the candidate is well known to the electorate and does not enjoy its confidence despite the endorsement given him or her by local CPSU officials. In such cases—there were more than two hundred in the 1961 and 1965 elections to local soviets—a second election must be held in those constituencies after a new candidate has been nominated. In elections to local soviets (below the union republic level) in 1975, of more than 2.2 million deputies only 68 failed to receive an absolute majority of the votes. In the 1987 local elections, with more than 2.3 million deputies elected, 1076 candidates failed to obtain a majority.[27] The odds of a candidate's being rejected by the voters are very small, but they do demonstrate that the Soviet nominating process is imperfect. The regime's principal leaders fare even better, for they are assured election not only to the U.S.S.R. Supreme Soviet but to republic soviets as well.

Recall of deputies is provided for both by the 1977 Constitution and by a law of October 30, 1959. Recall can be initiated by any of the public organizations that nominate deputies or by "assemblies of workers." Deputies can be recalled for having engaged in conduct unworthy of their position or for having lost the confidence of constituents (in practice, the confidence of the ruling hierarchy in the case of larger constituencies). Meetings of voters are convened in enterprises, institutions, farms, military units, and housing developments, and the recall proposal is voted on by a show of hands; a special election commission determines whether or not a majority of the voters in the constituency favor the recall. The practice of recall is another means of disciplining deputies and keeping them dependent.

---

[25]See Theodore Friedgut, *Political Participation in the USSR* (Princeton, N.J.: Princeton University Press, 1979), pp. 116–121, and Victor Zaslavsky and Robert J. Brym, "The Structure of Power and the Functions of Soviet Local Elections" in Everett M. Jacobs, ed., *Soviet Local Politics and Government* (London and Boston: George Allen & Unwin, 1983), pp. 70–71.

[26]A Canadian communist who studied at the Kiev Higher Party School of the Communist Party of Ukraine from 1963 to 1965 was told by a poll clerk: "We simply stuff ballots into the boxes and strike off the names of those who have not voted until there are enough to give the necessary ninety-nine percent." See John Kolasky, *Two Years in Soviet Ukraine* (Toronto: Peter Martin Associates Ltd., 1970), p. 46.

[27]*Izvestiia*, June 21, 1975, p. 2 and *Vedomosti Verkhovnogo Soveta SSSR* No. 26 (2412), July 1, 1987, p. 503. Of the 68 candidates rejected by voters in 1975, 64 were in village or settlement soviets, 3 in city soviets, and 1 in a raion soviet. Of the 1076 candidates rejected by voters in 1987, 74 were in raion soviets, 28 in city soviets, 5 in urban raion soviets, 105 in settlement soviets, and 864 in village soviets.

Soviet elections do serve certain functions despite their general failure to give the voter a choice between candidates, political parties, and alternative policies. The ritual of voting is maintained because the regime must hold elections of some kind in order to give itself the appearance of being democratic. Although the outcome of Soviet elections is never in doubt, the elected representatives who sit in the numerous soviets can claim to enjoy popular support, as demonstrated in their victory at the polls. The election campaign permits the Party to explain its policies and to justify the correctness of its actions. The holding of such plebiscitary elections enables the Party to claim that its policies have earned the overwhelming—and for their purposes unanimous—support of its subjects. By regularly holding such rituals of acclamation, the regime can assert that its mandate to rule has been renewed. Elections are also used as a means of supposedly demonstrating the "unparalleled moral-political unity" of Soviet society. It is probably for this reason that electoral contests, even between communist candidates, were not held as they would nullify this mass exercise in contrived unity. The elections also have a psychological significance if the voter is not permitted to boycott the balloting ritual but must participate and make a commitment to the regime. Thus, the voter is periodically reminded by means of this mass loyalty test and exercise in assent that there is no alternative to the Communist Party and its rule and that dissent is not permitted.

If Soviet elections require no manipulation, apart from assuring the high turnout, the same cannot be said of the nominating process, where a behind-the-scenes choice is actually made. At that stage an effort is made to select a candidate who will inspire public confidence and who has achieved recognition in his or her profession or vocation. The purpose is to select as deputies people who will generate support for the policies and contribute to their implementation. Deputies to the various soviets are not genuine legislators, insofar as they do not initiate bills and are not policy makers. However, the regime endeavors to nominate and elect to the soviets the "best people," who will then endorse the government at each level and approve its conduct. Nomination and election as a deputy is both a reward and a duty, but it does not confer power. Those deputies who hold administrative posts in the government and in the CPSU apparatus do wield power, but not by virtue of their elective positions as deputies. It is in the Party and government bureaucracies that decisions are made, and it is the elected soviets that are responsible for their fulfillment.

Gorbachev introduced limited and indirect electoral contests by forming some multimember constituencies on an "experimental" basis in the 1987 elections to local soviets. They comprised approximately one percent of the constituencies and were mostly at the village level but also included city and raion constituencies. Use of multimember constituencies (in which one or two candidates fail to get elected) provides limited choice in lieu of direct electoral contests between two opposing candidates. However, it could also mean erosion of the oligarchy's nomenklatura system if it ceased to be experimental. Genuine, as opposed to cosmetic, changes in the Soviet electoral system can provide a significant means for determining systemic change in the Soviet Union.

chapter 7

Administration: Central, Republic, and Local

The Soviet polity has what is probably the world's largest and most complex series of integrated bureaucratic structures. The Soviet bureaucracy functions by means of numerous ministries and related agencies, as well as government corporations and state-owned economic enterprises. Soviet society is highly administered, and the influence of the center is felt throughout the country. Each soviet below the republic level has an executive committee *(ispolkom)* that, in theory, supervises the administrative departments required by its particular jurisdiction and economy. In practice these departments are also subordinate to the corresponding body at the next higher level and indirectly are subordinate to the appropriate ministry or agency of union republic or All-Union jurisdiction. The size and scope of the Soviet administrative apparatus, its responsibility for managing the state-owned economy, and its many distinctive features set it apart from the more conventional administrative structures found in constitutional systems.

THE RUSSIAN ADMINISTRATIVE TRADITION

Historically, Russian public officials served an imperial political order at the discretion of the ruling autocrat or of persons capable of influencing, or acting in his or her name. Officials were not responsible to the public but to a regime upon which they were utterly dependent—but one that also gave them considerable authority in dealing with its subjects. Although their authority could be withdrawn abruptly should they be discredited, the powers exercised by local officials were sufficient to promote arrogance, arbitrariness, inefficiency, and corruption. The condition of the Russian bureaucracy was reflected in Russia's defeat in the Crimean War and in the Russo-Japanese War and in the events antecedent to the 1905 Revolution. The lack of an effective administrative apparatus resulted, furthermore, in the shortages of food and munitions that played such an important role in bringing about the Russian collapse in 1917.

Russians and the non-Russian subject peoples have traditionally been at the mercy of an officialdom against the excesses of which they have had little redress. The autocrat, whose good intentions they were willing to assume, was unapproachable in a distant capital but presumably would remove overbearing and corrupt officials once aware of their conduct. The centralism of the autocratic order and the nature of its officialdom deprived its subjects of any opportunity to identify effectively with the political order. Thus, there developed an attitude—often still evident in the Soviet Union—of viewing the regime, the administrative apparatus, the system of controls, and the rulers as "they." This term has been used to refer to the entire communist establishment and its all-pervasive bureaucracy that constantly pries, hinders, interferes, and makes unreasonable demands and that must be placated or deceived in various ways.

The distrust of bureaucracy and the "we"–"they" dichotomy have found expression both in classical Russian and in Soviet literature. The satirization of Russian provincial officialdom achieved prominence in Gogol's comedy, *The Inspector-General,* and the tradition was continued by Saltykov-Shchedrin, who was himself an official and therefore had to employ "Aesopean" language in his satires. The stories of Nikolai Leskov, who was also in the civil service, contain unflattering portraits of officials. The tradition of ridiculing the bureaucrat has been perpetuated under the Soviet regime by such writers as the humorist Mikhail Zoshchenko and the novelists Mikhail Bulgakov and Vladimir Dudintsev.

The Soviet regime has followed certain of the administrative patterns established by the imperial regime. The collegial form of ministry was introduced by Peter I and was used until the reign of Alexander I, when, in 1802, the collegium was initially reduced to subordinate status and, in 1811, abolished under the influence of Speransky. Significantly, Lenin restored the collegial principle in a form comparable to that existing between 1802 and 1811 with the collegium subordinate to the minister. Both the tsarist and Soviet regimes followed the principle of recognizing a division of functions but not a separation of powers. In neither the imperial nor the Soviet system has legal training figured prominently in preparing persons for public service.

In local government both regimes have exercised wide powers. The tsar appointed provincial governors, who enjoyed considerable autonomy although they could be arbitrarily dismissed. The Soviet counterpart of the provincial governor is the first secretary of the oblast' committee of the CPSU. Thus, the local administration has represented the central government more often than it has served as an agent of local assemblies.

THE SOVIET BUREAUCRACY

Although the Soviet regime abounds with Communist Party, government, and economic officials and managers, it finds the term "bureaucracy" distasteful because it stubbornly refuses to admit the obvious: that it actually is a form of "government by officials." Instead, the term *apparat* is used to refer to administrative structures and officialdom and is generally synonymous with Western usage of the term "bureaucracy," in a dispassionate and technical sense. Marxism viewed bureaucracy as a system of rule having a class basis, while Lenin held that socialism would put an end to bureaucracy, replacing it with a "democratic apparatus." Thus, in *State and Revolution* (1917), Lenin envisaged socialism as "accounting and control" with officials paid no more than workers and subject to instant recall. All were to become bureaucrats so that there would be no bureaucrats. Yet within five years Lenin, on December 30, 1922, was to lament the fact that the Soviet apparatus was "borrowed by us from tsarism and only barely annointed with Soviet chrism." Lenin also referred to "that truly Russian type, the Great Russian chauvinist, essentially a scoundrel and an oppressor, which is the typical Russian bureaucrat."[1]

In order to identify the unfavorable traits of officialdom, the Soviet lexicon employs the term *bureaucratism,* which is synonymous with the use of "bureaucracy," as an epithet. The phenomenon of bureaucratism, under attack since Lenin's time, includes red tape, delay, inefficiency, preoccupation with formalities and routine, apathy, "loss of contact with the masses," and neglect of the people's needs.[2] The Soviet press abounds with criticism of bureaucratism and such related practices as evasion of responsibility and falsification of reports. Bribery and reliance on "family-type relationships" *(semeistvennost')* that involve mutual accommodations at the regime's expense have been frequently condemned; "localism" *(mestnichestvo),* the promotion of local interests at the expense of the center, has also been a problem for the Soviet rulers. The Russian term *ochkovtiratel'stvo* is used extensively in the Soviet Union and means "throwing dust in someone's eyes"; its literal definition is "to smear someone's eyeglasses so as to obscure his vision" and is used to refer to efforts to hoodwink one's superiors and the regime. It is comparable to *pokazukha* or "window-dressing." The vice of *vedomstvennost'* ("departmentalism") has been acknowledged and added to the Russian language; the term means placing the interests of one's department ahead of those of superordinate agencies. *Administrirovanie* is condemned as rule by administrative fiat. Other abuses include nepotism, cronyism, pilfering, embezzlement, and bribery.

The need to combat such dysfunctional practices requires that the regime closely control personnel and be able to transfer it at will. This is done by means of the Party's ability to deploy administrative cadres through use of the nomenklatura system, under which there are lists of specific positions to be filled at the various administrative levels only with the approval of the corresponding Party body. The Ministry of Finance has a Central Administration of the Civil List *(Tsentral'noe shtatnoe upravlenie)* that determines personnel classification and

---

[1]V. I. Lenin, *Polnoe sobranie sochinenii,* 5th ed. (Moscow, 1964), XXXXV, p. 357.

[2]*Kratkii politicheskii slovar',* 2nd ed. (Moscow, 1969), p. 47. The third edition of this political dictionary claims that socialism makes possible the elimination of bureaucratism by "socialist democracy," "attracting the masses," and "criticism and self-criticism." See *Kratkii politicheskii slovar',* 3rd ed. (Moscow, 1983), p. 36.

fixes the number of employees and the size of the wage and salary fund. The Administration does not recruit personnel, as this is done by the agencies themselves, but it does set standards. The Finance Ministry also seeks to eliminate superfluous positions and administrative units both in the government and in the economy.[3] Soviet officials are subject to many restrictions. Superiors are responsible for the level of achievement of their subordinates, and both are responsible for disregarding orders and regulations that are contrary to the law.

Although the regime confers various awards and honors on state employees, it also insists that they bear full "administrative, disciplinary, criminal, and material responsibility" for those of their acts that are said to be illegal. State employees can be required to compensate with up to three months' salary for damage or loss inflicted on the state; this amount is fixed either by an administrative act or through a judicial determination. If state employees inflict loss or damage upon a citizen or public organization, they are liable only if their act involves "abuse of authority" *(zloupotreblenie vlasti),* nonfeasance, or neglect; however, this must be determined by a court. Officials are not liable if they can claim that they erred while acting in good faith, although they may still be subject to disciplinary action of some kind. In general, it is difficult for a Soviet citizen to obtain redress against the administrative acts of officials. The provisions in the 1977 Constitution (articles 57 and 58) that appear to protect citizens against officials who exceed their authority or infringe citizens' rights give to complainants the right to seek the aid of the courts. However, such judicial redress must be exercised "in conformity with the procedure and within the time limit established by law." Thus, Soviet courts are not likely to develop independently a body of law that will protect citizens against officials.

Soviet administration is unique not only because of its size but because it does not distinguish between public and private administration; consequently it is public administration *par excellence.* Soviet bureaucracy is a consequence of the Party's hostility to spontaneity and its belief that everything should be organized and nothing left to chance. Although the chief bureaucrats denounce bureaucratism, Soviet officialdom proliferates excessively, establishing unnecessary positions, turning out endless memoranda and communications, and seeking to justify its existence.[4] Because of its sheer magnitude Soviet bureaucracy manifests to a greater degree the pathology that often characterizes administration: endless delay, evasive responses, reluctance to accept responsibility because of fear of the possible consequences, arbitrariness, blind application of rules, and unresponsiveness to human needs. It is also distinctive because the Soviet administrator operates under a system of multiple controls of a magnitude and variety not encountered in more conventional polities. The rulers distrust the administrators and managers and have found it advisable to place them under frequent surveillance.[5] However, various forms of evasion and protective measures have been developed to outwit superiors and to conduct "business as usual."

---

[3]A. E. Lunev, ed., *Administrativnoe pravo* (Moscow: "Iuridícheskaia literatura," 1970), pp. 81–83.

[4]See *Khrushchev Remembers, The Last Testament* (Boston: Little, Brown, 1974), pp. 115–116.

[5]For further discussion of the Soviet bureaucracy, see the section on the bureaucratic model on pages 345–348.

TYPES OF CONTROLS

The surveillance of Soviet officialdom is conducted at all levels, both by Party and governmental bodies. While each of these inspection agencies is not operating in the same administrative unit simultaneously, it is reasonable to assume that Soviet administrators cannot be certain when they might be called to account and what the consequences might be. However, the size and complexity of the Soviet bureaucracy often work to the advantage of the administrator and to the disadvantage of the "control" bodies. It is not always possible for the latter to uncover the often subtle and concealed forms of evasion and corruption employed by administrators. While much remains undetected, the errant administrator is dealt with summarily when found out unless protected by powerful protectors.

Party Controls

Party loyalty and political reliability have always been important criteria in Soviet personnel assignments, although technical and professional qualifications have been given increased importance with the development of the economy. The notion of the politically neutral civil servant has been alien to Soviet public administration. However, the Party does not rest with the appointment of its members to all positions of trust and responsibility in the governmental and economic apparatus. They are subject to the surveillance of the primary party organizations whose role and functions were discussed in Chapter 4; for among those functions is the task of checking on the fulfillment of Party decisions. In production and commercial enterprises the primary party organization is required to advise the management on the means best suited to fulfill the concern's objectives; it is also required to inform the Party raikom or gorkom of conditions in the enterprise that require attention. In the state apparatus the primary Party organizations are expected to alert the superior Party body, so that it can deal with the problem through the appropriate governmental administrative channels. However, there is no assurance that a primary party organization will function effectively or that it will not engage in collusion either with plant management or with government officials.

By way of confirmation, Mikhail Gorbachev complained to the Twenty-seventh CPSU Congress in 1986 that the Central Committee needed to "resolutely enhance the role of the Party committees of ministries and departments." He conceded that Party committees in a number of ministries "are still using their right of supervision very timidly and cautiously and . . . are not catalysts of the new, of the struggle against departmentalism, paper-shuffling and red-tape."[6] This indicates that the loyalty of the government bureaucrat to the bureaucracy tends to override loyalty to the Party officialdom. The primary party organization becomes less the effective instrument of the Party organization and more a body that government officials can manipulate. The Party members are ministry officials, and their futures are more likely to be determined by higher ministry

---

[6]*Pravda,* February 26, 1986, p. 9.

officials than by the Party bureaucracy. Caution is more likely to reward the Party members than efforts to reform their superiors.

The Party and governmental bureaucracies are separate entities, and, in theory at least, the Party develops policies and monitors performance, while the government is charged with carrying out the policies. Yet there is an inescapable comingling of Party and government. This is seen in the membership of the Politburo and the Central Committee, wherein a "fusion" occurs. There is also, to a degree, an "interchangeability" of personnel. Prominent Party officials such as, for example, Aliev, Andropov, Chebrikov, and Ustinov have been transferred to key government positions in an effort to make certain that the Party's will is being heeded.

However, there also persists the danger of what Party officials have termed *podmena* (substitution)—the tendency of the Party to intervene excessively, to assume (or usurp) government functions and economic management, and to supplant government. The consequences of podmena were confirmed at the Twenty-seventh Party Congress when Moscow Party First Secretary Boris Yeltsin complained that Central Committee departments have tended to become "almost copies of ministries" with a "widespread duplication of Gosplan, [and] the Council of Ministers." Yeltsin contended that the Organizational and Party Work Department was neglecting its principal function—the selection of cadres and their evaluation—and was, instead, concerned with nearly everything else, including "railroad cars, fodder, and fuel."[7]

Although the Party presumably does not consciously seek to usurp governmental functions, it nevertheless is drawn into the web of management because of its unwillingness to delegate sufficient authority despite its being unable to oversee effectively the entire bureaucracy. Indeed, the Party has created more than it can effectively control.

Governmental Control Bodies

In the Soviet lexicon the term *control* is employed to mean verification in the nature of an audit or a check on performance and the fulfillment of decisions. It does not imply the ability of the control body to direct or restrain the administrative or production organization that is under its surveillance. Various bodies have exercised this function on behalf of the U.S.S.R. government since the early years of the Soviet regime. The Commissariat of Workers' and Peasants' Inspection *(Rabkrin),* headed by Stalin from 1919 to 1922, was the first such formal body. On Lenin's advice, it was subsequently merged with the Party's Central Control Commission, but both bodies later functioned separately; Rabkrin exercised financial "control" from 1926 to 1933, when this function was restored to the Commissariat of Finance. Rabkrin was abolished in 1934 by a decision of the Seventeenth Party Congress. As the economy developed, Rabkrin's efforts to intervene in all sectors proved ineffective.

---

[7]*Pravda,* February 27, 1986, pp. 2 and 3.

The reduced functions of Rabkrin were performed by a Commission of Soviet Control, attached to the U.S.S.R. Council of People's Commissars, which had its plenipotentiary representatives in the locales; these officials were not responsible to the union republic governments, as there was no comparable body within that jurisdiction. The All-Union Commission of Soviet Control was charged with overseeing the fulfillment of governmental decisions and functioned largely through the ministries. The Commission was itself renamed the Ministry of State Control and was later headed by the secret police official V. N. Merkulov (a lieutenant of Lavrentii Beria) in 1950–1953 and by V. M. Molotov in 1956–1957.

In August 1957, the Ministry was renamed Commission of Soviet Control, and similar bodies were established in the union republic councils of ministers. These agencies sought to find unused or hoarded reserves and to promote economies, eliminate shortcomings, and defend state interests. They could issue instructions to the organizations and enterprises subject to their inspection directing that they cease the violations and rectify the shortcomings uncovered. The commissions were also to inform the appropriate ministry and could impose financial penalties on persons responsible for losses suffered by an organization.

In November 1962, the Commission of Soviet Control was replaced by a Party-State Control Committee, which functioned until December 1965 and was headed by Aleksandr Shelepin, a CPSU Secretary and Politburo member. Despite its title, this body confined itself to the inspection of state agencies and did not inspect the Communist Party apparatus or replace the Party Control Committee. However, it did possess broad powers and could fine, demote, and remove officials.[8] It endeavored to develop "control from below" with mass participation by part-time volunteers numbering five million. This "control" arrangement was the offspring of Khrushchev's economic and Party reorganization of 1962 and could not long survive his ouster in 1964.

The fact that the Party-State Control Committee was headed by a prominent CPSU official like Shelepin raised the possibility that he could develop a personal power base in this mass organization possessing broad and discretionary inspection authority. During 1965, it became necessary to resolve the question of whether or not this central governmental inspection body would operate independently of the CPSU organization or whether local Party officials would truly control the local "control committees." Party Secretary Brezhnev won the conflict over control of appointments and made certain that the "control committees" would direct their efforts under the guidance of the Party.[9] Shelepin was eased into the lesser position of chairman of the All-Union Council of Trade Unions. In December 1965, the Party-State Control Committee was replaced by a "Committee of People's Control" headed by a Central Committee member.

---

[8] See Howard Swearer, "Who Controls Whom?" *Problems of Communism,* XII, No. 4 (July–August 1963), pp. 46–50; and Jan S. Adams, "People's Control in the Soviet Union," *Western Political Quarterly,* XX, No. 4 (December 1967), pp. 919–929.

[9] The nature and form taken by this conflict is documented in Christian Duevel, "The Dismantling of Party and State Control as an Independent Pillar of Soviet Power," *Bulletin, Institute for the Study of the USSR* (Munich), XIII, No. 3 (March 1966), 3–18.

Brezhnev asserted that this body would not inspect the work of Party organs. The chair of the Committee of People's Control is a member of the U.S.S.R. Council of Ministers.

Committees of People's Control also exist at the republic, oblast', raion, and city levels. In village soviets and in enterprises and on collective farms, there are "control groups and posts" that aid the Party and the administration. They are elected in open voting and function under the local control committee. The control function is designed to promote "state discipline" and legality. "Control committees" can request documents and issue instructions calling for the elimination of shortcomings. They can also issue reprimands and impose fines whenever the state has suffered a material loss, but the latter sanction is exercised only with the approval of an oblast' or republic control committee. Committee sanctions are limited to noncriminal offenses. The control function seeks to focus the light of publicity on managers and administrators and is designed to promote fulfillment of the economic plan. It also promotes a surrogate democracy, for it is conducted in the interests of the toilers and with their participation.[10]

The control function seeks to promote efficiency, reduce costs, increase labor productivity, improve quality, and increase output. Yet it can be asked whether these objectives can be accomplished more readily by delegating sufficient powers to management or by promoting the activities of a mass of controllers who often duplicate existing inspection and auditing arrangements. "People's control" has been known to disrupt operations; thus, it can be questioned whether such large numbers of controllers possess the knowledge and experience needed to audit complex operations and to introduce more efficient methods.

A number of other governmental agencies also perform specialized inspection functions. The State Planning Committee (Gosplan), found in the U.S.S.R. Council of Ministers and in those of the union republics, exercises broad inspection powers in determining fulfillment of the economic plan. It is also charged with enforcement of "state discipline" in production matters. Gosplan has the aid of the state committees for statistics (formerly the Central Statistical Administration), an agency of ministerial rank in the U.S.S.R. and republic councils of ministers, which collects statistical performance data and sets standards for evaluating accounting records.

Financial Controls

The promotion of economies is the responsibility of the U.S.S.R. Ministry of Finance and its counterparts in the union republic councils of ministers; the U.S.S.R. State Bank also exercises financial controls and promotes "financial discipline." The Control and Auditing Administration within the Ministry of Finance plays a key role in checking on the observance of the U.S.S.R. state budget. It also oversees the work of the state insurance system, the savings banks, and banks of long-term deposits. The accounts of all ministries and other agencies

---

[10]For a study of the system of "people's control committees," see Jan S. Adams, *Citizen Inspectors in the Soviet Union* (New York: Praeger, 1977).

and organizations are subject to audit. The union republic finance ministries also have control and auditing units, which inspect the accounts of the republic ministries and their subordinate organizations and enterprises.

The U.S.S.R. State Bank is responsible for overseeing the use of financial credits and the rate of accumulation of capital. In enterprises that are experiencing excessive losses, it can impose a special accounting regime for credits and disbursements and can insist that the agency responsible for the enterprise guarantee the loan. In the absence of such a guarantee the State Bank refuses to grant new credits and seeks recovery of funds already lent. It can declare such an enterprise to be insolvent if the special financial regime fails to restore solvency, and it can then use the enterprise's receipts to satisfy creditors.

Legal Controls

The principal role in the application of legal controls is played by the Procuracy. This is the centralized and unified system of state's attorneys that is headed by the Procurator-General of the USSR. This official is the government's chief legal officer, is elected for a five-year term by the U.S.S.R. Supreme Soviet, is responsible to the Supreme Soviet or its Presidium, and is, in theory at least, not a part of the executive. The Procurator-General appoints the procurators of the union republics, autonomous republics, provinces, and territories for five-year terms and confirms the appointment of area (okrug), district, and city procurators (who are appointed by the procurators of the union republics).

The Procuracy is authorized to exercise surveillance or "supervision" (nadzor) over all activities of ministries and their agencies to determine whether their acts are in accordance with Soviet law. This power extends to the operations of economic enterprises and to the organs of local government. The Procuracy can demand that any administrative agency submit to it any order, instruction, decision, regulation, ordinance, or other act to determine its legality. Such acts can be protested by the Procuracy, and the protest must be considered by the responsible ministry, agency, or superior body within ten days. However, the Procuracy is not empowered to annul orders and decisions of administrative bodies; in the event, though, that there is a violation of the criminal code, prosecution of officials can be instituted. It can also recommend that disciplinary measures be employed. The Procuracy is aided by the silent surveillance exercised by the Soviet security police. The Procuracy can submit representations to a ministry or to the Council of Ministers regarding the circumstances and conditions that lead to illegal acts, and that body is required to take action on the causes within one month.

The vagueness of the Procuracy's powers in dealing with administrative decisions that are based on a liberal interpretation of the law and its inability to discipline errant administrators directly limit its role as a guardian of "legality." However, its ability to influence the Soviet courts does give it an effective sanction whenever there is the possibility that a basis for criminal prosecution exists in a case. Since the Procuracy functions under the direction of the Communist Party's Administrative Organs Department and is also an agency of the Supreme Soviet and its Presidium, it can be expected to serve both Party and state interests. There is no system of administrative courts in which the aggrieved Soviet citizen can sue officials or obtain redress for alleged wrongs and damage suffered as a result of arbitrary acts. The citizen can protest to the official and to the Procuracy, but the latter can only present the matter to the Council of Ministers, which has the last word. Officials can be sued in the courts only for a limited group of acts, such as illegal dismissal of an employee, eviction from a dwelling, illegal imposition of disciplinary penalties, and inaccuracies in public records.[11]

A form of legal control is also provided by the system of state arbitration *(Gosarbitrazh)* established by Stalin in 1931 and which is not part of the regular judicial system. It provides a special type of administrative court that adjudicates disputes between economic enterprises concerning deliveries, accounts, the quality of goods, and the interpretation and fulfillment of contracts. Arbitration bodies are attached to each executive organ, from the U.S.S.R. and republic councils of ministers to the executive committees of oblast' soviets and of such cities as Moscow and Leningrad. The entire system of arbitration functions under the supervision of the Chief Arbiter of U.S.S.R. State Arbitration, who is appointed by the U.S.S.R. Supreme Soviet for a five-year term. Arbitral panels are appointed by the executive; when a dispute arises, each litigant designates a representative, and an arbiter is also named. Decisions of such panels are final, except that the chief arbiter in each jurisdiction, acting either on self-initiative or on a petition for review, can suspend a decision within one month. The chief arbiter reviews the legal basis and evidence for the decision and can then sustain it or modify or abrogate it or order a rehearing.[12] The review of an arbitral decision can also be undertaken by the executive agency to which the arbitration organ is attached. The costs of arbitration are borne by the litigants and determined by the arbitral body.

While legal principles are supposed to govern Soviet arbitration, it has in practice been influenced by criteria of economic policy and plan fulfillment. Arbitral bodies can declare contracts void in whole or in part if contrary to law and can also require performance under a contract. When evidence of serious violations of law is uncovered, the arbitration bodies refer the matter to the Procuracy. The arbitration body of the U.S.S.R. Council of Ministers takes only the most important cases involving institutions or organizations of different union republics or of All-Union subordination or those cases brought at the request of union republic councils of ministers; it also generalizes arbitration experience for the benefit of the lower arbitral bodies.

There is also a system of intraagency arbitration *(vedomstvennyi arbitrazh)*, under which disputes arising between enterprises and organizations of a particular ministry or agency are resolved by its own arbitral body; as in state arbitration, discussed above, the chief arbiter designates one arbiter, each party to the dispute appoints a representative, and together they arbitrate the dispute. A form of ad hoc arbitration *(treteiskii sud)* was introduced in 1960 and has acquired popular-

---

[11]A. E. Lunev, ed., *op. cit.* (above, n. 3), pp. 254–255.
[12]A. A. Dobrovol'skii, ed., *Arbitrazhnyi protsess v SSSR* (Moscow: izd-vo Moskovskogo universiteta, 1973), pp. 199–200.

ity. The dispute is often heard by one arbiter only who is acceptable to both parties and is either an economic management specialist or a lawyer. Decisions by ad hoc bodies are binding and enforceable by state arbitration bodies; they can be appealed to the chief arbiter only on the basis of their being contrary to law. The three types of arbitration keep property disputes between enterprises and state organizations out of the regular courts and also provide a fairly rapid means of administrative adjudication that functions under executive control. Arbitration also serves to uncover various administrative shortcomings.

The Soviets

In theory the standing commissions of the various elected soviets are regarded as able to exercise a form of control. They are specialized bodies whose number and membership vary with the size of the soviet; a village soviet will have several commissions, a raion or city soviet will have approximately 10, and an oblast' or krai soviet can have as many as 15. Commissions deal with such matters as local industry, budget and finance, education, cultural affairs, health, communal economy and welfare, and commerce. Although commissions as such have no special powers and are merely organs of the parent soviet, they can investigate any matter that comes within the competence of the soviet and verify the work of the institutions and enterprises responsible to the executive body of the particular soviet.

In practice, the role of the soviets as watchdogs over administrative agencies is severely circumscribed. There are several reasons for this. As part-time legislators, the deputies are not likely to acquire the kind of expertise needed to understand and scrutinize the ways of administrators. The budgetary powers of the lower soviets are limited, and their independent taxing powers are nonexistent; thus, the deputies cannot exercise the power of the purse that is normally used by a legislative appropriations committee over administrators.

The soviets are also limited by the nature of their system, which strictly subordinates lower soviets to higher soviets—and in practice subordinates them to the executive committee of the higher soviet. Since the executive and administrative organizations of each lower soviet are also subordinate to those of higher soviets, each administrative department of a soviet's executive committee can thus claim a certain degree of independence from its own soviet on the grounds that it is responsible to the department of the same name attached to a higher soviet and, ultimately, to a union-republican or All-Union ministry. The principle of "dual subordination"—subordination to both the soviet of an administrative unit's own jurisdiction and a higher administrative body—severely limits the soviet's role as a controlling organ.

The 1977 Constitution asserts that the "soviets of people's deputies . . . constitute a single system of organs of state authority" (Article 89). The emphasis on "state authority" is significant, for it effectively excludes the CPSU, which is formally not a part of the state and is an authority unto itself. Thus, the ultimate subordination of the soviets to the CPSU apparatus is implicitly sanctioned in the constitution. Yet the Party leadership has repeatedly sought to activate the more than 2.3 million deputies to the various soviets in an effort to obtain their aid in generating support for Party and government policies and in helping to monitor the performance of government officials and economic managers.

MINISTRIES AND RELATED AGENCIES

State ownership of the economy in the Soviet Union has made necessary the establishment of a great variety of ministries and other governmental agencies. Their number and the names of many of them have been subject to fairly frequent change despite the fact that they were established by constitutional amendment under the 1936 constitution. The 1977 constitution does not include lists of ministries by categories, as did the 1936 constitution. Instead, ministries are identified in the July 5, 1978, Law on the U.S.S.R. Council of Ministers, and it must be amended whenever there is any change in the name or status of a ministry. Originally, these bodies were called commissariats, at Trotsky's suggestion, in order to emphasize the regime's uniqueness and revolutionary nature. However, Stalin decided to adopt the "bourgeois" term *minister,* and this was done on March 15, 1946. The move was rationalized on the grounds that various local bodies were also termed commissariats and that it was advisable to use the conventional term *ministry* to clarify the status and competence of the union and republic agencies of government.

There are *three types* of ministries in the Soviet Union: the All-Union, Union-Republican, and Republic ministries. The All-Union ministries are to be found only in Moscow and are exclusively in the jurisdiction of the USSR; they function directly over the entire territory of the Soviet Union and do not operate through republic ministries of the same name, although they may have field offices. Examples of All-Union ministries are foreign trade, defense, merchant marine, railroads, and a variety of industrial ministries—including aviation industry, chemicals, electronics, shipbuilding, machine-building, and defense industry. The second type of ministry, the Union-Republican, is a joint type found both in the U.S.S.R. Council of Ministers and in the union republic councils of ministers. Each such ministry in Moscow functions in the field through the union republic ministries of the same name. The Union-Republican category includes such ministries as foreign affairs, culture, finance, public health, higher and specialized secondary education, communications, agriculture, internal affairs, light industry, and a variety of economic ministries. The third type of ministry is found exclusively at the republic level and includes social insurance, communal (municipal) economy, and vehicular transportation and highways.

The U.S.S.R. Council of Ministers consists of ministries of the first and second categories, while the union republic councils of ministers consist of ministries of the second and third type. Ministries have been transferred abruptly from one category to another. Foreign Affairs was in the first category until 1944, when it was placed in the second group. The Ministry of Justice was shifted from the second to the third category in 1956 and was abolished by 1963; however, it was reestablished as a ministry of the second type in September 1970 as part of an anticrime campaign. The Ministry of Internal Affairs (MVD) was transferred from the second to the third category in 1960 and was subsequently renamed Ministry for the Protection of Public Order (MOOP). However, in July 1966, MOOP was restored to the second category and became a joint Union-Republican ministry; and in 1968 it was again renamed the MVD. The practice of changing the status of ministries reflects the apparent need to enhance control by Moscow or to encourage local initiative in an attempt to find more effective solutions to problems.

Some ministries of the first and second type have been consolidated or divided at times. The regime has also employed a variety of "state committees" that are supra-agencies charged with planning, coordinating, and verifying the work of ministries dealing with common problems. Examples are Gosplan, the State Planning Committee, and *Gosstroi,* the State Committee for Construction, as well as the U.S.S.R. state committees for foreign tourism, standards, inventions and discoveries, forestry, and foreign economic relations. Those committees that are "of the Council of Ministers" have the status of ministries, while others have had subordinate status, indicating that they are "attached to the Council of Ministers."

The various special agencies that are below ministerial status include state committees, committees, main administrations, and a council. Such agencies are established by the Council of Ministers and not by the Supreme Soviet, as ministries are. The functions for which they are established are too specialized and of insufficient importance to be given ministerial status, and the heads of such agencies are not members of the Council of Ministers but have the right to speak at its meetings. The special agencies have included the State Committee on the Uses of Atomic Energy, the State Committee for Safety Inspection in Industry and Mining, the Committee for Physical Culture and Sports, the Main Administration for Geodesy and Cartography, and the Council for Religious Affairs.

The Committee of State Security provides an example of a "committee" that is actually a powerful ministry of the second (Union-Republican) type and that has subordinated to it "committees" of the same name in the republic councils of ministers. Cinematography, for instance, is a Soviet Governmental endeavor that has been at various times a separate ministry, a unit in the Ministry of Culture, and a state committee. The civil air fleet (*Aeroflot*—the government-owned Soviet commercial airline) was organized as a Main Administration (*glavnoe upravlenie*) attached to the Council Ministers until 1964, when it was given the status of an All-Union Ministry of Civil Aviation. These examples illustrate the variety of organizational forms available to the governmental leadership and the flexibility with which they are sometimes employed.

The importance of individual ministers varies with the ministries headed by them. Certain ministers have enjoyed rather long tenure and have a degree of technical expertise, while others have held ministerial posts on a "probationary" status. In general, a career in the governmental apparatus is not compatible with one in the Party apparatus, and it is relatively rare to find a Party secretary or Central Committee department head appointed to a ministership. Women have rarely served as ministers, although in the post-Stalin period they have headed the ministries of health and culture. Ministers are generally members of the

Central Committee of the Party and are usually deputies to the U.S.S.R. Supreme Soviet.

The minister bears sole responsibility for the conduct of the ministry's work before the Council of Ministers and is indirectly responsible to the Supreme Soviet. This is in accordance with the principle of "unitary headship" *(edinona-chalie)* advocated by Lenin, which is supposed to assure effective and rapid action and the fixing of responsibility. The principle of collegiality is also recognized and finds application in the institution of the collegium *(kollegiia),* which is found in each ministry. The collegium has from 9 to 11 members and consists of the minister (who presides over its meetings), several of the deputy ministers (usually numbering from two to five), and the heads of important departments. The collegium is expected to meet at least once every ten days to discuss important questions affecting the ministry's work, but it is not to involve itself in operational matters. Collegium decisions can be carried out only by an order *(prikaz)* issued by the minister, because the collegium as such has no authority. In the event of disagreement, the minister alone makes the decision but is required to inform the Council of Ministers of this. Members of the collegium can appeal the matter to the Council of Ministers, although the likelihood of this occurring is not great.[13]

THE QUESTION OF SOVIET "FEDERALISM"

The question of whether the Soviet Union can be regarded as a federal system is one of considerable importance for an understanding of the nature of the Soviet polity. If something resembling a federal system was adopted by Lenin and Stalin, it was in reluctant recognition of the linguistic and cultural diversity of the population and the vast size of the country over which they ruled. Of course, the federal device was also adopted in order to facilitate pursuit of the goals of military defense and expansion and to restore Moscow to the status of an "imperial" capital. Indeed, the 1977 Constitution (Article 73) provides for the admission of "new republics" to the USSR. The Soviet Union is at least a quasi-federal system insofar as it consists of constitutionally recognized territorial units (the union republics) that exercise certain functions, with the distribution of powers between the republics and the central government defined in the constitution.

However, there are many features of the Soviet system that in practice qualify or even nullify its federal character. It can be asked whether federalism, a political order that emerged in democratic systems, is possible under a system of party dictatorship that frequently denies political rights to those who openly question its policies. The application of the adjective "federal" to the Soviet Union is of limited validity if only because the meaning of the Russian term *soiuz* ("union," but sometimes translated as "federal") is vague and can be used to refer to a loose alliance of sovereign states or to a very close union; the choice of this

[13]N. A. Volkov, *Vysshie i tsentral'nye organy gosudarstvennogo upravleniia SSSR i soiuznykh respublik v sovremennyi period* (Kazan: izd-vo Kazanskogo universiteta, 1971), pp. 120, 124.

ill-defined term with reference to the Union itself and to union republics contributes to the lack of a precise definition of the powers of those republics.

In practice, Moscow has encroached upon the union republics in a variety of ways. The republics have no independent taxing power, although their ministries of finance are used to collect revenues for the taxation monopoly enjoyed by the Union. The budgets of the republics are subordinate parts of the unified All-Union budget that reflects the countrywide economic plan. The centralism that characterizes the Soviet taxation, planning, banking, and budgetary systems is also evident in the Communist Party organization, which expressly rejects federalism. The non-Russian-republic Party organizations enjoy no more real powers than do oblast' Party organizations within the Russian Republic. Such organizations are expected to carry out the will of the center even when this conflicts with the interests of their republic. Thus, centralism in the Party has vitiated Soviet federalism. If there is no sphere of activity that is immune to Moscow's ultimate control, the federalism is nominal at best. Genuine federalism gives the members of the federation complete independence within their own exclusive sphere that must remain inviolable if the federal compact is to be honored.

Soviet "federalism" is characterized by a division of powers that leaves few matters exclusively within the jurisdiction of the republics; it is a division that can be and has been shifted to the center's advantage with ease. The numerous powers that are directly exercised by Moscow through the All-Union ministries and indirectly through the joint Union-Republican ministries make it possible for the center to intervene in nearly all of the activities of the republics.[14] The republics are not even permitted to appoint their principal legal officers, the procurators, who are instead appointed by the U.S.S.R. Procurator-General; as a result Soviet centralism in the legal field is unparalleled.

The 1977 Constitution reflected a further shift in the division of powers at the expense of the union republics to the advantage of Moscow. The fact that the Constitution no longer lists the various ministries according to type means that the division of powers is less precise. The enumerated powers granted to the All-Union government in Article 73 are very broad and provide for a single governmental budget, "assurance of unity of legislative regulation over the territory of the U.S.S.R.," and include an elastic clause covering "other [unspecified] questions of All-Union significance" that Moscow can use to enhance its already ample jurisdiction. The 1977 Constitution does not contain any list of significant enumerated powers granted to the union republics. Republics are to participate in All-Union governmental bodies and have their own constitution; they can determine administrative divisions within their territory and cannot have their boundaries changed without their consent. The skewed nature of the division of powers is evident in a count of the total number of joint ministries (of the second category) among all the republics, which was 322 ministries and 88 state commit-

---

[14] I. N. Ananov, *Ministerstva v SSSR* (Moscow, 1960), p. 92, note, and p. 171, states that the U.S.S.R. Union-Republican ministries have at times brusquely interfered in the republic ministries of the same name, even to transferring personnel.

tees. By contrast, the total number of ministries of exclusively republic jurisdiction (the third category) was 172 ministries and 12 state committees.[15]

While the 1936 Constitution (Article 15) referred to the "sovereignty" of the union republics, the 1977 Constitution (Article 81) simply refers to their "sovereign rights," which are supposedly protected by the USSR. The noun *sovereignty* in the 1977 Constitution (Article 75) is limited to the USSR and is said to extend over its entire territory (which is said to be unitary) and to include the territory of the union republics. The right of union republics to enter into foreign relations, conclude treaties, exchange envoys, and participate in international organizations (Article 80) is greatly diminished or contradicted by Article 73, which gives the USSR the right to "establish the general order and coordination of the relations of union republics with foreign states and international organizations." No republic has exchanged ambassadors, and only Ukraine and Belorussia participate in international organizations; neither republic was permitted by Moscow to sign the 1975 Helsinki Final Act. The 1936 Constitution, as amended in 1944, contained a provision (Article 18B) that remained a dead letter but supposedly permitted union republics to maintain their own military formations and have defense ministries; no such provision was included in the 1977 Constitution.

Union republic institutions must conform to a common pattern imposed by the central government. With the adoption of the 1977 Constitution, the republics were told by Brezhnev that they would also be required to adopt new constitutions that would reflect the latest style of constitution drafting as practiced in Moscow.

The union republics are essential components of the Soviet administrative system and the economy. Thus, Soviet federalism has developed the institution of the Permanent Representation that each non-Russian union republic has in Moscow for its dealings with the U.S.S.R. Council of Ministers. In addition, the Iakut A.S.S.R. has a mission in Moscow because of the vast size of this republic's territory and its distance from the Soviet capital. These permanently staffed offices or missions represent the republics in the economic planning and budgetary processes and in the discussion of draft ordinances and regulations adopted by the U.S.S.R. Council of Ministers. They also provide a means of contact between the various union republics and a medium for the defense of republic interests.[16]

An important characteristic of genuine federalism is the right of the states or provinces to participate in the process of formal constitutional amendment in a role apart from their membership in the federal legislature. If a federal legislature alone has the right to amend the constitution, this can be detrimental to the component parts of the federation and can endanger their existence.[17] In the

---

[15]V. I. Semenkov and V. I. Shabailov, eds., *Ministerstva i gosudarstvennye komitety i vedomstva soiuznoi respubliki* (Minsk: "Nauka i tekhnika", 1984), p. 22.

[16]On the development and functions of this Soviet institution, see Peter J. Potichnyj, "Permanent Representations (Postpredstva) of Union Republics in Moscow," *Review of Socialist Law,* Vol. 7, issue 2 (June 1981), pp. 113–168.

[17]See William S. Livingston, *Federalism and Constitutional Change* (London: Oxford University Press, 1956), pp. 13–14, 298–302.

Soviet Union the Supreme Soviet or its Presidium amends the constitution and has done so on numerous occasions. The republics are accorded separate representation in the Soviet of Nationalities, but the republic governments and legislatures play no role in the amendment of the U.S.S.R. Constitution. Thus, there is no Soviet counterpart to the provision in the American amending process that requires three-quarters of the states to ratify amendments through their legislatures or by special conventions. By denying the governments or populations of the union republics a special and direct role in the amending process, the Soviet constitution fails to protect the republics' rights and maintain a fixed division of powers.

The federalism of the Soviet Union has been further attenuated by the fact that Moscow is the Union's capital. Instead of establishing a new capital on relatively neutral territory, in a separate federal district, Lenin selected the traditional seat of Russian despotism and absolutism as the seat of his regime. It is revealing that the Supreme Soviet of the Russian S.F.S.R. meets in the same chamber in the Kremlin in which the U.S.S.R. Supreme Soviet holds its joint sessions. While this fact may reflect the all too frequent Russian attitude expressed in the idiomatic phrase "vse ravno" ("it's all the same"), it also reveals a lack of appreciation of constitutional distinctions.[18] Indeed, the presence of a dominant member in the federation, like the Russian Republic, leads to an imbalance in the federal relationship and creates the condition for the subversion of the federal principle.

There is no right of judicial review that can be invoked by the union republics in defense of their powers against encroachments by the central government. The U.S.S.R. Supreme Court does not hear constitutional cases, and there is no judicial body above the All-Union government to which union republics can appeal in defense of their constitutional rights. The Presidium of the U.S.S.R. Supreme Soviet can annul decisions of the councils of ministers of the union republics "if they do not conform to law." Thus, the republics have no recourse when their interpretation of their constitutional powers might conflict with that of the central government. Nor are there any provisions governing the nature of the federal system that are specifically exempted from amendment.

Although federal systems vary greatly, they do share certain common characteristics. It is evident, therefore, that the Soviet Union possesses many features of a unitary system and falls short of qualifying as a genuine federal system.[19] Yet even a quasi-federal system such as the Soviet Union is comparable to authentic federalism in being a compromise between homogeneity and diversity, centralism and secession, integration and the preservation of identity. Such compromises are neither easily maintained nor necessarily stable and are reflected

---

[18]Certain U.S.S.R. ministries and agencies (e.g., internal affairs, communications, the KGB, and the state committee for television and radio) serve as Russian Republic ministries. See N. A. Volkov, *op.cit.* (above n. 13), p. 113, and V. I. Semenkov and V. I. Shabailov, *op. cit.* (above n. 15), p. 24.

[19]Theofil K. Kis, *Le fédéralisme soviétique, Ses particularités typologiques* (Ottawa: editions de l'Université d'Ottawa, 1973), pp. 174–175.

in changing institutional structures and in the kinds of tensions that have characterized ethnic relations in the Soviet Union.

REPUBLIC AND LOCAL ADMINISTRATION

Although the union republics are said to be "independent" and "sovereign"—
apart from the vast enumerated powers held by the central government—they
constitute an integral part of the countrywide administrative system. The majority of ministries are either joint (Union-Republican) or republic bodies; consequently, most of the business of Soviet government is conducted through ministries that are to be found in the republic councils of ministers. However, the
Union-Republican joint ministries function in conformity with directives issued
by the U.S.S.R. ministry of the same name in Moscow, and hence their administrative competence is subject to limitations and change because of their "dual
subordination" to the republic and to the Union.

The government and administration at the union republic level manifest
many of the features that characterize the central government. The unicameral
republic supreme soviets function in a manner similar to that of the U.S.S.R.
Supreme Soviet, meeting but twice a year in regular sessions; their presidiums,
while varying in size, investigate questions and complaints referred to them by
deputies regarding the activities of ministries and government agencies. The
presidiums issue decrees, interpret the laws of the union republics, and can
rescind ordinances and regulations issued by the republic councils of ministers
as well as the decisions of lower soviets. Councils of ministers of union republics
can rescind decisions and regulations of the executive committees of oblast' (and
krai) soviets as well as the orders and instructions of its own ministries.

The union republics are said to be "sovereign" and "independent," when
in fact they enjoy little more than autonomy. The autonomous soviet socialist
republics are said to possess "state-political autonomy" and to enjoy "self-government in internal affairs." Lesser autonomous units—such as the autonomous
oblast' and the national area *(okrug)*—are said to enjoy "administrative-political
autonomy," though they lack the status and trappings of statehood conferred on
soviet republics.

The autonomous soviet socialist republics have their own constitutions
(which must be approved by the supreme soviet of the union republic in which
they are located), supreme soviets, presidiums, supreme courts, and councils of
ministers. To these attributes of "nonsovereign statehood" can be added separate
representation in the U.S.S.R. Supreme Soviet's Soviet of Nationalities. However,
autonomous republics do not have the state seal and flag that union republics are
permitted to have. Unlike the union republics, the autonomous republics do not
possess the "right" to secede from the Soviet Union. Their councils of ministers
include a number of the ministries to be found in the union republics, such as
health, culture, education, social security, finance, the KGB, and others.

Most of the autonomous republics are in the Russian S.F.S.R. and vary
greatly in size of territory and population. Among the more populous autonomous republics are the Tatar, Bashkir, Daghestan, Chuvash, Komi, Mordovian,

Chechen-Ingush, and Karelian republics. Although six of the union republics were once autonomous republics or part of such republics, it is unlikely that others will be given such status. The presence of autonomous republics within the Russian S.F.S.R. does not make it a federation—despite the use (or semantic abuse) of the adjective "federated" in its name.[20] The claim that the Russian Republic is a federation is negated by the fact that it does not consist of coequal autonomous republics; the autonomous republics comprise but part of the R.S.F.S.R. and are not accorded separate and equal representation in its supreme soviet (representation is based exclusively on population). The lack of a bicameral legislature in the Russian Republic also confirms the spurious quality of its federation.

The "autonomous oblast' " is not to be confused with the ordinary oblast'. It represents a form of administrative autonomy based on the recognition of numerically small nationalities that occupy fairly large regions. It is subordinate to the government of a territory (krai) or directly to a union republic. The autonomous oblast' has a statute *(polozhenie)* that distinguishes it from the ordinary oblast' and provides for recognition of its nationality. Unlike the ordinary oblast', it has separate representation in the U.S.S.R. Soviet of Nationalities and can delimit its districts (raiony). Most autonomous oblasts' are in the R.S.F.S.R. and are included in territories (kraia). Thus, the Jewish Autonomous Oblast', which has attracted very few Jews, is located in the Khabarovsk krai on the Sino-Soviet frontier. Tuva, located on the frontier of the Mongolian People's Republic—and itself a "people's republic" prior to October 1944—became an autonomous oblast' when it joined the Russian Republic during World War II; in October 1961, it became the Tuvinian Autonomous Soviet Socialist Republic— one of several such Turkic republics.

The least of the ethnic autonomous administrative units is the "national area" *(okrug)*. They have been established for the numerically small peoples of the Soviet Far North and Far East, who inhabit large and sparsely populated areas. They are actually multinational units and are included within regular oblasti and kraia. Each such area has one deputy in the U.S.S.R. Soviet of Nationalities. It differs from the autonomous oblast' in not having a separate statute for its legal basis (instead, a single law pertains to all national areas). The administration of the krai or regular oblast' in which the national area is located exercises greater powers over it than are exercised by the krai over the autonomous oblast'.

The ordinary oblast' is the most numerous of the important units of Soviet administration, both in Party and governmental organization. The more than 120 oblasti and the far less numerous kraia (territories) occupy a crucial place in the hierarchy of Soviet administrative jurisdictions. They are subordinate to the union republic governments (in the R.S.F.S.R. and the other union republics that

---

[20]The adjective was initially introduced by Lenin in 1918 to provide a means of reintegrating seceded non-Russian territories while paying lip service to national self-determination. The formation of the USSR in 1922 rendered the federal form of the Russian Republic largely redundant, reducing it to a type of semantic abuse. See Walter R. Batsell, *Soviet Rule in Russia* (New York: Macmillan, 1929), pp. 61 and 81 and Chapter III.

are divided into oblasti); but they, in turn, are superordinate in relationship to the raiony (districts) and to the cities of oblast' subordination. The smaller union republics—like Estonia, Latvia, Lithuania, Moldavia, and Armenia—do not have oblasti but are divided into raiony. The raion (comparable to a county) has within its jurisdiction towns, the *poselok* (settlement), and villages. The workers' settlement is a populated area usually near a factory, mine, electric station, or railroad center.

Local administration functions in the name of the soviet or council that is popularly elected at each level in the administrative hierarchy. Formally known as the "soviets of workers' deputies" under the 1936 Constitution and as "soviets of people's deputies" under the 1977 Constitution, these bodies vary in size and in the frequency of their meetings. Oblast' and krai soviets have 100–300 deputies and meet at least once every three months. Raion (rural) soviets have 40–80 deputies, while poselok and village soviets are usually half that size; both hold bimonthly meetings. City soviets have from 50 to several hundred deputies, although the Moscow city soviet has more than 1100 members—far too many to function as a conventional city council. If the city is large enough to have boroughs (raiony), they also have soviets.

The local soviets must approve their annual budgets and the economic plan for their jurisdiction. They also determine the use to which land (all of which is state-owned) shall be put, although they cannot readily prevent location of a large factory dictated by central planners. The local soviets directly administer many important economic enterprises and provide a variety of public services. Each soviet elects an executive committee *(ispolkom)* that is a body of "dual subordination" being responsible both to its own soviet and—more significantly—to the executive committee of the next superior soviet, which can annul its decisions. The entire structure of soviets is rigidly hierarchical and is based on the subordination of one soviet to another. (See Figure 4.1, page 129.)

The executive committee serves as the interim decision-making body when its soviet is not in session—which is most of the time. It administers the local budget and is responsible for the fulfillment of the economic plan and for law enforcement. It directs the subordinate administrative agencies—the departments *(otdely)* and administrations *(upravleniia)* that are found in all soviets at and above the raion level. Although their number and nature vary, the departments and administrations at the oblast' level usually include the following: health, social security, education, finance, communal economy, culture, road construction and maintenance, trade, internal affairs (police), agriculture, local industry, and construction as well as a planning commission. Oblast' and krai departments and administrations are subordinate not only to their executive committee but to the appropriate union republic ministry. Departments of raion soviets are subordinate to the oblast' departments of the same name.

Oblast' and krai executive committees have organizational-instructional departments that inspect and oversee the work of subordinate soviets. "Instructors" are sent to the local soviets to organize elections and meetings of deputies with constituents and to train newly elected deputies—of whom there are many. These instructors conduct preparations for the infrequent sessions of the soviets and aid in the organization and work of the standing commissions. Deputies in the soviets are expected to explain the regime's policies to their constituents and to win their support; instructors check on the effectiveness with which deputies fulfill this task. Instructors also work with the staffs of subordinate soviets, conveying to them relevant decisions of the oblast' soviet executive committee and supervising their handling of complaints and requests received from citizens. They aid in the organization of the agendas of the executive committees. Seminars are organized for the chairs, vice-chairs, secretaries, and staffs of lower soviets in an effort to improve their qualifications.

City soviets and their executive committees are subordinate to the government of a raion, oblast', krai, or republic—depending upon their size and significance.[21] Municipal soviets in the larger cities are responsible for a wide range of activities and have administrations or departments for housing, housing renovation, capital construction, retail trade, various sectors of local industry, public health, water and sewage systems, gas, heat and electric power, streets and bridges, public transportation, parks, education, and social security. Municipal administration includes "culture"—the functioning of reading rooms, mass libraries, and museums; the organization of literary evenings, publishing, and the cinema; and the preservation of historical and artistic monuments. The soviets of cities provide such services as bathhouses, laundries and dry-cleaning shops, funeral services and operation of cemeteries and crematoria, repair shops for personal items (watches, shoes, radios), photo shops, pawnshops, and barber shops. They operate breweries, bakeries, hotels, and restaurants. Soviets also maintain records of vital statistics and direct the local law enforcement organization.

The administration or department of a local or city soviet is responsible both to its own executive committee and to the oblast' or union republic administrative unit that deals with the same subject matter. Dependence of local governmental bodies is especially evident in taxation and finance. Although the finance departments of local soviets collect all taxes, revenue policy is highly centralized because only the central government is empowered to levy taxes; local soviets enjoy no independent taxing power. The budget of each local soviet is merely a minute component of the total U.S.S.R. state budget administered under the U.S.S.R. and union republic ministries of finance. Local soviets are permitted by the central government to retain a stipulated portion of the taxes collected within their jurisdiction but are limited in what they can spend. Although each local soviet adopts a separate budget ordinance, decisions on expenditures are preempted as a result of their having been predetermined by higher echelons of government.

The Soviet administrative system is generally characterized by excessive centralization. The autonomy granted to local soviets, especially in fiscal matters,

---

[21]For a brief general description of Soviet municipal government, see B. Michael Frolic, "Decision Making in Soviet Cities," *American Political Science Review,* LXVI, No. 1 (March 1972), pp. 38–52. On the range of activities of Soviet local government, see the chapters by Carol W. Lewis, David T. Cattell, and Henry W. Morton in Everett M. Jacobs, ed., *Soviet Local Politics and Government* (London and Boston: George Allen & Unwin, 1983).

is tentative in addition to being circumscribed. The acts of soviets and of their administrative bodies and departments can readily be annulled both by higher soviets and their executive committees and by republic councils of ministers and ministries. Each superior soviet acquires a large administrative apparatus because, in addition to conducting its own business, it must concern itself with the work of all subordinate soviets. Such autonomy as is required by administrative necessity can readily be vitiated by the intervention of local Party officials who also hold key positions in the local soviets. Indeed, the local soviets are essential instruments for the fulfillment of Party decisions, although the local Party committee is supposed to guide but not supplant the local soviet.

However, local soviets have been known to lack both the authority and the financial resources to deal with many problems. Thus, city soviets have been confronted by powerful industrial enterprises whose managers are answerable to oblast' or republic officials or even directly to a U.S.S.R. ministry in Moscow. A ministry may establish a new factory and not provide adequate funds for housing, schools, utilities, stores, and other facilities, leaving municipal officials to cope with the situation as best they can. The city Party officials cannot always resolve disputes between city government and industrial managers, as a local Party secretary has limited influence on a ministry in Moscow.[22] Party, governmental, and industrial bureaucracies do not always function coordinately at the local level in the absence of intervention by higher authorities.

The Party has repeatedly sought to enlist the deputies of local soviets in monitoring activities and have them assume greater responsibilities for performance. However, there is an apparent reluctance on the part of the deputies. Soviet bureaucrats seek to protect themselves and to continue unhampered in their established ways and practices. Deputies, whose tenure is limited and whose participation may be involuntary, are often reluctant to challenge administrators and officials of local soviets who have various sanctions that can be employed to silence and punish local critics. This state of affairs and the resultant indifference to citizens' needs and complaints were acknowledged by Andrei Gromyko, who, as Chairman of the Presidium of the U.S.S.R. Supreme Soviet, is nominally responsible for the entire system of (government) soviets. At the Twenty-seventh CPSU Congress, Gromyko noted that "too often local soviet and economic bodies resolve questions of great concern to citizens only after the intervention, as it is sometimes said, 'from above' *(sverkhu).* However, there is an insufficiency of 'superior' [bodies] for the resolution of all these questions. The absolute majority come directly within the competence of local organs." He noted that "one is simply amazed, reading the individual and collective letters and complaints of citizens, sometimes signed by hundreds of persons: what is the source of this inattentiveness to their requests?" Gromyko preferred to have his question remain rhetorical and chose not to offer any explanation. Instead, he merely called for "sensitivity and concern" on the part of deputies and soviet officials instead of "callousness" *(cherstvost')* in dealing with visitors to government offices. He advised that "not a single citizen should leave without having seen a deputy."[23]

[22]See William Taubman, *Governing Soviet Cities* (New York: Praeger, 1973), pp. 111–112.
[23]*Pravda,* February 27, 1986, p. 6.

It is obvious that there is a great deal of apathy and disregard on the part of local officials in responding to citizens' complaints and requests. Ordinary deputies may choose avoidance and noninvolvement in an effort to complete their terms with the least unpleasantness and especially without antagonizing the local officials who are guilty of a cavalier attitude toward citizens. Solutions to many everyday problems lie beyond the capabilities and resources of the average deputy.

INTEREST ARTICULATION

The question of whether or not interest groups exist in the Soviet Union or play a significant role in Soviet policy making has elicited considerable discussion. The kinds of interest groups that exist in more pluralistic societies are based on the right of free association, which enables them to organize in order to press their demands by offering their conditional support to political parties (in the form of votes, money, and endorsements) in return for the adoption of specific public policies. Soviet theory does not readily allow for interest groups because it depicts Soviet society as being based on "social homogeneity" (article 19 of the 1977 Constitution) and alleges that the interests of the public and the Soviet state are basically identical. This position is testified to by the contrived unanimity found in voting in the Supreme Soviet or in elections designed to convey—however ineffectively—the alleged absence of conflict or of antagonistic groups in Soviet politics and society. Yet it is recognized that there are so-called "non-antagonistic contradictions" reflecting certain differences in Soviet society. M. S. Gorbachev told the Central Committee in January 1987 that under his predecessors "the social structure of society was depicted schematically as [being] devoid of contradictions and the dynamism of the diverse *(mnogoobraznykh)* interests of its various strata and groups."[24]

Soviet authorities have endeavored to prevent the formation of associations that are not officially sponsored. The Preamble to the CPSU Statutes forbids "group activity" *(gruppovshchina)* among Party members. Any unregulated public gathering is immediately suspect. Officially sanctioned groups are closely monitored and their leaders subjected to careful control and recall under the Party's nomenklatura system. The sole exceptions might be religious denominations that are barely tolerated and given only conditional recognition. Thus, the status and activities of the Russian Orthodox Church are greatly circumscribed when compared with those of the Catholic Church in Poland. Officially unrecognized religious groups certainly have interests—foremost among them their self-preservation—but are compelled to function underground and have no influence on policy. Such organizations as the Helsinki Groups, which monitor Soviet observance of the human rights provisions of the Helsinki Final Act, are regarded as "illegal" and have been hampered in every way. The fact that officially recog-

---

[24]*Izvestiia,* January 28, 1987, p. 1. Gorbachev subsequently observed that his "restructuring" of administrative bodies would be "effective only if it is able to unify and harmonize [*sic*] the diverse interests of our society, including the interests not only of enterprises and branches but also the interests of republics, territories and provinces, cities and districts or, as it is said, territorial interests" (*Pravda,* June 26, 1987, p. 5).

nized "social organizations" have been limited to inventors, athletes, life-saving, philately, the preservation of historical and cultural monuments, and the Red Cross and Red Crescent societies indicates the kinds of restraints imposed on the scope of organized group activity.

Whether or not we can speak of the existence of "interest groups" in the Soviet Union depends on how we define a group. If we require that such groups have formal organization and memberships, independent resources, group consciousness and shared attitudes, and the ability of members to interact freely, then the term can have but a qualified application to Soviet politics.[25] Yet interests do exist in view of the fact that Soviet society is differentiated. Examples that are frequently encountered include the various bureaucracies or institutional interest groups such as the Party apparatus, the government bureaucracy, the security police, and central planners. In addition, there are ethnic interests, economic managers, and agricultural and military interests that presumably seek benefits and concessions. Differences exist within and between the military services and among industrial managers as well as among Soviet intellectuals, some of whom favor more orthodox policies and tastes in the arts and in literature, while others are prepared to tolerate or actually advocate some degree of heterodoxy. Thus, occupational or professional groups can be divided and counterposed by the Party in its effort to remain dominant and the ultimate source of policy. Such an "interest group" as the Union of Writers has been used not to defend the interests of all writers—it has expelled dissident authors—but to promote conformity to artistic canons set down by Party ideologists. Yet it is conceivable that the Union could in certain circumstances defend the interests and artistic freedom of writers.

Interest articulation in the Soviet Union occurs in a context different from that of associational interest groups in more pluralist societies. Professional opinion of experts is sought by the leadership, especially when it may be divided on specific issues.[26] An example of disagreement within the leadership in the sixties and seventies was provided by the delay in adopting a new draft constitution. The less sensitive an issue may be—both politically and ideologically—the greater is the likelihood that specialized elites may be able to influence policy.[27] The greater diversification of Central Committee membership since the 1950s has also meant greater opportunity for interest representation when the circumstances of oligarchic rule make this possible.[28]

Interest articulation also occurs on a more modest scale in the various local

---

[25]For the most complete discussion, see H. Gordon Skilling and Franklyn Griffiths, eds., *Interest Groups in Soviet Politics* (Princeton, N.J.: Princeton University Press, 1971), especially Chapters 10 and 11.

[26]Khrushchev revealed the existence of pressures exerted by the military services on nuclear testing and by scientists favoring one or another project. For examples of disagreements between politicians and experts, see *Khrushchev Remembers, The Last Testament, op. cit.* (above, n. 4), Chapter 4.

[27]See Donald R. Kelley, "Interest Groups in the USSR: The Impact of Political Sensitivity on Group Influence," *Journal of Politics,* XXXIV, No. 3 (August 1972), pp. 860–888. See also Howard L. Biddulph, "Local Interest Articulation at CPSU Congresses," *World Politics,* XXXVI, No. 1 (October 1983), pp. 28–52.

[28]On the "cooptation" of specialist elite representatives with ties to groups, see Frederick Fleron, "Representation of Career Types in the Soviet Political Leadership" in R. Barry Farrell, ed., *Political Leadership in Eastern Europe and the Soviet Union* (Chicago: Aldine, 1970), pp. 108–139.

soviets when deputies are given an instruction *(nakaz)* at the time of the elections. Such instructions are formally adopted at meetings of voters and are recorded; they are also screened by local Party officials. They usually deal with such specific matters as housing repairs, street paving, extension of a water main, construction of some facility, or consumer complaints.[29] Local officials can always plead lack of funds or authority because of investment decisions made by central planners. A deputy can also formally make an inquiry *(zapros)* directed to the appropriate administrative official regarding a specific complaint. The executive committee of the soviet can reprimand officials and managers. However, an instruction from voters can also be rejected by the local soviet with an appropriate explanation. Soviet commentators have admitted that deputies' inquiries are not always heeded, and M. S. Gorbachev complained that the officials of local soviets seek to give orders to Party members and to deputies.[30]

A dissatisfied citizen can direct an inquiry or complaint to the press. The government newspaper *Izvestiia* reported that it receives approximately 500,000 letters per year on a wide range of subjects involving complaints and suggestions. The press publishes only a small number of such letters; but it also refers them to the appropriate officials, occasionally assigns journalists to verify and investigate the matter, and subsequently publishes a story prodding the responsible officials.

Interest articulation in the Soviet polity is more effectively exercised if it can be equated with the public interest and with the professed goals of the Party. Yet the essence of Soviet politics cannot be understood in terms of the interaction (conflict and collaboration) of associated interest groups. Issues rather than organized groups are at the core of Soviet interest articulation. Thus, there are differences of opinion regarding the future of nationalities and what is desirable and feasible in ethnic relations. The regime's inability to eliminate the individual agricultural plots of collective farmers indicates that the issue is of vital interest to those who would lose as a result of such action. The opposition encountered by Khrushchev from obkom secretaries as a result of the bifurcation of the oblast' Party organizations into separate agricultural and industrial committees (1962–1964) illustrates how a group can coalesce when threatened by a particular policy. Such diverse examples reflect the underlying play of interests that Soviet leaders cannot ignore. However, these interests, like many other phenomena in the Soviet polity, manifest themselves in uniquely Soviet ways. The central apparatus of the Party remains the ultimate aggregator of interests in its self-defined role. It does not perceive this role as being that of a mere broker acting as an intermediary. The Party has its own agenda and perception of the public interest.

---

[29]See James H. Oliver, "Citizen Demands and the Soviet Political System," *American Political Science Review,* LXIII, No. 2 (June 1969), pp. 465–475.

[30]*Izvestiia,* January 28, 1987, p. 4.

chapter 8

The Soviet Economy and Social Services

The wide scope of the many and diverse activities engaged in by the Soviet government gives to the polity a character very different from that of other industrial mass societies. The Soviet government forbids individuals or groups from owning the means of production or from engaging independently in entrepreneurial activities. The few exceptions are the collective farms, which are in theory agricultural cooperatives, and certain consumer and handicraft cooperatives, as well as family-operated "handicrafts and consumer services" not using hired labor. The use of any hired labor is regarded as "exploitation" and as "capitalism" producing "unearned income." By Soviet definition, when the state hires persons it does not engage in exploitation. State ownership of the means of production and of all land and natural resources has resulted in an economy that is a virtual state monopoly in all of its important aspects. The 1977 Constitution (Article 16) defines the Soviet economy as "a single public economic complex embracing all sectors of social production, distribution and exchange on the country's territory." The denial of freedom of economic enterprise, except on a most limited scale, has made nearly all citizens the equivalent of government employees, and very few are permitted to be self-employed.

The Soviet government is, indeed, a gigantic economic "conglomerate" or corporate "trust" that defies imagination. Its largest single source of revenue usually is the profits from economic enterprises. It is landlord to most of the country, having entered the housing business on a vast scale, especially in the cities. It owns all land and determines to what uses it can be put. It owns the entire banking system, operates all savings banks, and sells various kinds of insurance. It is a carrier having a monopoly on all forms of commercial transportation and has a single, state-owned airline for the entire country as well as for foreign routes. The Soviet regime owns the various communications media, including newspapers, magazines, and radio and television stations; if organizations subsidiary to the Communist Party have their own publications, they do not challenge the Party's monopoly position in the media, and their editors can be summarily replaced.

Yet the functions of Soviet government are not confined to state ownership of the economy and to profit making. State ownership is viewed as a means of achieving certain social ends and of effecting a transformation in human nature. Political objectives usually have primacy over economics, as economic policies have generally been designed to sustain the oligarchy's political power. The abolition of the stock market by the Soviet regime and the impossibility of private ownership of common stocks and of the means of production are viewed, for instance, as contributing to these ends. Centralized planning of a nationalized economy is but one of the means employed to promote the regime's objectives. There is much inculcation designed to persuade workers that their interests are, for all practical purposes, identical to those of the management of the state-owned enterprises. It is claimed that workers "own" the means of production, although in practice it is state ownership that raises the important question: Who "owns" the Soviet state and determines its policies? Trade unions are used to propagate the official view and cannot bargain collectively on behalf of workers for wage increases; strikes are not an activity of the Party-controlled trade unions, and there is no recognized right to strike.

The mobilization of labor has played an important role in the Soviet Union's impressive economic growth, which was discussed in Chapter 1. Although Soviet economic growth rates have slowed, large-scale projects continue to be undertaken. These include the development of new ports, great hydroelectric facilities on Siberian rivers as well as the 300-meter-high Nurek Dam in Tadjikistan, and the construction of the Baikal-Amur Mainline (BAM)—a new railway 3200 kilometers in length linking Central and Eastern Siberia along a shorter route that is well removed from the Chinese frontier. Yet other countries such as Brazil, the Federal Republic of Germany, and Japan have also experienced phenomenal economic growth rates by relying on private enterprise and on free market conditions. Thus, the Soviet economy, despite its many achievements, cannot be said to provide the sole model for rapid economic development.

ECONOMIC DECISION MAKING AND CONTROLS

The Soviet economy is sometimes described as a "command economy," by which is meant that all important decisions affecting the economy are determined by administrative directives issued by public officials rather than by the actions of consumers and of countless private individuals and corporations acting through the mechanism of the market. Centralized planning by the governmental bureaucracy made it possible to develop heavy industry at rapid tempos, although at the expense of light industry and consumer goods production. Such a command economy has been especially conducive to the development of the Soviet Union's military capabilities, as producers' goods and military hardware have been favored and subsidized by other sectors of the economy. Like the so-called capitalist countries, the Soviet Union accumulates and invests capital for economic return and development, but its capital is state-owned and is allocated among the various sectors of the economy on the basis of investment decisions made by planning officials. There is no market for capital in the Soviet Union, and capital is not raised through the sale of stocks as it is in other countries. High rates of capital formation and investment have been possible as a result of forced "savings" through low wages and deprivations imposed upon the population by the government's planners. Since capital in the Soviet Union is state-owned and is allocated by government officials, the system might be described as "state capitalism."

Economic planning per se is not unique to the Soviet Union. American, European, and Asian corporations engage in planning when deciding when and where to build a new factory or in adopting long-range production schedules. Governmental budgets in democratic countries are based on planning in that they often reflect deliberate choices affecting research and development or the granting of subsidies to a particular sector of the economy (e.g., the merchant marine or aircraft industry). However, the Soviet brand of planning is distinguished by its extensiveness and centralized nature, by the myriad of economic decisions made by the planners, and by the array of controls and devices available to them.[1] At times the Politburo has concerned itself with matters that in another country would be determined by a few businessmen, as is illustrated by Khrushchev's recounting of how he reported to the Politburo on the question of purchasing a license from an American firm for a bacon-producing plant and his colleagues rejected the proposal.[2] The Politburo has also taken up the matter of radio and television-set repairs and their inadequacy.[3]

Soviet planning is a consequence of a long-standing hostility toward market forces that are based on choice and demand. Trotsky expressed this view at the Party's Ninth Congress in 1920 when he declared: "We have killed the free market, exploitation, competition, speculation."[4] The Party has viewed the market as anarchic and wasteful and has preferred to rely as far as possible on bureaucratic determination of economic preferences and priorities. Yet it has also had to tolerate certain kinds of market situations, largely because of scarcities and unsatisfied demand and the inability of the planners to command all economic transactions and individual behavior.

---

[1]On the nature and problems of Soviet economic planning, see Abram Bergson and Herbert S. Levine, eds., *The Soviet Economy: Toward the Year 2000* (Winchester, Mass.: Allen & Unwin, 1983) and David A. Dyker, *The Future of the Soviet Economic Planning System* (Armonk, N.Y.: M. E. Sharpe, Inc., 1985). See also Fyodor I. Kushnirsky, *Soviet Economic Planning, 1965–1980* (Boulder, Colo.: Westview Press, 1982). For a critical view, see Marshall I. Goldman, *USSR in Crisis: The Failure of an Economic System* (New York: Norton, 1983).

[2]*Khrushchev Remembers, The Last Testament* (Boston: Little, Brown, 1974), pp. 141–142.

[3]*Pravda,* July 25, 1986.

[4]*Deviatyi s"ezd Rossiiskoi Kommunisticheskoi Partii, stenograficheskii otchet* (Moscow: Gosudarstvennoe izdatel'stvo, 1920), p. 90.

Financial and Budgetary Policies

Soviet planners have their decisions embodied in the central government's annual budget and in the subordinate budgets of the union republics. Unlike some "bourgeois" governments, the Soviet government claims to operate with a balanced budget and usually has a surplus at the end of the fiscal year. The apparent absence of government deficits is due to limited internal borrowing facilities, the lack of a market for capital, and the ability to impose rather heavy taxes; the government also has at its disposal the savings deposits in the State Bank. Former Soviet economist and CPSU member Igor Birman has contended that there are actually concealed deficits in the Soviet government budget. Such deficits can be covered through emissions of cash into circulation and by tapping the reserve funds of *Gosstrakh* (the state insurance monopoly that is a branch of the Ministry of Finance).[5] If chronic deficits are a feature of Soviet state budgets, they contribute to the steady growth of inflationary pressures in the economy. The budget provides the guidelines for the annual economic plan or, more correctly, series of plans, for there are financial, labor, output, and consumption plans as well as plans for separate regions. Planning is facilitated by a state monopoly of foreign trade that makes possible strict controls over imports and exports. Thus, Soviet foreign-exchange holdings are expended upon those imports that are essential to the fulfillment of the regime's economic objectives.

Soviet planners have at their disposal a wide variety of economic tools enabling them to exact sacrifices, stimulate economic growth rates, and determine what shall and shall not be produced by the state-owned factories. Prices and wages are controlled; arbitrarily fixed prices serve to encourage or discourage consumption of particular commodities and also serve as a form of indirect rationing. Consumption was postponed or limited for many years by the use of annual government loans from 1927 to 1957 that were compulsory for all practical purposes, as citizens usually feared the consequences of not subscribing. The Soviet government did not pay interest on the debt and failed to redeem these obligations in 1957, postponing repayment for two decades, although retirement of the debt finally commenced in 1974. However, citizens holding such government bonds have been able to participate in a state lottery—using the serial numbers of the bonds to identify winners—and thus obtain some "interest" if they have been fortunate enough to win.[6]

The Soviet government has employed drastic currency reforms and has revalued the ruble in order to reduce or wipe out accumulated savings. Thus, in December 1947 and in January 1961, a new ruble was introduced; in both reforms the new ruble was issued at the rate of 1:10 in relationship to the old ruble. In 1947 larger sums could be exchanged for the new ruble on the basis of reduced

---

[5]See Igor Birman, *Secret Incomes of the Soviet State Budget* (The Hague and Boston: Martinus Nijhoff, 1981). M. S. Gorbachev apparently confirmed this practice before the Central Committee in 1987 in referring to "the unfounded withdrawal [*iz'iatie*] for the budget of means [*sredstv*] belonging to enterprises and organizations." *Pravda,* June 26, 1987, p. 3.

[6]See James R. Millar, "History and Analysis of Soviet Domestic Bond Policy," *Soviet Studies,* XXVII, No. 4 (October 1975), pp. 598–614.

rates designed to eliminate large holdings of rubles, especially those accumulated as a result of the condition of the wartime and postwar economies. The 1961 currency reform was based on a fixed ratio of 1:10 and not on a scale of varying ratios, but persons with large ruble holdings were usually reluctant to exchange them so as not to arouse the interest of the security police in how such sums might have been acquired. Such drastic currency reforms also disposed of foreign ruble holdings and gave the ruble the appearance of a more substantial currency with a higher though artificial value in relationship to other currencies. Arbitrarily fixed foreign-exchange rates, as well as the Soviet price system, have been used to promote or discourage certain imports from, and exports to, particular countries.

The state banking monopoly provides an important means of effecting a variety of monetary controls, for money flows are seen as reflecting planning decisions. The State Bank of the U.S.S.R. *(Gosbank)* serves as the sole bank of emission issuing coin and paper currency; it provides a means of combating inflation by controlling the money supply (and the issuance of money is a vital factor in the economic plan). The State Bank also handles all foreign-exchange transactions and deals in gold and other precious metals; the Bank of Foreign Trade is its subsidiary. The State Bank and its numerous branches service the accounts of enterprises and enforce the economic plan; directors of enterprises must expend accounts as earmarked, and the Bank provides a means of ascertaining fulfillment of the *financial* plan in exercising "control by the ruble." It also provides short-term (one-year) credits to enterprises, but the State Bank official has little discretion in making loans because they must be for purposes provided for in the plan. Long-term credits for capital investment are extended by the Bank for Financing Capital Investments *(Stroibank),* which transfers such funds from the state budget and also serves as a control agency. The State Bank also operates approximately 78,000 savings banks throughout the country.

The need to raise large sums of capital and to control consumption has dictated Soviet taxation policies. The principal tax in the Soviet Union is the turnover tax *(nalog s oborota),* which is in fact a sales tax levied on a massive scale. It is an important source of the government's revenue and provides large quantities of needed capital. Prior to 1967 the turnover tax was the largest single source of revenue, but in that year it was exceeded by the government's share of the income from the profits of economic enterprises. These two sources together have provided as much as two-thirds of the revenue for the Soviet government's budget. The income tax has provided a modest share of less than 10 percent of the government's revenue. A variety of direct taxes and miscellaneous sources of revenue—such as profits from the sale of insurance by the government, a tax on bachelors and childless married persons, social-insurance revenues paid by enterprises, customs duties, automobile registration fees, and the like—provide additional funds.

The turnover tax is a largely hidden excise tax that is included in the sales price of commodities and manufactured articles. It was introduced by Stalin in 1931 and has survived. Rates are not generally publicized, but they are usually high, and the tax often constitutes half or much more than half of the total sales price. Such a tax absorbs much of the excess money that is more abundant than the supply of available goods. Thus, the turnover tax is a substitute for rationing. From the point of view of the regime, the turnover tax is preferable to the income tax because it is concealed, presumably less painful, and easily administered. It enables the regime to influence consumer preferences and consumption patterns and to limit demand by bringing it into balance with the available supply of consumer goods. Thanks to the turnover tax and to planners' decisions, the Soviet Union tends to remain a seller's market, although buyer resistance is evident at times.

PLANNING IN PRACTICE

Soviet finance is, by definition, public finance; and the revenues generated and the expenditures made reflect the government's current economic plan. While the central planning authorities in Moscow have the responsibility for setting longer-term economic goals, many decisions must be delegated to republic planning officials and to industrial managers. Thus, managers must determine the product mix and the specific quantities to be produced in particular colors, sizes, and styles. In practice, only the short-term operational plans (up to one year) can be detailed. Long-range planning can only set approximate production targets. For the most part the Soviet regime has relied on five-year plans, the first of which was introduced by Stalin in 1928. A seven-year plan was adopted in 1959, but was abandoned early in 1963 when it was decided to revert to the five-year-plan system. The twelfth five-year plan commenced in 1986.

The attempt to plan the manufacture of hundreds of thousands of items—indeed, probably ten million items, if one includes all components and parts—is a formidable undertaking to which task Soviet planners have not always been equal. The need to mobilize and allocate resources and to maintain a near-perfect balance between the various factors of production (capital, labor, transportation) requires that planning be based on accurate data and valid assumptions. In practice many imbalances have resulted, and Soviet planners and managers have not always been able to introduce new techniques. The high degree of centralization in Soviet planning has often resulted in inflexibility, excessive preoccupation with one or another sector of the economy, and high costs.

In industry, excessive preoccupation with increasing steel production led to a neglect of plastics and nonferrous metallurgy. A preference for huge plants ("gigantomania") led to a failure to develop smaller enterprises, which could provide the economy with greater flexibility. The fetish of economic self-sufficiency (autarky) resulted in the Soviet Union's exporting raw materials and surplus commodities rather than finished goods—despite the fact that the country is the world's second industrial power. It has been difficult for the Soviet Union to develop stable export industries that would provide adequate and regular means of earning foreign exchange. By stimulating exports the Soviet economy would, of course, be competing with foreign producers; innovation would moreover be promoted in ways not required by a domestic "captive" market. Insofar as the Soviet Union has retained a "closed economy," then, its domestic prices have borne little relationship to those of other countries and have not been permitted to determine decisions regarding what should be exported or imported.

Inflationary Pressures and Pricing Policy

It has frequently been claimed by Soviet spokesmen that only the capitalist world suffers from inflation, while the Soviet Union has allegedly solved the problem. Yet any rapidly developing (hyperactive) economy is subject to inflationary forces and disruption of the balance between the amount of money in circulation and the supply of available goods and services. The two postwar Soviet currency reforms testify to the presence of inflation. However, Soviet authorities have suppressed inflation to a considerable degree by wage restrictions, price controls in state retail stores, control of the money supply, and rather heavy taxation and high profits in certain sectors of the economy that absorb much of the excess currency.

Yet the planners have not been able to control wages as effectively as might be expected in a command economy. Wages have tended to creep upward in excess of the levels set in the economic plan and at a pace greater than increases in labor productivity. Factory directors, when faced with a labor shortage, are sufficiently resourceful to find ways of attracting workers by paying them at a higher scale through reclassification and other devices. There is also a great deal of "moonlighting"—due to Soviet efforts to control wages—with persons earning additional income in their spare time. The introduction of profitability as a criterion for judging management has promoted inflation by prompting higher estimates of production costs, which planners cannot always question. Khrushchev confirmed the common practice of increasing prices by introducing new brand names and replacing the less expensive item with a more expensive one that is not of higher quality despite the higher price.[7] Thus, the manager of a state-owned enterprise may be more concerned with maximizing profits than in producing a less expensive product.[8]

Soviet inflation is partly concealed through the use of artificially low prices for certain necessities such as rental housing, bread, and public transportation. Such items involve a government subsidy because the officially established prices cannot cover the costs. It is regarded as politically inadvisable to raise prices significantly on such necessities, as there would be public dissatisfaction or wages would have to be raised substantially. Thus, when Khrushchev adopted the politically unpopular but economically justified decision to raise prices of meat and milk products in 1962, he aroused much antagonism in the urban population, although the collective farmers benefited from the measure. In general, food prices have risen moderately in the state retail stores.

Yet citizens are willing to pay a price that may be several times higher in

---

[7]*Khrushchev Remembers, The Last Testament, op. cit.* (above, n. 2), p. 145.

[8]The padding of the Soviet citizen's television repair bill with unnecessary parts and labor in order to improve performance under the plan is apparently a fairly common practice, as explained in "Komu eto vygodno?" *Izvestiia,* February 4, 1975.

the legal collective farm market for fresh produce that is superior to what is often available in the state-owned food stores. Low official prices for meat sold in state stores does not assure an ample supply and may be quite specious. In a market economy higher prices would presumably lead to greater production of the scarce item and more effective satisfaction of demand in the long run. In fact, higher prices are paid by Soviet citizens when they seek a particular item and are willing to purchase it in the black or gray market at a premium price with no questions asked. The fact that savings deposits in state savings banks increased from 18.7 billion rubles in 1965 to 78.9 billion rubles in 1974 and 242.8 billion rubles in 1986 reflects an oversupply of money in relation to the quantity and quality of goods and services available. It also testifies to the existence of buyer resistance and to the ability of Soviet citizens to obtain additional income.

The lack of realistic and flexible prices has meant that the price structure reflects the preferences and decisions of economic planners and not market conditions. Thus the prices of products used by the Soviet "military-industrial complex" can be kept artificially low by means of a subsidy paid by those (civilian) sectors of the economy that must accept prices set deliberately high by planners. Production for the military establishment constitutes a *preferential internal economy* based on political considerations and the enhancement of great-power status. Administered prices can serve as regulators, but if they are deliberately set too low they lead to shortages and queues or can involve subsidization of an item in the civilian economy that remains in limited supply. Soviet official prices have not adequately identified scarcities in the economy and have not served so effectively as regulators as they would if they were to reflect consumer demand and market conditions.

The "Second Economy"

The existence of a wide range of semilegal and illegal economic activities that are beyond the economic plan has led foreign economists to employ the term *second economy* to refer to all such transactions. There are also legal activities that are conducted outside of the plan for personal advantage, such as the cultivation by collective farmers of their own individual plots of land. Other such activities include private tutoring, the sewing of clothes on individual order after hours by a tailor or seamstress, and the repairing of appliances, plumbing, or automobiles. Goods may be exchanged or cash paid or a commodity or article given in return for a service rendered. There is also speculation in the form of purchase of goods in quantity greater than required for one's own use in order to resell at a profit.

There are also cases of highly profitable clandestine manufacturing of small items that are difficult to obtain and for which there is a ready market. The materials used in such ventures are obtained from state-owned factories through illicit arrangements. The existence of bribery and corruption that are reported in the Soviet press and instances of outright theft from state-owned enterprises by rank-and-file workers and management indicate that the concept of "socialist property" does not serve as an effective deterrent. Indeed, state-ownership may even provide a rationalization for theft on the grounds that what is appropriated is not really owned by anyone if it belongs to the state and, in addition, the state owns everything in any case and will neither need nor miss the relatively small spoils.[9]

The "second economy" is a consequence of inadequacies in the official command economy. Such an unofficial, unplanned economy has arisen in response to a failure of the planners to supply the needs of the population whether in vegetables, consumer goods, spare parts, or necessary services. It is abetted by the relatively low official wages that often must be supplemented by additional sources of income, whether in the form of supplementary part-time work or illicit or semilegal small-scale commerce. Thus, collective and state farms were permitted to organize profitable, subsidiary small-scale enterprises that require little capital and that produce items for the consumer market. The "second economy" has produced a new sub-class of illicit "capitalists," many of whom employ bribery, theft, embezzlement, and side payments. Yet it is the pandemic corruption and illegality that have enabled the planned economy to function and survive.

The total scope of the "second economy" cannot be measured even by Soviet officialdom. It provides part of the explanation of why savings deposits have increased so dramatically and how Soviet citizens can pay higher prices for certain items and live beyond their apparent means. Earnings obtained in the unofficial economy can exceed any bonuses that an individual worker receives from an enterprise. The "second economy" has come to be tolerated to a large degree because it meets certain needs, although it possesses certain aspects of the NEP economy of the 1920s. Its existence indicates that the Soviet economy is less of a command economy in practice than it is in theory.

The Agricultural Problem

Soviet agriculture was radically transformed as a result of the collectivization campaign in the early 1930s that may have taken as many as 10 million lives.[10] The Ukrainian famine of 1932–33 probably took as many as 7 million lives and

---

[9]For information on the unofficial economy, see the results of interviews with former Soviet citizens in 1972–1973 conducted by Zev Katz and reported in *Soviet Economic Prospects for the Seventies: A Compendium of Papers Submitted to the Joint Economic Committee, Congress of the U.S.* (U.S. Government Printing Office, 1973), pp. 87–94. See also Konstantin M. Simis, *USSR: The Corrupt Society* (New York: Simon & Schuster, 1982) and Gregory Grossman, "The 'Second Economy' of the USSR" in Morris Bornstein, ed., *The Soviet Economy: Continuity and Change* (Boulder, Colo.: Westview Press, 1981), pp. 71–93. On the variety of Soviet markets, see Aron Katsenelinboigen, *Studies in Soviet Economic Planning* (White Plains, N.Y.: M. E. Sharpe, 1978), Chapter 7, "Market Colors and the Soviet Economy."

[10]Stalin, in a moment of frankness, informed Churchill of this horrendous statistic in August 1942. See Winston S. Churchill, *The Hinge of Fate* (Boston: Houghton Mifflin, 1950), p. 498. Corroborative evidence was provided by Stalin's suppression of the results of the 1937 census in an apparent effort to conceal the extent of the loss of life. According to the official census, 31,194,976 Ukrainians lived under Soviet rule in 1926, while the 1939 census gave a figure of 28,070,404—an apparent loss of 3.1 million, though it was actually greater, since the Soviet Ukrainian population had increased beyond 31 million between the 1926 census and the onset of the collectivization campaign. The Kazakhs were also severely affected by collectivization; according to the 1926 census, there were 3.96 million Kazakhs in that year, while in the 1939 census there were 3,098,800 and in 1959 they numbered 3.6 million. It is likely that the 1939 census results were inflated to conceal losses. For a carefully documented study of the famine and its consequences, see Robert Conquest, *The Harvest*

was genocidal in nature. The famine also affected the Volga and Kuban regions. Soviet authorities denied the existence of the famine and permitted no foreign relief efforts. That the famine was due to Soviet government policies and not to natural causes is obvious; its victims were the peasants who resisted collectivization while the urban population was assured a food supply with produce requisitioned from the starving countryside. The peasantry paid a disproportionate share of the cost of industrialization not only in loss of life but by being compelled to sell agricultural produce to the government below cost.[11] The lack of incentives for collective farmers and Stalin's refusal to invest sufficient capital in agriculture required the adoption of drastic measures by Khrushchev. These included such expensive crash programs as the cultivation of more than 100 million acres of virgin lands in West Siberia and Kazakhstan and the unsuccessful effort to grow corn (maize) in northern latitudes. Khrushchev increased significantly the money income of collective farmers, although he also sought to restrict the size of the private plots cultivated by them and to increase the number and size of the state farms *(sovkhozy)*.

Brezhnev sought to increase agricultural investment and chemical-fertilizer production, improve land, extend irrigation facilities, increase material incentives, and permit the private sector to function with fewer restraints despite the ideological bias against individual plots. Soviet agriculture is costly in terms of labor productivity; moreover, it involves nearly one-quarter of the labor force. Students, military personnel, and even scientists have been conscripted for work in the fields at harvest time. The private plots that are cultivated intensively provide a disproportionate share of agricultural produce. Although they constitute only 3 percent of the sown area, they have produced as much as 40 percent of the fruits and vegetables, nearly two-thirds of the potatoes, and as much as 30 percent of the meat and milk.[12] They provide striking testimony to the effectiveness of individual incentive and private endeavor. Yet the Soviet diet has remained disproportionately high in carbohydrates, with less than the desired level of protein consumption due to an inability to increase fodder production and the size of livestock herds. The failure to develop special breeds of cattle for meat and dairy production has hampered the efficient use of livestock. Faced with severe shortages of fodder and the specter of famine in 1963, 1972, and 1975, the Soviet leaders had to import billions of dollars worth of grain from "capitalist" countries and relied regularly on such imports in the 1980s. Yet the Soviet Union has continued to supply some East European countries with grain as part of the price of maintaining its hegemony.

---

of Sorrow: Soviet Collectivization and the Terror-Famine (New York: Oxford University Press, 1986). See also Roman Serbyn and Bohdan Krawchenko, eds., *Famine in Ukraine, 1932–1933* (Edmonton: University of Alberta, Canadian Institute of Ukrainian Studies, 1986). For eyewitness accounts of the Ukrainian famine, see Miron Dolot, *Execution by Hunger: The Hidden Holocaust* (New York: W. W. Norton, 1985), and the concluding chapter in Lev Kopelev, *The Education of a True Believer* (New York: Harper & Row, 1980). It is also described in Chapter 14 of Vasily Grossman, *Forever Flowing* (New York: Harper & Row, 1972).

[11]*Khrushchev Remembers, The Last Testament, op. cit.* (above, n. 2), pp. 112–113.

[12]D. Gale Johnson and Karen McConnell Brooks, *Prospects for Soviet Agriculture in the 1980s* (Bloomington: Indiana University Press, 1983), p. 6.

The Soviet agricultural problem is really a series of problems. Foremost among them is the country's climate, with its limited growing season in certain areas and the uncertainty of its rainfall, which provides a bountiful harvest one year and a deficit the next. One may wonder whether the Soviet Union's population may become too large for a country of such northern latitudes unless it is willing to import food paid for with foreign-exchange earnings. The Soviet leadership has repeatedly resorted to various panaceas that have involved them in controversial agricultural policies. In Stalin's time it espoused the Vil'iams (Williams) so-called grasslands theory of natural soil enrichment through the planting of cereal grasses and clover that would supposedly eliminate the need for mineral fertilizers and tilling of the soil.[13] Such issues as shallow plowing versus deeper tillage, collective farms versus state farms, and the size of agricultural labor crews (the smaller *zveno* or "link" work unit versus the larger brigade) have involved Soviet politicians in matters that could best be resolved through the use of rigorous experiments and scientific studies rather than by political fiat. The limitations of the Soviet approach to agriculture and the preoccupation of leaders with economic problems are seen in the fact that Khrushchev published eight volumes of speeches on agriculture without solving basic problems.

Yet the Party leadershp has insisted that it knows how agriculture should be organized. It has tended to favor extensive agriculture, bringing more marginal lands under cultivation instead of increasing labor productivity and crop yield per unit of land. This policy is seen in Khrushchev's virgin-lands program and in Brezhnev's decision to bring the nonblack earth-forest steppe area of the Russian S.F.S.R. under cultivation. Frequently, local Party officials, who are often engineers, have been given responsibility for agriculture without possessing the necessary training.[14]

However, more basic problems may be the size of Soviet farms and the inadequacy of incentives for the individual farm worker. Soviet farms may be too large; state farms have averaged more than 50,000 acres (21,000 hectares) in size, while collective farms are smaller, having about 15,000 acres (6,000 hectares). Farming necessarily involves monitoring of the crop on a daily basis if it is to be harvested properly. Fields and farms of excessive size, as well as centralized planning, make for inefficient agriculture. There is much spoilage and waste, and Soviet officials have exaggerated production figures.[15] Significant losses occur as a result of carelessness and inadequate transportation facilities and the resultant spillage from trucks and railroad cars; poor storage facilities and wasteful processing add to the losses. Farm workers may not have a sufficient interest at stake to give to the large fields the kind of attention that collective farmers give to their highly productive individual plots, which average only an acre in size. Thus, state subsidization of lower food prices and increased investments in agriculture cannot replace an effective program of individual incentives. Indeed official policies

---

[13]See the discussion in Zhores A. Medvedev, *The Rise and Fall of T. D. Lysenko* (Garden City, N.Y.: Doubleday Anchor Books, 1971), Chapter 5.

[14]*Khrushchev Remembers, The Last Testament, op. cit.* (above, n. 2), pp. 137–138.

[15]Khrushchev stated in 1970 that he did not trust the official Soviet agricultural statistics and observed that statisticians "conceal setbacks and tell the leadership what it wants to hear." *Ibid.,* pp. 131, 133, 139.

resulting in artificially low food prices are absorbing an excessive percentage of the gross national product.[16] Thus, Soviet farming is not only unprofitable but is overorganized by a centralized bureaucracy that has sought to impose detailed instructions concerning matters that should be left to the individual farmer or group of farmers to decide regarding what should be planted and when it should be harvested.

Although Mikhail Gorbachev was the first Soviet Party leader to possess formal training in agriculture, his prescriptions offered to the Twenty-seventh Party Congress in 1986 were singularly unimaginative. He conceded that a full supply of food for the country was a matter of the highest priority that required a "decisive breakthrough." Food stocks could be augmented by reducing losses during harvesting, transportation, storage, and processing. Yet he admitted that "today, as never before, agriculture needs people who are interested in working actively." He held out the promise of greater independence for collective and state farms and their freedom to dispose of a surplus at their own discretion once the state has fixed its purchase plans (demands) for a five-year period. Gorbachev also consolidated several state agencies into a new State Agro-Industrial Committee. He complained of farms having excessive debt and of their being subsidized; he demanded "economic accountability," asserting that farms must develop production and finance incentives with their own money. Soviet agriculture has been costly, and Gorbachev did not propose to make new investments but, instead, demanded that results come from "important changes in the style and methods of management of the agro-industrial complex."[17]

Organization and Incentives

The Soviet economy has undergone various reorganizations in the post-Stalin period. In 1957 Khrushchev established 105 regional economic councils that generally corresponded to the oblast' jurisdiction. He also reduced the number of central economic ministries on the assumption that each economic region would constitute a viable unit, with Party officials monitoring the economy more effectively. Closer ties were to develop between oblast' enterprises, which would supposedly result in greater efficiency and lower transportation costs. However, charges of "localism" were soon raised, and the number of regional economic councils was greatly reduced. In November 1962 Khrushchev divided most of the oblast' Party organizations into two separate committees for industry and agriculture, each headed by a first secretary. In this way Khrushchev sought to improve Party supervision over agriculture; he also dissolved the raion Party committee, replacing it with an agricultural production organization.[18]

[16]D. Gale Johnson and Karen McConnell Brooks, *op. cit.* (above, n. 12), p. 199.

[17]*Pravda*, February 26, 1986, pp. 4–5. Indicative of the agricultural problem and the flight from the countryside was M. S. Gorbachev's statement to the Central Committee in June 1987 that in the non-black earth region (in which Brezhnev had invested heavily) nearly 800,000 dwellings and the adjacent land had been abandoned. *Pravda,* June 26, 1987, p. 2.

[18]Khrushchev's reforms and reorganizations are discussed in William J. Conyngham, *Industrial Management in the Soviet Union* (Stanford, California: Hoover Institution Press, 1973). See also Barbara Ann Chotiner, *Khrushchev's Party Reform, Coalition Building and Institutional Innovation* (Westport, Conn.: Greenwood Press, 1984).

Khrushchev's ouster in October 1964 led to the abolition of his 1962 reorganization, which was highly unpopular with local Party officials. The single oblast' Party organization, headed by a single first secretary, was restored, as were the raion Party committees. The central economic ministries were also reestablished. Prior to Khrushchev's ouster, a public discussion had begun on the need for more effective criteria for determining plan fulfillment and efficiency. A proposal to employ profitability—the return on capital invested—was usually associated abroad with the name of Yevsei Liberman, although other prominent economists supported the measure.

The Brezhnev-Kosygin leadership introduced a reform in October 1965 that provided for sales and profitability as indicators of success. Direct contacts between enterprises and retailers were permitted, with delivery orders taken into account in the production plan. The remaining regional economic councils were abolished, and industrial ministries were reestablished. Special incentive funds were authorized, and it was recognized that price reforms would be necessary. Charges on the use of capital were introduced to prevent its being wasted or hoarded. Performance was to be measured on the basis of what was sold and on profit, although central planners were still to fix the volume and assortment of goods to be produced, the enterprise's wage fund, the amount of profit, the amount paid by the firm into the state budget, and the introduction of new technology.

If the 1965 reform had been carried through to its logical conclusion, profitability would have been the key criterion determining what was to be produced. Market conditions would determine prices and production in response to supply and demand. In practice, prices continued to be fixed administratively and often failed to reflect costs and scarcities. Plant managers were not given a great deal of autonomy, as too many key decisions affecting performance are still made by central planners and industrial ministries. Still another reorganization in April 1973 provided for the establishment of "production associations," to each of which a number of plants was subordinated with ministries confining themselves to planning, investment, and technological innovation.

With certain exceptions, the tendency has been to sacrifice economic flexibility and even the promise of increased productivity and greater profitability in order to maintain centralized control. The controls have, in turn, led to the development of evasive and protective tactics by managers. Accounts have frequently been padded in order to improve performance records. Managers have been known to underestimate their plant's productive capacity in order to prevent the fixing of a higher production quota. A lower quota is easier to fulfill, assures attainment of the production bonus, and makes next year's quota more readily attainable, as it is based on a percentage increase of that of the previous year. Hoarding of inventories of parts and supplies has been widespread because managers have not wished to be dependent on suppliers and have wanted to be in a position to fulfill their production quota. Such hoarding enhances the manager's bargaining position in dealing with other enterprises. Thus, plan fulfillment its made possible by evading the plan.

Technology and innovation have often lagged because managers have feared that production would decline (though only temporarily) and the economic plan be disrupted. The tendency of both planners and managers too often has been to continue to produce what has been manufactured in the past but at a higher rate of output. The development of new and improved products has suffered as a result. The official Soviet economy lacks the classical entrepreneur who is willing and able to take risks and induces others to share these risks. Such a person is an innovator who may profit handsomely but whose satisfaction may lie more in the success of accomplishment. The spark of entrepreneurship is not dead in the Soviet Union—as is evident in the "second economy"—but it persists in what is essentially a hostile environment. For it is the bureaucratization of the economy that is its dominant characteristic.

The Soviet economy has been characterized by disproportionate growth, overinvestment in certain sectors and underinvestment in others, growing demand as the population's purchasing power increases, the manufacture of producer goods having low profitability, and the neglect of consumer goods having high profitability. The state has tended to subsidize too many inefficient producers, and the returns on invested capital (often in the form of outright government grants rather than interest-bearing loans) have often been low. Capital, which Marx held not to be a source of value, has been known to lie idle rather than being put to work with dispatch.

Too often, Soviet planners have been guided by quantitative indices in measuring production and have ignored quality control and consumers' tastes. Large inventories of shoddy goods have accumulated. The inadequacy of the Soviet television set's longevity and warranty provisions became proverbial. The failure to manufacture automobile spare parts in sufficient quantities or to produce prescription lenses in adequate numbers reflects an indifference to the plight of the consumer. There is a shortage of service facilities such as tailor shops, dry cleaners, and shoe or watch repair shops. Entertainment facilities are very limited, and quality restaurants are not readily available; good chefs cannot open restaurants and make their fortune by pleasing their clientele. In these as in other areas, there is refusal to permit private ownership of consumer service facilities using hired labor, apparently on ideological grounds.

Soviet citizens have too often had to tolerate rude and surly sales personnel who care little whether the individual customer is satisfied or even makes a purchase. Although some self-service retailing has been introduced, there remains a need for more efficient merchandising methods. The ability to pay has not assured one's ability to buy, and it has often been useful to have friends in retail outlets, as sales personnel have been known to set aside scarce items for customers who pay a bribe or who return the favor.

One of the Soviet economy's problems has been the extensive use of labor, which is reflected in the important role played by women in certain sectors of the economy; women are present in large numbers in medicine and dentistry as well as in the textile industry, agriculture, and construction. The 1936 and 1977 Constitutions have stipulated that work is both a right and a duty. As a result the Soviet Union has dealt with the unemployment problem largely by "make work" measures and low wages with attendant featherbedding and overstaffing.

Plants tend to hire more workers to protect themselves against absenteeism, personnel turnover, and diversion of labor to civic tasks and the harvesting of crops.[19] It would appear that Soviet experience confirms C. Northcote Parkinson's First Law that "work expands so as to fill the time available for its completion."

The 1961 Party Program promised "the world's shortest and, concurrently, the most productive and highest-paid working day."[20] None of this was achieved, as promised, by 1981. The 1986 revised program offered another bold assertion: The Soviet Union would achieve "the highest world level in the productivity of social labor, quality of output, and productive efficiency."[21] Soviet workers are not usually well paid, with the exception of certain highly skilled personnel or those who are employed under hardship conditions in remote areas or whose work may involve high physical risk. Thus there is, especially in lower-paid workers, a tendency not to work too hard. The authorities unfailingly respond by having the media exhort workers to fulfill the economic plan. The Central Committee's apparatus has issued the most detailed instructions regarding the agricultural harvest—as though those concerned did not know how this should be done. As part of the effort to extract every last increment of labor at the lowest or at no cost, Soviet authorities employ the so-called "communist *subbotnik,*" or Saturday of labor contributed by workers without pay in April to commemorate the anniversary of Lenin's birth. Such labor is depicted as the true beginning of communism.

Yet labor productivity has suffered from the very serious problem of alcoholism, which is of great concern to the Soviet authorities. Consumption of alcohol on a per-capita basis has risen steadily so that the Soviet Union has become one of the world's leading consumers of alcohol in the form of spirits (hard liquor).[22] Such a high rate of consumption results in absenteeism, reduced labor productivity, industrial and traffic accidents, crime and delinquency, divorce and domestic conflict, and numerous medical problems. The Central Committee's report to the Twenty-sixth Party Congress characterized alcoholism as an "ugly phenomenon" and as a "serious problem."[23] Gorbachev at the Twenty-seventh Party Congress in 1986 claimed some limited success in the "struggle against drunkenness and alcoholism" but conceded that it was being waged "against traditions shaped and implanted over the centuries."[24] In an effort to stem the tide, the authorities have raised prices, limited the hours of sale, reduced

---

[19]The so-called Shchekino experiment (named after a chemical plant in Tula oblast') in the late 1960s provided for layoffs of personnel in an effort to increase production by using the savings to pay more to the workers who were retained. It was not very popular. For a more positive appraisal, see Peter Rutland, "The Shchekino Method and the Struggle to Raise Labour Productivity in Soviet Industry," *Soviet Studies* XXXVI, No. 3 (July 1984), pp. 345–365.

[20]*Programme of the Communist Party of the Soviet Union* (Moscow: Foreign Languages Publishing House, 1961), p. 87.

[21]*Partiinaia zhizn'*, Nos. 6–7, March–April 1986, pp. 109–110.

[22]Vladimir G. Treml, *Alcohol in the USSR: A Statistical Study* (Durham, N.C.: Duke University Press, 1982), pp. 69–70.

[23]*Izvestiia*, February 24, 1981, p. 8.

[24]*Pravda*, February 26, 1986, p. 6.

the alcohol content of vodka, attempted to substitute wine and beer sales for vodka, and launched a drive against the illicit production of alcohol *(samogon)*, which is fairly widespread in rural areas. The fact that the production of alcohol is a state monopoly—apart from samogon—and is highly lucrative, providing high turnover tax revenues and profits, presents the Soviet state with a dilemma that is both fiscal and moral.[25]

Despite such serious problems and shortcomings, Soviet planners have demonstrated the ability to concentrate resources on certain priority projects. Among these are the ability to engage in space exploration and to acquire a powerful military establishment; to develop supersonic aircraft and nuclear-energy facilities; to produce machine tools and some export items of adequate quality; and to build a modern merchant marine, nuclear-powered icebreakers, and hydrofoil rivercraft. However, as the Soviet economy seeks to develop greater diversifications of output and to satisfy consumer demands, it will require more sophisticated and accurate planning methods. To some degree the use of the most modern data-processing methods and the application of cybernetics can be expected to contribute to improved planning. The growing complexity of the task is reflected in the need to combat reduced growth rates and to make greater outlays for research and development and for automation.

Increasingly, planning requires an ability to revise priorities, rectify imbalances, and meet more diverse needs. It is one thing to maintain high growth rates and to keep increasing the production of electric power, steel, coal, and cement annually; but it is a very different task to retail large quantities of unpopular consumer goods or to produce the variety and quality of goods desired by consumers. An economic plan cannot readily anticipate changes in consumer tastes, and bureaucracy generally tends to stagnate rather than innovate.

The shortcomings of using quantitative fulfillment of the economic plan (in terms of gross output) as the index for measuring performance became increasingly evident during the 1960s. Yet to rely on profits and costs as providing a more effective index would mean permitting prices to reflect market conditions. Even if a novel species of "market socialism" should ultimately emerge in the Soviet Union, certain questions will still remain. For example, will employees in the state-owned enterprises identify with management? Will these enterprises be responsive to human costs (in contrast to financial costs) and be guided by the public interest (as against that of the enterprise) in such matters as air and water pollution and the interests and safety of the products' users? How are individual needs to be determined in a communist society? It is in terms of the answers to

---

[25]An interesting revelation was offered at the Twenty-seventh Party Congress by Party Control Committee Chairman Mikhail S. Solomentsev, who reported on an "unpunished violation of Party and state discipline": the joint 1972 decision of the Party and government on the struggle against drunkenness and alcoholism was ignored by "Gosplan and the ministry of finance and other ministries and agencies [who] instead of reducing . . . increased the production and sale of spirits." *Pravda,* March 1, 1986, p. 3. The quest for revenue and profit took precedence over compliance with the Party's decision, and the governmental bureaucracy was able to thwart the Party bureaucracy. M. S. Gorbachev revealed to the Central Committee that for most of four five-year plans the increase in Soviet national income was artificial, based on exports of petroleum at then-high world market prices and on "increasing the sale of alcoholic beverages." *Izvestiia,* February 19, 1988, p. 2.

questions such as these that the effectiveness of Soviet economic decision making must ultimately be judged.

Reform Versus "Restructuring"

The need for reform of the Soviet economy was comprehended by Iuri Andropov in 1983 when he launched a campaign against corruption and lax labor discipline. Relying on the policeman's approach, Andropov had citizens rounded up in public places to determine if they were absent from their work for legitimate reasons. He also adopted a Law on Labor Collectives (June 17, 1983) that obliged workers collectively to carry out Party decisions, fulfill government directives and contractual obligations, and increase productivity. The law provided for various sanctions, including demotion of workers to lower-paying positions, firing, denial of the right to an apartment, and refusal of any bonus. The Party could also use the "collective" to remove a manager. Andropov's reform efforts were cut short when his health failed.

The problem of reform was given even greater urgency by Mikhail S. Gorbachev, who, as General Secretary, used the Twenty-seventh CPSU Congress Central Committee Report to press for significant changes in the Soviet economy. However, Gorbachev was reluctant to use the term "reform" and, instead, called for a "restructuring of the Soviet economic mechanism and the system of management." Central to the "restructuring" *(perestroika)* was the goal of "acceleration" *(uskorenie),* which he defined as an increased rate of economic growth, greater productivity, improved quality of production, and more effective application of technology and automation. Gorbachev conceded that the Soviet economy was characterized by shortages, and he recited a veritable litany of admissions of failure. He admitted that there were "serious lags in machine building, the petroleum and coal industries, the electrical equipment industry, ferrous metallurgy, the chemical industry and capital construction."[26] He conceded that slow methods of construction meant that capital funds were "frozen" for long periods with no return on investment. Scientific discoveries and inventions have remained undeveloped and "find no practical application [in industry] for years, sometimes decades."[27] He complained of ministries erecting new factory buildings and equipping them with obsolete technology. Ministries were said to engage in "petty tutelage" and interfere in the day-to-day operations of enterprises. Energy and materials are wasted, and the Soviet Union must rely less on liquid fuels and more on gas and coal. Gorbachev admitted that unneeded jobs continue to exist and that persons are paid to continue producing goods that no one wishes to buy and that are "for the warehouse." Thus he conceded that the Soviet Union has "full employment" by wasting labor on unnecessary tasks and subsidizing workers.

Gorbachev argued that "enterprises' wage funds need to be tied directly to income from the sale of their output."[28] The increments to the labor force are no

---

[26]*Pravda,* February 26, 1986, p. 4.
[27]*Ibid.*
[28]*Ibid.,* p. 5.

longer what they were, and Gorbachev conceded that "we have begun to pay dearly for the extraction and delivery of every ton of petroleum, ore and coal. . . . We must economize in everything and everywhere—on the job and at home—and not take an indifferent attitude toward mismanagement and wastefulness."[29] He contended that increased income will have to come from increased labor productivity and reduced waste in the use of materials and energy.

Following the Twenty-seventh Congress, Gorbachev relied heavily on public exhortation, and he took to touring various parts of the country, giving speeches, and meeting with citizens in an effort to obtain support for economic "restructuring." He criticized government ministries and those officials who were apparently obstructing his efforts, but his basic theme was that Soviet citizens must support "restructuring" by working harder. Thus in Vladivostok, in an encounter with citizens, he defined "restructuring" as it applied to the ordinary citizen: "Everyone in his place must augment discipline, responsibility, creativity, productivity. Then we will unbind our Soviet flywheel."[30]

The effort to "restructure" the Soviet economy raises the question of how fundamental the "rebuilding" needs to be: whether or not it is sufficient to limit the effort to the "mechanism" and to management or whether it must concern itself with the very foundations of the economy. Tinkering with the "mechanism" cannot serve as a substitute for fundamental, systemic restructuring. Yet such basic restructuring would undoubtedly have numerous repercussions that would not be confined to the economic sphere. Thus if managers are to demonstrate greater initiative and innovation, they must be freed from the restrictions imposed upon them by the centralized ministries. However, if economic decentralization were to prove successful, it would probably result in demands for political decentralization, and this would threaten the Soviet oligarchy's monopoly of political power.

Gorbachev undertook to restore a degree of dynamism to the Soviet system, having conceded that it had lost tempo and had stagnated under his predecessors and that the central planning process had become an economic "braking system."[31] Yet reform efforts had been undertaken by Khrushchev and Brezhnev. In the case of Khrushchev the reforms were organizational and involved incentives; but they led to his ouster in the end, as he had reformed too much and, in the process, acquired too many enemies. Consequently Brezhnev followed the more cautious course of diluted and partial reform.

The obstacles to reform of the economy are numerous, and some are formidable. The "sacred cow" of centralized planning even prompted Gorbachev to favor "strengthening of the centralized basis" where it pertains to balance and proportionality in the economy and to ensure "the optimal combination of state, branch and regional interests."[32] Central planners and ministries are reluctant to surrender their prerogatives. Local Party officials may at best be ambivalent

---

[29] *Ibid.*, p. 5

[30] *Pravda,* July 27, 1986, p. 1.

[31] *Pravda,* April 9, 1986, p. 1 and *Izvestiia,* January 28, 1987, p. 1.

[32] *Pravda,* April 9, 1986, p. 2.

toward reform, as they are responsible for performance and may fear that reforms will affect performance and also reduce their authority. Managers may also be ambivalent, desiring increased authority but also being apprehensive regarding the increased demands that accompany reform measures. Reforms may not be popular if they require greater effort on the part of workers, especially if increased productivity is not accompanied by new incentives and rewards.

There are obstacles that can be said to be "cultural," in the sense of being behavioral and well ingrained. These include Gorbachev's admission concerning the uneven rate of work performance: "It is no secret that many enterprises at the beginning of the month spend more time standing idle than working. Thus at the end of the month a last minute rush begins, the result being poor quality articles. This chronic disease must be eliminated."[33] Gorbachev also acknowledged the existence of " 'pilferers' who do not consider it a crime to steal from their enterprise everything that comes their way, as well as all sorts of bribe-takers and rip-off artists."[34] Thus the widespread inertia and pandemic corruption in the Soviet economy and society need to be overcome before any reform efforts can be effective.

Symptomatic of the contradictions that characterize both the Soviet economy and "restructuring" efforts was Gorbachev's acknowledgement that "groups of people have appeared with pronounced private-ownership aspirations and a scornful attitude toward the interests of society."[35] Presumably he was referring to entrepreneurial groups within the "second economy" that are demonstrating entrepreneurial skills, flexibility, satisfaction of consumer needs, and the ability to take risks—all of which have been lacking in the official Soviet economy.

In an effort to improve consumer services, a "Law of the U.S.S.R. on Individual Work Activity" was adopted on November 19, 1986 to take effect on May 1, 1987. It specifically avoided the term "enterprise" and limited the activity to spare-time "individual labor of citizens and their families."[36] Hired labor is forbidden, although citizens can form cooperatives or voluntary associations; pensioners and housewives can participate full-time. Cooperatives must be self-financing and self-sustaining. Groups of individuals or cooperatives are encouraged to conclude contracts with state enterprises. Permitted "work activities" include: the making of clothing, footwear and haberdashery, fabrics, furniture and other wooden articles, carpets, pottery, toys, and household articles. Services permitted include: construction and building repair; livestock pasturing; repair of automobiles and other means of transportation, household appliances, radios and television sets, clothing, footwear, and furniture; photography; barber and hairdressing; typing; and transport services. Forbidden activities include the making of articles from fur or precious metals, weapons, toxic or narcotic articles or medicines, and duplicating equipment. Services that are forbidden include gam-

[33]*Pravda,* February 26, 1986, p. 5.
[34]*Ibid.*
[35]*Ibid.,* p. 6.
[36]For the text of the law, see *Pravda,* November 21, 1986, pp. 1, 3. The U.S.S.R. Council of Ministers subsequently issued unpublished instructions on October 23, 1987, forbidding publishing and printing cooperatives. See the *New York Times,* February 3, 1988.

bling, bathhouses, repair of weapons or articles made of precious stones, and the organization of entertainment. Individuals engaged in permitted "work activities" are obliged to obtain the necessary registration certificate or license and pay the required fees as well as income tax on all earnings. Supervision and registration of all such individual or family spare-time "businesses" and cooperatives are the responsibility of the executive committees of local soviets. That such a relatively wide range of handicraft and service activities should be permitted testifies to the failure of the official planned economy to satisfy consumer needs.

The adoption of a law on the state enterprise (June 30, 1987) was designed to reduce the role of the central bureaucracy in the economy and to eliminate what Gorbachev termed the " 'shadow' economy." It permitted the enterprise somewhat greater flexibility in employing economic stimuli, setting wage scales and employing material sanctions and incentives (including "allocating housing out of turn"), and entering into contracts with wholesale suppliers and purchasers. Yet enterprises are also subordinated to "higher level agencies," to which they must transfer part of their profits. Enterprises must be guided by control figures from above, orders placed by the state, five-year-plan goals, and contracts that they have concluded. They are expected to reduce the hoarding of supplies and to observe "technological discipline." They are required to pay charges for production assets, interest on borrowed capital, and fees for land, water, and minerals and to pay taxes on profits. They are expected to produce articles of high quality suitable for export.

The law on the state enterprise seeks to promote use of "economic methods" and motivation in lieu of administrative orders, prohibitions, and appeals. It acknowledges the possibility of financial insolvency and the need to dissolve certain enterprises. However, the law may seek to reconcile highly divergent positions and interests. Thus it seeks to combine "centralized management and the socialist self-management of the labor collective" (Article 6); the executive of an enterprise "expresses the interests of the state and the labor collective" (Article 6); and "the higher-level agency counteracts the monopoly tendencies of individual enterprises" (Article 9).

If economic reform must endeavor to reconcile and resolve certain contradictions, it can be questioned whether reform of the economy can provide the solution to the Soviet Union's numerous problems. Gorbachev equated "restructuring" with a "revolution" involving "social relations, the political system, the spiritual-ideological sphere, the style and methods of Party work of all our cadres."[37] Yet economic reforms have required priority and have been seen as providing the basis for solving other problems. Nevertheless, it can be questioned whether the necessary economic goals can be achieved without departing from the bases of socialism. Innovation is demanded in a system that has traditionally emphasized conformity and centralism. "Price flexibility" is called for, but there

---

[37]*Pravda,* August 2, 1986, p. 1. At the January 1987 Central Committee plenary session, Gorbachev defined "restructuring" as the "energetic deliverance of society from the distortions of socialist morality," "the profound renewal of all aspects of life," and the "transformation of the economic, social and spiritual [*dukhovnoi*] spheres." *Izvestiia,* January 28, 1987, p. 2.

is a reluctance to permit market forces to determine prices based on supply and demand. Authorities seek to eliminate wasteful and unneeded labor (overemployment), but this must be reconciled with the "guaranteed employment" provided for in the 1977 Constitution. Consumer satisfaction is advocated in an economy that has given priority to production for the military.

Politico-military considerations have determined Soviet priorities and have required the strictest centralized control over allocations of investment capital. A "new economic mechanism" is advocated, but it can include neither a free market for capital nor adequate decentralization of decision making regarding capital investment. A system that has consistently rewarded quantity of output is asked to employ qualitative criteria. Consumer needs are to be taken into account, although the discipline of the market is feared as disruptive and as dictating a different set of priorities. New technology is sought, but foreigners and foreign values are kept at arm's length. Joint ventures with capitalist foreign corporations are not excluded but are hampered with numerous restrictions and conditions. An act on joint enterprises adopted by the U.S.S.R. Council of Ministers on January 13, 1987, provided for amounts invested to be stated in rubles at the official rate of exchange (with the ruble greatly overvalued); the Soviet share must be at least 51 percent; the president and general director of each joint enterprise must be Soviet citizens; disputes are to be resolved in Soviet courts or by Soviet state arbitration; enterprises are to pay 30 percent of profits in taxes to the U.S.S.R. government; foreign partners must pay a 20 percent tax on their share of any profits transferred abroad; personnel of joint enterprises must be "fundamentally" *(v osnovnom)* Soviet, and enterprises must enter into agreements with Soviet trade unions; wages and benefits of Soviet personnel and social security taxes and insurance must be paid in accordance with Soviet law; and foreign employees must pay Soviet income tax. Joint enterprises are forbidden to provide any reports or information to any foreign organs or government agencies.[38]

The decision to tolerate joint enterprises revealed the urgency of the challenge, as did Gorbachev when he referred to "the crucial nature of the time we are living in, the fact that it is a turning point." Yet Gorbachev conceded that "all of our plans will be left hanging if they leave people indifferent, if we are unable to awaken the labor and public activeness of the masses, their energy and initiative."[39] He complained of the "people who neglect their duties and are indifferent to the interests of society: botchers, idlers, rip-off artists, writers of anonymous letters, red tape artists, bribe-takers."[40] Yet he also conceded the necessity of increasing workers' "material interest in making better use of public wealth and multiplying it" and observed that "it would be naive to assume that a sense of proprietorship *(chuvstvo khoziaina)* can be instilled through words."[41] However, his solution by means of "socialist self-management" simply reaffirmed

---

[38]The text of the act was published in *Izvestiia,* January 28, 1987, p. 6.
[39]*Pravda,* February 26, 1986, p. 9.
[40]*Ibid.*
[41]*Ibid.,* p. 5

the basic problem of ownership in the Soviet economy and the apparent inability to solve it.[42] In actual practice "social ownership" has meant no (or ill-defined) ownership and the apparent inability of workers to identify with the employer-state or develop any sense of co-proprietorship.

Gorbachev based his solution on the premise that workers' collectives can "establish order" in an enterprise and acquire the sense of being its "master" *(khoziain)* by holding management accountable for performance. Enterprises, under Gorbachev's prescription, would be self-financing and self-sustaining. "Levelling tendencies" in wages and in consumption *(uravnilovka)* would be abandoned. Gorbachev justified drastic prescriptions by depicting the Soviet economy in near-crisis terms at the January 1987 Central Committee plenary session. He advocated his program as a "radical turn [that is] necessary because there is no other course for us" and added: "It is impossible for us to retreat and there is nowhere to retreat."[43]

SOCIAL SERVICES

The Soviet polity in its post-Stalin variant could not base itself exclusively on the security police and other organs of repression and on propaganda. It has endeavored to raise real income and improve living standards and has rashly promised Soviet citizens that ultimately their material level of living will be the world's highest. Although Soviet living standards have been low compared with those of many industrial countries (in terms of housing, diet, clothing, automobile and appliance ownership, and various amenities), there is no reason to believe that the Soviet leadership is committed to the perpetuation of relative poverty. The Soviet regime has endeavored to provide its subjects with a variety of social services and benefits that are subsidized by the government and are paid for indirectly by the beneficiaries or by other citizens through low wages, the concealed turnover tax, and the profits of state-owned enterprises. Although capital-equipment accumulation and the production of producers' goods have been at the expense of the consumer and living standards have suffered in the "guns versus butter" dilemma, the regime has nevertheless been committed to "abundance" and to improving social services.[44]

Housing

Housing must be regarded as a social service because of the large amount of publicly owned and municipally administered apartment buildings. Since rents

---

[42]Alec Nove, *The Soviet Economic System,* 2nd ed. (Winchester, Mass.: Allen and Unwin, 1980), p. 50.

[43]*Pravda,* January 28, 1987, p. 2. Gorbachev repeated this warning to the Central Committee on February 18, 1988. See *Izvestiia,* February 19, 1988, p. 2.

[44]On Soviet living standards, see Janet G. Chapman, *Real Wages in Soviet Russia since 1928* (Cambridge: Harvard University Press, 1963), and Arvid Brodersen, *The Soviet Worker* (New York: Random House, 1966). See also the brief but pointed description of Soviet living standards by academician Andrei Sakharov in his *My Country and the World* (New York: Knopf, 1975), pp. 14–27.

are usually unrealistically low and cannot even finance the maintenance of housing structures, construction and repairs are subsidized by the government. It is little wonder, then, that Soviet housing—especially in the large cities—has been inadequate both in terms of the amount of per-capita living space and in the quality and variety of construction. If Soviet citizens often pay only nominal rents, their housing is frequently of a commensurate nature, and their choice of a dwelling is limited. Some citizens are able to obtain better housing from their place of employment, and those who have the financial means can join housing cooperatives that erect apartment buildings for their members. Individual dwellings can also be built, although they were prohibited in the larger cities in 1964.

Government-operated housing provides a means for claiming that Soviet workers have a real income that is greater than their money income because much of the housing cost (above the nominal rents paid by tenants) is really a form of social benefit. Of course, if Soviet workers were paid higher money wages and less housing were government-owned, there would probably be greater choice between various kinds of housing, and more money would be invested in the housing industry. However, the Soviet housing system has the possible added advantage, from the regime's point of view, of enabling officials to know who resides where, as this current information is kept by the local housing offices.

Soviet authorities undertook an unparalleled program of new housing construction after 1955, using prefabricated components in high-rise structures. Significant gains were made in increasing housing space per capita and in providing a substantial part of the population with new apartments. However, the stereotyped and cheap quality of much of this mass-produced housing has given it a monotonous appearance. Haste and lack of sufficient planning resulted in shoddy construction requiring major repairs, although much of it is still relatively new. Among problems faced is the need to provide revenues to finance repairs and maintenance—the alternative being a high rate of urban decay. Although the Soviet regime prefers government-operated housing, it has had to permit increased construction by housing cooperatives and by individuals in order to increase greatly the supply of available housing.

The goal of solving the Soviet housing problem has remained elusive. When agriculture required a greater share of investment beginning in the mid-1960s, it was at the expense of housing.[45] The 1961 CPSU Program promised that, by 1980, every Soviet family would have its own apartment or dwelling, but the promise was not fulfilled despite the construction of 54 million apartment units. The 1986 Program renewed the promise with the pledge that, by the year 2000, each Soviet family will have an apartment or house. To achieve this goal Gorbachev told the Twenty-seventh Congress that cooperative and individual housing should be encouraged. Since most urban housing is government-owned, there are problems

[45]Carol Nechemias and Donna Bahry, "The Soviet Union: Consumer Sector" in Alexander J. Groth and Larry L. Wade, eds., *Comparative Resource Allocation* (Beverly Hills, Calif.: Sage Publications, 1984), pp. 112–113.

regarding corruption in its allocation. It was conceded by Gorbachev that "serious improvements" are needed in allocation—because of bribery—and that the "poor quality of housing construction draws many complaints."[46] There is also a lack of special housing for the elderly.

Medical Care

The health of a country's population is a vital resource because it affects economic productivity and is an important factor in military capability. The Soviet government operates a centralized health service that functions through the ministries of health of the USSR and of the union republics. Medical care is provided for in each successive economic plan and in the annual governmental budgets. The system of medical care is financed from government revenues and taxation. Although the physician's services and hospital care are generally free to the patient, all Soviet taxpayers pay indirectly for medical care. Drugs for out-patient use and eyeglasses are paid for directly by the patient. All hospitals and clinics are state-owned or are operated by state-owned enterprises. The state trains all physicians, who then become salaried state employees.

The Soviet Union's system of medical care is impressive in a number of ways. The ratio of physicians to population is among the very highest in the world. Per-capita expenditures for medical treatment have risen. Epidemic and endemic diseases have been brought under control in a country in which malaria, cholera, and typhus were serious problems in the past. The number of hospital beds in relation to population has increased. Medical practice is conducted through district polyclinics that serve as out-patient facilities for several thousand persons and operate in two shifts in urban areas.

Despite many positive features, the Soviet system of public medical care has certain shortcomings. Thus, the patient cannot usually select the physician because they are simply assigned to each other; this tends at times to give the doctor-patient relationship an impersonal quality. Physicians of each specialty are expected to adhere to norms regarding the average number of patients they are to treat in an hour. Much Soviet general practice of medicine is highly routinized and based on bureaucratic observance of regulations issued by the ministry of health. The physician is placed in the position of having to certify medical excuses for employees and to determine who is malingering. Medical personnel, not the system of medical practice, are blamed for shortcomings. The system is highly bureaucratized, and many physicians serve as administrators. While standardization has certain advantages, it can also stifle innovation and medical research.[47]

The effectiveness of the public health system is weakened as a result of

---

[46]*Pravda,* February 26, 1986, p. 6.

[47]See Mark G. Field, *Soviet Socialized Medicine, An Introduction* (New York: Free Press, 1967), and his chapter "Soviet Urban Health Services: Some Problems and Their Sources" in Henry W. Morton and Robert C. Stuart, eds., *The Contemporary Soviet City* (Armonk, N.Y.: M. E. Sharpe, 1984), pp. 129–155.

various conditions of Soviet life. Among these is the general diet, which is high in carbohydrates and fats and low in protein; nor do crowded housing conditions promote health.[48] Admission to a hospital is not always an easy matter. A patient who is seriously ill and requires the services of a highly skilled specialist might find it preferable to pay for such medical care rather than rely on the government-operated system. By contrast, members of the Soviet elite are assured the best available medical care through a separate network of special facilities.[49] Although the medical profession is generally responsible for improving sanitary conditions and maintaining health standards, factory managers and economic planners often ignore medical recommendations regarding working and health conditions because of cost considerations. Soviet physicians are not paid very well, although they do not work the long hours that physicians in private practice in Western countries do. The system is staffed largely by female physicians, most of whom must also rear families and cannot devote much time to professional activities outside of office hours. Some Soviet physicians, especially highly skilled specialists, are able to conduct a limited private practice in their spare time; but the income from it is heavily taxed, and such practice is only tolerated.

While the polyclinics do provide primary medical care for ordinary ailments, the 1986 Party Program promised "a system of preventive medical examinations for the entire population." However, there is a shortage of diagnostic equipment and medical laboratory facilities. Medical supplies can be difficult to obtain, and certain pharmaceuticals can be bought more readily on the black market. There is a shortage of prosthetic devices and wheelchairs. Dentistry has been seriously neglected.

Soviet hospitals often provide indifferent care and lack adequate nursing and medical-support personnel. At times patients have found it necessary to pay gratuities to hospital personnel for ordinary services. Families of patients have been known to bring food, or the patient must purchase food. Yet it can be difficult to be discharged from a hospital because of administrative requirements, quotas, and endless regulations.[50] Soviet physicians tend to be paternalistic and tend not to inform patients sufficiently regarding the nature of their treatment. Yet higher-quality treatment requires additional payment, if only in the form of *blat* (better medical care given in return for an item in scarce supply or a gift) or a specific ruble fee. Thus, the Soviet state-operated system of medical care represents a mixed picture of achievements and serious defects.

---

[48]Khrushchev in his reminiscences describes food shortages in Moscow in 1970 and observes that "if it's bad in Moscow, it's worse in the provinces." *Khrushchev Remembers, The Last Testament, op. cit.* (above, n. 2), pp. 139–140.

[49]Mark G. Field, *op. cit.* (above, n. 47), pp. 94–96. Important Soviet leaders have been treated and have had surgery performed by prominent foreign medical specialists.

[50]See William A. Knaus, M.D., *Inside Russian Medicine* (New York: Everest House, 1981). The Supreme Soviet's Presidium, by a decree of August 25, 1987, acted swiftly and authorized mandatory testing for the disease AIDS (SPID, in Russian) and confinement for anyone endangering or infecting another person. See *Vedomosti Verkhovnogo Soveta SSSR,* August 26, 1987, No. 34 (2420), pp. 636–637.

Social Welfare

Work is an obligation of the individual that is enshrined in the Soviet constitution; consequently there is no unemployment compensation despite the fact that jobs may be scarce in areas in which economic development has been retarded as a result of decisions of planning bodies. In those areas that are plagued by a shortage of jobs, individuals who cannot find employment of the type sought have the choice of settling for a less desirable job or moving to an area in which jobs are in supply. It is assumed that unemployment compensation might discourage persons from working.

Various types of social benefits are provided through the union republic ministries of social security.[51] These include pensions for retired persons and for invalids and the permanently disabled, allowances to unmarried mothers for their children, institutional care for retarded and severely handicapped children, and various prosthetic devices for welfare recipients. Institutional care is also provided for the aged and disabled. The republic ministries of social security offer vocational rehabilitation to persons who are injured but can still be employed; placement facilities are also available for invalids, although in the Soviet Union, as in other countries, some reluctance is encountered in hiring the handicapped. The blind and deaf have separate membership organizations, the All-Union Society for the Blind (VOS) and the All-Union Society for the Deaf (VOG), which operate training and workshop facilities. Although these organizations function under the supervision of the republic ministries of social security, they come closest in the Soviet Union to being interest group organizations that seek to protect the well-being of their members.

Pensions and other forms of social insurance are financed by the Soviet employing enterprises and institutions as a percentage of the total payroll. However, there are minimum periods of employment, as well as different age requirements for men and women and for various industries, that must be met in order to qualify for a pension. Pension payments are part of the economic plan, and deficits are financed from the regular state budget. A worker who is ill or injured is paid a sickness benefit, the amount of which is determined by the length of employment, the level of one's earnings, and membership (or not) in a trade union. If one is injured in connection with one's work, full earnings are paid and trade union membership is not required. The principle of liability awards to compensate for harm and pain is not recognized; only the loss of wages is regarded as a basis for compensation.

Soviet trade unions perform various functions that prompt their inclusion with bodies responsible for welfare programs. The unions administer benefits paid to workers who are temporarily ill or disabled. In addition they operate numerous

---

[51]For a general survey and evaluation of Soviet welfare programs and policies based on a field study, see Bernice Q. Madison, *Social Welfare in the Soviet Union* (Stanford: Stanford University Press, 1968), as well as her article "Social Services for Families and Children in the Soviet Union Since 1967," *Slavic Review,* XXXI, No. 4 (December 1972), pp. 831–852. For a brief discussion of the range of benefits, see Alistair McAuley, *Economic Welfare in the Soviet Union: Poverty, Living Standards, and Inequality* (Madison: University of Wisconsin Press, 1979), Chapter 11.

resort facilities, sanatoria, and rest homes for convalescent care; it is the trade union organization that determines which members are entitled to use such facilities. Although the unions do not engage in collective bargaining for wage contracts, they do bargain with management over fringe benefits, factory-sponsored housing, bonuses, working conditions, and club and cafeteria facilities. Workers cannot be discharged by management without the union's approval; and unions, in general, seek to make the lot of workers more tolerable. However, unions may be more successful in protesting an individual's grievances and obtaining reinstatement, change in job classification, or vacation rights than in correcting endemic conditions that are a source of discontent. Indeed, the airing of workers' grievances in the press is more likely to bring results than is trade union intervention.[52]

Despite state-sponsored social welfare programs, many social ills persist in the Soviet Union, and welfare programs are needed in spite of the claims made for communism as a universal remedy. Poverty has not been abolished, although its most unfortunate consequences have been mitigated. Welfare services in rural areas are far below the level of those available in cities. Child allowances paid following the birth of a third child are modest and limited to the child's first five years, although single mothers receive slightly higher benefits. Soviet pensions and benefits for the elderly are inadequate and are generally well below the minimum wage—and this in a country in which food costs can be the largest single item in the average family's budget, at times constituting nearly half of its expenditures. However, Soviet pensioners have been aided considerably by low rents and free medical care. Collective farmers were excluded from the state pension system prior to 1965. While the Soviet Union may not be alone in neglecting retired persons, it is nevertheless evident that the Soviet system is not devoting adequate resources to pension benefits and welfare programs. Institutional facilities are often crowded and do not meet high construction standards. The Soviet version of the welfare state is not unlike its non-Soviet variants in that promises and expectations tend to exceed benefactions.

Soviet authorities are committed to providing a variety of social benefits. Yet there are pronounced differences in income and in living standards, and the Soviet general living standard has remained well below that of developed Western countries. The complaints of "social injustice" because of the "special benefits" *(blaga)* enjoyed by the Soviet elite reached the rostrum of the Twenty-seventh Party Congress.[53] In particular there is resentment that members of the elite have access to "closed" stores and do not have to stand in lines in order to make purchases.

As a welfare state the Soviet Union remains a modest undertaking. Yet organized private charity is nonexistent and forbidden in the Soviet Union; it is regarded as unnecessary, although the state is incapable of providing for all of

---

[52]This was one of the findings of a survey of industrial plants conducted in the Voronezh oblast'. See "U istoka konflikta," *Izvestiia,* October 22, 1975.

[53]Such complaints were especially evident in the address by the Moscow Party first secretary, Boris N. Yeltsin. *Pravda,* February 27, 1986, p. 3.

the unsatisfied human needs. Troubling questions and developments have marred the claims professed on behalf of the Soviet welfare state. Does a welfare state sell and derive huge profits from the sale of alcohol to its citizens? An unprecedented rise in the infant mortality rate in the 1970s led to a ban on the publication of statistics in 1974. A decline in male life expectancy from 66 to 62 years also occurred between 1965 and 1980. These startling developments have probably been due, in large part, to widespread alcoholism. In the case of infants, higher mortality has probably also been due to: widespread use of abortion (in lieu of contraceptive methods) and its attendant effects on pregnancy and premature delivery; inadequate prenatal and postnatal care; inadequate infant formulas; and large day care centers in which infants are vulnerable to infection.[54] Yet Soviet Central Asians, with their high birth rate, have to a large extent avoided both alcoholism and abortion—demonstrating once again that diversity is a characteristic of the Soviet Union.

The Soviet welfare state is the principal source of water and air pollution by state-owned industry, of inadequate water and waste-treatment facilities, and of excessive lead emissions. The deterioration of the country's land resources; soil erosion, due to improper agricultural and surface-mining practices; and lack of adequate conservation methods indicate the breadth of the obligations assumed by the modern welfare state. The awesome and lethal effects of radioactive fallout from the 1986 Chernobyl' nuclear disaster, not only in Ukraine and Belorussia but in various European countries and especially in Scandinavia, demonstrated the elusive nature of the concept of welfare and its impact beyond state frontiers and ethnic boundaries. Indeed, the diversity and complexity of the burdens placed on any welfare state may be even more pronounced in its Soviet version, which claims so much and assumes responsibilities that far exceed its capacities.

---

[54]Murray Feshbach, "A Different Crisis," *The Wilson Quarterly,* Winter 1981, pp. 117–125. See also Christopher Davis and Murray Feshbach, *Rising Infant Mortality in the U.S.S.R. in the 1970s,* International Population Reports, Series P-95, No. 74 (Washington, D.C.: U.S. Department of Commerce, Bureau of the Census, 1980).

chapter 9

Soviet Law
and the Judiciary

A study of the Soviet legal and judicial system could justifiably be included with the administrative system. For, in the highest degree, the Soviet system of justice is administered. The courts, law schools, judges, procuracy, and legal profession all function as parts of an integrated system that is administered under the close guidance of the ruling Communist Party. The constitutional provision that "judges and people's assessors are independent and subject only to the law" (Article 155) provides no real assurance of judicial independence. Because of its limited tenure and its being subject to recall during its five-year term of office, the judiciary has little independence. If judges can readily be removed because of their "errors," or if they can be "transferred to other work," they are hardly independent. Indeed, Soviet judges are little more than civil servants. The fact that judges of the U.S.S.R. Supreme Court are elected for only five years is indicative of the status of the Soviet judiciary. The Soviet legal and judicial system can be regarded as administered because the judiciary is closely supervised; the higher courts and Communist Party directives provide the lower courts with instructions regarding judicial policy (leniency or harshness in sentencing) in certain types of cases. The Ministry of Justice also keeps the judiciary under surveillance. The contents of the legal codes of the union republics also reflect the centralism of a highly administered system, for they must conform to general principles laid down in Moscow and adopted by the U.S.S.R. Supreme Soviet.

THE RUSSIAN LEGAL TRADITION
AND THE MARXIST VIEW OF LAW

Russian legal and judicial institutions developed in the shadow of autocracy. Although Imperial Russia had a ponderous collection of detailed laws (the *Svod*

Zakonov Rossiiskoi Imperii), this fact did not make it less of an autocracy. Thus, Russia did not cultivate the ideal of the *Rechtsstaat,* in which the government itself must be subordinate to a fundamental law. Instead, there developed an instrumental view of law that reproached the West for being preoccupied with "legalisms" rather than pursuing "truth" and "justice." The implication of this point of view is that a regime that claimed to represent "truth" and "justice" could ignore legal niceties and procedural safeguards and could justify its every action by the allegedly virtuous nature of its motives. This has led to a situation in which the Soviet rulers have made themselves the sole judges of the legality of their conduct—except when they have quarreled among themselves and the judgment of the victorious faction has prevailed. It has given continuing meaning to the old Russian proverb: "Law is like a wagon tongue, it goes wherever you turn it." It is this quality of a traditional indifference toward the law as a binding force that may have prompted one Soviet commentator to observe approvingly that Soviet laws are "not a collection of congealed norms, but are characterized by pliability."[1]

Russian legal practice has meant ignoring laws at times. Thus, popular election of judges of the People's Courts was provided for in the 1936 Constitution but went unheeded for more than a decade. Although Soviet citizens are supposedly guaranteed a public trial, there have been instances of closed trials, and in certain cases the prosecution and the security police have been known to pack the courtroom with spectators hostile to the defense.[2] The 1977 Constitution (Article 157) permits closed trials. At times in the law there has been neglect, as when the antiquated legal codes of the 1920s were not replaced with revised codes until the early 1960s. All decisions of the U.S.S.R. Supreme Court have not been published, and there have been times when Soviet judges have not been certain how particular types of cases should be decided. Much of Soviet administrative law is secret, as all administrative regulations are not published, and citizens may have no way of knowing what their rights are. The Communist Party has also been known to issue secret instructions to legal officials.[3]

Russian law acquired a codified form comparable to, yet different from, other continental legal systems that were influenced by Roman law. The Soviet rulers initially attempted to apply the tenets of Marxism-Leninism to what was supposed to be a legal system of a new type. In the Marxist view, law is little more than a phase of politics reflecting economic relationships and is a weapon in the class struggle designed to promote the interests of a particular ruling class rather than to achieve justice. It was naively assumed that, with the advent of Communist Party rule (in the name of the "proletarian masses"), the need for law would

---

[1]A. I. Lepeshkin, A. I. Kim, N. G. Mishin, and P. I. Romanov, *Kurs sovetskogo gosudarstvennogo prava* (Moscow, 1962), II, p. 409.

[2]For examples, see Viacheslav Chornovil, *The Chornovil Papers* (New York: McGraw-Hill, 1968). The Ukrainian historian Valentyn Moroz was also tried behind closed doors on November 17–18, 1970, in Ivano-Frankivsk. See his statement to the court in *Report from the Beria Reserve: The Protest Writings of Valentyn Moroz* (Toronto: Peter Martin Associates Ltd., 1974), pp. 116–121. Moroz was sentenced to nine years' imprisonment and five years of exile principally because the KGB sought to punish him for writing *Report from the Beria Reserve.*

[3]See the relevant sources discussed in Robert Sharlet, "Politics of Soviet Law," *Problems of Communism,* XXXV, No. 1 (January–February 1986), pp. 54–60.

decline, as "exploitation" and class conflict would supposedly be eliminated and state functions would be assumed by "society." The notion of the "withering away" of the state also contributed to the belief that law and courts would disappear along with standing armies, money, bureaucracy, and crime.

Lenin's regime dissolved the courts, dismissed government attorneys, and disbanded the organized bar. A rough brand of justice was meted out by local, popularly elected courts in ordinary cases and by revolutionary tribunals designed to combat counterrevolution. Any citizen enjoying civil rights could serve as a prosecutor or defense counsel.

It soon became evident, however, that a system of regular courts was necessary along with legal counsel and codes. As a result, the judicial and legal institutions that had been discarded so hastily had to be reestablished, albeit in a form designed to promote the interests of the Soviet state. However, the tendency to view law and courts as temporary, if necessary, nuisances persisted—as did the notion of the gradual withering away of the state.

The principal spokesman for this latter viewpoint and the leading Soviet jurist in the 1920s and early 1930s was Eugene B. Pashukanis. His advocacy of the withering away of the Soviet state even led him to predict that 1937 would be a turning point in this process because all economic classes would supposedly disappear by then. However, it was in that year that Pashukanis was denounced for his errors in the important field of legal theory. One of these errors was his statement that the Soviet state had commenced to wither away from the first moment of its existence. Contending that law had resulted from exchange in the free marketplace and had reached its most developed form under the bourgeoisie, he suggested that it could be expected to disappear with the last remnants of the bourgeoisie. Pashukanis's heresy was his unwillingness to regard the state as the source of law; and when he finally did so, he still regarded Soviet law as bourgeois in form though socialist in content. For this he was accused of the philosophical error of separating form from substance and of confusing the similarity in terminology between bourgeois and Soviet legal codes with similarity in form. His heresy was his failure to regard Soviet law as socialist in both form *and* substance. He had also ignored the "capitalist encirclement" of the USSR—which played a prominent role in Stalin's thought—and its logical consequence in the form of a (Soviet) state of unprecedented strength.[4]

Stalin's insistence that the Soviet state would not wither away in the condition of "capitalist encirclement" but would make laws required that Pashukanis be replaced by a new legal theorist. This role was bestowed upon Andrei Vyshinsky, a Menshevik who converted to Bolshevism and who became the high priest of Soviet jurisprudence after a career as a law professor and as chief prosecutor in Stalin's purge trials. Vyshinsky had the task of eliminating Pashukanis's influence from the law schools and from legal publications. Soviet socialist law was declared to be socialist in both form and substance and to express the

---

[4] For a brief firsthand account of circumstances in the Moscow Juridical Institute at the time of Pashukanis's removal, see John N. Hazard, *Recollections of a Pioneering Sovietologist* (New York: Oceana Publications, 1984), pp. 23–25.

will of the entire people. The role of law and the state was to be enhanced and not diminished, and legal norms would protect socialist property and assure its defense against foreign and domestic enemies. Law was to serve as a weapon in the "struggle against the remnants of capitalism" in life and in the minds of men and as a means of educating the masses in "socialist discipline." It was subsequently conceded by Lev N. Smirnov, President of the U.S.S.R. Supreme Court, that, during the period of Vyshinsky's leadership, "in a number of instances the Supreme Court of the U.S.S.R. as well as other judicial organs permitted violations of socialist legality."[5]

THE SOVIET LEGAL SYSTEM

One of the basic characteristics of the Soviet view of law is to regard it as an instrument of the state and as an executor of state policies. The term *zakonnost'*, which is usually translated as "legality," implies an ordering and strengthening of the state rather than the notion of law as the means of circumscribing the role of the state and protecting the individual. Law exists to further state interests, and the courts and the Procuracy are regarded as the instruments through which this is accomplished. The Soviet Union's legal system is therefore based on a variety of legal codes that are adopted through legislation but that are also supplemented and amended by means of decrees and orders of a normative nature.[6] Thus, while the codes possess a certain conciseness, clarity, and simplicity, they must also be viewed as incomplete repositories of the law that can be substantially modified and even negated by new enactments and by judicial practice, as well as by the intervention of the Communist Party.

The Soviet regime's policy regarding capital punishment illustrates well the fluid quality of Soviet law. The death penalty, while initially abolished for a brief period, was originally applied only to crimes against the state; but by 1932, it was extended to the theft of state and collective farm property in the absence of mitigating circumstances. On May 26, 1947, a decree of the Presidium of the U.S.S.R. Supreme Soviet abolished the death penalty, supposedly because of the "exceptional devotion" of the population toward the Soviet regime. However, the death penalty was restored on January 12, 1950, for treason, espionage, and sabotage; in 1954, it was extended to persons committing murder under aggravating circumstances. In a series of subsequent enactments, capital punishment was extended to a number of other crimes, including so-called economic crimes (counterfeiting, embezzlement, bribery, black market activities, and speculation in foreign currencies) committed under aggravating circumstances. Per-

---

[5]L. N. Smirnov, V. V. Kulikov, and B. S. Nikiforov, eds., *Verkhovnyi sud SSSR* (Moscow: "Iuridicheskaia literatura, 1974), p. 15.

[6]For general treatments of the Soviet legal system, see William E. Butler, *Soviet Law* (London: Butterworths, 1983), as well as Harold J. Berman, *Justice in the USSR,* rev. ed. (New York: Vintage Books, 1963); Wayne R. La Fave, ed., *Law in the Soviet Society* (Urbana: University of Illinois Press, 1965); and Edward L. Johnson, *An Introduction to the Soviet Legal System* (London: Methuen, 1969). For a more detailed work, see Samuel Kucherov, *The Organs of Soviet Administration of Justice: Their History and Operation* (Leiden: E. J. Brill, 1970).

sons convicted of economic offenses earlier were executed in 1961 even though the death penalty was not applicable at the time they were convicted. The criminal codes of 1960 retained application of the death penalty in a variety of crimes ranging from espionage and terrorist acts to rape, bribery, and attempting to take the life of a policeman.[7] Capital punishment has also been applied to individuals accused of having collaborated with Nazi Germany during World War II—more than four decades after the alleged offense was said to have occurred. Such obsessive application of the death penalty for political reasons has occurred in the absence of any statute of limitations for that category of offense. Yet many other serious (nonpolitical) crimes are punishable with sentences of no more than ten years, with a fifteen-year maximum for "especially dangerous recidivists." The severity of the punishment and the types of crimes to which it has been applied have varied but cannot be said to have been generally and progressively lightened under the Soviet regime.

Soviet law as code law has required the preparation of numerous codes and manuals dealing with criminal law, criminal procedure, civil law, civil procedure, family law, agrarian law, labor law, housing law, and administrative law. The revision of the codes in the early 1960s reflected a tendency to strengthen and regularize legal procedures in force since the abolition of the special three-man administrative tribunals of the secret police in September 1953. Thus, confession alone was no longer regarded as an adequate proof of guilt as it had been under Stalin and Vyshinsky. The principle of analogy was abandoned; under this principle it was possible for judge and prosecutor to find a person guilty of a "crime" not specifically mentioned in the criminal code but analogous to specific criminal acts. However, the Soviet codes, despite their detail, contain certain vague provisions, such as those regarding "crimes against the state," "subverting or weakening the Soviet authority," "participation in an anti-Soviet organization," and circulating "slanderous fabrications which defame the Soviet state and social system."[8] Conviction on a charge of "anti-Soviet agitation and propaganda" can result in a sentence of up to seven years with or without an additional period of exile of two to five years. Thus it is possible to treat any criticism of the authorities or of Communist Party policy as a criminal offense, since the criminal code, in effect, nullifies any constitutional provision regarding freedom of speech, press, and assembly.

THE SOVIET COURTS

The Soviet judicial system has a fairly simple structure because there is a single integrated system rather than parallel hierarchies of All-Union ("federal") and republic courts. The U.S.S.R. Supreme Court is the sole regular court of non-republic jurisdiction. All other (lower) courts function within particular territo-

---

[7]See Harold J. Berman, *Soviet Criminal Law and Procedures; The RSFSR Codes* (Cambridge: Harvard University Press, 1966), pp. 61–62.

[8]*Ibid.*, pp. 178–181.

rial jurisdictions in the union republics. Soviet courts are collegial. The court of first instance in more than 90 percent of the civil and ordinary criminal cases is the People's Court, the judges of which are the only jurists popularly elected in the Soviet Union. Judges in all higher Soviet courts are elected by the corresponding soviet; thus, the judges of an oblast' court are elected by the oblast' soviet, while the members of the supreme court of a union republic are elected by the republic's supreme soviet.

The People's Court functions at the district (raion) or municipal level, and the number of judges attached to it is determined by the volume of cases heard. Judges must be at least twenty-five years old, and approximately 95 percent are members or candidate-members of the CPSU. Of the 12,122 professional judges of the People's Court elected in June 1987, 44.5 percent were women and 29 percent were elected for the first time. Judges are elected for a five-year term (increased from a three-year term in 1958) without opposition. Soviet judges do not wear robes, and there is a degree of informality in the courtroom that is sometimes obtained at the expense of judicial dignity and respect for the law. It is possible to have a graduate fresh out of law school sent to a remote area to be "elected" as a judge. Soviet judges do not create law but only apply existing statutory law (codes, statutes, and decrees) to specific cases. Judicial precedent is not recognized because it would make the judiciary a less flexible instrument and hinder changes in governmental policy as applied in the courts.[9]

A distinctive feature of Soviet courts is the institution of the assessor (zasedatel'), or temporary lay judge, designed to introduce an element of popular participation in the judicial process through judgment by one's "peers." It is used in lieu of the jury system, although assessors are given some lectures along with a handbook on the law. For every elected professional judge in the people's courts there are 70 to 80 assessors; consequently more than 700,000 persons are author-

---

[9]A quasi-judicial institution, outside of the formal structure of the Soviet judiciary, is the so-called Comradely Court, which is not bound by legal codes or procedural requirements. It deals with antisocial acts and attitudes including drunkenness, use of foul language, poor workmanship, and failure to fulfill family obligations, but not with any truly criminal offenses, and also takes up minor quarrels between citizens. It can levy small fines and determine minor claims for damages (up to 50 rubles, if both parties consent) but often simply issues reprimands or demands a public apology and attempts to conciliate petty disputes. The Comradely Courts are held in housing developments, on collective and state farms, and in factories; there are usually three lay "judges," who are elected at public meetings in each locale or institution. Comradely Courts follow a highly informal procedure without lawyers and with the audience actually participating. They are designed to promote "communist morality" and supposedly provide a model for the Soviet court of the future. They are seen as "educational" rather than punitive bodies and seek to bring about embarrassment by one's peers and a sense of guilt through public shaming; they reflect the Soviet subordination of the individual to the collective. Cases can be brought by trade union committees or by volunteer police aides (druzhiny), citizens, or the court itself. Such courts cannot enforce their rulings if a penalty or damage award is involved but must then invoke the authority of the regular People's Court to assure execution of decisions that are then subject to review. Comradely Courts function under the supervision of the executive committees of the local soviets; cases can be appealed to the local soviet or to the trade union committee. Comradely Courts were first established by Lenin but fell into disuse under Stalin; they were revived in 1959 by Khrushchev. For a graphic and detailed firsthand account of the Comradely Courts' activities and of the workings of the People's Courts, see George Feifer, *Justice in Moscow* (New York: Simon & Schuster, 1964).

ized to sit on the judicial bench.[10] Half of the assessors are women, and there is a high rate of turnover, with many limited to a single term.

Each case—whether criminal or civil, other than the hearing of appeals—is heard by a judge and two assessors. Assessors are, in theory, the judge's equals and enjoy all the rights of a judge while serving and can interrogate witnesses and litigants. Assessors determine questions of law and of fact and differ from a jury, which would determine only questions of fact; there are no juries in Soviet courts. In theory the two assessors can outvote the presiding judge, who is the last to express himself and vote, although the judge's knowledge and experience may influence the assessors. A member of the bench who disagrees with the verdict must still sign it; he or she can record a minority opinion in a written dissent that is not made public, although it becomes a part of the judicial record and can figure in the appeal of a case.[11]

Panels of assessors for the People's Courts are elected at public assemblies by open voting. The 1977 Constitution increased the terms of assessors from two to two and one-half years; assessors hear cases for only two weeks out of the year and do not receive a special salary for their services but are paid by their employers. They are to be found not only in the People's Courts but in all higher courts, including the U.S.S.R. Supreme Court, and participate whenever the higher courts serve as courts of first instance but not when appeals are being heard. Assessors for the higher courts are elected by the corresponding soviet. Assessors, like judges, are subject to recall by the bodies of voters or by the soviets that elected them.

Soviet judicial procedure is generally flexible and is in keeping with the unprepossessing physical attributes of the average Soviet courtroom. Cases are usually handled with dispatch and at times even with haste because, in criminal cases, the court is presented with a lengthy case record and the testimony of witnesses compiled by the pretrial investigator *(sledovatel')*. The court's task is to determine the validity of the investigator's findings, thus in a sense the actual trial is little more than an appeal from a de facto "conviction" rendered by the prosecution. Yet it is the court's responsibility to determine guilt or innocence and to render, at least in theory, a judgment not unduly influenced by the prosecution.

Soviet courts employ the inquisitorial procedure common to the Western European continental civil law systems; it is designed to establish the facts of the case with a minimum of procedural delay—although this is not always in the defendant's interests. Many civil cases are heard without lawyers. The Soviet judge plays an active role in the proceedings—unlike the relatively passive role of the judge in the British and American courts. Judges question witnesses, civil plaintiffs, and the accused and at times may give the appearance of a prosecutor rather than a judge. The court can summon witnesses and elicit expert testimony on its own initiative—apart from testimony provided by the prosecution and the

---

[10]Vladimir Terebilov, *The Soviet Court* (Moscow: Progress Publishers, 1973) pp. 43 and 110. Cf. V. Terebilov, "Sovetskii narodnyi sud," *Izvestiia,* April 14, 1982.

[11]*Ibid.,* p. 44.

defense. The rules governing evidence admissible in Soviet courts are very broad and flexible, and judges are empowered to determine freely what evidence is admissible and relevant; there are no formal rules regarding exclusion of evidence or providing for evaluation of specific kinds of evidence. Hearsay is admitted only if the source is identifiable. Indeed, Soviet courts seek to obtain all kinds of biographical data regarding the defendant that would be treated as inadmissible in a British or American court. There is little likelihood of a mistrial on the grounds that certain evidence was admitted.

Soviet courts permit a form of popular participation in trials in addition to that provided by the two lay assessors who sit with the judge. Since 1958, Soviet judicial practice has provided for community accusers and community defenders, who participate along with the defense counsel and prosecution when admitted to the trial by the court. Such accusers and defenders represent "public" or "social" (voluntary) organizations, as distinct from governmental bodies; they speak in the name of the "collective" that they represent and can urge either clemency, leniency, or severe punishment. If the "collective" can testify to the defendant's good character and record, this can be an advantage. Other aspects of Soviet judicial procedure are not always to the defendant's advantage. Thus, while the 1960 R.S.F.S.R. Code of Criminal Procedure gives the accused the "right to give testimony," it does not explicitly grant the right to remain silent on the grounds of possible self-incrimination. Indeed, the Soviet court can compel relatives (including spouses) to testify against the accused; it does not recognize professional confidence (of a physician or clergyman) as grounds for refusing to testify. Only legal counsel or physically or mentally incapable persons may not be interrogated as witnesses.

Litigant's right of appeal is limited in the Soviet Union to one appeal only—the court of next instance. Thus a case originating in the People's Court can be appealed to the oblast' or other regional court (at the krai, autonomous republic, autonomous oblast', or national area level). However, in union republics that are not divided into oblasti, cases are appealed directly from the People's Court to the union republic supreme court. Few cases go beyond the union republic supreme court. The U.S.S.R. Supreme Court is primarily an appellate court, but it hears cases on appeal only if they are taken to it by the Procuracy (under its right to "protest" decisions) or if the President of the Court decides to exercise its broad powers of supervision *(nadzor)* over all lower courts. Appeal in its Soviet version can actually be to the defendant's disadvantage because the appellate court can remand the case for retrial, and the court of first instance can impose a heavier sentence or retry the defendant for a graver offense. Appeals are generally handled with dispatch. Review of a case under the supervision powers of the Procuracy or of a higher court (on the initiative of its presiding judge) is not a public proceeding. The parties to a case do not attend it, nor does legal counsel participate unless requested to do so, as review is based on the case record. Thus, court decisions can be reopened, and this introduces an additional element of uncertainty into the Soviet judicial system.

The U.S.S.R. Supreme Court is a large body and includes the presidents of the supreme courts of the fifteen union republics. It is divided into civil, criminal, and military divisions and acts as a court of first instance only in the most important cases. Espionage cases of importance are tried before the Military Division of the U.S.S.R. Supreme Court, which also supervises a separate system of military tribunals for service-connected offenses.[12] The Criminal Division acts as a court of first instance when it is desired to publicize a case, as in August 1972 when it tried and convicted managers and engineers of a Minsk radio and television plant and personnel of a Leningrad design institute. It held them responsible for an industrial explosion in a new facility that resulted in loss of life. This was the sole case tried by the Criminal Division in a decade.[13] However, the Criminal Division of the U.S.S.R. Supreme Court in 1987 acted as a court of first instance in the trials of: several officials held responsible for the Chernobyl' nuclear power plant explosion and fire; two Soviet ship captains found guilty of a marine collision that resulted in the death of several hundred persons in the sinking of an old Soviet passenger ship; and the West German civilian pilot who overflew the Soviet Union and landed his plane near Moscow's Red Square.

The Supreme Court sits in plenary session at least once every four months to supervise its divisions and to pass final judgment on their rulings. Plenary sessions are also convened for the purpose of issuing general legal interpretations *(rukovodiashchie raziasneniia)* that are binding upon all lower courts. Such sessions must be attended by the U.S.S.R. Procurator-General, who can protest any decisions of the Supreme Court's three divisions or of a union republic supreme court. The plenary session may decide to refer questions of interpretation to the Presidium of the U.S.S.R. Supreme Soviet. The Presidium of the Supreme Soviet can offer guidance to the Supreme Court, in response to the Court's reporting to it, but does not involve itself in specific cases.[14] The Supreme Court has various departments and a staff of researchers supervised by its President. A Scientific-Consultative Council of legal specialists and scholars meets several times each year and assists the Court. Its members study drafts and aid in the preparation of the guiding interpretations that are issued to lower courts. They can even participate in plenary sessions of the Supreme Court but are not involved in the adjudication of specific cases.[15] Thus the U.S.S.R. Supreme Court seeks to systematize judicial practice and promote more uniform application of the law.

The work of the courts is also monitored by the U.S.S.R. Ministry of Justice and those of the union republics reestablished in 1970. The ministry participates in the election of judges and promotes improved professional standards for the bench, monitors the activities of the legal profession, and proposes to the U.S.S.R. Supreme Court specific legal interpretations. It also collects judicial statistics, conducts research, and codifies legislation. It publishes a popular magazine, *Man*

[12]The case of A. N. Filatov, who spied for the United States, was tried before the Military Division in July 1978. See M. A. Marov, "Otshchepenets" in L. N. Smirnov, S. I. Gusev, et al., eds., *Vysshii sudebnyi organ SSSR* (Moscow: "Iuridicheskaia literatura," 1984), pp. 244–248.

[13]L. N. Smirnov et al., *op. cit.* (above, n. 5), pp. 22f, 417–421.

[14]Nikolai F. Chistiakov, *Verkhovnyi Sud SSSR* (Moscow: "Nauka," 1984) pp. 72–73.

[15]I. D. Melikhov, "Nauchno-konsul'tativnyi sovet pri Verkhovnom Sude SSSR," in L. N. Smirnov et al., *op. cit.* (above, n. 12), pp. 230–237.

and the Law, and also uses other media to publicize and explain new laws.[16] It is evident that Soviet judges are not left to their own devices but are under the unremitting tutelage of the Communist Party, the Presidium of the Supreme Soviet, the Ministry of Justice, and the Procuracy.

THE PROCURACY

The Soviet legal system is unique in its institution of the Procuracy, which performs a variety of functions. It is difficult to find in other legal systems a single institution that merges so many diverse functions. The Procuracy is specifically charged with guarding "socialist legality" and with making certain that public officials observe the law and fulfill the government's directives. This aspect of the Procuracy was discussed in Chapter 7 in the section dealing with legal controls over administration. The Procuracy is "a single and centralized system" (Article 4 of the November 30, 1979, Law on the U.S.S.R. Procuracy). Local procurators are made independent of the local soviets and of their officials; this is said to assure strict observance of the law. However, this arrangement is more effective as a rationale for centralism than as a means of creating a responsible officialdom. The entire system of states' attorneys is headed by the U.S.S.R. Procurator-General, who is elected by the Supreme Soviet for a term of five years and who appoints republic, oblast', and krai procurators and confirms those of lesser rank, who are appointed by union republic procurators. The 1977 Constitution reduced the term of office of the U.S.S.R. Procurator-General from seven to five years.

The Procuracy is best understood in terms of its being a pre-Soviet institution established by Peter I in 1722, abolished by Lenin in 1918, and restored in 1922. Indeed, the Soviet Procuracy has much in common with the tsarist Procuracy of the eighteenth century. Peter I was interested in promoting autocratic centralism and in combating those who resisted his administrative reforms; he viewed his General Procurator "as Our eye, and lawyer in matters of state." Thus, the Soviet practice of having the Procuracy exercise supervision over administrative acts and serve as an organ of control had its origins in Peter's imperial brand of tsarism.

The other functions of the Soviet Procuracy include advising the executive bodies of the various soviets and prosecuting persons who are alleged to have violated the law. The Procuracy approves the arrest of persons by the ordinary and security police forces; the Soviet substitute for a bench warrant, the Procuracy's approval is not issued by a court and can be given after the fact of arrest. Prosecution for criminal offenses is the responsibility of the Procuracy, and it also supervises the pretrial investigation of persons charged with such offenses. Yet it is known that the Procuracy in Stalin's time failed to control the security police, and the question of the degree to which the Procuracy imposes legal norms and due process upon the KGB is not readily answered. Indeed, collusion between the Procuracy and the security police is very possible.

---

[16]V. Terebilov, *op. cit.* (above, n. 10), pp. 84–85.

The relationship of the Procuracy to the Soviet courts is an unusual one, and in many ways the Procuracy is more important than the judiciary. The Procuracy is actually a large, centralized judicial bureaucracy that exercises considerable supervision *(nadzor)* over the courts. It is responsible for the legality and validity of all court judgments, decisions, rulings, and decrees. The Procuracy is constantly scrutinizing judicial acts to determine whether or not they are "legal" and meet with its approval. Procurators can enter civil suits at any time to urge the court to adopt a particular decision on the grounds that it is in the interests of the state or security, although this practice is a common feature of code law systems. In general, the Procuracy is less concerned with the rights of individual citizens and has regarded itself as fulfilling the "historic tasks" of the Party, enforcing "state discipline," and protecting "socialist property."[17]

The Procuracy's influence over judicial practice is especially evident in its role in appealing court decisions. If the Procuracy is not satisfied with a decision in a civil or criminal case, it can protest it to a higher court and continue protesting under its powers of supervision. However, presidents of supreme courts can also initiate reviews of cases. Even an acquittal can be protested and the higher court can vacate the judgment. Supreme courts of union republics and of the USSR cannot meet in plenary session in the absence of the republic procurator or the U.S.S.R. Procurator-General. If the U.S.S.R. Procurator-General is of the opinion that a decision or interpretation by the U.S.S.R. Supreme Court taken in plenary session is not in accordance with the law, he is obliged to take the matter to the Presidium of the U.S.S.R. Supreme Soviet.[18] He can also propose to the Supreme Court that it issue new instructions regarding judicial practice. Only the Presidium of the Supreme Soviet can rescind orders and instructions issued by the Procurator-General.

Among the Procuracy's other functions is the supervision of the execution of all criminal sentences and the supervision of detention facilities, prisons, and prison colonies. It also publishes a journal, *Socialist Legality,* which is indicative of its role as a fountainhead of judicial doctrine. The Procuracy receives complaints from citizens and has been likened to the ombudsman in other systems, but the analogy is not very apt because the ombudsman's role is not performed well by states' attorneys. Indeed, one can ask whether the procurator, as the government's legal counsel and prosecutor, can really fulfill the role of "guardian of legality." In many ways a truly independent judiciary is in a better position to perform this vital function if legality must be protected not only against encroachments by individuals but by government as well. The fact that the Procuracy maintains its own investigative branch conflicts with its responsibility for supervision over the observance of legality. The President of the U.S.S.R. Supreme Court, Vladimir I. Terebilov, noted pointedly: "In my opinion, for justice it would be better if the investigative apparatus existed outside of the

---

[17]Roman A. Rudenko, ed., *Na strazhe sovetskikh zakonov* (Moscow: "Iuridicheskaia literatura," 1972), pp. 32f, 36, 44.

[18]L. N. Smirnov et al., *op. cit.* (above n. 5), p. 172. This power was incorporated into Article 40 of the 1979 law on the Procuracy.

Procuracy. In this way the procurator would not in words but in fact accomplish supervision over the legality, completeness and objectivity of investigations."[19]

THE LEGAL PROFESSION

Although Lenin distrusted lawyers despite the fact that he himself was trained in the law, the Soviet regime has not been able to dispense with their services. The Soviet legal profession includes judges and procurators, as well as those engaged directly in legal practice. Practicing lawyers are of two types: the *advokat,* who is a trial lawyer, and the *iuriskonsul't,* who is the Soviet version of a corporation counsel and is employed by government agencies and economic enterprises. The iuriskonsul't is confined largely to administrative law and labor law but does enter the courtroom when enterprises are involved in litigation with a citizen. Since disputes between enterprises and economic organizations regarding property and contracts are resolved by arbitration bodies, the iuriskonsul't practices law before them.

The advokat serves as defense counsel in criminal cases and as counsel for plaintiff or defendant in civil suits and also prepares documents and gives legal advice to clients. The Soviet courts hear civil suits dealing with evictions, inheritance claims, payment of alimony, libel, reinstatement in place of employment, and almost every other conceivable matter; thus, under these circumstances, lawyers have much to do.[20]

The practice of law is conducted through legal-consultation offices that function under the jurisdiction of collegiums of advocates organized on a territorial basis. The collegiums are supposedly "voluntary" organizations, by which is meant that they are not agencies of the state, although they are under the supervision of the courts, union republic councils of ministers, and regional and local executive bodies. The Soviet advokat cannot practice privately but must be a member of a legal "collective" or consultation office and a member of the local (city or regional) collegium. Disbarment is by administrative action, and the courts do not participate directly in the procedure, as they do in the United States.

Soviet lawyers, although they include persons of wit, intellectual subtlety, and rhetorical talent, do not enjoy the high fees received by many American attorneys and trial lawyers specializing in criminal law and in personal liability suits involving generous awards and commissions. The Soviet legal profession is

---

[19]"Pravosudie i vremia," *Izvestiia,* October 25, 1986, p. 3. Judge Terebilov suggested that the investigative function could be placed in the MVD, in a separate state committee, or in the Ministry of Justice.

[20]The Soviet Union also has a system of *state notaries* for the purpose of preparing and certifying documents (including sales and other agreements and wills), taking depositions, and attesting to matters of fact and record. Notaries are under the jurisdiction of the ministries of justice and their oblast' departments (including appointment and removal), and notarial offices are state organs. Notaries also accept documents for safekeeping and hold sums of money and valuable papers in trust for transfer. Fees, fixed by law, are charged for nearly all notarial services, and a register is kept of all notarial acts. Notaries must have a certain minimum of legal training and experience because they are required to determine the legality of all transactions and agreements notarized. Notarial activities are important and are well defined in Soviet law. See Nina I. Avdeienko and Muza A. Kabakova, *Notariat v SSSR* (Leningrad: Izd-vo Leningradskogo' Universiteta, 1984).

closely regulated by the state, and the fees for various types of legal service are fixed by law and are very reasonable. The fees are paid to the legal consultation office and not directly to the advokat; they are then apportioned among the lawyers. A limited number of routine legal services must be performed gratis for certain specified categories of clients. Nevertheless, the Soviet advokat earns at least as much or more than the highly skilled Soviet worker and may even obtain a generous gratuity from an especially appreciative client, although this practice can have unpleasant consequences and lead to disbarment.

The advokat, furthermore, often enjoys a far better income than does the Soviet judge or ordinary procurator, neither of whom is well paid. Indeed, the judge of the People's Court often aspires to enter legal practice as an advokat or iuriskonsul't. A barrier separates the advokat from the procurator and judge because the latter are more often than not serving the Soviet state and its policies, while the advokat is endeavoring to protect the rights and interests of a client and is doing this for remuneration. So long as civil litigation and criminal prosecution persist in the Soviet Union and the defendant is said to have certain rights, the advokat will play an indispensable role in the administration of justice.

Apart from the matter of remuneration, the Soviet polity has circumscribed the role of the legal profession in a variety of other ways. As befits a planned and state-owned economy, it controls the size of the enrollments in law schools and limits the number of persons permitted to practice law. It also prescribes the curricula of law schools and endeavors to influence the character and ethos of the legal profession. Lawyers, the Procuracy, and the courts are periodically mobilized to combat those practices and forms of conduct that the Communist Party leadership regards as especially undesirable or as a threat to the regime's stability.

Yet the advokat is inevitably in conflict with the regime and with its officials, including the Procuracy and the security police, when endeavoring to protect a client and when the client's interests and those of the Soviet state are at variance. The state claims that the Procuracy must prosecute the guilty but must also protect every last innocent person suspected of having broken the law. Since it is unlikely that even a dictatorial regime seeks to punish innocent persons for ordinary crimes, it then becomes a question of whether or not there are adequate procedural safeguards to protect the accused from the chronic suspiciousness and desire to convict that often characterize the agencies of detection and prosecution. In theory the investigator is supposed to conduct an "impartial" examination of the case and is to serve as the suspect's "defense counsel" while simultaneously determining whether there are sufficient grounds to convict. If the procurator is convinced that such grounds exist and that the suspect is guilty, the latter is placed on trial. Yet the Soviet investigating official *(sledovatel')* is not under the jurisdiction of the court and is in a position to abuse the powers of his office.

In any judicial system the rights of the accused depend on access to, and effectiveness of, legal counsel available to the defense. The Soviet lawyer's role as defense counsel in criminal cases is circumscribed and has been hampered by the inability to help a client at an early stage in the proceedings. In Soviet procedure the suspect is denied access to legal counsel during the initial inquiry and pretrial investigation. It is only after the investigation of the case has been completed to a significant degree and the procurator has confirmed the indictment that defense counsel can enter the case. Only if the accused is a minor or under a physical or psychiatric handicap can he or she have access to legal counsel during the investigation. Thus, by the time the investigation is completed and the case against the accused is developed, both defense counsel and defendant are at a disadvantage. There is no Soviet counterpart of the legally required American practice of informing detained persons of their right to consult a lawyer before responding to any questions.

Although Soviet judicial procedure contains many aspects of a fair trial and appears to permit defendants their "day in court," the right to legal counsel is not absolute. This is especially true in political trials and in cases involving interests of state. In ordinary cases, defense counsel may present a spirited defense; but when the Procuracy, a dependent judge, and the Communist Party regime make it patently clear that a defendant must be convicted for reasons of state, defense counsel is likely to offer a halfhearted defense limited to pleading for leniency on the grounds of mitigating circumstances. The situation is made even more disadvantageous, especially for the political defendant, by the absence of a free press that would report on the arbitrary activities of procurators, judges, and assessors.

The Soviet lawyer practices law before courts that seek to shame the defendant and that employ procedures designed to render the accused contrite. Soviet law has therefore been termed "parental law" by Professor Harold J. Berman. Soviet judges often employ a didactic approach, with the courts expected to help make the "new Soviet person," who will presumably be worthy of communism. Thus, the Soviet lawyer is caught in conflicting roles; he or she is an aide to a court that seeks to reeducate while punishing and is also expected to serve the client as an advocate.[21] In certain circumstances also, the confidential nature of the lawyer-client relationship involves ambiguities and can therefore be violated; an individual is not free to select specific counsel, for instance, and a lawyer doesn't have a choice of cases. Soviet lawyers are not members of a free profession as ordinarily understood, and they do not possess the equivalent of a countrywide bar association. Yet many of their number continue an old tradition of civic courage and seek to defend the individual against the state and against miscarriages of justice perpetrated by the courts.

THE DIALECTICS OF SOVIET LEGALITY

The concept of the dialectic, with its emphasis on contradiction and the play of opposites, seems especially relevant to any appraisal of the Soviet legal system. In certain respects Soviet law has developed from its unsatisfactory role in the

---

[21]For revealing accounts of the Soviet legal system and the legal profession by former practitioners, see Olimpiad S. Ioffe, *Soviet Law and Soviet Reality* (Dordrecht: Martinus Nijhoff, 1985), and Dina Kaminskaya, *Final Judgment: My Life as a Soviet Defense Attorney* (New York: Simon and Schuster, 1982).

Stalinist period. More lawyers are being trained, and nearly all judges possess legal education even though there is no formal requirement to that effect. There is greater reliance on the regular courts. The law of tort has been extended, although liability is a limited concept in Soviet practice and does not include punitive damages or financial awards for pain and suffering. Libel suits can be brought against a newspaper editor, although the plaintiff must be satisfied with a retraction or correction rather than a monetary award. Efforts have been undertaken to provide some degree of legal accountability on the part of state officials.

Yet such salutary developments have been partially nullified by abuses of judicial power and by arbitrariness on the part of the Procuracy. Such abuses have occurred whenever purported interests of state have challenged the exercise of individual rights. While in some Western countries the executive can lose in court despite claims of executive privilege and national security, in the Soviet Union such an outcome is unlikely because Soviet courts do not rule on the constitutionality of executive or legislative acts. Soviet courts are pliable instruments and the Soviet leadership is not held accountable before the bar of justice. For example, the de-Stalinization of Khrushchev's time and the "restoration of socialist legality" never involved trials of security police officers, prison camp commanders, and informers whose infamous activities resulted in the death and suffering of countless victims. When the police chief Beria was secretly tried and executed, it was not for crimes committed against individual Soviet citizens but for allegedly being a "British agent."

Such a basic right as the freedom to emigrate is recognized only for foreigners in the 1977 Constitution (Article 38), which grants "the right of asylum to foreign citizens persecuted for defending the interests of the workers and the cause of peace, for participating in a revolutionary and national liberation movement, or for progressive sociopolitical, scientific or other creative activity." Soviet citizens are denied this right except for the purpose of reuniting family members. Soviet authorities expend large sums to prevent citizens from leaving the country—contrary to the United Nations Universal Declaration of Human Rights—maintaining special border zones with electronic detection devices, barbed wire, large numbers of watchdogs, and belts of plowed-up no-man's-lands.[22] In September 1973 the Soviet Union did ratify the International Covenant on Civil and Political Rights, which recognized that "everyone shall be free to leave any country, including his own." However, the Soviet criminal code (Article 64 of the RSFSR Criminal Code) includes under its definition of "treason": "flight abroad or refusal to return from abroad to the U.S.S.R."[23] Although a substantial number of Jewish citizens of the USSR as well as some Germans were permitted to emigrate by the Brezhnev regime as a result of persistent demands and international pressure, other Soviet nationalities were

---

[22]For a description of Soviet border controls and the complex procedures to which Soviet citizens are subjected when obtaining permission to travel abroad, see Zhores A. Medvedev, *The Medvedev Papers* (London and New York: Macmillan and St. Martin's Press, 1971), pp. 174–254.

[23]Harold J. Berman, *op. cit.* (above, n. 7), p. 178.

not accorded such consideration, and many Soviet Jews who wished to emigrate were denied permission.

The willingness to ignore constitutional rights is seen in the case of the Ukrainian lawyers who were arrested in 1961 and whose plight was concealed for more than half a decade because they were convicted in a closed trial on the flimsiest of evidence. Levko H. Lukianenko, a graduate of the University of Moscow Law Faculty and a Party member, Ivan Kandyba, and another lawyer in a group of seven Ukrainians (four of whom were Communist Party members) were given sentences of ten to fifteen years for seeking to exercise constitutional freedoms, including the right to advocate the secession of Ukraine from the Soviet Union through constitutional and peaceful means and to combat bureaucratism and Russian chauvinism. The defendants claimed to favor a Soviet political system in an independent Ukraine and a socialist economy.[24] That Soviet lawyers should understand the law literally and not regard it as fictitious was more than the Party and KGB (security police) authorities could bear, and it resulted in extraordinary sentences. Lukianenko originally received the death sentence, which was later commuted to fifteen years. Released in 1976, Lukianenko defended the rights of Orthodox Christians and became a member of the Ukrainian Helsinki Group. Rearrested in 1977, he was sentenced to ten years of imprisonment and five years of internal exile. Kandyba, released in 1976, was harassed for five years and then rearrested in 1981; he also received a sentence of ten years' imprisonment and five years' internal exile for his activities in the Ukrainian Helsinki Group.

Soviet citizens who have sought to publicize and protest the arbitrary actions of the KGB and Procuracy have suffered for their efforts. When Viacheslav Chornovil, a Ukrainian journalist, collected materials on the secret closed trials of twenty Ukrainian intellectuals who had been tried in 1965–1966—subsequently published abroad as *The Chornovil Papers*—he was tried for "anti-Soviet agitation and propaganda" in 1967 and again in 1972, when he was sentenced to seven years of imprisonment and five years of internal exile in Iakutia. As a result of fabricated charges, he was sentenced to an additional five years of exile for having joined the Ukrainian Helsinki Group.

Another example of Soviet judicial arbitrariness is provided by the case of the microbiologist Nina Strokata, who defended her husband, Sviatoslav Karavans'ky, refusing to divorce him and denounce him publicly when advised to do so by the KGB. She was herself arrested and given a four-year sentence at a closed trial in May 1972 for allegedly disseminating anti-Soviet literature.[25] Aleksandr

---

[24]For this and related cases, see Michael Browne, ed., *Ferment in the Ukraine* (New York: Praeger, 1971), pp. 31–93.

[25]The case of Karavans'ky is of special interest, as he was originally sentenced to 25 years in 1945 when accused of spying for the Romanians. He was released in December 1960 and acquired recognition as a journalist and translator but was rearrested in 1965 without any judicial proceeding and was ordered to serve the remaining 8 years and 7 months of the 25-year sentence, although the maximum prison sentence under the law was only 15 years at that time. In 1970 at a closed trial held in the Vladimir Prison, he was sentenced to an additional 5 years in prison and 3 years in a hard-labor camp for protest writings prepared as a prisoner. Karavans'ky's sentence to a total of 33 years
(continued)

Solzhenitsyn was spared a prison sentence only because he was internationally known. Yet when he prepared a massive compilation of the excesses perpetrated by the Soviet security police, under the title of *The Gulag Archipelago,* he was arrested, expelled from the country in February 1974, and deprived of Soviet citizenship by administrative action without any judicial proceeding or hearing.

The Soviet physicist and Nobel peace laureate Andrei Sakharov was, by purely administrative action, exiled with his wife to the city of Gorky and placed under house arrest from 1980 to 1987.[26] Another landmark in Soviet jurisprudence was the arrest in 1981 of Oksana Meshko at the age of 76 for alleged "anti-Soviet agitation and propaganda" and her sentence to six months of imprisonment and five years of exile in the cold, dank, and totally isolated settlement of Aian on the Sea of Okhotsk. This was probably considered "mild" punishment for an elderly former teacher who had served as acting head of the Ukrainian Helsinki Group; Meshko had been wrongly imprisoned from 1947 to 1956 and had been rehabilitated in the latter year.

One of the most reprehensible cases in Soviet judicial practice has been that of Iuri Shukhevych-Berezynskyi, who was arrested in 1947 at the age of 14 and subjected to two decades of confinement in the infamous Vladimir prison—an initial ten-year sentence was doubled. During five years in exile, he undertook to write memoirs of his prison experience. In 1972 he was sentenced to five years in prison, five years in a labor camp, and five years in exile. Shukhevych's "crime" was his refusal to denounce his late father, Roman Shukhevych, who had commanded the Ukrainian Insurgent Army (UPA), a guerrilla force that had opposed the Soviets in Western Ukraine during and after World War II. In the course of his imprisonment, Iuri Shukhevych lost his sight.[27]

The physical mistreatment of political prisoners has been confirmed by Anatoly (Nathan) Shcharansky, who was imprisoned from 1978 to 1986. He testified that the KGB has used "torture by hunger and by cold" and would vary caloric intake from 900 to 1500 calories per day in order to weaken the prisoner.[28] Prisoners are also compelled to work under unhealthy and physically hazardous conditions.[29] There is also a sordid record of victimized dissidents and political prisoners who have died in highly questionable circumstances as a result of mistreatment or who were victims of foul play.[30]

apparently set a record for length of incarceration for alleged political offenses. Both Karavans'ky and Strokata were ultimately able to immigrate to the United States. The political prisoner Danylo Shumuk was imprisoned for a total of 31 years, serving three sentences between 1945 and 1982 as well as 5 years of internal exile after which he was permitted to emigrate in 1987.

[26]For Sakharov's own account of his mistreatment at the hands of the KGB, see his letter in *U.S. News and World Report,* February 24, 1986, pp. 29–35 and March 3, 1986, pp. 34–37.

[27]*Sobranie dokumentov samizdata,* Vol. II, *Arkhiv samizdata,* AS No. 154.

[28]*New York Times,* February 14, 1986, pp. 1, 6.

[29]For a comprehensive account of Soviet punitive methods used against political prisoners, see Jaroslaw M. Bilocerkowycz, *Soviet Ukrainian Dissent: A Study of Political Alienation* (Boulder, Colo.: Westview Press, 1988), Chapter 7. For more detail see his Ph.D. dissertation, University of Washington, 1983, Chapter 7.

[30]For example, the Ukrainian painter Alla Horska was murdered in 1970. The popular Ukrainian composer Volodymyr Ivasiuk was murdered in 1979 (presumably because he refused to lend his talents to political purposes, as demanded by the authorities). Political prisoners who have died while

Unfortunately, such instances of abuse or neglect of procuratorial powers and abdication of judicial responsibility have been too numerous. They testify to the influence of the KGB as a consequence of the Party's reliance upon it for intelligence and the resultant perceptions of threats and dangers. The KGB may have a vested interest in exaggerating such dangers. As a vast bureaucratic organization, the KGB can be heavy-handed and not very efficient, though brutal and ruthless in its methods.[31] It is simultaneously feared (by many but not by all) and despised for its surveillance activities, provocations, threats and annoyances, searches and use of entrapment devices, blackmail, and intimidation. It has been known to arrange an individual's loss of employment, eviction from housing, physical beating, and other forms of harassment and reprisal. It is obsessed with obtaining confessions and expressions of recantation and guilt rather than establishing objective truth. This is seen in its practice of occasionally conducting show trials according to a scenario prepared by its own interrogators acting as scriptwriters.[32] It is also evident in the efforts to "convert" political prisoners and in several instances of public recantations arranged for the media.

A reprehensible practice employed during the Brezhnev period has been the incarceration of political and religious dissidents in psychiatric facilities. With the cooperation of unethical psychiatrists, the KGB has simply had such persons declared "mentally ill," thus avoiding even the pretense of a closed trial or the risk of the defendant's making embarrassing statements at a public trial. The political "patient" and detainee cannot appeal the verdict of such a medical commission and can be given debilitating drugs and kept in a helpless condition indefinitely.[33] The patient is "cured" if he renounces his views. By equating sanity

---

in the custody of Soviet prison authorities include Estonian chemist, faculty member at Tartu University, and former Party member Jüri Kukk (in 1981 at age 40); Ukrainian writer and film director Helii (Yevhen) Sniehirov (in 1978 at age 51); teacher and Ukrainian Helsinki Group member Oleksiy Tykhy (in 1984 at age 57); journalist Valery Marchenko (in 1984 at age 37); Ukrainian poet Vasyl Stus (in 1985 at age 47); and Anatoly Marchenko (in 1986 at age 48). See Ludmilla Alexeyeva, *Soviet Dissent* (Middletown, Conn.: Wesleyan University Press, 1985), pp. 39, 53–54, 94–95. See also Rein Taagepera, *Softening without Liberalization in the Soviet Union, The Case of Jüri Kukk* (Lanham, Md.: University Press of America, 1984). For a description of the circumstances of Sniehirov's death in a KGB prison, see the account by Wasyl Hrishko in Helii Sniehirov, *Naboyi dlia rozstrilu ta inshi tvory* (New York and Toronto: Sniehirov Fund and Novi Dni, 1983), pp. 40–48.

[31]On the conduct of KGB officers during interrogations and in the prisons and labor camps, see *The Chornovil Papers* and Valentyn Moroz, *op. cit.* (above, n. 2) and Michael Browne, *op. cit.* (above, n. 24).

[32]This practice is testified to by Greville Wynne, codefendant with Colonel Oleg Penkovskiy in a May 1963 espionage trial, who states that testimony was rehearsed on the basis of a script. See Greville Wynne, *Contact on Gorky Street* (New York: Atheneum, 1968), pp. 98–139.

[33]For an account of conditions among political prisoners in psychiatric facilities, see the testimony of the Ukrainian mathematician-cyberneticist Leonid Pliushch, who was imprisoned in a Dnipropetrovsk hospital with about sixty other political prisoners. *Le Monde* (Paris) and the *New York Times,* February 4, 1976. Pliushch was arrested in January 1972 and was placed in the psychiatric institution (or *psykhushka,* as it is termed in the vernacular) in July 1973, where he spent two and one-half years. He was released in January 1976 largely as a result of foreign protests, including that of the French communist newspaper *L'Humanité,* and was permitted to emigrate together with his wife and sons. See Leonid Plyushch, *History's Carnival: A Dissident's Autobiography* (New York: Harcourt Brace Jovanovich, 1979). For another well-known case of psychiatric abuse, see (General) Petro Grigorenko, *Memoirs* (New York: Norton, 1982. See also Zhores A. and Roy

(*continued*)

with political conformity and by subjecting political dissidents to cruel and humiliating treatment, Soviet jurisprudence has distinguished itself in a dubious manner.

While the Soviet media have readily condemned the imprisonment of so-called "democratic elements" (usually communists) in selected noncommunist countries, they have remained silent concerning the harsh treatment meted out to political dissidents in the Soviet Union. Yet ironically, political prisoners in the Soviet Union have stated that they have had greater "inner freedom" while in prison or in labor camps and more freedom of expression than does the Soviet citizen who is not incarcerated. The CPSU seeks to defend its double standard with the assertion that the Party's interests are those of Soviet society. However, it appears that the venality and corruption that have come to permeate so much of Soviet society have also affected the organs of law enforcement. Thus, the removal from office of U.S.S.R. minister of internal affairs Nikolai Shchelokov in June 1983, after 14 years in that post, and his deprivation of general's rank and arrest were due to corruption. It appears that the courts were also affected to some degree by corruption. In a sense the Party itself suborns the judicial process and the procuratorial function by making Party membership and discipline qualifications for holding judicial office. If the president of the U.S.S.R. Supreme Court and the Procurator-General of the USSR are both full members of the Party's Central Committee, it is not simply honorific but at the very least represents a subliminal partisanship, although these high officials might also wish to uphold a professional legal standard.

Thus Soviet law serves as a legal instrument of the sole political party in all judicial proceedings of any political significance, enabling it to judge but not be judged. This aspect of Soviet law detracts from the many ways in which the legal system functions in a conventional manner, especially in ordinary civil and criminal cases. Viewed dialectically, Soviet law is not a homogeneous phenomenon but is characterized by contradiction, a condition of flux, and the conflicting views of those who see it either as a standard to be upheld or as an instrument to be utilized.

A. Medvedev, *A Question of Madness* (New York: Knopf, 1971) and the testimony of Alexander S. Yesenin-Volpin, the appeal of Vladimir Bukovsky, and supporting documentation in *Abuse of Psychiatry for Political Repression in the Soviet Union,* hearing held before a subcommittee of the Committee on the Judiciary, U.S. Senate, September 26, 1972 (Washington, D.C.: Government Printing Office, 1972, reprint ed., New York: Arno Press, 1973). For a study undertaken in the Soviet Union, see Alexander Podrabinek, *Punitive Medicine* (Ann Arbor, Mich.: Karoma Publishers, 1980). See also Sidney Bloch and Peter Reddaway, *Psychiatric Terror: How Soviet Psychiatry Is Used to Suppress Dissent* (New York: Basic Books, 1977) and their *Soviet Psychiatric Abuse: The Shadow over World Psychiatry* (Boulder, Colo.: Westview Press, 1985). For a brief study that includes documentary materials, see Harvey Fireside, *Soviet Psychoprisons* (New York: Norton, 1979).

chapter *10*

Soviet Political Socialization and Its Limitations

In claiming to be a system led by men endowed with a knowledge of Marxism-Leninism and in assuming a special role in history, the Soviet polity has not left political socialization to chance. Socialization involves the training of citizens, political learning, and the perpetuation of prevailing political values, norms, attitudes, and accepted practices. In the Soviet Union it is designed to maintain the official political culture and ideology, as described in Chapter 3, and to eliminate or repress those cultural traits, discussed in Chapter 2, and "bourgeois" values deemed to be incompatible with it.

Soviet political socialization as defined by the CPSU reflects certain basic themes. Children from the earliest years in a nursery are made aware of Lenin's image as liberator and deliverer of humanity. Lenin as well as Leninism is depicted as an "immortal" entity. Soviet socialization seeks to obtain acceptance of authority and established institutions, recognition of the leading role of the CPSU, and the unquestioned wisdom of its current leadership and its loyalty to Lenin's teachings. In addition to conformity and allegiance to the Soviet state, it promotes belief in the superiority of the collective and the subordination of the individual to the group. It stresses the virtue of work and of being an activist.

It propagates the notion that the Soviet Union is superior to other countries, has greater experience in constructing "developed socialism" and in "building communism," and represents the future. Soviet socialization promotes the declared advantages of state-ownership and condemns the alleged evils of private gain and individual advantage. It seeks to propagate Soviet "patriotism" and condemns "nationalism" (especially its non-Russian forms) while claiming that

271

the Soviet state represents "socialist internationalism." Thus non-Russian Soviet citizens are supposed to accept the notion of a "Soviet people" and the submergence of ethnic values and differences that set them apart from the Soviet (Russian) mass. The socialization process is designed to foster a secularism that finds its justification in the profession of humanism and in atheism.

The consequences of the socialization process have been depicted in highly critical terms by former Soviet citizens who have been political dissidents. Thus, physicist and Moscow human-rights activist Iuri Orlov has observed: "It's very important to note here something that Westerners simply don't understand. Living in the Soviet Union is like living in a large underground labor camp. You are deformed as a person. This process of deforming a personality begins in the kindergarten and it doesn't end even if a man becomes a scholar and academician. The process continues."[1] Another former Soviet citizen has described the "new Soviet person" in the following terms: "It is not the new person about which Soviet propaganda calls out—the convinced builder of communism, the fighter for peace infinitely dedicated to the Party and the people, the bearer of the new socialist morality. . . . But there has been created a new person—one with a distorted perception of the world and with a suppressed ability to protest."[2]

Yet Soviet citizens who accept the socialization process by accommodating to it undoubtedly perceive it in more positive terms. Here one must distinguish between the real and apparent (or partial) "true believers," the latter able to function simultaneously on different levels of perception and expression: the public (or official) and the private (or personal) level, with "correct" verbal or written statements carefully separated from inner thoughts and silent doubts that must remain repressed. Yet one must be active and responsive to "political education" if one wishes to obtain a promotion, improved housing, or other rewards or be granted permission to journey abroad.

Soviet socialization extends beyond such agents as the family, the schools, peer groups, and the mass media. It includes the entire *official* cultural sphere and the effort to mobilize writers and artists. It is viewed as a continuing process, and it is assumed that backsliding can occur. The apparent need for constant vigilance against corrupting alien ways and dangerous thoughts has prompted the regime to maintain a vast program of ideologically oriented adult-education courses.[3] The *Znanie* (Knowledge) Society is also used to provide millions of lectures on political and other topics, and these are attended by citizens who wish to be certain that they are thinking "correctly" and that their perception of important events is "accurate." Yet there are many who resist or even reject outright the substance of socialization, although they may preserve the necessary forms and be adept at responding with the appropriate answer.

---

[1] *U.S. News and World Report,* October 20, 1986, p. 23.

[2] Isak Geiber, "Liudyna 'novoho typu'," *Suchasnist* (Munich), November 1983 (No. 271), p. 71.

[3] See Ellen Propper Mickiewicz, *Soviet Political Schools, The Communist Party Adult Instruction System* (New Haven: Yale University Press, 1967).

AGENTS OF SOCIALIZATION

The Family

Initially, the Soviet regime adopted a hostile attitude toward the family as the principal instrument of socialization. It apparently took seriously Marx's and Engels' prediction that the family was essentially a "bourgeois" phenomenon and was therefore obsolete; socialization would be accomplished more readily and more effectively in state institutions for the rearing of children. Lenin's government reduced marriage to a simple act of registration and made divorce easily accomplished by a simple declaration by one of the spouses made at the civil registry office. Abortion was fully legalized, and the distinction between legitimate and illegitimate children was eliminated. The Soviet regime made an effort to undermine the conventional urban family, fearing that it could be used to develop antiregime attitudes. The presence of several millions of homeless children in the post-revolutionary period gave the state an opportunity to experiment in institutional child rearing. The undertaking proved to be costly, however, and the results far from satisfactory.

As the country concentrated on rapid industrialization, it was decided to strengthen parental authority and to stress the family's responsibilities as an agent of socialization. Juvenile delinquency and low moral standards contributed to the change in policy. Beginning in 1935 parents were held responsible for the acts of their children, and abortion was forbidden in 1936 except for narrowly defined medical reasons. In 1944 divorce was made difficult and costly and could be obtained only in the courts and not, as previously, in registry offices. Abortion was legalized again in 1955 and made available on demand. Divorce was simplified somewhat in 1965 so that the court of first instance, the People's Court, could grant divorces and determine questions of custody, alimony, and property settlement; and the cost of divorce was also reduced.

Although allowances are paid by the state to families having more than three children, most mothers find it necessary to work because prices and wages in the Soviet Union are such as to compel a family to have two sources of income. Pregnant women are given maternity leave for 112 days under the social insurance system—for two months prior to and following the birth of the infant.[4] Preschool nurseries are numerous, and since 1960 extended-day schools have been developed to keep children occupied after classes until parents can take them home in the late afternoon or evening. Thus children are exposed from an early age to nonfamilial rearing and are influenced by the collective. This is in accordance with the Soviet practice of stressing the rights of society and of restraining the individual's interests, desires, and feelings—subordinating them to what are said to be social ends.

That the regime continued to be dissatisfied with the family as the agent of socialization was evident in the establishment of boarding schools *(internaty)* by Khrushchev. However, these schools tended to attract "problem children" and

---

[4]Paid leave for maternity was reduced from 112 days to 70 days in 1938 and the more liberal benefit was not restored until 1956.

were quite costly to operate. Thus, the upbringing of children in an institutional environment has not been the panacea that Engels thought it would be in proposing that society care for children. The less costly extended-day school does not eliminate the family's role; but, like the boarding school, it reflects the regime's unwillingness to rely exclusively upon the family in the crucial area of socialization.[5]

Yet the Soviet family has an important role to play, since socialization begins in childhood and children are given considerable attention and affection. Parents tend to advocate adjustment, accommodation, and compliance in their children as the price to be paid for a successful career. Nevertheless, difficulties can arise when a parent may be a "freethinker" or when a parent or grandparent may regard religious teachings as desirable in a child's upbringing. The experiences of other family members with the regime may shape one's attitudes; much depends on how closely knit a family is. Nor are elite Party members' families always spared difficulties; children of the elite have been known to resist the socialization process in a manner somewhat akin to that of the wellborn early Bolsheviks who, like Lenin, refused to identify with parental values and their own social class. Indeed, the rebellious and spoiled offspring of members of the Soviet establishment are a common phenomenon.

The Soviet family suffers from many ills, especially in the urban milieu. The shortage of adequate housing has often created or contributed to family crises. The fact that many mothers work and must also perform household chores (which men do not wish to share) and spend much time purchasing food means that children are frequently deprived of the warm maternal nurturing that is important in the development of a child's personality and attitudes. Although the regime does not publish statistics on the problem, juvenile delinquency occurs with sufficient frequency—and among those who are not deprived in a material sense—to indicate that the family is subject to great pressures and strains. Parents may have incompatible work schedules and may not even be able to take their vacations simultaneously. Divorce, illegitimacy, sexual promiscuity, conjugal infidelity, alcoholism, and suicide occur often enough to testify to the weaknesses and failings of the "new Soviet person." Between 1950 and 1974 the Soviet divorce rate increased sevenfold, while the marriage rate declined.[6] At the

---

[5]See H. Kent Geiger, *The Family in Soviet Russia* (Cambridge: Harvard University Press, 1968); Barbara Holland, ed., *Soviet Sisterhood* (Bloomington: Indiana University Press, 1985); and Gail Warshofsky Lapidus, *Women in Soviet Society: Equality, Development and Social Change* (Berkeley: University of California Press, 1978).

[6]The ratio of divorces to marriages per 1000 of population since 1950 has changed as follows (from *Narodnoe khoziaistvo SSSR v 1974 godu* [Moscow: "Statistika," 1975], p. 48, *Narodnoe khoziaistvo SSSR v 1984 g.* [Moscow: "Finansy i statistika," 1985], p. 32, and *Narodnoe khoziaistvo SSSR za 70 let* [Moscow: "Finansy i Statistika," 1987], p. 404).

Year	Divorces	Marriages
1950	0.4	11.6
1960	1.3	12.1
1965	1.6	8.7
1966	2.8	8.9
1974	2.9	10.3
1980	3.5	10.3
1986	3.4	9.8

Twenty-seventh Party Congress in 1986, Gorbachev conceded that "there are a good many unhappy families" and that this "has a negative effect on the rearing of children and also on the morale of men and women and their work and public activity."[7] In asserting that the stable family is one of society's "most important foundations," Gorbachev acknowledged it to be a vital instrument of socialization, although it must be supplemented by other agents.

Education

In the Soviet Union the distinction is made between upbringing or rearing *(vospitanie)* and education *(obrazovanie)*. While both family and school are expected to contribute to upbringing, formal education is exclusively the province of the state-operated school system. Private education—with the exception of a few theological seminaries—is not permitted. The state assumes total responsibility for education because trained manpower is an important asset, and the schools can contribute significantly to the regime's success and perpetuation. Apart from providing the personnel needed for the country's economy, the educational system endeavors to provide a communist unbringing and the inculcation of communist values and Soviet patriotism. The history of the CPSU and Marxist-Leninist philosophy are required subjects.

Education is a social benefit to those who are enabled to study in that it is free, although Stalin did impose tuition for secondary and higher education in 1940 that was not abolished until 1956. Living expenses of college and university students are frequently provided for by state scholarships, and as a result the authorities have a means of controlling student conduct and of promoting conformity.

Soviet university and college graduates must also accept employment for up to three years where assigned—often to undesirable positions—as a condition of receiving financial aid. Although many Soviet citizens have completed only eight or nine years of schooling, the complete secondary education has become commonplace. In 1984 it was decided to add one year to secondary schooling, making it a total of eleven or twelve years, depending on the individual republic. Secondary schools teach difficult subjects, and there are some urban schools in which much of the instruction is given in a foreign language as well as special schools for the arts and music. Soviet education is highly centralized, although it is administered through the union republic governments. Curricula are standardized, and textbooks are prescribed by administrators and reflect a basic uniformity throughout the country, especially in the subjects most closely related to political socialization.

There is an effort to make vocational secondary education more attractive because of a recognized limit to the number of young persons that can be given higher education and commensurate employment opportunities (with the attendant higher living standards). Such an effort, when undertaken by Khrushchev, proved to be abortive because it required students to obtain direct work experience in industry or agriculture, make education more practical and less theoreti-

---

[7] *Pravda,* February 26, 1986, p. 6.

cal, and make manual labor more socially acceptable. Khrushchev's reform aroused resistance from factory directors, who did not care to have part-time students in their plants, as well as opposition from parents and teachers. The declining percentage of Soviet secondary-school graduates admitted to higher education and the use of competitive examinations have meant that advantaged youths could more readily meet admission requirements. Thus the sons and daughters of the Soviet intelligentsia and political elite are overrepresented in higher education.[8]

While education is free and in theory accessible to all, in practice admission to higher education is limited to those who can compete effectively or whose families have influence and means. In addition to not being entirely accessible, Soviet higher education is specialized and does not offer a liberal arts education. Most Soviet institutions of higher education are polytechnical or specialized institutes, including those for medicine, teacher-training, engineering, law, agronomy, construction, foreign languages, economics (including business administration), and conservatories of music. Institutes specialize in applied sciences and the training of practitioners. The less numerous universities offer training in the pure and theoretical sciences and in the humanities. Many Soviet students in higher education are enrolled in part-time correspondence courses in special, tuition-free correspondence-course institutes.

The enrollments in higher and specialized education are based on the manpower needs of the economic plan. Despite centralization and the regime's assumption of responsibility for education, there are disparities in the system, especially between rural and urban schools. Secondary schooling in rural areas is often inadequate and below urban standards. The general emphasis on scientific and technical training in Soviet education means that certain subjects in the humanities and social sciences are neglected or are taught in a biased manner. Yet it is such bias and the banning of interpretations and evidence that conflict with Marxist-Leninist ideology that give to Soviet political socialization its special character.

Peer Groups

Probably the most significant fact regarding Soviet peer groups is that they are not voluntary and spontaneous bodies but are institutional and sponsored. By contrast, in other societies peer groups tend to be private associations. Soviet children's peer groups are the units of the Little Octobrists and Pioneers, discussed in Chapter 5, which can lead to membership in the Komsomol (League of Communist Youth). They function in the classroom and in nonschool activities and teach the importance of collective effort, the sharing of things and experiences, and one's responsibility to the group. Children are not left to their own devices but are made aware of the sanctions that can be used by the group: exclusion, public criticism, and shaming as well as commendations and awards.

---

[8]See Murray Yanowitch & Wesley A. Fisher, eds., *Social Stratification and Mobility in the U.S.S.R.* (White Plains, N.Y.: International Arts & Sciences Press, 1973), Chapter 13.

They are trained to discipline each other and to show respect for adults. It has been observed that Soviet schoolchildren learn hypocrisy at an early age as a result of their being taught to give "correct" answers even if they are at variance with personal experience or conviction.[9]

There are many other peer groups, including primary (communist) party organizations, local branches of the mass auxiliary organizations, and such specialized and select groups as the Unions of Writers of the various union republics. In each case their purpose is to attempt to elicit conformity in support of officially determined values and policies. Yet there also exist smaller, more exclusive groups, informal associations of like-minded persons, including dissidents who have published the clandestine journals *The Chronicle of Current Events, Glasnost'*, and *The Ukrainian Herald*.

The Soviet regime has faced several difficulties in utilizing peer groups. Consequently, it has not been able to recruit all citizens into the relevant groups. Thus the Komsomol membership includes only about half of the population that is eligible. There is also the problem of waning interest and commitment on the part of those who do join. Some Soviet Ukrainian survey data indicate that parents, and especially mothers, are more influential than teachers, the school, and peers as agents of socialization. Thus the institutionalized peer group with official status tends to lose influence.[10] The problem of boredom, the tedious nature of Soviet political indoctrination, and the tendency to exercise excessive control have seriously affected the performance of the Komsomol. Even the socialization of the elite has its limits, as reflected in the alienation of CPSU members and their expulsion from the Party's ranks despite the requirements of ideological training. Idealism, in the sense of fostering visionary perceptions that conflict with reality, can readily be transformed into cynicism if the claims and assertions on which political socialization are based prove to be wanting.

Communications Media

The most significant fact concerning Soviet communications media is that they are official organs either of the Soviet government or the Communist Party of the Soviet Union or one of its subordinate units or of public organizations directly controlled by the Party. The fact that all printing plants, radio and television stations, news agencies, newsprint suppliers, and cinema studios are government-owned testifies to the subordination of the media to political ends. The dissemination of Soviet newspapers and magazines is centralized in *Soiuzpechat'* (the Chief Administration for the Dissemination of the Press), a department in the Ministry of Communications that collects subscriptions and operates newsstands.

The content of the Soviet news media is effectively controlled by TASS (Telegraphic Agency of the Soviet Union), which is an official governmental body

---

[9]See David K. Shipler, *Russia: Broken Idols, Solemn Dreams* (New York: Penguin Books, 1984), pp. 113–118.

[10]See Charles D. Cary, "Peer Groups in the Political Socialization of Soviet Schoolchildren," *Social Science Quarterly*, LV, No. 2. (September 1974), pp. 451–461.

attached to the U.S.S.R. Council of Ministers. TASS often issues important announcements on behalf of the Soviet government. It provides the bulk of articles of more than local significance that appear in the local party and government press organs subscribing to the TASS service. TASS sends Soviet correspondents on foreign assignments and selects the news despatches from foreign media—usually those that confirm Soviet stereotypes of the non-Soviet world. It also prepares special, secret background reports on foreign countries and their leaders along with digests of the foreign media for use by Soviet leaders.[11]

The *Novosti* (News) Press Agency (APN) was established in 1961 to provide news and feature articles, commentaries, and photographs about Soviet life primarily for dissemination in foreign countries; it also publishes books, brochures, magazines, and a variety of visual materials in foreign languages. The Novosti Agency claims to be "commercial" and unofficial. Finally there are, in addition to TASS, subordinate official news agencies for the non-Russian union republic, such as RATAU for Ukraine, BELTA for Belorussia, GRUZTAG for Georgia, UZTAG for Uzbekistan, and others. However, these republic news agencies do not deal directly with non-Soviet news agencies and have no foreign correspondents.[12]

The Soviet journalistic profession is under direct Communist Party control; much of its membership is in the Party and is subject to its discipline. Nor does the Party hesitate to replace those editors with whose performance it is dissatisfied.

Another means of control is through the Union of Journalists of the USSR—founded in November 1959 to give a special status to the writers of the press, periodicals, radio, and television and to enable the Party to mobilize and utilize their talents more effectively. Soviet journalists are in effect government or Party functionaries.

The leading Soviet newspaper is *Pravda,* official organ of the Communist Party of the Soviet Union, founded by V. I. Lenin in 1912. *Pravda,* which means "truth," is appropriately named if one bears in mind that it truthfully reflects the current line of the Soviet Communist Party. *Pravda*'s importance lies in the fact that it gives the cue to Party members and to other Soviet media and also prints in full Party decrees and key speeches. The official organ of the Soviet government is *Izvestiia (The News).*

Other Soviet newspapers with large circulations include *Komsomol'skaia Pravda,* official organ of the Central Committee of the League of Communist Youth, and *Trud (Labor),* official organ of the Central Council of Trade

---

[11]This practice is confirmed in *Khrushchev Remembers, The Last Testament* (Boston: Little, Brown, 1974), pp. 313, 321.

[12]For a thorough study of Soviet journalism, see Mark W. Hopkins, *Mass Media in the Soviet Union* (New York: Pegasus, 1970). See also Theodore E. Kruglak, *The Two Faces of TASS* (Minneapolis, Minn.: University of Minnesota Press, 1962), and Gayle Durham Hollander, *Soviet Political Indoctrination, Developments in Mass Media and Propaganda since Stalin* (New York: Praeger, 1972). For a study of popular responses to the Soviet media, see Ellen Propper Mickiewicz, *Media and the Russian Public* (New York: Praeger, 1981). On the origins of the Soviet establishment media, see Peter Kenez, *The Birth of the Propaganda State: Soviet Methods of Mass Mobilization, 1917–1929* (New York: Cambridge University Press, 1985).

Unions—as well as the *Literaturnaia Gazeta (Literary Gazette),* published by the Union of Writers. Other newspapers are published for teachers, children, sportsmen, medical workers, farmers, military personnel, civil defense workers, and "cultural workers." In all more than 8000 newspapers are published in the Soviet Union, ranging from *Pravda* and more than 25 other press organs of an all-Union nature through approximately 150 union republic newspapers in various languages down to small collective farm and factory organs.

Soviet newspapers have been limited in size to six or eight pages per issue and have relatively little foreign news. Though containing little advertising, there is no dearth of exhortatory and remonstrative articles, especially in the fields of economic affairs and ideology; detailed production statistics and claims are regarded as front-page news and readers are advised to produce more. In contrast, the Soviet press frequently fails to publish accounts of events that are regarded as newsworthy in many other countries. It often lacks human interest and the titillating details regarding personalities and political scandals found in the press in many other countries. Much of the Soviet press is characterized by an official optimism, and news stories are often didactic in tone. Feature articles, essays, editorials, and commentary tend to overshadow news reporting. Lengthy Party and government resolutions that dominate the central press hardly make for interesting reading. Headlines often praise or condemn and read more like slogans; commentary is frequently combined with news reporting. Soviet journalists write very critically of certain foreign countries but hesitate to apply the same standards of criticism to their own country. There is no *open* debate in the Soviet press on Party policies or on military or foreign policy, although cryptic or indirect expressions of disagreement are published on occasion. Journalists do seek to expose local instances of maladministration and serious social problems— often with prompting in the form of letters to the editor. A form of investigative journalism has developed, and it is possible to vent grievances against selected officials.

During the 1960s, the Soviet press tended to become more competitive, making an effort to be less dull and to heed readers' interests and preferences to a greater degree. The periodical press also acquired greater acceptance, and academic journals could even sponsor printed discussions. Yet what is published still is printed always with a purpose—not merely to inform or entertain. The objectives of communist journalism were stated succinctly by Lenin as early as May 1901 in an editorial published in *Iskra* (no. 4): "A newspaper is not only a collective propagandist and a collective agitator; it is also a collective organizer."[13] This statement, frequently quoted in Soviet journalistic circles, is equally applicable to Soviet radio and television, which also seek to indoctrinate and mobilize the population in addition to providing entertainment.

The Soviet radio network is distinctive in that many of the receivers are

---

[13]V. I. Lenin, *Polnoe sobranie sochinenii,* 5th ed. (Moscow: Gospolitizdat, 1961), V, 11. M. S. Gorbachev repeated Lenin's statement at the January 1987 Central Committee plenary session in support of the role of the press and media in his use of *glasnost'* (openness) to promote his "restructuring" program. *Izvestiia,* January 28, 1987, p. 3.

simple wired speakers connected to a closed circuit, over which a broadcast is retransmitted from a conventional radio receiver. This system has had several advantages from the point of view of the government: it is inexpensive; it prevents the listener from receiving foreign radio broadcasts; it compels the subscriber to the local radio service to listen to the limited program offering or forgo use of the service; in public places the loudspeaker cannot be turned off by the listener. However, Soviet citizens may purchase conventional radio receivers and have been doing so in increasing numbers; there are also ham radio operators, who sometimes have difficulties with the authorities. All broadcasting and telecasting facilities and programming are controlled by the State Committee for Television and Radio Broadcasting, attached to the U.S.S.R. Council of Ministers, which supervises bodies of the same name in the union republics. Soviet television, though less accessible than that of Western Europe, the United States, and Canada, has developed rapidly; it appears to be the prime source of news on international affairs for Soviet citizens. Among its principal shortcomings have been limited programming and very restrictive choice, although there are cultural programs as well as films and sports events.

The media are employed to maintain closed intellectual and information systems in an effort to impose tastes and opinions, regulate the dissemination of political information, and isolate citizens from ideologically harmful news, opinions, and values. Soviet customs officials and border guards have been known to confiscate publications from foreign tourists and from Soviet citizens returning home. Vast sums have been spent in efforts to jam certain foreign radio broadcasts, as many Soviet citizens own shortwave receivers. (Shortwave broadcasting is used in the Soviet Union because of the country's expanses.) The Soviet Union has sought an international ban on the transmission of foreign telecasts from space satellites not authorized by the receiving country. Soviet law requires the registration of mimeograph machines and of all other reproducing devices by the Interior Ministry.[14] Soviet authorities have arrested and sentenced persons for possessing foreign or Soviet books and publications that have been consigned to the closed special collections in libraries that are accessible only to certain officials and scholars. This practice of long standing reflects the Soviet effort to ban whatever contradicts or challenges the current Party line, whether in historiography, international relations, or domestic policy.

The Central Committee Report by Gorbachev to the Twenty-seventh Party Congress stated that the "Central Committee sees the media as an instrument of creativity, as a spokesman for the Party's overall point of view which is incompatible with departmentalism and localism."[15] He criticized the mass media for pursuing the "fortuitous and the sensational." Yet he also complained of "dullness, sluggishness" and delays in disseminating the news. Of course the delays are a consequence of official censorship and the unwillingness of media officials to take chances in second-guessing the censors' version of "accuracy" in the news.

Yet one can question the effectiveness of restrictive measures and efforts to

---

[14]A. E. Lunev, ed., *Administrativnoe pravo* (Moscow: "Iuridicheskaia literatura," 1970), p. 532.
[15]*Pravda,* February 26, 1986, p. 10.

monopolize the media. If Soviet citizens rely upon word-of-mouth information or if they listen to foreign radio broadcasts in the various languages of the Soviet Union, it is because they lack complete confidence in the Soviet media. Experience has taught them that news is frequently suppressed, distorted, manipulated, and orchestrated. The phenomenon of uncensored clandestine publication, known as *samizdat* (self-publication), has been a response to these conditions.

Thus, the Party's claimed monopoly of the media is not complete, and the efforts to monopolize the socialization process are less than entirely successful. The results are evident in several important areas: in nationality policy and the efforts to promote assimilitory practices and the notion of the "Soviet people"; in questions of conscience and the attempt to eradicate religious belief; and in the effort to control the content of culture, especially in literature and the arts.

SOVIET NATIONALITY POLICY: THEORY AND PRACTICE

The interaction of communism and nationalism has been one of the salient features of the twentieth century and has profoundly influenced developments both within the international communist movement and in the CPSU. The problem of resolving national differences in a manner that would serve the interests of the communist cause was of concern to Lenin and Stalin and has required the attention of their successors. The Soviet rulers have had to govern a multinational state and lead an ethnically mixed Communist Party. Since the communist world expanded in the aftermath of World War II, the Soviet Union has had to deal with other ruling Communist parties and cope with the disruptive effects of various forms of national communism.

Nationalism and Communist Theory

The founders of Marxism, Marx and Engels, assumed that the interests of the international proletarian class struggle would make nation-states and nationalism obsolete. In the *Communist Manifesto* they asserted that "the workingmen have no country" and contended that "national differences and antagonisms between peoples are daily more and more vanishing, owing to the development of the bourgeoisie, to freedom of commerce, to the world market, to uniformity in the mode of production and in the conditions of life corresponding thereto."[16] Thus Marx and Engels approved of some national movements and disapproved of others. The German and Italian national movements were regarded as "progressive" because they led to the integration of small principalities into larger economic units. The Polish and Hungarian national movements were viewed favorably because they were aimed at Russian autocracy and at the rule of the Hapsburgs; Irish nationalism was regarded as beneficial because it was directed against the British Empire and the center of capitalism. However, Marx and Engels did not approve of Czech or South Slavic nationalisms because of their

---

[16]Emile Burns, ed., *A Handbook of Marxism* (New York: International Publishers, 1935), p. 43.

failure to support the revolutions of 1848; and the founders of Marxism, further-more, supported the Ottoman Empire as a bulwark against Imperial Russia. Thus, Marxism provided its Russian followers with a purely instrumental and opportunistic approach to national claims, recognizing only those national move-ments that might further the cause of the revolution.

Lenin and his Bolsheviks had to face the fact that the Russians were in a minority in their own empire and recognize that the grievances of the non-Russian subject nationalities could be utilized in the struggle against the tsarist autocracy. While Lenin would not recognize the principle of nationality in his Bolshevik Party organization, he did recognize the right of national self-determi-nation for such non-Russian peoples as the Poles, Finns, Ukrainians, and others, including freedom of secession from the Russian Empire. Lenin branded Russia a "prison-house of nations," and he quoted Marx and Engels approvingly: "A people who oppresses other peoples cannot itself be free."[17] He held that Russians had to cease oppressing other nationalities and permit the free cultural develop-ment of the non-Russian peoples, abandoning the policies of russification and economic exploitation. While recognizing that Russia was a colonial power. Lenin nevertheless cherished the illusion that there could be an "international culture" of the world's toiling masses that would be reflected in the "unity and fusion of the workers of all nations."[18] "National culture" was regarded as a weapon of the bourgeoisie designed to weaken the class struggle.

Lenin apparently believed that the struggle against capitalism would in itself lead to an automatic "solution" of the problem of national oppression. He naively thought that after the overthrow of the old order, Russian workers and peasants would somehow, as if by means of a miraculous transformation, acquire an immunity against the Russian great-power chauvinism that was supposedly the monopoly of Russian "capitalists, landowners and exploiters." True to his centralist convictions, Lenin advocated only the right of secession of the non-Russian nationalities but not its practice. He assumed that the right of self-determination would not be exercised and that, instead, there would occur a merger of nationalities into a large centralized state under the leadership of the messianic Russian proletariat. Thus, Lenin remained essentially in the Russian centralist tradition, arguing for the alleged "advantages of large states." He wished to restore the "Empire" but with a different socioeconomic order. Yet he recognized that if you "scratch some communists you find a Great Russian chauvinist" and warned: "He [the Russian chauvinist] sits in many of us and must be combatted."[19] In the end Lenin saw Russian great-power chauvinism as the chief danger, and he conceded that Russians were guilty of numerous injustices in their treatment of non-Russian peoples.

Stalin, in his theoretical writing on the nationality problem in 1913, gener-

---

[17]V. I. Lenin, *Polnoe sobranie sochinenii,* 5th ed. (Moscow, 1961), XXVI, p. 108.
[18]*Ibid.,* XXIV, p. 10.
[19]*Ibid.,* XXXVIII, pp. 183–184. Lenin made these statements at the Eighth Party Congress on March 19, 1919.

ally followed Lenin's line and wrote under the latter's tutelage. Stalin defined the nation as an aspect of "the epoch of rising capitalism" and contended that the doom of capitalism would sound the death knell of the nation. While recognizing in the short run the right of nations to autonomy, federalism, or even to secession, Stalin contended that the solution in each case had to be consistent with "the concrete historical conditions in which a given nation finds itself" and suggested that such conditions were subject to change.[20] Thus the Party was to reserve the right to determine when and where application of the "right" of national self-determination was expedient or inexpedient. Stalin noted: "If the dialectical approach to a question is necessary anywhere, it is required here in the nationality question."[21] Ultimately Lenin and Stalin were to hold that self-determination could be decided only by the "proletariat" or "toiling population" of a nation—obviously on the advice of the Communist Party—in terms of whether exercise of the right was "revolutionary" or "counterrevolutionary." They never satisfactorily explained why a national movement had to be "bourgeois" and could not be "proletarian" or "socialist"—except to assert that nationalism was associated with capitalism, although they subsequently conceded that it could play a role in the antiimperialist movement of colonial peoples.

The Development of Soviet Nationality Policy

The establishment of the Soviet regime by the Bolshevik Party prompted most of the non-Russian nationalities to secede and establish independent states in 1917–1918. They took seriously the Bolshevik claim to respect the right of national self-determination but were soon confronted with the opposition of the Russian minority in the non-Russian areas and with the intervention of such armed forces as Lenin's government could muster. The Bolsheviks, furthermore, had an abundance of agitators who preached the class struggle and who endeavored to equate each non-Russian national movement with the non-Russian and Russian "national bourgeoisie," claiming that all must be subordinate to the "revolutionary centers" of Petrograd and Moscow. Lenin reluctantly let go of Finland, Poland, Estonia, Latvia, Lithuania, Bessarabia, and Kars and Ardahan but refused to part with most of Ukraine and the other non-Russian territories.

Thus, what was said to be a civil war, and the national conflicts between Russians and the non-Russian subject peoples, became intertwined. However, it was Russian military forces that by 1920–1921 imposed Soviet rule upon the non-Russian peoples. Lenin and Stalin had both expressed opposition to a federal system, but the realities of the relations between the nationalities and the intense resistance offered to Soviet rule led them to modify their position. By December 1919, after twice failing to establish a Soviet regime in Ukraine exclusively by armed invasion and preaching the class struggle, it became evident to Lenin that an effort had to be made to enable the Soviet regime to become "indigenous" in

---

[20]I. V. Stalin, *Sochineniia* (Moscow, 1946), II, p. 313.
[21]*Ibid.,* p. 314.

each non-Russian republic. The policy of "indigenization" *(korenizatsiia)* was designed to build popular support for the regime by promoting use of non-Russian languages and personnel in public administration and by furthering non-Russian cultural development.

However, this policy met with resistance from the more doctrinaire Bolsheviks and from Russians who had conveniently attached themselves to the new regime. As a result, Lenin at the end of 1922 had grave misgivings regarding the practices that had developed in the regime's nationality policy. On December 30–31, 1922, Lenin dictated notes in which he stated frankly that Russian chauvinism had reared its head and that Soviet bureaucrats were behaving like scoundrels and bullies and committing "acts of violence and insults" at the expense of non-Russians.[22] The poor state of Lenin's health did not permit him to attempt to reorient Soviet policy, however. Stalin had to concede a nominal federalism with the formation of the U.S.S.R. in January 1923, even though he had repeatedly, along with Lenin, denounced the federal principle. Many non-Russian communists, on the other hand, had advocated a *confederation* of Soviet republics with a weaker center instead of a federal union, but they had failed to prevail against the Party's commitment to centralism.[23] Although nationality conflicts persisted even within the CPSU, the non-Russian nations did make certain gains during the 1920s in terms of education; official use of their languages; and an enhanced, if still very modest, role in the Party.

As Stalin's control of the Party took hold, there began a gradual but relentless shift in Soviet nationality policy. Thus, as early as April 1926, Stalin warned that in view of the "weakness of the basic Communist cadres in Ukraine," the movement for the development of Ukrainian national culture was often led by noncommunist intellectuals and would alienate Ukrainian culture from "general Soviet culture and social life."[24] At that time Stalin was already defending the right of Russian minorities in the non-Russian republics to oppose and actually hinder the process of indigenization and to claim special privileges for themselves. Yet throughout the 1920s and at the Sixteenth CPSU Congress in June 1930, Stalin continued to insist that in the area of nationality policy Russian chauvinism was a more dangerous deviation than local (non-Russian) nationalism. This formulation was in accordance with Lenin's dictum on the need to distinguish between the nationalism of the oppressing nation and the nationalism of the oppressed nation, between the large nation and the small nation.[25]

---

[22]For the text of Lenin's notes, first published in the Soviet Union in 1956, see Robert Conquest, ed., *Soviet Nationalities Policy in Practice* (New York: Praeger, 1967), pp. 144–147. See also Richard Pipes, *The Formation of the Soviet Union,* rev. ed. (New York: Atheneum, 1968), Chapter 6 and especially pp. 263–293. Lenin's secretary, Lidiia Fotieva, confirmed (following Stalin's death) that Lenin, in the winter of 1922–1923, was greatly concerned over the "Georgian question," which had become a test case of Soviet nationality policy. See L. A. Fotieva, *Iz vospominanii o V. I. Lenine* (Moscow: Politizdat, 1964), pp. 63–66, 68, 70, 72, 74, 77.

[23]See the quoted communication from Anastas Mikoyan regarding use of the confederate form in Mikhail I. Kulichenko, *Obrazovanie i razvitie SSSR* (Erevan: "Aiastan," 1982), pp. 115–116.

[24]I. V. Stalin, *Sochineniia* (Moscow, 1948), VIII, pp. 149–154.

[25]Conquest, *op. cit.* (above, n. 22), p. 146.

By the time of the Seventeenth CPSU Congress—in January 1934—Stalin in effect reversed the Leninist line by asserting that the question of which nationalism was the greater danger was "a formal and therefore an empty controversy" and that "the major danger is the deviation against which one has ceased to fight."[26] Thus, the advantage was to be given to the large nation; and Stalin undertook a revival of purely Russian national heroes, including (St.) Alexander Nevsky, Ivan IV (the Terrible), and Peter I (the Great). The Marxist school of Russian historiography (headed by Mikhail Pokrovsky) was condemned for having denigrated Russian national heroes and for depicting Russian expansionism and colonialism not as "progressive" phenomena but as the predatory exploits of the Russian land-owning and commercial ruling class. Russian subjugation of non-Russian peoples was now reinterpreted with the so-called "lesser evil" formula, which justified Russian imperialism and its gains as a "lesser evil" than British or other imperialisms. Russian annexation of non-Russian peoples allegedly prevented their coming under British or other rule (influence) and brought them into contact with the supposedly superior Russian culture. Since the Russian Empire was to become the Soviet Union, its territorial gains ultimately became "progressive," as they resulted in communist rule over the peoples involved, while British imperial rule would have simply led to national independence (after 1945). Thus Stalin sponsored an official Soviet Russian nationalism that depicted his regime as the embodiment of Russian national interests while it continued to lay claim to the loyalties of those who might be inspired by the slogans of "revolutionary internationalism."

To this end Stalin had developed in May 1925 the formula that defined the cultures of the various peoples of the Soviet Union as "national in form and socialist in content." By 1930 this formula gained acceptance at the Sixteenth CPSU Congress, and it provided a convenient means of condemning as "bourgeois nationalism" those aspects of a particular "national form" that the regime condemned. While claiming to support the "flourishing" of national cultures, Stalin also asserted that the Soviet regime favored their fusion into a single culture with a single common language. Although the development of such fusion was a long-range goal, it was hardly a consolation to those among the non-Russian peoples who wished to preserve their national identity.

Soviet nationality policy as explicated by Stalin's successors has been similar to Stalin's policy regarding socialist content and national form. The 1961 CPSU Program asserted that "the Party neither ignores nor exaggerates national characteristics" but also advocated the "closer drawing together" of all Soviet nationalities "until complete unity is achieved" with common (communist) cultural traits. The (national) boundaries of the union republics—which often correspond to ethnic frontiers—were said to be "increasingly losing their former significance," but it was conceded that the "obliteration of national distinctions, and especially of language distinctions" will require more time than the obliteration of class distinctions.

---

[26]I. V. Stalin, *Sochineniia* (Moscow, 1951), XIII, p. 362.

The 1986 Program omitted the provision on the declining significance of national boundaries but provided for "increasing the material and spiritual potential of each republic within the framework of the single public economic complex." It continued to claim that "the resolution of the nationalities question is an outstanding achievement of socialism" and that national oppression and inequality have been eliminated and "friendship and brotherhood of all nations and nationalities have been established."[27] The 1986 Program contained the usual contradictory statements. It called for the "developing of a single culture of the Soviet people socialist in content, diverse in national forms and internationalist in spirit." Socialist nations and nationalities are supposed to experience both "flourishing and undeviating convergence" on the basis of "voluntariness." There is to be "free development of native languages and their equal use by all Soviet citizens will continue to be assured," but (non-Russian) Soviet citizens are required to master the Russian language, "which Soviet people have voluntarily adopted as the means of communication between nationalities." There is to be "neither artificial prodding nor restraining of urgent (*nazrevshikh*) tendencies of development," which, it is claimed, will "bring about the complete unity of nations in the remote historical future."[28] Thus, the Russian authors of the 1986 Party Program continue in the tradition of homogenization and linguistic russification with the use of Russian as a *lingua franca* and as the principal means of effecting the unity, if not the actual fusion, of nations.

Nationality Policy in Practice

It is the avowed purpose of the Soviet regime to endeavor to control the content of the non-Russian national cultures—and that of the Russians as well—while attempting to promote greater cultural homogenization by employing assimilatory practices. Various manifestations of non-Russian nationalism are condemned as "bourgeois"—despite the supposed absence of a bourgeoisie in the Soviet Union—while the "single family" of nations that is said to be the "Soviet people" in practice assumes a Russian rather than an "international" form. However, the relations between nationalities in the Soviet Union are far too complex to be characterized by a simple formula, and the elimination of everyone's national identity—except that of the Russians—is not a readily realizable goal.[29]

Soviet nationality policy has varied markedly. It has included the development of alphabets for isolated and numerically small northern peoples, the estab-

---

[27]*Partiinaia zhizn'*, No. 6–7 (March–April), 1986, pp. 100, 122.

[28]*Ibid.*, p. 122.

[29]For a treatment of Soviet nationality policy, see Erich Goldhagen, ed., *Ethnic Minorities in the Soviet Union* (New York: Praeger, 1968), as well as the special issue of *Problems of Communism*, XVI, No. 5 (September–October 1967) and Edward Allworth, ed., *Soviet Nationality Problems* (New York: Columbia University Press, 1971), as well as his *Nationality Group Survival in Multi-Ethnic States* (New York: Praeger, 1977). See also Jeremy R. Azrael, ed., *Soviet Nationality Policies and Practices* (New York: Praeger, 1978).

lishment of extensive systems of primary and secondary schools using non-Russian languages as the media of instruction, and the organization of national theaters, choirs, ballet companies, dancing troupes, and instrumental groups. The Soviet regime has given non-Russians access to higher education. It has also provided them with higher standards of public health and with a significant degree of economic development.

Soviet policy has also included mass deportations, the arrests and mistreatment of large numbers of non-Russian intellectuals, and the use of cruel and unconscionable measures against less numerous peoples, such as the Crimean Tatars, Chechens, Kalmyks, and others—measures that border on genocide.[30]

Language, education, the arts, and culture are interrelated areas in which nationality policy can be evaluated most readily. A people's language is one of its priceless treasures; and whenever the use and development of the native language is restricted, there is a corresponding impoverishment in the diversity and richness of human experience. A non-Russian Soviet citizen has the choice, language-wise, of using and defending his native tongue and refusing to use Russian *or* becoming bilingual by acquiring fluency in Russian in addition to his native language *or* opting for identification with the dominant Russian ethnic group and sending his children to Russian schools. While the use of one's native language is supposedly a constitutional right in the Soviet Union, the non-Russian who insists upon this right in "inappropriate" places is likely at the very least to arouse suspicion or to be accused of "bourgeois nationalism" and encounter humiliating and discriminatory treatment or worse. Although instruction in the non-Russian languages is available in primary and secondary schools, it is

---

[30]For example, see Robert Conquest, *The Soviet Deportation of Nationalities* (London: Macmillan; and New York: St. Martin's Press, 1960). During World War II seven nationalities were deported *en masse* from their territories and had their republics dissolved: the Chechens, Ingushi, Crimean Tatars, Kalmyks, Balkars, Karachai, and Volga Germans. Khrushchev criticized most of these deportations in his 1956 "secret speech," and the republics were restored except those of the Crimean Tatars and Volga Germans. The Volga Germans were "rehabilitated" and absolved of guilt by decree on August 29, 1964, and Stalin was blamed for their deportation: but they were not permitted to return from Central Asia and Siberia to the land that they had inhabited since the eighteenth century. The Crimean Tatars were absolved by a decree of September 5, 1967, but were forbidden to return to the Crimea. On the efforts of the Crimean Tatars to return to their homeland see Peter J. Potichnyj, "The Struggle of the Crimean Tatars" in Ihor Kamenetsky, ed., *Nationalism and Human Rights, Processes of Modernization in the USSR* (Littleton, Colo.: Libraries Unlimited, Inc. for the Association for the Study of Nationalities, Inc., 1977), pp. 228–243.

Khrushchev offered a most revealing observation regarding the failure of Soviet nationality policy in discussing the deportations. He noted: "the Ukrainians avoided meeting this fate only because there were too many of them and there was no place to which to deport them. Otherwise he [Stalin] would have deported them also." Stalin's dislike of the Ukrainians was prompted by widespread opposition among them that for several years during and after World War II took the form of guerrilla warfare conducted in Western Ukraine by the UPA (Ukrainian Insurgent Army). Khrushchev, in discussing the "struggle against the Ukrainian nationalists" and the UPA, conceded that in 1949 "the Carpathian Mountains were literally out of bounds for us because from behind every bush, from behind every tree, at every turn of the road, a [Soviet] government official was in danger of a terrorist attack." *Khrushchev Remembers, The Last Testament, op. cit.* (above, n. 11), p. 95. See also John A. Armstrong, *Ukrainian Nationalism,* 2nd ed. (New York: Columbia University Press, 1963), Chapters 6 and 13; also see Yaroslav Bilinsky, *The Second Soviet Republic: The Ukraine after World War II* (New Brunswick, N.J.: Rutgers University Press, 1964), Chapter 4.

markedly less available in higher education.[31] Thus, the 1977 Constitution (Article 45) provides for the "opportunity to study in school *(v shkole)* in the native language" with no assurance of such an opportunity in higher education. In the case of Yiddish and Hebrew, no instruction is available.[32] Most important, if Russian is the language of instruction in much of higher education, the graduates of non-Russian secondary schools are placed at a disadvantage in admissions examinations; discrimination is evident both in language use and in the ethnic composition of student bodies in higher education.

Cultural development is circumscribed in various ways, not all of which are subtle.[33] Russian loan-words—especially in technological and sociopolitical fields—are imposed upon the non-Russian languages, for in the Soviet Union linguistics is not far removed from politics. The Slavic Cyrillic alphabet has been imposed upon the Turkic and other non-Slavic peoples. The repertoires of non-Russian artistic companies are controlled and are required to include Russian offerings. Important historical and architectural monuments have been destroyed or permitted to fall into disrepair; archives have been destroyed.[34] Non-Russian Soviet historians cannot treat the history of their own peoples objectively if doing so directly challenges the biased tenets of Russian national historiography as propounded by the Soviet regime. Persistent efforts have been made to distort and truncate and deny when possible the "collective memory" that, for non-Russian peoples, is a nation's history and the basis for its sense of identity and distinctiveness. Such policies have been criticized as fostering ethnocide.

The numbers of copies of published non-Russian literary and historical works and textbooks have been deliberately limited; the circulation of certain magazines and journals has been impeded and their sale on newsstands limited, while Russian publications are generally available in unrestricted quantities. Once non-Russians leave their own republic, they are often subjected to greater cultural deprivation even if they reside in compact groups. Thus, Ukrainians who reside in the Russian S.F.S.R. are not permitted to have their own schools or publish

---

[31]It is evident that fluency in Russian improves an individual's life chances and educational and career opportunities. Khrushchev developed the formula of Russian as "the second native language" for non-Russians, although this has prompted the question of why Russians should also not be required to have a second native language. See Yaroslav Bilinsky, "Education of the Non-Russian Peoples in the USSR, 1917–1967: An Essay," *Slavic Review,* XXVII, No. 3 (September 1968), pp. 411–437, as well as his article "Expanding the Use of Russian or Russification?" *Russian Review,* XL, No. 3 (July 1981), pp. 317–332. For an examination of some of the methodological problems and issues involved in the study of Soviet nationality policy and the retention of ethnic identity, see Brian Silver, "Social Mobilization and the Russification of Soviet Nationalities," *American Political Science Review,* LXVIII, No. 1 (March 1974), pp. 45–66.

[32]Despite this linguistic discrimination, Soviet authorities in April 1983 organized a Soviet Public Anti-Zionist Committee headed by Colonel-General Daniil Dragunskii. See B. Putrin, ed., *Sovetskii narod podderzhivaet* (Moscow: izd-vo Novosti, 1983) and "V klevetnicheskom zapale," *Izvestiia,* June 21, 1983.

[33]The entire range of discriminatory policies and practices is discussed in detail with ample documentation by the Soviet Ukrainian literary critic Ivan Dzyuba in his work *Internationalism or Russification?* (London: Weidenfeld and Nicolson, 1968). Although Dzyuba was arrested in April 1973 and after a half year of imprisonment was persuaded by the KGB to condemn his own work, it remains a valid indictment of Soviet nationality policy.

[34]For example, see Titus D. Hewryk, *The Lost Architecture of Kiev* (New York: The Ukrainian Museum, 1982).

their own newspapers. Yet the Russian minority in Ukraine and in other non-Russian republics is given every conceivable cultural advantage (schools, publications, films, radio, television, theaters, university education in the Russian language) as well as political advantages. As if to add insult to injury, Soviet citizens who are not Russian must pay taxes to finance the cultural privileges that Russians enjoy in most non-Russian republics.

Although most of the nationalities have their own republics, they are not assured control over their economic development or republic governments, for political rights are as circumscribed as cultural rights. While it is true that industry has been introduced into non-Russian areas that were economically underdeveloped, the division of labor is determined by the planners in Moscow and has often resulted in highly skewed development. Thus, Uzbeks are required to grow cotton, which they must sell at a price set in Moscow, and are not permitted to develop a full-scale textile industry or to diversify their republic's economy sufficiently.[35] Uzbek cotton is used to supply textile mills in the Russian Republic.

Russians dominate the CPSU Politburo and have a near-monopoly on positions in the Secretariat, although non-Russians are elected to the Central Committee. Prominent posts in the Party and governmental and KGB organizations of the non-Russian republics are held by Russians. The Russian leadership of the CPSU has deliberately promoted the mingling of peoples by population transfers that have been both involuntary and economically induced through investment policies, by not maintaining adequate employment opportunities in all parts of the non-Russian republics, and by sending Russians and Ukrainians to settle in the various non-Slavic republics.

At the same time the Soviet system has developed non-Russian cadres of Party and government officials, intelligentsias, and economic and technical personnel. The cadres include semidenationalized or deraciné types who are nominally of non-Russians nationality and adequately bilingual but whose careerist inclinations make them fairly reliable executors of the center's commands. There are also non-Russian officials who seek to gain for their republics such advantages as they can—often employing the most ingenious arguments—while giving the appearance of complete dedication to Moscow's prescriptions. However, non-Russian communist leaders can be removed, as is demonstrated in the case of Petro Shelest, CPSU Politburo member and Ukrainian Party first secretary. Shelest had defended the use of the Ukrainian language and had succeeded temporarily in preventing the arrests or demotions of certain Ukrainian intellectuals in 1970–1971. However, he was summarily removed from Ukraine in May 1972 and demoted to the position of a U.S.S.R. deputy premier; he was dropped from the Politburo in 1973. Shelest was subsequently accused of "national narrow-mindedness," of having glorified and idealized the pre-Soviet Ukrainian past and of having encouraged a "spirit of self-satisfaction, of self-esteem."[36]

---

[35]See Grey Hodnett, "Technology and Social Change in Soviet Central Asia: The Politics of Cotton Growing," in Henry W. Morton and Rudolf L. Tökés, eds., *Soviet Politics & Society in the 1970s* (New York: Free Press, 1974), pp. 60–117.

[36]See Lowell Tillett, "Ukrainian Nationalism and the Fall of Shelest," *Slavic Review,* XXXIV, No. 4 (December 1975), pp. 752–768.

It appears that the readiness with which even the slightest manifestations of non-Russian nationalism are condemned indicates a concern that any major concession granted to ethnic demands or genuine equality of the union republics would entail great risks and place the Union itself in jeopardy. The implied assumption in Soviet nationality policy is that the non-Russian peoples are incapable of governing themselves or that some dire fate will befall them in the absence of Moscow's tutelage. Charges that Ukrainian "bourgeois nationalism" was in alliance with Zionism and Maoism reflect the concern of the Soviet leadership that the issues involved in the area of nationality policy have very broad ramifications. Assertions concerning the "voluntary" nature of the Union and such official slogans as "eternal friendship" and "together forever" may prove to be as valid as those of Stalin's time regarding the "monolithic" nature of the communist world.

The regime's nationality policy has yet to run its full course, and it has generated reactions that have on occasion prompted modifications and some concessions. Parents, teachers, linguists, and non-Russian intellectuals as well as some CPSU officials have resisted the regime's language policy, for instance. Encyclopedias and new journals have appeared in the non-Russian languages, and the non-Russian component in the CPSU membership has increased. The Soviet regime has had to republish the literary classics of the non-Russians and permit them a contemporary literature. If the regime has been able to promote bilingualism among many non-Russians, this cannot be equated with their becoming Russian. Indeed, the presence in the various republics of Russians, who often show little respect for the indigenous population's history, language, and culture (and who do not always conceal their arrogance), breeds resentment—as does the invidious official formula that has depicted the Russians as the "elder brother" to the non-Russian nationalities. The latter are frequently—and annoyingly—reminded of their alleged cultural "debt" to the Russians. In many ways the deplorable condition described by the great Ukrainian poet Taras Shevchenko in his poem "The Caucasus" (1845) still prevails:

> We teem with prisons and with peoples beyond all counting!
> From Moldavian to Finn
> In all languages each keeps his silence . . .

Yet Shevchenko in that same poem also counseled: "Struggle and you shall overcome," as if to foresee the restiveness of non-Russians that has become increasingly evident.

It is impossible to determine to what extent the Soviet regime's efforts to denationalize and russify non-Russians will succeed. Soviet census data reveal the phenomenon of millions of persons who give Russian as their native language but who refuse to identify with the Russian nationality. The Russians, as a result of their own declining birthrate and rapid increases in the populations of the Turkic peoples, are themselves apparently becoming a minority nationality in the USSR—albeit one with a dominant plurality. Under the pressures of demographic decline, Russians may have to rely on Communist ideology, despite its being an increasingly ineffective bonding agent of empire. The alternative of "Russianism" claiming to be "internationalism" is not likely to be viable in the long run if Russians fail to endear themselves to non-Russian subject peoples.

The fact that Russians have found themselves increasingly on the defensive in their dominant position vis-à-vis non-Russians has prompted Kremlin policy makers to intensify in particular the repressive measures employed against the Ukrainians. The unenviable position of Ukrainians as a target is due to their numbers. As the second-most-numerous nationality, they occupy a crucial position, which means that every effort is made to render them compliant. If Ukrainians can be reduced to the status of auxiliaries of the Russians, the empire could be prolonged and Russian domination sustained. Ukrainians by their very numbers represent a greater potential threat; the fact that they have been overrepresented among political dissidents and have been treated with special severity testifies to their pivotal position as a target.

When M. S. Gorbachev became General Secretary, he inherited a nationalities problem that was said to have been "solved." Yet at the Twenty-seventh Congress he acknowledged that "contradictions are inherent in any development, and they are also inevitable in this sphere." He conceded that "in this area the striving for national exclusiveness, localism, and parasitical sentiments have still not been overcome and at times become painfully evident." He denounced "attempts . . . made in certain works of literature and art and in scholarly works to present in idyllic tones reactionary-nationalistic and religious vestiges that are at variance with our ideology."[37]

Gorbachev assumed the Party leadership without knowledge of, and personal experience in, any of the non-Russian republics, having spent 23 years in Stavropol Territory and six years in Moscow. His apparent indifference to the nationalities problem was evident in the extreme brevity of his treatment of the subject at the Twenty-seventh Congress. From the beginning Gorbachev manifested an insensitivity that can be explained only in terms of ignorance or a deliberate flaunting of the General Secretary's "Russianness." Thus, he offended Ukrainians when he repeatedly referred to the Soviet Union as "Russia" during a visit to Kiev on June 25, 1985, and only belatedly corrected himself. He also proceeded to purge leading Party cadres in the Central Asian republics and introduce Russians into key posts—presumably to deal with corruption.[38] When he removed Kazakh first secretary Dinmukhamed Kunaev (and replaced him with a Russian, Gennadii Kolbin), large-scale street riots broke out in Alma Ata on December 17–18, 1986, with loss of life, injury, and destruction to buildings and vehicles.

Following the Alma Ata disorders, Gorbachev found it necessary to discuss nationalities issues at the January 1987 Central Committee plenary session. He asserted that "there is not a single question of principle . . . that can be resolved without taking into account [the fact] that we live in a multi-national country." He referred to the "events in Alma Ata," which, he said, required "serious

---

[37]*Pravda,* February 26, 1986, p. 6.
[38]See Yaroslav Bilinsky, "Nationality Policy in Gorbachev's First Year," *Orbis,* XXX, No. 2 (Summer 1986), pp. 331–342.

analysis." Shaken by these events, Gorbachev found it necessary to invoke Lenin's formula on the need to "exercise special sensitivity and circumspection in everything that pertains to the development of nationalities relations, that affects the interests of each nation and nationality, the national feelings of people, [and] in a timely manner resolve questions that arise in this sphere." Yet he also called for a "struggle against any manifestations of national limitation and conceit, nationalism and chauvinism, localism, Zionism, and anti-Semitism." However, he could only propose to counter the "nationalist contagion" *(povetriia)* with "internationalism" and "internationalist upbringing."[39]

Those non-Russian peoples who are sufficiently numerous and who retain an awareness of their past that includes periods of national independence, cultural renaissance, and armed resistance to Russian rule cannot be entirely subdued by efforts to stunt their cultural development. They cannot but ask why nationalism should be regarded by Soviet leaders as "progressive" in Asia, Africa, and Latin America but condemned as "bourgeois" among non-Russians in the Soviet Union. It is natural for non-Russian Communist Party cadres to desire greater authority in their own republics at Moscow's expense. There is considerable evidence indicating that ethnic tensions, antagonisms, and frustrations persist within the Soviet Union and that the regime has not "solved" its nationality problem despite the official claims regarding the "friendship of peoples."

COMMUNISM AND CONSCIENCE

Freedom in matters of conscience implies the right of individuals to determine for themselves or within groups their attitudes and personal beliefs regarding right and wrong, fairness and justice, and moral goodness. It also implies the existence of a pluralistic society in which diverse beliefs are tolerated by mutual understanding within the framework of generally accepted rules of conduct.

In contrast, communist doctrine dictates that beliefs regarding such matters must be determined for society by the Communist Party, which, according to Lenin's dictum, is "the intelligence, honor and conscience of our epoch."[40] The notion of a morality transcending social classes is specifically rejected. Morality is viewed as a class phenomenon based upon property interests, with the ruling class imposing moral principles designed to serve its interests. An allegedly exploiting class seeks to impose its own moral code designed to promote, disguise, and rationalize its particular interests and dupe the exploited class. Thus what is "moral" is that which advances the interests of the ruling class of the future, which has "history" on its side. For communists—who see themselves as a new ruling class whose avowed purpose is the unity of humanity and the abolition of

---

[39]*Izvestiia,* January 28, 1987, p. 3. Several weeks later, Gorbachev noted that "the nationality question requires special attention" and "a respectful attitude toward national feelings, history, culture, and the language of all peoples, for full and actual equality." He stated: "We live in a multi-national country and inattentiveness to these questions is dangerous." He conceded that each national intelligentsia "is studying the roots of its origins [and] at times it leads to the deification of history . . . and not only of what is progressive." *Izvestiia,* February 15, 1987, p. 2.

[40]V. I. Lenin, *Polnoe sobranie sochinènii,* 5th ed. (Moscow, 1962), XXXIV, p. 93.

all ruling classes—doctrines of morality must not hinder the pursuit of their objectives and the defeat of their enemies. Yet Marxism-Leninism is claimed to be the source of a new morality and to provide a code of conduct. The communist attitude toward religious belief is related to that taken toward the class enemy. Religious faith is viewed crudely as nothing more than a rationalization of the interests of the old ruling classes designed to make the exploited forget who is exploiting them. Thus, religion is regarded by communists as an "opiate" used to make the exploited submissive and satisfied with their lot, and the clergy are regarded as servants of the "exploiters." Religious belief and membership in the Communist Party are incompatible. It is assumed by communists that religious belief is a "remnant of capitalism" that should disappear once changes in the economic base and in the mode of production have made its presence unnecessary in the Marxist superstructure. Once exploitation has been eliminated and alienated humanity supposedly restored to its true condition, Marxist-Leninists contend that there should be no need for religion.

Lenin's intense hostility toward religion can be understood in terms of his having regarded it as the principal tool of the bourgeoisie in the class struggle. In this sense communist atheism must be distinguished from the atheism found among the bourgeoisie or that of the Enlightenment. However, there are problems with Lenin's simplistic understanding of the role of religion in history. Apart from the question of the validity of atheism and whether it ennobles or debases humanity and promotes moral conduct, communism fails to explain certain facts of religious history that do not accord with its scheme of historic development. Religion has transcended historical epochs in spite of its allegedly being part of a changing superstructure dependent upon the mode of production; thus Christianity has persisted from the slaveholding epoch through feudalism and capitalism and possibly into communism. If religion is supposedly an instrument of the ruling class, why did Christianity begin not with rulers but with the poor and enslaved? Similarly, many religious leaders have not identified themselves and their churches with the ruling class or with a particular economic order but have opposed them or have been indifferent to such purely secular matters.

Yet atheism is an essential component of communist belief and is derived from its philosophical materialism. For communist doctrine only the material world exists, and man is viewed as nothing more than an earthly, physical being who is part of the matter of which the universe consists. In denying what cannot be perceived by the physical senses, communism confines itself to the human flesh and to the satisfaction of physical appetites and material needs. In its obsession with man, society, and economic development, it rejects the possibility of divine creation or intercession or the need for spiritual solace as a response to human weakness and limitations.

Dialectical materialism holds that only matter itself is eternal and infinite, having neither a beginning nor an end, and that the source of its movement is internal and spontaneous (auto-dynamism). Matter is said to be infinite both in time and in space, and the universe is held to be self-contained and its own cause. Indeed, dialectical materialism's insistence upon self-movement is derived from its denial of all that is divinely ordained and its refusal to recognize God. It ignores the questions of how the material world came into being and how it could exist and be ordered without a prime mover and a first cause. Instead, science is substituted for religious belief and is held by communists to be incompatible with belief in God. The role of mystery—whether in life or in death—is not recognized.

Science is seen as holding the key to a complete understanding of the material universe, of which man is regarded as a part. Communist atheism reflects a refusal to believe in anything higher than humanity—except the communist movement itself. Religion is equated with superstition and condemned as falsehood and obscurantism. Thus, Soviet "scientific atheism," with its emphasis on conscious development and belief in progress, claims to be creating a paradise on earth in contrast to Christ's injunction: "My Kingdom is not of this world" (St. John 18:36).

In politicizing matters of conscience, Soviet communism has demonstrated that it is itself a creed claiming to be a complete system of thought. Its atheism is actually a pseudo-religious phenomenon, in that it requires a fervently held belief that God does not exist. Paradoxically, it is unbelief based on belief that God does not exist. Indeed, it is ironic that communist rulers should combat so intensively something that is alleged not to exist. Communism rejects the Christian injunction to render unto Caesar what is Caesar's and unto God what is God's and instead makes an unlimited claim on the human personality, which, in a sense, justifies its being termed a totalitarian system. In claiming to give meaning to life and to explain all social phenomena and possess absolute truth, Marxism-Leninism can hardly tolerate competing creeds or systems of thought, whether these be Christianity, Judaism, Islam, or Buddhism. If communist ideology were nothing more than a political theory or a socioeconomic doctrine, it would at least be indifferent toward religious belief but would not be so totally dedicated to its eradication.[41]

One of the early acts of Lenin's regime was to separate church and state in February 1918 by disestablishing the Russian Orthodox Church and secularizing education. A variety of tactics have been employed against the Church, including acts of sacrilege and the physical destruction of church buildings or their conversion into clubs, theaters, or warehouses; lectures and propaganda designed to promote atheism; and divisive measures in supporting reformist and sectarian movements and "progressive" clergy against the traditional Church. The decree of disestablishment also nationalized all church property and made religious bodies entirely dependent upon the government in obtaining use of church buildings. Many clergymen experienced deprivations and oppression, and many were executed. At times the crudest kinds of blasphemous propaganda have been employed in an effort to discredit religious belief.

World War II saw the Soviet regime hard pressed for support, and in September 1943, Stalin arrived at a modus vivendi of sorts with the Russian

---

[41]Aleksandr Solzhenitsyn, in his Templeton Prize Address delivered in the London Guildhall in May 1983, observed that "militant atheism is the 'central pivot' of communist policy." He contended that the Soviet rulers, in order to achieve their ends, need to render their subjects devoid of religious faith and nationhood. See Aleksandr Solzhenitsyn, "Men Have Forgotten God," *National Review,* July 22, 1983, pp. 872–876.

Orthodox Church, permitting it to reestablish a central organization and to elect a Patriarch—the first in two decades. This concession was related to the upsurge of Russian nationalism during the war and to the fact that the Russian Church had demonstrated its loyalty to Stalin's regime; it was also prompted by the spontaneous religious revival that had occurred in the large area under German military occupation. The dictator was also interested in demonstrating to Westerners that "freedom of religion" existed in the Soviet Union, and he undoubtedly recognized that the Moscow Patriarchate could serve as a useful instrument in foreign policy. Two councils were established under the U.S.S.R. Council of Ministers—one for Russian Orthodox Church affairs and the other for the "affairs of religious cults." In 1966 they were merged into a single Council for Religious Affairs headed, ironically, by a Party member who must be an atheist.[42]

The Council for Religious Affairs operates through offices at the oblast' and republic levels, and its officials closely monitor and regulate the activities of all religious denominations. The law under which the Council operates has not been published, so it is difficult for believers to challenge the legality of purely administrative acts perpetrated by the Council's officials. Strictly speaking, it is not a council but a bureaucratic organ charged with the task of harassing religious believers and controlling the activities of clergymen of all denominations. The Council's principal administrative weapon is its authority to "register" all religious bodies and congregations, which gives it a licensing power. Unlicensed congregations are not permitted, and those that are "registered" can be deprived of any right to exist. Twenty lay persons supposedly have the right to organize a congregation, but their requests and appeals can be ignored with impunity.[43] Since the government possesses legal title to all religious edifices and even articles of worship, it can repossess them at any time, and a congregation has little or no recourse, even in the courts. Thus the legal status of Soviet religious bodies and congregations is obscure and uncertain, and their legal rights can be very tenuous. Revised regulations made public in 1986 apparently permit registered religious societies (the "twenty") to exercise the rights and obligations of judicial persons, including the acquisition of real property by purchase or construction. Children above the age of ten are said to be allowed to participate voluntarily in religious services with parental permission.[44]

---

[42]The most thorough study of Soviet policy toward religious bodies is Walter Kolarz, *Religion in the Soviet Union* (New York: St. Martin's Press, 1962). For a brief treatment, see Bohdan R. Bociurkiw, "Church-State Relations in the USSR." *Survey,* No. 66 (January 1968), pp. 4–32.

[43]Vladimir A. Kuroyedov, chairman of the Council for Religious Affairs of the U.S.S.R. Council of Ministers, conceded that "there still occur isolated [sic] instances when certain local organs permit incorrect actions in relationship to the church and believers." Yet he also observed that religious "extremists" are prosecuted. See "Sovetskii zakon i svoboda sovesti," *Izvestiia,* January 31, 1976. For a graphic account of the tension and conflict between the spiritual and the profane in the Soviet Union, see Aleksandr Solzhenitsyn's "The Easter Procession" in Michael Glenny (trans.), *Stories and Prose Poems* (New York: Farrar, Straus & Giroux, 1971), pp. 125–131.

[44]See "Prava i obiazannosti religioznogo obshchestva," *Zhurnal Moskovskoi Patriarkhii,* No. 1, 1986, p. 80. A poignant document that describes the forms of harassment that the "plenipotentiary" (head) of the Council's oblast' office can employ against parishes and the diocesan bishop is the letter to Brezhnev by Bishop Feodosii (Dikun) of the Poltava Diocese in Ukraine, dated October 26, 1977.

(continued)

As a result of Khrushchev's and Brezhnev's intensified campaign against religion, the number of functioning, officially recognized congregations was greatly reduced. Detailed official statistics are not published, and the gross figures that occasionally appear in Soviet publications have been inconsistent and unreliable. To foreign audiences Soviet officials seek to convey the impression of freely functioning religious denominations, except for prosecution of those who allegedly seek to use religion for "political purposes directed against the interests of the Soviet state." However, those officials in charge of the antireligious campaign go about their business and must claim success for their various operations.

The Soviet authorities have employed a variety of techniques in combating religious belief. Church buildings have been converted into museums of atheism; and most churches, synagogues, mosques, monasteries, and seminaries have been closed. Religious instruction of children is forbidden, and clergymen have been imprisoned for providing such instruction. Churches cannot conduct Sunday schools or sponsor religious study groups for the laity. The 1936 Soviet constitution provided for "freedom of religious worship and freedom of antireligious propaganda" (Article 124) and, in effect, implicitly forbade the active propagation of religion. The ban on the teaching of religion and on proselytizing persists in the 1977 Constitution (Article 52), which "guarantees freedom of conscience, that is the right to confess any religion or to confess none, to perform religious exercises or to conduct atheistic propaganda." It is explicitly stated (in Article 52) that "the school is separated from the church," so all religious schools are outlawed except for several seminaries that train limited numbers of clergy under the watchful eyes of Soviet officials. Religious literature cannot be published and sold freely, and the limited editions of the Bible and of prayer books have been insufficient to satisfy the demand. Congregations can be accused of "disturbing public order" and can be subjected to administrative restrictions and pressures designed to bring about their closing.[45] Religious processions away from church premises are banned. Churches cannot undertake any charitable activities. Congregations cannot impose dues or other requirements on members. Periodic efforts are made to discredit clergymen; police agents have been known to enter

---

These harassments include: refusal to permit necessary repairs to parish churches, threats of physical harm and other sanctions against outspoken believers, refusal to permit clergy to substitute for each other, interference in the bishop's right to ordain candidates for the priesthood by limiting their number, the closing of churches by force, and use of the local press to incite and justify excesses by atheists and to offend the sensibilities of religious believers. The letter also reveals that parishes have been required to contribute "voluntarily" substantial amounts to Soviet "state funds" such as the "peace fund" and the fund for the "renovation of historical monuments." See Feodosii, episkop Poltavskii i Kremenchugskii, "Pis'mo L. I. Brezhnevu o polozhenii pravoslavnoi tserkvi v Poltavskoi eparkhii," AS No. 4456 in *Materialy samizdata, vypusk No. 40/81* (October 30, 1981).

[45] A vague article (227) in the Criminal Code of the Russian Republic provides for punishment of up to five years of imprisonment or exile with or without confiscation of property for "organizing or directing a group, the activity of which, carried on under the appearance of preaching religious beliefs and performing religious ceremonies, is connected with causing harm to citizens' health or with any other infringements of the person or rights of citizens, or with inducing citizens to refuse social activity or performance of civic duties, or with drawing minors into such group." Participation in such a group can result in a sentence of up to three years. *Soviet Criminal Law and Procedure, The RSFSR Codes,* translated by Harold J. Berman and James W. Spindler (Cambridge: Harvard University Press, 1966), p. 230.

the clergy and engage in acts of provocation and subsequently commit apostasy. In the case of the Russian Orthodox Church, the regime is in a position to control episcopal appointments (and has even removed diocesan bishops from office), interfere in its internal administration, and censor its publications that are printed on the government's presses.

Although the Russian Orthodox Church experienced renewed repression in the 1960s, it continued to be useful to the regime in communist-inspired international "peace" movements and in the World Council of Churches and elsewhere, where it has endeavored to further the interests of Moscow's foreign policy. An anomalous situation has developed in which the church is separated from the state and its activities severely circumscribed, although churchmen must proclaim to the non-Soviet world that the churches enjoy complete freedom while endorsing Soviet foreign policy objectives and demonstrating their "patriotism" and loyalty to a government that seeks their destruction. It is this paradoxical plight of the clergy of the Moscow Patriarchate that prompted a group of Orthodox Christian believers to comment with bitterness on the clergy's relations with Soviet authorities: "They [the clergy] are cowardly, but they do not fear God."[46]

If the Russian Orthodox Church is treated with less intolerance, the same cannot be said of other denominations. The Ukrainian Autocephalous Orthodox Church has been suppressed and its hierarchy liquidated. The Ukrainian Catholic Church was compelled to go underground in 1946 and its hierarchy was arrested; its primate, Josyf Cardinal Slipyj, was held in prison camps and experienced eighteen years of untold tribulations until released in 1963, when he was permitted to reside abroad.[47] The Islamic, Judaic, and Buddhist faiths have also experienced severe restrictions. Judaism in particular suffered as a result of the Soviet regime's attacks on Zionism and the state of Israel; it has been forbidden to have any central organization or sustained contacts with coreligionists abroad.

The propagation of atheism is an essential part of the Soviet socialization process, and vast sums are spent on it apart from the repressive measures that are employed. The 1986 Party Program calls for "atheistic upbringing" and "condemns attempts to use religion to the detriment of the interests of society and the individual." Religion is to be overcome by "increasing people's labor and public activity, their enlightenment and the wide dissemination of new Soviet

---

[46]*Sobranie dokumentov samizdata,* Vol. 26, AS No. 891, p. 474.

[47]On the oppression of the Ukrainian churches, see: *Ukraine: A Concise Encyclopaedia* (Toronto: University of Toronto Press, 1971) II, pp. 161–198; Yaroslav Bilinsky, *op. cit.* (above n. 30), pp. 99–110; Fedir Bulbenko, "The Ukrainian Orthodox Church and Moscow: Rebirth and Golgotha," *The Ukrainian Quarterly,* XXIX, No. 4 (Winter 1973), pp. 358–379. See also Bohdan R. Bociurkiw, "The Ukrainian Autocephalous Orthodox Church, 1920–1930: A Study in Religious Modernization" in Dennis Dunn, ed., *Religion and Modernization in the Soviet Union* (Boulder, Colo.: Westview Press, 1977), and Frank E. Sysyn, "The Ukrainian Orthodox Question in the USSR," *Religion in Communist Lands,* II, No. 3 (Winter 1983), pp. 251–263 as well as Vasyl Markus, "Religion and Nationalism in Ukraine" in Pedro Ramet, ed., *Religion and Nationalism in Soviet and East European Politics* (Durham, N.C.: Duke University Press, 1984), pp. 59–81, and Vasyl Markus, "Religion and Nationality: The Uniates of the Ukraine" in B. R. Bociurkiw and J. W. Strong, eds., *Religion and Atheism in the U.S.S.R. and Eastern Europe* (Toronto: University of Toronto Press, 1975), pp. 101–122.

rituals and customs."[48] Atheism is the dialectical counterpart of a state church, with the state committed, instead, to an antichurch position. "Scientific atheism" is taught in the schools, and there are professorships in it at the college level. There are special courses to train atheist lecturers, as well as conferences and seminars. The media, films, and debates are used; an extensive literature is published and is often criticized for its limited effectiveness.[49] Civic rituals have been developed to compete with the religious ceremonies of baptism, confirmation, marriage, and the religious funeral. These have included granting a memento to newborn infants and the issuance of the internal passport ceremony at the age of sixteen. "Wedding palaces" have been established to give the Soviet civil marriage some of the splendor and beauty of the religious marriage ceremony.[50] Parents who wish to have their child baptized must register and present their passports; the clergyman must report all baptisms to the local office of the Council for Religious Affairs. As a result parents are later subjected to harassment at their place of employment. Church weddings must also be reported in this way. Believers are subjected to measures that range from being given gratuitous advice to ridicule and scorn and even possible loss of employment if they persist in their "erroneous" beliefs.

Religious belief persists in the Soviet Union despite many decades of repression, and believers have often protested the illegal acts of Soviet authorities restricting the right of religious worship. In Lithuania, for example, such protests have contained hundreds and even thousands of signatures, and the clandestine *Chronicle of the Lithuanian Catholic Church* appeared in 67 issues between 1972 and 1985. Religion can be practiced in the privacy of one's home, and the Islamic faith, in particular, can be practiced without mosques and clergymen. Estimates of the number of religious believers range from 15 to 30 percent of the population and may be conservative, for religion is a highly personal matter on which it is not always easy to obtain data. In certain areas, as in the Central and Western Ukraine, the density of believers is far higher. Evangelical Baptists have gained members to a greater degree than has Orthodoxy. Protestantism, with its more active personal participation of believers, lack of strict hierarchy, and emphasis on Scriptural teachings and homiletics, has been more effective in resisting or circumventing Soviet government controls and restrictions and has developed "unregistered" congregations. Pentecostalists, Seventh-Day Adventists, and Jehovah's Witnesses have acquired adherents.

Religious affiliation—whether covert or declared—is also a form of dissent, and in the case of non-Russians it can serve as a means of maintaining cultural and ethnic identity. There may be more secret than overt believers, and agnostics may outnumber the convinced atheists. Thus, many millions of Soviet citizens of all ages reject the official socialization prescription in matters of conscience.

---

[48]*Partiinaia zhizn'*, No. 6–7 (March–April), 1986, p. 129.

[49]See David E. Powell, *Antireligious Propaganda in the Soviet Union: A Study in Mass Persuasion* (Cambridge, Mass.: The M.I.T. Press, 1975), especially Chapters 7 and 8.

[50]For a description of the Soviet effort to establish civic rituals, see Christel Lane, *The Rites of Rulers, Ritual in Industrial Society—The Soviet Case* (London: Cambridge University Press, 1981), Chapters 5–8.

THE POLITICS OF CULTURE

In the Russian Empire literature was used as a form of political expression and reflected the alienation of the intelligentsia—a phenomenon that was brilliantly portrayed in Dostoevsky's novel *The Demons (The Possessed)*. Lenin viewed the intelligentsia as a disruptive element and tended to distrust it while also seeking to use it. Stalin is said to have defined writers as "engineers of human souls" in depicting their role in the socialization process. Khrushchev, in forced retirement, distinguished between the "technological intelligentsia" and the "creative intelligentsia" (writers, artists, and composers) and conceded that the latter are "very troubled" and work under difficult conditions.[51] Yet it was Russian political practice that created difficulties for Pushkin, Lev Tolstoy, and Maxim Gorky and provided a precedent for the Soviet regime's mistreatment of the Nobel laureates in literature, Boris Pasternak and Aleksandr Solzhenitsyn.

The Soviet authorities seek to control the content of literature in accordance with the doctrine of "socialist realism" that became official policy in 1934. "Socialist realism" resulted from the attempt to apply to the arts Lenin's concept of *partiinost'* (party-mindedness). According to this doctrine, the writer and artist are expected to depict "reality" in terms of a "class approach" in order to promote the communist cause. Often the result has been insipid and synthetic literature that is didactic and optimistic with a "positive hero" and a happy ending extolling the "builders of communism." Literature and the arts are viewed not only as activity comparable to economic production—as, for example, the manufacturing of tractors or washing machines—but as potentially harmful and requiring constant supervision. The writer has difficulty portraying life as it is with its occasions of senselessness, misery, pain, personal tragedy, cruelties, unfaithfulness, and coarseness in human conduct. The doctrine of "socialist realism" does not recognize alienation except in capitalist countries. It condemns the mystical along with sensuality and the erotic, and it rejects suicide, pessimism, the ironic, and the melancholic. It is obsessed with humanity's knowing and striving, consciously fulfilling historical tasks, and glorifying the masses. Writers who seek to depict Soviet life honestly run the risk of being accused of permitting themselves to be used by enemy propaganda. If writers endeavor to be truly creative, they can be accused of ideological errors and of seeking to subvert the Soviet system. Satirists can find it dangerous should they direct their satire against certain subjects or practices.

The techniques employed to control writers have varied greatly and have included prosecution and confinement to prison camps, as in the case of Andrei Siniavsky and Iulii Daniel' in 1966, as well as confinement to mental hospitals. Intimidation and vilification have been employed against Anna Akhmatova, Mikhail Zoshchenko, Boris Pasternak, and many others; official criticism has been levelled against individual writers. By owning all publishing houses, the regime can refuse to publish certain works, as for example, the novels of Aleksandr Solzhenitsyn, who spent a decade in Stalin's concentration camps and in

---

[51]*Khrushchev Remembers, The Last Testament, op. cit.* (above, n. 11), Chapter 5.

exile. While his *One Day in the Life of Ivan Denisovich* was published in 1962 because it was useful to Khrushchev, his novels *The Cancer Ward* and *The First Circle* could be published abroad only, although they have circulated clandestinely and even among Soviet officials in a limited edition apparently published by the security police. Pasternak's novel *Doctor Zhivago* and the works of many other Soviet authors have had to be published abroad.

When authors are published, the authorities are not above bowdlerizing the texts of their manuscripts and removing entire passages that they deem to be politically inexpedient or ideologically harmful or even rewriting and adding entire passages.[52] However, the regime prefers to have authors engage in self-censorship. This is accomplished through the U.S.S.R. Union of Writers and its affiliates in the union republics, established by Stalin in 1932 as part of the effort to regiment the arts. In order to receive recognition and enjoy the status of an author or literary critic, each writer must be a member of the Union. Membership is the equivalent of the regime's "licensing" authors. The Union reprimands errant writers; distributes awards and perquisites, including vacations and travel abroad; and supposedly defends authors' rights. However, the Union has failed to defend the creative rights and professional interests of Soviet writers against the demands of the Communist Party.[53] The poet Evgenii Evtushenko expressed the plight of the Soviet writer in his poem "Winter Station" (1956) when he observed: "And what is a writer now? Not master, but a keeper of thought."

If self-censorship proves to be ineffective, the regime can generally rely on the politically responsible editors of journals, newspapers, and publishing-house directors to publish only what serves the Party's interests. Nearly every Soviet publication bears a code number referring to the individual censor who represents the organization still known as *Glavlit* (the Chief Administration of Literary and Publishing Affairs). This organization, officially renamed the Chief Administration for the Protection of State Secrets, is responsible for determining that an approved publication does not contain any classified material. Decisions on the publication of controversial writings are taken only at the highest Party organizational levels. As a result publication of individual issues of journals has been delayed while the decision was pending. The journalism profession serves as a watchdog through the Union of Soviet journalists established in 1959.

In the arts, the Union of Soviet Composers includes both composers and musicologists and determines which persons and what kinds of music shall be accorded professional recognition. The Union decides what will be published and performed. The CPSU condemns "formalism" and modernism in music and

---

[52]The Soviet writer Anatolii Kuznetsov, who defected in Great Britain in 1969, provided graphic proof of this practice when he brought with him on film the *unexpurgated* texts of his works published in the Soviet Union in expurgated form. See his personal account in the *New York Times,* August 7, 1969, pp. 1 and 14 and the complete version of his *Babi Yar, A Document in the Form of a Novel,* by A. Anatoli (Kuznetsov) (New York: Farrar, Straus & Giroux, 1970), which indicates the original censored 1961 version, the passages deleted by censors in 1966, and also portions added.

[53]The Union's inability to defend writers and the nature of Soviet literary censorship are discussed in Aleksandr Solzhenitsyn's letter of May 16, 1967, addressed to the Fourth All-Union Congress of Soviet Writers. For the full text, see *Bulletin of the Institute for the Study of the USSR* (Munich), XV, No. 8 (August 1968), pp. 39–43.

endeavors to have composers incorporate political themes into their music and combat "alien ideology." It keeps a close watch on the Union and its leadership. In painting and sculpture, the controls are exercised through the Union of Soviet Artists, which enforces official aesthetic standards and rewards conformity. Loss of membership in the Union can mean loss of an assured income, a studio, commissions for new works, and the right to exhibit in museums and exhibitions. The state-owned museums have been reluctant to purchase art that does not conform to the canons of "socialist realism." In general, it is "art for the people," art that can be understood by the masses and conveys a political message that is sanctioned. Nonrepresentational and abstract art has been able to exist largely in a semiunderground. Works of art in unorthodox styles are sold by artists to private collectors who are often also members of the Soviet cultural and scientific elite.

The U.S.S.R. Ministry of Culture, which operates through republic ministries and departments of culture attached to local soviets, is responsible for the arts and supervises concert organizations, theaters, museums, libraries, cultural exchanges with foreign countries, and even circuses. It controls the repertoires of artistic performing companies and maintains special schools for the training of artists and performers. It controls the U.S.S.R. Academy of Arts and publishes the newspaper *Sovetskaia Kul'tura (Soviet Culture)* as well as specialized journals. Painter and sculptor Ernst Neizvestnyi has observed that "it is not a ministry that is concerned that there be culture—it is an agency that is concerned that there not be culture, it is essentially a police agency, one more censor."[54]

In literature and the arts, as in other areas, official policies encounter resistance. Prominent writers have remained silent, refusing to write, or do translations. Manuscripts that the censors will not approve for publication circulate, often surreptitiously, in limited, usually typewritten, editions. Although Aleksandr Solzhenitsyn could be expelled by the Writers' Union in November 1969, his literary stature and his talents could hardly be diminished by such an arbitrary act—as testified to by his being awarded the 1970 Nobel Prize for literature. Writer Mykola Rudenko did not fare so well, although he had been a Party member and secretary of the Party organization in the Ukrainian Union of Writers. He abandoned Marxism-Leninism, became a religious believer, and founded and headed the Ukrainian Helsinki Group, sacrificing all of the material advantages and perquisites of a recognized writer. As a result, in 1977 he was sentenced to seven years in prison camp and five years in internal exile and also had his personal archive seized by the KGB—this despite his being a severely wounded veteran of World War II whose wound had never fully healed. Thus, the lot of the openly nonconforming writer is a very difficult one.

Neizvestnyi has conceded that "the Procrustean bed . . . has been lengthened" although it remains Procrustean.[55] Yet he has acknowledged that there are "grooves" or "slots" *(pazy)* in the system that the artist can utilize. The practical needs of the system, as well as its efforts at image-building abroad, can conflict

---

[54]Ernst Neizvestnyi, *Govorit Neizvestnyi* (Frankfurt am Main: Possev-Verlag, 1984), p. 137.
[55]*Ibid.*, p. 136.

with ideological officialdom and its demands, and the artist can take advantage of this and of administrative oversights that occur. Censorship policies can vary; what might be censored in one jurisdiction is passed in another. Obedient writers and artists are permitted a certain degree of latitude. In a field such as architecture, considerable creative freedom has developed since Stalin imposed his own peculiar version of "neo-classicism." Although the inducements to conformity and the various other methods of control are much in evidence, they have neither stifled artistic creativity entirely nor produced the kinds of art and literature that fully meet the Party's expectations.

chapter 11

Soviet Foreign Policy

The emergence of the Soviet Union as one of the great powers can be viewed against the record of the Russian Empire of the tsars. The acquisition by the tsars of the world's largest territorial mass under a single sovereignty was an essential antecedent to the Soviet Union's foreign policies. Although Imperial Russia suffered humiliating defeat in the Russo-Japanese War of 1904–1905 and had advocated international "disarmament" as early as 1899 at the Hague Conference because of its own weakness, it nonetheless succeeded in retaining its vast holdings until the advent of the 1917 Revolution brought the Empire to an end. Once the Soviet regime established itself in the ethnically Russian territories, it succeeded ultimately in reacquiring all of its lost territories except Poland, Finland, Kars, and Ardahan (the latter came under Russian rule in 1878 but were regained by Turkey in 1918).

The Soviet Union's great-power status cannot be explained simply in terms of its numerous territorial acquisitions, for its influence has extended well beyond the Soviet frontiers. Initially Moscow had the advantage of the fact that the Western Powers, although disapproving of Lenin's regime, were too exhausted following World War I to undertake an effective military effort to support the forces opposed to Soviet rule. Another advantage enjoyed by the Bolsheviks lay in the disunity from which the various anticommunist forces suffered, while Lenin and Stalin were able to identify with Russian national interests. The ability to utilize foreign Communist parties in obtaining support for Soviet foreign-policy undertakings (by means of strikes, demonstrations, and propaganda) provided an advantage that was of particular value when the Soviet Union was weak.

World War II provided the Soviet leadership with its most significant opportunity. Although Moscow was sought after as an ally by the French and Czechs in 1934 and by the British in 1939, it signed a nonaggression pact with Nazi Germany on August 23, 1939. This pact precipitated World War II and enabled the Soviet regime to annex lands with a non-Russian population of more than 22 million. Not only were Estonia, Latvia, and Lithuania regained—along with Bessarabia and Western Belorussia—but the Soviet Union also acquired the Western Ukrainian lands (Eastern Galicia, Northern Bukovina, and Carpatho-Ukraine—the latter in 1945) that had not been part of the Russian Empire. Thus the Pact not only postponed for twenty-two months Soviet entry into World War II, but it offered territorial gains that were to survive both the Pact and the war.

After the Soviet Union became involved in the war as a result of the Nazi invasion of June 22, 1941, it had the advantage—despite a year and a half of retreats—of having the Germans pursue brutal occupation policies that offered no real alternative to Soviet rule. American Lend-Lease aid, valued at nearly $12 billion and offered unconditionally, also contributed significantly to Soviet victory, although the Soviet sacrifice of approximately 24 million lives and much physical destruction meant that the great-power status came at a great cost. The total defeat of Germany and Japan, and the weakened condition of France and Italy following the war, resulted in a United States–Soviet bipolarity in place of the multipolar international system of the prewar period and redounded to Moscow's advantage. The inability of the Western Powers to prevent the establishment of communist regimes in eight East European countries and in North Korea led to the emergence of a Soviet bloc under Moscow's leadership. Growing Soviet industrial might and scientific and technological achievements were testified to by the detonation of a Soviet atomic bomb in 1949. This was followed by Soviet development of a hydrogen bomb in 1953 and the acquisition of ballistic-missile and space-flight capabilities. As a great power, the Soviet Union in the mid-1950s also became a money lender and an exporter of conventional weapons.[1]

The Soviet Union's admission to great-power status has been the result of the regime's policies in that human and material resources were mobilized and military capabilities enhanced in support of this objective. However, it was also made possible by the policies (and errors) of others, from which the Soviet Union has profited. Thus, the failure of the Western Powers and of Nazi Germany to

---

[1]General works on Soviet foreign policy include the unique work by Louis Fischer, *The Soviets in World Affairs* (reprinting; Princeton, N.J.: Princeton University Press, 1951); Max Beloff, *The Foreign Policy of Soviet Russia* (London: Oxford University Press, 1947 and 1949); Jan Librach, *The Rise of the Soviet Empire*, rev. ed. (New York: Praeger, 1965); Alvin Z. Rubinstein, ed., *The Foreign Policy of the Soviet Union,* 3rd ed. (New York: Random House, 1972); Jan F. Triska and David D. Finley, *Soviet Foreign Policy* (New York: Macmillan, 1968); Adam B. Ulam, *Expansion and Coexistence: The History of Soviet Foreign Policy, 1917–1973,* 2nd ed. (New York: Praeger, 1974); Kurt London, ed., *The Soviet Impact on World Politics* (New York: Hawthorn Books, 1974); and the various writings of George F. Kennan. See also Joseph L. Nogee and Robert H. Donaldson, *Soviet Foreign Policy since World War II,* 2nd ed. (New York: Pergamon Press, 1984), and Alvin Z. Rubinstein, *Soviet Foreign Policy since World War II, Imperial and Global,* 2nd ed. (Boston: Little, Brown, 1985).

pursue limited objectives in World War II and the American demand that Germany surrender unconditionally were advantageous to Moscow and resulted in a Soviet military presence in Central Europe. The USSR was spared having to fight a war on two fronts simultaneously against Germany and Japan. Allied military strategy employed during the war also contributed to Soviet gains—as did concessions made to Stalin (mostly at China's expense) at the Yalta Conference on the basis of faulty estimates of the Japanese ability to prolong the war.

OBJECTIVES OF SOVIET FOREIGN POLICY

Like any great power, the Soviet Union seeks to preserve and, if possible, enhance its security and the area under its influence and to prosper. At the very least, it wishes to retain its domains and to persuade other countries—especially Japan and the People's Republic of China—to recognize its various acquisitions and accept its current frontiers. In addition to this minimal objective, Moscow seeks to extend its influence wherever possible, even if at times this is accomplished at the expense of the local Communist Party. However, it has generally been willing to do this only when the risks and costs have been acceptable and in the absence of a nuclear confrontation. The goal of increased influence has often been referred to as "world communism" (the establishment of new communist regimes), although since 1955 Moscow has been more interested in influencing the foreign policies of "capitalist" states and of "bourgeois national anticolonialist" regimes in Africa and Asia than in establishing a host of new communist governments. The Soviet leaders value great-power status and are willing to devote inordinate amounts of time to receiving foreign heads of state and government and ministers of external affairs, as well as foreign communist leaders and delegations.

A third Soviet objective is to divide its "capitalist" opponents by driving wedges between them and by disrupting alliance systems established to deter the possible threat of communist aggression. Moscow has always sought to isolate whatever state it regards as its principal enemy. Great Britain was cast in this role in the 1920s, Nazi Germany in the 1930s, and the United States after World War II. Related to this goal is the continuing Soviet effort to isolate the Federal Republic of Germany from the NATO alliance and prevent its obtaining nuclear weapons. If noncommunist regimes can be kept weak and divided, Soviet power is enhanced. By encouraging nonalignment in Africa, Asia, and Latin America, Moscow seeks to isolate the United States.

A fourth objective of the Soviet Union is to retain some degree of primacy and leadership in the communist world, especially among the East European states and over as many nonruling Communist parties as possible. For example, Hungary was not permitted to leave the Warsaw Pact and adopt neutral status under the UN in November 1956. Moscow also seeks to defeat or reduce the Chinese challenge to its leadership of the international communist movement and to render ineffective the Yugoslav attitude that encourages polycentrism (the existence of several communist centers). A fifth Soviet objective has been to minimize risks and generally to avoid serious involvement on more than one of its several fronts at any given time. Thus in April 1941, it sought a neutrality pact with Japan as the danger of involvement in the European war increased. Moscow has pursued a policy of expansionism by military means, as in 1939–1945, only when it has involved little risk and been directed against weak victims. It has as an alternative taken advantage of proxy military forces, as when Stalin used the International Brigades in the Spanish Civil War and when Brezhnev used Cuban troops in Angola and Ethiopia.

MOTIVE FACTORS AND TACTICS

Soviet foreign policy may be said to have several motive factors, although it is unwise to isolate any of these determinants; it is, instead, preferable to view them as an amalgam of interests, drives, and responses. One determinant is identified as the "national interest" syndrome, although it is somewhat inaccurate to refer to the national interests of a multinational state like the USSR. However, what is usually meant is that the national interests of the Russians, as those of the dominant ethnic group within the USSR, have presumably been furthered by the Soviet regime. This explanation of Soviet conduct in international relations assumes that communist doctrinal writings do not determine Soviet policy in all its aspects and that the Soviet Union employs conventional diplomacy rather than revolutionary warfare. Moscow is said, in this view, to base its policies more on what is feasible and practicable and only secondarily on what might be ideologically desirable.[2]

Geopolitical and strategic factors might be said to explain certain parallels between tsarist Russian and Soviet policies and the fact that Russia was a problem for its neighbors long before the Soviet rulers appeared on the scene. Thus, the tsarist regime acquired a sphere of influence in Northern Iran in 1907, and the Soviet regime sought such a sphere in 1945–1946. The tsars and Catherine II were

---

[2]The issue of "national interest" versus doctrinal considerations is discussed by R. N. Carew Hunt, Samuel L. Sharp, and Richard Lowenthal, *Problems of Communism,* VII, No. 2 (March–April 1958), p. 10–30. The discussion is reprinted in DeVere E. Pentony, ed., *Soviet Behavior in World Affairs* (San Francisco: Intext, 1962), and in Alexander Dallin, ed., *Soviet Conduct in World Affairs* (New York: Columbia University Press, 1960). Of course, the simple assertion that a country's foreign policy has but one purpose, namely to promote the "national interest," raises the question of how it is to be defined both in the abstract and in practice and whether this criterion can be used to justify the violation of treaty obligations and whether or not decisions do in fact serve that interest. Thus, was it really in the "national interest" of the USSR to wage war against Finland in 1939–1940 in violation of treaty obligations? Was it in Moscow's interest to sever relations with Communist Yugoslavia in 1948 or to promote the dispute with China? Was it in the Soviet interest to intervene militarily in Afghanistan in 1979 in an attempt to deal brutally with a fierce anticommunist insurgency?

A related question may be raised regarding the extent to which the Nazi regime in Germany promoted German national interests. Thus, it would be necessary to distinguish between those of Hitler's actions and policies that might be said to have furthered German interests and those that had a clearly detrimental effect; the problem for the student of *Realpolitik* would be to determine the year in which Hitler "went wrong" and committed gross errors (rather than mere blunders) that proved to be irreparable. In other words, how many errors of judgment or breaches of faith can be perpetrated in the name of the national interest without bringing about a debacle or placing the entire system in question?

obsessed with obtaining the Turkish Straits, and the Soviet regime also sought military bases in the Dardanelles between 1945 and 1953. Both regimes annexed Estonia, Latvia, Lithuania, and Bessarabia; Alexander II attempted to establish Bulgaria as a Russian satellite in 1877, and the Soviets succeeded in doing so after World War II. The tsarist regime supported liberation wars of the Balkan peoples against Turkish rule, while the Soviet regime has sought to aid such wars on a broader scale. Both regimes sought to annex Western Ukraine. Tsarist interests in Korea, Manchuria, Sakhalin, and the Kurile Islands preceded Soviet demands involving those areas.[3]

A second determinant, or series of determinants, is derived from the Soviet view of international politics, which is based largely on ideological tenets. In general, this view, insofar as it is expressed in terms of Marxism-Leninism, assumes a certain level of tension and conflict as a "normal" condition in the relations between states. This is a logical corollary of the view that class conflict is the prime mover of history and that the class struggle should be extended into the realm of interstate relations. However, tension should be kept within limits and not be permitted to involve Soviet foreign policy in unplanned or high-risk military conflicts or in "adventurist" undertakings or confrontations; it should also lead to deterrence of military actions on the part of "capitalist" countries, especially the United States. The tense and hostile condition of international relations has been viewed in Moscow as a natural consequence of the dialectical materialist outlook and the "struggle of opposites"; the conflict between countries governed by capitalist and socialist ruling classes is seen as an unfolding of the dialectic and as the hallmark of "progress" and of historical development.

The Soviet leaders perceive themselves as exponents and executors of a "peace-loving foreign policy," *even though they generally view international politics as a species of warfare conducted by other than purely military means.* To the extent that they are guided by ideological considerations, they view their foreign policies as based on the "science" of Marxism-Leninism and as taking into account the "laws of social development." The Soviet leadership views the international situation as developing in terms of historical forces interpreted by them as operating in their favor in the long run, despite certain setbacks, necessary retreats, and postponements. The 1961 CPSU Program states categorically: "The United States, the strongest capitalist power, is past its zenith and has entered the stage of decline."[4] The 1986 Program offers a somewhat different appraisal: "U.S. imperialism is the citadel of international reaction. The threat of war emanates from it, above all. In laying claim to world domination, it arbitrarily declares entire continents [to be] zones of its 'vital interests.' " The prediction was stated

---

[3]On continuities in tsarist and Soviet foreign policy, see Barbara Jelavich, *St. Petersburg & Moscow: Tsarist & Soviet Foreign Policy, 1814–1974* (Bloomington Ind.: Indiana University Press, 1974). For a comparison of various aspects of tsarist and Soviet foreign policy, see Ivo J. Lederer, ed., *Russian Foreign Policy: Essays in Historical Perspective* (New Haven: Yale University Press, 1962).

[4]*Programme of the Communist Party of the Soviet Union* (Moscow: Foreign Languages Publishing House, 1961), p. 31.

in general terms: "The dialectic of development is such that the very means that capitalism employs in order to strengthen its position inevitably lead to the exacerbation of all its profound contradictions. Imperialism is parasitic, decaying and dying capitalism, the eve of the socialist revolution."[5]

The noncommunist world is said to be suffering from the malaise discussed by Lenin in his *Imperialism, the Highest Stage of Capitalism.* Capitalism is said to be in its "ripest" and last stage when it is allegedly driven to obtain colonies. This "need" to exploit dependent peoples that lack investment capital supposedly leads to "inevitable" conflict between capitalist states. Communist states are by their own self-serving definition not imperialistic or given to promoting conflict, because of their claim to have abolished capitalism.[6] Wars and militarism are said to be bred by capitalism, and the danger of war is said to exist as long as capitalism is not removed from the face of the earth. At the same time, capitalism and its species of imperialism are said to be in decline due to continuing crises. Two world wars, said to have resulted from two general crises of world capitalism, have led to the establishment of communist regimes ruling at least one-third of the human race and constituting a "whole system of socialist states."

The increased strength of communist states is said to deter capitalist states from precipitating World War III. Indeed, a general nuclear war has been declared not to be inevitable by Soviet spokesmen—at least since 1956—although

---

[5] *Partiinaia zhizn',* No. 6–7 (March–April), 1986, p. 104.

[6] This self-deluding viewpoint (which is also used to mislead others) ignores the residual imperialism that has characterized both the Soviet Union and China as legatees of the Russian and Han empires. It also fails to explain the disagreements and overt conflicts that have developed between communist regimes, as, for example, between China and the Soviet Union, the Soviet Union and Albania, the Soviet Union and Yugoslavia, the Soviet Union and Romania (over Bessarabia and Romania's desire to industrialize fully), the Soviet Union and Czechoslovakia, China and Vietnam, and Albania and Yugoslavia. Lenin's definition of imperialism as a characteristic of capitalism failed to explain the many forms of imperialism that preceded capitalism (those of the Assyrians, the Greeks and Romans, Spain, Portugal, and Sweden). With respect to the weaknesses in this definition, it is important to note that Lenin published *Imperialism, The Highest Stage of Capitalism* in Switzerland in 1916 and based it largely on data from the last quarter of the nineteenth and the first decade of the twentieth centuries. He relied heavily on data from Germany, where banking and industry had coalesced to an exceptional degree. For discussions of various theories of imperialism, see Archibald P. Thornton, *Doctrines of Imperialism* (New York: Wiley, 1965), E. M. Winslow, *The Pattern of Imperialism* (New York: Columbia University Press, 1948), Benjamin J. Cohen, *The Question of Imperialism* (New York: Basic Books, 1973), and Anthony Brewer, *Marxist Theories of Imperialism* (Boston: Routledge and Kegan Paul, 1980).

According to Lenin, monopoly finance capitalism tended to stagnate and retard technological progress. Yet such advances as the x-ray, the internal combustion and diesel engines, radio, electronics and the transistor, radar, antibiotics, nuclear energy, jet propulsion, xerography, cybernetics, and computers were developed under bourgeois "capitalism."

In defining imperialism in terms of the need to export capital, Lenin ignored the fact that Russia acquired a vast empire over a period of four centuries and did not export capital in the process; indeed, while the Empire was being completed, the Russians were importing capital from France, Belgium, and Great Britain. The Leninist theory of imperialism also fails to take into account the fact that in the 1930s such countries as Japan and Italy undertook to establish empires despite the fact that they were poor in capital and had no need to export it. It ignores the fact that colonies have usually been economic liabilities and have attracted fewer investments than have noncolonies. In reducing imperialism to a single cause, Lenin failed to comprehend a complex phenomenon that has spanned many centuries.

wars of liberation have been viewed as both desirable and inevitable.[7] Thus, the wars in Korea, Vietnam, and Algeria; the advent of the Castro regime in Cuba; and guerrilla operations in various countries have elicited Soviet support. They are seen as a vital counter in the changing balance of international forces that is said to be occurring to the Soviet Union's advantage. Although the 1977 Soviet Constitution (Article 28) states that "in the U.S.S.R. war propaganda is forbidden," advocacy of so-called liberation wars has been encouraged.

However, the Soviet views on the demise of capitalism have not prompted the leadership to adopt a fixed timetable for foreign-policy operations and revolutionary strategy. Indeed, Soviet tactics have varied markedly, and dual policies have frequently been pursued as if to exemplify the dialectic in action. Thus, Moscow could negotiate simultaneously with Nazi Germany and with Great Britain during 1939 in the period preceding the Nazi-Soviet Pact. Similarly, Stalin endeavored to negotiate with the Germans in 1943 in an apparent attempt to withdraw from the war and only went to Teheran to confer with Churchill and Roosevelt after these efforts failed to produce the appropriate response from Hitler.[8] While supposedly developing common postwar policies for Germany with the United States and Britain in 1943–1944, the Soviet Union organized and utilized a Free Germany National Committee, part of which served as the nucleus for the Communist East German regime established subsequently by Soviet occupation authorities. The Kremlin has simultaneously wooed Wall Street and American businessmen with promises of trade while denouncing the defense policies of an American government that is said to be the "instrument" of a "military-industrial complex" and Wall Street.

Other examples of Soviet tactical flexibility can be cited. Moscow has had cordial relations with Third World countries that have suppressed local Commu-

---

[7]Khrushchev explicated this viewpoint in an official address delivered on January 6, 1961 (see Pentony, *op. cit.* [above, n. 2], pp. 242–248): "There will be wars of liberation as long as imperialism exists, as long as colonialism exists. These are revolutionary wars. Such wars are not only possible but inevitable . . ." (p. 245). The 1961 CPSU Program states: "The CPSU and the Soviet people as a whole will continue to oppose all wars of conquest, including wars between capitalist countries, and local wars aimed at strangling people's emancipation movements, and consider it their duty to support the sacred struggle of the oppressed peoples and their just anti-imperialist wars of liberation." *Programme of the Communist Party of the Soviet Union* (Moscow: Foreign Languages Publishing House, 1961), p. 58. The 1986 Program is less explicit. It characterizes "the present era" as "an era of socialist and national-liberation revolutions" and asserts that the "replacement of capitalism by socialism" can be accomplished in "peaceful or nonpeaceful" ways. *Partiinaia zhizn'*, No. 6–7 (March–April), 1986, pp. 105, 107. These statements reaffirm the position expressed by Stalin in a letter of January 17, 1930, to Maxim Gorky. In it, Stalin stated that the Soviet Union opposed imperialist wars but was "*for* a liberating, anti-imperialist revolutionary war." I. V. Stalin, *Sochineniia* (Moscow, 1949), XII, 176 (italics in original). See also P. H. Vigor, *The Soviet View of War, Peace, and Neutrality* (London & Boston: Routledge and Kegan Paul, 1975), for an analysis based on textual and policy statements.

[8]Stalin is said to have used the Soviet embassy in Stockholm and a Swedish businessman as go-between in exploring possible terms for a separate peace. The German contact was Peter Kleist of the Foreign Ministry, who has provided an account of his efforts in *Zwischen Hitler and Stalin, 1939–1945* (Bonn: Atheneum, 1950). The effort failed because of Hitler's objections and Stalin's demand for better terms for a separate peace as the Soviet military situation improved during 1943. The circumstantial evidence pointing to Stalin's interest in a separate peace and the measures taken to that end are carefully documented in Vojtech Mastny, "Stalin and the Prospects for a Separate Peace in World War II," *American Historical Review,* 77, No. 5 (December 1972), pp. 1365–1388.

nist parties (as in Egypt, Iraq, and Indonesia). While supporting the regime in Iraq that followed the overthrow of the monarchy in 1958, the Soviet Union also sought to utilize the Kurdish national movement against the Baghdad government. The classic example of dual policy was that of the 1920s, when the Kremlin established diplomatic relations with various countries while working for the overthrow of their governments (as in Germany and Estonia) and playing host to the Communist International.[9] In July 1971 Soviet diplomats were involved with local communists in an abortive coup to overthrow President Jaafar Nimeri's government in the Sudan. In 1977 the Soviet Union had to abandon a dual policy and sacrifice its alliance with Somalia in order to arm Ethiopia and acquire a more important ally in the Horn of Africa.

Moscow's foreign policy tactics have also changed abruptly at times, as when the Soviet Union decided to join general disarmament talks in 1927 and became a member of the League of Nations in 1934 after having condemned both efforts for years. In 1955 a decision was taken to attempt a reconciliation with Communist Yugoslavia and Tito's regime after having denounced his leadership and his loyalty to communist ideology since 1948. The attitude toward socialist parties has varied; they have often been branded "social fascists," "social traitors," and "opportunists" and at other times have been sought as allies in a "popular front" tactic.

The variety and flexibility of such tactical undertakings lend a measure of credence to the contention that Soviet conduct is rational and is based on a "scientific" ideology. However, there is also an irrational component (or residue) in Soviet conduct, which is testified to by the fact that Soviet leaders have repeatedly expressed their commitment to grandiose goals; it is also evident in the Sino-Soviet dispute. Their view of the historical process is both utopian and at times megalomaniacal—at least in its verbal expression, the Party has claimed a monopoly on truth and wisdom. The distinctiveness of the lexicon of Soviet leaders makes it difficult to communicate with them. Their extensive preoccupation with enemies and their view of international relations as an extension of the class struggle and of ideological conflict can be viewed as reflecting a tendency to suffer from mass paranoia. There is also a fear of being "contaminated" by the part of the "bourgeois" world that is "evil" and "unclean."[10]

---

[9]Lenin provided relevant advice on tactical measures and splitting efforts in his *"Left Wing" Communism, An Infantile Disorder* (1920): "A more powerful enemy can be conquered only by exerting the utmost effort and by *necessarily,* most carefully, solicitously, cautiously, and skillfully taking advantage of every 'rift,' even the smallest, among the enemies, of every antagonism of interest among the bourgeoisie of various countries, between various groups or types of bourgeoisie within different countries, by taking advantage of every, even the smallest, opportunity of gaining a mass ally, even though this ally be only temporary, vacillating, unstable, unreliable and conditional. Those who have not understood this have not understood a particle of Marxism, or of scientific contemporary socialism *in general.*" V. I. Lenin, *Polnoe sobranie sochinenii,* 5th ed. (Moscow, 1963), XLI, p. 55 (italics in original).

[10]Various (Bolshevik) syndromes of this type are discussed in Nathan Leites, *A Study of Bolshevism* (Glencoe, Ill.: Free Press, 1953). See also Leites' *Kremlin Moods* (Santa Monica, Calif.: RAND Corporation Memorandum RM-3535-ISA, 1964). For a provocative discussion of the role of rationality and irrationality in Soviet conduct, see Gerhart Niemeyer, *Deceitful Peace* (New Rochelle, N.Y.: Arlington House, 1971).

Soviet diplomacy and political warfare have sought to identify and utilize the "contradictions" that are said to characterize the "capitalist" world. Stalin, at the Fifteenth Party Congress, identified five groups of contradictions: (1) the contradictions between the proletariat and the bourgeoisie within capitalist countries; (2) the contradictions between imperialism and the liberation movements in colonies and dependent countries; (3) the contradictions between the victorious capitalist countries and the vanquished capitalist countries; (4) the contradictions between the victorious capitalist countries; and (5) the contradictions between the Soviet Union and the capitalist countries as a whole.[11] Sixty years later, at the Twenty-seventh Party Congress, M. S. Gorbachev reaffirmed and refined these groups of contradictions. He identified as the first and most important group that one which is "connected with *relations between the states of the two systems, of the two formations*"—capitalism and socialism. He asserted that "the contradictions *between labor and capital* are becoming exacerbated," and he also identified "new outbreaks of interimperialist contradictions," as in the case of "a new knot of contradictions *between transnational corporations and the national-state form of the political organization of society.*" He further identified "three principal centers of contemporary imperialism—the U.S.A., Western Europe and Japan [which] are full of obvious and concealed contradictions." Although "changes in the correlation of forces will continue in the system of imperialism," Gorbachev admitted that "one hardly expects that in the real conditions of today's world the established complex of economic, military-political and other common interests of the three 'centers of power' can be broken up." He conceded that "in the next few decades . . . new capitalist 'centers of power' may appear." He also identified a *"new, complicated and active complex of contradictions [that] has formed between imperialism and the developing countries and peoples."*[12]

Despite the peculiarities of the Soviet mentality and its pronouncements, it is necessary to recognize the existence of an additional determinant of Soviet foreign policy. This is the ability of other powers to exercise some degree of influence on Soviet policy in particular situations. While it is recognized that the Soviet leadership will attempt to exercise initiative at advantageous times and places of its own choosing, it has on occasion been confronted with conditions, created by other powers, which have required revision of Soviet policy or even abandonment of a Soviet position that had been held tenaciously.

Among examples of such situations are the Soviet decision to recognize the Federal Republic of Germany in 1955 (after having ignored its existence for six years), the abandonment of the policy of ignoring the Japanese Peace Treaty of 1951, and the launching in 1956 of an attempt to influence Tokyo's foreign policy. Consistent and firm policies on the part of the states concerned led to modification in Soviet policy. Stalin's decision not to press the civil war in Greece in 1946–1947 was another such instance, as was the Soviet withdrawal from Northern Iran in 1946 under pressure. Khrushchev retreated on Berlin after delivering to the Western powers in November 1958 a six-month ultimatum demanding their

---

[11]I. V. Stalin, *op. cit.* (above, n. 7), VII, pp. 262–263.
[12]*Pravda,* February 26, 1986, pp. 2–3 (italics in original).

withdrawal from West Berlin. Khrushchev also abandoned his efforts to place intermediate-range ballistic missiles in Cuba in October 1962—again as a result of American firmness.

Retreats in the face of unanticipated obstacles or underestimated risks appear to be acceptable to the Soviet rulers whenever they do not involve vital interests. Yet the definition of "vital interests" has varied with the degree to which Soviet leaders have been able to employ credible threats and to persuade other powers that there is no room for compromise at Soviet expense or at the expense of countries, regimes, or movements that the Soviet Union regards as being within its sphere of influence. Thus, communist regimes were prevented from collapsing in North Korea in 1950 and in Hungary in 1956. Hungary's efforts to obtain neutral status, and to withdraw from the Warsaw Pact and revert to a coalition government (including socialists), were suppressed by Soviet troops in November 1956; and Imre Nagy, who had voiced these demands, was executed along with other leaders. Yet at other times communist regimes have been sacrificed: that of Bela Kun in Hungary in 1919; that in Iranian Azerbaidjan in 1946 while the area was under Soviet occupation; the Finnish communist shadow regime established in December 1939 behind Soviet military lines; and the Arbenz regime in Guatemala in 1954. Nor could the Soviet Union rescue either the Allende government in Chile, when it was overthrown by the military in September 1973, or the Marxist regime in Grenada in October 1983. In each instance various factors entered into the decision; these included an estimate of relative capabilities made by the Soviet leadership, the risks involved in intervening and the likelihood of a confrontation, the consequences likely to ensue in the event of nonintervention, and the immediacy of domestic concerns or higher priority foreign policy goals as opposed to further foreign involvement.

THE SOVIET VIEW OF INTERNATIONAL LAW

The use of international law has figured prominently in Soviet foreign-policy pronouncements. Other states have been accused of violating international law, while it is claimed that the Soviet Union always acts in accordance with such law. Soviet writers on the subject attempt to further Soviet interests and do not ignore political considerations. Initially, the Soviet regime rejected international law as a "bourgeois" instrument (in accordance with the Marxist notion of law as a tool of the ruling class) but soon recognized that it could be useful in furthering Soviet interests. As a result there is an abundant Soviet literature on international law, with textbooks, monographs, theoretical works, and collected documents. The subject is widely taught on the graduate level in the Soviet Union and is essential in the training of Soviet diplomats and foreign-trade officials.

The Soviet Union views international law as subordinate to domestic law and regards states as the sole subjects of international law (excluding international organizations from this category). States are seen as sovereign entities, and the doctrine of sovereignty is utilized as a weapon against alleged "imperialist encroachments." However, with the granting of independent statehood to numerous colonies following World War II, Soviet ideologists devised the concept of neocolonialism to apply to selected new states regarded as economically (and politically) dependent upon capitalist states. Soviet spokesmen have advocated the right of national self-determination if its exercise has not been at Moscow's expense; in the latter case there is no advocacy. The Soviet Union has been an outspoken advocate of the primacy of states' domestic jurisdiction (especially its own) and has frequently objected to alleged encroachments by international bodies.

In the field of maritime law Soviet authorities recognize the open seas, although the regime has extended its territorial waters at their expense. It treats as interior maritime waters such bodies of water as the White Sea, the Gulf of Riga, the Sea of Azov, and certain Arctic waters (the Kara, Laptev, East Siberian, and Chukchi Seas). Non-Soviet vessels have generally been excluded from these waters except in accordance with conditions set down by Soviet authorities. The Barents Sea is placed in the category of open seas. The Soviet Union has led other states in extending territorial waters to the twelve-mile limit in stages commencing with a decree of May 24, 1921, and has exercised sovereignty in them as well as in the air space above them. The base line in determining the twelve-mile limit is the line of low tide or a line across the mouths of bays and inlets. In practice the Soviet Union has extended its waters well beyond the twelve-mile limit. For example, on July 21, 1957, the Soviet Foreign Ministry announced that henceforth the Bay of Peter the Great in the Sea of Japan would be considered as Soviet "interior waters."[13] Despite the protests of the United States, Great Britain, and Japan, Moscow in effect extended its territorial waters far out to a line passing through the Sea of Japan for a distance of more than 100 miles. On December 10, 1976, a 200-mile fishing zone was proclaimed by a decree of the Presidium of the U.S.S.R. Supreme Soviet in response to similar measures adopted by other countries. As a result of the growth of Soviet maritime interests there is greater interest in the open seas and concern regarding extension of territorial waters in important straits.

Another distinctive feature of Soviet policy is that regarding the legal status of the so-called closed seas. The Baltic and Black seas, as well as the Sea of Okhotsk and the Sea of Japan, are placed in this category; it is contended that the regime for closed seas and the straits leading to them is to be determined by a treaty concluded between the littoral states. Although such seas are open to commercial vessels, it is the Soviet view that they are not international maritime routes and must be treated separately from the open seas.[14] The Soviet position has not gained general acceptance.

The Soviet Union has adopted very different positions regarding Arctic and Antarctic waters. By a decree of April 15, 1926, it claimed all islands in the Arctic sector lying north of the Soviet landmass (excluding Spitzbergen-Svalbard and Bear Island). Although the Arctic Sea is not claimed, the Kara, Laptev, East

---

[13]G. L. Shmigel'skii and V. A. Iasinovskii, *Osnovy sovetskogo morskogo prava* (Moscow: izd. "Morskoi Transport," 1959), p. 29.

[14]The Sea of Okhotsk has been classified with interior maritime waters by some Soviet lawyers. See the discussion in William E. Butler, *The Soviet Union and the Law of the Sea* (Baltimore: The Johns Hopkins Press, 1971), Chapter 4.

Siberian, and Chukchi seas are claimed as "historic bays" and are said to be under exclusive Soviet jurisdiction.[15] In the case of the Antarctic and its waters, a sector theory would not be to the Soviet Union's advantage; instead, the Soviet government has contended that it has an interest in the area based on whaling and on the explorations conducted by F. F. Bellingshausen and M. P. Lazarev in 1820–1821. Thus, Moscow contests Norway's claim to Peter I and Alexander I Islands. The Soviet position on the Antarctic received general recognition in the Antarctic Treaty of December 1, 1959. Although the treaty places territorial claims in abeyance, it provides for use of the Antarctic for peaceful and exclusively scientific purposes.

In the field of law dealing with airspace, the Soviet Union has been a staunch defender of its own sovereignty and has denied the right of innocent passage to foreign aircraft in the airspace above its territorial waters without special permission. Foreign aircraft—military and civilian—have been shot down at various times. The most flagrant instance was the shooting down of Korean Air Line's flight 007 on September 1, 1983, and resultant killing of 269 persons. In recent years agreements have been concluded granting foreign commercial airlines flight routes into and across the Soviet Union on a reciprocal basis.

The Soviet desire to retain freedom of action and be judge in its own cause is evident in the position adopted on international arbitration and on participation in the International Court of Justice. Although tsarist Russia favored the principle of international arbitration, the Soviet government has not been willing to submit to an international arbitral body political disputes in which it is a party; the USSR is not a member of the Permanent Court of Arbitration at The Hague. As a consequence of increased foreign commercial contacts, the Soviet Union has been willing to agree to third-country arbitration of business disputes. Although the Soviet Union did join the League of Nations, it refused to recognize the Permanent Court of International Justice, which existed from 1920 to 1946, regarding it as an "instrument of the aggressive policies of the great imperialist powers."[16]

As a result of joining the United Nations, the Soviet Union became a signatory of the Statute of the International Court of Justice (ICJ). However, it has not seen fit to accept the jurisdiction of the ICJ in the adjudication of any disputes to which it has been a party. It is the Soviet contention that only disputes of a purely *legal* character should be submitted to the ICJ and that *political* questions should be taken up in the United Nations Security Council and General Assembly. A Soviet judge has always been elected to the ICJ, in accordance with the tenet that it should represent the principal legal systems and civilizations.

---

[15]The U.S. Coast Guard icebreaker *Northwind* penetrated the eastern and central Soviet Arctic waters in 1963 (from Bering Strait to Cape Cheliuskin and Vil'kitskii Strait) and traversed the Kara Sea in 1965. Although Soviet naval vessels and military aircraft kept the *Northwind* under constant surveillance, it was not hindered in its scientific task of oceanographic surveying. However, two U.S. icebreakers were prevented from passing through the Vil'kitskii Strait in August 1967, when the Soviet Foreign Ministry declared that the Strait is within Soviet territorial waters and such passage would be a violation of Soviet frontiers. The U.S. Department of State protested the Soviet assertion and claimed the right of innocent passage for foreign vessels.

[16]N. N. Polianskii, *Mezhdunarodnyi sud* (Moscow: izd. Akad. Nauk SSSR, 1951), p. 24.

However, during the Korean War (1950–1953), the Soviet judge (Sergei B. Krylov and later Sergei A. Golunskii) did not participate in the work of the Court. Soviet judges have frequently dissented from the Court's findings. In general, the Soviet leadership views the judges of the ICJ as "representatives" of sovereign states and appears to doubt that members of an international tribunal can be truly impartial in adjudicating disputes involving state interests.

THE SOVIET VIEW OF INTERNATIONAL ORGANIZATIONS

Soviet policy toward international bodies had its origins in hostility and contempt expressed toward the League of Nations because it was associated with the allegedly unjust Treaty of Versailles and was regarded as a tool of the victorious "imperialist" states in World War I. The Soviet decision to join the League in September 1934 led to disappointment when Soviet membership did not prevent the collapse of the European security system. Nor was Moscow endeared to the defunct League when it became the sole member-state to be expelled—as an aggressor due to the Soviet attack on Finland in November 1939.

The Soviet Union, the Ukrainian S.S.R., and the Belorussian S.S.R. became charter members of the United Nations in 1945. Although superficially the Soviet Union was regarded as having obtained "three votes" in the United Nations (as a result of a decision taken at the Yalta Conference), in reality three separate memberships were obtained, despite the fact that Ukraine and Belorussia joined the world organization while being union republics within the U.S.S.R.[17] Ukrainian and Belorussian memberships were also obtained in the international specialized agencies.

Soviet spokesmen in international organizations have championed state sovereignty and the equality of member states while simultaneously defending the veto power exercised by any one of the five permanent members of the Security Council in deciding "substantive" issues as opposed to procedural matters. The doctrine of the sovereignty and the equality of states has been used to denounce alleged U.N. efforts to interfere in the domestic affairs of communist states— although Soviet spokesmen have not hesitated to advocate UN intervention in Southwest Africa (Namibia) and Puerto Rico in the name of "anticolonialism." The UN was viewed initially as a security organization designed to maintain the military victory won in 1945; indeed, the successor to the League was named for the victorious World War II military alliance. The logical consequence was the principle of the unanimity of the "Big Five"—the permanent members of the Security Council—a synonym for the "veto." Thus, no decision could be binding and enforceable unless it had the support of the great powers. It was assumed erroneously that the foreign ministers of the great powers would first resolve an issue in closed negotiations and then present their decisions to the UN.

---

[17]The motives, causes, and consequences of multiple Soviet membership in international bodies are discussed in Vernon V. Aspaturian, *The Union Republics in Soviet Diplomacy* (Geneva: No. 36 in the Publications of the Graduate Institute of International Studies, Librairie E. Droz, 1960); see especially Chapters 4 and 8 and the appendices.

In defending the veto, the Soviet Union has advocated a strict and "legalistic" interpretation of the UN Charter. It has insisted upon the soundness and legitimacy of the veto provision. Soviet judges in the ICJ and Soviet spokesmen in the UN have therefore repeatedly objected to the Court's interpreting the Charter and statutes of the specialized agencies in advisory opinions; they have insisted that Charter interpretation involves political and not legal questions. The generally rigid Soviet view of the Charter prompted Soviet spokesmen to object to efforts to resort to the General Assembly when action was prevented in the Security Council by a Soviet veto. However, as the number of African and Asian member-states increased, the communist states were less isolated; and Moscow in the mid-1950s lost its reluctance to utilize the Assembly.

The veto has not been a monopoly of the Soviet Union and is actually a symptom of tension rather than its cause. Many Soviet vetoes were employed in opposing membership applications, as on December 13, 1955, when the Soviet Union used it fifteen times in denying membership. By June 1962, the Soviet Union had employed the veto one hundred times. If the other four permanent members of the Council have not employed the veto with the same frequency, it is because they were able to rely on other devices to protect their interests. It is also significant that Moscow could veto any effort to expel it from the UN since such a proposal must be based on a Security Council recommendation and would be a substantive issue. Nor can the Charter be amended formally without the consent of the five permanent members.

The Soviet Union does not regard the UN as a "world government" in embryo and has frequently opposed modest efforts to enhance the UN Secretary-Generalship. It organized a campaign against Secretary-General Trygve Lie in 1950, for instance, when he supported the UN effort to repel North Korean aggression against the Republic of Korea. In 1960–1961 a Soviet effort to discredit Secretary-General Dag Hammarskjöld resulted from his active role in the UN effort to restore order in the Congo. A Soviet attempt to reduce the influence of Western states in the Secretariat led to an unsuccessful proposal, advanced by Khrushchev in September 1960, to replace the Secretary-General with a three-man body representing Western, communist, and third-force states.[18]

Soviet presence in the UN Secretariat professional staff was limited to about one-tenth of its quota at the outset, even though Moscow, Ukraine, and Belorussia have been contributing approximately 13 percent of the budget. The limited number of Soviet personnel resulted from Soviet policy and was due initially to a lack of qualified personnel and to Stalin's desire to limit official contacts with the non-Soviet world. Yet Soviet officials have usually held the key post of UN Under-Secretary of Political and Security Council Affairs. In 1959 Moscow demanded more professional Secretariat positions for Soviet citizens. However, a major difficulty has been the turnover in Soviet personnel as the result of a high rate of recall, usually after several years' service, as well as the fact that Moscow

---

[18]For a treatment of the campaign against Hammarskjöld, see Alexander Dallin, *The Soviet Union at the United Nations* (New York: Praeger, 1962), Chapters 9, 10, and 11. See also John G. Stoessinger, *The United Nations and the Superpowers,* 3rd ed. (New York: Random House, 1973).

does not permit the Secretariat to recruit Soviet citizens directly but offers its own candidates. The Soviet Union has generally offered the UN the services of its own diplomats and other personnel, who are subsequently reassigned to its own service. In addition, Soviet officials in the UN Secretariat have repeatedly been accused by the United States of engaging in espionage activities and have been expelled from the country.[19]

Increased Soviet interest in the Secretariat was preceded by a decision to join or rejoin a number of the specialized agencies. Originally the Soviet Union, Ukraine, and Belorussia had joined such bodies as the Universal Postal Union, the International Telecommunications Union, the World Health Organization, and the World Meteorological Union. In 1949 they withdrew from the World Health Organization because of dissatisfaction over the amount of financial aid received from it but subsequently rejoined it. The Soviet Union originally adopted a hostile attitude toward the International Labor Organization (ILO), the United Nations Educational Scientific and Cultural Organization (UNESCO), and the International Refugee Organization (which functioned from 1947 to 1951, resettling refugees who the Soviet Union demanded be forcibly repatriated). It also refused to join the International Monetary Fund, the World Bank, and the Food and Agricultural Organization. However, in 1954 the three Soviet states joined UNESCO and ILO (the Soviet Union had joined ILO in 1935 but was expelled in 1940). The decision to end the boycott was probably motivated by a desire to obtain additional channels of contact with African, Asian, and Latin American countries and gain their support for Soviet policy positions. In UNESCO an effort was made to obtain recognition for communist viewpoints in cultural matters. The ILO had participated in an ad hoc committee that investigated forced labor (including Soviet concentration camps) during 1951–1953; thus Moscow may have concluded that its absence from the ILO was disadvantageous. The USSR also joined the Inter-Governmental Maritime Consultative Organization in 1958 and the International Civil Aviation Organization in 1970. Soviet representatives have sought to politicize some of the specialized agencies by introducing extraneous issues.

The Soviet leadership is power conscious and has had no illusions regarding the UN; it has not relied upon the UN as more than an auxiliary instrument of Soviet policy. It does not desire a strong UN, but neither does it wish to see the organization destroyed. Nor does the Soviet Union wish the UN to act in a manner contrary to Soviet interests; the organization's effectiveness is to be limited to areas in which Soviet interests are advanced. It does not wish to be bound by UN decisions of which it does not approve or have the organization resolve disputes between communist states. The Soviet Union

---

[19]The extensive use of the U.N. Secretariat for Soviet espionage purposes has been amply confirmed by the former Soviet diplomat Arkady Shevchenko, who had the rank of ambassador and who served as U.N. Under-Secretary-General from 1973 to 1978. See Arkady N. Shevchenko, *Breaking with Moscow* (New York: Ballantine Books, 1985), Chapter 21. Soviet personnel in the U.N. Secretariat are also a source of hard currency for the Soviet government, as they are required to surrender a considerable portion of their salaries—the "kickback" being a condition of their appointment. *Ibid.*, pp. 173–174.

has advocated a narrow construction of the Secretary-General's powers on the assumption that they might be used to the Soviet Union's disadvantage. It refused to help finance UN peacekeeping forces in the Near East and the Congo despite an advisory opinion of the ICJ in July 1962 that held the costs of such operations to be part of the expenses of the organization and an obligation of membership. In the Soviet view peacekeeping costs incurred by action of the Assembly and in the absence of a Security Council decision are "illegal" and contrary to the Charter. When a general financial crisis ensued (affecting the entire UN budget and causing the UN to issue bonds), an American effort in 1965 to deprive the three Soviet UN members of their right to vote in the Assembly failed to gain the support of a majority. Yet the Soviet intervention in Afghanistan was repeatedly condemned in the General Assembly by Third World countries throughout the 1980s.

Soviet participation in the UN is advantageous in view of its permanent membership in the Security Council. The organization provides a forum in which Soviet doctrines, policies, and professions of support for peace can be expounded. The Soviet anticolonial campaign was indicative of the attraction of such proposals for newer member-states as well as of Soviet willingness and ability to utilize the Assembly to discredit the policies of other powers, especially the United States. The UN organization and the numerous delegations in attendance serve as sources of information that may be of use to the Soviet Foreign Ministry. The UN has also provided an area of contact in which meaningful negotiations can occur, as when the Berlin Blockade was lifted in 1949. M. S. Gorbachev sought to make greater use of the UN both in the interests of greater international stability (which he regarded as essential for his domestic "restructuring") and in enhancing Soviet influence in international bodies.

THE COMMUNIST MOVEMENT AND SOVIET FOREIGN POLICY

From its very inception the Soviet leadership anticipated the establishment of other communist regimes as proof that the Russian Revolution was the harbinger of a worldwide revolutionary movement. Indeed, it was Lenin's belief that such regimes were essential if the Soviet regime was to survive. However, efforts in 1919 to establish communist regimes in Hungary, Bavaria (Munich), Estonia, Latvia, and Lithuania were unsuccessful, just as an attempt to impose communism upon Finland had failed in 1918. However, Lenin's regime succeeded in surviving and even attempted to bring communist rule to Western Ukraine, Western Belorussia, and Poland in the summer of 1920, though without success.

The conviction that Moscow had become the capital of the world proletariat prompted Lenin to establish the Comintern, or Third International, in March 1919. Since there were few Communist parties in existence outside of Russia and most of the foreign "representatives" were prisoners of war who remained in Russia or foreign admirers of Bolshevism, the founding congress was more a tribute to Lenin's persistence and Russian staging than proof that Europe was about to be inundated by the tide of world revolution. Indeed, the German Party's delegate held that it was premature to found such an organization and abstained in the voting.[20]

As more Communist parties were formed with the secession of the left wing of the socialist movement, the Comintern assumed organizational form. The 21 Conditions that parties had to accept to gain admission to the Comintern were adopted by the Second Congress in 1920. The requirements included commitment to the "dictatorship of the proletariat" and a revolutionary course; removal of "reformists" and "opportunists"; and establishment of a parallel illegal (covert) organization, even in bourgeois countries in which the Communist Party enjoyed legal status. Parties were to conduct agitation both in the armed forces of "bourgeois" countries and among the "rural proletariat and the poorest peasants" and infiltration of trade unions, cooperatives, and "other mass workers' organizations." Member-parties were obliged to purge their ranks of "petty-bourgeois elements" periodically, to give "unconditional support to any Soviet republic in its struggle against counterrevolutionary forces," and to accept all Comintern decisions as binding.

The fact that Comintern headquarters were in Moscow, that Russian communists or agents headed its Executive Committee and various commissions, and that Soviet funds were at its disposal to subsidize the various parties meant that the Soviet Communist Party would exercise a dominant influence in the organization. The highly centralized character of the Comintern meant that there was no equality of parties. The CPSU actively intervened in the internal affairs of other Communist parties—including the German Party—removing its leadership in 1921, 1923, and 1925. Non-Soviet Communist parties were compelled by Stalin to become involved in the Soviet power struggle during the 1920s, and those leaders who supported Stalin's rivals were removed. Efforts to seize power in Germany in March 1921 and in October 1923 failed, as did attempts in Bulgaria in 1923 and in Estonia during December 1924. Comintern policy in China failed in 1927, when Chiang Kai-shek moved to crush the Chinese Communist Party. The Comintern was further discredited by the skepticism with which Stalin viewed it and by the fact that many foreign communists residing in the Soviet Union perished in the purges. Infiltration and espionage were practiced against the various parties in accordance with Russian secret-police methods. The Kremlin also took the drastic step of dissolving the Polish and Korean Communist parties in 1938, and the Yugoslav Party came close to being dissolved. Thus, the interests of other parties were repeatedly subordinated to those of the Soviet regime. The Nazi-Soviet Non-Aggression Pact of August 23, 1939 (which communists throughout the world found difficult to explain because they had been denouncing Nazi

---

[20]For an eyewitness account of the founding congress by the Comintern's First Secretary, see Angelica Balabanoff, *Impressions of Lenin* (Ann Arbor: University of Michigan Press, 1964), pp. 70–71. See also Stanley Page, *Lenin and World Revolution* (New York: New York University Press, 1959).

Germany and calling for a "united front against fascism" during the preceding five years), resulted in the total disgrace of the Comintern.[21]

Stalin had the Comintern dissolved by its own Executive Committee in May 1943, probably because of the wartime international situation and the desirability of fostering the impression that Moscow was abandoning the policy of world revolution. It is ironic that Soviet foreign policy and the communist movement should have enjoyed greater successes following the Comintern's dissolution. Despite numerous failures, the Comintern trained thousands of foreign communists in special schools in the Soviet Union. Its agents fought in civil wars in Spain, Greece, and elsewhere; conducted political strikes and agitational activities; fulfilled espionage assignments; and assisted Soviet intelligence in various ways.[22] Tested cadres were developed to promote Soviet domestic and foreign policies in the mass media of other countries. Although most of the approximately 90 Communist parties in the world were small, the Kremlin could assume that in nearly every country it had some supporters upon whom it could rely.

The formal dissolution of the Comintern was useful because it lent some credence to the Soviet assertion that the various Communist parties are independent and do not act on orders from Moscow. The Soviet military victory in 1945 led to the establishment of communist regimes in eight Eastern and Central European countries. This, together with the victory of the Chinese communists in 1949 and the creation of communist regimes in North Korea and North Vietnam, laid the groundwork for profound changes in the entire communist movement. Stalin endeavored to maintain Soviet control by founding the Cominform, or Communist Information Bureau, in September 1947 at a meeting in Poland. The Cominform comprised nine Communist parties: the CPSU and the Polish, Yugoslav, Romanian, Czechoslovak, Hungarian, Bulgarian, French, and Italian parties. Asian Communist parties were not represented, nor was the Socialist Unity (Communist) Party of East Germany (its presence would have divulged Soviet objectives in Germany prematurely). The Albanian Party of Labor did not join the Cominform because of its dependence upon the Yugoslav Communist Party at that time.

The fact that the Cominform encountered difficulties less than a year after its founding has obscured somewhat the purposes that Stalin set for it. Although its strident anti-Americanism was much in evidence, the Cominform was not a successor to the Comintern. Its limited and predominantly East European membership indicated its role as a device for integrating and consolidating Soviet domination over the new regimes. The inclusion of the Italian and French parties was probably related to the Soviet effort to obstruct the American Marshall Plan for Europe's economic recovery. In 1947 the Yugoslavs were given the task of criticizing the two West European parties for their ineffectiveness. The location

---

[21]The best general work on the Comintern is Günther Nollau, *International Communism and World Revolution: History and Methods* (New York: Praeger, 1961). See also Franz Borkenau, *World Communism* (reprinting; Ann Arbor: University of Michigan Press, 1962), and E. H. Carr, *Twilight of the Comintern, 1930–1935* (New York: Pantheon, 1983).

[22]The entire range of Comintern activities and controls is discussed in Nollau, *ibid.,* Chapter 4.

of Cominform headquarters in Belgrade probably reflected Stalin's intention of using the organization to control the Yugoslav regime of Marshal Tito.[23] The Cominform had limited but important functions; its newspaper, *For a Lasting Peace, For a People's Democracy,* was controlled by the CPSU and was used to communicate directives and shifts in the line to various Communist parties.

The Soviet decision to expel Yugoslavia from the Cominform in June 1948 and to transfer the headquarters to Bucharest was to have far-reaching consequences, which Stalin's subsequent sanctions to bring Tito to heel and Khrushchev's effort to effect a reconciliation in May 1955 could not undo. The Yugoslav Party had been accused of adopting a "nationalistic attitude"; and the evidence does indicate that Tito resisted Soviet controls, wished to establish a communist Balkan federation, and was utilizing the Greek "civil war" to that end. Alleged supporters of Tito in the various East European countries were brought to trial as Soviet controls tightened. The death of Stalin made possible the decision to attempt to attract Yugoslavia back into the communist fold, but the Soviet admission that Tito was "building socialism" also had the effect of rewarding heresy. Khrushchev's 1956 "secret speech" denigrating Stalin and his public proclamation that there were "various roads to socialism" led to disillusionment and confusion. Foreign communists wondered what Khrushchev and his associates were doing while Stalin committed his crimes and were at a loss for a Marxist explanation of the "cult of personality." The speech also resulted in the Hungarian rebellion of October 1956 and the replacement of the Polish communist leadership (the restoration of "Titoist" Wladyslaw Gomulka). Khrushchev's speech also elicited dissatisfaction from the Chinese communists, who objected to the unilateral Soviet decision to criticize Stalin's excesses—a decision regarding the historical heritage of communism and affecting the entire movement but not the result of joint deliberations.

The Chinese had other grievances as well and resented the Soviet unwillingness to grant their party—the world's largest Communist Party—an effective veto over decisions. In return for such a veto Beijing was willing to recognize the primacy of the CPSU. The limited nature of Soviet economic aid to China and the 1959 Soviet decision to terminate nuclear-development aid were also causes of resentment. Basic to the rivalry was the question of which party would provide the most effective and relevant model and achieve purer communism. Mao Zedong's contempt for Khrushchev as a theoretician and revolutionary and the fact that Mao had brought communist rule to the world's most populous country and oldest extant culture—accomplishing this with little Soviet aid and against Stalin's advice—contributed to Beijing's combined sense of frustration and superiority. When Khrushchev failed to seize the initiative in the (Soviet-precipitated) Berlin crisis of 1959–1961 and sought, instead, a limited détente with the United States, China's fears of betrayal were apparently confirmed. Beijing became convinced that Moscow was not using its alleged

---

[23]For a participant's account of the founding of the Cominform, see Eugenio Reale, "The Founding of the Cominform" in Milorad M. Drachkovitch and Branko Lazich, eds., *The Comintern: Historical Highlights* (New York: Praeger, 1966), pp. 253–268.

military superiority in dealing with the United States. The deterioration of relations between the two largest Communist parties was intensified by Khrushchev's unilateral decision to excommunicate Albania from the communist movement in October 1961. The Albanian leadership, for its part, was embittered by the new conciliatory Soviet policy on Yugoslavia (a traditional Albanian enemy) and by the anti-Stalin campaign. China welcomed its new Balkan ally. Romania utilized the Sino-Soviet dispute to adopt a "neutralist" stance within the communist world and to insist upon its right to rapid and diverse industrial development despite Soviet advocacy of a more specialized Romanian economy. The Soviet occupation of Bessarabia also served as a source of grievance for Romanian communists. China's sense of betrayal was confirmed by the Nuclear Test Ban Treaty signed in Moscow in August 1963. China became the second communist nuclear power in October 1964.

No longer could Moscow demand and obtain the unqualified obedience of all of the world's Communist parties. It had been an easy matter to cope with the Trotskyite deviation of the 1920s because the Trotskyites controlled no country, army, or state apparatus. Communist deviationists who led ruling parties and had their own bureaucracies, armies, and security police could not be disciplined easily and brought to heel by Moscow—especially if they had obtained power with little or no Soviet aid. The Soviet claim to a monopoly on Leninism, while condemning those who disagree as "sectarians," "revisionists," or "dogmatists," lost its effectiveness. The variety of deviations and brands of communist doctrines ("Trotskyism," "Bukharinism," "Stalinism," "Titoism," "Khrushchevism," "Maoism," and Togliatti's "polycentrism")—all descended from Leninism—undermined Moscow's authority and its claim to primacy.

By January 1959, the CPSU had to recognize that Communist parties were "equal and independent." However, the Sino-Soviet disagreement made it impossible to establish policy-making bodies and practices for the so-called Socialist Commonwealth that would be acceptable to all; nor was there agreement on voting (and veto) rights. The dissolution of the defunct Cominform in April 1956 eliminated the sole formal organizational expression of Soviet hegemony. The conferences of Communist parties held in Moscow in November 1957 and in November–December 1960 were not effective and only served to conceal differences. More limited multilateral conferences have also been held. Under the circumstances the CPSU has had to rely upon a variety of devices in attempting to exercise leadership of other Communist parties. These devices include the CPSU's Central Committee section dealing with other Communist parties. High Soviet leaders have attended the congresses of many other parties, and those parties regularly send nonvoting delegates to CPSU Congresses in Moscow. Such exchanges of representatives provide ample opportunity for efforts at persuasion.

Communists are expected to be ideologically schooled and to understand the need for tactical flexibility and sensitivity to new "cues" emanating from Moscow. Apart from official Soviet publications and secret circulars sent to other parties, the theoretical journal *Problems of Peace and Socialism* has been published since 1958 in numerous foreign languages in an effort to promote Moscow's influence.[24] Other channels of information and aid to foreign Communist parties are provided by Soviet embassies, commercial missions, journalists, and special emissaries with appropriate cover. Small parties have been supported by Soviet subsidies and have usually remained loyal to Moscow.

The Soviet disputes with Yugoslavia, China, and Albania exposed the falsity of the oft-repeated claim that international communism was a monolithic movement. Nationalism has served as the principal eroding force, and communist leaders have plotted against each other. Armed border conflicts have broken out between China and the Soviet Union and between China and Vietnam—rendering hollow the "socialist internationalism" that communists have so ardently claimed to profess. The brutal Soviet occupation of Afghanistan in the 1980s and the bloody and cruel war waged against the Moslem insurgents has had a corrupting effect on relations among communist parties. Communist leaders in Afghanistan (1979), Grenada (1983), and South Yemen (1986) have murdered each other in what can only be termed gangland style.[25] Such examples make the term "communist fraternalism" an oxymoron and may have prompted members of the Soviet Politburo to ask themselves serious questions regarding the search for allies and influence in the Third World.

The Soviet Union has been confronted with economic, political, and ideological demands from its communist allies. Insofar as Moscow has retained its ability to attract the support of foreign communists, this has been due more to Soviet military capability, industrial might, and economic wealth than to ideological purity. Communist regimes have taken on ever more diverse, exotic, and bizarre forms—rule by military leaders in Ethiopia and Poland; the genocidal Khmer Rouge despotism in Kampuchea in 1975–1979; the attempt at dynastic communism in North Korea; the Vietnamese "garrison state," fully mobilized and heavily armed but with an impoverished, run-down civilian economy; and the divided and discredited Afghan Peoples Democratic Party, which had to be maintained by Soviet military forces. Thus, Moscow's claim to leadership in an increasingly divided communist world has brought some advantages, but it has also imposed costly and questionable burdens.

THE FOREIGN MINISTRY

Soviet foreign policy is not exclusively the concern of the U.S.S.R. Ministry of Foreign Affairs. The Ministry is under the supervision of the Council of Ministers, and the premier (or Chairman of the Council) plays an important role in Soviet diplomacy. However, all important foreign-policy decisions emanate from the Central Committee's Politburo and are based on recommendations and studies made in the Central Committee departments responsible for foreign affairs and

---

[24]The English language edition, *World Marxist Review,* is published in Toronto, although the editorial offices are in Prague.

[25]In South Yemen a shootout on January 13, 1986, left the meeting room of the Politburo of the Yemen Socialist Party blood-spattered and littered with corpses. There ensued 12 days of violent street fighting, which resulted in thousands of deaths and great destruction stemming from the enormous amounts of weaponry that had been provided by the Soviet Union. See the *New York Times,* February 9, 1986.

in the Foreign Ministry. The Ministry has a special relationship with the Politburo and Party apparatus because of the highly important matters with which
it is charged.

Although the Foreign Ministry does not bear final responsibility for the
making of foreign policy, its political reporting and research are of inestimable
value to the Party officials who make the ultimate decisions. The Ministry is
organized along functional and geographic lines; the former include units concerned with protocol, the press, treaty and legal matters, and the like. The
Minister is advised by a collegium of approximately twelve members, who are first
deputy ministers, deputy ministers, or heads of important divisions within the
Ministry. However, the Minister bears full responsibility for the Ministry and
cannot be overruled by the collegium, although it can appeal to the Council of
Ministers or the Central Committee in the event that it disagrees.

The Soviet Union has had a limited number of foreign ministers, as several
have held the post a decade or longer and have provided a remarkable degree of
continuity. Trotsky, a revolutionary who had no taste for diplomacy, served as
Commissar of foreign affairs for several months. Georgii Chicherin, a gifted
aristocrat and tsarist diplomat who had resigned from the Empire's foreign service
in 1904 after seven years and had joined the Marxist movement, held the post from
April 1918 until 1930. He was succeeded by Maxim Litvinov, also an old revolutionary, who headed the foreign office from 1930 to 1939, when he was removed
prior to the negotiation of the Nazi-Soviet Pact. Viacheslav Molotov served as
Foreign Minister from 1939 to 1949 and again from 1953 to 1956. Andrei Vyshinsky, Stalin's chief prosecutor and former professor of law and rector of
Moscow University, held the post from 1949 to 1953. The Minister with briefest
tenure, next to Trotsky's, was Dmitrii Shepilov, a Party official who served from
June 1956 to February 1957 but broke with Khrushchev. Andrei Gromyko—a
career diplomat and former Soviet ambassador to the United States, the United
Kingdom, and the UN—succeeded Shepilov and served from 1957 to 1985.

Soviet Foreign Ministers have usually attained at least full membership in
the CPSU Central Committee. Trotsky, Molotov, and Gromyko became full
members of the Politburo, while Vyshinsky and Shepilov were alternate members.
Molotov enjoyed full Politburo membership because he was also head of government. Chicherin achieved Central Committee membership only in 1925, and
Litvinov attained it in 1934—long after they became heads of the foreign office.
Gromyko became a Central Committee member in 1956 as a First Deputy
Foreign Minister and attained full membership in the Politburo only in 1973.
Eduard Shevardnadze attained Politburo full membership in July 1985 when he
succeeded Gromyko. The Foreign Minister who is not a Politburo member can
probably avoid committing himself on many issues—especially those that con-
cern domestic politics—and, unlike Shepilov, can possibly avoid certain pitfalls.
Yet the importance of foreign policy would appear to make full Politburo membership for the Foreign Minister desirable.

Soviet career diplomats must be Communist Party members and are trained
at the Foreign Ministry's Diplomatic Academy and the Moscow State Institute
of International Relations (MGIMO). All key diplomatic posts are filled only

with the approval of the Central Committee apparatus. The Soviet diplomatic service's subordinate status was made especially evident when Stalin, at the end of World War II, ordered Foreign Ministry personnel to be put in uniform, complete with shoulder boards, rank insignia, and gold braid. The abandonment of the uniform and the restoration of the business suit in 1954 was followed by the infusion of Party and government functionaries into the diplomatic service. Although the service was severely purged in the late 1930s (and new personnel had to be drafted into it from other fields), the ouster of Molotov and Shepilov did not lead to the removal of career diplomats. However, career diplomats have usually not been entrusted with Soviet embassies in communist-ruled countries; these ambassadorships have usually gone to Party officials.

The role of Soviet diplomats is circumscribed and deals more with the implementation of policy than with policy making. Nor does the Soviet leadership rely exclusively upon diplomats for reporting on developments abroad. Although the ambassador reports to the Foreign Ministry, the military attachés report to the Chief Directorate of Intelligence (GRU), and the commercial counselor reports to the Ministry of Foreign Trade. The Party's representative, the secretary of the primary party organization within the embassy, who uses a diplomatic post as a cover, reports directly to the Central Committee in Moscow. The KGB, the secret police, has its personnel in all Soviet embassies and also receives reports. The Central Committee apparatus sifts and evaluates all reports for use by the Politburo. In addition to providing multiple channels of communication, this system also facilitates the use of Soviet embassies for intelligence and espionage purposes, and encourages mutual surveillance. The extent of such activity was illustrated by the British government's expulsion in September 1971 of 90 Soviet diplomats and other personnel and refusal to grant re-entry to 15 other persons, all of whom were said to be engaged in espionage activities. The scope of the network was revealed by a KGB defector and resulted in the largest single expulsion of Soviet agents from a foreign country.[26] France expelled 47 Soviet diplomats in April 1983 on charges of espionage activities. Although the influence of Soviet diplomats on the Politburo may be limited, they have nevertheless acquired enhanced status, appropriate linguistic training, and a standard of professionalism as a result of the Soviet Union's emergence as a great power.

SOVIET DIPLOMATIC TECHNIQUE

The Soviet diplomat is trained to regard diplomacy as part of a total strategy in which each of the skirmishes or encounters fought has its place. It undoubtedly was with this in mind that Stalin reminded his generals and marshals in June 1945, following their military victory over Nazi Germany, that a shrewd foreign policy is worth several army corps. Soviet diplomats are carefully instructed, their plenipotentiary powers are usually rigidly circumscribed, and they are backed by a powerful propaganda machine. They are not likely to mediate between the position of their government and that adopted by a foreign government. They do

---

[26]The *New York Times,* September 25, 1971.

not readily reveal the areas in which they are permitted to negotiate, and this makes it very difficult for their counterparts. Their skill in engaging in delaying tactics and in repetitiousness is renowned. They can be abusive or pleasant, urbane, and polite as the situation or their instructions might demand. They are not troubled by inconsistencies. Thus, they think nothing of advocating the struggle against colonialism for Namibia but not for Lithuania, Moldavia, Ukraine, or Uzbekistan.

Negotiations are employed not only to reach agreements. Soviet diplomacy frequently seeks to confuse and disarm its opponents by exploiting the "contradictions" said to exist between the various capitalist states. The popular-front tactic or the "anti-imperialist struggle" are cases in point. Soviet diplomacy attempts to exploit the greed and fears of particular countries. It attempts to utilize interest groups in other countries—as for example, appealing to businessmen to have their governments lift trade or loan-guarantee restrictions—and is not likely to be undercut by Soviet interest groups. Soviet foreign policy has taken full advantage of the mass media in pluralistic and democratic societies in an effort to pressure other governments into offering greater concessions. Negotiating tactics and positions have been synchronized with massive public relations campaigns.

Negotiations have been employed to prevent agreement if the Soviet Union has been seeking to buy time. The peace talks conducted with the Central Powers by Trotsky at Brest-Litovsk early in 1918 provide a classic example of this tactic. Other examples are the negotiations for an Austrian State Treaty, in which Moscow stalled from 1947 to 1954 in more than 260 negotiating sessions; various disarmament meetings; the Korean truce talks (1951–1953), and negotiations on German reunification since 1946. The Test Ban Treaty took five years to negotiate; the SALT II Agreement took seven years. Extraneous issues are introduced, and on occasion Soviet diplomats have even walked out or absented themselves. Opponents are accused of engaging in obstructionist tactics, and diplomatic conferences have been used to "unmask" or discredit them and to impugn their motives. Repeatedly the Soviet Union has engaged in negotiations with no intention of offering a *quid pro quo;* it has treated as "negotiable" only concessions offered by others and has usually been reluctant to offer genuine concessions in return. Thus, what is claimed as the Soviet Union's is not generally subject to negotiation.

Soviet diplomacy has frequently been related to propaganda considerations, and the use of the diplomatic conference as a propaganda sounding board can remain a side effect even when Moscow is pursuing negotiations seriously. The precedent of subordinating diplomacy to propaganda was set when Lenin's government, in one of its first acts, published the secret Anglo-Russian and Franco-Russian agreements of World War I regarding the planned division of spoils. Soviet spokesmen have frequently appealed directly to peoples over the heads of their governments. Soviet diplomatic notes have often told foreign governments what Moscow thinks their peoples to be thinking and what *their* national interests are. The notes can be lengthy, and their purpose is not only to communicate with other governments but to influence public opinion. This objective has been especially evident when the Soviet government has published diplomatic communications before they have been translated and studied by the governments to which they are addressed. Yet Soviet diplomats are quite capable of negotiating seriously and in secret when it suits their purposes.

Soviet leaders have employed a variety of diplomatic methods ranging from summit meetings and state visits (including calls on the Pope by Foreign Minister Gromyko and chief of state Podgorny, despite the regime's hostility to the Catholic Church) to threats. The threat of Soviet "volunteers" and the vulnerability of London and Paris to H-bombs succeeded in October 1956 in compelling Anglo-French and Israeli withdrawal from Egypt. During the October 1973 Arab-Israeli hostilities, a Soviet threat of intervention on behalf of Egypt brought American acquiescence in an Israeli withdrawal. The use of a specific threat by Khrushchev in November 1958 to sign a separate peace treaty with the East German communist regime within six months backfired when Presidents Eisenhower and Kennedy called his bluff. Khrushchev then repeatedly extended the ultimatum and lost credibility by not transferring to East German authorities control of the access routes to West Berlin as he had threatened to do. Yet Soviet aims in Germany were attained as a result of the election of Willy Brandt's Social Democratic government and its decision to acquiesce in Germany's partition and recognize the communist German Democratic Republic.

The various characteristics of Soviet diplomacy have made it difficult to negotiate with Moscow. The Soviet belief that persistence pays was evident when the Western Powers accepted the uninspected Nuclear Test Ban Treaty in 1963 (although the Soviet Union offered a paper concession in agreeing to the exception for underground tests). Perseverance was also rewarded with the signing of the Soviet-West German Treaty of August 12, 1970, which provided for renunciation of force and recognition of existing frontiers. The Soviet insistence upon a regime for the Antarctic was vindicated in the Antarctic Treaty of December 1959, which embodied the provisions of a Soviet *aide memoire* of June 7, 1950, sent at a time when the Soviet Union was excluded from talks dealing with that subcontinent. The rewards of a persistent pursuit of policy objectives were evident in Soviet conduct at the Yalta and Potsdam conferences, which were very advantageous for Moscow. Soviet persistence has also obtained diplomatic immunity for its consular and foreign-trade officials.

SOVIET FOREIGN TRADE POLICY

The system of central economic planning has as its logical consequence the state monopoly of Soviet foreign trade, although planners have tended to dislike such trade insofar as it requires them to deal with external factors that they cannot control. World trade involves too many variables to suit the communist economic planners. As a result, controls are maintained over all imports and exports, and foreign trade serves both as an instrument of Soviet foreign policy in the pursuit of political objectives and as a means of promoting internal economic development. If the Soviet Union has not in the past been a highly important factor in world trade, this has been due to its traditionally having followed a policy of autarky, or economic self-sufficiency, so as not to be permanently dependent upon other countries for essential items. Yet foreign trade has played a vital role in obtaining imports of entire factories and vehicle assembly plants from Western Europe and the United States to remedy shortcomings in the Soviet economy; the Soviet Union has furthermore sought from the West "strategic commodities"— goods that add appreciably to a country's capabilities. The state foreign-trade monopoly has also sought to protect the Soviet Union from fluctuations of prices and output in the world's markets and to reduce the country's dependence for political-military reasons.

The system of controls is administered by the U.S.S.R. Ministry of Foreign Trade and is based on fixed foreign-exchange rates. The ruble is not freely convertible into other currencies and is exchanged only under controlled conditions; nor is the ruble backed by gold in practice, although it is said to have an official gold content. The need to manage the limited supply of foreign exchange and to exploit every possible means of earning foreign currency and regulate imports has led to the establishment of numerous specialized Soviet foreign-trade organizations. Each has headquarters in Moscow, is known as an All-Union Association *(Vsesoiuznoe Ob"edinenie),* and has an abbreviated special designation. Thus V/O "Vneshposyltorg" sells consumer goods, household appliances, and automobiles for delivery in the Soviet Union to persons purchasing such with foreign currency. The organization also operates special stores in the Soviet Union in which only hard currencies are accepted from Soviet citizens and foreign tourists. Soviet trade organizations are often represented abroad by a single Soviet commercial agency, as, for example, in the United States, where the Amtorg Trading Corporation oversees Soviet imports and exports.

Soviet foreign trade has been complicated by the use of exchange rates and domestic prices that are arbitrary. Export prices are also manipulated; the use of bilateral trade agreements with other countries and the trade organizations' practice of selling at prices that differ from those charged domestically serve to keep the Soviet Union competitive in many areas. Soviet foreign trade has been conducted in Western currencies and in world prices as determined by capitalist markets; the official rate of exchange for the ruble is not relevant, as it does not represent the currency's real value. Soviet foreign trade is part of the economic plan, and it is conducted on the basis of decisions made by state agencies. Yet Soviet businessmen, despite the fact that they are government employees, have sought to buy cheaply and sell dearly—except where political considerations or bureaucratic interests might prompt them to do otherwise.[27]

The Soviet Union has not been eager to trade extensively with the Western industrial states except to obtain valuable equipment and items not readily manu-

---

[27]The problems of Soviet foreign trade are discussed in Alan A. Brown and Egon Neuberger, eds., *Trade and Planning* (Berkeley and Los Angeles: University of California Press, 1967), and in Frederic L. Pryor, *The Communist Foreign Trade System* (Cambridge: MIT Press, 1963; Greenwood Press, 1982 reprint ed.). On the organization and functioning of the Soviet Ministry of Foreign Trade, see John Quigley, *The Soviet Foreign Trade Monopoly* (Columbus: Ohio State University Press, 1974). For a case study in extra-economic aspects of foreign trade, see Philip S. Gillette, "Armand Hammer, Lenin and the First American Concession in Soviet Russia," *Slavic Review,* XL, No. 3 (Fall 1981), pp. 355–365.

factured by domestic producers. Most Soviet foreign trade has been with other communist states. Soviet exports include such items as petroleum, furs, caviar, machine tools, aircraft, merchant ships, hydroelectric equipment, forest products, natural gas, manganese, and industrial diamonds. Some of the most useful Soviet imports have been obtained from countries that have little need for Soviet export items. For example, beginning in 1963 the Soviet Union contracted to import at great cost large shipments of grain from Australia, Canada, and the United States. Such purchases have resulted in balance of payments difficulties. The Soviet Union has attempted to cope with trade deficits by increasing its exports and foreign-exchange earning activities wherever possible and also selling gold for hard currencies to purchase needed imports. Despite condemnation of South Africa for apartheid, the Soviet Union has frequently sold its diamonds on the world market under agreements with the South African DeBeers organization in order to obtain the highest price.[28] It has also participated in a quasi-cartel for gold sales.

The Soviet Union is probably the world's second largest producer of gold (surpassed only by South Africa), although the size of its annual production is a state secret. This has made it possible for Moscow to remain aloof from the International Monetary Fund in dealing with balance-of-payments difficulties. The Soviet government sells gold through commercial banks that it controls in London, Paris, Frankfurt, Vienna, Luxembourg, and Zurich; the London bank (known as the Moscow Narodny Bank) has branch offices in Beirut and Singapore. The banks are also used to sell other precious metals, to finance trade credits, and to deal in foreign exchange.

Yet the Soviet Union prefers not to sell gold and attempts to earn foreign exchange by a variety of means. It sells raw materials that, however, are not always well located for export markets. It benefited from the rise in oil prices following the Arab oil embargo of 1973–1974 but had to absorb losses when petroleum prices fell in the 1980s. Foreign markets for machinery are sought but are difficult to develop whenever Soviet producers cannot meet rigid specifications of foreign buyers and provide spare parts and servicing of equipment sold. The Soviet government promotes tourism and has entered the cruise business. There is even a law firm in Moscow *(Iniurkollegiia)* that specializes in private international-law cases and claims estates of persons who die abroad on behalf of Soviet citizens who purport to be heirs of the deceased. Extremely high import duties have been imposed on gift parcels sent to Soviet citizens from abroad by relatives. A most important source of foreign exchange are long-term loans obtained from foreign banks at attractive interest rates and sometimes guaranteed by "bourgeois" governments. Although there is a possibility of its foreign debt becoming excessive, the Soviet Union has had a good financial record in paying debts (apart from those involving political issues such as the Lend-Lease settlement dating from World War II).

Although the Soviet Union has contracted large foreign debts to finance

---

[28]See Kurt M. Campbell, *Soviet Policy toward South Africa* (New York: St. Martin's Press, 1986), Chapter 5.

needed imports of technology, it has also been active as a lender and seller of arms to select countries. In the mid-1950s Moscow began to offer credits to a limited number of states that included Afghanistan, Egypt, Syria, India, Indonesia, Burma, Iraq, and Yemen. The Soviet claim was that developing countries could obtain low-interest loans in Moscow without accepting the allegedly onerous conditions attached by international and capitalist lending agencies. The State Committee for Foreign Economic Relations was established to oversee the new loan program and to save African and Asian lands from the predatory grasp of neocolonialism—which allegedly sought to subvert their political independence by making them economically dependent upon Wall Street. Moscow also undertook to sell arms, beginning with sales to Egypt and Afghanistan, as a means of countering Western military aid and alliance systems.

Soviet objectives in the foreign-loan program have been to reduce, if not entirely eliminate, the influence of the capitalist states in Asia, Africa, and Latin America. By depriving these states of their colonial territories and areas of investment, capitalism will be correspondingly weakened. In this way "contradictions" between the imperialist powers can be intensified as the competition for markets and investments increases. The Soviet Union is also interested in limiting the influence and membership of Western-sponsored defensive alliances. The Soviet Union hopes that the states receiving loans will support, or at least not obstruct, Soviet foreign-policy undertakings and resolutions in the UN and in the international specialized agencies. Moscow also assumes that the export of Soviet capital and technology will promote the adoption of the Soviet model for modernization and rapid industrialization. While the Soviet Union seeks to use the "national bourgeoisie" of the borrowing countries in the struggle against "monopolies" and imperialism, it also seeks to promote conditions that will lead to the emergence of Communist parties and, ultimately, communist regimes. Although the Soviet financial investment in developing countries is more political and strategic than economic in nature, it serves to underscore Moscow's continuing interest in world trade and its ability to extend credits and to place on the market, or withhold from it, large quantities of goods and armaments as well as services.

CONDITIONS OF COEXISTENCE: *RAZRIADKA* AND BEYOND

The Soviet assertion that the ultimate triumph of communism is possible without resorting to cataclysmic thermonuclear warfare has required a refurbishing of the concept of "peaceful coexistence." Although the term "coexistence" was employed by Lenin and Stalin, its more recent usage involves a redefinition of the means to be employed in the contest between the American and Soviet superpowers. According to the new definition, economic competition and political-ideological struggle are to be accompanied by a search for new allies and an effort to enlarge the ranks of the uncommitted countries. Although outright war is to be avoided in the relations between "states with different social systems," it has been said that there "can be no peaceful coexistence when it comes to internal processes of the class and national-liberation struggle in the capitalist countries or in the colonies."[29] The "peaceful coexistence" formula is designed to contribute to the immobilization of the Soviet Union's antagonists, while the communist cause is to be advanced by a variety of means that fall short of thermonuclear war. Thus, "coexistence" cannot be based on a static condition but must reflect a changing international situation that is supposedly developing in the Soviet Union's favor.

If there remains much of the "two camps" doctrine in the "coexistence" concept, the Soviet Union can still be said to desire a modicum of stability in international relations. To this end it has maintained a limited dialogue with its various antagonists and has entered into limited agreements, such as the Test Ban Treaty of August 1963; the Austrian State Treaty of May 1955; the Antarctic Treaty of December 1, 1959; the Space Treaty of 1967; the 1968 Treaty on the Non-Proliferation of Nuclear Weapons; the strategic-arms-limitations agreements of 1972, 1974, 1979, and 1987; and a number of lesser agreements concluded with the United States. Yet it has also utilized conflicts and rivalries between various countries, mounted diplomatic offensives, and become involved in various regional international crises. It has maneuvered at the expense of unstable countries and has endeavored to split the bourgeoisie when there has been little chance of establishing a communist regime in a country. The Soviet leadership has also sought to capitalize upon divergent interpretations and analyses (in Western circles) concerning what Soviet policy actually is, thus contributing to confusion and indecision among its adversaries.

Coexistence has also been complicated and even endangered by the various crises precipitated by direct action or by use of proxies. Thus the Berlin Blockade of 1948–1949, the Korean War of 1950–1953, the Berlin crises of 1958–1961, and the Cuban missile crisis of October 1962 all threatened the international balance of forces and gave meaning to the Soviet definition of "coexistence." Subsequent Soviet decisions to arm the Vietcong guerrillas in order to overthrow the Republic of (South) Vietnam and to become actively involved in the international politics of the Near East by arming certain Arab countries served to underline the fact that, for Moscow, coexistence has a dynamic that distinguishes it from a static balance of power.

In the Soviet view, established communist regimes must be maintained in power even at great cost and in the face of open revolt, as in Hungary in October–November 1956 and in East Germany in June 1953. This view was reaffirmed in the so-called Brezhnev doctrine of 1968, which asserted the claim of the Soviet Union to intervene militarily in a "fraternal" country in which there allegedly is a deviation from the "common laws governing socialist construction" or a "threat to the cause of socialism." If Soviet policy makers vacillated initially in Poland and Hungary in 1956 and in the decision to occupy Czechoslovakia militarily in August 1968, in the end they did not hesitate to employ military forces to preserve these regimes. Finland in 1940 and Iranian Azerbaidjan and Kurdistan in 1946 (where Soviet-sponsored regimes were abandoned) are rare exceptions to a policy that has sought to aid and protect even the weakest

---

[29]From the Report of the Central Committee to the 23rd CPSU Congress, as delivered by Brezhnev on March 29, 1966. See *XXIII S" ezd KPSS* (Moscow, 1966), I, p. 44.

communist regime. It was the weakness and internal divisions of the Afghan communist regime and its inability to cope with a popular rebellion based on an Islamic backlash that prompted the costly Soviet military intervention in Afghanistan in the 1980s. Marxist regimes in Angola, Ethiopia, Kampuchea, Mozambique, and Nicaragua also found themselves combating insurgency movements, much to Moscow's consternation. Indeed, Soviet leaders are obsessed by "imperialism's" alleged efforts to organize "counter-revolutionary coups." Thus, while Gorbachev at the Twenty-seventh Congress acknowledged Afghanistan to be a "bleeding wound," he blamed it on "counter-revolution and imperialism." By Soviet "logic" Soviet troops were killing Afghans in the name of Afghan sovereignty and "fraternal assistance" while "imperialism" was allegedly violating that sovereignty by aiding a mass rebellion.

In the 1970s Soviet spokesmen introduced the phrase "relaxation of international tension" *(razriadka mezhdunarodnoi napriazhënnosti)* as a counterpart to the term detente that had acquired currency in the West in reference to efforts to improve relations with the Soviet Union. The Russian term *razriadka* has various meanings and is also used to refer to the spacing out of letters in typography or to the discharging or unloading of a firearm. In Soviet practice and in official pronouncements regarding razriadka, there are very specific limitations in the concept, and it is not to be confused with rapprochement, a settlement of all major issues that divide two countries, or with an alliance, or entente.

The Soviet Union has supported razriadka because it brought certain advantages. First, it meant recognition of Soviet parity or better in nuclear weapons and recognition of the frontiers of communist states, including Soviet territorial gains resulting from World War II. The 1986 Party Program asserts that "the establishment of military-strategic parity between the USSR and the United States and between the Warsaw Treaty Organization and NATO was a historic achievement of socialism."[30] This was said to be due to the emergence of "the world system of socialism" as well as "a fundamental change in the correlation of forces in the international arena." It was claimed that no question of world politics can be resolved without the "socialist commonwealth."[31] A second advantage of razriadka is that it contributes to reducing the risk or likelihood of World War III. Third, it has the possible advantage of reducing Western military efforts and contributing to a certain apathy or euphoria and even antimilitary attitudes and possibly a false sense of security in "capitalist" countries. It could be perceived as a means of disarming one's adversary or reducing his ability to employ military means. Fourth, it contributed to a climate in which "capitalist" countries are willing to provide the Soviet Union with modern technology, investment capital, and grain as well as long-term financial credits enabling the Soviet economy to deal with certain of its problems and also concentrate on increasing its military capabilities. A fifth advantage of razriadka is that it contributes to the image of the Soviet Union as a peaceful state governed by reasonable men and diverts attention from such unattractive aspects of Soviet conduct as the persecu-

---

[30]*Partiinaia zhizn'*, No. 6–7 (March–April 1986), p. 100.
[31]*Ibid.*, p. 102.

tion of religious believers, the arrest of political dissidents, and the suppression of ethnic grievances. A sixth advantage is that it contributes to Soviet efforts to isolate the People's Republic of China and to be in a better position to attempt to intimidate Beijing. Seventh, it could enable the Soviet Union to avoid the costly development and deployment of certain weapons systems, insofar as other states might agree to limit their deployment. Yet the 1972 and 1974 agreements on anti-ballistic missiles (ABM) gave the Soviet Union an advantage because, in the end, the United States chose not to exercise its option to erect an ABM system around Washington, D.C., while the Soviet Union retained such a system around Moscow.

An eighth advantage of razriadka was stated in General Secretary Brezhnev's Central Committee Report to the Twenty-fifth CPSU Congress. He asserted that détente was accompanied by a further growth in the "world revolutionary process" and the "deepening crisis of capitalism." Thus, coexistence and razriadka are said to actually further the revolutionary struggle. Brezhnev, in explaining the Soviet Union's "solidarity . . . with the struggle of other peoples for freedom and progress," reiterated that:

> *razriadka,* peaceful coexistence concern interstate relations. This means first of all that disputes and conflicts between countries must not be decided by means of war, by use of force or threats of force. *Razriadka* in no sense abolishes nor can it abolish or change the laws of class struggle. Nor can one expect communists in conditions of *razriadka* to become reconciled to capitalist exploitation or monopolists to become supporters of the revolution.[32]

Thus detente is seen as promoting "socialism" and the "national liberation struggle," though Brezhnev also warned against predicting the "automatic collapse" of capitalism and conceded that it still possessed "considerable reserves" but that "it is a society without a future."[33] The 1986 Party Program states that "the exploiter world of capitalism . . . is still strong and dangerous but is already past its zenith."[34]

Razriadka was not to be confused with pacifism, as communists have never claimed to be pacifists. Soviet leaders have always contended that certain kinds of wars are "just" and "revolutionary," and they have supported civil wars and resistance to imperialism and neocolonialism. The 1986 Party Program defined revolution as "the logical *(zakonomernyi)* result of social development and the class struggle in a given country." Yet the program also stated that neither revolution nor counterrevolution should be "exported," and the Soviet Union, it declares, "resolutely opposes attempts to forcibly halt and turn back the course of history."[35]

The 1986 Program emphasized the concept of "peaceful coexistence" more than razriadka-détente. It declared that "the historical dispute between the two

[32]*Izvestiia,* February 25, 1976, p. 4.
[33]*Ibid.*
[34]*Partiinaia zhizn', op. cit.* (above, no. 30), p. 102.
[35]*Ibid.,* p. 137.

opposing social systems into which the world is divided today can and must be solved by peaceful means." It called for "normal, stable relations between the Soviet Union and the U.S. . . . on the basis of the greatest possible mutual trust. Differences in social systems and ideologies are no reason for strained relations." Yet the program also defined "the present era" as one of "the transition from capitalism to socialism and communism and of the historic competition of two world social and political systems, an era of socialist and national liberation revolutions." It confidently declares: "For all its unevenness, complexity and contradictory nature, mankind's movement toward socialism and communism is inexorable."[36]

The Party Program, like the pronouncements of Soviet leaders, must be understood as a dialectical document whose provisions may be "contradictory" and are designed to cover a variety of contingencies and to enable Soviet leaders to deal with opportunities as well as necessities. Ideological coexistence was firmly ruled out under Brezhnev, and the 1986 Program declared "the extension of the ideological contradictions between the two systems in the sphere of . . . [inter-state] relations to be impermissible."[37] However, this provision still left ample room for ideological warfare in the "non-inter-state" areas of the class struggle and the "world revolutionary process."

Nevertheless, Gorbachev expressed opposition to the policy of "military confrontation" and sought to carry razriadka-détente beyond a modest reduction in international tension and advocated a "mature razriadka." In asserting that "nuclear weapons bear the threat of a hurricane [*smerch*] capable of wiping humankind from the face of the earth,"[38] Gorbachev also stated that the Soviet Union was presenting its proposals "directly to world opinion, to the peoples." To this end the Soviet Union sought to induce what might be termed a mass nuclear neurosis in Western countries with the aid of "non-communist trends and organizations including religious ones that speak out against nuclear war."[39] Thus, pacifists and other well-intentioned groups in Western countries are to be used to induce a paralysis of will or to advocate concessions and the signing of agreements on Soviet terms as an alternative to supposedly risking nuclear devastation.

Although the nuclear "balance of terror" has been said to have prevented a nuclear war between the major powers, Gorbachev's Central Committee Report to the Twenty-seventh Congress apparently rejected the doctrine of strategic deterrence known as mutual assured destriction (MAD). The Report asserted: "Security cannot be built ad infinitum on fear of retribution, that is on the doctrine of 'deterrence' or 'terror.'" Gorbachev denounced the "absurdity and immorality of the situation in which the entire world becomes a nuclear hostage."[40] In particular, he singled out for criticism the (anti-ballistic missile) Strategic Defense Initiative of the United States as "a stimulus to a continued arms race

---

[36]*Ibid.*, p. 108.
[37]*Ibid.*, p. 138.
[38]*Pravda*, February 26, 1986, p. 7.
[39]*Ibid.*, p. 8.
[40]*Ibid.*, p. 7

and as an obstruction on the path to radical disarmament."[41] However, it was contended by Gorbachev's Western critics that the Soviet Union was itself seeking to deploy an anti-ballistic-missile territorial-defense system.

The notion of razriadka entails certain problems and contradictions. It must be viewed as part of a larger strategy that seeks to avoid nuclear global war while pursuing various initiatives, utilizing proxies, and maintaining pressure against the class enemy, "reaction," capitalism, the "monopolies," and imperialism. It includes an apparent double standard that permits the Soviet Union to intervene in a civil conflict, as in Angola in 1976 with Cuban troops, while condemning efforts of other countries to aid the forces that Moscow is bent on destroying. Another example is the right claimed by the Soviet Union to intervene militarily in other "socialist" countries, as it did in Czechoslovakia in 1968 when it removed the government of Alexander Dubček, while "capitalist" countries are not accorded such a right. Thus the Soviet Union would not coexist with a Czechoslovakia led by a communist like Dubček, while the United States was fully expected to coexist with a communist Cuba governed by Fidel Castro. While Soviet spheres of interest or areas of hegemony are to be accorded recognition, there is apparently no reciprocal recognition of the spheres of influence of other states or of the Monroe Doctrine. While Gorbachev could claim to be seeking a "mature détente," he also characterized the United States as "the mother country of imperialism"[42] and as "the locomotive of militarism."[43] While the Soviet leadership has claimed to "act from principled positions," it has been reluctant to acknowledge or respect the principles of others.

Nor is there reciprocity under the Helsinki Final Act (Declaration) of the 1975 Conference on Security and Co-operation in Europe, to which the Soviet Union has attributed such great importance as having recognized the inviolability of existing frontiers, renunciation of threats of force, and peaceful settlement of disputes. Although the Soviet Union pledged at Helsinki to "facilitate the freer and wider dissemination of information of all kinds,"[44] it invokes the sovereignty argument and claims that any effort to challenge its own domestic information quasi-monopoly is "intervention in the internal affairs" of the Soviet Union or is viewed as "anti-Soviet demagogy."[45] Razriadka is also characterized by another contradiction: while the Soviet Union has sought a reduction in international tension, it has simultaneously reinforced internal political controls. Concern expressed in foreign countries on behalf of human rights in the Soviet Union or on the right to emigrate has been viewed as contrary to the spirit of razriadka.

Among the obstacles to improved relations with the Soviet Union is its proclivity for waging wars of nerves, engaging in intimidation, vilifying its critics,

---

[41]*Ibid.*, p. 8.
[42]*Ibid.*, p. 2.
[43]*Ibid.*, p. 7.
[44]U.S. Department of State, *Conference on Security and Co-operation in Europe, Final Act* (Helsinki, 1975), p. 117. The Final Act was declared "not eligible for registration" by the United Nations as a treaty but was transmitted to the U.N. Secretary-General for circulation as an official U.N. document. It has been characterized as a political statement of intent that is not legally binding.
[45]*Izvestiia*, February 25, 1976, p. 3.

and wanting to settle old scores. There is an underlying arrogance that finds expression in the (Russian) preoccupation with *slava* (glory and self-glorification) and *mogushchestvo* (might). This may be due, in part, to the fact that Soviet power is unidimensional—based essentially on military capabilities.[46] Indeed, the very existence of more prosperous democratic societies in the West among the NATO countries, Austria, Sweden, and Switzerland constitutes a "threat" of sorts to the Soviet system in the eyes of its suspicious rulers.

In seeking to absolve themselves of any responsibility for international tensions and conflicts, the Soviet leaders have sought to attribute all of the world's ills—including the arms race—to "imperialism." Yet the Soviet Union has itself initiated and exacerbated certain stages of the arms race. Thus, it led in the development and reliance upon the long-range ballistic missile as a response to the U.S. Strategic Air Command. The Soviet Union deployed the first operational ABM (anti-ballistic missile) system and developed an anti-satellite weapon. It also developed a fractional orbital bombardment system (FOBS). The Soviet Union developed the unique SS-18 missile, tremendous throw-weight, and the world's largest nuclear warheads. It led in deploying the first intercontinental mobile ballistic missiles, the SS-24 and SS-25.

Détente deteriorated in the late 1970s, but the process began with the Soviet decision to supply North Vietnam and the Vietcong guerrilla movement. The Soviet Union also decided to take advantage of perceived American weakness and the crippling of the U.S. executive branch following the resignation of President Richard Nixon. Soviet involvement in Angola and Ethiopia with Cuban forces, the arming and penetration of the Marxist Sandinista regime in Nicaragua, the support of the Vietnamese invasion of Kampuchea and of various insurgency movements (including that in El Salvador), and the Soviet invasion of Afghanistan—all led to the undoing of détente.

Such Soviet actions apparently reflect a desire to demonstrate Soviet superiority and the validity and viability of the Soviet system. It can be asked whether the Soviet leaders are not tempted to expand Soviet influence as a means of demonstrating that "the future belongs to socialism." Thus, a craving for recognition and prestige complements an obsession to reaffirm revolutionary credentials on the part of a system that has lost its revolutionary élan.

The various undercurrents that flow beneath the surface of the razriadka policy make it very difficult to arrive at binding agreements. One of the reasons for this is that the Soviet leaders have difficulty in accepting perpetuation of the status quo. Gorbachev's Central Committee Report to the Twenty-seventh Congress stated that "the world is in a process of rapid changes and it is beyond anyone's power to maintain an eternal status quo in it."[47] As dialecticians, the Soviet leaders appear to reject on philosophical grounds the notion of any stable or lasting equilibrium and are very cognizant of the "correlation of forces" *(sootnoshenie sil)* that is said to be developing in the Soviet Union's favor. In

---

[46]See Paul Dibb, *The Soviet Union: The Incomplete Superpower* (Champaign: University of Illinois Press, 1986).

[47]*Pravda,* February 26, 1986, p. 7.

philosophical terms they regard movement and change (of matter) as absolute and treat stability and rest *(pokoi)* as relative and temporary and the consequence of certain conditions. Temporary conditions of equilibrium are acknowledged, but equilibrium is always linked to movement ("movement within equilibrium") and is considered to be undergoing change.[48] Thus the Soviet view of the status quo is one of anticipating change and development and its being replaced by a qualitatively new condition.

If Marxist-Leninist philosophy can provide a degree of comfort and reassurance to the Soviet leadership, the realities of the Soviet position have been a source of discomfort and apprehension. Despite its nuclear arsenal and military power, the Soviet Union has found itself in an isolated position with small-state allies that must be kept under constant surveillance and cajoled into the various common ventures undertaken in the name of the "socialist commonwealth." The tragic fate of Afghanistan in the 1980s at the hands of the Soviet military demonstrated graphically the dangers and misfortune that can befall a country that becomes dependent on the Soviet Union militarily and economically, as Afghanistan did beginning in the 1950s. The fact that two such different countries as the United States and China should have shared such great difficulties in dealing with the Soviet Union is also a reflection of Moscow's relative isolation. Although the Soviet Union succeeded to a large extent in obtaining recognition of its conquests and frontiers in Europe under the Helsinki Final Act, it has had difficulty in obtaining recognition of its frontiers and position in East Asia because of its intransigence in disagreements with China and Japan. China remains for the Soviet Union a great imponderable—a preplexing problem that refuses to disappear and that is a source of great embarrassment as a result of Beijing's having termed Soviet policy "social imperialism" and the Soviet leaders "revisionist new tsars."

Caught between its Chinese Marxist-Leninist antagonists or rivals and its "capitalist" opponents, the Soviet Union has little choice but to attempt to isolate one or the other side and thus prevent its own isolation. The size and destructive power of the Soviet nuclear arsenal make it necessary to include the Soviet Union in any effort to reduce or balance the world's weapons systems. Thus, coexistence is unavoidable because the stakes involve the question of nuclear war. Yet coexistence will not endure unless it is based on countervailing power among the principal contenders in weaponry, scientific research, technological ability, intelligence, and propaganda. Given an appropriate strategic balance, coexistence should lead to greater discourse, and it, in turn, might facilitate the resolution of the various contradictions that have characterized the Soviet Union's relations with noncommunist countries.

---

[48]A. P. Sheptulin, ed., *Materialisticheskaia dialektika kak nauchnaia sistema* (Moscow: izd-vo Moskovskogo universiteta, 1983), p. 49.

chapter 12

The Soviet Polity: Problems and Prospects

Attempts to predict the future development of the Soviet polity have not been especially successful in the past. Changes in the regime's policies have frequently been misinterpreted, as when the NEP was viewed as a restoration of capitalism or when Stalin's policy of industrialization and "socialism in one country" was erroneously regarded as a Russian species of isolationism. The 1936 Constitution was misunderstood by some as the harbinger of a new democracy. The military alliance of World War II was at the time mistakenly viewed by many as heralding a new era of international cooperation between the Soviet Union and the Western democracies. The impact of the various reforms undertaken by the post-Stalin regimes was frequently exaggerated. While each of these events was significant, the tendency was to anticipate consequences that did not ensue.

If the record of Soviet development is strewn with inaccurate predictions and dubious assumptions, such failures have been due principally to an apparent inability to understand the basic nature of the Soviet system. Although the system is subject to change, such change is limited by the system's parameters. However, if we are to understand the prospects for change, it is necessary to define the characteristics of the Soviet polity. This can be done most readily by examining a number of models. Such a comparison of models also provides an overview of the Soviet polity and both summarizes and categorizes our knowledge of the system.

A model is an effort to represent reality or important aspects of reality even though the complexity of reality cannot be captured and made static. Each model has a logic of its own, and each simplifies to a degree in emphasizing a particular facet or set of traits that characterizes the system. Each model is based on a particular interpretation of the system and provides a different insight into the nature of the Soviet polity, but each must exclude certain variables while emphasizing others. Models facilitate inquiry and understanding, help to clarify controlling assumptions and hypotheses, and aid in the identification of traits. In addition to aiding cognition, models help to measure change in a system and aid in the development of expectations regarding the probable outcomes of its political process.

In this chapter, six different systemic models are examined: the totalitarian, the authoritarian, the bureaucratic, the oligarchic, the modernization, and the imperial. Each of these models raises fundamental questions. Each, taken alone, tends to project a single line of development, even though development usually proceeds on a number of planes and results from the interaction of many factors. No single model can be a faithful reproduction of an entire polity, because no model fits the data completely and precisely.

It is preferable to have more rather than fewer models because there is always the likelihood that preoccupation with a single model will distort one's perception of the system under investigation. Observers who concentrate upon a particular model, therefore, tend to replicate the error of the Marxist-Leninists in projecting a single line of development and adopting a deterministic approach. The validity and relevance of a particular model may vary over time, and no single model provides *the* key to an understanding of the Soviet political system in its entirety. Indeed, models are most useful when they are juxtaposed and compared. Together they provide a multidimensional image or series of images that depict the Soviet polity with greater accuracy.

SIX MODELS

The Totalitarian Model

The totalitarian model of the Soviet polity derives from the fact that the Soviet Union emerged both as an original species of totalitarian dictatorship and as the quasi-prototype of the Italian Fascist regime of Mussolini and of Hitler's National Socialist movement. Lenin, as the embodiment of the first great revolution of the twentieth century and as organizer of a "party of a special type" and master propagandist, provided a model for the fascist and Nazi dictators. Totalitarian regimes constitute a special type of polity because of certain characteristics. The term "totalitarian" is derived from the desire of such regimes to bring under their control the totality of human existence and to equate the polity with the totality of society. Such a regime endeavors to claim as much of the whole person as it can. It seeks to maximize and monopolize political power for the sole ruling "party" while politicizing as many sectors of social, economic, and cultural activity as possible. In addition to claiming total political power, it must centralize the exercise of power so that it remains dictatorial. For, if there is any significant devolution of such power, it quickly ceases to be dictatorial.

The totalitarian model possesses at least *ten* unique but related characteristics apart from the general definition discussed above.[1] These may be summarized as follows:

1. A mass "party" or movement—which remains a small minority of the population despite its numerically large membership—provides the principal means by which totalitarian rulers impose their will upon society and provide purposeful leadership. The "party" provides the means for recruiting persons into the political elite and has specialized courses and schools to train its members. It takes over the state, transforming the latter into its own instrument, usurping its sovereignty, and employing its authority in an arbitrary manner. The state is reduced to the role of fulfilling decisions adopted by the movement or in the latter's name. Thus the totalitarian movement extends beyond the state. The "party" renews itself and develops a following that has a stake in the system's perpetuation.

2. An ideology provides an essential legitimizing and rationalizing device that gives the regime a quasi-intellectual basis. It enables totalitarian rulers to justify the most repressive measures in the name of professed millenarian goals that include establishment of a totally new social order and the remaking of humanity.[2] The ideology rejects previous sociopolitical forms and values, and the rulers endeavor to predict and to make the future by appealing to "historical necessity" and "destiny" and offering a total solution to human problems. The doctrine's tenets are propagated through the mass media, educational institutions, and the arts.

3. The totalitarian system also endeavors to justify itself and its methods in terms of ambitious undertakings, huge monuments, grandiose construction projects, and military power. It seeks to mobilize the population and exact sacrifices in the name of a revolutionary cause that claims moral justification on the basis of huge investments and concrete achievements, such as the construction of dams, canals and steel mills, space exploration, expansionism, and its ability to coerce. It often acts arbitrarily, recognizing no legal limitations on its rule.

4. Organizations other than the "party" are controlled by the totalitarian movement, for the latter refuses to share power. No strictly voluntary or private organizations are permitted to function, because the movement insists upon controlling all avenues of advancement in order to make the individual dependent and more willing to serve it. It denies autonomy to the individual and to groups and persistently presses its claims. By preventing the development of a pluralistic society based on free and voluntary associations, the regime can extend itself into nearly all of society. Thus, it requires a high degree of involvement and commitment on the part of its subjects but does not permit them any choice

---

[1] All efforts to define and analyze totalitarianism owe a debt to the work of Carl J. Friedrich and Zbigniew Brzezinski, most of whose six traits of totalitarianism are incorporated into the ten characteristics presented here.

[2] For a penetrating discussion of the professed totalitarian goals of the Nazis and communists and their effect on policies, see Ihor Kamenetsky, "Totalitarianism and Utopia," *Chicago Review,* XVI, No. 4 (1964), pp. 114–159.

between parties and leaders. It is the antithesis of privacy and individualism. It eliminates the distinctions between public and private, between the social and the political.

5. The totalitarian movement retains ownership of the economy—or direct control over it—and endeavors to subordinate economic decision making to its will through total or near-total planning. It limits the amounts and kinds of property that individuals can acquire. This gives it an ability to distribute or withhold material satisfactions in ways that reinforce its political power. By being the sole or ultimate employer, the totalitarian regime is in a position to enforce conformity. The purpose of economic policy is to enhance political and military power.

6. The totalitarian system retains a monopoly on the media of mass communication (the press, radio, television, and cinema) for the purpose of attempting to impose uniformity of openly expressed opinion. It endeavors to condition, or "program," the individual to repeat stereotyped answers to prepared questions. It seeks to seal off the population from alien influences and certain kinds of news in order to prevent its being "contaminated" and permits relatively few of its subjects (and even of its officials) to travel abroad. To the extent that such measures are successful, it remains a closed society.

7. If persuasion, exhortation, and indoctrination are inadequate, the totalitarian regime possesses a security police to intimidate and, if necessary, coerce actual or potential opponents into submission. It maintains a large and costly coercive apparatus manned by specialists in the "technology of violence," whose task it is to eliminate or isolate the regime's most dangerous enemies and to break the will of lesser opponents. If necessary, it maintains concentration or forced labor camps for political opponents. The security-police apparatus and the "party" merge in the totalitarian movement.

8. While endeavoring to homogenize social and political life, totalitarian rulers also seek to atomize society in order to render helpless the individual citizen. Through intimidation they limit the ability of individuals to create informal opposition groups. Individuals are constantly reminded of their subordination to the collectivity. By employing psychological terror the rulers induce fear and endeavor to impress upon their subjects the lack of any alternative system and the futility and danger of opposition. Through networks of spies, agents, and informers who practice denunciation, the totalitarians seek to infiltrate everywhere, creating distrust and impotence among their subjects. Yet atomization of society is accompanied by the requirement of mass involvement and activism and the claim of mass support.

9. The totalitarian movement tends to thrive on tension and is preoccupied with enemies—both internal and external as well as real and imagined. It preaches vigilance and espouses a "plot theory" of history that requires it to extirpate the "evil" personified by its enemies— whether foreign or domestic. Tension is sustained by means of periodic campaigns against "counterrevolutionaries," "reactionaries," and other enemies. The overly ambitious nature of the movement's goals requires reliance upon scapegoats, who are blamed for failures.

10. To remain totalitarian the movement must retain its dynamic and

expansionist quality. It must deliver self-proclaimed successes in order to justify its claim to rule. If it becomes quiescent and loses its revolutionary vision and zeal by resting on its laurels, it may retain power and preserve its viability as a political system, but it will lose its totalitarian quality. It must retain the outward commitment and active involvement of a high percentage of its population in order to maximize the number of its active collaborators and passive supporters.

The above characteristics comprise a totalitarianism of an "ideal" type, and each of these characteristics will not be present in the same degree. It must be borne in mind that there are definite limits to totalitarianism and that it often possesses a synthetic quality that gives to its extravagant claims and pretences only the semblance of reality. Many of its goals are unrealizable, and its performance often falls short of expectations. It endeavors to control too many aspects of life and undertakes more than it can accomplish. The regime's orders are not always carried out, and it encounters resistance. It is unable to eradicate entirely the old society and the political culture that it sought to replace with a new social and political order. The totalitarian system tends to overburden its centralized decision-making apparatus, overcommits its resources, loses flexibility, and ultimately elicits apathy from many of its subjects.[3] Indeed, the full-blown totalitarian system is unlikely to perpetuate itself or outlive its founder-leader and can be regarded as a form of political aberration.

The applicability of the totalitarian model to the Soviet Union has been questioned, especially since Stalin's death. Although the model does not require that the movement be headed by a despotic charismatic leader, the dominant personalities of Stalin and Hitler made it appear that rule by one man was an essential attribute of totalitarianism. Thus the advent of rule by committee in the Soviet Union was interpreted by some observers as a sign of the erosion of its totalitarianism. Other developments that have been interpreted in a similar way are the persistence of religious belief and the growth of religious sectarianism; tourism and the failure of the regime to prevent foreign influences such as rock music and clothing styles as well as radio broadcasts from penetrating the country; the "de-Stalinization" campaign and the limited criticism at times of some of Stalin's crimes; and economic reorganization and greater reliance on the profit motive. Further evidence of the Soviet regime's inability to exercise total control is provided by the circulation of illicit literature and of typed manuscripts of works that it will not publish, restiveness among youth, the persistence of the peasant's private plot and black-market activities, and a greater tendency of courageous individuals and of oppressed groups like the Crimean Tatars, Jews, and others to protest the regime's policies. The totalitarian regime's communications monopoly is not complete insofar as the official media do not always enjoy

---

[3]See Karl W. Deutsch, "Cracks in the Monolith: Possibilities and Patterns of Disintegration in Totalitarian Systems," in Carl J. Friedrich, ed., *Totalitarianism* (Cambridge: Harvard University Press, 1954), pp. 308–333. See also Hans Buchheim, *Totalitarian Rule: Its Nature and Characteristics* (Middletown, Conn.: Wesleyan University Press, 1968), especially Chapter 7, and Karl W. Deutsch, *The Nerves of Government* (New York: Free Press, 1969), Chapter 13.

credibility, individuals tend to rely on word of mouth communication and foreign broadcasts, and rumors circulate with great rapidity. It has also become increasingly evident that the Communist Party is not monolithic (despite its claims to be such) because of factionalism, intraparty conflict, and shifting coalitions.

Yet there are certain characteristics and policies of the Soviet regime that give to the totalitarian model a certain degree of relevance. It is revealing that prominent domestic critics of the Soviet regime, including Andrei Sakharov and others, have referred to it as totalitarian. Those who, on the basis of firsthand experience, have felt the heavy hand of Soviet repression have found the term "totalitarian" both relevant and acceptable in contrast to foreign intellectuals who question it. The fact that the system readily survived Stalin's death indicates that certain basic systemic features transcended the personal qualities of the individual dictator. If the Stalinist "cult of personality" was condemned in 1956 and in 1961 and 1987, it found a counterpart in the cult of the Communist Party that depicts itself as the sole repository of truth and wisdom. Despite relaxation of controls in certain sectors at times, the Party has refused to share power and has persisted in imposing the official ideology. The search for enemies of various kinds and the manifestation of hostility and self-proclaimed destiny have survived Stalin. The efforts to combat religious belief persist. The Party still seeks to prescribe what writers and artists may create and to impose its aesthetic standards upon the public. It insists upon its right to define "truth" and to employ censorship. It employs severe repressive measures against any manifestation of politically deviant behavior and values. There persist too many instances of what George F. Kennan has termed the "congenital untruthfulness" of the Soviet regime.

The totalitarian model has been questioned by some on the grounds that the adjective "totalitarian" has been applied to different kinds of regimes; yet it has also been argued that, despite certain differences, such regimes are "basically alike."[4] The same criticism might be employed regarding the use of such adjectives as "democratic," "constitutional," and "parliamentary" in discussing types of political systems. If we were to abandon these terms on the grounds that "pure" types do not exist in practice, we would be impoverishing our vocabulary or be compelled to search for synonyms. The specific criteria used to define the totalitarian regime need not be present in each such regime in the same degree. It is even possible to define a regime as "semitotalitarian," "near-totalitarian," or "quasi-totalitarian" because of its unwillingness to abandon the claim to total power, remaining totalitarian in intent despite increasing difficulties encountered in attempting to exercise that claim. If a regime is becoming less totalitarian, the

---

[4]See Carl J. Friedrich and Zbigniew K. Brzezinski, *Totalitarian Dictatorship and Autocracy*, rev. ed. (Cambridge: Harvard University Press, 1965), especially Chapter 2. For a discussion of the validity of the model, see Carl J. Friedrich, Michael Curtis, and Benjamin R. Barber, *Totalitarianism in Perspective: Three Views* (New York: Praeger, 1969), as well as Leonard Schapiro, *Totalitarianism* (New York: Praeger, 1972). Roy D. Laird, in *The Soviet Paradigm* (New York: Free Press, 1970), proposes to substitute for totalitarianism the notion of the Soviet Union as a "monohierarchical" polity based on an all-encompassing bureaucracy dominated by the CPSU, which controls advancement by cooptation from above, rules by claiming to be the repository of all truth, and severely restricts the scope of privacy and of private activity in society.

model is still useful because it can provide a standard against which to evaluate change.

Critics of the totalitarian model have argued that it is too value-laden and that the term was used by some in a pejorative sense during the cold war. In fact the term "totalitarian" was applied by various scholars in the 1930s to the regimes headed by Stalin, Mussolini, and Hitler. Soviet totalitarianism under Stalin from 1935 to 1953 was as full-blown a species as one could find, while the Soviet system under Khrushchev and Brezhnev became less totalitarian. Certainly Stalinism and its legacy cannot be understood fully without reference to the model. It also has relevance for Nazi Germany, China under Mao Zedong, Albania under Enver Hoxha, and the Khmer Rouge regime in Kampuchea (1975–1979) under Pol Pot.

It has also been argued that a quasi "totalitarianism by consent" is possible with tyrannical majorities or even pluralities imposing coercive and highly restrictive legislation and publicly pronounced moral judgments on a population without the use of terror. The distinctions between public and private, compulsory and voluntary, collective and individual become increasingly blurred in such a society. The totalitarian model is discomforting, especially to those who are convinced that greatly enhanced state authority is more likely to be used for beneficent purposes than for creating a society that is overshadowed by the heavy hand of government. Even if Soviet totalitarianism should become purely vestigial, the model has value beyond the study of a particular system by serving as a reminder of the consequences of excessive statism.

The Authoritarian Model

A variety of dictatorships can be subsumed under the broad category provided by this model, yet each stands apart from the totalitarian dictatorship. The authoritarian regimes have been far more numerous than the totalitarian variety. The authoritarian model has been applied to Spain under Franco, to Turkey under Ataturk, to Portugal under the Salazar-Caetano dictatorships, and to a variety of tutelary and military regimes in developing countries.

The authoritarian regime includes conservative dictatorships and the single-party nationalist revolutionary post-colonial regimes in Asia and Africa, some of which have sought to effect radical social and economic transformations. It can be autocratic—with a single dictator, oligarchic, or based on a military *junta*. If such a regime is based principally on the dictator's control of the police in the absence of a ruling party, it is most aptly called a "police state" in a very literal sense. Authoritarian systems can range from the relatively benign to the brutal, but all seek to enhance state authority.

In the authoritarian regime, state authority is not effectively checked through institutions that exercise countervailing political power, but it frequently accepts self-limitation. The authoritarian dictatorship differs from the totalitarian species in numerous ways. It is repressive rule, but it is not total and permits a modicum of social pluralism. Although the authoritarian regime usually operates under a one-party system, the ruling party sets limits to its role, pursuing reasonable or even modest goals and remaining within the framework of the nation-state. It does not ordinarily suffer from delusions of grandeur or seek to remake humanity and all of society. It does not regard itself as the embodiment of the will of history and as a model for other countries. The authoritarian regime may have some form of ideology, but it is usually vague and does not play a vital role. If there is no ruling party, the regime may be based on the police, the army, or the bureaucracy.

An authoritarian regime does not endeavor to mobilize the entire population and penetrate all segments of society. A degree of pluralism is permitted, with some de facto subsystem autonomy for churches, trade unions, business corporations, and cultural bodies so long as they do not become directly involved in political matters. The press is controlled but can remain in private hands subject to self-censorship and the risk of the publisher's losing the license to operate. The authoritarian regime may or may not operate a command economy (or can have a quasi-command economy) but usually permits a variety of entrepreneurship, including private ownership and state-operated enterprises. It does not forbid private educational institutions. The authoritarian regime seeks to restrict freedom in the name of the national good but does not abolish it entirely. It does not rely extensively on indoctrination, for it is not committed to total revolutionary goals and to an ideology that attempts to explain the cosmos. Although authoritarian rulers can exercise power arbitrarily, they have been known to tolerate opposition in certain circumstances.

Authoritarian regimes have been far more numerous than the totalitarian species of dictatorship, which has been limited to such countries as Germany, the Soviet Union, China, and Albania. It is possible that a communist regime need not be totalitarian, as has been demonstrated by the experience of some of the East European countries. Thus, a regime that does not collectivize agriculture or actively persecute religion but does permit limited private entrepreneurship and a modest degree of freedom of expression qualifies more as an authoritarian than as a totalitarian polity. The authoritarian model was applicable to the Soviet Union during the NEP period of the 1920s.

Numerous developments since Stalin's death point to a post-totalitarian system that falls somewhat short of being genuinely authoritarian. In order to become authoritarian, the Soviet polity would have to deemphasize ideology and permit a greater degree of pluralism and freedom of association, greater latitude to religious bodies, religious instruction to children, less press censorship, private ownership of at least some of the means of production, importation of more foreign literature, greater artistic freedom, and greater freedom to emigrate. Yet the long pre-Soviet experience of Russians with authoritarian rule would suggest that the authoritarian model is likely to be relevant for the study of the Soviet polity.

The Bureaucratic Model

In this model the Soviet regime is viewed as a "bureaucracy writ large," sharing certain traits with such large bureaucratic organizations as the military, the modern giant corporation with its many subsidiaries, and the governmental agencies of the so-called democratic welfare-state.[5] Like any bureaucracy, that of the Soviet Union is based on specialization of functions, expertise, hierarchy, and career service. The Soviet bureaucracy can be regarded as one of a species, all members of which suffer from a pathology. However, in the case of the Soviet Union, the pathological aspects are more extensive, and their consequences more evident. This is due to the fact that the scope of Soviet bureaucracy is unusually broad, since all Soviet administration is public administration; it is also attributable to the general lack of extraadministrative restraints imposed on Soviet officialdom. The self-perpetuating nature of Communist Party rule makes the bureaucracy dependent upon the Party's leadership, but it also often permits the bureaucrat to abuse power at the expense of the citizen.

Efforts to liken the Soviet bureaucracy to a modern giant corporation raise as many questions as they endeavor to answer. It has been suggested that the CPSU rank-and-file membership plays the role of stockholder—albeit in a more active capacity than that of shareholders of a capitalist corporation—and that the Central Committee, Politburo, and Secretariat together serve as a "board of directors," while the role of "corporate management" is fulfilled by the Soviet government (the Council of Ministers).[6] Although such analogies do serve to stimulate efforts at more precise role definition, they neglect certain differences between the Soviet bureaucracy and the corporation. Generally speaking, the corporation's board of directors is less influential than management, although the board can remove the managers should the corporation's condition require such action. A corporation's stockholders, should they become sufficiently aroused, can change the board of directors, while the Soviet counterpart in the analogy is a self-perpetuating "board" that is not removed at a Party Congress ("stockholders' meeting") but undergoes change as a result of internal power struggles and personnel shakeups. The ethos of the Soviet "corporation" differs from that of the Western economic corporation; there is a basic difference between the Soviet political corporation and an American sutomobile or manufacturing concern both in ideology and in the objectives pursued by each.

The Soviet "corporate system" is unique in another respect. There are a number of bureaucracies in the Soviet Union: Communist Party, governmental, economic, military, security police, and the like. In place of a single unified bureaucracy there are parallel and, at times, competing and conflicting bureaucracies. Thus, the military intelligence (GRU) and the intelligence apparatus of the secret police (KGB) compete with each other. However, the dominant role of the CPSU bureaucracy and its leadership tends to relegate the other bureaucracies to the status of subsidiary "corporations" whose autonomy is usually tentative and conditional. For all responsible Soviet bureaucrats are Communist Party

[5]This model has been expounded in Alfred G. Meyer, *The Soviet Political System: An Interpretation* (New York: Random House, 1965), Chapter 8.

[6]*Ibid.*, pp. 112–115, 134, 198, pp. 467–468. Also see Alfred G. Meyer, "USSR, Incorporated," *Slavic Review,* XX, No. 3 (October 1961), pp. 369–376, as well as the article by Zbigniew Brzezinski on "The Nature of the Soviet System," pp. 351–368, which applies the totalitarian model, and the commentary of Robert C. Tucker, reprinted in Donald W. Treadgold, ed., *The Development of the USSR: An Exchange of Views* (Seattle: University of Washington Press, 1964).

members and subject to Party discipline. Nor can Soviet bureaucrats readily "sell out" within the system and transfer loyalties and services to a competing corporate bureaucracy, as Western counterparts can. Although personnel transfers occur, they are usually under the supervision of the CPSU apparatus and in accordance with the nomenklatura system. Yet the Soviet governmental and economic bureaucracies have been known to obstruct Party directives. The Politburo and Central Committee can adopt resolutions and issue directives, but the way in which they will be fulfilled depends on local soviet (governmental) officials.

Despite such dissimilarities, there is utility in the bureaucratic model of Soviet political reality. The model serves to challenge the image of the Soviet system as a smoothly functioning monolith.[7] Like others of its species, the Soviet bureaucracy is obsessed with organizational matters and, because of the many demands made upon it, has experienced various reorganizations. Although it is based on rules and regulations (the criteria of bureaucracy known as precision and objectivity), these can and do become ends in themselves and cease to be means for the fulfillment of organizational objectives. When rules must be evaded or violated in order to achieve the desired results, this has been tolerated by the Communist Party. If such practices do not produce the desired results, however, the responsible official is vulnerable to removal or a worse fate.

The frequent imposition of unreasonable goals and the periodic harassment of subordinates have necessitated their adopting surreptitious practices, especially in reporting on inventories, productive capacity, and actual production. Despite the preoccupation with formal organization, Soviet bureaucracy has fostered informal organization in order to cope with its tasks and to maintain necessary communication channels apart from the official lines. Yet it has also fostered evasion of responsibility as well as resistance to innovation and the stifling of initiative, as established structures have sought to preserve their prerogatives and pursue settled routines. Soviet bureaucracy has not escaped conflict; this has taken the form of conflict within and between organizations as well as between staff and line organizations and the center and the locale (or headquarters and the field). The Soviet principle of "dual subordination" means that many administrative organizations are responsible to the executive of the soviet in whose jurisdiction they function as well as to superior bodies in the chain of command; this results in a certain degree of confusion in Soviet administration.

The pathology of Soviet bureaucracy goes beyond the usual inflexibility (in applying rules), lack of imagination, the application of old solutions to new problems, self-perpetuation (an organization continues to exist when the need for it no longer exists), and proliferation. It has prompted indecision apart from the lethargy, inertia, indifference, and delay from which all bureaucracies suffer. Indeed, it has been noted by foreign observers having experience in dealing with Soviet officials that it is difficult to find anyone with (sufficient) authority in what is said to be an authoritarian system. The typical Soviet official seeks to avoid

---

[7]The nature of the Soviet economic bureaucracy is discussed in John A. Armstrong, "Sources of Administrative Behavior: Some Soviet and Western European Comparisons," *American Political Science Review,* LIX, No. 3 (September 1965), pp. 643–655.

responsibility (or fears assuming it) and usually prefers to refer a matter to a higher level. This phenomenon is known as *perestrakhovka* (over-insuring)— making certain that your superior bears responsibility for the decision. It leads to innumerable delays, and it also compounds the problem of the accountability of officials.

The bureaucratic model is useful insofar as it directs attention to the relationship between the various bureaucratic structures and the form that each is assuming in its development. It is important, moreover, to observe whether or not the Soviet bureaucratic behemoth will continue to attempt to influence all human activity and to equate itself with society. Will the Party bureaucracy grant greater autonomy to its subsidiary bureaucracies, creating a kind of political holding company of highly autonomous units, or will it retain a tight control? Will segments of the non-Party bureaucracy continue to serve as objects of criticism, performing the function of a lightning rod by directing the criticism away from the Communist Party apparatus and confining it to the *implementation* of policies, while leaving the Party's policies immune? While the various bureaucracies perform many vital functions and the regime relies heavily on specialists of various kinds, does this necessarily render the Party bureaucracy dependent? Will the Party retain the ability and the will to create new bureaucratic organizations that will compete with and undercut those on whom it may become too dependent? Will the Party bureaucracy itself become subject to checks of the kind that it has imposed on non-Party bodies? The usefulness of the bureaucratic model is that it promotes greater awareness of such questions.

The Oligarchic Model

Although "oligarchy" is a term of Greek origin and represents a form of classical political experience discussed by Aristotle in his *Politics,* it is a concept rarely employed by contemporary social scientists, who concern themselves with political elites. In its Greek meaning, "oligarchy" is government by the few, who are usually wealthy, rule in their own interests, and form a plutocracy; oligarchy was regarded by Aristotle as a corruption of aristocracy (government by the best). In the twentieth century the concept of oligarchy received attention in the work of Roberto Michels dealing with political parties. Writing in 1911, Michels viewed all larger organizations as oligarchies "based upon the competence of the few" and having a professional leadership and a full-time staff of paid bureaucrats because of the sheer size of such organizations. Although Michels developed his so-called iron law of oligarchy prior to the emergence of Communist parties as we know them, he applied it to democratic and socialist parties and even to anarchist organizations. Thus for Michels, all organizations tend to become oligarchic in practice—even those that profess democratic values. As the size of the party and its apparatus increases, it suffers loss of purpose and dynamism, and the organization becomes an end in itself.

The concept of oligarchy is relevant in two ways to an understanding of Soviet politics. It is relevant in Michel's sense and applicable to the Communist Party of the Soviet Union, in which the rank-and-file membership has no real voice in the selection of the organization's leaders and is not even presented with a choice in an electoral contest or in the Party Congress. The concept is also relevant in a broader sense in that, whenever it has not been ruled by an individual leader such as Lenin or Stalin, the Soviet polity can be defined as a dictatorship by a committee. Even a collegial dictatorship can be dominated by a single leader, who can be a *primus inter pares* or something more.

Some of the ground rules for the Soviet version of the game of oligarchical politics as practiced in the CPSU Politburo were discussed in Chapter 5, together with types of career patterns. Of course there is much that is not known about the relationships between the individual members of the Soviet oligarchy of approximately 25 members who hold positions in the Politburo and/or Secretariat. Yet it is clear that the oligarchy is not monolithic and that cleavages do develop. Some members seek to replace or subordinate others in order to enhance their own role and status within the collegial dictatorship. Problems must be dealt with, and they become an integral part of power struggles. Improvisation, reorganization, and the search for more effective policies occur in spite of power struggles, but they also play a key role in such internal conflicts. Disagreements over specific policy issues can lead to open conflict within the ruling oligarchy, especially when accompanied by a confrontation of personal and/or group interests that can be cast in terms of what is ideologically "correct." The members of the Soviet oligarchy are not equal, and some members of the Politburo undoubtedly have greater influence than others.

The role of the chief oligarch, the General Secretary of the CPSU, is of great consequence. This official's power base in the Secretariat confers enormous advantages with its control over key personnel appointments and much vital information and with the force of precedent behind it. The ease with which Brezhnev succeeded in upstaging his fellow oligarchs in foreign affairs before becoming head of state in 1977 provides an example. In undertaking state visits abroad, receiving prominent foreign visitors, conducting summit-level negotiations personally, and even signing important treaties that should have been signed by the head of state or head of government, Brezhnev demonstrated the primacy of his Party office. There is always the potential for a chief oligarch to go beyond the role of arbiter and to arouse suspicion, assume too many responsibilities, demean colleagues, and attempt to impose rather than seek a consensus. Conversely, a chief oligarch may be selected because of relative weakness and an inability to present a threat to fellow oligarchs—in which case apparent innocuousness has even been an advantage. A lackluster chief oligarch is likely to permit the other oligarchs a high degree of freedom of action and not interfere in their separate fiefdoms. However, if the chief oligarch should arrogate too much authority or press too hard for policies that fellow oligarchs find questionable or unsound, he risks the danger of ouster.

Oligarchical rule is potentially unstable.[8] The lack of a clearly defined and

---

[8]The oligarchic model is implicit in the published studies of Myron Rush, Sidney Ploss, Robert Conquest, Carl Linden, and Robert C. Tucker, although their works reflect different interpretations of data and events.

constitutionally established line of succession and the absence of a formal order of ranking within the Politburo in accordance with offices held make for instability. Thus, oligarchy at worst can mean political crises, palace revolutions, and coups. At best, oligarchy can mean maneuvering between oligarchs for control over power bases represented by subsystem bureaucracies, and it can be slow and cumbersome. It can mean jockeying for influence over key groups within the Central Committee membership, insofar as that body is recognized as an arbitral organ to which "appeals" are taken as a last resort when all other efforts to resolve conflict within the Politburo fail. Since oligarchies tend to be based on coalitions, there is a strong likelihood that such coalitions can be temporary and reflect disparate interests but can at the same time be held together by fear of potential rivals and opposition to alternative policies.[9]

If an oligarchy manages to remain stable, it runs the risk of stagnating and becoming corrupt, as was the case under Brezhnev. His career was extended by his fellow oligarchs, who sought to extend their own careers or use the additional time to their own advantage in preparing for the succession struggle. Indeed, the oligarchy can reflect the Soviet phenomenon of *semeistvennost'* ("family relations") once its members settle into a pattern in which they tolerate each others' failures and vices.

An oligarchy is a committee and can hardly provide inspiring leadership. It tends to be irresponsible, as it is difficult to affix responsibility within any committee. In trying to avoid crises and preserve whatever equilibrium the oligarchy has, the oligarchs may be reluctant to admit newcomers. They thus tend to opt for a pattern of mutual accommodation with resultant inertia, drift, and delay in decision making. There is also the potential for the oligarchy—or at least the Politburo—to default by depending increasingly on the initiative and the informational and policy-structuring resources of the Secretariat, thus greatly enhancing the status of the General Secretary and chief oligarch.

The status and tenure of individual oligarchs can be uncertain, as is testified to by the fate of various Politburo and Secretariat members who have been quietly removed and demoted, "exiled" abroad as ambassadors, or forcibly retired. This has been done without benefit of press conferences, television interviews, or even statements of "resignation." Junior oligarchs can be especially vulnerable. The dispensability of individual oligarchs can even apply to the chief oligarch, for the oligarchy has been able to function in his absence. The late 1970s and early 1980s demonstrated how the oligarchy and the bureaucracies can enable the Soviet polity to function with a weak or debilitated chief oligarch, albeit at the price of indecision or disagreement.

It is obvious that membership in the Soviet oligarchy is not based on the acquisition or possession of wealth—a criterion that figures so prominently in the classical definition of the concept. Yet qualification for Politburo membership

---

[9]William Riker, in his *The Theory of Political Coalitions* (New Haven: Yale University Press, 1962), offers the hypothesis that all coalitions tend to be only of such a minimal size as is needed to win in order to minimize the "price" paid for allies. Riker also contends that coalitions have a tendency to overspend for allies, and this leads to weakness and the ultimate decline of the coalition.

depends upon the manifestation of other skills. The question of whether or not the Soviet oligarchs rule for corrupt and selfish purposes—as classical oligarchs presumably did—does not make the model irrelevant. To the extent that the Soviet rulers are dedicated to the pursuit of communist goals and do not enjoy an excess of material satisfactions ostentatiously displayed, it might be argued that they do not qualify as "oligarchs" because they are not ruling in their own personal interests. However, it must be borne in mind that the Soviet oligarchy as such is ruling in its *collective* self-interest and engaging in *collective* self-aggrandizement. It is a self-perpetuating oligarchy, even though individual oligarchs may come and go. Although it may reorganize itself periodically, the Soviet oligarchy does not surrender the power of the CPSU, in whose name it rules.

Yet no modern oligarchy can rule exclusively in its own interest. The Soviet oligarchy must share perquisites and satisfactions with subgroups because it requires their support if its near-total mobilization efforts are to be effective. It depends not only upon the CPSU bureaucracy but upon the governmental bureaucracy as well. While the latter is always represented in the inner ruling circle, it has not provided the Chairman of the Council of Ministers with an organizational power base that could lead to domination of the oligarchy. Thus the careers of Rykov, Molotov, Malenkov, Bulganin, Kosygin, and Tikhonov have indicated that the governmental bureaucracy has not been sufficiently homogeneous and interest-oriented to constitute a viable alternative to the Party-dominated oligarchy. Yet the possibility remains that the Soviet oligarchy may become increasingly diverse and more representative of various social strata, ethnic groups, professional and economic interests, and society generally. A key question is whether it will become more accountable to the Central Committee (as well as to the Soviet public and the Supreme Soviet) and less of a self-perpetuating body.

The Modernization Model

The concept of "modernization" implies a highly differentiated large-scale society based on industrialism and technology, literacy, a highly variegated division of labor, and increasing urbanism. It assumes a steady rate of economic growth, with rising per-capita consumption and adequate surpluses for investment. The modern society is highly stratified, characterized by social mobility as well as by physical mobility, and said to create a qualitatively different political system distinguished from traditional systems. The notion of "secularization" is also associated with modernization and is said to be synonymous with increasing rationality and an empirical and pragmatic approach to problem solving. Presumably the "modernized" polity is one that is capable of dealing with change and of adapting itself and achieving goals. It might be said to be in perpetual transformation as a result of its highly developed capacity for innovation.

Personalities are of less importance in modernized than in traditional political systems, and doctrinal considerations supposedly play a declining role in policy formulation. Attitudes are more dependent upon social class; the mass media and the educational system are important in the formulation of attitudes and beliefs. It is usually assumed that modernization, in addition to promoting the advent of more "rational" political norms, makes necessary a greater degree of popular involvement and participation in politics. Modernity is said to imply democracy and egalitarianism. The roles of public opinion and of mass persuasion are enhanced. Demands made upon the system are said to be more effectively articulated. There supposedly is a desire to achieve and to enjoy greater personal freedom and the ability to make rational choices.[10] In its long-range impact, modernization supposedly leads to the emergence of new modal personality traits and behavior patterns, which in the case of the Soviet Union would differ from those outlined in Chapter 2.

The concept of "modernization" is sufficiently broad and vague to be applicable to a number of different systems. It includes not only a variety of mature industrial societies (the United States, Great Britain, Germany, and Japan), but also countries that are still pursuing that maturity. The concept can be criticized on the grounds that it reflects a cultural bias and is derived largely from North American and West European experience. It can also be questioned whether all industrial urban societies are sufficiently alike to be subsumed under a single, all-embracing concept. To equate all forms of industrialism—to the exclusion of differences between political cultures and their distinctive structures—may not be representative of scientific sophistication. Yet such a concept—one that is supposedly applicable to a variety of systems that are said to be becoming increasingly similar—possesses a certain appeal comparable to those qualities of Marxism that have attracted some intellectuals. It reflects a belief in "progress" and the notion that humanity is moving inexorably toward a common future.

Whether or not all things are to be remade by the ubiquitous process of "modernization," it cannot be denied that the Soviet Union has been "modernized" in many respects and that the process is likely to continue. In support of this contention, one can cite the industrialism of the Soviet Union, its urbanism, its efforts to acquire a degree of affluence, its managerial bureaucracy, and its development of education and the mass media. The Soviet polity has also developed an impressive scientific establishment and has lavished resources on such scientific installations as those at Akademgorodok, the "science city" near Novosibirsk. The Soviet Union is also characterized by a substantial degree of physical and social mobility.

However, several serious reservations should be taken into account in any evaluation of the modernization model as the key to predicting the future of the Soviet polity. There is the basic question of whether many attributes of modernization may be only a veneer—especially when acquired in haste and adopted only by a part of the population. Do established institutional structures and practices that reflect attitudes and values acquired over generations readily yield to the new "superstructure" that reflects the modernized "base" of the society? Thus, the

---

[10]See Edward Shils, *Political Development in the New States* (The Hague: Mouton, 1962). The communist view of modernization in the social and political spheres is at variance with that of Western liberal proponents of the modernization model. See Vernon V. Aspaturian, "Marxism and the Meaning of Modernization" in Charles Gati, ed., *The Politics of Modernization in Eastern Europe: Testing the Soviet Model* (New York: Praeger, 1974), especially pp. 16–19.

oligarchical crises and coups of June 1957 and October 1964 and the 1982 power struggle would appear to have been anomalies in the modernized Soviet polity, which possesses the world's second largest industrial system. Yet they did occur, and the emergence of rational political norms and quasi-constitutional practices in the Soviet Union may require many years. Indeed, it might be more accurate to regard modernization as constituting part of a hybrid polity that also incorporates features of other models.

There is another disturbing aspect of the modernization model's simplicity and of the halcyon consequences that are supposed to ensue from it. The modernization model tends to rule out the possibility that neo-totalitarianism can emerge in a truly modernized society and polity. Yet the totalitarian dictators did promote technical innovation, grandiose construction projects, and modernization in addition to expending vast sums on their military establishments. Some proponents of the modernization model have endeavored to solve this problem by simply classifying Nazi Germany and Stalin's regime as "transitional" systems.[11] It is usually assumed that modernization, by definition, means a decline in authoritarianism. However, it can be questioned whether the problem of modern authoritarianism can be disposed of so neatly once and for all. There is also the fact that the instruments of science and technology—which are essential to modernization—are ideologically "neutral" and can be employed by a variety of regimes in pursuit of conflicting and mutually exclusive goals. It can be questioned whether the tools of modernization will actually produce the kind of stereotyped liberal-democratic polity envisaged by some of the model's proponents. The model may also underestimate the social pathology and the varieties of deviant behavior that follow in the wake of modernization if traditional mores are destroyed and not replaced. Modernization is an elusive concept, and there can be no certainty regarding its outcome. Modernity can assume various forms, including strange amalgams of the modern and the traditional. In addition, modernization, if carried too far, can prompt a reaction or even a fierce backlash. Ultimately, the attempt to "modernize" the "modern" (or post-modern) can breed its dialectical counterpart.

Yet what is stressed in the modernization model is the ability to adapt and to adjust the system to enable it to cope with the constant growth and rapid change that the modernizers themselves initiated. Thus, modernization is characterized by a *perpetuum mobile* of its own creation. However, ceaseless innovation can acquire a dysfunctional character unless there is a capacity for "systemic transformation" that makes it possible to satisfy changing demands made upon the system.[12] What is frequently neglected is the Soviet polity's substantial regulative capability, which has enabled it to deflect, blunt, suppress, or modify the demands made upon it by its subjects. However, if urbanization and industrial-

---

[11]It has been argued that Hitler's and Stalin's regimes were incapable of genuine modernization and adaptation to change because of their reliance upon dogma and terror. For example, see Manfred Halpern, "The Revolution of Modernization in National and International Society" in Carl J. Friedrich, ed., *Nomos VIII, Revolution,* Yearbook of the American Society for Political and Legal Philosophy (New York: Atherton Press, 1966), especially pp. 192–193, 210.

[12]*Ibid.,* pp. 211–213.

ism, in their Soviet variant, result in serious strains, mass frustration, and alienation with which the rulers cannot cope, then the system's ability to qualify as
"modern" may be questioned. Soviet modernity is distinctive in its political
controls and the suppression of pluralism and criticism of leaders, the degree of
concentration of political power, and the preoccupation with ideologically correct
policies.

The modernization model provides a rationale for two related hypotheses:
(a) the "convergence" thesis, which represents the Soviet Union as becoming
increasingly like other industrial societies and which foresees a substantial degree
of convergence between the Soviet Union and the United States; and (b) the
"technocracy" thesis, which foresees an increasingly "rational" Soviet leadership
as a result of the emergence of a new class of elite members possessing technical
training.

The convergence thesis has assumed several forms and has been based on
different kinds of data as interpreted by its various proponents. The thesis has
been advocated in differing degree by such observers as the late Pitirim Sorokin,
W. W. Rostow, Raymond Aron, and John K. Galbraith. At least a partial
convergence has been advocated by such prominent Soviet physicists as Andrei
D. Sakharov and Piotr Kapitsa.[13]

Sorokin, a Russian émigré sociologist, was one of the first advocates of
convergence—basing his thesis on the Soviet-American military alliance of World
War II—and contended that Americans and Russians shared certain important
traits and values. Thus, he seriously contended that there existed a "mutual
mental, cultural and social congeniality" between Russians and Americans allegedly based on their occupying vast continents, their ethnic diversity, and the
"essentially democratic structure of their basic sociocultural institutions."[14]
When this alleged congeniality failed to prevent the advent of the cold war
between the Soviet Union and the United States after 1945, Sorokin subsequently
sought to explain events in terms of the "stupidity" and "blindness" of Soviet and
American leaders.[15]

---

[13]Sakharov expressed his advocacy in an essay (not published in the Soviet Union) that is
critical of the Soviet regime's policies. See Andrei D. Sakharov, *Progress, Coexistence, and Intellectual
Freedom* (New York: Norton, 1968). Kapitsa endorsed Sakharov's thesis in an interview reported in
the *New York Times* of October 9, 1969.

[14]Pitirim A. Sorokin, *Russia and the United States,* 2nd ed. (London: Stevens and Sons, 1950),
pp. 4, 10–12, 34–35, 41. Sorokin's controversial work, based on highly selective data and marred by
special pleading, was first published in 1944. Sorokin was undoubtedly influenced by Stalin's reliance
upon Russian nationalism during and after World War II and by the development of a more stratified
Soviet society, with greater emphasis upon traditional values and norms as in family law, military
rank, wartime concessions to the Russian Orthodox Church, and the like. For a critique of Sorokin's
views on Soviet-American relations, see the paper by Alex Inkeles in Philip J. Allen, ed., *Pitirim A.
Sorokin in Review* (Durham, N.C.: Duke University Press, 1963), pp. 225–246, as well as Sorokin's
reply on pp. 461–469.

[15]Allen, *ibid.,* pp. 468–469. In the second edition of *Russia and the United States* (1950),
Sorokin contended that the Soviet-American conflict was attributable, not to a lack of "congeniality,"
but to the fact that in 1945 the two countries emerged as the most powerful. In a somewhat Tolstoyan
vein, he also attributed wars and international tensions to the "disintegrating sensate order" based
on "sensory, material hedonistic values" rather than on "creative love or altruism" (pp. 169 and 174).
Sorokin shifted the grounds for his thesis and insisted that lasting peace—and, by implication,

Another variant of the convergence thesis is based on the contention by John K. Galbraith and others that the Western and Soviet economies and social systems are becoming more similar. It is argued that both systems share the same technology and management requirements, if not the same ideology, and will thus supposedly become more similar in spite of ideological differences. In support of the thesis, it is contended that the nationalization (socialization) of parts of the economies of Western Europe as a result of state ownership of certain sectors, the emergence of the welfare state, and greater reliance on economic planning are moving Western economic and social systems closer to the Soviet model. One might also cite the growth of surrogate socialism in the United States with its constantly rising public expenditures designed to reduce inequality of income and provide social benefits and government-owned or subsidized housing. It is also contended that the Soviet model is changing as a result of a decline of the command economy and the rise of a "socialist market economy" that is more consumer-oriented. The granting of somewhat greater initiative to the Soviet economic firm and greater reliance on the profit criterion are also cited in support of convergence, as is the doctrine of peaceful coexistence. Sorokin went as far as to argue that "liberties and rights" were increasing in Soviet Russia (after 1953) and declining in the United States as the two systems allegedly proceeded toward "mutual convergence."[16]

It is not difficult to observe in the Soviet Union many characteristics of a "modern" society apart from industrialism, science, and technology. Such phenomena as Western dance styles and popular music and dress, alcoholism and other forms of addiction, juvenile delinquency, the weakening of the family, the numerous tensions of urban living, and the search for affluence and hedonistic pursuits are generally evident. Indeed, at least some of the proponents of convergence see the Soviet Union experiencing an *embourgeoisement,* with its attendant corpulence, conformity, and accommodation and the gradual corruption of revolutionary ideals and goals. Thus, there are many features that, viewed superficially, would tend to lend credence to the convergence thesis.

In criticism of the thesis, one can cite the hostility to it on the part of *official* Soviet spokesmen, who have insisted that the socioeconomic and political superstructure of the Soviet system differs qualitatively from that of the "nonsocialist" systems. In their view state-ownership is the essential difference—however, the owning state must not be bourgeois but communist. Thus, it is claimed that the

---

convergence—could occur only in the event of "a fundamental reintegration and transvaluation of most of the contemporary culture values" as well as "effective promulgation and inculcation among all states, nations, and social groups of a set of fundamental norms and values which shall be universally binding" (p. 201).

[16]In Philip J. Allen, ed., *op. cit.* (above, n. 14), p. 465. Sorokin's most extreme exposition of the convergence thesis is to be found in his article, "Mutual Convergence of the United States and the USSR to the Mixed Sociocultural Type," *International Journal of Comparative Sociology,* I, No. 2 (September 1960), 143–176. There he argued that detotalitarianization was inevitable once the emergencies and crises that gave birth to it had subsided. He contended—on the basis of highly selective evidence and sheer imaginative speculation—that convergence between the United States and the U.S.S.R. was rapidly occurring in such areas as science, philosophy, ethical and legal systems, education, sports and recreation, fine arts, religion, marriage and the family, the economic system, and the political system. His exposition probably ignored far more than it revealed.

"relations of production" in the Soviet Union differ from those of the mixed (private and socialist) Western economies and that there is a qualitative difference between the two systems. In evaluating the official Soviet rejection of the convergence thesis, one can question its self-serving assumption that non-Soviet workers are employed by "exploiters," while Soviet workers work "for themselves" because "their" state owns the factories and farms. If the Soviet rulers continue to combat the idea of convergence to a mixed type of system on ideological grounds, viewing it as a tool of the "monopolists," this in itself is a significant input in the total interaction of factors. Communism's adherents hold that *it*—and not some synthesis of Soviet and Western industrialism—is the epitome of "modernization." Of course, doctrinaire communists have their own version of convergence, as represented in the old slogan "All roads lead to Communism" and in the 1986 CPSU Program, which contends that socialist countries are converging.

The convergence thesis, as usually expounded in the West, reflects a form of economic determinism that regards the forces of production as the principal determinant of a political system. In sharing a similar economic base, two countries would acquire similar superstructures. Some advocates of convergence may have engaged in projection—desiring that the Soviet system become more like Western systems—on the assumption that such a development will promote coexistence and aid the cause of international cooperation and world peace. Convergence is often a matter of belief rather than of scientific evidence; it is often expounded by those who want it to occur and who confuse the desirable with the inevitable in attempting to predict the Soviet future in terms relevant only to Western experience.

The concept of convergence can be criticized on a variety of grounds.[17] It can be questioned whether science, technology, and the factory system inevitably produce a single unified type of industrial system that results in a common political system. It might be argued, instead, that science and technology are neutral instruments that have served such diverse political systems as Nazism, communism, the American system, several French republics, Japanese militarism, and the British and other parliamentary systems. One is prompted to ask why Germany, Great Britain, the United States, and Japan—possessing essentially similar industrial systems and technologies during the period between the two world wars—did not "converge" and develop similar political structures but, instead, went to war. Does shared technology really lead to a convergence of values as they affect political freedoms, individual rights, and constitutional government? The notion of convergence in its extreme form ignores every quality and condition that causes a people to stand apart. It ignores everything that is unique about a country's political system and its values.

---

[17]For a broad criticism, see Bertram D. Wolfe, "The Convergence Theory in Historical Perspective," *An Ideology in Power* (New York: Stein & Day, 1969), pp. 376–394. See also Zbigniew Brzezinski and Samuel P. Huntington, *Political Power: USA/USSR* (New York: Viking Press, 1964), as well as Leon Gouré, Foy D. Kohler, Richard Soll, and Annette Stiefbold, *Convergence of Communism and Capitalism: The Soviet View* (University of Miami, Center for Advanced International Studies, 1973). For a comparative critical treatment, see Wilbert E. Moore, *World Modernization: The Limits of Convergence* (New York: Elsevier, 1979).

The convergence thesis can also be questioned on other grounds. Even if one assumes the existence of a number of highly similar industrial systems, this in itself does not guarantee that their interests will be identical or highly similar and that there will be an absence of conflict. Similar systems—whether "converged" industrial or authoritarian—can diverge when their vital interests conflict. There is no assurance that converged or converging systems will necessarily be more compatible.

Instead of positing a simple and inevitable process of convergence, it might be more realistic to distinguish between *limited,* or *partial,* and *total* convergence and between specific areas of convergence and divergence. Thus, full convergence would presumably require the Soviet Union to abolish censorship of the news media and literature, provide for electoral contests and free elections, abandon state-sponsored propagation of atheism, permit a wide variety of free entrepreneurial activity, and restore intellectual and artistic freedom.

Although two countries may have steel mills, computers, nuclear reactors and engineering institutes, comparable levels of electric-power consumption and per-capita income and the like, one can still ask whether the presence or absence of free labor unions is not a matter of vital significance. Is it not important to determine whether both converging systems have an independent press and other free media, more than one political party, and free elections? Is it not essential to ask whether ownership of all the means of production is in state hands and the government is, in effect, the sole employer? Thus, two countries that are allegedly converging may be very similar in certain respects and significantly different in other respects. In knowledge of sociopolitical phenomena, as in all else, understanding comes as a result of the ability to recognize distinctions rather than through the formulation of simple equations.

The other hypothesis derived from the modernization model regards the Soviet Union as increasingly governed by a new class of "technocrats" consisting of persons with scientific and technological training and including the members of the managerial elite. The technocracy thesis has its origins in James Burnham's *The Managerial Revolution* (1941), in which rule by a new elite of managers was foreseen. As applied to the Soviet Union, the thesis foresees the displacement of the Party apparatus official and ideocrat by engineers, scientists, mathematicians, economic managers, and planners. Thus, rule by CPSU secretaries and *apparatchiki* is to be replaced by that of the scientific, technical, and professional intelligentsia. These persons, it is argued, as a result of their specialized training—in which criteria of scientific objectivity and rationality predominate—will bring to Soviet politics an outlook totally different from that of the old-style Party bureaucrat. It is also contended that a modern economy, in requiring large amounts of capital and careful calculation in determining how it is to be invested, promotes a rationality that will find an application in Soviet politics as well.[18]

In support of the thesis, it is contended that the Soviet regime must rely

---

[18]The technocracy thesis found expression in W. W. Rostow's *The Dynamics of Soviet Society* (New York: Norton, 1952), p. 196. For a fuller exposition, see Albert Parry, *The New Class Divided: Science and Technology versus Communism* (New York: Macmillan, 1966).

increasingly on the expertise possessed by the technical and scientific intelligentsia. It requires their services in administrative positions and as consultants; and therefore presumably their political influence can be expected to increase. Additional evidence cited in support of the thesis is the technical training of more recent Soviet leaders. Thus Khrushchev's successors—Brezhnev, Podgorny, Kosygin, Tikhonov, and Ryzhkov—were graduates of various engineering institutes. Increasingly CPSU and Soviet governmental officials have been appointed from the ranks of graduates of technical and other specialized institutes. Yet, in contrast, Andropov, Chernenko, and Gorbachev had non-engineering training.

The technocracy thesis can be criticized on the grounds that scientists, technicians, and managers—despite their grievances against CPSU bureaucrats and the Party's meddling in "their" work—do not constitute a homogeneous and cohesive group. The Party, it can be argued, will dominate so long as it can keep the technocrats divided and docile and provide them with sufficient rewards. Although the technocrats can win concessions from a Party that seeks to keep them productive but politically impotent, it can be questioned whether they can succeed entirely in taking over the CPSU. It is quite possible that many in the technical and managerial elite are satisfied to be left alone to pursue their professional specialties and may not aspire to rule the country, being satisfied with having influence in certain policy matters. Many technocrats have a rather specialized competence, and their narrow professional training may not prepare them to play the role of the generalist required of those who do aspire to rule. It can also be questioned whether the rational criteria and methods of objective inquiry emphasized in technical and scientific training necessarily carry over into the realm of political experience and practice. There is no assurance that engineers and scientists are more politically sophisticated or immune to being doctrinaire than other persons; they may be no less gullible and no more discriminating when dealing with matters that lie outside their professional expertise.

While the Party has relied heavily on the managerial and technical intelligentsia, it has also insisted that those whom it promotes to responsible political and executive positions be politically schooled. To this end, the CPSU maintains a network of special Party schools whose graduates are deemed better qualified than other people for leadership posts. So long as acceptability to the Party apparatus in charge of personnel remains an important—though not the sole—criterion for advancement, it is not likely that the technocrats will take over completely. Yet even if the Party leadership and bureaucracy are increasingly staffed with persons trained originally as engineers or managers, it can be contended that they undergo a metamorphosis of sorts when they abandon engineering or business administration—as they do fairly early in their careers—and become professional Party officials. In any society, the scientist who becomes a bureaucrat or the scholar who becomes an administrator often undergoes a change in attitudes, perspectives, and loyalties as a result of having changed roles. Professional Soviet politicians—irrespective of their background, training, and early career experiences—can reasonably be expected to preserve the system in its *basic* aspects rather than to subvert it.[19]

Thus, while it is likely that the technically skilled will hold important posts, in accordance with the technocracy thesis, it cannot be stated with certainty that a quasi-constitutional system will result. It cannot be assumed that technocrats are democrats and that civil liberties and intellectual and artistic freedom will flourish because of their dominance. Yet there is value in the modernization model to the degree that it fosters a less static view of the Soviet polity and emphasizes adaptability and the system's developmental character.

The modernization model also prompted efforts to apply the concepts of "pluralism" and "corporatism" to the study of the Soviet polity.[20] These efforts elicited considerable debate and were offered as alternatives to a (monistic) totalitarian model. "Pluralism" implies the existence of voluntary organizations that are highly autonomous, competitive, and self-directing. In its original usage in British political theory, it represented a challenge to the doctrine of state sovereignty. The effort to relate "pluralism" to Soviet politics was limited largely to the attempt to identify Soviet governmental and economic institutions that are bent on pursuing and protecting their organizational interests with a minimum of Communist Party intervention and control. Thus, "pluralism" in a restricted sense is compatible with the bureaucratic model. Critics of the "pluralist" approach point to the partocracy (the party-state), the prevalence of the nomenklatura system, the requirements of Soviet ideology, and the Party's (monistic) insistence that only recognized groups are to be permitted to function legally. The concept of "pluralism" in the Soviet context had serious limitations, as it was not really a systemic model. However, it was employed to portray what was perceived to be a neglected aspect of the Soviet political process.

"Corporatism" was also proposed as a model for the Soviet system, although the concept was central to the fascist system developed in Italy by Benito Mussolini. Corporatism is a system of state-authorized recognition of economic and social interests by means of officially designated corporate entities. These bodies ("corporations") are compulsory, nonautonomous, differentiated by function, monopolistic in representation of their respective sectors, and organized hierarchically. Through them the party-state bureaucracies promote an official consensus and obtain their cooperation in the pursuit of officially planned goals and objectives. Corporatism, like pluralism, omits certain central attributes of the Soviet polity. It is essentially a regulatory device designed to mobilize the economic and social sectors, but it could become a model for the Soviet system if Party controls and ideology were to become sufficiently diluted.

---

[19]George Fischer has argued that a Soviet system that is both "monist" and modern, rather than "pluralist," is a possible development. Such a system would reject the autonomy of subunits and groups and would be based on "public power" (not shared with private groups) and exercised by politicians ruling a highly centralized polity. See George Fischer, *The Soviet System and Modern Society* (New York: Atherton Press, 1968).

[20]For the relevant literature, see the contributions of Susan Gross Solomon, Jerry F. Hough, and Archie Brown, in *Pluralism in the Soviet Union, Essays in Honour of H. Gordon Skilling,* ed. by Susan Gross Solomon (London: Macmillan, 1983).

The Imperial Model

The adjective "imperial" elicits a variety of responses because of its association with the historical bureaucratic and autocratic empires that have existed since ancient times. The term *imperial*—which is even employed in commercial advertising in certain countries—is often used to convey a sense of opulence, splendor, substance, quality, and permanence. In political parlance "imperial" often connotes the notion of pomp, ostentation, and military might. Despite the diverse meanings and connotations of the term, it will be employed here in a highly specific sense with reference to the Soviet polity.

The model of the imperial order is relevant to an understanding of the Soviet polity for a variety of reasons. The sheer extent and size of the Soviet Union's territory and the inclusion in it of a number of non-Russian nations subjugated by the Russian Empire would alone make the imperial model relevant. It is an irrefutable historical fact that the Russian nation has battened upon other nations as a result of its vast territorial acquisitions and assimilatory policies. Geographically and culturally the USSR can be viewed not as a single country but as a group of countries comprising a multinational empire or as the world's last colonial empire. An imperial polity aspires to universality, seeking to influence and, if possible, control other countries and to enjoy deference and "greatness" as a world leader while claiming to be acting in the interests of humanity. Russian professions of universalism (both religious and secular) have been used to justify the claim to empire. Thus, it is significant that the state seal of the USSR should include a globe with hammer and sickle superimposed upon all of Eurasia, Africa, the Near East, the Arctic and Greenland, and the North Atlantic and Indian Oceans. The record of Soviet foreign policy provides much evidence in support of the imperial model.

Because size of territory and population are essential criteria, very few modern polities can be said to qualify for the imperial model. The Soviet Union is one of the few because it is the world's largest territory under a single sovereignty and the third most populous country. However, there are other essential criteria. The imperial polity is highly centralized and is ruled from a single center wielding concentrated power. Internal order and unity are imposed, and diversity is suppressed in the effort to homogenize the population. Subject peoples are regarded as incapable of governing themselves. A swollen imperial bureaucracy often acts irresponsibly and arbitrarily and ultimately becomes incompetent; its members are servile in dealing with superiors, harsh and condescending toward subordinates and the public. The dominant nationality takes full advantage of its preferred status, and the center flourishes at the expense of the dependencies and peripheries. It seeks to isolate its subjects and limits contacts with foreigners and with other cultures. Yet it may also seek to influence events in remote parts of the world and overcommit itself in foreign ventures that are pursued at the expense of domestic interests and concerns.

Although the imperial regime makes a fetish of bigness, regarding it as a virtue, the imperial polity need not be imperialistic in the sense of actively undertaking new ventures in pursuit of self-aggrandizement. It may simply be a megastate that wishes to retain its gains. However, the burdens of the imperial polity are many for its size, and the hypertrophy of its state and bureaucracy results in certain consequences. The imperial polity is costly and wasteful. Heavy taxes are imposed, and substantial military and police establishments must be maintained in order to retain conquests and great-power status and inspire fear in the population. Bigness leads to the sacrifice of quality for quantity. Corruption and venality, peculation and pilfering contribute to the growth of cynicism and moral breakdown. The imperial system conceals its defects and growing incompetence by means of secretiveness and mendacity as well as by extravagant claims, while the means for effecting them diminish. Vast resources are squandered on grandiose public monuments glorifying military exploits and imperial power in a desperate and vain attempt to claim omnipotence and immortality. Military might may combine with serious domestic problems to form an incongruous combination. The imperial polity loses credibility and acquires a reputation for hypocrisy as its actions fail to correspond with its noble words, and its universal aims and grandiose pretensions are made hollow by its practices.

Imperial systems can acquire a grotesque character that is intensified as the ruling class becomes effete, commits more serious errors, and fails to solve problems. The imperial polity is unstable because it attempts to embrace too many and too much.[21] The sheer size, diversity, and complexity of the imperial system ultimately make it unmanageable. In the end it overextends itself, and its acquisitive capabilities exceed its digestive capacities. Its unity has a synthetic quality. Imperial polities are difficult to identify with because of their vastness and heterogeneous nature; as loyalty becomes more formal, indifference and apathy grow, civic virtue declines, and the rulers are referred to as "they."

Imperial systems are vulnerable to decay and are mortal. They may disintegrate because (a) they attempt to govern too large an area from a single center and overextend themselves; (b) they fail to integrate disparate populations; or (c) the ruling element in the end suffers a failure of nerve and resultant paralysis in the face of crisis as a result of having become inflexible, corrupt, and ineffective. Yet the decline of an imperial regime may take a long time, and empires have been known to survive in debility for lengthy periods despite widespread internal decay and decomposition.

The imperial model does not find a ready reception among those observers who assume that the adjective "imperial" went out of use in World War I following the collapse of the Austro-Hungarian and Russian Empires. The model is also resisted by those who look approvingly upon any large political system and the alleged advantages of bigness and who favor centralism and the integration or even the homogenization of peoples and cultures in the name of humanistic universalism and "progress." Other critics of the imperial model regard the Soviet Union as a modernizing system not to be equated with the depravities and despotism of the corrupted historical universal empires, despite Stalin's excesses.

---

[21]The late Max Hayward characterized the USSR as "a grotesque conglomerate for which the main raison d'être is a concept of imperial defense inherited from the Tsars." Foreword to *Ferment in the Ukraine,* ed. by Michael Browne (New York: Praeger, 1971), p. xi.

Still others see the model as a threat to "eternal Russia." Those who may be overwhelmed by the outwardly impressive panoply of Soviet power and its grandiose claims cannot imagine its degeneration and, instead, view it as stable, permanent, and invincible. Yet the semblance of success may actually presage and conceal decline as the internal contradictions of empire dialectically transform success into failure. An imperial order may appear to be at the apogee of its power and grandeur when it is in actuality well into its decline.

There are weighty reasons for not discarding the imperial model.[22] Numerous large polities have suffered breakdown and dissolution in the past. The Russian Empire experienced total collapse in 1917–1919 and was resurrected as the Soviet Union only in the name of the "new legitimacy" provided by its newly adopted creed of Marxism-Leninism. Of course, if the Russian S.F.S.R. were to exercise its constitutional right and secede from the Soviet Union, the model would lose much of its relevance.[23] However, such a development is unlikely; and the Russians, by denying their subject peoples the right to national self-determination, pay the high price of subjecting themselves to a dictatorship that preserves the imperial patrimony. As the eminent historian Hugh Seton-Watson has observed:

> Under Communist rule, Russia has remained an empire. . . . The evidence shows that the Soviet leaders are afraid of anti-Russian nationalism among their own subjects. Relaxation of the dictatorship might lead to dangerous separatist movements. It would thus seem that the multinational nature of the Soviet Union is an important obstacle to the extension of liberties. The Russian citizen is in the predicament from which the citizens of other empires have suffered. By depriving Ukrainians, Letts, Tatars or other peoples of their liberty, the Russian substantially reduces his own chances of winning liberty.[24]

If all empires in the end experience hubris—the arrogance and self-deception that precedes downfall—the Soviet Union cannot be expected to remain immune to the processes of maturation, although hubris may serve to conceal debility and decay.

The price paid for empire by the Russians has far exceeded that of having to live under a repressive political order designed to preserve the imperial system

---

[22]The imperial model is evident in implicit or explicit form in the works of such scholars as Richard Pipes, Robert Conquest, the late Hugh Seton-Watson, Robert G. Wesson, Hélène Carrère d'Encausse, Alexandre Bennigsen, S. Enders Wimbush, the late Walter Kolarz, and the late Georgii Fedotov. On the historical empires see Robert G. Wesson, *The Imperial Order* (Berkeley and Los Angeles: University of California Press, 1967).

[23]The 1978 Constitution of the Russian S.F.S.R. provides for its sovereignty (Article 68) and for its "right freely to secede from the U.S.S.R." (Article 69). *Izvestiia,* April 13, 1978, p. 2.

[24]Hugh Seton-Watson, "The Evolution of Communist Dictatorship," *Modern World, Annual Review of International Relations,* VI (Düsseldorf and Vienna: Econ-Verlag, 1968), 63. Georgii Fedotov also noted that Muscovy's autocratic order was the price that Russia paid for its expansion and that the "imperial way of life" based on force was incompatible with liberty. See Georgii P. Fedotov, *Novyi grad, sbornik statei,* ed. Iu. P. Ivask (New York: izd-vo im. Chekhova, 1952), pp. 198 and 244. Aleksandr Solzhenitsyn has observed that "the aims of a great empire and the moral health of the people are incompatible" and that empire inflicts spiritual harm. *Letter to the Soviet Leaders* (New York: Harper & Row, 1974), p. 41.

and hold restive subject peoples within its grip. The existence of the Soviet imperial order has actually meant a diminution or loss of original identity by the Russians. The new orthodoxy of Marxism-Leninism has even meant partial abandonment of the ethnic name "Russian." Soviet authorities have found it necessary to employ as an adjective "fatherland" *(otechestvennyi)*—with reference, for example, to machine building, medicine, and music—in lieu of "Russian" or any other ethnic adjective and even in lieu of the adjective "soviet." Thus, Russians have been unable to acquire genuine nationhood as part of the USSR, and Russia, in a sense, has been submerged in the Union that is the new empire. Ironically, the Russian S.F.S.R. has a foreign ministry but is not even a member of the United Nations and as such has less formal international recognition than Ukraine and Belorussia, although the Union-empire has membership.

Another cost of empire has been its impact on Russian traditions if, as Aleksandr Solzhenitsyn contends, the Russian "national way of life" and the "Russian national character" are disappearing under Soviet rule and if "Russian nationhood is being destroyed without pity" by Soviet leaders who nevertheless claim to be of Russian nationality.[25] Solzhenitsyn has argued that the Soviet form of Russian is actually "a sullied and bastardized form of the Russian language."[26] If so, this is also part of the price of empire as the Russian language ceases to be the possession of Russians who cannot prevent its corruption by non-Russian users. Indeed, Russians themselves corrupt their language with neologisms, lexical barbarisms, and foreign loan-words. Ironically, Russians have been learning English in substantial numbers despite the claim that Russian was becoming an international language. Yet it can be asked whether Russian might eventually become a language like English, French, German, or Spanish—one that is not associated with nationhood or statehood and will cease to be a means of identifying nationality.

An additional price is paid for empire as the metropole and the imperial capital are subjected to inundation by subject peoples and alien elements. They lose their original character and come to represent a strange mixture of peoples and cultures and cease to be the exclusive domain of the dominant ethnic group. Russians may also cease to endear themselves as they interact with subject peoples. The fear of fragmentation of the empire engenders suspiciousness and obsession with security. It also engenders blindness as Russians fail to understand the national ideals of subject peoples. Solzhenitsyn sensed the extraordinary cost of empire when, in his essay "Repentance and Self-Limitation in the Life of Nations" (in *From under the Rubble*), he counseled his people to withdraw and engage in self-examination in an effort to find themselves and divest themselves of the heavy burdens of empire.

The Soviet polity reflects many of the characteristics of the imperial mentality. It glorifies itself and its might and claims to be the embodiment of a new order.

---

[25] Aleksandr Solzhenitsyn, *The Mortal Danger: How Misconceptions about Russia Imperil America,* 2nd edition (New York: Harper & Row, 1981), p. 28. Originally in *Foreign Affairs,* LVIII, No. 4 (Spring 1980), p. 811.

[26] *Ibid.,* p. 109. Originally in *Foreign Affairs,* LIX, No. 1 (Fall 1980), p. 199.

Its demands on its subjects for loyalty and obedience have exceeded those of most other polities. However, the principal value of the imperial model lies in its promoting a greater awareness of the concealed fissures in the Soviet polity, which may result in the system's fragmentation under appropriate conditions.

THE CHALLENGES OF CHANGE

Each of the six models discussed in the preceding section is based on a body of empirical data, and each represents a distinctive theory of the Soviet polity. Of course there is always the Procrustean danger of cutting or stretching data to fit a particular model. Yet a model need not be entirely compatible with reality in order to be of use. It is therefore useful to juxtapose models and to be confronted with more than one model, because it would be simplistic to insist that only one model has validity and that all others be discarded as irrelevant.[27] Thus, a rigid totalitarian model, taken alone, can be as misleading as a modernization model that depicts a democratic, peace-loving, humanistic, and reasonable Soviet Russia of the future. Political reality is far too complex to be understood in terms of a single theoretical model.

Each of the models is relevant, and taken together they need not be mutually exclusive. Thus, a totalitarian regime is bureaucratic and can be oligarchic as well as imperial. An oligarchic regime can be based on a bureaucracy and can be authoritarian as well as modernizing and imperial. At a given point in time, then, the Soviet polity may be defined as a hybrid or amalgam of several models.

Efforts to predict the future development of the Soviet polity are, like all predictions, conditional and depend upon the outcome of important events and fortuitous occurrences that have yet to take place. It is safe enough to predict change, but predicting the quality and extent of change is another matter. While no particular line of development, however remote or unlikely, should be excluded, it is probably safe to assume that the Soviet regime will not develop along a smooth evolutionary course free of crises.

The numerous changes that have occurred since the mid-1950s probably portend greater change. Among these changes are the greater, if not always effective, articulation of group interests, usually of an institutional rather than of an associational nature. Group interests that lack a formal organization are expressed through the limited circulation of petitions, some of which have been signed by persons of distinction. Appeals and protests have also been presented to officials by courageous individuals who seek changes in specific policies. While it is presumably safe to protest water pollution, the postal service, and the destruction of certain historical and architectural monuments, criticism of the regime's

---

[27]For a discussion of various typologies and problems of method in the study of Soviet politics, see Frederic J. Fleron, Jr., ed., *Communist Studies and the Social Sciences* (Chicago: Rand McNally, 1969), especially the papers by Fleron and by H. Gordon Skilling, T. H. Rigby, Robert S. Sharlet, Erik P. Hoffmann, and William A. Welsh. See also Zbigniew Brzezinski, ed., *Dilemmas of Change in Soviet Politics* (New York: Columbia University Press, 1969). For a somewhat controversial and revisionist view, see Stephen F. Cohen, *Rethinking the Soviet Experience: Politics and History since 1917* (New York: Oxford University Press, 1985).

policies in the sensitive areas of censorship, nationality policy, and the powers of the union republics has involved considerable personal risk and even arrest. If acts of open resistance can be dealt with by the KGB, acts of passive resistance by the many are a problem of a different order. Thus, a restive population confronts an oligarchy that desires to retain power, cope with the most acute problems, and grant only the bare minimum of concessions.

The Soviet polity can be viewed as a system that seeks to mobilize and direct human effort and material resources in pursuit of certain ends. Like any system it generates outputs in the form of decisions, priorities, programs, policies, propaganda, rewards, and deprivations. It must also reckon with inputs in the form of interests, demands, values, and expectations, while at the same time it seeks to create support for the system through the generation of more effective outputs. The effort to control or modify such inputs as increased demands is necessary if the system is not to be subjected to excessive stress. If the system is to survive, it must possess a capacity to restructure itself and to innovate.

Thus, maintenance of the system requires an increased learning and adaptive capacity on the part of the leadership. The maintenance of a Stalinist system could be based on support generated through terror, isolation, and indoctrination. However, as the environmental context of the polity changes as a result of modified outputs, the quantity and nature of the demands with which it is confronted also change. In seeking self-maintenance, a system that adopts enough new policies and reforms actually may undergo a qualitative change so that, in "maintaining" itself, it actually becomes a different system. Whether or not the Soviet polity undergoes such a qualitative change will depend ultimately upon the problem-solving abilities of its leaders.

The problems that confront the Soviet leadership are many and varied. By taking responsibility for the entire economy, it must also assume ultimate blame for failures. Antiquated retailing practices inspire little confidence. The chronic inadequacy of Soviet agriculture, the lack of adequate incentives, reliance on extensive farming rather than increased yields, the livestock shortage, and the waste of manpower all testify to the need to reevaluate the entire system. The shortage of adequate recreational facilities, quality eating establishments, and variety in housing and styles, along with the absence of the numerous other physical amenities that make life more tolerable, results in popular dissatisfaction. Yet more important than per-capita consumption levels is the quality of life. A polity that claims to have created a "new person" and that preaches a boundless optimism inevitably raises expectations that are difficult to fulfill. The persistence and growth of numerous social ills testifies to the regime's inability to mobilize the population fully.

The system also faces problems of a political nature. Apathy and alienation have grown as a result of the tiresome nature of political indoctrination, the irrelevance of much of the rhetoric for solving the country's problems, and the prying into matters of a personal nature. Ideological incantations are of little help. Many Soviet citizens seek *pokoi*—to be left alone—and desire to withdraw by cultivating personal interests, enjoying leisure, and acquiring material possessions. An excessively bureaucratized youth movement elicits waning enthusiasm at best and utter indifference at worst. The attempts to muzzle critics and domestic opponents prompted the late writer Anatolii Kuznetsov to despair: "My God, to what has the unfortunate country come if even the elementary demand 'Observe the Constitution' or 'Do not imprison innocent persons in the camps' is the height of political struggle, courage and heroism?"[28] However, in the long run the failure to observe constitutional norms can only result in a loss of confidence.

Yet the problem of establishing and observing meaningful norms also plagues the Soviet ruling elite itself. It is undoubtedly an improvement to have the members of the elite cease executing each other for political errors and ideological deviations, but the price exacted from the defeated is humiliating silence, in return for which they receive a pension or demotion. However, so long as basic procedures and relationships within the Soviet inner ruling circle remain vague and unstructured, there is the possibility of intrigue and new political crises and instability. The Soviet polity has no clearly defined and undisputed chief executive, and the relationship between the CPSU General Secretaryship and the Chairmanship of the Council of Ministers is not constitutionally defined. The powers of the General Secretary are not specified in the Party Statutes, and the term of office is not fixed. Nor are the powers of the Politburo and the Central Committee delineated in relationship of the Secretariat. There is no legally defined line of succession in either the Party or government leadership.

Foreign observers have identified with considerable accuracy the Soviet Union's major problems, at least since the late Stalinist period when the Harvard Project on the Soviet Social System (Refugee Interview Project) identified the principal stresses and strains within the Soviet polity at a time when the Soviet Union was closed to foreign scholars.[29] Many of its findings were confirmed in Khrushchev's efforts to reform the system. The frankness with which General Secretary M. S. Gorbachev addressed the Soviet Union's numerous unresolved problems at the Twenty-seventh Party Congress in 1986 was unusual, as it revealed the crisislike nature of the situation that he inherited from his predecessors. He subsequently acknowledged that 15 to 17 years had been "lost" in failing to address the question of "scientific-technical progress."[30] Yet Gorbachev's "restructuring" and "acceleration" could not be implemented easily or quickly and did not provide sufficiently specific formulas or blueprints. However, he did appear to recognize that everything could not be managed from Moscow, that there is need for greater public expression and criticism in dealing with problems, and that "restructuring" cannot succeed without popular commitment and broad public support.

---

[28]In a letter of September 6, 1969, addressed to the playwright Arthur Miller in his capacity as International President of the P.E.N. Reproduced in *Po Sovetskomu Soiuzu* (Radio Liberty), No. 312, October 17, 1969, pp. 1–6.

[29]See Raymond A. Bauer, Alex Inkeles, and Clyde Kluckhohn, *How the Soviet System Works* (Cambridge: Harvard University Press, 1956; 1960 reprint), as well as Alex Inkeles and Raymond A. Bauer, *The Soviet Citizen* (Cambridge: Harvard University Press, 1959; reprint ed. New York: Atheneum, 1968).

[30]"Ubezhdennost'—opora perestroiki," *Izvestiia,* February 15, 1987, p. 1.

Indeed, the factor of public support was crucial, as Gorbachev exhorted Soviet citizens to work harder and be more productive and asserted that "the people are the principal active face of restructuring."[31] He conferred with writers and addressed media representatives and heads of social-science faculties in an attempt to enlist their support. He released academician Andrei Sakharov from house arrest and exile in Gorky, in return for which the famed physicist offered his conditional and cautious support.

Gorbachev undertook to propagate the notion of "socialist democracy" in January 1987, proposing that "workers' collectives" vote for the directors of enterprises. This measure was depicted as associating workers with the responsibilities and obligations of management in an effort to commit them to higher production goals. The full development of the practice of voting for managers on the basis of some form of competition could result in the dismantling of the Party's nomenklatura system—unless all candidates had the Party's approval. Gorbachev was critical of the Party's cadres policies and demanded both the infusion of "new forces" and the replacement of leaders who were incapable of innovating and coping with new tasks and changing conditions. In a Central Committee resolution, Gorbachev succeeded in applying the "fresh forces" and "constant replenishment" principles to the Central Committee itself (as if to threaten those of its members who questioned the soundness or even the necessity of his policies) in his effort to make certain that the "process of renewal will not be interrupted."[32] Indeed, the "decisive criterion for evaluating cadres" was said to be their "relationship to restructuring" (to Gorbachev's policies).[33] Yet Gorbachev and the Central Committee also advocated greater use of "non-Party comrades" and women in "responsible posts."[34]

Gorbachev's purpose in advocating glasnost' was not to promote civil liberties or freedom of speech as understood in the Western democracies. It was made clear that glasnost' was to be "an important instrument of restructuring, an instrument of democracy."[35] It could be argued that glasnost' was also designed to intimidate and silence Gorbachev's critics and detractors in the Soviet establishment. Presumably if the hoary Bolshevik "principle" of "criticism and self-criticism" had been honored and had meaning in practice, it would not have been necessary to introduce the slogan of glasnost'. The term *glasnost'* in its most literal translation means "vocality" or "publicity," although it has been commonly translated as "openness." Gorbachev did not select the more literal and less used term *otkrytost'*, which would connote true openness as well as frankness.

---

[31]*Ibid.*

[32]"O perestroike i kadrovoi politike partii," *Izvestiia,* January 29, 1987, p. 1.

[33]*Ibid.,* p. 2.

[34]*Ibid.,* p. 1

[35]"Plenum TsK KPSS o razvitii demokratii," *Izvestiia,* February 2, 1987, p. 1. Gorbachev stated frankly in Khabarovsk that glasnost' was needed to assure fulfillment of the decisions of the Twenty-seventh Congress. *Pravda,* August 2, 1986, p. 2. Subsequently, in addressing the Central Committee, M. S. Gorbachev defined "democratism" largely in instrumental terms as providing a greater role for the governmental soviets, promoting participation, initiative, and involvement, and as a means of "overcoming . . . passivity, civic colorlessness, apathy, unselfreliant thinking." *Izvestiia,* February 19, 1988, p. 2.

Warnings were issued that democracy does not mean a lack of order, discipline, and responsibility. It would be a most remarkable change if glasnost' were to be more than a tactic or device and if it were extended to include frank and explicit reports on disagreements and debates within the Politburo or to live television coverage of Central Committee plenary sessions.

Basic problems of glasnost' have been Soviet obsession with secrecy and a reluctance to accept the information revolution effected by computerization, word processing, information retrieval, printers, and copying machines. Although Soviet leaders desire innovation and creativity, these qualities are not likely to flourish in a system that is unwilling to accept the information revolution with all of its implications. Thus, Gorbachev at the Twenty-seventh Party Congress complained of "a special form of aggression, of information imperialism, that tramples on the sovereignty, history, and culture of peoples."[36] By "information imperialism" Gorbachev meant Western radio broadcasts beamed to the Soviet Union, which he termed "psychological warfare." In broadening the over-stretched concept of "imperialism," Gorbachev was confirming the Soviet mistrust of freedom of information and their insistence that only information judged by them to be "aseptic" can be safely exchanged.

Gorbachev's Herculean efforts—though undertaken with far less than Herculean strength—invite comparison with previous reform efforts. The kinds of basic "restructuring" undertaken by Peter I and Stalin were effected by coercion and brutal methods; they also had as their purpose the enhancement of military power. Whether six-hour-long speeches by the Soviet leader and lengthy Central Committee resolutions can actually effect fundamental change can be questioned.

Gorbachev's pronouncements and his efforts at reform invite comparison with N. S. Khrushchev's efforts at system "restructuring." Both leaders quickly grasped the need for change, were able to identify problems, and sought to accomplish change rapidly with a "magic formula." However, Gorbachev is said to have conceded (in a moment of frankness in a closed meeting) that: "Generations will have to pass before we can really restructure."[37] Gorbachev was somewhat more cautious in promising benefits and constantly stressed the "complexity, difficulty and dialectical nature" of his "restructuring." Gorbachev contended that each Soviet citizen had to "restructure" himself or herself, in contrast to Khrushchev's administrative reforms and ideological bombast. Yet both leaders shared a form of "iconoclasm": Khrushchev's denunciation of Stalin and Gorbachev's criticism of the Party's failures, especially in his indictment of its cadres (personnel) policies. Gorbachev depicted the Party as having lost discipline and a sense of responsibility and as being tolerant of "all-forgivingness" *(vseproshchenie)* and "permissiveness" *(vsedozvolennost')* and of drunkenness in primary

---

[36] *Pravda,* February 26, 1986, p. 10.
[37] See the *samizdat* account (No. AS 5785) of Gorbachev's meeting with 30 Soviet writers on June 19, 1986, first published in *L'Unita,* October 7, 1986, and subsequently in *Radio Liberty Research Bulletin,* October 29, 1986, No. 44 (3405), RL 399/86 and also in *The Samizdat Bulletin,* No. 164 (December 1986), pp. 4–5.

party organizations.[38] Thus, both Khrushchev and Gorbachev offered revelations and admissions that were shattering, controversial, and de-ideologizing. Yet Khrushchev had a profound impact on the Soviet system despite the fact that he was ousted and his various administrative reforms were aborted or rescinded.

The previous editions of the present work (in 1971 and 1978) contended that the Soviet polity needed to "restructure itself." Yet the kind of fundamental reform that is needed in the Soviet Union would require the presence of a genuinely charismatic leader, a popularly perceived crisis, and a broad public consensus concerning the need for basic reform. These conditions prompt comparison with the situation in France in 1958. In that crisis General Charles de Gaulle, a truly charismatic figure, was able to name his own terms for assuming the French Presidency and to create the Fifth Republic with a strong executive and a very different constitution. A currency reform and new economic policies resulted in a dramatic rebirth of the French economy. It would appear that only comparable leadership and comparably radical solutions could resolve the Soviet Union's problems.

Efforts at reform are made necessary by change and the effort to cope with it, but they can also prompt even greater change. Reform can be fraught with uncertainty, and there is the risk that fear of excessive change will lead to the aborting of reforms. The leader advocating reforms may not be sufficiently empowered to carry them out and to overcome those entrenched forces that resist reform. If reforms are not actually aborted, there remains the possibility that they will not be consummated and will prove to be of only limited effectiveness. Promises can outpace performance. Yet if reforms are to a large extent fulfilled, there remains the potential danger that they will have raised popular expectations beyond the ability to satisfy them and thus generate new demands. There is also the danger that in an ideocratic, oligarchic, and imperial system of the Soviet type, reforms can have unanticipated consequences or side effects.

Thus, Gorbachev's advocacy of "socialist democracy," the election of managers, and electoral contests for deputies to soviets and for Party secretaries from the raion to the republic levels could lead to greater demands. His proposal was motivated by a desire to make officials more accountable for their performance as a means of correcting the failures of the Party's cadres (personnel) policies and of enforcing discipline. However, elections can be dangerous unless one can control their outcome. Similarly, glasnost'—if not accompanied by censorship limits and taboos—can generate demands that it be applied to the oligarchy itself and to public discussion of the goals of Soviet military and foreign policy, an end to the jamming of foreign radio broadcasts, and greater access to foreign publications. Yet reform at the very least might restore a system sufficiently to enable it to prolong its existence, postponing its demise. Reform can

---

[38]*Izvestiia,* January 28, 1987, p. 2. Robert G. Kaiser has contended that Gorbachev's admission of the Party's failures has meant the "collapse of the Soviet pretence" that Soviet socialism is the wave of the future, that the correlation of forces has shifted in its favor, and that Soviet ideology is confirmed by events. See Robert G. Kaiser, "The Soviet Pretence," *Foreign Affairs,* Vol. 65, No. 2 (Winter 1986–1987), pp. 236–251.

modify a system's superstructure just enough to reduce the contradictions between the political superstructure and its socioeconomic base, enabling it to
survive somewhat longer.

The profundity of Soviet internal contradictions is also reflected in the
potential for violence within the system. Terrorist bombings have occurred in the
Soviet capital. An unsuccessful attempt on Brezhnev's life occurred in the Kremlin on January 22, 1969. The minister of internal affairs of the Azerbaidjan
Republic and two of his subordinates were shot and killed in June 1978. The head
of the government of the Kirghiz Republic was murdered in December 1980.
Such violent acts could be isolated instances or portents of a new "time of
troubles."

There also lurks in the background the possibility, however remote, of a
military takeover. Although Russian tradition and experience have not favored
military takeover, the realistic observer, who seeks to recognize every significant
contingency, would not rule it out. Such a development would require certain
conditions.[39] If a direct military coup is not likely, military rule could result from
the Party's civilian leadership's defaulting and its authority becoming eroded with
the prospect of a threatened collapse. A prominent military figure could become
Party General Secretary or chairman of the Supreme Soviet's Presidium with the
latter position becoming the new focus of leadership. A Soviet marshal could
assume control as a result of a profound domestic crisis, serious foreign military
involvement, or a leadership crisis involving succession or a deadlocked power
struggle. Precedent for professional military figures' becoming communist party
leaders was provided by Poland and Ethiopia. The military could rule either
through the Party, with officers assuming key positions in the oligarchy, or
through the hierarchy of soviets and their executive committees if the Party and
its apparatus were in disarray.

Although such an outcome may appear to be unlikely, the military's key
role in the Soviet system gives it unparalleled advantages. It has served as an agent
of adult socialization, inculcating patriotism and promoting use of the Russian
language. Military power has served as a means of justifying and legitimizing the
Soviet system. Its role in maintaining internal order and Soviet dominance over
the Warsaw Pact allies, in dealing with backsliding communist regimes, and in
containing China make it the mainstay of the system. However, a military take-
over—even if undertaken to hold the empire together and preserve Russian
dominance—would probably prove to be temporary at best. A Russian-dominated military serving essentially Russian imperial interests would have difficulty
maintaining a multi-national empire in which Russians are steadily losing
ground. This would be especially difficult if the military alternative were to be
dominated by chauvinistic Russian officers.

If the Party's effectiveness has diminished, this has been due not only to its

---

[39]See Roman Kolkowicz, "Military Intervention in the Soviet Union: Scenario for Post-
Hegemonial Synthesis" in Roman Kolkowicz and Andrzej Korbonski, eds., *Soldiers, Peasants and
Bureaucrats: Civil-Military Relations in Communist and Modernizing Societies* (London and Boston:
George Allen & Unwin, 1982), pp. 109–138.

huge size but to certain structural, operational, and programmatic characteristics. At the Twenty-seventh Party Congress, then–Moscow City Party Committee first secretary Boris Yeltsin posed several painful, indeed damning, questions: "Why is it that at congress after congress we keep raising the very same problems? Why has there appeared in our Party vocabulary the patently alien word 'stagnation'? Why is it that after so many years we are unable to deracinate from our life the roots of bureaucratism, social injustice, [and] malfeasance?"[40] Yeltsin attributed these shortcomings to an inability to make objective evaluations of circumstances and to confront the "bitter truth." However, it would appear that there are deeper causes. The Party has fallen victim to its own principle of "democratic centralism," which has effectively silenced any open criticism of a policy once adopted and not yet abandoned.[41] The fear of factionalism has resulted in a refusal to acknowledge even a loyal opposition and the silencing of minority criticism. In Soviet usage, "criticism" is to be directed not at adopted policies but to the means used to carry out policies; and current Party leaders seek to avoid criticism of themselves. Thus, self-reform under a communist oligarchy is a very difficult undertaking. While oligarchs can and do disagree, the general policy adopted by the oligarchy has not been subjected to the continuing scrutiny of an institutionalized opposition or even a "devil's advocate." Gorbachev declined to conduct a public debate with those who, he claimed, were conducting an uncompromising struggle against his policies and methods.

The Russian record of reform efforts is not very reassuring. The reforms of Peter I and the expansionism of Catherine II left the Empire in a backward status in the nineteenth century. The would-be reforms of Alexander I ended in the chauvinism and reaction of Nicholas I. The reforms of Alexander II succeeded only in the short run and could not prevent military defeat at the hands of Japan and the 1905 Revolution. The reforms of 1905–1907 were largely negated by the Stolypin reaction. The imperial regime imposed prohibition of vodka in 1914 but was unable to prevent its own demise. The reform efforts of Khrushchev in the 1950s and of Kosygin in the 1960s cannot be said to have been successful. One of the most significant facts concerning the Russian Empire/USSR is that it experienced total collapse in 1917 and near collapse in 1905 and 1941. The impact of these experiences on the Soviet rulers can hardly be exaggerated.

Yet the problems of the Soviet leadership may be more profound and may actually be of an essentially moral quality. Evidence for this is to be found not only in the widespread corruption but in repeated statements by Gorbachev in which the decline in moral values is acknowledged and attributed to "social corrosion" and to "servility and eulogizing" *(ugodnichestvo i slavoslovie)*. Gorbachev conceded that the quality of Party membership had been sacrificed for quantity and that "dishonest, intrusive and self-interested" persons had acquired

---

[40]*Pravda,* February 27, 1986, p. 2.

[41]For a discussion of the impact of the concept of "democratic centralism," see Ronald Tiersky, *Ordinary Stalinism, Democratic Centralism and the Question of Communist Political Development* (Boston: George Allen & Unwin, 1985), especially Chapters 2 and 3.

the Party card for their own advantage. The "social corrosion" was described by Gorbachev as involving

> a decline in interest in public affairs, a display of skepticism and lack of spiritual- ity, a lowering of the role of moral stimuli in work. There grew strata of people, among the youth as well, for whom the purpose of life is reduced to material well-being, to gain by any means. Their cynical position, acquiring increasingly militant forms, poisoning the consciousness of those around them, begot a wave of consumerism. Indicative of the decline in social mores, there occurred an increase in drunkenness, the spread of narcotics addiction and an increase in crime.[42]

Gorbachev acknowledged that "restructuring" required "strengthening of the moral health of society." Yet it can be asked whether the vices and moral failings of Soviet society are not in some degree the consequence of philosophical materialism and Leninist moral relativism. There is something profoundly ironic about Gorbachev's and other Soviet philosophical materialists' acknowledging a spiritual void in Soviet society and employing the adjective "spiritual" *(du- khovnoe)* in referring to desired social conditions and the quality of life. It is not surprising that there persists in the Soviet Union a debate over the source of moral conduct: atheists arguing that it is a natural consequence of atheism; others seeking to attribute it to values that are cultural and even nonsecular in origin; and religious believers contending it results from articles of religious faith.

Moral decay, malaise, and degeneration inevitably raise the question of their cause. One explanation, offered by the Russian philosopher Nicolas Berdyaev, warns against the limitations of humanism:

> Its belief in the self-sufficiency of man has brought about its own crisis, which may turn out to be the final undoing of man. Dostoevsky and Nietzsche alike have shown that this crisis marks an inversion whereby humanism issues in anti-humanism.[43]

The cruelty of such an unanticipated and undesired dialectic can only prompt thought concerning how the Soviet moral and spiritual condition can be or is likely to be resolved.

The Soviet Union is a difficult country to govern. Its nuclear arsenal cannot be used to solve its internal problems, and it may be of declining effectiveness in

---

[42] *Izvestiia*, January 28, 1987, p. 2. There is added irony in the fact that the Twenty-seventh Party Congress eliminated from the Party Statutes (Article 58) the "moral code of the builder of communism" at the very time that moral decay was being acknowledged. This lofty statement, introduced by Khrushchev in 1961, was abandoned presumably because the failure to observe its demanding precepts had become so obvious as to make the code an embarrassment. For the text of the defunct code, see *Resolutions and Decisions of the CPSU*, Robert H. McNeal, general ed., Vol. 4, *The Khrushchev Years, 1953–1964*, Grey Hodnett, ed., (Toronto: University of Toronto Press, 1974), p. 279.

[43] Nicolas Berdyaev, *Dream and Reality: An Essay in Autobiography* (New York: Macmillan, 1951), p. 180. See also his *The Fate of Man in the Modern World* (Ann Arbor: University of Michigan Press, 1961), Chapter 2.

intimidating neighboring states. The Soviet leadership has not been truly responsible because it need not give a complete accounting nor have its policies fully debated at specific intervals in terms of alternative policies. It remains a self-perpetuating oligarchy. The line between the expression of dissent and "treason" has remained ill defined.

The maintenance of the Soviet polity is complicated by certain fundamental internal contradictions. The need for reform and "restructuring" conflicts with demands for restoration and nostalgic evocation of the past, when there was "order." It is a polity that attempts to satisfy the growing individual needs of its subjects while being tempted to pursue costly and chimeric foreign and domestic goals. The CPSU seeks to remain an elite vanguard while being confronted with the need to renew itself by absorbing more of the ruled and identifying with their aspirations. It seeks to co-opt groups, lest they develop outside its tutelage, but is unwilling to grant them the full recognition and standing that genuine co-optation would entail. It seeks to profess "internationalism" while employing policies and practices that have denied the equality of nations and peoples. It is torn between the need for (and the fear of) decisive and dynamic individual leadership and the recourse to a dull and faceless "collective" rule of colorless functionaries. Thus, the CPSU is caught between the desire to prevent the abuse of political power and the continuing need to base itself on the centralization of power. It is confronted with growing demands for autonomy and the inertia of its commitment of centralism.

The presence of profound contradictions within the Soviet polity imposes serious limitations upon its development. The problem-solving abilities and far-sightedness of Russian political leaders—whether tsars or their successors—have not been very impressive, and there is no assurance that the Soviet leadership will not continue to offer its subjects a patchwork of improvised policies and partial solutions. No political system can escape the ultimate consequences of its excesses and extravagance and of the quality of its leadership. The Soviet polity is no exception.

Selected Bibliography

The titles listed here for the various chapters of this book represent but a fraction of the voluminous literature on the Soviet polity now available in English. Detailed bibliographical works that can profitably be consulted include the following:

The American Bibliography of Slavic and East European Studies, published annually for the American Association for the Advancement of Slavic Studies.

Bochenski, Joseph et al., eds., *Guide to Marxist Philosophy* (Chicago: Swallow Press, 1972).

Foreign Affairs Bibliography, 1932–1972, 4 vols. (New York: Bowker, 1945, 1955, 1964, 1976).

Hammond, Thomas T., ed., *Soviet Foreign Relations and World Communism: A Selected, Annotated Bibliography of 7,000 Books in 30 Languages* (Princeton, N.J.: Princeton University Press, 1965).

Horak, Stephan M., ed., *Guide to the Study of the Soviet Nationalities: Non-Russian Peoples of the USSR* (Littleton, Colo.: Libraries Unlimited, 1982).

———, *Russia, the USSR, and Eastern Europe: A Bibliographic Guide to English Language Publications, 1964–1974* (Littleton, Colo.: Libraries Unlimited, 1978).

———, *Russia, the USSR, and Eastern Europe: A Bibliographic Guide to English Language Publications, 1975–1980* (Littleton, Colo.: Libraries Unlimited, 1982).

———, *The Soviet Union and Eastern Europe: A Bibliographic Guide to Recommended Books for Small- and Medium-Sized Libraries and School Media Centers* (Littleton, Colo.: Libraries Unlimited, 1985).

Horecky, Paul L., ed., *Russia and the Soviet Union: A Bibliographic Guide to Western-Language Publications* (Chicago: University of Chicago Press, 1965).

Kolarz, Walter, ed., *Books on Communism: A Bibliography,* 2nd ed. (New York: Oxford

University Press, 1964). The first edition (1959) was prepared by R. N. Carew Hunt and was a continuation of Philip Grierson's *Books on Soviet Russia* (1943).

Lachs, John, ed., *Marxist Philosophy: A Bibliographic Guide* (Chapel Hill: University of North Carolina Press, 1967).

Shapiro, David, ed., *A Select Bibliography of Works in English on Russian History, 1801–1917* (Oxford: Basil Blackwell, 1962).

Vigor, P. H. ed., *Books on Communism and the Communist Countries: A Selected Bibliography* (London: Ampersand, 1971).

Important collections of documents and reference sources are:

Berman, Harold J. and Quigley, John B., Jr., eds., *Basic Laws on the Structure of the Soviet State* (Cambridge: Harvard University Press, 1969).

Current Soviet Policies, 9 vols. (New York and Columbus, Ohio: 1953, 1957, 1960, 1962, 1973, 1977, 1981, 1986). Documentary records of the 19th, 20th, 21st, 22nd, 23rd, 24th, 25th, 26th, and 27th CPSU Congresses. Translated by the *Current Digest of the Soviet Press.*

Daniels, Robert V., ed., *A Documentary History of Communism* (New York: Random House, 1960; rev. ed. in 2 vols., University Press of New England, 1984).

McNeal, Robert H.; Elwood, Ralph Carter; Gregor, Richard; Hodnett, Grey; and Schwartz, Donald V., eds., *Resolutions and Decisions of the Communist Party of the Soviet Union, 1898–1981,* 5 vols. (Toronto: University of Toronto Press, 1974 and 1982).

Prominent Personalities in the USSR (Metuchen, N.J.: Scarecrow Press, 1968). Previous volumes were entitled *Who's Who in the USSR* (1962 and 1966 editions) and *Biographic Directory of the USSR* (1958).

Schulz, Heinrich et al., eds., *Who Was Who in the U.S.S.R.* (Metuchen, N.J.: Scarecrow Press, 1972). Biographical data on 5015 prominent Soviet historical personalities.

Soviet Law and Government (a quarterly published since 1962 by International Arts and Sciences Press).

Soviet Statutes and Decisions (a quarterly published since 1964 by International Arts and Sciences Press).

Triska, Jan F., ed., *Soviet Communism: Programs and Rules* (San Francisco: Intext, 1962).

Yearbook on International Communist Affairs (Stanford: The Hoover Institution), published annually beginning in 1967.

The following periodicals offer significant articles in the form of analysis or documentation of Soviet developments:

Aussenpolitik (English edition)
Bulletin of the Institute for the Study of the USSR (Munich, 1954–1971)
Canadian-American Slavic Studies/Revue Canadienne-Americaine d'etudes Slaves
Canadian Slavonic Papers/Revue Canadienne des Slavistes
Current Digest of the Soviet Press
Digest of the Soviet Ukrainian Press (*Suchasnist',* Munich, 1957–1977)
Foreign Affairs
Harriman Institute Forum (Columbia University)
Harvard Ukrainian Studies
Journal of Ukrainian Studies (University of Alberta)
Nationalities Papers

Orbis (Foreign Policy Research Institute, University of Pennsylvania)
Problems of Communism (United States Information Agency)
Religion in Communist Lands (Keston College)
Religion in Communist Dominated Areas
Review of Socialist Law (University of Leyden)
Russian Review
Samizdat Bulletin
Slavic Review (formerly *American Slavic and East European Review*)
Soviet Analyst, A Fortnightly Newsletter (London)
Soviet Economy
Soviet Nationality Survey (London)
Soviet Studies (University of Glasgow)
Soviet Union and the Middle East: A Monthly Summary and Analysis of the Soviet Press
 (Soviet and East European Research Centre, The Hebrew University, Jerusalem)
Soviet Union/Union Sovietique
Studies in Comparative Communism
Studies in Soviet Thought (Institute of East-European Studies, University of Fribourg,
 Switzerland, and the Center for East Europe, Russia, and Asia at Boston College)
Studies on the Soviet Union (Institute for the Study of the U.S.S.R., Munich 1957–1971)
Survey: A Journal of Soviet and East European Studies (London)

Among the various general histories of Imperial Russia and the Soviet Union that merit attention are those by Jesse D. Clarkson, Herbert Ellison, Michael T. Florinsky, Sidney Harcave, David MacKenzie and Michael W. Curran, Anatole Mazour, Richard Pipes, Nicholas V. Riasanovsky, Hugh Seton-Watson, Ivar Spector, B. H. Sumner, George Vernadsky, and Warren B. Walsh. The works of the Polish historians Henryk Paszkiewicz and Jan Kucharzewski and of the Ukrainian historian Mykhailo Hrushevsky, which challenge basic tenets in Russian national historiography, also merit attention.

The several books of readings on the Soviet political system vary considerably in emphasis and scope. Samuel Hendel, ed., *The Soviet Crucible,* 5th ed. (North Scituate, Mass.: Duxbury Press, 1980), includes Soviet materials and a variety of analyses and commentaries. Joseph L. Nogee, ed., *Man, State, and Society in the Soviet Union* (New York: Praeger, 1972), offers selections on political and social structures and problems. William G. Andrews, ed., *Soviet Institutions and Policies: Inside Views* (New York: Van Nostrand, 1966), consists exclusively of Soviet documents and official statements. Randolph L. Braham, ed., *Soviet Politics and Government* (New York: Knopf, 1965), juxtaposes Soviet statements with selections from the writings of various Western scholars. Harry G. Shaffer, ed., *The Soviet System in Theory and Practice,* 2nd ed. (New York: Ungar, 1984), presents Soviet and Western (Marxist and non-Marxist) views on a wide variety of issues. Richard Cornell, ed., *The Soviet Political System* (Englewood Cliffs, N.J.: Prentice-Hall, 1970), consists of selections from the writings of various Western analysts.

For accounts of daily life and conditions in the Soviet Union by foreign correspondents—though often limited by a Moscow-bound perspective—see the relevant works of Michael Binyon, Robert G. Kaiser, Kevin Klose, Elizabeth Pond, David K. Shipler, and Hedrick Smith.

Chapter 1 The USSR: A Multinational Empire

Akiner, Shirin, *Islamic Peoples of the Soviet Union* (London: Kegan Paul International, 1983).

Armstrong, John A., *Ideology, Politics, and Government in the Soviet Union: An Introduction,* 4th ed. (Lanham, Md: University Press of America, 1986).

Bennigsen, Alexandre and Wimbush, S. Enders, *Muslims of the Soviet Empire: A Guide* (Bloomington: Indiana University Press, 1986).

Black, Cyril E., ed., *The Transformation of Russian Society: Aspects of Social Change since 1861* (Cambridge: Harvard University Press, 1960).

The Cambridge Encyclopedia of Russia and the Soviet Union, ed. by Archie Brown, John Fennell, Michael Kaser, and H. T. Willetts (New York: Cambridge University Press, 1982).

Cole, J. P., *Geography of the Soviet Union* (London: Butterworths, 1984).

Daniels, Robert V., *Russia: The Roots of Confrontation* (Cambridge: Harvard University Press, 1985).

Dmytryshyn, Basil, *USSR: A Concise History* 4th ed. (New York: Scribner, 1984).

Encyclopedia of Ukraine, ed. by Volodymyr Kubijovyc, 5 vols. (Toronto: University of Toronto Press, 1984–).

Fitzsimmons, Thomas et al., *USSR: Its People, Its Society, Its Culture* (New Haven: HRAF Press, 1960; reprint, Greenwood Press, 1974).

Hosking, Geoffrey, *The First Socialist Society: A History of the Soviet Union from Within* (Cambridge: Harvard University Press, 1985).

Hunczak, Taras, ed., *Russian Imperialism: From Ivan the Great to the Revolution* (New Brunswick, N.J.: Rutgers University Press, 1974).

Kolarz, Walter, *Russia and Her Colonies* (New York: Praeger, 1953; reprint, Shoestring Press, 1967).

Lane, David, *The End of Social Inequality? Class, Status and Power under State Socialism* (London: George Allen & Unwin, 1982).

Lang, David Marshall, *A Modern History of Georgia* (New York: Praeger, 1962).

Lensen, George Alexander, ed., *Russia's Eastward Expansion* (Englewood Cliffs, N.J.: Prentice-Hall, 1964).

Matthews, Mervyn, *Class & Society in Soviet Russia* (N.Y.: Walker & Co., 1972).

———, *Privilege in the Soviet Union: A Study in the Elite Life-Styles under Communism* (London: Allen & Unwin, 1978).

Medish, Vadim, *The Soviet Union,* 3rd ed. (Englewood Cliffs, N.J.: Prentice-Hall, 1987).

Mickiewicz, Ellen, ed., *Handbook of Soviet Social Science Data* (Riverside, N.J.: Free Press, 1973).

Pelenski, Jaroslaw, *Russia and Kazan: Conquest and Imperial Ideology (1438–1560s)* (The Hague: Mouton, 1974).

Pierce, Richard A., *Russian Central Asia, 1867–1917: A Study in Colonial Rule* (Berkeley: University of California Press, 1960).

Pipes, Richard, *The Formation of the Soviet Union: Communism and Nationalism, 1917–1923,* rev. ed. (Cambridge: Harvard University Press, 1964).

Seton-Watson, Hugh, *The New Imperialism,* 2nd ed. (New York: Capricorn Books, 1971).

———, *The Decline of Imperial Russia* (London: Methuen, 1952; reprint, Westview Press, 1985).

———, *The Russian Empire, 1801–1917* (New York: Oxford University Press, 1967).

Symons, Leslie and Dewdney, J. C. et al., *The Soviet Union: A Systematic Geography* (Totowa, N.J.: Barnes & Noble, 1983).

Treadgold, Donald W., ed., *The Development of the USSR: An Exchange of Views* (Seattle: University of Washington Press, 1964).

———, *Twentieth Century Russia,* 6th ed. (Boulder, Colo.: Westview Press, 1987).

Ukraine: A Concise Encyclopaedia, ed. Volodymyr Kubijovyč, 2 vols. (Toronto: University of Toronto Press, 1963 and 1971).

Wheeler, Geoffrey, *The Modern History of Soviet Central Asia* (New York: Praeger, 1964; reprint, Greenwood Press, 1975).

Chapter 2   Soviet Political Culture and the Russian Political Tradition

Anderson, Thornton, *Russian Political Thought: An Introduction* (Ithaca, N.Y.: Cornell University Press, 1967).

Avrich, Paul, *The Russian Anarchists* (Princeton, N.J.: Princeton University Press, 1967; reprint, Greenwood Press, 1980).

Billington, James H., *The Icon and the Axe: An Interpretive History of Russian Culture* (New York: Knopf, 1966; reprint, Random House, 1970).

Brown, Archie, *Political Culture and Communist Studies* (London: Macmillan, 1984).

Cherniavsky, Michael, *Tsar and People: Studies in Russian Myths* (New Haven: Yale University Press, 1961).

Gaucher, Roland, *Opposition in the USSR, 1917–1967* (New York: Funk & Wagnalls, 1969).

Gorer, Geoffrey and Rickman, John, *The People of Great Russia: A Psychological Study* (New York: Norton, 1962).

Hingley, Ronald, *The Russian Mind* (New York: Scribner, 1977).

Kline, George L., *Religious and Anti-Religious Thought in Russia* (Chicago: University of Chicago Press, 1969).

Lampert, Evgenii, *Sons against Fathers: Studies in Russian Radicalism and Revolution* (New York: Oxford University Press, 1965).

———, *Studies in Rebellion: Belinsky, Bakunin and Herzen* (New York: Praeger, 1957).

Mead, Margaret, *Soviet Attitudes Toward Authority* (New York: McGraw-Hill, 1951; reprint, Greenwood Press, 1979).

Miller, Wright, *Russians as People* (New York: Dutton, 1961).

Pipes, Richard, ed., *The Russian Intelligentsia* (New York: Columbia University Press, 1961).

Pyziur, Eugene, *The Doctrine of Anarchism of Michael A. Bakunin* (Chicago: Regenery, 1968).

Shatz, Marshall S., *Soviet Dissent in Historical Perspective* (New York: Cambridge University Press, 1981).

Szamuely, Tibor, *The Russian Tradition* (New York: McGraw-Hill, 1975).

Utechin, S. V., *Russian Political Thought* (New York: Praeger, 1964).

Venturi, Franco, *Roots of Revolution: A History of the Populist and Socialist Movements in Nineteenth Century Russia* (New York: Knopf, 1960).

Von Laue, Theodore H., *Why Lenin? Why Stalin? A Reappraisal of the Russian Revolution, 1900–1930,* 2nd ed. (Philadelphia: Lippincott, 1971).

Walicki, Andrzej, *A History of Russian Thought from the Enlightenment to Marxism* (Stanford: Stanford University Press, 1979).

White, Stephen, *Political Culture and Soviet Politics* (London: Macmillan, 1979).

Chapter 3   The Ideological Heritage

Acton, H. B., *What Marx Really Said* (New York: Schocken Books, 1967).

Anderson, Thornton, ed., *Masters of Russian Marxism* (Englewood Cliffs, N.J.: Prentice-Hall, 1963).

Baron, Samuel H., *Plekhanov: The Father of Russian Marxism* (Stanford: Stanford University Press, 1963).

DeGeorge, Richard T., *Patterns of Soviet Thought: The Origins and Development of Dialectical and Historical Materialism* (Ann Arbor: University of Michigan Press, 1970).

———, *Soviet Ethics and Morality* (Ann Arbor: University of Michigan Press, 1969).

Drachkovitch, Milorad M., ed., *Marxist Ideology in the Contemporary World: Its Appeal and Paradoxes* (New York: Praeger, 1966).

Feuer, Lewis S., *Marx and the Intellectuals* (Garden City, N.Y.: Doubleday, 1969).

Graham, Loren, *Science and Philosophy in the Soviet Union* (New York: Knopf, 1972).

Gregor, A. James, *A Survey of Marxism* (New York: Random House, 1965).

Hammond, Thomas T., *Lenin on Trade Unions and Revolution, 1893–1917* (New York: Columbia University Press, 1957; reprint, Greenwood Press, 1974).

Hunt, R. N. Carew, *The Theory and Practice of Communism*, 5th ed. (New York: Macmillan, 1958).

Institute of Philosophy, U.S.S.R. Academy of Sciences, *The Fundamentals of Marxist-Leninist Philosophy* (Moscow: Progress Publishers, 1974).

Jaworskyj, Michael, ed., *Soviet Political Thought: An Anthology* (Baltimore: Johns Hopkins Press, 1968).

Medvedev, Zhores A., *The Rise and Fall of T. D. Lysenko* (New York: Columbia University Press, 1969).

Meyer, Alfred G. *Leninism* (Cambridge: Harvard University Press, 1957; reprint, Westview Press, 1986).

Scanlan, James P., *Marxism in the USSR: A Critical Survey of Current Soviet Thought* (Ithaca, N.Y.: Cornell University Press, 1985).

Wesson, Robert G., *Why Marxism? The Continuing Success of a Failed Theory* (New York: Basic Books, 1976).

Wetter, Gustav A., *Dialectical Materialism,* rev. ed. (New York: Praeger, 1958; reprint, Greenwood Press, 1973).

———, *Soviet Ideology* (Boulder, Colo.: Westview Press, 1985; published originally as *Soviet Ideology Today* in 1966 by Praeger).

Wolfe, Bertram D., *Marxism: One Hundred Years in the Life of a Doctrine* (New York: Dial Press, 1965; reprint, Westview Press, 1985).

Zemtsov, Ilya, *Lexicon of Soviet Political Terms* (Fairfax, Va: Hero Books, 1984).

Chapter 4   The Communist Party of the Soviet Union: Development and Organization

Armstrong, John A., *The Politics of Totalitarianism* (New York: Random House, 1961).

Balabanoff, Angelica, *Impressions of Lenin* (Ann Arbor: University of Michigan Press, 1964).

Carr, Edward Hallett, *A History of Soviet Russia: The Bolshevik Revolution, 1917–1923,* 3 vols. (New York: Macmillan, 1950, 1951, 1953); *The Interregnum, 1923–1924* (New York: Macmillan, 1954); *Socialism in One Country, 1924–1926,* 3 vols. (New York: Macmillan, 1958, 1959, 1964).

Chamberlin, William Henry, *The Russian Revolution, 1917–1921,* 2 vols. (New York: Macmillan, 1952; published originally in 1935).

Cohen, Stephen F., *Bukharin and the Bolshevik Revolution: A Political Biography, 1888–1938* (New York: Knopf, 1973; reprint, Oxford University Press, 1980).

Daniels, Robert V., *The Conscience of the Revolution* (Cambridge: Harvard University Press, 1960).

Deutscher, Isaac, *The Prophet Armed: Trotsky, 1879–1921; The Prophet Unarmed:*

Trotsky, 1921–1929; The Prophet Outcast: Trotsky, 1929–1940 (New York: Oxford University Press, 1954, 1959, 1963; reprint, 1980).

——, *Stalin: A Political Biography,* 2nd ed. (New York: Oxford University Press, 1967).

Haimson, Leopold H., *The Russian Marxists and the Origins of Bolshevism* (Cambridge: Harvard University Press, 1955).

Heer, Nancy Whittier, *Politics and History in the Soviet Union* (Cambridge: MIT Press, 1971).

Leites, Nathan, *A Study of Bolshevism* (Glencoe, Ill.: Free Press, 1953).

Pipes, Richard, ed., *Revolutionary Russia* (Cambridge: Harvard University Press, 1968).

Rabinowich, Alexander, *Prelude to Revolution: The Petrograd Bolsheviks and the July 1917 Uprising* (Bloomington, Ind.: Indiana University Press, 1968).

Randall, Francis B., *Stalin's Russia: An Historical Reconsideration* (New York: Free Press, 1965).

Reshetar, John S., Jr., *A Concise History of the Communist Party of the Soviet Union,* rev. ed. (New York: Praeger, 1964).

Rigby, Thomas H., ed., *Stalin* (Englewood Cliffs, N.J.: Prentice-Hall, 1966).

Schapiro, Leonard, *The Communist Party of the Soviet Union,* rev. ed. (New York: Random House, 1971).

——, *The Origin of the Communist Autocracy: Political Opposition in the Soviet State— First Phase, 1917–1922* (Cambridge: Harvard University Press, 1955; reprint, 1977).

——, and Reddaway, Peter, eds., *Lenin: the Man, the Theorist, the Leader* (New York: Praeger, 1967).

Smith, Edward Ellis, *The Young Stalin: The Early Years of an Elusive Revolutionary* (New York: Farrar, Straus & Giroux, 1967).

Sukhanov, N. N., *The Russian Revolution 1917: A Personal Record,* ed. Joel Carmichael (New York: Oxford University Press, 1955; reprint, Princeton University Press, 1980).

Treadgold, Donald W., *Lenin and His Rivals* (New York: Praeger, 1955; reprint, Greenwood Press, 1976).

Tucker, Robert C., *Stalin as Revolutionary, 1879–1929: A Study in History and Personality* (New York: Norton, 1973).

Tumarkin, Nina, *Lenin Lives: The Lenin Cult in Soviet Russia* (Cambridge: Harvard University Press, 1983).

Ulam, Adam B., *The Bolsheviks: The Intellectual and Political History of the Triumph of Communism in Russia* (New York: Macmillan, 1965).

——, *Stalin: The Man and His Era* (New York: Viking Press, 1973).

Williams, Robert C., *The Other Bolsheviks: Lenin and His Critics, 1904–1914* (Bloomington: Indiana University Press, 1986).

Wolfe, Bertram D., *Khrushchev and Stalin's Ghost* (New York: Praeger, 1956; reprint, Greenwood Press, 1983).

——, *Three Who Made a Revolution* (New York: Dial Press, 1948; reprint, Stein and Day, 1984).

The functioning of the CPSU is dealt with in the following works:

Avtorkhanov, Abdurakhman, *The Communist Party Apparatus* (Chicago: Henry Regnery, 1966).

Fainsod, Merle, *How Russia Is Ruled,* rev. ed. (Cambridge: Harvard University Press, 1963).

——, *Smolensk under Soviet Rule* (Cambridge: Harvard University Press, 1958).

Hill, Ronald and Frank, Peter, *The Soviet Communist Party,* 3rd ed. (Winchester, Mass.: Allen & Unwin, 1986).

Hough, Jerry and Fainsod, Merle, *How the Soviet Union Is Governed* (Cambridge: Harvard University Press, 1979).

Stewart, Philip D., *Political Power in the Soviet Union: A Study of Decision-Making in Stalingrad* (Indianapolis: Bobbs-Merrill, 1968).

Chapter 5　　The Communist Party and the Structure of Power

Bialer, Seweryn, *Stalin's Successors: Leadership, Stability and Change in the Soviet Union* (New York: Cambridge University Press, 1980).

Breslauer, George, *Khrushchev and Brezhnev as Leaders: Building Authority in Soviet Politics* (Winchester, Mass.: Allen & Unwin, 1982).

Conquest, Robert, *Power and Policy in the U.S.S.R.* (New York: St. Martin's Press, 1961).

Crankshaw, Edward, *Khrushchev: A Career* (New York: Viking Press, 1966).

Dallin, Alexander and Westin, Alan F., eds., *Politics in the Soviet Union: 7 Cases* (New York: Harcourt Brace Jovanovich, 1966).

Dornberg, John, *Brezhnev: The Masks of Power* (New York: Basic Books, 1974).

Frankland, Mark, *Khrushchev* (New York: Stein & Day, 1967).

Gehlen, Michael P., *The Communist Party of the Soviet Union: A Functional Analysis* (Bloomington, Ind.: Indiana University Press, 1969).

Harasymiw, Bohdan, *Political Elite Recruitment in the Soviet Union* (London: Macmillan Press in association with St. Antony's College, Oxford, 1984).

Juviler, Peter H. and Morton, Henry W., eds., *Soviet Policy-Making: Studies of Communism in Transition* (New York: Praeger, 1967).

Kelley, Donald R., ed., *Soviet Politics in the Brezhnev Era* (New York: Praeger, 1980).

Khrushchev, Nikita S., *Khrushchev Remembers* and *Khrushchev Remembers, The Last Testament* (Boston: Little, Brown, 1970 and 1974). Translated and edited by Strobe Talbot.

Laird, Roy D., *The Politburo: Demographic Trends, Gorbachev, and the Future* (Boulder, Colo.: Westview Press, 1986).

Linden, Carl A., *Khrushchev and the Soviet Leadership, 1957–1964* (Baltimore: Johns Hopkins Press, 1966).

———, *The Soviet Party-State: The Politics of Ideocratic Despotism* (New York: Praeger, 1983).

Lowenhardt, John, *The Soviet Politburo* (Edinburgh: Canongate, 1982).

Medvedev, Roy A. and Zhores, A., *Khrushchev: The Years in Power* (New York: Columbia University Press, 1976; reprint, Norton, 1978).

Narkiewicz, Olga A., *Soviet Leaders: From the Cult of Personality to Collective Rule* (New York: St. Martin's Press, 1986).

Nogee, Joseph L., ed., *Soviet Politics: Russia after Brezhnev* (New York: Praeger, 1985).

Pistrak, Lazar, *The Grand Tactician: Khrushchev's Rise to Power* (New York: Praeger, 1961).

Ploss, Sidney I., *Conflict and Decision-Making in Soviet Russia: A Case Study of Agricultural Policy, 1953–1963* (Princeton, N.J.: Princeton University Press, 1965).

Rigby, Thomas H., *Communist Party Membership in the U.S.S.R., 1917–1967* (Princeton, N.J.: Princeton University Press, 1968).

Rush, Myron, *The Rise of Khrushchev* (Washington, D.C.: Public Affairs Press, 1958).

Schueller, George K., *The Politburo* (Stanford: Stanford University Press, 1951; reprinted in Harold D. Lasswell and Daniel Lerner, eds., *World Revolutionary Elites* (Cambridge: M.I.T. Press, 1965).

Simmonds, George W., ed., *Soviet Leaders* (New York: Crowell, 1967).

Swearer, Howard R. and Rush, Myron, *The Politics of Succession in the USSR* (Boston: Little, Brown, 1964).

Tatu, Michel, *Power in the Kremlin: From Khrushchev to Kosygin* (New York: Viking Press, 1968).

Voslensky, Michael, *Nomenklatura: The Soviet Ruling Class* (Garden City, N.Y.: Doubleday, 1984).

Regarding the Komsomol, see:

Fisher, Ralph T., Jr., *Pattern for Soviet Youth* (New York: Columbia University Press, 1959).

Kassof, Allen, *The Soviet Youth Program: Regimentation and Rebellion* (Cambridge: Harvard University Press, 1965).

The activities of the Soviet secret police are discussed in:

Conquest, Robert, *The Great Terror: Stalin's Purges of the Thirties,* rev. ed. (New York: Macmillan, 1973).

Corson, William R. and Crowley, Robert T., *The New KGB: Engine of Soviet Power* (New York: William Morrow, 1985).

Deriabin, Peter and Gibney, Frank, *The Secret World* (Garden City, N.Y.: Doubleday, 1959; reprint, Ballantine, 1982).

Hingley, Ronald, *The Russian Secret Police: Muscovite, Imperial Russian and Soviet Political Security Operations* (New York: Simon & Schuster, 1970).

Knight, Amy W., *The KGB: Police and Politics in the Soviet Union* (Winchester, Mass.: Allen & Unwin, 1988).

Levytsky, Boris, *The Uses of Terror: The Soviet Secret Service, 1917–1970,* 3rd ed. (London: Sidgwick and Jackson, 1971).

Poretsky, Elisabeth K., *Our Own People* (Ann Arbor: University of Michigan Press, 1970).

Richelson, Jeffrey T., *Sword and Shield: The Soviet Intelligence and Security Apparatus* (Cambridge, Mass.: Ballinger Publishers, 1986).

Wolin, Simon and Slusser, Robert M., eds., *The Soviet Secret Police* (New York: Praeger, 1957; reprint, Greenwood Press, 1975).

Rositzke, Harry A., *The KGB: The Eyes of Russia* (Garden City, N.Y.: Doubleday, 1981).

Among the more important works on the Soviet Military are:

Armstrong, John A., ed., *Soviet Partisans in World War II* (Madison: University of Wisconsin Press, 1964).

Bialer, Seweryn, ed., *Stalin and His Generals: Soviet Military Memoirs of World War II* (New York: Pegasus, 1969; reprint, Westview Press, 1984).

Colton, Timothy J., *Commissars, Commanders, and Civilian Authority: The Structure of Soviet Military Politics* (Cambridge: Harvard University Press, 1979).

Erickson, John, *The Soviet High Command: A Military-Political History, 1918–1941* (New York: St. Martin's Press, 1962; reprint, Westview Press, 1984).

Garthoff, Raymond L., *Soviet Military Policy: An Historical Analysis* (New York: Praeger, 1966).

Gouré, Leon, *The Siege of Leningrad* (Stanford: Stanford University Press, 1962).

Kolkowicz, Roman, *The Soviet Military and the Communist Party* (Princeton, N.J.: Princeton University Press, 1967; reprint, Westview Press, 1985).

Penkovskiy, Oleg, *The Penkovskiy Papers* (Garden City, N.Y.: Doubleday, 1965; reprint, Ballantine, 1982).

Chapter 6   The Central Government

Carson, George Barr, Jr., *Electoral Practices in the USSR* (New York: Praeger, 1955).

Churchward, L.G., *Contemporary Soviet Government,* 2nd ed. (New York: American Elsevier Publishing Co., 1975).

Crowley, Edward L. et al., eds., *Party and Government Officials of the Soviet Union, 1917–1967* (Metuchen, N.J.: Scarecrow Press, 1969).

D'Encausse, Hélène Carrère, *Confiscated Power: How Soviet Russia Really Works* (New York: Harper & Row, 1982).

Feldbrugge, F. J. M., *The Constitutions of the USSR and the Union Republics: Analyses, Texts, Reports* (Alphen aan den Rijn, The Netherlands, and Winchester, Mass.: Sijthoff & Noordhoff International Publishers, 1979).

Gripp, Richard C., *Patterns of Soviet Politics,* rev. ed. (Homewood, Ill.: Dorsey Press, 1967).

Hazard, John N., *The Soviet System of Government,* 5th ed. (Chicago: University of Chicago Press, 1980).

Mote, Max E., *Soviet Local and Republic Elections* (Stanford: The Hoover Institution, 1965).

Schuman, Frederick L., *Government in the Soviet Union,* 2nd ed. (New York: Crowell, 1967).

Sharlet, Robert, *The New Soviet Constitution of 1977: Analysis and Text* (Brunswick, Ohio: King's Court Communications, Inc., 1978).

Towster, Julian, *Political Power in the USSR, 1917–1947* (New York: Oxford University Press, 1948; reprint, Greenwood Press, 1975).

Unger, Aryeh L., *Constitutional Development in the USSR: A Guide to the Soviet Constitutions* (New York: Pica Press, 1981).

Vanneman, Peter, *The Supreme Soviet: Politics and the Legislative Process in the Soviet Political System* (Durham, N.C.: Duke University Press, 1977).

Chapter 7   Administration: Central, Republic, and Local

Azrael, Jeremy R., *Managerial Power and Soviet Politics* (Cambridge: Harvard University Press, 1966).

Berliner, Joseph, *Factory and Manager in the USSR* (Cambridge: Harvard University Press, 1957).

Davies, Robert W., *The Development of the Soviet Budgetary System* (New York: Cambridge University Press, 1958; reprint, Greenwood Press, 1979).

Granick, David, *The Red Executive* (Garden City, N.Y.: Doubleday, 1960; reprint, Ayer Co., 1979).

Hough, Jerry F., *The Soviet Prefects: The Local Party Organs in Industrial Decision-Making* (Cambridge: Harvard University Press, 1969).

Hutchings, Raymond, *The Soviet Budget* (Albany: State University of New York Press, 1983).

Moses, Joel C., *Regional Party Leadership and Policy-Making in the U.S.S.R.* (New York: Praeger, 1974).

Skilling, H. Gordon and Griffiths, Franklyn, eds., *Interest Groups in Soviet Politics* (Princeton, N.J.: Princeton University Press, 1971).

Regarding Soviet local government, see:

Cattell, David T., *Leningrad: A Case Study of Soviet Urban Government* (New York: Praeger, 1968).

Jacobs, Everett M., ed., *Soviet Local Politics and Government* (London and Boston: Allen & Unwin, 1983).

Lewis, Carol W. and Sternheimer, Stephen, *Soviet Urban Management: With Comparison to the United States* (New York: Praeger, 1979).

Morton, Henry W. and Stuart, Robert C., eds., *The Contemporary Soviet City* (Armonk, N.Y.: M. E. Sharpe, Inc., 1984).

Savas, E. S. and Kaiser, J. A., *Moscow's City Government* (New York: Praeger, 1985).

Taubman, William, *Governing Soviet Cities: Bureaucratic Politics & Urban Development in the USSR* (New York: Praeger, 1973).

Chapter 8   The Soviet Economy and Social Services

Amann, Ronald and Cooper, Julian, eds., *Industrial Innovation in the Soviet Union* (New Haven: Yale University Press, 1982).

────── and Davies, R. W., eds., *The Technological Level of Soviet Industry* (New Haven: Yale University Press, 1977).

Berliner, Joseph S., *The Innovation Decision in Soviet Industry* (Cambridge: M.I.T. Press, 1976).

Bornstein, Morris, ed., *The Soviet Economy: Continuity and Change* (Boulder, Colo.: Westview Press, 1981).

Colton, Timothy J., *The Dilemma of Reform in the Soviet Union,* 2nd ed. (New York: Council on Foreign Relations, 1986).

Dyker, David A., *The Future of the Soviet Economic Planning System* (Armonk, N.Y.: M. E. Sharpe, Inc., 1985).

Feiwel, George R., *The Soviet Quest for Economic Efficiency: Issues, Controversies and Reforms,* 2nd ed. (New York: Praeger, 1972).

Goldman, Marshall I., *Environmental Pollution in the Soviet Union: The Spoils of Progress* (Cambridge: M.I.T. Press, 1975).

Greer, Thomas V., *Marketing in the Soviet Union* (New York: Praeger, 1973).

Gregory, Paul R. and Stuart, Robert C., *Soviet Economic Structure and Performance,* 3rd ed. (New York: Harper & Row, 1986).

Hutchings, Raymond, *Soviet Economic Development,* 2nd ed. (New York: New York University Press, 1983).

Kaser, Michael, *Soviet Economics* (New York: McGraw Hill, 1970).

Millar, James R., *The ABC's of Soviet Socialism: The Soviet Economic Experiment, 1917–1980* (Champaign-Urbana: University of Illinois Press, 1981).

Munting, Roger, *The Economic Development of the USSR* (New York: St. Martin's Press, 1982).

Newcity, Michael A., *Taxation in the Soviet Union* (New York: Praeger, 1986).

Nove, Alec, *The Soviet Economic System,* 3rd ed. (Winchester, Mass.: Allen & Unwin, 1986).

Ryavec, Karl W., *Implementation of Soviet Economic Reforms: Political, Organizational and Social Processes* (New York: Praeger, 1975).

Regarding Soviet agriculture, the following works are of special importance:

Joravsky, David, *The Lysenko Affair* (Cambridge: Harvard University Press, 1970).

Laird, Roy D. and Betty A., *Soviet Communism and Agrarian Revolution* (Baltimore: Penguin Books, 1970).

Millar, James R., ed., *The Soviet Rural Community: A Symposium* (Urbana: University of Illinois Press, 1971).

Osofsky, Stephen, *Soviet Agricultural Policy: Toward the Abolition of Collective Farms.* (New York: Praeger, 1974).

Stuart, Robert C., ed., *The Soviet Rural Economy* (Totowa, N.J.: Rowman and Allenheld, 1984).

Wädekin, Karl-Eugen, *The Private Sector in Soviet Agriculture,* translated by Keith Bush (Berkeley: University of California Press, 1973).

Regarding social services and living standards, the following are important:

Andrusz, Gregory D., *Housing and Urban Development in the U.S.S.R.* (Albany: State University of New York Press, 1985).

Field, Mark G., *Soviet Socialized Medicine: An Introduction* (New York: Free Press, 1967).

Herlemann, Horst G., ed., *The Quality of Life in the Soviet Union* (Boulder, Colo.: Westview Press, 1987).

Madison, Bernice Q., *Social Welfare in the Soviet Union* (Stanford: Stanford University Press, 1968).

Matthews, Mervyn, *Poverty in the Soviet Union: The Life-styles of the Underprivileged in Recent Years* (New York: Cambridge University Press, 1986).

McAuley, Mary, *Labor Disputes in Soviet Russia, 1957–1965* (New York: Oxford University Press, 1969).

Osborn, Robert J., *Soviet Social Policies: Welfare, Equality, and Community* (Homewood, Ill.: Dorsey Press, 1970).

Potichnyj, Peter J., *Soviet Agricultural Trade Unions, 1917–1970* (Toronto: University of Toronto Press, 1972).

Schapiro, Leonard and Goodson, Joseph, eds., *The Soviet Worker: Illusions and Realities* (New York: St. Martin's Press, 1981).

Sorenson, Jay B., *The Life and Death of Soviet Trade Unionism, 1917–1928* (New York: Atherton Press, 1969).

Chapter 9 Soviet Law and the Judiciary

Berman, Harold J., *Justice in the USSR,* rev. ed. (Cambridge: Harvard University Press, 1963).

———, ed., *Soviet Criminal Law and Procedure: The RSFSR Codes* (Cambridge: Harvard University Press, 1966).

Butler, William E., ed., *Basic Documents on the Soviet Legal System* (Dobbs Ferry, N.Y.: Oceana, 1983).

———, *Soviet Law* (London: Butterworth & Co. Publishers, 1983).

Celmina, Helene, *Women in Soviet Prisons* (New York: Paragon House, 1985).

Chalidze, Valery, *Criminal Russia: Essays on Crime in the Soviet Union* (New York: Random House, 1977).

————, *To Defend These Rights* (New York: Random House, 1974).

Feldbrugge, F. J. M., Van den Berg, G. P., and Simons, W. B., eds., *Encyclopedia of Soviet Law,* 2nd ed. (Dordrecht, The Netherlands: Martinus Nijhoff, 1985).

Gray, Whitmore, ed., *Soviet Civil Legislation* (Ann Arbor: University of Michigan School of Law, 1965).

Grzybowski, Kazimierz, *Soviet Legal Institutions: Doctrines and Social Functions* (Ann Arbor: University of Michigan Press, 1962; reprint, W. S. Hein, 1982).

Hazard, John N., *Law and Social Change in the USSR* (London: Stevens, 1953; reprint, Hyperion, 1980).

————, *Managing Change in the USSR: The Politico-Legal Role of the Soviet Jurist* (New York: Cambridge University Press, 1983).

————, *Settling Disputes in Soviet Society: The Formative Years of Legal Institutions* (New York: Columbia University Press, 1960; reprint, Octagon, 1978).

————, Butler, William E., and Maggs, Peter B., *The Soviet Legal System: Fundamental Principles and Historical Commentary,* 3rd ed. (Dobbs Ferry, N.Y.: Oceana, 1977).

———— and Butler, William E., *The Soviet Legal System: The Law in the 1980s* (Dobbs Ferry, N.Y.: Oceana, 1984).

Juviler, Peter H., *Revolutionary Law and Order: Politics and Social Change in the U.S.S.R.* (New York: The Free Press, 1976).

La Fave, Wayne R., ed., *Law in Soviet Society* (Urbana: University of Illinois Press, 1965).

Morgan, Glenn G., *Soviet Administrative Legality: The Role of the Attorney General's Office* (Stanford: Stanford University Press, 1962).

Prisoners of Conscience in the USSR: Their Treatment and Conditions: An Amnesty International Report, 2nd ed. (London: Amnesty International Publications, 1980).

Shifrin, Avraham, *The First Guide Book to Prisons and Concentration Camps in the Soviet Union,* 2nd ed. (New York: Bantam Books, 1982).

Chapter 10 Soviet Political Socialization and Its Limitations

Atkinson, Dorothy, Dallin, Alexander, and Lapidus, Gail Warshofsky, eds., *Women in Russia* (Stanford: Stanford University Press, 1977).

Bereday, George Z. F. and Pennar, Jaan, *The Politics of Soviet Education* (New York: Praeger, 1960; reprint, Greenwood, 1976).

Bronfenbrenner, Urie, with the assistance of Condry, John C., Jr., *Two Worlds of Childhood: U.S. and U.S.S.R.* (New York: Russell Sage Foundation and Basic Books, 1970).

Hollander, Gayle, *Soviet Political Indoctrination: Developments in Mass Media & Propaganda since Stalin* (New York: Praeger, 1972).

Hopkins, Mark W., *Mass Media in the Soviet Union* (New York: Pegasus, 1970).

Lapidus, Gail Warshofsky, *Women in Soviet Society: Equality, Development, and Social Change* (Berkeley: University of California Press, 1980).

Matthews, Mervyn, *Education in the Soviet Union: Policies and Institutions since Stalin* (Winchester, Mass.: Allen & Unwin, 1982).

Sorrentino, Frank M. and Curcio, Frances R., *Soviet Politics and Education* (Lanham, Md: University Press of America, 1986).

Walker, Gregory, *Soviet Book Publishing Policy* (New York: Cambridge University Press, 1978).

Among the works on Soviet nationalities and nationality policy, the following merit attention:

Allworth, Edward, ed., *Central Asia: A Century of Russian Rule* (New York: Columbia University Press, 1967).
————, *Soviet Nationality Problems* (New York: Columbia University Press, 1971).
Armstrong, John A., *Ukrainian Nationalism,* 2nd ed. (New York: Columbia University Press, 1963; reprint, Libraries Unlimited, 1980).
Azrael, Jeremy R., ed., *Soviet Nationality Policies and Practices* (New York: Praeger, 1978).
Bacon, Elizabeth E., *Central Asians under Russian Rule: A Study in Cultural Change* (Ithaca, N.Y.: Cornell University Press, 1966 and 1980).
Barghoorn, Frederick C., *Soviet Russian Nationalism* (New York: Oxford University Press, 1956; reprint, Greenwood, 1976).
Bennigsen, Alexandre and Broxup, Marie, *The Islamic Threat to the Soviet State* (New York: St. Martin's Press, 1983).
Bilinsky, Yaroslav, *The Second Soviet Republic: The Ukraine after World War II* (New Brunswick, N.J.: Rutgers University Press, 1964).
Borys, Jurij, *The Sovietization of Ukraine, 1917–1923: The Communist Doctrine and Practice of National Self-determination,* revised ed. (Edmonton, Alberta: Canadian Institute of Ukrainian Studies, 1980).
Browne, Michael, ed., *Ferment in the Ukraine: Documents by V. Chornovil, I. Kandyba, L. Lukyanenko, V. Moroz, and Others* (New York: Praeger, 1971).
Bruchis, Michael, *Nations, Nationalities, Peoples: A Study of the Nationality Policies of the Communist Party in Soviet Moldavia* (Boulder, Colo.: East European Monographs, 1984).
Caroe, Sir Olaf, *Soviet Empire, The Turks of Central Asia and Stalinism,* 2nd ed. (New York: St. Martin's Press, 1967).
Chornovil, Vyacheslav, ed. and comp., *The Chornovil Papers* (New York: McGraw-Hill, 1969).
Connor, Walker, *The National Question in Marxist-Leninist Theory and Strategy* (Princeton, N.J.: Princeton University Press, 1984).
Conquest, Robert, *The Harvest of Sorrow: Soviet Collectivization and the Terror-Famine* (New York: Oxford University Press, 1986).
————, *The Nation Killers: The Soviet Deportation of Nationalities* (London: Macmillan, 1970).
Dmytryshyn, Basil, *Moscow and the Ukraine, 1918–1953* (New York: Bookman Associates, 1956).
Dzyuba, Ivan, *Internationalism or Russification? A Study in the Soviet Nationalities Problem* (London: Weidenfeld and Nicolson, 1968).
Farmer, Kenneth C., *Ukrainian Nationalism in the Post-Stalin Era: Myth, Symbols and Ideology in Soviet Nationalities Policy* (The Hague and Boston: Martinus Nijhoff, 1980).
Fisher, Alan, *The Crimean Tatars* (Stanford: Hoover Institution Press, 1978).
Gilboa, Yehoshua A., *The Black Years of Soviet Jewry, 1939–1953* (Boston: Little, Brown, 1971).

Gitelman, Zvi Y., *Jewish Nationality and Soviet Politics: The Jewish Sections of the CPSU, 1917–1930* (Princeton, N.J.: Princeton University Press, 1972).

Goldhagen, Erich, ed., *Ethnic Minorities in the Soviet Union* (New York: Praeger, 1968).

Humphrey, Caroline, *Karl Marx Collective* (New York: Cambridge University Press, 1983).

Kamenetsky, Ihor, ed., *Nationalism and Human Rights: Processes of Modernization in the U.S.S.R.* (Littleton, Colo: Libraries Unlimited, Inc., 1977).

Karklins, Rasma, *Ethnic Relations in the USSR: The Perspective from Below* (Winchester, Mass.: Allen & Unwin, 1985).

Katz, Zev, Rogers, Rosemarie, and Harned, Frederic, eds., *Handbook of Major Soviet Nationalities* (New York: The Free Press, 1975).

Kochan, Lionel, ed., *The Jews in Soviet Russia since 1917,* 3rd ed. (New York: Oxford University Press, 1978).

Kolasky, John, *Education in Soviet Ukraine: A Study in Discrimination and Russification* (Toronto: Peter Martin Associates, 1968).

Kostiuk, Hryhory, *Stalinist Rule in the Ukraine: A Study of the Decade of Mass Terror, 1929–1939* (New York: Praeger, 1960).

Krawchenko, Bohdan, *Social Change and National Consciousness in Twentieth-Century Ukraine* (New York: St. Martin's Press, 1985).

———, ed., *Ukraine after Shelest* (Edmonton, Alberta: Canadian Institute of Ukrainian Studies, 1983).

Kreindler, Isabelle T., ed., *Sociolinguistic Perspectives on Soviet National Languages: Their Past, Present and Future* (Berlin and New York: Mouton, 1985).

Low, Alfred D., *Lenin on the Question of Nationality* (New York: Bookman Associates, 1958).

Lubachko, Ivan S., *Belorussia under Soviet Rule, 1917–1957* (Lexington: University Press of Kentucky, 1972).

Lubin, Nancy, *Labour and Nationality in Soviet Central Asia* (London: Macmillan in association with St. Antony's College, Oxford, 1984).

Mace, James E., *Communism and the Dilemmas of National Liberation: National Communism in Soviet Ukraine, 1918–1933* (Cambridge: Harvard Ukrainian Research Institute, 1983).

Massell, Gregory J., *The Surrogate Proletariat: Moslem Women and Revolutionary Strategies in Soviet Central Asia, 1919–1929* (Princeton, N.J.: Princeton University Press, 1974).

Matossian, Mary Kilbourne, *The Impact of Soviet Policies in Armenia, Nineteen Twenty to Nineteen Thirty-Six: A Study of Planned Cultural Transformation* (Leiden: E.J. Brill, 1962; reprint, Hyperion, 1981).

Mazlakh, Serhii and Shakhrai, Vasyl', *On the Current Situation in the Ukraine,* ed. Peter J. Potichnyj, intro. Michael M. Luther (Ann Arbor: University of Michigan Press, 1970).

Misiunas, Romuald J. and Taagepera, Rein, *The Baltic States: Years of Dependence, 1940–1980* (Berkeley: University of California Press, 1983).

Parming, Tönu and Järvesoo, Elmar, eds., *A Case Study of a Soviet Republic: The Estonian SSR* (Boulder, Colo.: Westview Press, 1978).

Pinkus, Benjamin, *The Soviet Government and the Jews, 1948–1967: A Documented Study* (New York: Cambridge University Press, 1984).

Potichnyj, Peter J., ed., *Ukraine in the Seventies* (Oakville, Ont.: Mosaic Press, 1975).

Rakowska-Harmstone, Teresa, *Russia and Nationalism in Central Asia: The Case of Tadzhikistan* (Baltimore: Johns Hopkins Press, 1970).

Rywkin, Michael, *Moscow's Muslim Challenge, Soviet Central Asia* (Armonk, N.Y.: M. E. Sharpe, 1982).

Sawyer, Thomas E., *The Jewish Minority in the Soviet Union* (Boulder, Colo.: Westview Press, 1979).

Schwarz, Solomon M., *The Jews in the Soviet Union* (Syracuse, N.Y.: Syracuse University Press, 1951; reprint, Ayer, 1972).

Sullivant, Robert S., *Soviet Politics and the Ukraine, 1917–1957* (New York: Columbia University Press, 1962).

Tillett, Lowell R., *The Great Friendship: Soviet Historians on the Non-Russian Nationalities* (Chapel Hill: University of North Carolina Press, 1969).

Vakar, Nicholas P., *Belorussia: The Making of a Nation* (Cambridge: Harvard University Press, 1956).

Vardys, V. Stanley, ed., *Lithuania under the Soviets: Portrait of a Nation, 1940–1965* (New York: Praeger, 1965).

The following works relating to Soviet policy in the area of religion are important:

Bourdeaux, Michael, *Opium of the People: The Christian Religion in the U.S.S.R.,* 2nd ed. (London: Mowbrays, 1977).

Curtiss, John S., *The Russian Church and the Soviet State, 1917–1950* (Boston: Little, Brown, 1953).

Ellis, Jane, *The Russian Orthodox Church: A Contemporary History* (Bloomington: Indiana University Press, 1986).

Fletcher, William C., *Nikolai: Portrait of a Dilemma* (New York: Macmillan, 1968).

———, *The Russian Orthodox Church Underground, 1917–1970* (New York: Oxford University Press, 1971).

———, *Soviet Believers: The Religious Sector of the Population* (Lawrence, Kansas: Regents Press of Kansas, 1981).

———, and Strover, Anthony J., eds., *Religion and the Search for New Ideals in the USSR* (New York: Praeger, 1967).

Kolarz, Walter, *Religion in the Soviet Union* (New York: St. Martin's Press, 1962).

Lane, Christel, *Christian Religion in the Soviet Union: A Sociological Study* (Albany: State University of New York Press, 1978).

Marshall, Richard H., Jr.; Bird, Thomas E.; and Blane, Andrew, eds., *Aspects of Religion in the Soviet Union, 1917–1967* (Chicago: University of Chicago Press, 1971).

Pospielovsky, Dimitry, *The Russian Church under the Soviet Regime,* 2 vols. (Crestwood, N.Y.: St. Vladimir's Seminary Press, 1984).

Powell, David E., *Antireligious Propaganda in the Soviet Union* (Cambridge, Mass.: M.I.T. Press, 1975).

Vardys, V. Stanley, *The Catholic Church, Dissent and Nationality in Soviet Lithuania* (Boulder, Colo.: East European Quarterly, 1978).

Important works dealing with literature and censorship include the following:

Blake, Patricia and Hayward, Max, eds., *Dissonant Voices in Soviet Literature* (New York: Pantheon, 1962).

Brown, Deming, *Soviet Russian Literature since Stalin* (New York: Cambridge University Press, 1977).

Brown, Edward J., *Russian Literature since the Revolution* (Cambridge: Harvard University Press, 1982).

Dunham, Vera S., *In Stalin's Time: Middleclass Values in Soviet Fiction* (New York: Cambridge University Press, 1979).

Ehrenburg, Ilya, *Memoirs: 1921–1941, The War: 1941–1945, Post-War Years: 1945–1954* (Cleveland: World Publishing Company, 1964, 1965, 1967).

Friedberg, Maurice, *A Decade of Euphoria: Western Literature in Post-Stalin Russia, 1954–1964* (Bloomington: Indiana University Press, 1977).

Hayward, Max, ed., *On Trial: The Soviet State versus "Abram Tertz" and "Nikolai Arzhak"* (New York: Harper & Row, 1966).

————, *Writers in Russia, 1917–1978,* edited and with an introduction by Patricia Blake (San Diego: Harcourt Brace Jovanovich, 1983).

Hosking, Geoffrey, *Beyond Socialist Realism* (New York: Holmes and Meier, 1980).

Shanor, Donald R., *Behind the Lines: The Private War against Soviet Censorship* (New York: St. Martin's Press, 1985).

Spechler, Dina, *Permitted Dissent in the USSR: Novy mir and the Soviet Regime* (New York: Praeger, 1982).

Starr, S. Frederick, *Red and Hot: The Fate of Jazz in the Soviet Union, 1917–1980* (New York: Oxford University Press, 1983).

Swayze, Harold, *Political Control of Literature in the USSR, 1946–1959* (Cambridge: Harvard University Press, 1962).

Chapter 11 Soviet Foreign Policy

Adomeit, Hannes, *Soviet Risk-taking and Crisis Behavior* (Winchester, Mass.: Allen & Unwin, 1982).

Aspaturian, Vernon V., *The Union Republics in Soviet Diplomacy* (Geneva: Droz, 1960; reprint, Greenwood Press, 1984).

Barghoorn, Frederick C., *The Soviet Cultural Offensive* (Princeton, N.J.: Princeton University Press, 1960; reprint, Greenwood, 1976).

————, *Soviet Foreign Propaganda* (Princeton, N.J.: Princeton University Press, 1964).

Beloff, Max, *The Foreign Policy of Soviet Russia, 1929–1941,* 2 vols. (London: Oxford University Press, 1947–1949).

Bialer, Seweryn, ed., *The Domestic Context of Soviet Foreign Policy* (Boulder, Colo.: Westview Press, 1981).

Bishop, Donald, *The Roosevelt-Litvinov Agreements: The American View* (Syracuse, N.Y.: Syracuse University Press, 1965).

Brzezinski, Zbigniew K., *The Soviet Bloc: Unity and Conflict,* rev. ed. (Cambridge: Harvard University Press, 1967).

Cornell, Richard, *Youth and Communism: An Historical Analysis of International Communist Youth Movements* (New York: Walker, 1965).

Dailey, Brian, and Parker, Patrick J., eds., *Soviet Strategic Deception* (Stanford: Hoover Institution Press, 1987).

Dallin, Alexander, *The Soviet Union at the United Nations* (New York: Praeger, 1962; reprint, Greenwood, 1976).

Dallin, David J., *Soviet Espionage* (New Haven: Yale University Press, 1955).

————, *Soviet Foreign Policy after Stalin* (Philadelphia: Lippincott, 1961; reprint, Greenwood, 1975).

Degras, Jane, ed., *The Communist International, 1919–1943,* 3 vols. (New York: Oxford University Press, 1956, 1960, 1965; reprint, F. Cass, 1971).

————, *Soviet Documents on Foreign Policy, 1917–1941,* 3 vols. (New York: Oxford University Press, 1951–1953; reprint, Octagon, 1978).

Donaldson, Robert H., ed., *The Soviet Union in the Third World: Successes and Failures* (Boulder, Colo.: Westview Press, 1981).

Edmonds, Robin, *Soviet Foreign Policy: The Brezhnev Years* (New York: Oxford University Press, 1983).

Ellison, Herbert J., ed., *The Sino-Soviet Conflict: A Global Perspective* (Seattle: University of Washington Press, 1982).

———, ed., *Soviet Policy toward Western Europe: Implications for the Atlantic Alliance* (Seattle: University of Washington Press, 1983).

Eudin, Xenia J. and Fisher, Harold H., eds., *Soviet Russia and the West, 1920–1927: A Documentary Survey* (Stanford: Stanford University Press, 1957) and Eudin, Xenia J. and North, Robert C., eds., *Soviet Russia and the East, 1920–1927: A Documentary Survey* (Stanford: Stanford University Press, 1957).

Eudin, Xenia J. and Slusser, Robert M., eds., *Soviet Foreign Policy, 1928–1934; Documents and Materials,* 2 vols. (University Park, Pa.: Pennsylvania State University Press, 1967).

Fischer, Louis, *The Soviets in World Affairs,* 2 vols. (1929; reprint, Princeton University Press, 1951).

Fletcher, William C., *Religion and Soviet Foreign Policy, 1945–1970* (New York: Oxford University Press, 1973).

Freedman, Robert O., *Soviet Policy Toward the Middle East Since 1970* (New York: Praeger, 1975).

Garthoff, Raymond L., *Detente and Confrontation: American-Soviet Relations from Nixon to Reagan* (Washington, D.C.: Brookings Institution, 1985).

Gehlen, Michael P., *The Politics of Coexistence: Soviet Methods and Motives* (Bloomington: Indiana University Press, 1967; reprint, Greenwood Press, 1980).

Gelman, Harry, *The Brezhnev Politburo and the Decline of Detente* (Ithaca, N.Y.: Cornell University Press, 1984).

Goodman, Elliot R., *The Soviet Design for a World State* (New York: Columbia University Press, 1960).

Goren, Roberta, *The Soviet Union and Terrorism,* edited by Jillian Becker, introduction by Robert Conquest (Winchester, Mass.: Allen & Unwin, 1984).

Gouré, Leon, *War Survival in Soviet Strategy: USSR Civil Defense* (Miami, Fla.: University of Miami, Center for Advanced International Studies, 1976).

Griffith, William E., *Albania and the Sino-Soviet Rift* (Cambridge, Mass.: M.I.T. Press, 1963).

———, *The Sino-Soviet Rift, Analyzed and Documented* (Cambridge, Mass.: M.I.T. Press, 1964).

Grzybowski, Kazimierz, *Soviet Public International Law, Doctrines and Diplomatic Practice* (Durham, N.C.: Rule of Law Press, 1970; reprint, W. S. Hein, 1982).

Hammond, Thomas T. and Farrell, Robert, eds., *The Anatomy of Communist Takeovers* (New Haven: Yale University Press, 1975).

Hoffmann, Erik P. and Fleron, Frederic J., eds., *The Conduct of Soviet Foreign Policy,* 2nd ed. (New York: Aldine, 1980).

Holzman, Franklyn D., *International Trade Under Communism—Politics & Economics* (New York: Basic Books, 1976).

Horelick, Arnold L. and Rush, Myron, *Strategic Power and Soviet Foreign Policy* (Chicago: University of Chicago Press, 1966).

Hosmer, Steven T. and Wolfe, Thomas W., *Soviet Policy and Practice toward Third World Conflicts* (Lexington, Mass.: Lexington Books, 1983).

Jamgotch, Nish, ed., *Sectors of Mutual Benefit in U.S.-Soviet Relations* (Durham, N.C.: Duke University Press, 1985).

Jones, Christopher D., *Soviet Influence in Eastern Europe: Political Autonomy and the Warsaw Pact* (New York: Praeger, 1981).

Kanet, Roger E., ed., *The Soviet Union and the Developing Nations* (Baltimore, Md: The Johns Hopkins University Press, 1974).

Kaplan, Steven S., et al., *Diplomacy of Power: Soviet Armed Forces as a Political Instrument* (Washington, D.C.: Brookings Institution, 1981).

Kaznacheev, Aleksandr, *Inside a Soviet Embassy: Experiences of a Russian Diplomat in Burma* (Philadelphia: Lippincott, 1962).

Kennan, George F., *Russia and the West under Lenin and Stalin* (Boston: Little, Brown, 1961).

Kolkowicz, Roman and Mickiewicz, Ellen Propper, eds., *The Soviet Calculus of Nuclear War* (Lexington, Mass.: Lexington Books, 1986).

Kubálková, Vendulka and Cruickshank, Albert, *Marxism and International Relations* (New York: Oxford University Press, 1985).

Kulski, Wladyslaw W., *The Soviet Union in World Affairs: A Documented Analysis, 1964–1972* (Syracuse, N.Y.: Syracuse University Press, 1973).

Laird, Robbin F. and Hoffmann, Erik P., eds., *Soviet Foreign Policy in a Changing World* (New York: Aldine De Gruyter, 1986).

Laqueur, Walter, ed., *The Pattern of Soviet Conduct in the Third World* (New York: Praeger, 1983).

Lederer, Ivo J., ed., *Russian Foreign Policy: Essays in Historical Perspective* (New Haven: Yale University Press, 1962).

Leebaert, Derek, ed., *Soviet Military Thinking* (Winchester, Mass.: Allen & Unwin, 1981).

Mayer, Peter, *Cohesion and Conflict in International Communism* (The Hague: Martinus Nijhoff, 1968).

McKenzie, Kermit E., *Comintern and World Revolution, 1928–1943: The Shaping of Doctrine* (New York: Columbia University Press, 1964).

McLane, Charles B., *Soviet Strategies in Southeast Asia* (Princeton, N.J.: Princeton University Press, 1966).

Mosely, Philip E., *The Kremlin and World Politics* (New York: Random House, 1960).

Nogee, Joseph L. and Donaldson, Robert H., *Soviet Foreign Policy since World War II* (Elmsford, N.Y.: Pergamon Press, 1984).

Pipes, Richard, *U.S.-Soviet Relations in the Era of Detente* (Boulder, Colo.: Westview Press, 1981).

Porter, Bruce D., *The USSR in Third World Conflicts: Soviet Arms and Diplomacy in Local Wars, 1945–1980* (New York: Cambridge University Press, 1984).

Rosser, Richard F., *An Introduction to Soviet Foreign Policy* (Englewood Cliffs, N.J.: Prentice-Hall, 1969).

Rubinstein, Alvin Z., *The Soviets in International Organizations* (Princeton, N.J.: Princeton University Press, 1964).

———, *Soviet Foreign Policy since World War II, Imperial and Global,* 2nd ed. (Boston: Little, Brown, 1985).

Rush, Myron, ed., *The International Situation and Soviet Foreign Policy: Reports of Soviet Leaders* (Columbus, Ohio: Charles E. Merrill, 1970).

Saivetz, Carol R. and Woodby, Sylvia, *Soviet-Third World Relations* (Boulder, Colo.: Westview Press, 1985).

Schmid, Alex P. with Berends, Ellen, *Soviet Military Interventions since 1945* (New Brunswick, N.J.: Transaction Books, 1985).

Schwartz, Morton, *The Foreign Policy of the USSR: Domestic Factors* (Encino, Calif.: Dickenson Publishing Co., 1975).

Scott, William F. and Scott, Harriet Fast, *The Soviet Control Structure: Capabilities for Wartime Survival* (New York: Crane Russak, 1983).

Seton-Watson, Hugh, *From Lenin to Khrushchev: The History of World Communism,* 2nd ed. (New York: Praeger, 1960; reprint, Westview Press, 1985).

Shulman, Marshall D., *Stalin's Foreign Policy Reappraised* (Cambridge: Harvard University Press, 1963; reprint, Westview Press, 1985).

Sloss, Leon and Davis, M. Scott, eds., *A Game for High Stakes: Lessons Learned in Negotiating with the Soviet Union* (Cambridge, Mass.: Ballinger, 1986).

Slusser, Robert M., *The Berlin Crisis of 1961: Soviet-American Relations and the Struggle for Power in the Kremlin, June–November, 1961* (Baltimore: Johns Hopkins University Press, 1973).

Smolansky, Oles M., *The Soviet Union and the Arab East Under Khrushchev* (Lewisburg, Pa.: Bucknell University Press, 1974).

Timmermann, Heinz, *The Decline of the World Communist Movement* (Boulder, Colo.: Westview Press, 1987).

Triska, Jan F. and Finley, David D., *Soviet Foreign Policy* (New York: Macmillan, 1968).

Triska, Jan F. and Slusser, Robert M., *The Theory, Law and Policy of Soviet Treaties* (Stanford: Stanford University Press, 1962).

Ulam, Adam B., *Dangerous Relations: The Soviet Union in World Politics, 1970–1982* (New York: Oxford University Press, 1983).

———, *Expansion and Coexistence: The History of Soviet Foreign Policy, 1917–1973,* 2nd ed. (New York: Praeger, 1974).

Urban, Joan Barth, *Moscow and the Italian Communist Party: From Togliatti to Berlinguer* (Ithaca, N.Y.: Cornell University Press, 1986).

Valenta, Jiri and Potter, William C., eds., *Soviet Decisionmaking for National Security* (Winchester, Mass.: Allen & Unwin, 1984).

Valkenier, Elizabeth Kridl, *The Soviet Union and the Third World: An Economic Bind* (New York: Praeger, 1983).

Warth, Robert D., *Soviet Russia in World Politics* (New York: Twayne, 1963).

Wesson, Robert G., *Soviet Foreign Policy in Perspective* (Homewood, Ill.: Dorsey Press, 1969).

Zagoria, Donald S., *The Sino-Soviet Conflict, 1956–1961* (Princeton, N.J.: Princeton University Press, 1962).

———, ed., *Soviet Policy in East Asia* (New Haven: Yale University Press, 1982).

Zimmerman, William, *Soviet Perspectives on International Relations, 1956–1967* (Princeton, N.J.: Princeton University Press, 1969).

Chapter 12 The Soviet Polity: Problems and Prospects

Alexeyeva, Ludmilla, *Soviet Dissent: Contemporary Movements for National, Religious, and Human Rights* (Middletown, Conn.: Wesleyan University Press, 1985).

Allworth, Edward, ed., *Ethnic Russia in the U.S.S.R., The Dilemma of Dominance* (New York: Pergamon Press, 1980).

Amalrik, Andrei, *Will the Soviet Union Survive until 1984?* (New York: Harper & Row, 1970; revised and expanded edition, 1981).

Bialer, Seweryn, *The Soviet Paradox: External Expansion, Internal Decline* (New York: Knopf, 1986).

Bilocerkowycz, Jaroslaw, *Soviet Ukrainian Dissent: A Study of Political Alienation* (Boulder, Colo.: Westview Press, 1988).

Brown, Archibald H., *Soviet Politics & Political Science* (London: Macmillan, 1974).

Brumberg, Abraham, ed., *In Quest of Justice; Protest and Dissent in the Soviet Union Today* (New York: Praeger, 1970).

Brzezinski, Zbigniew and Huntington, Samuel P., *Political Power: USA/USSR* (New York: Viking Press, 1963; reprint Greenwood Press, 1982).

Connor, Walter D., *Deviance in Soviet Society; Crime, Delinquency and Alcoholism* (New York: Columbia University Press, 1972).

Conquest, Robert, ed., *The Last Empire: Nationality and the Soviet Future* (Stanford, Calif.: Hoover Institution Press, 1986).

D'Encausse, Hélène Carrère, *Decline of an Empire; The Soviet Socialist Republics in Revolt* (New York: Harper & Row, 1981).

Dunlop, John B., *The Faces of Contemporary Russian Nationalism* (Princeton, N.J.: Princeton University Press, 1983).

Feldbrugge, F. J. M., *Samizdat and Political Dissent in the Soviet Union* (Leyden: A. W. Sijthoff, 1975).

Fleron, Frederic J., ed., *Communist Studies and the Social Sciences* (Chicago: Rand McNally, 1969).

Gilison, Jerome M., *The Soviet Image of Utopia* (Baltimore: Johns Hopkins University Press, 1975).

Hammer, Darrell P., *Russian Nationalism and Soviet Politics* (Boulder, Colo.: Westview Press, 1987).

Hoffmann, Erik P. and Laird, Robbin F., *Technocratic Socialism, The Soviet Union in the Advanced Industrial Era* (Durham, N.C.: Duke University Press, 1985).

Hollander, Paul, *Soviet and American Society: A Comparison* (New York: Oxford University Press, 1973).

Inkeles, Alex and Bauer, Raymond A., *The Soviet Citizen: Daily Life in a Totalitarian Society* (Cambridge: Harvard University Press, 1959).

Johnson, Chalmers, ed., *Change in Communist Systems* (Stanford: Stanford University Press, 1970).

Kanet, Roger E., ed., *The Behavioral Revolution and Communist Studies* (New York: Free Press, 1970).

Kassof, Allen, ed., *Prospects for Soviet Society* (New York: Praeger, 1968).

Kelley, Donald R., *The Politics of Developed Socialism: The Soviet Union as a Post-Industrial State* (New York: Greenwood Press, 1986).

Menze, Ernest A., ed., *Totalitarianism Reconsidered* (Port Washington, N.Y.: Kennikat Press, 1981).

Pap, Michael, ed., *Russian Empire: Some Aspects of Tsarist and Soviet Colonial Practices* (Cleveland, Ohio: Institute for Soviet and East European Studies, John Carroll University and Ukrainian Historical Association, 1985).

Perlmutter, Amos, *Modern Authoritarianism* (New Haven: Yale University Press, 1981).

Parrott, Bruce, *Politics and Technology in the Soviet Union* (Cambridge: M.I.T. Press, 1983).

Ra'anan, Uri and Perry, Charles M., eds., *The USSR Today and Tomorrow: Problems and Challenges* (Lexington, Mass.: Lexington Books, 1987).

Rush, Myron, *Political Succession in the USSR,* rev. ed. (New York: Columbia University Press, 1965).

Simirenko, Alex, *Professionalization of Soviet Society,* edited by Cheryl A Kern-Simirenko (New Brunswick, N.J.: Transaction Books, 1982).

Solzhenitsyn, Aleksandr et al., *From Under the Rubble* (Boston: Little, Brown, 1975).

Taagepera, Rein, *Softening without Liberalization in the Soviet Union: The Case of Jüri Kukk* (Lanham, Md: University Press of America, 1984).

Tökés, Rudolf L., ed., *Dissent in the USSR: Politics, Ideology and People* (Baltimore: Johns
  Hopkins University Press, 1975).
Wesson, Robert G., *The Aging of Communism* (New York: Praeger, 1980).
———, *The Russian Dilemma,* rev. ed. (New York: Praeger, 1986).
Wimbush, S. Enders, ed., *Soviet Nationalities in Strategic Perspective* (New York: St.
  Martin's Press, 1985).
Yanov, Alexander, *The Russian Challenge and the Year 2000* (Oxford: Basil Blackwell,
  1987).

Political Novels

The novels listed here are of varying literary quality, convey different degrees of information regarding life in the Soviet Union, and emphasize particular aspects of the system or
a historical period. A political novel is obviously not significant as a source of empirical
data, for it may deviate from historical fact and may exaggerate or minimize an event or
development. Yet the novel can in its own way be more "true" for certain purposes than
a body of empirical data. Fiction can serve as a means of perceiving and interpreting reality
more accurately. If novels do not provide *the* key to an understanding of the Soviet polity,
they can lay bare a problem, scrutinize a facet of the structure, capture the temper of a
period, and convey something of the ethos of the system. Few works are literary classics
or near-classics, but even literature that is not great can still be read with profit. Unfortunately something can be muted or even lost in translation. Yet, despite all such caveats
the political novel can serve as an important collateral source that offers many insights.

Abramov, Fyodor, *One Day in the "New Life"* (New York: Praeger, 1963), originally
    entitled *Round and About,* deals with the frustrations and disillusionment of a
    communist chairman of a collective farm and offers a realistic depiction of Soviet
    rural life.
Aitmatov, Chingiz, *The Day Lasts More than a Hundred Years* (Bloomington: Indiana
    University Press, 1983), is set in Kazakhstan and stresses historical memory, ethnic
    and cultural identity, traditional values, and religiosity as well as mind control and
    conflicts in values.
Aksenov, Vasilii, *The Island of Crimea* (New York: Random House, 1983), is a political
    fantasy and satire depicting the Crimea as an independent democracy, led by former
    White Guards, that seeks to "rejoin" the Soviet Union.
Bulgakov, Mikhail, *Heart of a Dog* (New York: Grove Press and Harcourt Brace
    Jovanovich, 1968), is a biting satire at the expense of Soviet officialdom, written
    in 1925.
Chukovskaya, Lydia, *The Deserted House* (New York: Dutton, 1967), conveys the tribula-
    tions of a courageous Leningrad widow during the nightmare of the Stalin terror.
Dudintsev, Vladimir, *Not by Bread Alone* (New York: Dutton, 1957), tells of an impracti-
    cal inventor who does battle with the Soviet bureaucracy, which is depicted in all
    its grossness.
Ehrenburg, Ilya, *The Thaw* (Chicago: Henry Regnery, 1955), is important chiefly for its
    depicting conditions in the immediate post-Stalin period and its daring to deal with
    such forbidden themes as official art versus nonconformist free art and individuals
    seeking to regain a measure of spontaneity following the Stalinist "freeze."
Gouzenko, Igor, *The Fall of a Titan* (New York: Norton, 1954), is a large-scale novel

dealing with the demise of Maxim Gorky and was written by a famous defector who uncovered a Soviet spy ring in Canada in 1945.

Grossman, Vasily, *Forever Flowing* (New York: Harper & Row, 1972), contrasts the suffering and thoughts of a returning political prisoner with the successful career of his relative who makes numerous compromises; the Soviet author debunks the Lenin myth.

————, *Life and Fate* (New York: Harper & Row, 1986), is a historical, epic novel of the Soviet system under stress; completed in 1960, the novel was nearly destroyed by the KGB but was rescued almost by chance and published abroad posthumously.

Koestler, Arthur, *The Age of Longing* (New York: Macmillan, 1951), which depicts the pessimistic temper of Western Europe in the early 1950s and the politics of the European intelligentsia, also provides a characterization of a certain type of Soviet official and of the communist mentality.

————, *Darkness at Noon* (New York: Macmillan, 1940), is a near-classic based on the Moscow purge trials and the ritual of confession as performed by an old revolutionary.

Kuper, Yuri, *Holy Fools in Moscow* (New York: Quadrangle, 1974), provides glimpses into the Soviet bohemian world of persons who have jobs but do not work, free-lance prostitutes, thieves, and artists—reflecting the boredom and seamy side of life.

Nekrasov, Victor, *Kira Georgievna* (New York: Pantheon Books, 1962), is a not entirely successful novella about the life story of a sculptress, the three men in her life, and the return of her first husband from twenty years of imprisonment and Siberian exile; it conveys the passivity and fatalism of much of Soviet life.

Pasternak, Boris, *Doctor Zhivago* (New York: Pantheon Books, 1958), is a historical novel that depicts the Russian Revolution in terms of personal life histories against a broad canvas and offers a harsh judgment on revolution and civil war.

Salisbury, Harrison E., *The Northern Palmyra Affair* (New York: Harper & Row, 1962), deals with Leningrad in Stalin's time under siege and in the postwar period—depicting the Soviet bureaucracy, the purges, and day-to-day life.

Serge, Victor, *The Case of Comrade Tulayev* (Garden City, N.Y.: Doubleday, 1950), offers a grim and dramatic account of the excesses of the Stalinist dictatorship in the 1930s by an old revolutionary and Trotskyite who left the Soviet Union in 1936.

Sholokhov, Mikhail, *And Quiet Flows the Don* (New York: Knopf, 1941), *The Don Flows to the Sea* (New York: Knopf, 1941), *Seeds of Tomorrow* (New York: Knopf, 1935). Also published as *Virgin Soil Upturned. Harvest on the Don* (New York: Knopf, 1961). These novels all deal in an earthy manner with the revolution and civil war in the Don River region and with the realities of collectivization and opposition to it; the author, the CPSU's leading writer-member, has been awarded the Nobel Prize, has served the regime, and remained in its good graces.

Solzhenitsyn, Aleksandr, *Cancer Ward* (New York: Dial Press, 1968), offers vivid contrasts of freely speaking characters brought together in a hospital in 1955 and depicts the injustices inflicted upon the hero, Kostoglotov, a victim of Stalinism deprived of nearly everything at the age of thirty-four.

————, *The First Circle* (New York: Harper & Row, 1968), is a story of imprisoned scientists and intellectuals conducting research in 1949 while incarcerated and stresses the deception and irony of Stalinism.

————, *Lenin in Zurich* (New York: Farrar, Straus & Giroux, 1976), is part of a multivolume historical novel on the Russian Revolution and depicts Lenin in European exile in very unattractive terms.

————, *One Day in the Life of Ivan Denisovich* (New York: Dutton, 1963; Praeger, 1963) depicts the relentless struggle of an ordinary man for physical and spiritual survival in a concentration camp, as seen through the eyes of the prisoner; the novel created great controversy after Khrushchev permitted its publication; the two English translations differ markedly.

Suslov, Ilya, *Here's to Your Health, Comrade Shifrin* (Bloomington: Indiana University Press, 1977), by means of satire, describes the gradual disillusionment of a Soviet journalist.

Tarsis, Valerii, *The Bluebottle* (New York: Knopf, 1963), contains this and another novella, *Red and Black,* by a bitterly satirical anticommunist writer who became completely alienated and was permitted to leave the Soviet Union in 1966.

———, *Ward 7: An Autobiographical Novel* (New York: Dutton, 1965), deals with the practice of incarcerating political dissenters in mental hospitals.

Tertz, Abram (Andrei Siniavsky), *The Trial Begins* (New York: Pantheon Books, 1960), treats with biting irony the police and prosecuting authorities, generational conflict, the clichés and jargon of Marxism-Leninism, and the problem of ends and means. A later edition (University of California Press, 1982) includes the author's essay *On Socialist Realism,* which depicts it as a contradiction in terms.

Voinovich, Vladimir, *The Life and Extraordinary Adventures of Private Ivan Chonkin* and *Pretender to the Throne, The Further Adventures of Private Ivan Chonkin* (New York: Farrar, Straus & Giroux, 1976 and 1981), provide a satirical treatment of a Soviet soldier in Stalin's time and of suspicion, denunciation, and treachery combining the humorous, bizarre, and grim aspects of Soviet life.

Wilson, Mitchell, *Meeting at a Far Meridian* (Garden City, N.Y.: Doubleday, 1961), deals with an American physicist in Moscow and with the Soviet scientific establishment; the author became one of the most popular American novelists in the Soviet Union.

Yurasov, Vladimir, *Parallax* (New York: Norton, 1966), is a partly autobiographical novel by a former Soviet army officer who defected and who depicts postwar Stalinism in the USSR and Germany in terms of the careers of one officer who defects and another who returns home.

Zamiatin, Eugene, *We* (New York: Dutton, 1924, 1952). A Russian precursor of George Orwell depicts the hypertrophy of totalitarianism in a famous utopian novel.

Zinoviev, Alexander, *The Yawning Heights* (New York: Random House, 1979), is a cutting satire, likened to that of Swift, that depicts the absurdities, moral bankruptcy, and corrupted language and thought patterns of officials and citizens of the mythical country of Ibansk (for which the author was expelled from the Soviet Union).

Zoshchenko, Mikhail, *Nervous People and Other Satires* (New York: Pantheon, 1963).

———, *Scenes from the Bathhouse and Other Stories of Communist Russia* (Ann Arbor: University of Michigan Press, 1961). These are difficult-to-translate novellas and humorous stories by the boldest of Soviet satirists, who stressed the ironic and absurd in Soviet life and was attacked by Politburo member Andrei Zhdanov in 1946.

Glossary

administrirovanie bureaucratic rule by administrative fiat.

advokat member of a group of lawyers engaged in the practice of law.

Agitprop Department of Propaganda and Agitation of the CPSU Central Committee.

agitpunkt (agitatsionnyi punkt) a propaganda station or agitation center used in elections or other campaigns.

aktiv the leading cadres and most active members of an organization or society, including the CPSU.

apparat the administrative apparatus of the Soviet state or of the CPSU.

artel' a voluntary association of persons engaged in production, as in agriculture, manufacturing, or fishing, and having a claim to a share of its income.

blat an illicit or questionable economic transaction, often in the form of barter, entered into in order to fulfill production quotas; in conversational usage, influence ("pull") or protection.

Cheka the original Soviet secret police organization.

Chekist a member of the Cheka or of any of its successor organizations.

chistka literally "cleansing" or purging of personnel.

dekret decree, a term used prior to 1936, when it was replaced by *ukaz*.

domkom (domovyi komitet) house committee, a voluntary but elected body that organizes activities in housing developments.

DOSAAF (Dobrovol'noe obshchestvo sodeistviia armii, aviatsii i flotu) The Voluntary Society for Assistance to the Army, Air Force, and Navy—the Soviet civil defense organization.

druzhiny volunteer semiofficial organizations of aides to the police.

edinonachalie single command or one-man control and responsibility in management and administration.

fartsovshchik black-market operator who often trades in foreign goods and currencies.

gebist colloquial term for KGB official.

General'nyi Prokuror SSSR the Procurator (Attorney) General of the USSR.

glasnost' translated as "openness"—but more literally as "vocality"—and advocated by M. S. Gorbachev as a means of directing public attention to the failings of his predecessors and as a method of mobilizing popular support for Gorbachev's reforms by permitting limited discussion of various issues and problems.

Glavlit (Glavnoe upravlenie po delam literatury i izdatel'stv) Chief Administration of Literary and Publishing Affairs. The term is still employed to refer to the successor organization responsible for censorship, the Chief Administration for the Protection of State Secrets in the Press.

glavnoe upravlenie   chief administration.

gorispolkom (gorodskoi ispolnitel'nyi komitet)   the executive committee of a city soviet.

gorkom (gorodskoi komitet)   committee of a city CPSU organization.

gorod   city.

gorraikom   borough (urban district) CPSU committee.

Gosarbitrazh   the system of state arbitration bodies that resolve disputes involving property and fulfillment of contracts between enterprises.

Gosbank (Gosudarstvennyi Bank)   the State Bank of the USSR.

Gosplan SSSR (Gosudarstvennyi Planovyi Komitet)   State Planning Committee of the USSR.

GUITU (Gosudarstvennoe upravlenie ispravitel'no-trudovykh uchrezhdenii)   The Chief Administration for Corrective-Labor Institutions, successor to *GULag*.

GULag (Glavnoe upravlenie lagerei)   The Chief Administration for (prison) Camps, a branch of the Soviet police establishment; often used to refer to the entire Soviet system of oppression.

ispolkom (ispolnitel'nyi komitet)   executive committee.

iuriskonsul't   legal counsel in the permanent employ of an enterprise or institution.

izbiratel'nyi okrug   constituency or election district.

KGB (Komitet Gosudarstvennoi Bezopasnosti)   Committee of State Security, the secret police.

khoziain   boss, master, "owner"—used to refer to Stalin but not applied exclusively to him.

khuliganstvo   activity that grossly violates social order, indicating a lack of respect for society; rowdyism, ruffianism.

kolkhoz (kollektivnoe khoziaistvo)   collective farm.

kollegiia   a board of officials summoned for consultation; also used to refer to a group of lawyers engaged in legal practice.

kombinat   a form of economic organization that unites various related branches of industry or production into a single enterprise.

Komsomol (Kommunisticheskii soiuz molodezhi)   Young Communist League.

KPSS (Kommunisticheskaia partiia Sovetskogo Soiuza)   Communist Party of the Soviet Union (CPSU).

krai   territory.

kraiispolkom (kraevoi ispolnitel'nyi komitet)   executive committee of a territory soviet.

kraikom (kraevoi komitet)   committee of a territory CPSU organization.

kulak   literally "fist," used to refer to a "wealthy" peasant who allegedly exploited hired labor.

kul't lichnosti   the cult of personality, based on an exaggerated emphasis on the role of an individual in history; a euphemism usually employed to refer to the less attractive features of Stalin's regime.

melochnaia opeka   petty tutelage, excessive interference by ministries in the activities of subordinate enterprises.

mestnichestvo   localism, placing the interests of one's locale ahead of those of the state or the center.

militsiia   the ordinary Soviet police.

ministerstvo   ministry of the USSR, a union republic, or an autonomous republic.

MVD (Ministerstvo Vnutrennikh Del)   Ministry of Internal Affairs.

nalevo   "on the side" or "under the counter" dealings, sometimes illicit activities and earnings.

narodnyi sud people's court.

narodnyi zasedatel' people's assessor, a lay person who serves as a temporary member of all Soviet courts hearing civil and criminal cases but who does not participate in appellate proceedings.

natsional'nyi okrug an ethnically distinctive part of an *oblast'* or *krai* constituting a separate administrative and territorial subdivision such as that of the Chukchi.

NEP (Novaia Ekonomicheskaia Politika) New Economic Policy initiated by Lenin in 1921.

nesun pilferer, one who "carries off" state property, usually small items in short supply.

notariat the system of state-operated notarial offices.

ob"edinenie a type of super-firm to which related plants, factories, and construction and technological organizations are subordinated or that embraces entire sectors of an industry (as chemicals, forest products).

obkom (oblastnoi komitet) committee of a CPSU province organization.

oblast' province.

oblispolkom (oblastnoi ispolnitel'nyi komitet) executive committee of a province soviet.

okrug area (either electoral or ethnic).

Oktiabriata Little Octobrists, Communist children's organization for those in the seven-to-nine age group.

otdel department (or section), usually of the CPSU Secretariat or of a ministry.

OVIR (Otdel viz i registratsii inostrannykh grazhdan) The Department for Visas and Registration of Foreign Citizens (in the Ministry of Internal Affairs).

partiinost' party-mindedness in terms of acts and teachings that promote the CPSU's objectives.

pervichnaia partiinaia organizatsiia primary party organization.

piatiletka five-year plan, usually for economic development.

Pionery the Young Pioneers, Communist children's organization for ages ten to fifteen.

plenum plenary session of a body, such as the Central Committee; one attended by all members.

politruk (politicheskii rukovoditel') political instructor.

poselok settlement, often referred to as a *rabochii poselok* (workers' settlement) or a *dachnyi poselok* (settlement of suburban homes).

postanovlenie an ordinance or act issued by the Supreme Soviet or its Presidium or by a council of ministers in fulfillment of a law; also refers to acts adopted by a plenary session of the U.S.S.R. Supreme Court.

predsedatel' chairman.

prezidium presidium or presiding council.

pripiska the practice of adding or embellishing data concerning plan fulfillment and performance records; inflation or attribution by exaggeration.

priusadebnyi uchastok collective farmer's household garden plot.

profsoiuz (professional'nyi soiuz) trade union.

prokuratura the unified system of state attorneys.

propiska registration document or residence permit.

propusk pass or permit needed to gain entry.

protektsiia patronage, influence, wire-pulling.

rasporiazhenie a regulation of an operational character issued by a council of ministers or by a local soviet, usually directing an agency to undertake certain actions.

raiispolkom (raionnyi ispolnitel'nyi komitet) executive committee of a district soviet.

raikom (raionnyi komitet) committee of a district CPSU organization.

raion district, either rural or an urban borough.

reshenie the decision of a soviet or its executive body.

samizdat (self-publication) clandestine reproduction of writings that would not pass official Soviet censorship.

samokritika self-criticism.

seksot (sekretnyi sotrudnik) secret collaborator of, or informer for, the secret police.

selo village.

sel'sovet (sel'skii sovet) village soviet.

semeistvennost' family relations or "nepotism," denoting collusion and a closeness between officials for mutual protection.

shabashnik spare-time worker or "moonlighter."

shablon cliché and stereotyped, overly used practice.

shefstvo sponsorship or patronage, as of a factory vis-à-vis a school or library; also used to refer to the mentor-protégé relationship in politics.

sledovatel' investigating official, interrogator conducting preliminary investigation in criminal cases.

Sovet Ministrov Council of Ministers.

Sovet Natsional'nostei Soviet (Council) of Nationalities, a chamber of the U.S.S.R. Supreme Soviet.

Sovet Soiuza Soviet (Council) of the Union, a chamber of the U.S.S.R. Supreme Soviet.

Sovet Stareishin Council of Elders.

sovkhoz (sovetskoe khoziaistvo) state farm.

sovnarkhoz (sovet narodnogo khoziaistva) economic council.

sovnarkom (sovet narodnykh komissarov) executive and administrative body that was renamed the Council of Ministers in 1946.

stukach police informer, "stool-pigeon."

tekhnikum vocational or technical school.

tolkach a "pusher," one who expedites business transactions and serves as a factory representative.

tovarishcheskii sud comradely court.

Ts K Central Committee of the CPSU or of a union republic.

uchastok election precinct or polling place.

ukaz decree issued by Presidium of Supreme Soviet.

val gross output as the principal indicator of economic performance.

vedomstvennost' "departmentalism" or giving priority to the interests of one's agency (*vedomstvo*) or department.

Verkhovnyi Sovet Supreme Soviet of the USSR, a union republic, or an autonomous republic.

Verkhovnyi Sud Supreme Court.

vuz (vysshee uchebnoe zavedenie) higher educational institution, usually of a specialized nature.

zakon statute or law.

zampolit (zamestitel' komandira po politicheskoi chasti) deputy military commander for political affairs.

ZhEK (Zhilishchno-ekspluatatsionnaia kontora) housing-operations office that manages and maintains urban housing projects owned by the government or state-owned enterprises.

z/k (zakliuchënnyi) prisoner.

zveno smallest unit of Young Pioneers, also a small work unit ("link") on a collective farm.

Index